Honoring America

For Americans, the flag has always had a special meaning. It is a symbol of our nation's freedom and democracy.

Flag Etiquette

Over the years, Americans have developed rules and customs concerning the use and display of the flag. One of the most important things every American should remember is to treat the flag with respect.

- The flag should be raised and lowered by hand and displayed only from sunrise to sunset. On special occasions, the flag may be displayed at night, but it should be illuminated.

- The flag may be displayed on all days, weather permitting, particularly on national and state holidays and on historic and special occasions.

- No flag may be flown above the American flag or to the right of it at the same height.

- The flag should never touch the ground or floor beneath it.

- The flag may be flown at half-staff by order of the president, usually to mourn the death of a public official.

- The flag may be flown upside down only to signal distress.

- The flag should never be carried flat or horizontally, but always carried aloft and free.

- When the flag becomes old and tattered, it should be destroyed by burning. According to an approved custom, the Union (stars on blue field) is first cut from the flag; then the two pieces, which no longer form a flag, are burned.

The American's Creed

I believe in the United States of America as a Government of the people, by the people, for the people, whose just powers are derived from the consent of the governed; a democracy in a republic; a sovereign Nation of many sovereign States; a perfect union, one and inseparable; established upon those principles of freedom, equality, justice, and humanity for which American patriots sacrificed their lives and fortunes.

I therefore believe it is my duty to my Country to love it; to support its Constitution; to obey its laws; to respect its flag, and to defend it against all enemies.

The Pledge of Allegiance

I pledge allegiance to the Flag of the United States of America and to the Republic for which it stands, one Nation under God, indivisible, with liberty and justice for all.

The Star-Spangled Banner

O! say, can you see, by the dawn's early light,
What so proudly we hail'd at the twilight's last gleaming?
Whose broad stripes and bright stars, thro' the perilous fight,
O'er the ramparts we watched were so gallantly streaming?
And the rockets' red glare, the bombs bursting in air,
Gave proof thro' the night, that our flag was still there.
O! say, does that Star-Spangled Banner yet wave
O'er the land of the free and the home of the brave?

On the shore, dimly seen thro' the mist of the deep,
Where the foe's haughty host in dread silence reposes,
What is that which the breeze, o'er the towering steep,
As it fitfully blows, half conceals, half discloses?
Now it catches the gleam of the morning's first beam,
In full glory reflected now shines on the stream.
'Tis the Star-Spangled Banner. O long may it wave
O'er the land of the free and the home of the brave.

And where is that band who so vauntingly swore,
That the havoc of war and the battle's confusion
A home and a country should leave us no more?
Their blood has wash'd out their foul footstep's pollution.
No refuge could save the hireling and slave
From the terror of flight or the gloom of the grave,
And the Star-Spangled Banner in triumph doth wave
O'er the land of the free and the home of the brave.

O thus be it e'er when free men shall stand
Between their lov'd home and war's desolation,
Blest with vict'ry and peace, may the Heav'n-rescued land
Praise the pow'r that hath made and preserv'd us a nation.
Then conquer we must, when our cause it is just,
And this be our motto, "In God is our Trust."
And the Star-Spangled Banner in triumph shall wave
O'er the land of the free and the home of the brave.

Glencoe

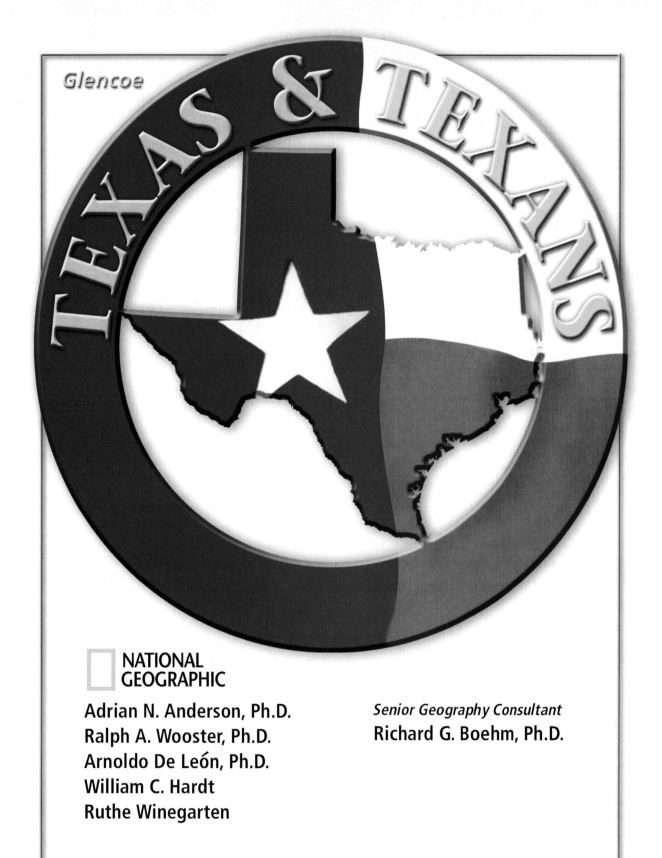

TEXAS & TEXANS

NATIONAL
GEOGRAPHIC

Adrian N. Anderson, Ph.D.
Ralph A. Wooster, Ph.D.
Arnoldo De León, Ph.D.
William C. Hardt
Ruthe Winegarten

Senior Geography Consultant
Richard G. Boehm, Ph.D.

Mc Graw Hill **Glencoe**
McGraw-Hill

New York, New York   Columbus, Ohio   Chicago, Illinois   Peoria, Illinois   Woodland Hills, California

Authors

The National Geographic Society, founded in 1888 for the increase and diffusion of geographic knowledge, is the world's largest nonprofit scientific and educational organization. Since its earliest days, the Society has used sophisticated communication technologies, from color photography to holography, to convey geographic knowledge to a worldwide membership. The School Publishing division supports the Society's mission by developing innovative education programs—ranging from traditional print materials to multimedia programs including CD-ROMS, videos, and software.

Adrian N. Anderson, Ph.D. is professor of History at Lamar University. Previously, he taught at San Antonio College and Texas Tech, his alma mater. Dr. Anderson is the coauthor with Rupert Richardson, Ernest Wallace, and Carey D. Wintz of *Texas: The Lone Star State.*

Ralph A. Wooster, Ph.D. is professor of History at Lamar University. An award-winning teacher, Dr. Wooster is the author or editor of many books and articles on Texas and Civil War history. He is the past president of the Texas State Historical Association, East Texas Historical Association, and Texas Association of College Teachers.

Arnoldo De León, Ph.D. is professor of History at Angelo State University. He has authored numerous books about Mexican Americans and Texas. He is a fellow of the Texas State Historical Association and a member of the Texas Institute of Letters.

William C. Hardt is a 30-year veteran of the Aldine ISD and has conducted workshops on teaching Texas history. An award-winning teacher, he is the author of *A Shared Past: Texas and the United States Since Reconstruction* and *Twentieth-Century Texas.*

Ruthe Winegarten is the author of many books, including the award-winning *Texas Women, A Pictorial History: From Indians to Astronauts* and *Black Texas Women: 150 Years of Trial and Triumph.* She is a faculty associate at the University of Texas at San Antonio.

Senior Geography Consultant
Richard G. Boehm, Ph.D. holds the Jesse H. Jones Distinguished Chair in Geographic Education. He directs the Grosvenor Center for Geographic Education at Southwest Texas State University and is co-director of the Texas Alliance for Geographic Education. He is the author of several best-selling textbooks.

The authors wish to acknowledge their indebtedness to the director and staff of **The Bob Bullock Texas State History Museum** in Austin, Texas, for their cooperation in developing "The Story of Texas" features in this edition of *Texas and Texans.*

About the Cover: Shown are the six flags of Texas (the United States, Republic of Texas, Confederate States of America, Mexico, France, and Spain) and the dome of the Capitol in Austin, Texas.

Printed in the United States of America
Send all inquiries to:

Glencoe/McGraw-Hill, 8787 Orion Place, Columbus, Ohio 43240-4027
ISBN 0-07-823967-2 (Student Edition) ISBN 0-07-823968-0 (Teacher Wraparound Edition)

1 2 3 4 5 6 7 8 9 027/043 05 04 03 02

Consultants & Reviewers

Academic Consultants

Randolph Campbell, Ph.D.
Department of History
University of North Texas
Denton, Texas

Ty Cashion, Ph.D.
Department of History
Sam Houston State University
Huntsville, Texas

Donald Chipman, Ph.D.
Department of History
University of North Texas
Denton, Texas

Dallas Cothrum, Ph.D.
Department of History
University of Texas at Tyler
Tyler, Texas

Ricky F. Dobbs, Ph.D.
Department of History
Texas A&M University
Commerce, Texas

Stephen L. Hardin, Ph.D.
Department of History
Victoria College
Victoria, Texas

Charles Martin, Ph.D.
Department of History
University of Texas at El Paso
El Paso, Texas

Sara Massey, Ph.D.
Institute of Texan Culture
San Antonio, Texas

Ken B. McCullough, Ph.D.
Department of History
Blinn College
Brenham, Texas

Phyllis McKenzie
Institute of Texan Culture
University of Texas at San Antonio
San Antonio, Texas

Heather Newsome
Center for Private Enterprise
Baylor University
Waco, Texas

Jane Phares, Director
Petroleum Museum
Midland, Texas

Merline Pitre, Ph.D.
College of Liberal Arts
Texas Southern University
Houston, Texas

Marc Sanders, M.A.
University of Phoenix
Austin, Texas

Jack Sheridan, Ph.D.
Professor Emeritus
University of Texas
Houston, Texas

James A. Wilson, Ph.D.
Department of History
Southwest Texas State University
San Marcos, Texas

Teacher Reviewers

Brenda Beaven
Texas History Teacher
Montgomery Jr. High School
Montgomery ISD

Candy Collins
Government Teacher
Pine Tree High School
Pine Tree ISD

James Ellis
Social Studies Department
   Chair
Humble High School
Humble ISD

Roseann Ferguson
Social Studies Chair
Austin Academy
Garland ISD

Ann Fisher
Texas History Teacher
Riverwood Middle School
Humble ISD

Carol Hanson
Texas History Teacher
Spring Forest Middle School
Spring Branch ISD

Michelle Hickey
Texas History Teacher
Riverwood Middle School
Humble ISD

Jeanie Jackson
Hughes Springs High School
Hughes Springs ISD

Mattie Johnson
Texas History Teacher
J.P. Elder Middle School
Ft. Worth ISD

Rene Kozarsky
Texas History Teacher
Timberwood Middle School
Humble ISD

Debbi Lindamood
Texas History Teacher
Marsh Middle School
Castleberry ISD

Sarah Matt
Social Studies Teacher
Marsh Middle School
Castleberry ISD

Tara Musslewhite
Texas History Teacher
Atascocita Middle School
Humble ISD

Larry R. Renfro
Texas History Teacher
University Middle School
Waco ISD

Anna Reyna
Texas History Teacher
Canyon Vista Middle School
Round Rock ISD

Marsha Richards
Member
Daughters of the Republic
   of Texas
Kingwood, Texas

Ann Robinson
Chapter President
Daughters of the Republic
   of Texas
Kingwood, Texas

Anna Shepeard
Texas History Teacher
Creekwood Middle School
Humble ISD

Brent Truitt
Texas History Teacher
Bowman Middle School
Plano ISD

Charles D. Wilson
Texas History Teacher
Florence Middle School
Florence ISD

Contents

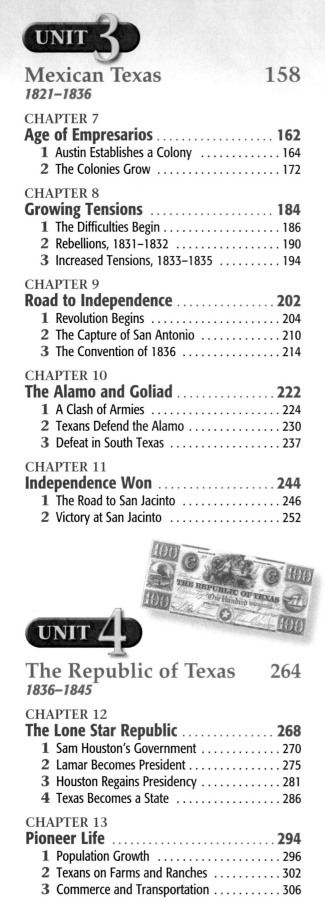

Contents

Features

CHAMPION BARB WIRE!

(Pat. Nov. 4th, 1879.)

Infringes no patents. Galvanized after being made, it is Indestructible. Is the most visible and effective,

and the **Least Dangerous** Barb Wire known. " A rod for every pound." Send for circular and sample to 119,121,125,127 **HAZARD MANUFACTURING CO.**, No. 87 Liberty Street, New York.

Two Viewpoints

Economics & History

Only in Texas

Causes and Effects

Features

Primary Source Quotes

A variety of quotations and excerpts throughout the text express the thoughts, feelings, and life experiences of people—past and present.

Primary Source Quotes

Charts & Graphs

Land Provisions of the Constitution of 1836

Category	Amount of Land Received
Head of family living in Texas before March 2, 1836	4,605 acres
Head of family coming to Texas between 1836 and October 1837	1,208 acres
Head of family coming to Texas between November 1837 and 1842	640 acres
Veterans (people with experience in the armed forces) arriving in Texas before August 1836	4,605 acres
Additional bequests to disabled veterans; veterans of San Jacinto; heirs (those who inherit) of soldiers killed at the Alamo, Goliad, other battles	Various amounts
African Americans	None
Native Americans	None
Married women	None

NATIONAL GEOGRAPHIC Maps

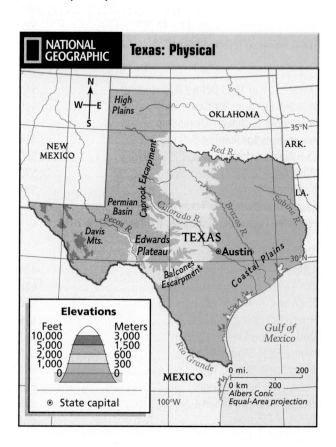

NATIONAL GEOGRAPHIC **Texas: Physical**

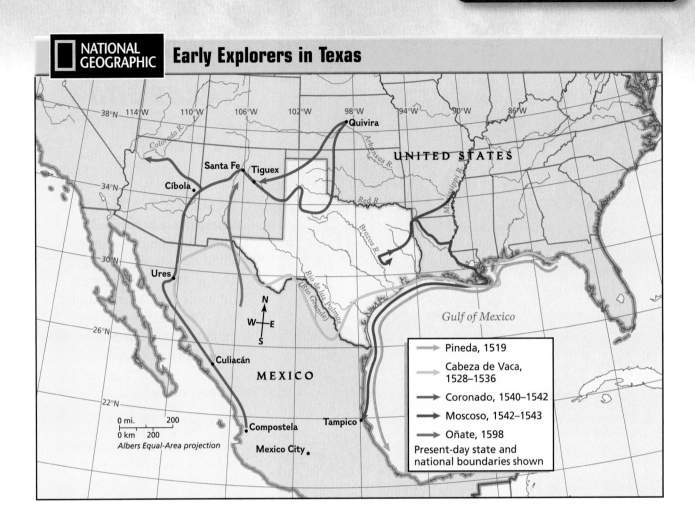

NATIONAL GEOGRAPHIC Early Explorers in Texas

Legend:
- Pineda, 1519
- Cabeza de Vaca, 1528–1536
- Coronado, 1540–1542
- Moscoso, 1542–1543
- Oñate, 1598
- Present-day state and national boundaries shown

0 mi. 200
0 km 200
Albers Equal-Area projection

How Do I Study History?

As you read *Texas and Texans*, you will be given help in sorting out all the information you encounter. This textbook organizes the events of your state's past and present around 10 themes. A theme is a concept, or main idea, that appears again and again throughout history. By recognizing these themes, you will better understand events of the past and how they affect you today.

Themes in *Texas and Texans*

Culture and Traditions
Being aware of cultural differences helps us understand ourselves and others. This text explores the way different peoples contributed to the arts, beliefs, customs, language, and technology of Texas. It helps explain why the state motto, "Friendship," is appropriate.

Continuity and Change
Recognizing our historic roots helps us understand why things are the way they are today. This theme includes political, social, religious, and economic changes that have influenced the way Texans think and act.

Geography and History
Understanding geography helps us understand how humans interact with their environment. Texas succeeded in part because of its rich natural resources and its vast open spaces. In many regions, the people changed the natural landscape to fulfill their ambitions.

Individual Action

Responsible individuals have often stepped forward to help lead the republic and the state. Texas's strong family values helped create such individuals. These values spring in part from earlier times when the home was the center of many activities, including work, education, and daily worship.

Groups and Institutions

Identifying how political and social groups and institutions work helps us work together. From the beginning, Texans formed groups and institutions to act in support of their economic, political, and religious beliefs.

Science and Technology

Texans have always been quick to adopt innovations. The state was settled and built by people who gave up old ways in favor of new. Texans' lives are deeply influenced by technology, the use of science and machines. Perhaps no advancement shaped early modern life as much as the railroad. Understanding the role of science and technology helps us see their impact on our society and the roles they will play in the future.

Government and Democracy

Understanding the workings of government helps us become good citizens. Texans embrace democracy as "government of the people, by the people, for the people." As Sam Houston said, "Be free men that your children may bless their father's name."

Economic Factors

The free enterprise economy of Texas is consistent with the state's history of rights and freedoms. Freedom of choice in economic decisions supports other freedoms. Understanding the concept of free enterprise is basic to studying Texan—and American—history.

Global Connections

Being aware of global interdependence helps us make decisions and deal with the difficult issues we will encounter.

Civic Rights and Responsibilities

For a democratic system to survive, its citizens must take an active role in government. The foundation of democracy is the right of every person to take part in government and to voice one's views on issues. An appreciation for the struggle to preserve these freedoms is vital to the understanding of democracy.

Using the Themes

You will find Section Themes at the beginning of every section of your text. At the end of each section, you are asked questions that help you put together all that you have read. Then you will better understand how ideas and themes are connected across time—and to see why history is important to you today.

TEKS & TAKS Preview

A GUIDE FOR STUDENTS AND PARENTS

Succeeding in Grade 7 Social Studies

Welcome to Grade 7 Social Studies and *Texas and Texans*. Get ready to explore your state's fascinating history and the rich diversity of its land and people. It should be an exciting journey.

In this course, you will study the full sweep of Texas history, from the early Native American societies through the eras of European mission-building and colonization, Mexican Texas, the Texas Revolution, the Republic of Texas, Texas statehood, the Civil War and Reconstruction, the late 19th century, and the 20th century. You will witness the people, events, and issues that shaped each era. You will also study the geography of Texas, its impact on history, and changes in Texans' way of life. Further, you will explore the structure and levels of Texas government and what it means to be citizen of Texas.

On the following pages you will find:

- **The Texas Essential Knowledge and Skills (TEKS) for Social Studies Grade 7.** The TEKS are the things you should learn and be able to do as

you take the course. As a preview, you may want to read over the TEKS with your parents or caregivers. Many of the names and terms may not be familiar to you at first, but together with your family you can outline some steps you can take to learn them. You may also plan to review these TEKS from time to time to help the things you learn fall into place.

- **Information about Texas Assessment of Knowledge and Skills (TAKS).** Students take the TAKS test for Social Studies at Grades 8, 10, and 11. (For an overview of these tests, see pages TEKS 14–15.) As a seventh grader, you can be looking ahead to the Grade 8 Social Studies TAKS. This test is based on the content in Grade 8 Social Studies, which covers United States history from the early colonial period through Reconstruction. However, there are many ways you can be preparing for TAKS now. For example, critical thinking skills you will be tested on are the same as those you will be practicing and using in Grade 7. Use the **TAKS Preparation Handbook** beginning on page 670 of this textbook to help you sharpen your test-taking skills. You can review the complete TAKS objectives by visiting the *Texas and Texans* Web site at <u>texans.glencoe.com</u>

The importance of the knowledge and skills you gain this year extends well beyond your classroom. After all, as a Texan you learn about your state's history not simply to know names and dates, but rather to become better citizens—of Texas and of the United States of America. Studying state history helps you build upon your understanding of the importance of patriotism, your role in a free-enterprise society, and your appreciation for the basic democratic values of our nation. We hope that this textbook will help you succeed as a student and an informed citizen of your state and your country.

◀ *State Capitol, Austin*

History

7.1 The student understands traditional historical points of reference in Texas history. The student is expected to:

(A) identify the major eras in Texas history and describe their defining characteristics;

(B) apply absolute and relative chronology through the sequencing of significant individuals, events, and time periods; and

(C) explain the significance of the following dates: 1519, 1718, 1821, 1836, 1845, and 1861.

7.2 The student understands how individuals, events, and issues prior to the Texas Revolution shaped the history of Texas. The student is expected to:

(A) compare the cultures of Native Americans in Texas prior to European colonization;

(B) identify important individuals, events, and issues related to European exploration and colonization of Texas, including the establishment of Catholic missions;

(C) identify the contributions of significant individuals including Moses Austin, Stephen F. Austin, and Juan Seguín during the colonization of Texas;

(D) identify the impact of the Mexican federal Constitution of 1824 on events in Texas;

(E) trace the development of events that led to the Texas Revolution, including the Law of April 6, 1830, the Turtle Bayou Resolutions, and the arrest of Stephen F. Austin; and

(F) contrast Spanish and Anglo purposes for and methods of settlement in Texas.

7.3 The student understands how individuals, events, and issues related to the Texas Revolution shaped the history of Texas. The student is expected to:

(A) explain the roles played by significant individuals during the Texas Revolution, including George Childress, Lorenzo de Zavala, James Fannin, Sam Houston, Antonio López de Santa Anna, and William B. Travis; and

(B) explain the issues surrounding significant events of the Texas Revolution, including the battle of Gonzales, the siege of the Alamo, the convention of 1836, Fannin's surrender at Goliad, and the battle of San Jacinto.

(B) analyze the causes of and events leading to Texas statehood.

7.4 The student understands how individuals, events, and issues shaped the history of the Republic of Texas and early Texas statehood. The student is expected to:

(A) identify individuals, events, and issues during the Republic of Texas and early Texas statehood, including annexation, Sam Houston, Anson Jones, Mirabeau B. Lamar, problems of the Republic of Texas, the Texas Rangers, the Mexican War, and the Treaty of Guadalupe-Hidalgo; and

7.5 The student understands how events and issues shaped the history of Texas during the Civil War and Reconstruction. The student is expected to:

(A) explain reasons for the involvement of Texas in the Civil War; and

(B) analyze the political, economic, and social effects of the Civil War and Reconstruction in Texas.

▼ *The Alamo and surrounding buildings, San Antonio*

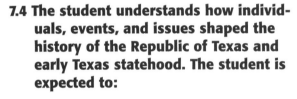

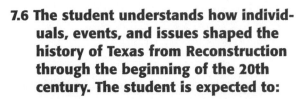

7.6 The student understands how individuals, events, and issues shaped the history of Texas from Reconstruction through the beginning of the 20th century. The student is expected to:

(A) identify significant individuals, events, and issues from Reconstruction through the beginning of the 20th century, including the factors leading to the expansion of the Texas frontier, the effects of westward expansion on Native Americans, the development of the cattle industry from its Spanish beginnings, the myth and realities of the cowboy way of life, the effects of the growth of railroads, the buffalo soldiers, James Hogg, Cynthia Parker, and Spindletop; and

(B) explain the political, economic, and social impact of the cattle and oil industries and the development of West Texas resulting from the close of the frontier.

7.7 The student understands how individuals, events, and issues shaped the history of Texas during the 20th century. The student is expected to:

(A) define the impact of "boom and bust" and trace the boom-and-bust cycle of leading Texas industries throughout the 20th century, including farming, oil and gas, cotton, cattle ranching, real estate, and banking;

(B) evaluate the Progressive and other reform movements in Texas in the 19th and 20th centuries;

(C) trace the civil rights and equal rights movements of various groups in Texas in the 20th century and identify key leaders in these movements, including James Farmer, Hector P. García, Oveta Culp Hobby, and Lyndon B. Johnson;

(D) analyze the political, economic, and social impact of major wars, including World War I and World War II, on the history of Texas; and

(E) trace the emergence of the two-party system in Texas during the second half of the 20th century.

Geography

7.8 The student uses geographic tools to collect, analyze, and interpret data. The student is expected to:

(A) create thematic maps, graphs, charts, models, and databases representing various aspects of Texas during the 19th and 20th centuries; and

(B) pose and answer questions about geographic distributions and patterns in Texas during the 19th and 20th centuries.

7.9 The student understands the location and characteristics of places and regions of Texas. The student is expected to:

(A) locate places and regions of importance in Texas during the 19th and 20th centuries;

(B) compare places and regions of Texas in terms of physical and human characteristics; and

(C) analyze the effects of physical and human factors such as climate, weather, landforms, irrigation, transportation, and communication on major events in Texas.

▼ *Guadalupe Mountains National Park*

7.10 The student understands the effects of the interaction between humans and the environment in Texas during the 19th and 20th centuries. The student is expected to:

(A) identify ways in which Texans have adapted to and modified the environment and analyze the consequences of the modifications; and

(B) explain ways in which geographic factors have affected the political, economic, and social development of Texas.

7.11 The student understands the characteristics, distribution, and migration of population in Texas in the 19th and 20th centuries. The student is expected to:

(A) analyze why immigrant groups came to Texas and where they settled;

(B) analyze how immigration and migration to Texas in the 19th and 20th centuries have influenced Texas;

(C) analyze the effects of the changing population distribution in Texas during the 20th century; and

(D) describe the structure of the population of Texas using demographic concepts such as growth rate and age distribution.

Economics

7.12 The student understands the factors that caused Texas to change from an agrarian to an urban society. The student is expected to:

(A) explain economic factors that led to the urbanization of Texas;

(B) trace the development of major industries that contributed to the urbanization of Texas; and

(C) explain the changes in the types of jobs and occupations that have resulted from the urbanization of Texas.

7.13 The student understands the interdependence of the Texas economy with the United States and the world. The student is expected to:

(A) analyze the impact of national and international markets and events on the production of goods and services in Texas;

(B) analyze the impact of economic phenomena within the free enterprise system such as supply and demand, profit, government regulation, and world competition on the economy of Texas; and

(C) analyze the impact of significant industries in Texas such as oil and gas, aerospace, and medical technology on local, national, and international markets.

▼ *Cattle amongst bluebonnets, Texas Hill Country*

Government

7.14 The student understands the basic principles reflected in the Texas Constitution. The student is expected to:

(A) identify how the Texas Constitution reflects the principles of limited government, checks and balances, federalism, separation of powers, popular sovereignty, and individual rights; and

(B) identify the influence of ideas from the U.S. Constitution on the Texas Constitution.

7.15 The student understands the structure and functions of government created by the Texas Constitution. The student is expected to:

(A) describe the structure and functions of government at municipal, county, and state levels;

(B) identify major sources of revenue for state and local governments; and

(C) describe the structure and governance of Texas public education.

Citizenship

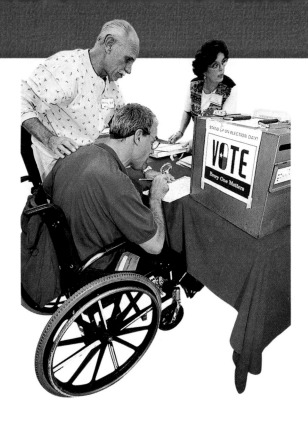

7.16 The student understands the rights and responsibilities of Texas citizens. The student is expected to:

(A) summarize the rights guaranteed in the Texas Bill of Rights; and

(B) identify civic responsibilities of Texas citizens.

7.17 The student understands the importance of the expression of different points of view in a democratic society. The student is expected to:

(A) identify different points of view of political parties and interest groups on important Texas issues;

(B) describe the importance of free speech and press in a democratic society; and

(C) express and defend a point of view on an issue of historical or contemporary interest in Texas.

7.18 The student understands the importance of effective leadership in a democratic society. The student is expected to:

(A) identify the leadership qualities of elected and appointed leaders of Texas, past and present, including Texans who have been President of the United States; and

(B) analyze the contributions of Texas leaders such as Henry B. González, Phil Gramm, Barbara Jordan, and Sam Rayburn.

▼ *Padre Island National Seashore*

Culture

7.19 The student understands the concept of diversity within unity in Texas. The student is expected to:

(A) explain how the diversity of Texas is reflected in a variety of cultural activities, celebrations, and performances;

(B) describe how people from selected racial, ethnic, and religious groups attempt to maintain their cultural heritage while adapting to the larger Texas culture; and

(C) identify examples of Spanish influence on place names such as Amarillo and Río Grande and on vocabulary in Texas, including words that originated from the Spanish cattle industry.

Science, Technology, and Society

7.20 The student understands the impact of scientific discoveries and technological innovations on the political, economic, and social development of Texas. The student is expected to:

(A) compare types and uses of technology, past and present;

(B) identify Texas leaders in science and technology such as Roy Bedichek, Walter Cunningham, Michael DeBakey, and C.M. "Dad" Joiner;

(C) analyze the effects of scientific discoveries and technological innovations, such as barbed wire, the windmill, and oil, gas, and aerospace industries, on the developments of Texas;

(D) evaluate the effects of scientific discoveries and technological innovations on the use of resources such as fossil fuels, water, and land;

(E) analyze how scientific discoveries and technological innovations have resulted in an interdependence among Texas, the United States, and the world; and

(F) make predictions about economic, social, and environmental consequences that may result from future scientific discoveries and technological innovations.

▶ *Lighthouse Rock at Palo Duro Canyon State Park*

Social Studies Skills

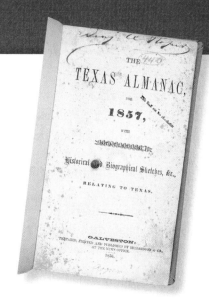

7.21 The student applies critical-thinking skills to organize and use information acquired from a variety of sources including electronic technology. The student is expected to:

(A) differentiate between, locate, and use primary and secondary sources such as computer software, databases, media and news services, biographies, interviews, and artifacts to acquire information about Texas;

(B) analyze information by sequencing, categorizing, identifying cause-and-effect relationships, comparing, contrasting, finding the main idea, summarizing, making generalizations and predictions, and drawing inferences and conclusions;

(C) organize and interpret information from outlines, reports, databases, and visuals including graphs, charts, time lines, and maps;

(D) identify points of view from the historical context surrounding an event and the frame of reference that influenced the participants;

(E) support a point of view on a social studies issue or event;

(F) identify bias in written, oral, and visual material;

(G) evaluate the validity of a source based on language, corroboration with other sources, and information about the author; and

(H) use appropriate mathematical skills to interpret social studies information such as maps and graphs.

7.22 The student communicates in written, oral, and visual forms. The student is expected to:

(A) use social studies terminology correctly;

(B) use standard grammar, spelling, sentence structure, and punctuation;

(C) transfer information from one medium to another, including written to visual and statistical to written or visual, using computer software as appropriate; and

(D) create written, oral, and visual presentations of social studies information.

7.23 The student uses problem-solving and decision-making skills, working independently and with others, in a variety of settings. The student is expected to:

(A) use a problem-solving process to identify a problem, gather information, list and consider options, consider advantages and disadvantages, choose and implement a solution, and evaluate the effectiveness of the solution; and

(B) use a decision-making process to identify a situation that requires a decision, gather information, identify options, predict consequences, and take action to implement a decision.

A Guide to TAKS

Overview

In June 1999, Senate Bill 103 was signed into law establishing a new statewide testing program. The new program, called TAKS, has been designed to follow the state curriculum, the Texas Essential Knowledge and Skills (or TEKS). TAKS includes several changes from the previous testing program:

- It expands both the grades that are tested and the subject areas that are covered. The chart on the next page shows the full TAKS testing program for Grades 3–11.

- Students are required to pass a new Exit Level exam given at the 11th grade in order to graduate from high school. The new Exit Level exam includes four subject areas: mathematics, English language arts, science, and social studies.

Social Studies TAKS

Students take TAKS Social Studies tests at Grades 8, 10, and 11. While the specific knowledge and skills tested at each level vary, all the tests cover these broad content areas:

1. Issues and events in U.S. history.
2. Geographic influences on historical issues and events.

▼ *Johnson Space Center, Houston*

3. Economic and social influences on historical issues and events.

4. Political influences on historical issues and events.

5. Use of critical thinking skills.

Following is a general description of the Social Studies TAKS tests:

- **Grade 8.** This test includes only TEKS from Social Studies Grade 8, the history of the United States from the early colonial period through Reconstruction.

- **Grade 10.** The Grade 10 TAKS test is meant to provide information on how students are progressing in social studies, but is not a graduation requirement. The test includes content taught in Social Studies Grade 8, World History Studies, and World Geography Studies. Because students have the option of taking either World History or World Geography as part of the minimum high school requirements, the test planners incorporated World History and Geography TEKS that are very similar or identical in both courses.

- **Grade 11 Exit Level.** The Grade 11 exam includes the content areas covered in the Grade 10 test (early American history, world history, and world geography), but the majority of TEKS are drawn from United States History Since Reconstruction, the required high school American history course. Passing this test is required for graduation.

◀ *Mission San José, San Antonio*

TAKS Testing
(Implementation 2003–2005)

Grade 3	Grade 4	Grade 5	Grade 6	Grade 7	Grade 8	Grade 9	Grade 10	Grade 11	Grade 12
ENGLISH-VERSION ASSESSMENT									
Reading	Reading	Reading	Reading	Reading	Reading	Reading			
	Writing			Writing			English Language Arts	English Language Arts	
Math	Math	Math	Math	Math	Math	Math	Math	Math	
		Science					Science	Science	
					Social Studies		Social Studies	Social Studies	
SPANISH-VERSION ASSESSMENT									
Reading	Reading	Reading	Reading						
	Writing								
Math	Math	Math	Math						
		Science							
READING PROFICIENCY TESTS IN ENGLISH FOR LEP STUDENTS									
RPTE	RPTE	RPTE			RPTE				
ALTERNATIVE ASSESSMENT FOR SPECIAL EDUCATION STUDENTS									
Reading	Reading	Reading	Reading	Reading	Reading	Reading			
	Writing			Writing			English Language Arts		
Math	Math	Math	Math	Math	Math	Math	Math		

Source: Texas Education Agency: Department of Curriculum, Assessment & Technology

REFERENCE ATLAS

NATIONAL GEOGRAPHIC

ATLAS KEY

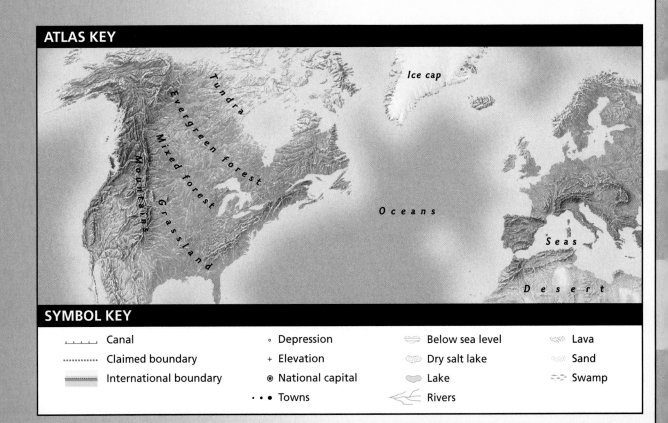

SYMBOL KEY

Canal	∘ Depression	Below sea level	Lava
Claimed boundary	+ Elevation	Dry salt lake	Sand
International boundary	⊛ National capital	Lake	Swamp
• • Towns	Rivers		

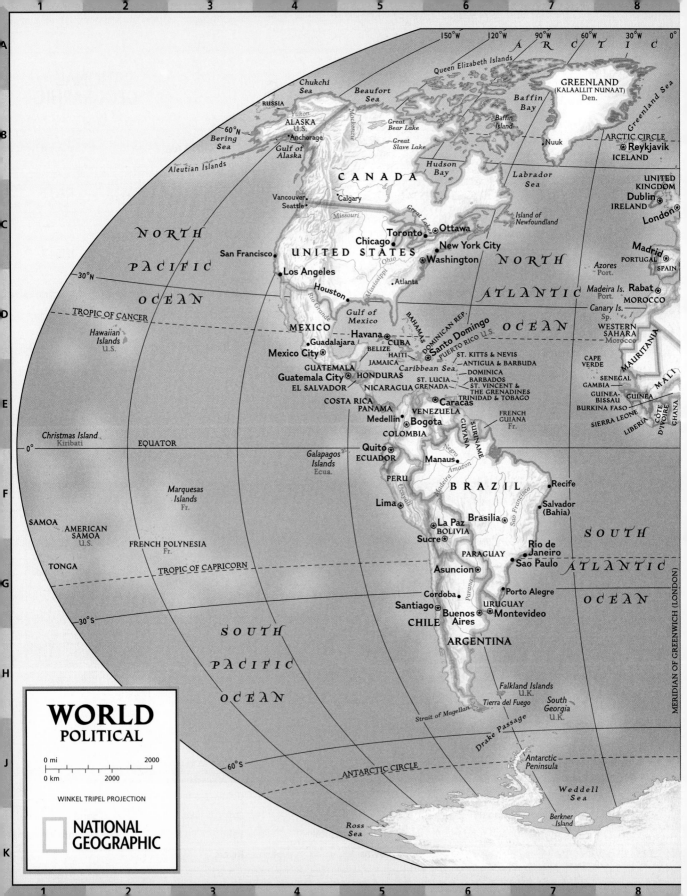

WORLD
POLITICAL

0 mi   2000

0 km   2000

WINKEL TRIPEL PROJECTION

NATIONAL GEOGRAPHIC

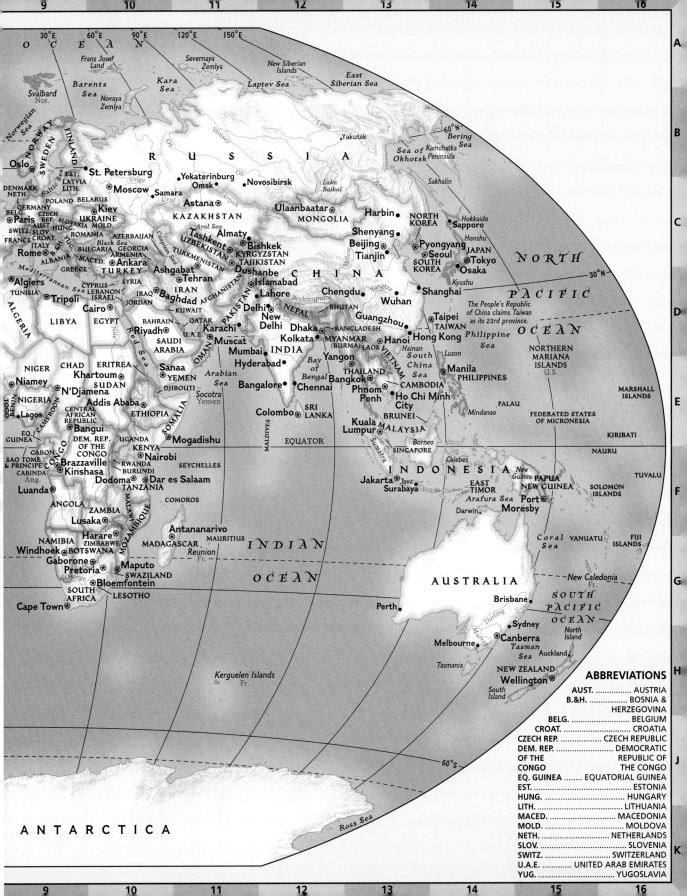

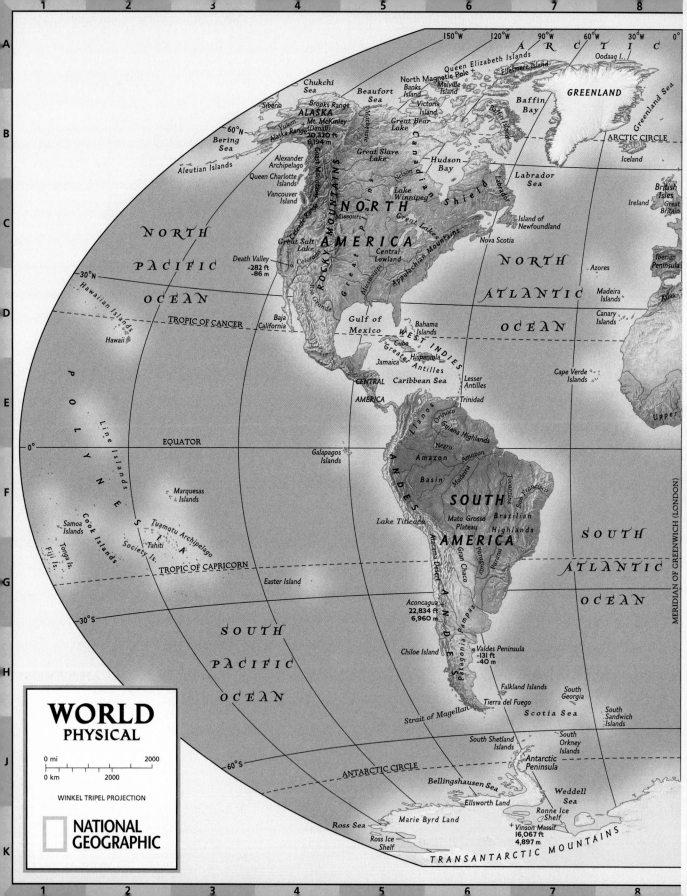

WORLD
PHYSICAL

0 mi   2000

0 km   2000

WINKEL TRIPEL PROJECTION

NATIONAL
GEOGRAPHIC

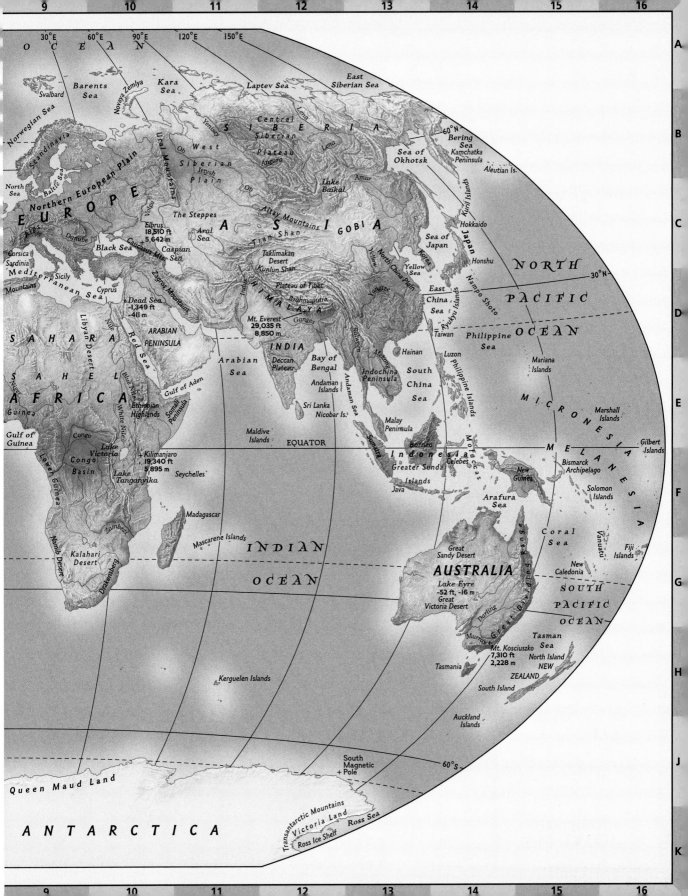

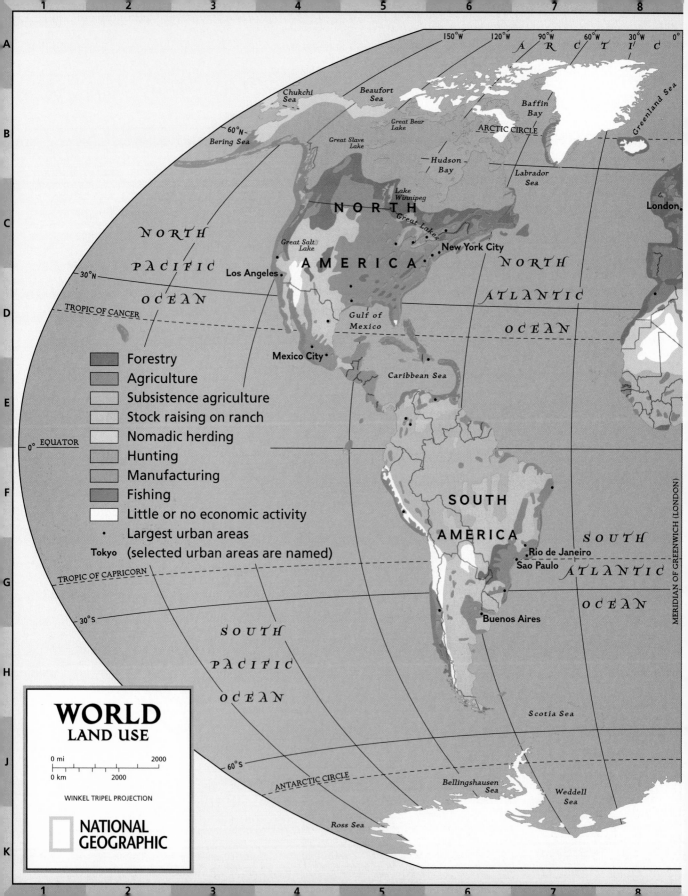

WORLD
LAND USE

0 mi   2000

0 km   2000

WINKEL TRIPEL PROJECTION

NATIONAL GEOGRAPHIC

Legend:
- Forestry
- Agriculture
- Subsistence agriculture
- Stock raising on ranch
- Nomadic herding
- Hunting
- Manufacturing
- Fishing
- Little or no economic activity
- · Largest urban areas
- Tokyo (selected urban areas are named)

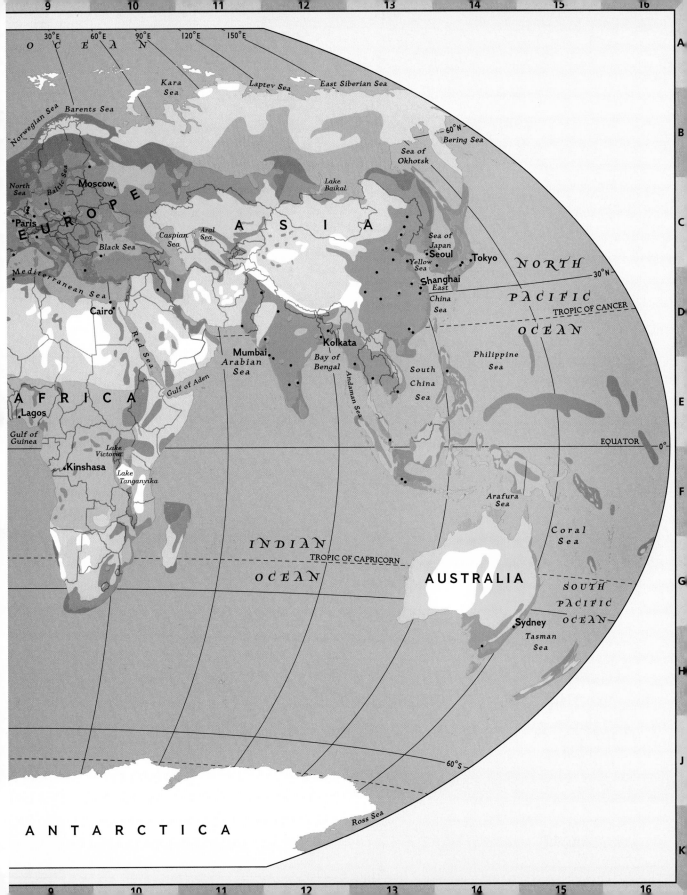

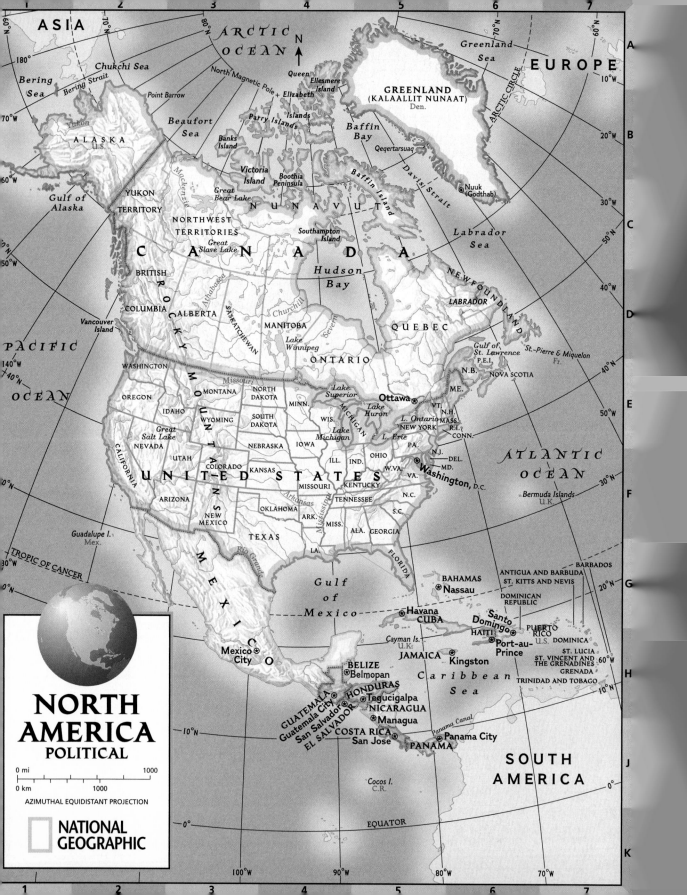

NORTH AMERICA
POLITICAL

0 mi   1000
0 km   1000

AZIMUTHAL EQUIDISTANT PROJECTION

NATIONAL GEOGRAPHIC

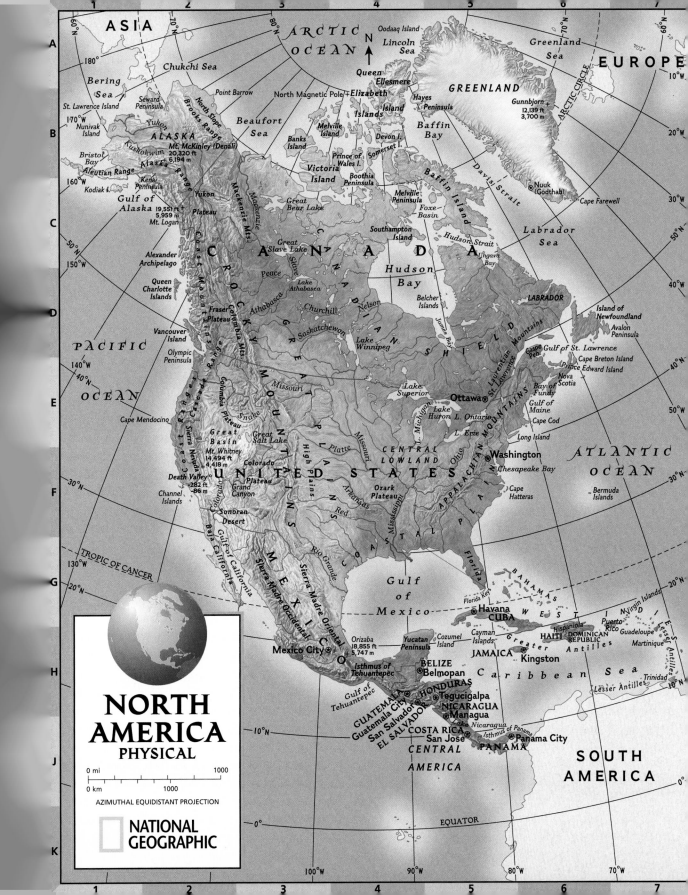

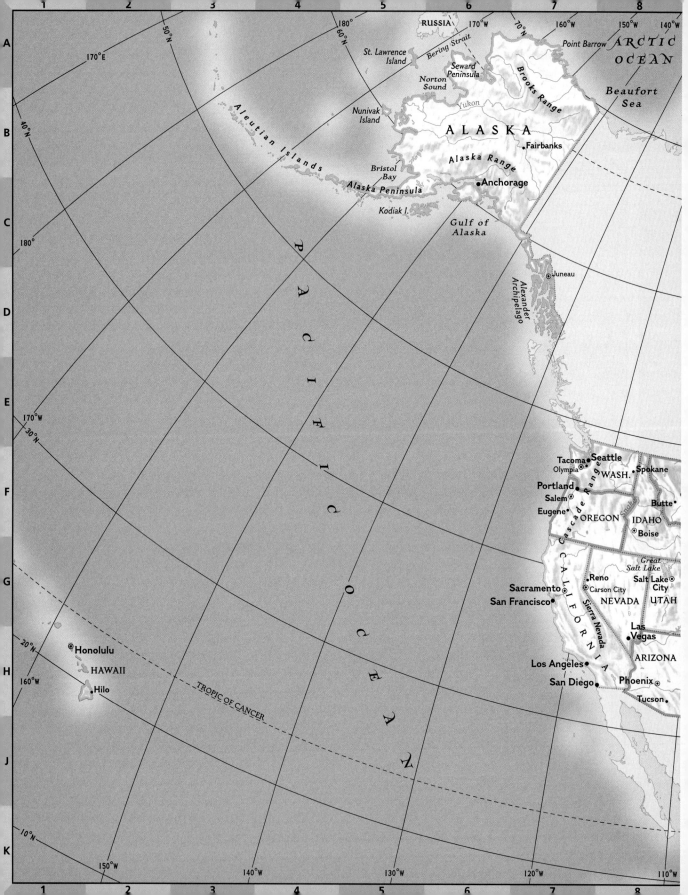

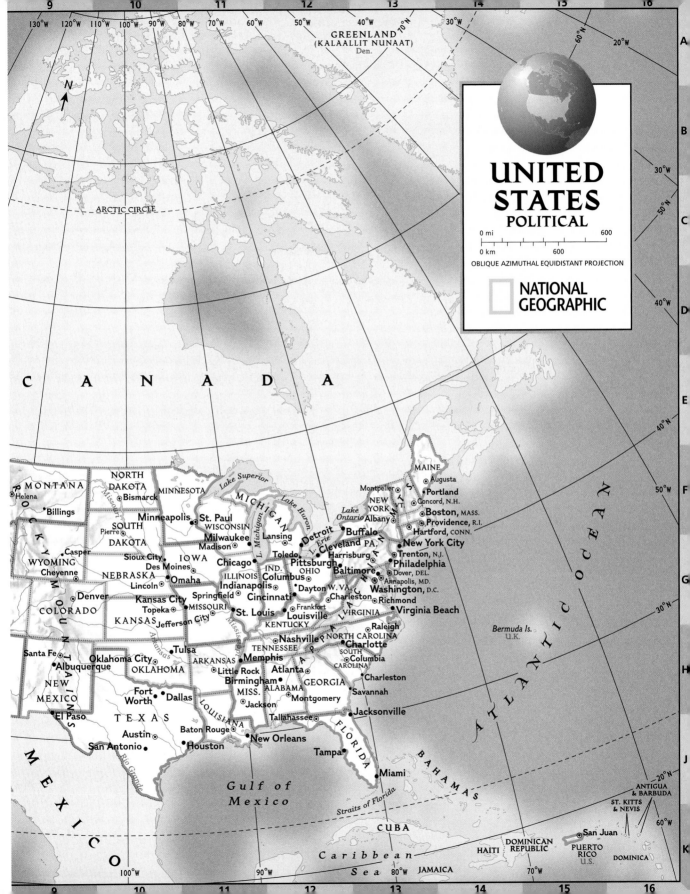

GREENLAND
(KALAALLIT NUNAAT)
Den.

N

ARCTIC CIRCLE

UNITED STATES
POLITICAL

0 mi ⊢————————⊣ 600
0 km ⊢————————⊣ 600

OBLIQUE AZIMUTHAL EQUIDISTANT PROJECTION

NATIONAL
GEOGRAPHIC

C A N A D A

MONTANA
• Helena
• Billings

NORTH
DAKOTA
Bismarck
MINNESOTA

Lake Superior

MICHIGAN

Lake Huron

MAINE
Augusta
Montpelier
Portland
Concord, N.H.
NEW
YORK
Boston, MASS.
Albany
Providence, R.I.
Hartford, CONN.

SOUTH
DAKOTA
Pierre
Minneapolis
St. Paul
WISCONSIN
Madison
Milwaukee
Lansing

Lake
Ontario

Detroit
L. Erie
Buffalo
Cleveland
PA.
New York City

WYOMING
Casper
Cheyenne
Sioux City
IOWA
Des Moines
Chicago
ILLINOIS
IND.
Columbus
OHIO
Toledo
Pittsburgh
Harrisburg
Trenton, N.J.
Philadelphia
Dover, DEL.

NEBRASKA
Omaha
Lincoln
Indianapolis
Dayton
Cincinnati
W. VA.
Annapolis, MD.
Washington, D.C.

COLORADO
Denver
Kansas City
MISSOURI
Springfield
St. Louis
Louisville
KENTUCKY
Charleston
Richmond
VIRGINIA
Virginia Beach

Topeka
KANSAS
Jefferson City
Frankfort

Santa Fe
Tulsa
Raleigh
NORTH CAROLINA
Nashville
TENNESSEE
Charlotte

Albuquerque
Oklahoma City
OKLAHOMA
ARKANSAS
Memphis
Little Rock
Atlanta
SOUTH
Columbia
CAROLINA

NEW
MEXICO
Birmingham
MISS.
ALABAMA
GEORGIA
Charleston

El Paso
Fort
Worth
Dallas
Jackson
Montgomery
Savannah

T E X A S
LOUISIANA
Tallahassee
Jacksonville
FLORIDA

Austin
Baton Rouge
New Orleans
San Antonio
Houston
Tampa

Gulf of
Mexico
Miami

M E X I C O

Rio Grande

Missouri

L. Michigan

Mississippi

Arkansas

ROCKY MOUNTAINS

APPALACHIAN MOUNTAINS

ATLANTIC OCEAN

Bermuda Is.
U.K.

BAHAMAS

Straits of Florida

CUBA

DOMINICAN
REPUBLIC
HAITI
San Juan
PUERTO
RICO
U.S.
ANTIGUA
& BARBUDA
ST. KITTS
& NEVIS

DOMINICA

C a r i b b e a n   S e a

JAMAICA

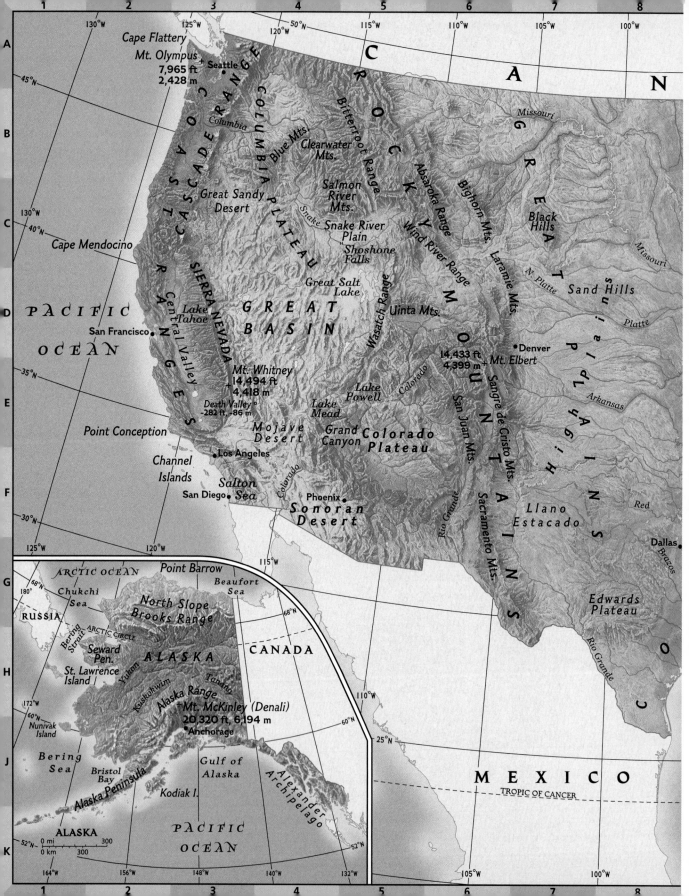

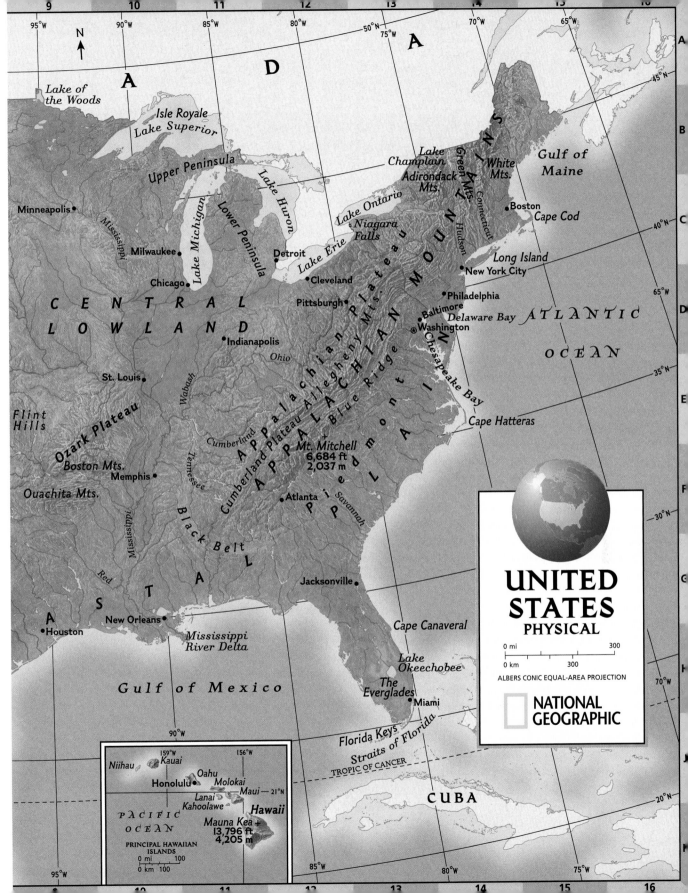

UNITED STATES
PHYSICAL

ALBERS CONIC EQUAL-AREA PROJECTION

NATIONAL GEOGRAPHIC

Lake of the Woods

Isle Royale
Lake Superior

Upper Peninsula

Minneapolis

Milwaukee

Chicago

Lake Michigan

Lower Peninsula

Lake Huron

Detroit

Cleveland

Lake Erie

Niagara Falls

Lake Ontario

Lake Champlain

Adirondack Mts.

Green Mts.

White Mts.

Gulf of Maine

Boston

Cape Cod

Connecticut

Hudson

Long Island

New York City

Philadelphia

Baltimore

Delaware Bay

Washington

Chesapeake Bay

ATLANTIC OCEAN

CENTRAL LOWLAND

Mississippi

Indianapolis

Ohio

St. Louis

Wabash

Flint Hills

Ozark Plateau

Boston Mts.

Memphis

Ouachita Mts.

Tennessee

Mississippi

Red

Black Belt

Appalachian Plateau

Allegheny Mts.

Cumberland Plateau

Cumberland

Blue Ridge

APPALACHIAN MOUNTAINS

Mt. Mitchell
6,684 ft
2,037 m

Atlanta

Savannah

Piedmont

COASTAL

Cape Hatteras

Pittsburgh

Jacksonville

New Orleans

Houston

Mississippi River Delta

Gulf of Mexico

Cape Canaveral

Lake Okeechobee

The Everglades

Miami

Florida Keys

Straits of Florida

TROPIC OF CANCER

CUBA

CANADA

PRINCIPAL HAWAIIAN ISLANDS

Niihau
Kauai 159°W
Oahu
Honolulu
Molokai
Lanai
Kahoolawe
Maui — 21°N
156°W

Hawaii

Mauna Kea +
13,796 ft
4,205 m

PACIFIC OCEAN

0 mi 100
0 km 100

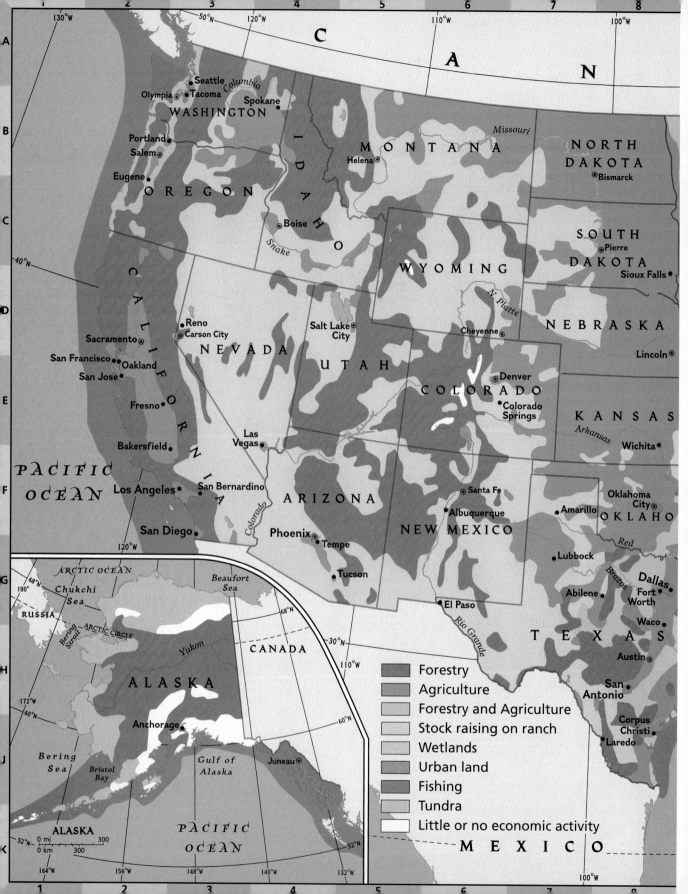

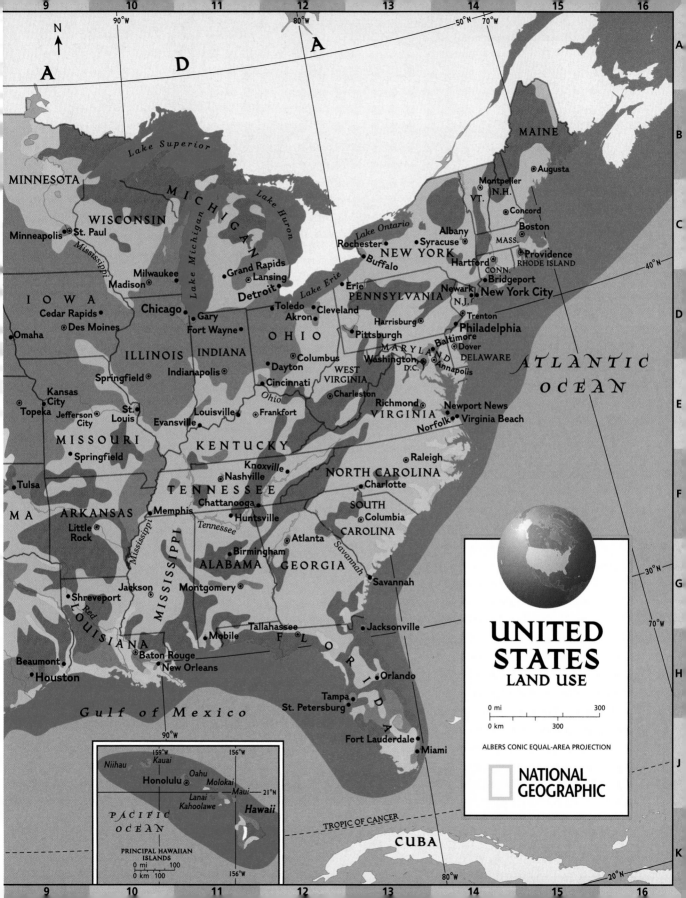

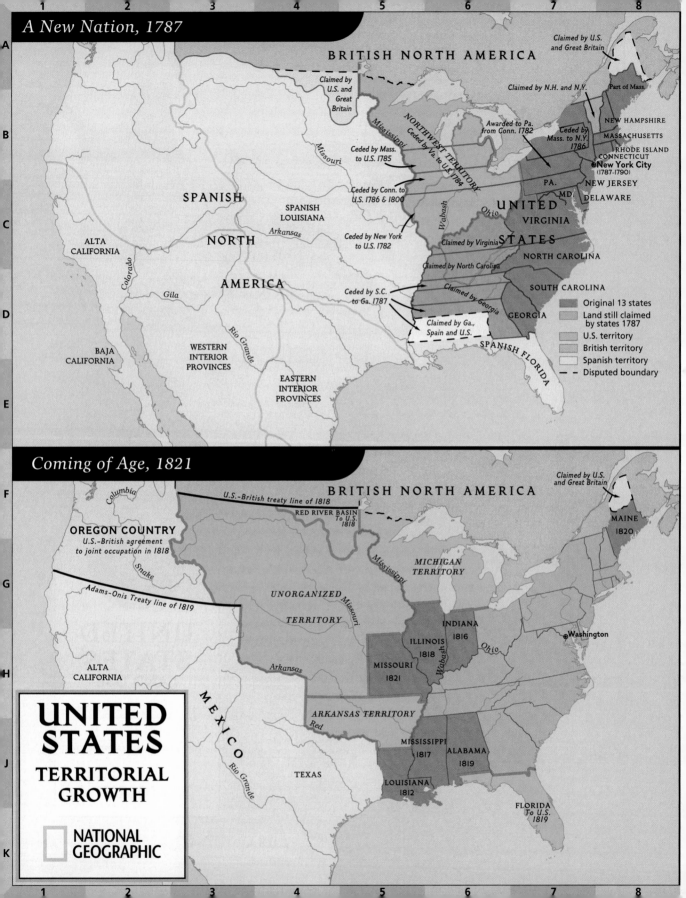

A New Nation, 1787

BRITISH NORTH AMERICA

Claimed by U.S. and Great Britain

Claimed by U.S. and Great Britain

Claimed by N.H. and N.Y.

Part of Mass.

Mississippi

NORTHWEST TERRITORY
Ceded by Va. to U.S. 1784

Missouri

Ceded by Mass. to U.S. 1785

Awarded to Pa. from Conn. 1782

Ceded by Mass. to N.Y. 1786

NEW HAMPSHIRE

MASSACHUSETTS

RHODE ISLAND
CONNECTICUT

New York City
(1787-1790)

PA.

NEW JERSEY

MD.

DELAWARE

Ceded by Conn. to U.S. 1786 & 1800

SPANISH

NORTH

AMERICA

SPANISH
LOUISIANA

Arkansas

UNITED

VIRGINIA

STATES

Ceded by New York to U.S. 1782

Wabash

Ohio

Claimed by Virginia

ALTA
CALIFORNIA

Colorado

Gila

NORTH CAROLINA

Claimed by North Carolina

SOUTH CAROLINA

Claimed by Georgia

GEORGIA

Ceded by S.C. to Ga. 1787

BAJA
CALIFORNIA

Rio Grande

WESTERN
INTERIOR
PROVINCES

EASTERN
INTERIOR
PROVINCES

Claimed by Ga., Spain and U.S.

SPANISH FLORIDA

Original 13 states

Land still claimed by states 1787

U.S. territory

British territory

Spanish territory

Disputed boundary

Coming of Age, 1821

Columbia

U.S.-British treaty line of 1818

BRITISH NORTH AMERICA

RED RIVER BASIN
To U.S. 1818

Claimed by U.S. and Great Britain

MAINE
1820

OREGON COUNTRY
U.S.-British agreement to joint occupation in 1818

Snake

Mississippi

MICHIGAN
TERRITORY

Adams-Onis Treaty line of 1819

UNORGANIZED

TERRITORY

Missouri

INDIANA
1816

ILLINOIS
1818

Washington

Ohio

ALTA
CALIFORNIA

Arkansas

MISSOURI
1821

Wabash

ARKANSAS TERRITORY

Red

MEXICO

MISSISSIPPI
1817

ALABAMA
1819

Rio Grande

TEXAS

LOUISIANA
1812

FLORIDA
To U.S.
1819

UNITED STATES
TERRITORIAL GROWTH

NATIONAL GEOGRAPHIC

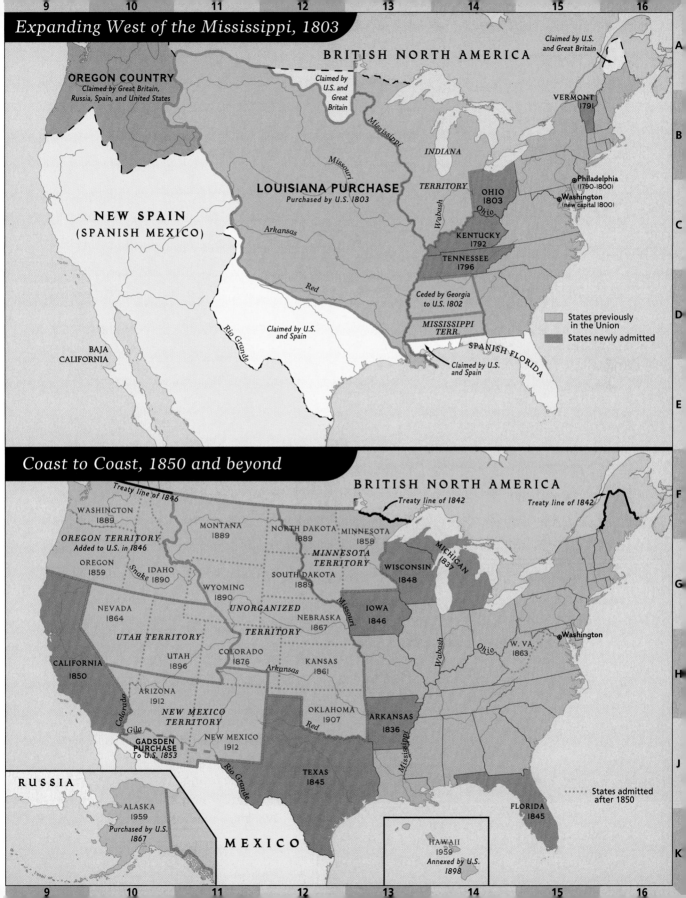

Expanding West of the Mississippi, 1803

OREGON COUNTRY
Claimed by Great Britain, Russia, Spain, and United States

BRITISH NORTH AMERICA

Claimed by U.S. and Great Britain

Claimed by U.S. and Great Britain

VERMONT 1791

INDIANA

NEW SPAIN (SPANISH MEXICO)

LOUISIANA PURCHASE
Purchased by U.S. 1803

TERRITORY

OHIO 1803

Ohio

Philadelphia (1790–1800)

Washington (new capital 1800)

KENTUCKY 1792

Missouri

Mississippi

Arkansas

Wabash

TENNESSEE 1796

Red

Ceded by Georgia to U.S. 1802

MISSISSIPPI TERR.

Rio Grande

Claimed by U.S. and Spain

SPANISH FLORIDA

BAJA CALIFORNIA

Claimed by U.S. and Spain

States previously in the Union

States newly admitted

Coast to Coast, 1850 and beyond

BRITISH NORTH AMERICA

Treaty line of 1846

Treaty line of 1842

Treaty line of 1842

WASHINGTON 1889

MONTANA 1889

NORTH DAKOTA 1889

MINNESOTA 1858

OREGON TERRITORY
Added to U.S. in 1846

OREGON 1859

Snake

IDAHO 1890

SOUTH DAKOTA 1889

MINNESOTA TERRITORY

MICHIGAN 1837

WISCONSIN 1848

WYOMING 1890

NEVADA 1864

UTAH TERRITORY

UNORGANIZED TERRITORY

NEBRASKA 1867

Missouri

IOWA 1846

Washington

CALIFORNIA 1850

UTAH 1896

COLORADO 1876

KANSAS 1861

Arkansas

Wabash

Ohio

W. VA. 1863

ARIZONA 1912

Colorado

Gila

GADSDEN PURCHASE
To U.S. 1853

NEW MEXICO TERRITORY

NEW MEXICO 1912

OKLAHOMA 1907

Red

ARKANSAS 1836

Mississippi

RUSSIA

Rio Grande

TEXAS 1845

ALASKA 1959
Purchased by U.S. 1867

MEXICO

HAWAII 1959
Annexed by U.S. 1898

FLORIDA 1845

States admitted after 1850

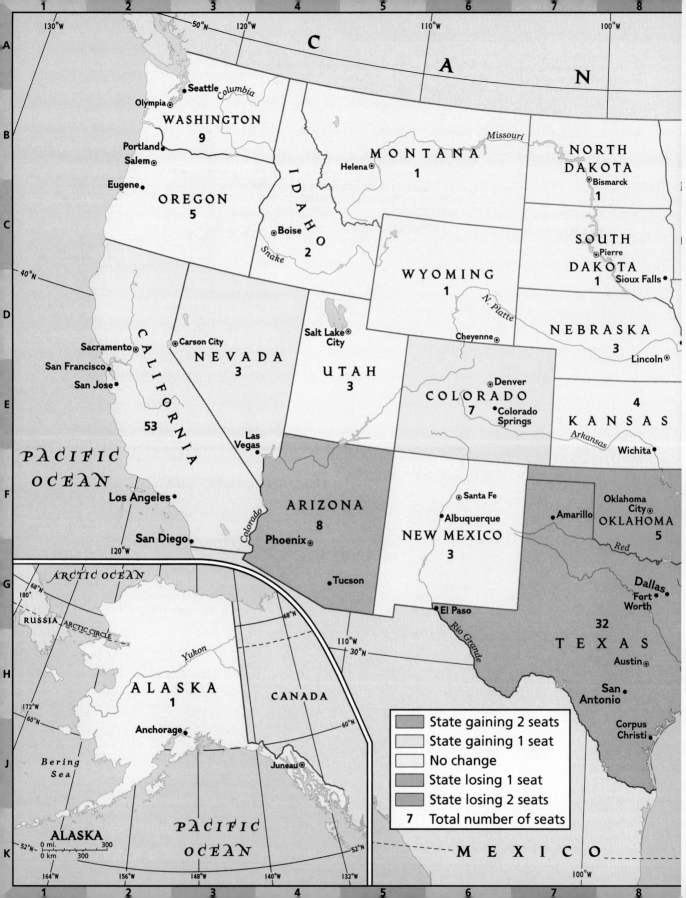

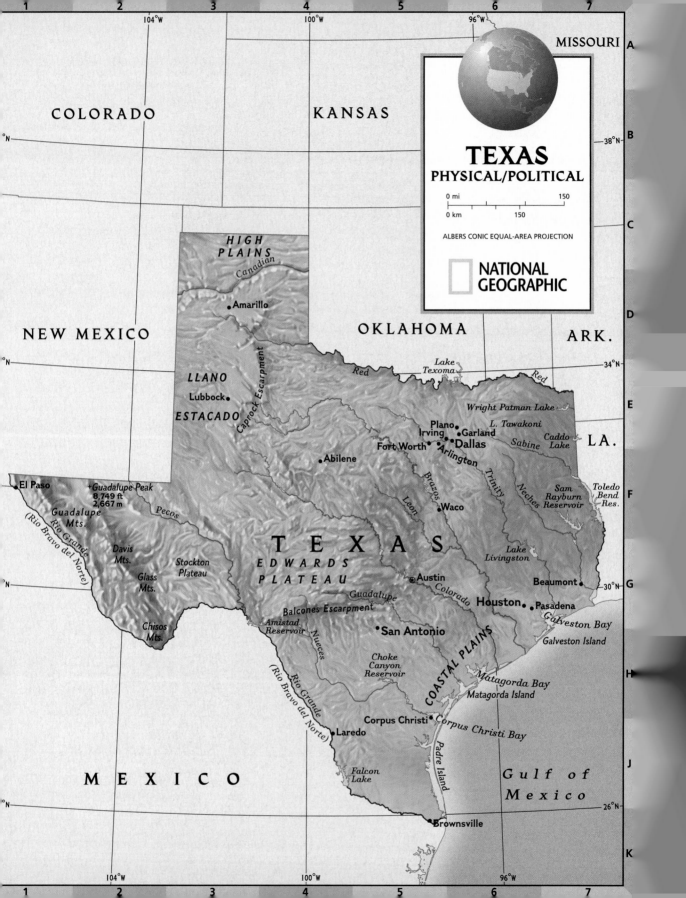

TEXAS
LAND USE

0 mi — 150
0 km — 150

ALBERS CONIC EQUAL-AREA PROJECTION

NATIONAL GEOGRAPHIC

MISSOURI

COLORADO

KANSAS

NEW MEXICO

OKLAHOMA

ARK.

LA.

T E X A S

MEXICO

Gulf of Mexico

Legend:
- Forestry
- Agriculture
- Forestry and Agriculture
- Stock raising on ranch
- Wetlands
- Urban land
- Fishing

Cities and places:
Amarillo · Lubbock · Wichita Falls · Sherman · Texarkana · Denton · Lewisville · Plano · L. Tawakoni · Garland · Irving · Mesquite · Fort Worth · Dallas · Arlington · Sabine · Caddo Lake · Longview · Tyler · Abilene · El Paso · Guadalupe Peak 8,749 ft 2,667 m · Odessa · Midland · Waco · San Angelo · Killeen · Temple · Bryan · College Station · Lake Livingston · Beaumont · Port Arthur · Pasadena · Austin · Houston · Texas City · Galveston · Galveston Island · San Antonio · Amistad Reservoir · Victoria · Matagorda Bay · Matagorda Island · Choke Canyon Reservoir · Corpus Christi · Corpus Christi Bay · Laredo · Padre Island · Falcon Lake · McAllen · Harlingen · Brownsville · Sam Rayburn Reservoir · Toledo Bend Res. · Wright Patman Lake · Lake Texoma

Rivers and water:
Canadian · Red · Pecos · Rio Grande (Rio Bravo del Norte) · Brazos · Leon · Trinity · Neches · Colorado · Guadalupe · Nueces

Latitude/Longitude:
104°W · 100°W · 96°W · 38°N · 34°N · 30°N · 26°N

Geography Handbook

Padre Island ▶
National Seashore

▲ Palo Duro
Canyon

Wildflowers of Texas ▶
Hill Country

What Is Geography?

The story of Texas begins with geography—the study of the earth in all of its variety. Geography describes the earth's land, water, and plant and animal life. It is the study of places and the complex relationships between people and their environments.

Geography of Texas

Texas is a land of startling physical differences. It is also a state of diverse groups of people. A study of geography can help explain how Texas acquired its diversity.

Texas—with a total land area of 267,277 square miles (430,316 sq. km)—is the second-largest state in size. Only Alaska is bigger.

Location

Texas has four major geographical regions. It shares borders with four other states—Louisiana, Arkansas, Oklahoma, and New Mexico. An international boundary between Texas and Mexico and the Gulf of Mexico form the southern and southeastern borders.

Our State's Growth

Within the borders of Texas stretch a rich variety of landscapes—forests, hot deserts, sandy beaches, rolling prairies, Hill Country lakes, and majestic mountains. Because of its large size and diverse environments, Texas throughout its history has offered many opportunities to people from other states and countries. Over the centuries people from Mexico, Europe, Africa, Asia, and other parts of the Americas have journeyed here. Today nearly 21 million people make their homes in Texas.

▼ El Capitan rises to 8,085 feet

NATIONAL GEOGRAPHIC

Texas: Physical

N
W—E
S

High Plains

OKLAHOMA

35°N

NEW MEXICO

Red R.

ARK.

Caprock Escarpment

Permian Basin

Pecos R.

Colorado R.

Brazos R.

Sabine R.

LA.

Davis Mts.

Edwards Plateau

TEXAS

⊙ Austin

Coastal Plains

30°N

Balcones Escarpment

Elevations

Feet	Meters
10,000	3,000
5,000	1,500
2,000	600
1,000	300
0	0

⊙ State capital

Rio Grande

Gulf of Mexico

MEXICO

0 mi. 200
0 km 200
Albers Conic Equal-Area projection

100°W

How Does Geography Influence History?

G eographic factors—landforms, waterways, natural resources—have shaped Texas's history. Here are some examples of geography's influences in history that are highlighted in Texas and Texans.

Unit 1 The Geography of Texas Texas geography is closely linked to its history. Location, resources, and climate have made it attractive to people for thousands of years.

Unit 2 Explorers and Settlers Texas's location made it an ideal meeting ground for various cultures. Arriving Spanish explorers both blended and clashed with Native American cultures. When France sent an expedition out under the explorer La Salle, Spain moved quickly to establish missions and presidios.

Unit 3 Struggle for Independence Geography played a vital role in the Battle of San Jacinto, the greatest military victory in the history of Texas. Incredibly, Sam Houston led about 800 soldiers across a flat prairie without being seen. Santa Anna and his troops were camped almost a mile away, hidden behind a natural rise in the terrain. The low ridge protected the Mexicans from Houston's artillery, but it also hid the Texans from view. When the Texas soldiers marched directly toward Santa Anna's army, the ridge hid them until they were within 200 yards (183 m) of the camp.

Unit 4 The Republic of Texas The vast reaches of Texas attracted land-hungry settlers from the United States and other countries. Texans of Anglo, German, Czech, and Irish nationality—along with Tejanos of Mexican heritage—played important parts in creating a new republic.

Unit 5 The Lone Star State Mexico's refusal to acknowledge Texas's annexation to the United States led to the Mexican–American War. As part of the South and a neighbor of Mexico, Texas played a key role in supplying arms and money to the Confederacy.

Unit 6 Growth and Development Fertile soils and grassy plains allowed ranching and farming to develop rapidly. To overcome problems caused by the sheer size of Texas and the distance between population centers, railroads helped Texans move their products across the state and nation.

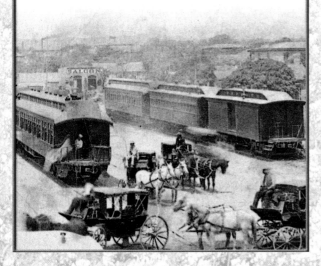

Unit 7 Early Twentieth Century The discovery of oil and the oil boom that followed resulted in great industrial expansion. Today Texas is dealing with the results of that oil boom as thousands of abandoned wells are located and plugged. Left alone, the wells can affect the environment.

Unit 8 Into the Modern Era The theme of human-environmental interaction is the focus of this unit. The change from a rural agricultural state to a technological urban society had both benefits and costs. Traffic, pollution, and threatened plant and animal life are all challenges facing Texans today.

Unit 9 Government of Texas Recent economic booms have increased migration into Texas. Houston and Dallas–Fort Worth are among the largest cities in the country. Meeting the needs of diverse populations is one of the biggest challenges facing the Texas legislature.

I Study Geography?

To understand how our world is connected, some geographers have broken down the study of geography into five themes. **The Five Themes of Geography** are (1) location, (2) place, (3) human-environment interaction, (4) movement, and (5) regions.

Six Essential Elements

Recently, geographers have begun to look at geography in a different way. They break down the study of geography into **Six Essential Elements,** which are explained below. Being aware of these elements will help you sort out what you are learning about geography.

Element 1

The World in Spatial Terms

Geographers first take a look at where a place is located. **Location** serves as a starting point by asking "Where is it?" Knowing the location of places helps you develop an awareness of the world around you.

Element 2

Places and Regions

Place has a special meaning in geography. It means more than where a place is. It also describes what a place is like. These features may be physical characteristics such as landforms, climate, and plant or animal life. They may also be human characteristics, including language and way of life.

To help organize their study, geographers often group places or areas into regions. **Regions** are united by one or more common characteristics.

Element 3

Physical Systems

When studying places and regions, geographers analyze how **physical systems**—such as hurricanes, volcanoes, and glaciers—shape the earth's surface. They also look at communities of plants and animals that depend upon one another and their surroundings for survival.

Element 4

Human Systems

Geographers also examine human systems, or how people have shaped our world. They look at how boundary lines are determined and analyze why people settle in certain places and not in others. A key theme in geography is the continual **movement** of people, ideas, and goods.

Element 5

Environment and Society

"How does the relationship between people and their natural surroundings influence the way people live?" This is one of the questions that the theme of **human-environment interaction** answers. This theme also shows how people use the environment and how their actions affect the environment.

Element 6

The Uses of Geography

Knowledge of geography helps people understand the relationships among people, places, and environments over time. Understanding geography, and knowing how to use the tools and technology available to study it, prepares you for life in our modern society.

Using Globes and Maps

Photographs from space show the earth in its true form—a great ball spinning around the sun. The most accurate way to depict the earth is as a globe. A globe gives a true picture of the relative size and shape of landmasses and bodies of water. Globes accurately show distance and direction between places.

A map is a flat drawing of all or part of the earth's surface. Maps can show small areas in great detail. People use maps to locate places, plot routes, and judge distances. Maps can also display information such as political boundaries, population densities, or even voting returns.

Hemispheres

To locate places on the earth, geographers use a system of imaginary lines that crisscross the globe. The Equator divides the earth into "half spheres," or **hemispheres.** Everything north of the Equator is in the Northern Hemisphere. Everything south of the Equator is in the Southern Hemisphere.

Another imaginary line runs from north to south. Find this line—called the **Prime Meridian** or the Meridian of Greenwich—on a globe. Everything east of the Prime Meridian for 180 degrees is in the Eastern Hemisphere. Everything west of the Prime Meridian for 180 degrees is in the Western Hemisphere.

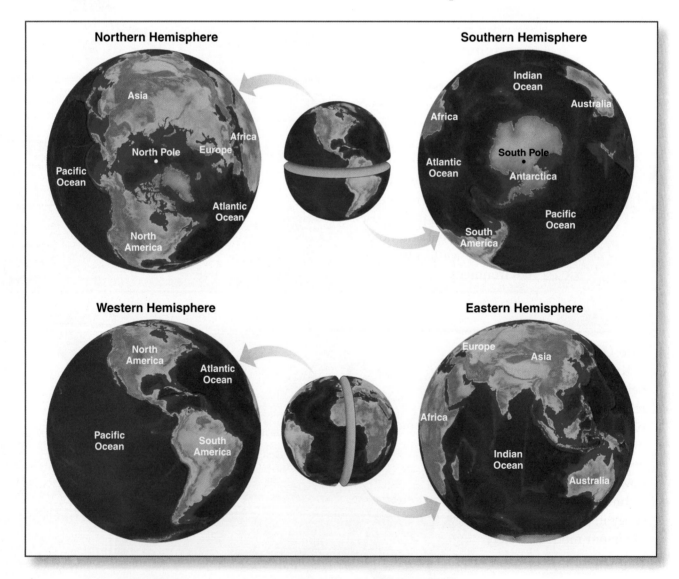

Northern Hemisphere
Asia
Africa
Europe
North Pole
Pacific Ocean
Atlantic Ocean
North America

Southern Hemisphere
Indian Ocean
Australia
Africa
South Pole
Atlantic Ocean
Antarctica
Pacific Ocean
South America

Western Hemisphere
North America
Atlantic Ocean
Pacific Ocean
South America

Eastern Hemisphere
Europe
Asia
Africa
Indian Ocean
Australia

Latitude and Longitude

The Equator and the Prime Meridian are the starting points for two sets of lines used to find any location. Parallels show **latitude,** or distance measured in degrees north and south of the Equator. The letter *N* or *S* following the degree symbol tells you if the location is north or south of the Equator.

Meridians run from pole to pole and crisscross parallels. Meridians show **longitude,** or distance measured in degrees east (E) or west (W) of the Prime Meridian. Opposite the Prime Meridian at 180° is the International Date Line.

Two important parallels in between the poles are the **Tropic of Cancer** ($23\frac{1}{2}$°N latitude) and the **Tropic of Capricorn** ($23\frac{1}{2}$°S latitude). The Arctic Circle lies at $66\frac{1}{2}$°N latitude and the Antarctic Circle lies at $66\frac{1}{2}$°S latitude.

Absolute Location

Lines of latitude and longitude cross each other in the form of a **grid system.** You can find a place's absolute location by naming the latitude and longitude lines that cross exactly at that place. For example, the city of Tokyo, Japan, is located at 36°N latitude and 140°E longitude.

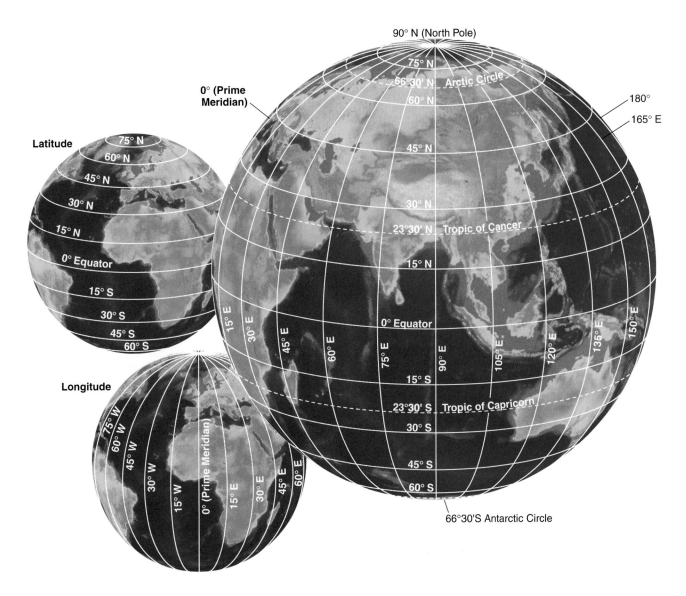

Using Globes and Maps

Why Use Maps?

Globes are the best, most accurate way to show the round earth. Using a globe has its difficulties, though. First, a globe is too big and awkward to carry around. Also, a globe cannot show you the whole world at one time. For these reasons, geographers use maps also. A map is made by taking data from a round globe and placing it on a flat surface. It is important to remember that the earth's features, which are shown accurately on a globe, become distorted when the curves of a globe become straight lines on a flat map.

Map Projections

Imagine taking the whole peel from an orange and trying to flatten it on a table. You would either have to cut it or stretch parts of it. Mapmakers face a similar problem in showing the surface of the round earth on a flat map. When the earth's surface is flattened, big gaps open up. To fill in the gaps, mapmakers stretch parts of the earth. They choose to show either the correct shapes of places or their correct sizes. It is impossible to show both. As a result, mapmakers have developed different **projections,** or ways of showing the earth on a flat piece of paper. Each projection has its strengths and weaknesses. None is a completely accurate representation of the earth, but all prove useful in one way or another.

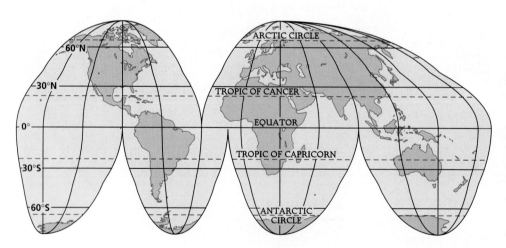

Goode's Interrupted Equal Area Projection

◀ This projection looks something like a flattened orange peel might look. Goode's Interrupted Equal Area projection shows continents close to their true shapes and sizes. Distances —especially in the oceans— are less accurate. This projection would be helpful if you wanted to compare land area data about the continents.

Mercator Projection ▶

The Mercator projection shows land shapes fairly accurately, but not size or distance. Areas that are located far from the Equator are quite distorted on this projection. Alaska, for example, appears much larger than it does on a globe. The Mercator projection does show true directions, however. This makes it very useful for sea travel.

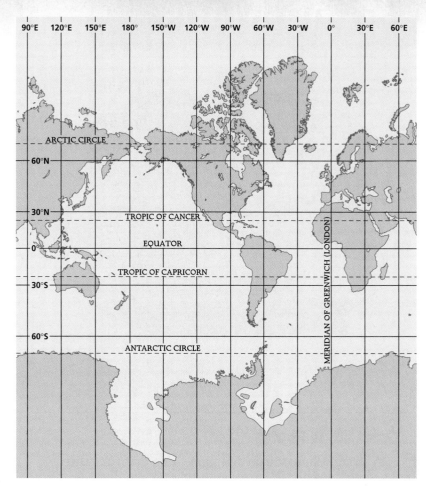

▼ Robinson Projection

A map using the Robinson projection shows size and shape with less distortion than does a Mercator map. Land on the western and eastern sides of a Robinson map appear much as they do on a globe. The areas most distorted on this projection are near the North and South poles. You may notice that many atlases use Robinson projections.

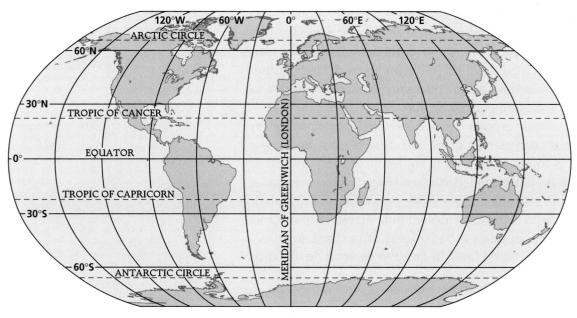

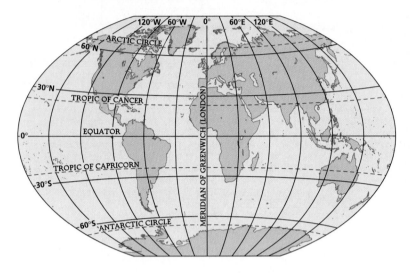

Winkel Tripel Projection

Mapmakers are always looking for a more accurate way to show the round earth on flat paper. The Winkel Tripel projection gives a good overall view of the continents' shapes and sizes. You may notice a close similarity between the Winkel Tripel and Robinson projections. Land areas in a Winkel Tripel projection are not as distorted near the poles as they are in the Robinson projection. In 1998 the National Geographic Society began using the Winkel Tripel projection for its reference maps of the world.

Great Circle Routes

A straight line of true direction—one that runs directly from west to east, for example—is not always the shortest distance between two points on Earth. This is due to the curvature of the earth. To find the shortest distance between any two places, take a piece of string and stretch it around a globe from one point to the other. The string will form part of a *great circle*, or imaginary line that follows the curve of the earth. Traveling along part of a great circle is called following a **great circle route.** Ship captains and airline pilots use great circle routes to reduce travel time and save fuel.

The idea of a great circle shows one important difference between using a globe and using a map. Because a globe is round, it accurately shows great circle routes, as shown on the partial globe (see Map B). However, on a flat map, such as the Mercator projection (see Map A), the great circle distance (dotted line) between Tokyo and Los Angeles appears to be far longer than the true direction distance (solid line). In fact, the great circle distance is 345 miles (555 km) shorter.

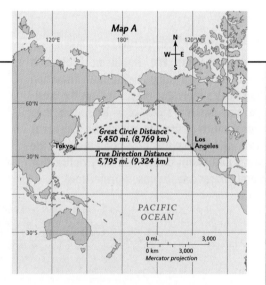

Map A

Great Circle Distance
5,450 mi. (8,769 km)

True Direction Distance
5,795 mi. (9,324 km)

PACIFIC OCEAN

0 mi. 3,000
0 km 3,000
Mercator projection

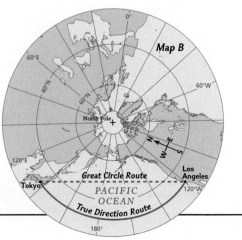

Map B

North Pole

Great Circle Route

Los Angeles

Tokyo

PACIFIC OCEAN

True Direction Route

Maps include several important tools to help you interpret the information shown. Learning to use these map tools will help you read the symbolic language of maps more easily.

Map Key Cartographers use a variety of symbols to represent map information. The **map key** explains the lines, symbols, and colors used on the map. It might include the symbols used for roads, highways, railroads, cities and towns, natural resources, etc. The map on this page shows the various climate regions of the United States. The key shows what colors are used to represent each of the climate regions.

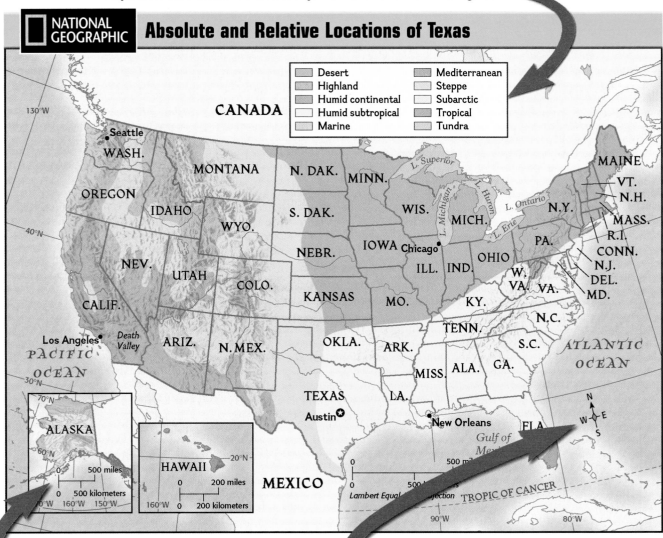

NATIONAL GEOGRAPHIC

Absolute and Relative Locations of Texas

	Desert		Mediterranean
	Highland		Steppe
	Humid continental		Subarctic
	Humid subtropical		Tropical
	Marine		Tundra

Lambert Equal Area Projection

Scale Every map is a representation of a part of the earth. The **scale bar** shows the relationship between map measurements and actual distance. Scale can be measured with a ruler to calculate actual distances in standard or metric measurements. On this inset map, 3/8 inch equals 500 miles.

Compass Rose An important first step in reading any map is to find the **compass rose**. It shows where the cardinal directions—north, south, east, and west—are positioned. Sometimes a compass rose may point in only one direction because the other directions can be determined in relation to the given direction.

Using Graphs, Charts, and Diagrams

A **graph** *is a way of summarizing and presenting information visually. Each part of a graph gives useful information. First read the graph's title to find out its subject. Then read the labels along the graph's axes—the vertical line along the left side of the graph and the horizontal line along the bottom of the graph. One axis will tell you what is being measured. The other axis tells what units of measurement are being used.*

Bar Graphs

Graphs that use bars or wide lines to compare data visually are called **bar graphs.** Look carefully at the bar graph below, which explains how Texas state budgeted funds are distributed. The vertical axis shows the amount of money (in billions of U.S. dollars). The horizontal axis identifies various departments that receive state funding. By comparing the length of the bars above each state department, you can quickly compare the relative amount of money received by different departments.

The dotted line at the top of the bar graph indicates the total budgeted amount. This allows comparison not only between various departments, but as part of the whole budget. For example, education receives something less than half of the State of Texas budget for 2002–2003. Bar graphs are especially useful for comparing quantities.

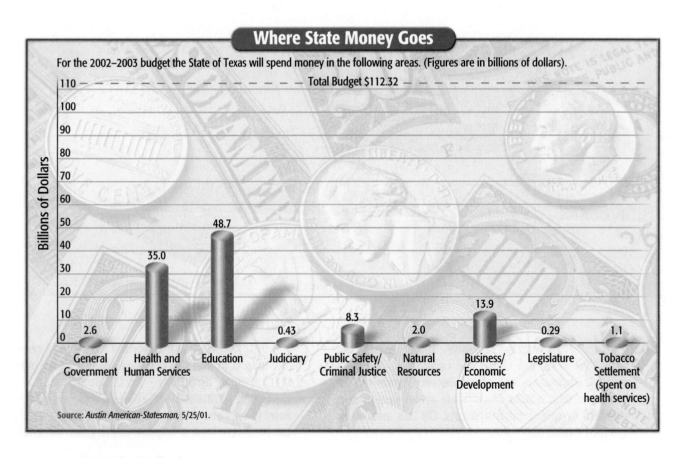

Where State Money Goes

For the 2002–2003 budget the State of Texas will spend money in the following areas. (Figures are in billions of dollars).

Total Budget $112.32

Billions of Dollars

General Government	Health and Human Services	Education	Judiciary	Public Safety/ Criminal Justice	Natural Resources	Business/ Economic Development	Legislature	Tobacco Settlement (spent on health services)
2.6	35.0	48.7	0.43	8.3	2.0	13.9	0.29	1.1

Source: *Austin American-Statesman, 5/25/01.*

Line Graphs

A **line graph** is a useful tool for showing change over a period of time. The title tells you the subject being measured. The amounts being measured are plotted on the grid above each year, and then are connected by a line. Line graphs sometimes have two or more lines plotted on them.

This line graph shows the number of students in the Texas school population from 1850 to 1950. The vertical axis lists the numbers of students and the horizontal axis identifies the years. Put your finger on the year 1910 and run it up to where it meets the solid line. Look to the left and you will see that the spot where the vertical and horizontal lines meet is between 800 and 1000. Approximately 920 times 1000 (or 920,000) students were enrolled in Texas schools in 1910.

Line graphs also allow you to see trends. School population increased at a fairly steady rate until 1930 when the school population

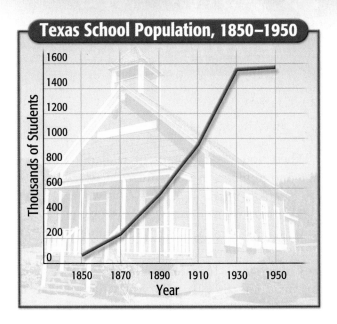

Texas School Population, 1850–1950

leveled off and stayed constant for the next twenty years. The graph does not tell you why this occurred, however. For that, more research is needed.

Circle Graphs

You can use **circle graphs** when you want to show how the whole of something is divided into its parts. Because of their shape, circle graphs are often called **pie graphs** or **pie charts.** Each "slice" represents a part of a percentage of the whole "pie."

Like bar graphs, circle graphs present a visual representation of ratio or proportion. Circle graphs are most effective when there are a limited number of elements being compared. On the circle graph at left, the whole circle represents the population of the Spanish settlements in Texas in 1790. The graph shows us immediately that males made up a larger part of the population. For every 55 males living in Spanish colonial settlements in Texas in 1790, there were only 45 females.

Population of Spanish Settlements, 1790

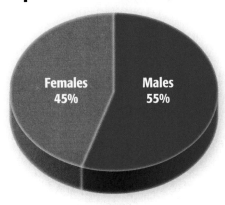

Females 45%

Males 55%

Using Graphs, Charts, and Diagrams

Charts

When you want to present related facts and numbers in an organized way, you can use a **chart.**

The most common type of chart is a **table.** A table arranges data, especially numbers, in rows and columns for easy reference. To interpret a table, first read the title. It tells you what information the table is presenting. Next read the labels at the top of each column and on the left side of the table. They explain what the numbers or data on the table are measuring.

The table above compares the size of districts in Texas before the "one-man, one-vote" law was passed. The column on the far left tells that the information in the other columns all refers to a particular district number.

Sometimes charts are used to summarize information in a concise way and to show the relationship between various elements. The table below summarizes the major roles of each branch of Texas government. It also illustrates that no branch is higher than the other—they are equal parts of the government. This allows you to review material and to compare main ideas easily.

District Size Before Redistricting in 1953

District	Representative	Home	Population of District
1	Wright Patman	Texarkana	276,945
4	Sam Rayburn	Bonham	227,735
5	J. Frank Wilson	Dallas	614,799
6	Olin Teague	College Station	228,112
8	Albert Thomas	Houston	806,701
20	Paul Kilday	San Antonio	500,460

The Three Branches of Texas Government

Legislative Branch	Judicial Branch	Executive Branch
What they do:	What they do:	What they do:
Make the laws of the state.	Interpret the laws of the state.	Enforce the laws of the state.
Who they are:	Who they are:	Who they are:
• Senate (31 members) • House of Representatives (150 members)	• Supreme Court • Court of Criminal Appeals • District Courts • County Courts • Commissioners Courts • Justice of the Peace Courts	• Governor • Lieutenant Governor • Secretary of State • Comptroller of Public Accounts • Commissioner of the General Land Office • Commissioner of Agriculture • Attorney General

Flow Charts

A **flow chart** shows the order of how things happen, or how they are related to each other. One popular type of flow chart illustrates cause and effect. This cause-and-effect chart illustrates causes of Spain's renewed interest in settling Texas.

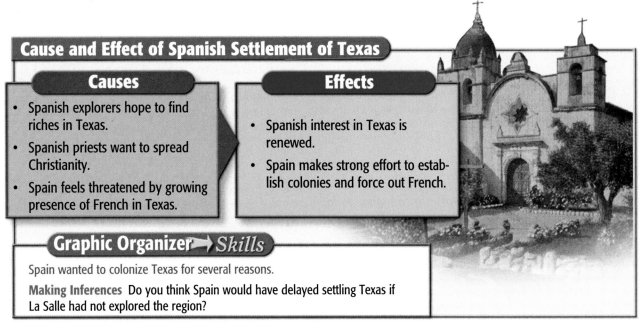

Cause and Effect of Spanish Settlement of Texas

Causes
- Spanish explorers hope to find riches in Texas.
- Spanish priests want to spread Christianity.
- Spain feels threatened by growing presence of French in Texas.

Effects
- Spanish interest in Texas is renewed.
- Spain makes strong effort to establish colonies and force out French.

Graphic Organizer → Skills

Spain wanted to colonize Texas for several reasons.

Making Inferences Do you think Spain would have delayed settling Texas if La Salle had not explored the region?

Diagrams

Diagrams are drawings that show steps in a process, point out the parts of an object, or explain how something works. The diagram below is an elevation profile. It shows an exaggerated profile, or side view, of the land as if it were sliced and you were viewing it from the side. This elevation profile of Texas shows low areas and mountains. The line of latitude at the bottom tells you the line along which this profile was "sliced."

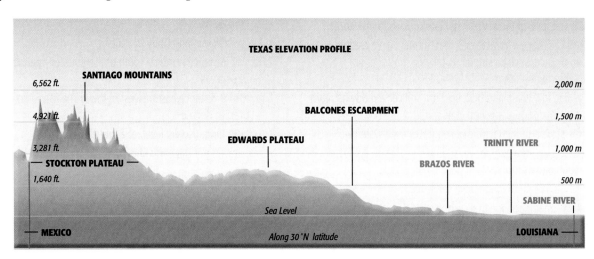

TEXAS ELEVATION PROFILE

SANTIAGO MOUNTAINS
6,562 ft.   2,000 m

                                    BALCONES ESCARPMENT
4,921 ft.   1,500 m

                        EDWARDS PLATEAU   TRINITY RIVER
3,281 ft.   1,000 m
STOCKTON PLATEAU   BRAZOS RIVER
1,640 ft.   500 m

                                                                          SABINE RIVER
                            Sea Level

MEXICO   LOUISIANA
                    Along 30°N latitude

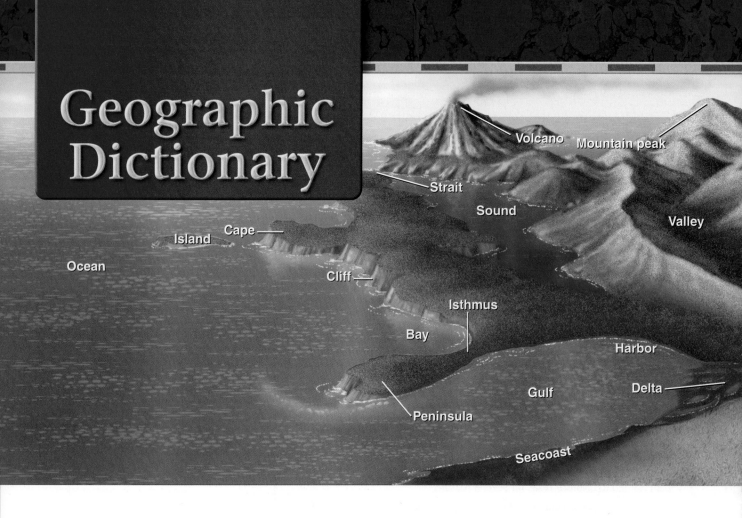

Geographic Dictionary

Volcano
Mountain peak
Strait
Sound
Valley
Island
Cape
Ocean
Cliff
Isthmus
Bay
Harbor
Peninsula
Gulf
Delta
Seacoast

absolute location exact location of a place on the earth described by global coordinates

basin area of land drained by a given river and its branches; area of land surrounded by lands of higher elevations

bay part of a large body of water that extends into a shoreline, generally smaller than a gulf

canyon deep and narrow valley with steep walls

cape point of land that extends into a river, lake, or ocean

channel wide strait or waterway between two landmasses that lie close to each other; deep part of a river or other waterway

cliff steep, high wall of rock, earth, or ice

continent one of the seven large landmasses on the earth

cultural feature characteristic that humans have created in a place, such as language, religion, housing, or settlement pattern

delta flat, low-lying land built up from soil carried downstream by a river and deposited at its mouth

divide stretch of high land that separates river systems

downstream direction in which a river or stream flows from its source to its mouth

elevation height of land above sea level

Equator imaginary line that runs around the earth halfway between the North and South Poles; used as the starting point to measure degrees of north and south latitude

glacier large, thick body of slowly moving ice

gulf part of a large body of water that extends into a shoreline, generally larger and more deeply indented than a bay

harbor a sheltered place along a shoreline where ships can anchor safely

highland elevated land area such as a hill, mountain, or plateau

hill elevated land with sloping sides and rounded summit; generally smaller than a mountain

island land area, smaller than a continent, completely surrounded by water

isthmus narrow stretch of land connecting two larger land areas

lake a sizable inland body of water

latitude distance north or south of the Equator, measured in degrees

longitude distance east or west of the Prime Meridian, measured in degrees

lowland land, usually level, at a low elevation

map drawing of the earth shown on a flat surface

meridian one of many lines on the global grid running from the North Pole to the South Pole; used to measure degrees of longitude

mesa broad, flat-topped landform with steep sides; smaller than a plateau

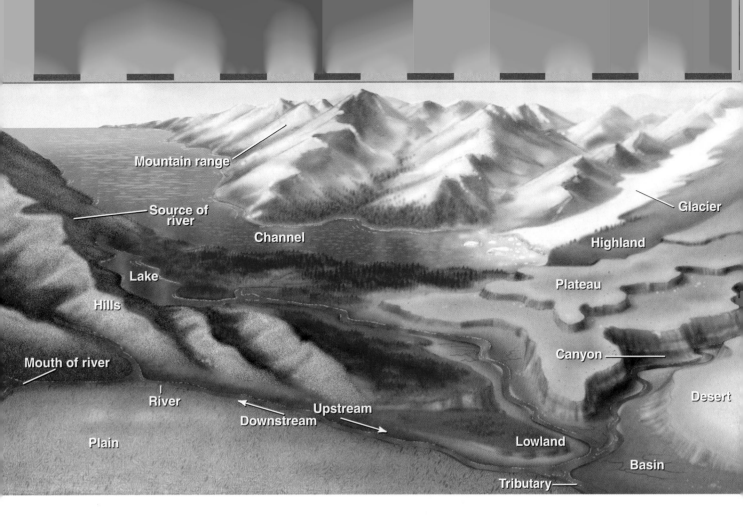

Mountain range

Source of river

Channel

Glacier

Highland

Lake

Plateau

Hills

Canyon

Mouth of river

Desert

River

Upstream

Downstream

Plain

Lowland

Basin

Tributary

mountain land with steep sides that rises sharply (1,000 feet or more) from surrounding land; generally larger and more rugged than a hill

mountain peak pointed top of a mountain

mountain range a series of connected mountains

mouth (of a river) place where a stream or river flows into a larger body of water

ocean one of the four major bodies of salt water that surround the continents

ocean current stream of either cold or warm water that moves in a definite direction through an ocean

parallel one of many lines on the global grid that circle the earth north or south of the Equator; used to measure degrees of latitude

peninsula body of land jutting into a lake or ocean, surrounded on three sides by water

physical feature characteristic of a place occurring naturally, such as a landform, body of water, climate pattern, or resource

plain area of level land, usually at a low elevation and often covered with grasses

plateau area of flat or rolling land at a high elevation, about 300–3,000 feet high

Prime Meridian line of the global grid running from the North Pole to the South Pole through Greenwich, England; starting point for measuring degrees of east and west longitude

relief changes in elevation over a given area of land

river large natural stream of water that runs through the land

sea large body of water completely or partly surrounded by land

seacoast land lying next to a sea or ocean

sea level position on land level with surface of nearby ocean or sea

sound body of water between a coastline and one or more islands off the coast

source (of a river) place where a river or stream begins, often in highlands

strait narrow stretch of water joining two larger bodies of water

tributary small river or stream that flows into a large river or stream; a branch of the river

upstream direction opposite the flow of a river; toward the source of a river or stream

valley area of low land between hills or mountains

volcano mountain created as liquid rock or ash erupts from inside the earth

Reading for Information

Think about your textbook as a tool that helps you learn more about the world around you. It is an example of nonfiction writing—it describes real-life events, people, ideas, and places. Here is a menu of reading strategies that will help you become a better textbook reader. As you come to passages in your textbook that you don't understand, refer to these reading strategies for help.

✔ Before You Read

Set a Purpose
- Why are you reading the textbook?
- How does the subject relate to your life?
- How might you be able to use what you learn in your own life?

Preview
- Read the chapter title to find what the topic will be.
- Read the subtitles to see what you will learn about the topic.
- Skim the photos, charts, graphs, or maps. How do they support the topic?
- Look for vocabulary words that are bold-faced. How are they defined?

Draw From Your Own Background
- What have you read or heard concerning new information on the topic?
- How is the new information different from what you already know?
- How will the information that you already know help you understand the new information?

Question

- What is the main idea?
- How do the photos, charts, graphs, and maps support the main idea?

Connect

- Think about people, places, and events in your own life. Are there any similarities with those in your textbook?
- Can you relate the textbook information to other areas of your life?

Predict

- Predict events or outcomes by using clues and information that you already know.
- Change your predictions as you read and gather new information.

Visualize

- Pay careful attention to details and descriptions.
- Create graphic organizers to show relationships that you find in the information.

Look for Clues As You Read

Comparison and Contrast Sentences

- Look for clue words and phrases that signal comparison, such as similarly, just as, both, in common, also, and too.
- Look for clue words and phrases that signal contrast, such as on the other hand, in contrast to, however, different, instead of, rather than, but, and unlike.

Cause-and-Effect Sentences

- Look for clue words and phrases such as because, as a result, therefore, that is why, since, so, for this reason, and consequently.

Chronological Sentences

- Look for clue words and phrases such as after, before, first, next, last, during, finally, earlier, later, since, and then.

After You Read

Summarize

- Describe the main idea and how the details support it.
- Use your own words to explain what you have read.

Assess

- What was the main idea?
- Did the text clearly support the main idea?
- Did you learn anything new from the material?
- Can you use this new information in other school subjects or at home?
- What other sources could you use to find more information about the topic?

UNIT ★

1

The Geography of Texas

Why It Matters

As you study Unit 1, you will learn about the geography of Texas. Geographers are interested in the places where events occur. They ask, "Where?" Historians are interested in events as they occur in time. Among the questions they ask is, "When?" Both geographers and historians want to know "Why?" It is, perhaps, the most important question of all. For you to understand why events in Texas history occurred, you will need to understand both where events occurred and when they occurred.

Primary Sources Library

See pages 684–685 for primary source readings to accompany Unit 1.

Wildflowers and yucca plants thrive at the foot of Nugent Mountain in Big Bend National Park.

"*Texas is, in many respects, the most eligible part of North America.*"

—*Mary Austin Holley (1784–1846)*

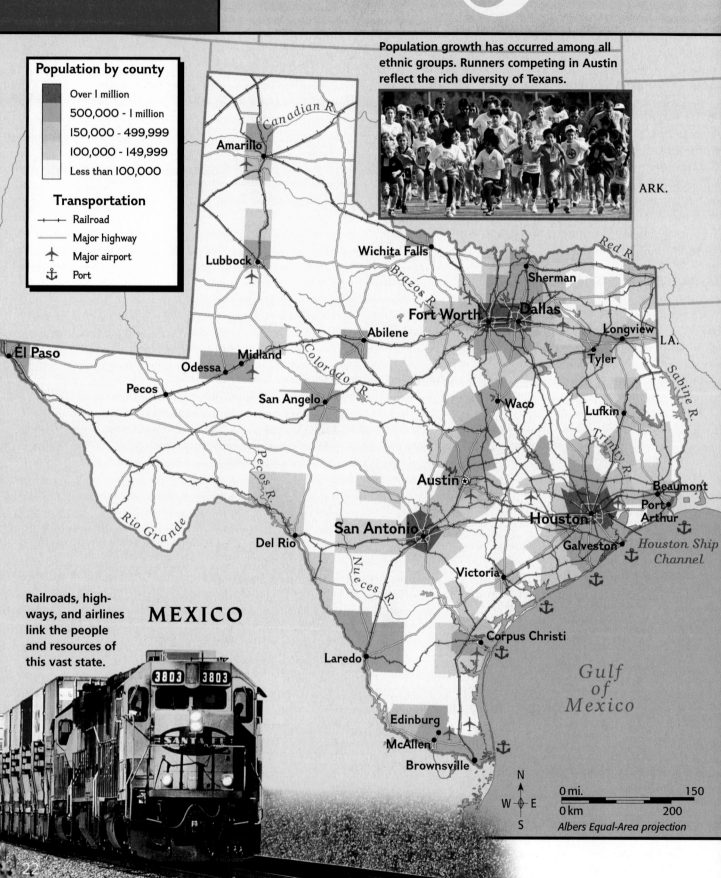

Population by county

- Over 1 million
- 500,000 - 1 million
- 150,000 - 499,999
- 100,000 - 149,999
- Less than 100,000

Transportation

- ┼┼ Railroad
- ── Major highway
- ✈ Major airport
- ⚓ Port

Population growth has occurred among all ethnic groups. Runners competing in Austin reflect the rich diversity of Texans.

ARK.

Canadian R.

Amarillo

Lubbock

El Paso

Pecos

Odessa

Midland

San Angelo

Del Rio

MEXICO

Railroads, highways, and airlines link the people and resources of this vast state.

Rio Grande

Pecos R.

Nueces R.

Colorado R.

Brazos R.

Wichita Falls

Sherman

Fort Worth

Dallas

Abilene

Longview

Tyler

Red R.

LA.

Sabine R.

Waco

Lufkin

Trinity R.

Austin ✪

Beaumont

Port Arthur

Houston

Galveston

Houston Ship Channel

San Antonio

Victoria

Corpus Christi

Laredo

Gulf of Mexico

Edinburg

McAllen

Brownsville

3803 3803

SANTA FE

N
W ✛ E
S

0 mi.   150
0 km   200
Albers Equal-Area projection

Modern skyscrapers dot the night skyline of Dallas. Dallas is the second largest city in Texas. Combined with Fort Worth and other neighboring communities, it forms the state's largest metropolitan area.

MISSISSIPPI

A drilling ship probes for oil off the Texas coast. The oil industry has stimulated population growth.

The rapidly growing population of Texas is expected to double in the next 50 years.

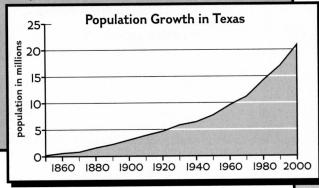

Population Growth in Texas

population in millions

25
20
15
10
5
0

1860 1880 1900 1920 1940 1960 1980 2000

POPULATION PATTERNS

Today eight out of ten Texans live in urban areas. The largest, most crowded cities developed in the eastern part of Texas. People originally settled there because they found moist, fertile lowlands where they could grow crops. Later, the discovery of oil, natural gas, and other resources attracted workers to the region. Slightly more than half of all Texans live in the metropolitan areas of Houston, Dallas–Fort Worth, and San Antonio.

More than four million people representing many different cultures have settled in and around Houston. Originally a cotton-shipping port, the city expanded rapidly after railroads were built and oil was discovered nearby. Today Houston is one of the busiest ports in the country and a leading petrochemical center.

Dallas and Fort Worth, located in the heart of a rich agricultural region, have expanded toward each other. Like Houston, Dallas started out as a cotton market and grew dramatically when oil was found. Fort Worth, originally a military outpost, mushroomed into a large cattle-shipping center after railroads were constructed. Today Dallas–Fort Worth has evolved into a single large metropolitan area with a wide variety of industries, including oil refining, aircraft and electronic equipment manufacturing, and food processing.

Good transportation is key to population growth. Many railroads and highways in south central Texas meet in San Antonio. It has been a commercial center since its early days of selling supplies to cowboys as they started north to sell cattle. The population of San Antonio jumped dramatically when the military established bases and training facilities there during World War II.

Vast transportation and communication networks link Texas's major metropolitan areas to the people and resources of smaller towns and cities throughout the state and the rest of the world.

LEARNING from GEOGRAPHY

1. Where do most of the people in Texas live today?
2. How do you think railroads and highways have affected settlement patterns in the state? How have settlements affected railroads and highways?

23

CHAPTER 1

Land of Contrasts

Why It Matters

Texas is a diverse state in many different ways, including its landscapes and climate. Knowing about the basic geographical features of Texas provides a good context for learning about the history of Texas.

The Impact Today

Understanding geography helps us to understand events that shape our lives today. Although people modify their environment through technology, all societies are dependent upon a natural resource base. The location of those resources influences where Texans live and how they make a living.

c. 600 million B.C.
★ Broad, shallow seas covered much of Texas

c. 300 million B.C.
★ Ouachita Mountains uplifted across Texas; seas receded

c. 1 billion B.C.
★ Llano Uplift formed

Texas

United States — *c. 1 billion B.C.* — *c. 600 million B.C.* — *c. 200 million B.C.*

World

c. 190 million B.C.
• Dinosaurs and flowering plants covered North America

Guadalupe Mountains National Park contains some of the most dramatic landscape in Texas.

FOLDABLES™
Study Organizer

TAKS PRACTICE

Summarizing Information Study Foldable
Make this foldable to help you summarize what you learn about the geography of Texas by focusing on six key words and phrases.

Step 1 Fold a sheet of paper in half from side to side.

Fold it so the left edge lays about $\frac{1}{2}$ inch from the right edge.

Step 2 Turn the paper and fold it into thirds.

Step 3 Unfold and cut the top layer only along both folds.

This will make three tabs.

Step 4 Now cut each of the three tabs in half and label as shown.

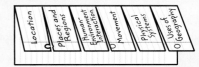

Location | Places and Regions | Human-Environment Interaction | Movement | Physical Systems | Uses of Geography

Reading and Writing As you read the chapter, write definitions and examples under the appropriate tabs of your foldable to learn why Texas is called a "Land of Contrasts."

TEXAS HISTORY Online

Chapter Overview
Visit the texans.glencoe.com Web site and click on **Chapter 1—Chapter Overviews** to preview chapter information.

c. 140 million B.C.
★ *Seas covered Texas again*

c. 65 million B.C.

c. 2 million B.C.

c. 65 million B.C.
• *Rocky Mountains began to form*

c. 2 million B.C.
• *Ice Age began*

Understanding Texas Geography

Guide to Reading

Main Idea
Geographers look at a variety of topics as they learn about a place.

Key Terms
geography, environment, location, absolute location, relative location, place, region, human-environment interaction, movement, cultural diffusion, diameter

Reading Strategy
Organizing Information Complete a chart like the one shown here by explaining the importance of the elements below.

Geographical Elements	Importance
Places/Regions	
Human-Environment Interaction	
Movement	

Read to Learn
• what questions geographers ask.
• about absolute and relative location.
• why people need to understand the geography of their area.

Section Theme
Geography and History Geography explains why people live where they do and why certain events occurred where they did.

Preview of Events

♦ *c. 600 million* B.C.
— Broad, shallow seas cover much of Texas

♦ *c. 300 million* B.C.
— Ouachita Trough forms

A
Texas Story

The first Texas Almanac

The *Texas Almanac* was published for the first time in 1857 in Galveston. It was a reference book that provided information about the climate, government, and law. It was also intended as a guide to help people moving to Texas. The *Texas Almanac* is still published every two years. Instead of merely telling about Texas, it has become part of Texas culture.

Six Geographical Questions

Do you live in a large city, in a small town, or on a farm or ranch? What language or languages do you speak? Is the food you eat grown nearby or brought in from elsewhere? These questions have to do with geography. Almost every detail of your life is affected by geography. The foods you eat, the things you do for fun, the type of house you live in, and the clothes you wear are all influenced by where you live. If you live in Amarillo, for example, you need warmer winter clothes than if you live in Brownsville.

Geography deals with the present by helping to explain why people live the way they do. Geography also helps explain the past—why certain events occurred. Whether you are studying Texas or the world, the past or the present, a knowledge of geography is essential.

When you study places and events in Texas, ask yourself these six questions: (1) Where is the place? (2) What is the place like? (3) How is the place similar to and different from other places? (4) How do the people who live there interact with their surroundings, or **environment?** (5) How are those people in that place linked with other people and places? (6) How does geography relate to the past, present, and future of that place? These questions reflect the six essential elements of the national standards in geography: location, places and regions, human-environment interaction, human systems, physical systems, and uses of geography.

Reading Check **Evaluating** How is a knowledge of geography useful to people?

Location

Location answers the question "Where is it?" For example, where is Houston? Houston is located near the eastern border of Texas, a state in the United States of America.

There are two types of location: absolute and relative. **Absolute location** refers to the exact position of a place on the earth's surface. It is identified by latitude and longitude 📖 *(see the Geography Handbook, pages 1–17).* Absolute location can be considered as a place's "global address." Look at the map on page 28 and identify the absolute location for the southernmost point in Texas.

Relative location is the position of a place in relation to other places. Austin is located 182 miles *south* of Dallas and 78 miles *north* of San Antonio. A place may be described with many relative locations. When describing relative location, you may use terms like *south of, located next to, between,* and *in the same region.*

The relative location of Texas has been one of the most important factors in the state's development. On the southeast coast, the warm waters of the **Gulf of Mexico** wash Texas beaches. Today, the Gulf of Mexico provides jobs to thousands of Texans who work in the fishing, oil, tourist, and shipping industries.

TEXAS HISTORY *Online*

Student Web Activity Visit the texans.glencoe.com Web site and click on **Chapter 1—Student Web Activity** to learn how geographers use GIS to study the economy.

Texas's relative location places it along the border of Mexico. This long border has deeply affected Texas history and in the future may be the single most important factor in the state's economic and social development. According to U.S. Census figures, the Mexican American population of Texas stood at over 32.5 percent in April of 2000 and is expected to continue growing.

Texas's location in the south central part of the United States makes it attractive to many kinds of businesses. Its relatively moderate climate and central location make it an ideal place for airline and product distribution operations serving the entire United States.

Reading Check **Examining** How does the relative location of Texas affect the state's economy?

Exploring **Geography**

Route 66 is a famous highway that once connected Los Angeles to Chicago. Today, only parts of it still exist. What is Adrian's location relative to Los Angeles and Chicago?

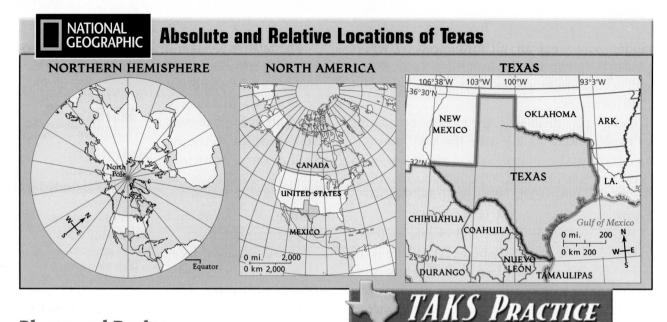

Absolute and Relative Locations of Texas

NORTHERN HEMISPHERE NORTH AMERICA TEXAS

Places and Regions

Geographers also look at places and regions. Place refers to those features and characteristics that give an area its own identity or personality. Places have physical characteristics—such as landforms, climate, plants, and animals—and human characteristics—such as language, religion, architecture, music, politics, and way of life.

To make sense of all the complex things in the world, geographers often group places or areas into regions. Regions are areas that are united by one or more common characteristics. When many places share similar characteristics, they form a region. In addition to physical and human characteristics, regions may be defined by their business needs. For example, Mexico trades heavily with United States border towns along the Rio Grande to form an economic region.

Human-Environment Interaction

The study of geography includes looking at human-environment interaction, or the relationships linking people to their surrounding environment. Throughout history, people have cut forests and dammed rivers to build farms and cities. Some of these activities have led to air and water pollution. The physical environment affects human activities as well. The type of soil and amount of water in a place determines if crops can be grown. Earthquakes and floods also affect human life.

TAKS Practice

Relative location affects the politics, society, and economy of a place.
Understanding Location *How does Texas's nearness to Mexico affect the state's economic development?*

Human Systems

Geographers also examine human systems, or the way people go about shaping the world. They look at how boundary lines are determined and analyze why people settle in certain places and not in others. An important theme in geography is the continual movement of people, ideas, and goods. People bring ideas and culture from one place to another. Sometimes those ideas are widely accepted in the new location, changing the culture. This process is called cultural diffusion. Other aspects of movement and human systems include trade and urbanization (the growth of cities).

Physical Systems

Why do some places have mountains and other places have flat deserts? When studying places and regions, geographers analyze how physical systems—such as volcanoes, glaciers, and hurricanes—interact and shape the earth's surface. They also look at ecosystems, or communities of plants and animals that are dependent upon one another and their particular surroundings for survival.

The Uses of Geography

Understanding geography and knowing how to use the tools and technology available to study it help prepare you for life in our technological society. Individuals, businesses, and governments depend upon geography and maps of all kinds on a daily basis. Computer software, such as the **Geographic Information System** (GIS), allows us to make informed decisions about using our physical and human environment. If, for example, a company wanted to log in a forest where a rare species of birds nested, they could enter nesting and logging data into the computer. GIS would be used to determine what areas had to be protected and which could be cut.

Sizing Up Texas

Texas is the second largest state in the United States. Only Alaska is bigger. Of the other states, only California and Montana are even half as large as Texas. The state stretches 801 miles (1,289 km) from the northwest corner of the Panhandle to the extreme southern tip near Brownsville. It is 773 miles (1,244 km) from the easternmost bulge of the Sabine (suh•BEEN) River in Newton County to the westernmost point near El Paso.

The total surface area of Texas is 267,277 square miles (692,247 sq. km). This includes both land and water. If you wanted to hike around the boundaries of Texas, you would have to walk 3,822 miles (6,150 km). That is almost two and one-half times the distance from Dallas to New York City! Texas is as large as the states of New York, Pennsylvania, Ohio, Illinois, Connecticut, Rhode Island, Massachusetts, Vermont, New Hampshire, New Jersey, and Maine combined. Even then, Texas still has land to spare. Texas makes up about 7 percent of the total area of the United

TWO VIEWPOINTS

Rural Past or Urban Future?

Although this high-speed rail system plan was defeated, conflict continues between urban and rural interests. Read the two views below and then answer the questions.

A City Point-of-View Supports High-Speed Rail System

There are countless numbers of good ideas that have fallen by the wayside because skeptics thought they would never work. The Texas High-Speed Rail project, the first bullet train system for North America, should not become one of them. The Texas project would connect the state's biggest cities, provide thousands of jobs and put Texas on the map in a dramatic way.

—Editorial, *Dallas Morning News*

Small Town Opposition

We realized that this is not good for Westphalia. Many residents are concerned because the rail's route run[s] about 2,000 feet from a 100-year-old Catholic church that is the town's focal point. Many residents fear that the train tracks will cut off access from one section [of their property] to another. They also fear that noise from the train will hurt cattle.

During peak hours, a train will pass every 15 minutes and generate about 107 decibels at 25 feet.

—*Dallas Morning News*

Learning From History

1. Why are many rural residents opposed to the rail system?

2. What are some of the special needs of big city populations?

People of Texas

Roy Bedichek 1878-1959

Roy Bedichek was a naturalist who was inspired by the vast Texas landscape. Early in his career, he taught English in high schools in Houston and San Angelo. Later, after working at University of Texas, Bedichek traveled around the state visiting schools, often writing about his travels. At times, he would camp out. This experience got him interested in wildlife, especially birds. In 1946, he retreated to Friday Mountain Ranch in Austin, where he wrote *Adventures With a Texas Naturalist.* His next two books, *Karánkaway Country* and *Educational Competition*, were recognized as books of the year in Texas. Bedichek had a gift for describing the world around him.

States. The state is larger than many nations, including Ecuador, France, Italy, Spain, Germany, Poland, Kenya, Japan, and Vietnam.

Sometimes the vast distances between cities pose problems for Texans. The following examples will help you understand how big Texas is. El Paso is closer to the Pacific Ocean than it is to Houston. A circle 500 miles (805 km) in diameter—with El Paso as its center—would include the capitals of three Mexican and two American states, but not Austin. Amarillo is closer to the capitals of New Mexico, Colorado, Kansas, and Oklahoma than it is to that of Texas. Residents of the village of Lajitas (lah•HEE•tahs), in the Big Bend area, live nearly 100 miles (161 km) from the nearest high school. Some students must spend 4 hours each day on a school bus. Understandably, people in these far-flung parts of Texas sometimes have closer business and social ties with the people of other states than they do with fellow Texans.

✓ Reading Check **Explaining** How do long distances pose problems for some Texans?

SECTION 1 ASSESSMENT

Checking for Understanding

1. **Using Key Terms** Write a short paragraph explaining how location, place, and region are related.
2. **Reviewing Facts** How do you describe a place's relative location?

Reviewing Themes

3. **Geography and History** How does the physical environment affect human activities?

Organizing to Learn

4. **Categorizing** Create a web like the one shown here and list the physical and human characteristics of your hometown or neighborhood.

Critical Thinking

5. **Identifying** Are there examples of cultural diffusion in your community? What are they?

TAKS PRACTICE

Supporting Generalizations Explain whether you think there is more movement of people, ideas, and goods today than in the past. Support your answer with examples.

Natural Resources

Guide to Reading

Main Idea
Texas contains a number of different landforms and an abundance of natural resources.

Key Terms
plain, barrier island, escarpment, fault, plateau, aquifer, savanna, grassland

Reading Strategy
Classifying Information Complete a chart like the one shown here.

Major Rivers	Major Minerals

Read to Learn
• about major landforms and water resources.
• about natural vegetation.
• about Texas's mineral resources.

Section Theme
Economic Factors The land's resources affect economic activities in an area.

Preview of Events

◆ *c. 240 million B.C.*
Gulf of Mexico begins to develop

◆ *c. 65 million B.C.*
Earthquakes create Balcones Escarpment

Piney Woods of Texas

A
Texas Story

"The northern counties of the state embrace what is usually called the wheat region of Texas . . . Eastern Texas is the great timbered region of the state . . . The counties between the Colorado and San Antonio Rivers possess the advantage of being better adapted to stock-raising and wool growing . . . the region extending from San Antonio to the Rio Grande is capable of supporting stock sufficient to supply the whole United States . . . "
—*The Texas Almanac and Emigrant's Guide to Texas,* 1869

Viewing Texas

Imagine flying over the widest part of Texas in a straight line from the south to the north and then from the east to the west. During these two flights, the face of Texas would change dramatically.

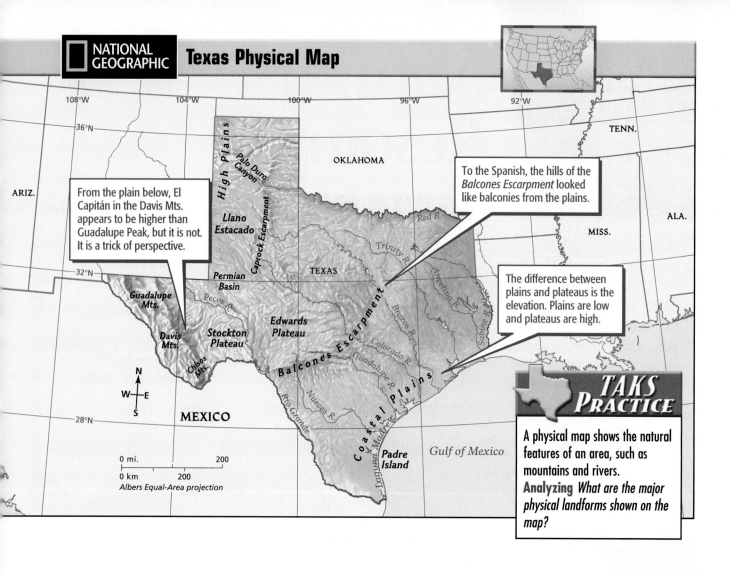

NATIONAL GEOGRAPHIC

Texas Physical Map

From the plain below, El Capitán in the Davis Mts. appears to be higher than Guadalupe Peak, but it is not. It is a trick of perspective.

To the Spanish, the hills of the *Balcones Escarpment* looked like balconies from the plains.

The difference between plains and plateaus is the elevation. Plains are low and plateaus are high.

High Plains

Palo Duro Canyon

Llano Estacado

Caprock Escarpment

Permian Basin

Pecos

Guadalupe Mts.

Davis Mts.

Chisos Mts.

Stockton Plateau

Edwards Plateau

Balcones Escarpment

Red R.

Trinity R.

TEXAS

Brazos R.

Colorado R.

Guadalupe R.

Angelina R.

Sabine R.

Rio Grande

Nueces R.

Coastal Plains

Laguna Madre

Padre Island

Gulf of Mexico

MEXICO

OKLAHOMA

ARIZ.

TENN.

ALA.

MISS.

N W E S

0 mi. 200
0 km 200
Albers Equal-Area projection

108°W 104°W 100°W 96°W 92°W
36°N 32°N 28°N

TAKS PRACTICE

A physical map shows the natural features of an area, such as mountains and rivers.
Analyzing What are the major physical landforms shown on the map?

The southernmost point in Texas lies on a mostly level **plain.** Plains may be gently rolling and even have low hills. The southern tip of Texas is very near sea level where Texas meets the Gulf of Mexico. Running along the coast a few miles offshore is Padre Island. This long thin strip of land covered with sand dunes is a **barrier island** protecting the mainland shore from ocean waves. Between Padre Island and the mainland is Laguna Madre, a large sheltered bay. Laguna Madre is a rich fishing area.

Moving northward from the Brownsville area, you will see that the land slowly rises, as it begins to gently roll. This part of Texas is covered with a tough and prickly mixture of mesquite trees, cacti, blackbrush, and other plants that thrive in a dry, hot climate. Large areas of South Texas are also covered with grasses. In spring, great masses of bluebonnets, Indian blankets, Indian paintbrushes, and other wildflowers carpet the land.

Cutting across Texas in a great curving arc is an **escarpment,** or long cliff. The **Balcones** (bal•KOH•neez) **Escarpment,** formed millions of years ago by a giant earthquake, follows a weak part of the earth's crust called a **fault.** In the distant past, the land sank east and south of the fault. North and west of it, the land rose many feet, forming the escarpment.

The Balcones Escarpment marks the beginning of a region of Texas known as the **"Hill Country."** This part of Texas is a **plateau,** or tableland, covered with small trees and brush. Hills on the rim of the plateau were formed by streams cutting and smoothing over the plateau's limestone edges. There are more streams and rivers in this part of Texas than in any other. This region is also known for the massive wildflower displays that blanket its slopes in spring.

The land gradually gets flatter and higher as you travel northwest. One abrupt change disrupts this plains region. The **Caprock**

Escarpment slashes south to north from Big Spring to Pampa. Palo Duro and Tule Canyons, great gashes in the Caprock, hold some of the most beautiful scenery in Texas.

A trip starting at the easternmost point in the state would also begin on a plain. Again, the level of the land gently rises as you travel westward. After crossing the Balcones Escarpment and the hilly central region, you finally reach the plains to the west.

West Texas has landforms that do not appear in other parts of the state. Most noticeable are the mountains. Texas has 91 mountains more than one mile high, and all of them are in West Texas. The highest point in the state, **Guadalupe Peak,** rises 8,749 feet (2,667 m) above sea level and is part of the Guadalupe Mountains National Park in Culberson County.

✓ Reading Check **Contrasting** What noticeable difference in land level occurs as you travel westward?

Texas's Water Resources

Hardly anywhere is water more precious than in the hot, arid, and rapidly growing region of the Southwest United States. Texas faces many of the concerns shared by people in this region.

Increasing demands for water are straining the ecosystems of communities along rivers and near dams. There are few new water sources available to the many businesses and homes that have been built here in the past decades.

The Gulf of Mexico is a major water resource of Texas. Both commercial and sports fishing boats ply its waters. Also important are the many bays found along the Texas coast. These bays serve as nurseries for fish, shrimp, oysters, crabs, and birds. They are also important fishing areas. Emptying into the bays, however, are rivers often polluted by wastes and chemicals from cities, factories, and fields. Because of this pollution, seafood from some Texas bays is sometimes declared unsafe to eat.

Rivers of Texas

Texas's river systems vary widely from region to region. Because it receives little rainfall, South Texas has few rivers. The **Rio Grande** forms most of Texas's southern boundary. Between 15 and 30 million years ago, forces within the earth caused the crust to drop forming a rift, or gash, more than 5 miles deep in places. The basins of the rift filled with the runoff of rain and snow to form inland seas. Earthquakes caused the seas to

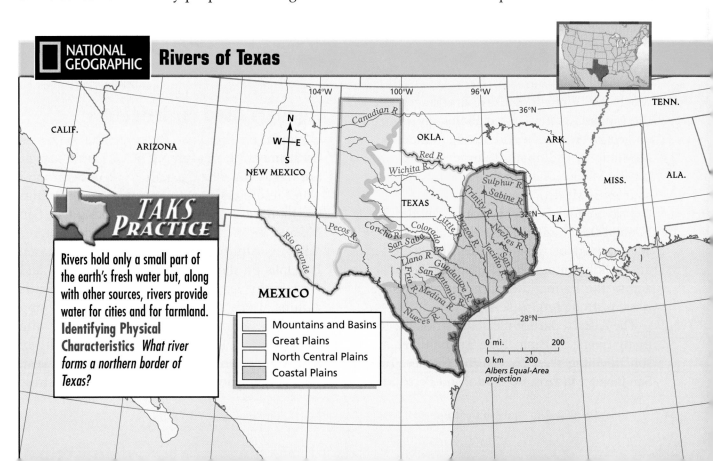

NATIONAL GEOGRAPHIC **Rivers of Texas**

TAKS PRACTICE

Rivers hold only a small part of the earth's fresh water but, along with other sources, rivers provide water for cities and for farmland. **Identifying Physical Characteristics** *What river forms a northern border of Texas?*

Mountains and Basins
Great Plains
North Central Plains
Coastal Plains

Albers Equal-Area projection

Caddo Lake

Exploring **Geography**

Named for the Caddo Indians, Caddo Lake is noted for its giant cypress trees. A dam was built in 1971, and the lake was designated a national wetlands region in 1993. What is the purpose of creating dams along rivers and lakes in Texas?

overflow, and the Rio Grande was formed. In hopscotch fashion, the river connected basin after basin, finally reaching the ocean about a half-million years ago. The beds of the ancient seas now form the fertile valleys through which some parts of the river runs.

The Rio Grande actually carries little water compared to other rivers of its length. The nearly 2,000-mile-long (3,218 km) river is one of the longest in the United States and the 24th longest river in the world. Rising in the San Juan Mountains of southern Colorado, it ends at the Gulf of Mexico. Most of the river's water is from sources in Mexico.

Two major rivers are found in the Texas Panhandle. The Red River flows eastward and acts as part of the boundary between Texas and Oklahoma. The Canadian River cuts across the Panhandle from west to east as it runs north of Amarillo.

The eastern part of the state is notable for its many rivers. Starting at the Sabine River, a person traveling west crosses the Neches, Trinity, San Jacinto, Brazos, Colorado, and Pecos Rivers.

Texas rivers are sometimes called "wrong-way" rivers because they carry water from the dry part of the state, where it is needed, to the southeastern part, which normally has plenty of water. Texas is like a giant tabletop that has been tipped from northwest to southeast. Because the land is higher in the northwest, almost all the rivers in Texas run to the southeast. To keep precious water from running unchecked into the Gulf of Mexico and to control floods, many rivers in Texas have been dammed, forming lakes.

Texas Lakes Have Many Uses

Texas has nearly 200 major lakes. All but one were formed when rivers were dammed. Only **Caddo Lake** in East Texas began as a natural lake. Even this lake, however, now holds waters backed up by a dam. Surprisingly, Texas ranks third behind Alaska and Minnesota in the surface area of its inland waters.

Originally built for flood control and water conservation, Texas lakes have taken on more roles. Most lake water is still used for irrigation, but surface waters (drawn primarily from lakes) provided about 60 percent of the needs of cities and towns in 1997 and most of the water used in manufacturing. For many years, lakes have supplied about 40 percent of Texas's water needs.

✓ **Reading Check** **Identifying** What are the two major rivers in the Texas Panhandle?

Aquifers Used for Irrigation

North of the Frio River is the Balcones Escarpment, an area famous for its many springs. Springs occur where aquifers, or underground water reservoirs, meet the surface. Large springs are found at San Antonio, New Braunfels, San Marcos, and Austin. These springs depend on the **Edwards Aquifer,** which gets its water from rain that falls on the Hill Country to the north and west. In dry years, the water level in the Edwards Aquifer drops so much that some springs stop flowing. Enormous amounts of water are pumped from the aquifer to supply the city of San Antonio and to irrigate farms to the west. This, combined with drought, applies great stress to the Edwards Aquifer. Rainfall refills this aquifer, however, creating a dependable source of water that can be used for years to come.

Another major aquifer with declining water levels is the **Ogallala** (oh•gah•LAH•lah) **Aquifer.** It lies under the Texas High Plains and cannot be refilled easily or quickly by rainfall. More than 5 million acres (2,025,000 hectares)—an area larger than New Jersey—are irrigated by the aquifer. Conservation programs and efforts to replenish the aquifer have been put into effect, but the future of the aquifer remains a matter of concern.

Soil Is a Valuable Resource

The rich soil of Texas is one of its most valuable resources. Huge areas of the state can be used for farming. Tons of cotton, watermelons, and spinach are harvested each year. Other leading crops include wheat, rice, corn, soybeans, vegetables, and peanuts.

Land that is not suited for farming can still be used for ranching. The state of Texas usually leads the nation in the number of cattle, sheep, and goats raised, and in the amount of wool and mohair (goat hair) clipped. Together, ranching, farming, and related businesses produce about $40 billion in income for the people of Texas each year.

✓ **Reading Check** **Comparing** How is an aquifer different from a dammed lake?

Three Vegetation Regions

In general, Texas has three types of natural vegetation regions: forests, savannas, and grasslands. Three major forest regions are found in Texas, all in the eastern third of the state where rainfall is greatest. Hardwood trees, long-leaf pines, and oak-hickory forests can be found that are about the size of Indiana.

Texas forests are an important natural resource. Timber is one of the top cash crops in Texas, usually outranked only by cotton. The lumber, plywood, and paper industries provide more than one-fourth of the manufacturing jobs in East Texas.

Exploring **Geography**

Water from the Edwards Aquifer comes to the surface at Barton Springs in Austin *(left)*. Water from the Ogallala Aquifer is pumped to the surface for irrigation *(below)*. Identify some uses for aquifer water.

Austin ★

Ogallala Aquifer

Texas also has several savanna regions. Far West Texas is a desert shrub savanna. Only short grasses and small shrubs grow here, except in the mountains and along streams. This region supports only limited grazing of animals. Most of the center of Texas has savanna areas. The soil here is rocky, and the land is sometimes rugged.

The third vegetation region in Texas is grasslands. Early settlers established farms on the grasslands because they had to clear only a few trees before crops could be planted. Texas cities today echo the patterns of the early settlers. The grasslands stretching from Dallas to San Antonio and the grassy prairies around Houston are the most heavily settled regions.

Texas Leads in Energy Production

The main minerals in Texas are petroleum, natural gas, coal, sand, and gravel. Texas also produces building stone, such as limestone and granite. Gypsum is mined in many places in the state. It is used to manufacture drywall, a material used in construction. Texas is a leading producer of salt, mainly from mines near Grand Saline in Van Zandt County. Sand, crushed stone called gravel, clay, and coal are mined in East Texas.

Petroleum and natural gas are the most important mineral resources. Oil or gas has been found in all but 23 counties. As of 2001, the value of oil and gas produced in Texas is about $17 billion annually. These resources are important to

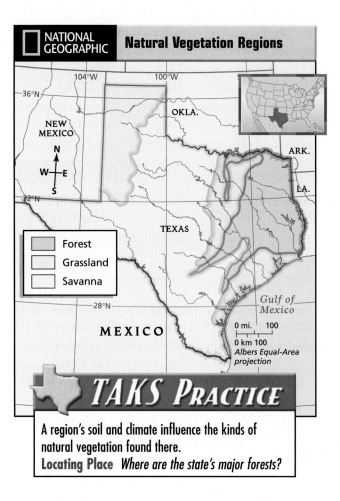

NATIONAL GEOGRAPHIC **Natural Vegetation Regions**

Forest
Grassland
Savanna

Gulf of Mexico

0 mi. 100
0 km 100
Albers Equal-Area projection

TAKS PRACTICE

A region's soil and climate influence the kinds of natural vegetation found there.
Locating Place *Where are the state's major forests?*

the state and to the country. One-fourth of all the energy produced in the entire history of the United States has been produced in Texas.

✓ Reading Check **Examining** In what ways are Texas forests an important natural resource?

SECTION 2 ASSESSMENT

Checking for Understanding

1. **Using Key Terms** Describe a trip through Texas using the following words: plain, barrier island, escarpment, fault, plateau, and grassland.
2. **Reviewing Facts** What river forms most of the southern boundary of the state?

Reviewing Themes

3. **Economic Factors** How do Texans use land not suited for farming?

Organizing to Learn

4. **Identifying** Complete a chart like the one shown below and identify a major river found in each region.

Region	River
Panhandle	
East Texas	
West Texas	
South Texas	

Critical Thinking

5. **Describing** In which natural vegetation region would you most like to live? What would that area look like?

TAKS PRACTICE

Understanding Geography Why are the three major forest regions all found in the eastern third of Texas?

TAKS Skillbuilder

Understanding a Map Key

Why Learn This Skill?

Maps can show many kinds of information, including climate, cities, vegetation, and elevation. The information on maps is often shown by various symbols such as numbers, colors, lines, circles, and other shapes and pictures. To understand what the map is showing, look at the map key, or legend, which explains what the symbols mean.

Also included in the legend may be two other kinds of information. First, a compass rose is often placed on maps to point out the directions north, south, east, and west. Second, a scale is included to show the relationship between distance on the map and distance on the ground.

Learning the Skill

To use a map key correctly, follow these steps:
• Check the compass rose to determine the directions on the map.
• Check the scale of distance.
• Study all the symbols in the legend and find examples of each one on the map.

Practicing the Skill

Study the map and the map key. Then answer the following questions.

❶ In which direction is Austin from Dallas?

❷ Which city is shown in the far west part of Texas?

❸ How far is Brownsville from San Antonio?

❹ Traveling at 50 miles per hour, about how long would it take to drive from Dallas to Brownsville?

❺ How many interstate highways meet at Houston?

❻ What is the value of the type of geographical information that you have learned in this map exercise?

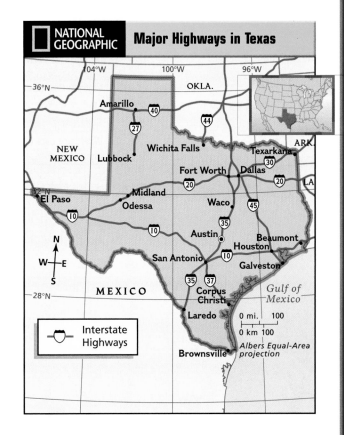

NATIONAL GEOGRAPHIC **Major Highways in Texas**

TAKS PRACTICE

Understanding a Map Key   Draw a simple map of your classroom. Create a map key that includes symbols for desks, doorways, and other room features. Add a compass rose showing true directions. Create a scale that reflects true measurements of the classroom. Compare your map to those of your classmates to see how many different symbols were developed.

Glencoe's **Skillbuilder Interactive Workbook,** Level 1, provides instruction and practice in key social studies skills.

The Climate of Texas

A
Texas Story

Early Texas farmer

". . . Texas contains, beyond any other state of the Union, the advantages of . . . climate, a soil of unsurpassed fertility, adapted to the production of all the most valuable staples, together with great mineral resources. This may seem to some an extravagant assertion, but it will be readily admitted by all who know any thing of this highly favored country."
—*The Texas Almanac and Emigrant's Guide to Texas,* 1869

Absolute Location Affects Climate

The absolute location of Texas has important effects on its climate. Texas lies in what are called the middle latitudes, the region about midway between the equator and the North Pole. Because Texas is not very far north of the equator, it has mild winters. Even in Amarillo, the temperature rises above freezing most winter days. Because of the great north-to-south spread of the state, however, the climate of South Texas is much warmer than that of North Texas. In the Brownsville area, for example, farmers can expect freezing weather to occur perhaps only one or two days a year. South Texas is a popular winter vacation spot for many people because of its warm climate.

Despite its overall warmth, Texas is subject to periods of cold weather. In fact, the Texas climate has a reputation for being highly unpredictable. Tornadoes, hurricanes, dust storms, and northers may strike. Northers are sudden blasts of cold air that extend south from Canada and sweep across the plains. There are no mountains or other landforms to block these northers. They can drop temperatures below freezing, but they rarely last for more than two or three days. A powerful norther in 1899 froze Corpus Christi Bay so solidly that people could walk on it. A party of surveyors near Palo Duro Canyon in the Panhandle experienced a norther in December 1887:

❝It caught us in a few minutes. With a rush of ice cold wind, a snarl like an angry beast, an awful roar, changing into a long drawn out wail which continued to rise and fall—the yellow norther of the plains struck and enveloped us.

The air was full of ice needles that drove into the exposed flesh and stuck, but did not seem to melt. The snow seemed to parallel the ground in its flight; yet the plains grass was covered by it in a few minutes and it rolled along the ground with the wind. That wind didn't turn aside. When it hit you it just kept [going] right on through your body, as though your flesh offered no obstruction to it. There wasn't a hill between us and the North Pole and that wind must have come all the way—and gathering power at every jump.

We had been sweating ten minutes before. Now we pulled the wagon sheet over us huddling under it. But the wind and cold . . . cut and stung despite the cover.❞

Texas's absolute location affects its climate in another way. The middle latitudes are a meeting place of cool air moving from the north and moist warm air moving from the Gulf of Mexico. Especially in the spring and fall, violent storms sometimes result from this mixing of cold and warm air. Thunderstorms may bring heavy rain, lightning, and sometimes hail the size of baseballs. Tornadoes may form, causing tremendous damage or injury when they touch ground.

Texas has an average of 118 tornadoes each year. April, May, and June are the peak months of the tornado season, although the storms can strike in any month. When tornadoes strike cities, they can be particularly destructive. The greatest outbreak of tornadoes in Texas history occurred in September 1967, when a hurricane generated 115 tornadoes, 67 of them in one day.

 **Reading Check** **Explaining** Name two ways Texas's absolute location affects climate.

🧭 *Exploring* **Geography**

Tornadoes, like this one that touched down in Pampa, occur in Texas most often in April, May, and June. The twisting tail, called a funnel, acts like a suction tube. How might tornadoes affect the economy of Texas?

Relative Location Also Affects Climate

The location of Texas relative to the Gulf of Mexico has a major influence on the climate of the state. Most of the year, winds blow inland from the south, southeast, or southwest for 200 miles (322 km) or more. These ocean breezes cool the land in summer and warm it in winter. Moisture from the Gulf of Mexico is the source of most of the rain that falls on the state. The city of Orange in East Texas averages 59 inches (150 cm) of rainfall per year. Farther west, winds blow across the deserts and mountains of Mexico before entering Texas. This drier air brings less rainfall. El Paso, for example, averages less than 8 inches of rain per year.

The Gulf is so far from some areas of Texas that it has little effect on climate there. Wichita Falls and other cities across the middle of the state broil in the summer sun. Similarly, winter temperatures in the Panhandle or in the Dallas–Fort Worth area get little warming from Gulf breezes.

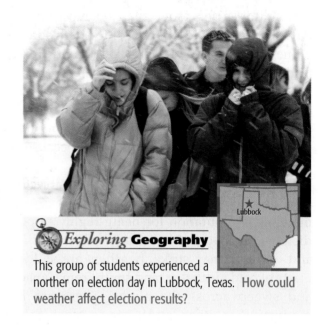

Exploring **Geography**

This group of students experienced a norther on election day in Lubbock, Texas. How could weather affect election results?

The location of Texas next to the Gulf of Mexico—with its hundreds of miles of coastline—has negative effects, too. Destructive storms sometimes sweep in from the Gulf and do great damage to the state. The hurricane of Galveston in 1900 left more than 6,000 dead, and great storms

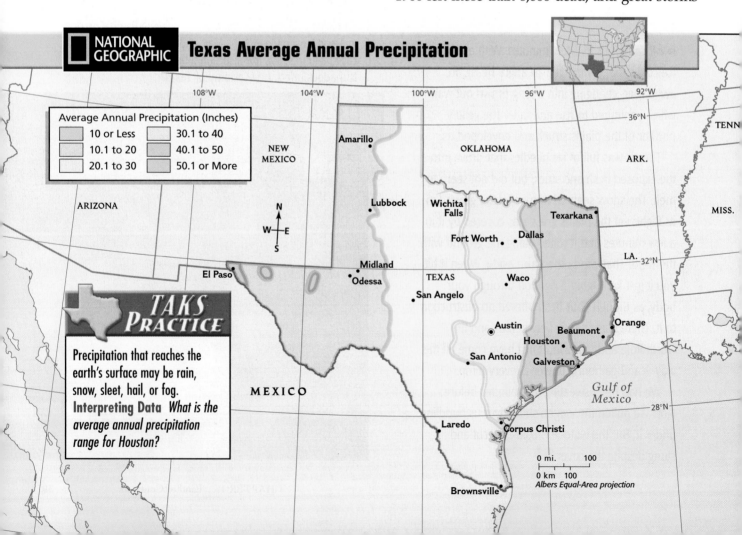

NATIONAL GEOGRAPHIC Texas Average Annual Precipitation

Average Annual Precipitation (Inches)

- 10 or Less
- 10.1 to 20
- 20.1 to 30
- 30.1 to 40
- 40.1 to 50
- 50.1 or More

TAKS PRACTICE

Precipitation that reaches the earth's surface may be rain, snow, sleet, hail, or fog. **Interpreting Data** *What is the average annual precipitation range for Houston?*

struck Corpus Christi in 1916, 1919, and 1970. Houston was struck by a hurricane in 1983.

Any part of the state can be affected by hurricanes. In 1921 a hurricane moved from Mexico across south and central Texas, causing the greatest flood in the state's history. During that storm, more than 36 inches (91 cm) of rain fell at Thrall in 18 hours—setting a record for rainfall in American history.

Elevation and Climate Patterns

Besides absolute and relative location, the Texas climate is also affected by elevation. In general, the temperature cools about 3 degrees for each 1,000-foot (305-m) rise in elevation. Similarly, the average temperature rises as elevation decreases. This fact affects the Texas climate in several ways.

If distance from the ocean were the only factor determining climate, El Paso would be the warmest city in the state. This is not the case, however. Because El Paso lies at an average elevation of about 3,700 feet (1,128 m), its temperatures are generally cooler than cities at a lower elevation but located at about the same latitude.

The warmer temperatures at lower elevations help Texans in winter. Northers that chill residents of Amarillo, at an elevation of about 3,650 feet (1,113 m), warm as they blow south. By the time a

TEXAS FICTION

Anyone who thinks Texas weather is all dry is "all wet." The image of Texas as a parched, sunbleached wasteland persists in the popular imagination, but more of Texas is humid than dry. The state's three largest cities, Houston, Dallas, and San Antonio, have average relative humidity percentages of 77, 65, and 67, respectively. Houston gets 45 inches of precipitation a year, more than Boston; Chicago; Washington, D.C.; New York City; or even Key West, Florida.

norther reaches Austin, at an elevation of approximately 500 feet (152 m) above sea level, the temperature may be 20°F (7°C) warmer.

Elevation also affects rainfall. Warm air holds more moisture than cool air. The mountains of West Texas receive more rainfall than the surrounding desert because moisture-filled air moving up the mountains is cooled. As the air becomes cooler and less able to hold moisture, some of the moisture falls as rain. The Davis Mountains receive almost 19 inches (48 cm) of rain a year. The lower desert several miles away gets only 12 to 14 inches (30 to 36 cm).

✓ **Reading Check** **Explaining** How does elevation affect climate?

SECTION 3 ASSESSMENT

Checking for Understanding

1. **Using Key Terms** Define *norther* and *middle latitudes*.
2. **Reviewing Facts** On average, how many tornadoes does Texas experience each year?

Reviewing Themes

3. **Geography and History** If you like cool summer temperatures, where in Texas should you live? Where should you live if you like warm winter temperatures?

Organizing to Learn

4. **Comparing** Complete a chart like the one shown below and write the positive and negative effects of the state of Texas being located near the Gulf of Mexico.

Positive Effects	Negative Effects

Critical Thinking

5. **Evaluating Location** How does the mild climate of South Texas favorably affect the economy of that part of the state?

TAKS PRACTICE

Analyzing Climate Texas experiences many types of weather. What type of weather conditions occur in the middle latitudes?

Chapter Summary

Land of Contrasts

Main Idea
The six elements of geography are:

- Location
- Places and regions
- Human-environment interaction
- Human systems
- Physical systems
- Uses of geography

Main Idea
The major landforms in Texas are:

- Plains
- Escarpments
- Plateaus
- Mountains

Main Idea
Texas's water resources include:

- Gulf of Mexico
- Rivers and man-made lakes
- Aquifers

Main Idea
Natural vegetation regions are:

- Forests
- Savannas
- Grasslands

Main Idea
Important mineral resources in Texas include:

- Coal
- Natural gas
- Petroleum

Reviewing Key Terms

Write the definition of each key term. Then list a geographical place, or name, to which the term relates.

1. plain
2. barrier island
3. escarpment
4. fault
5. plateau
6. aquifer
7. savanna
8. grassland

Reviewing Key Facts

9. Describe the size of Texas, north to south and east to west.
10. How was the Balcones Escarpment formed?
11. Identify where mountains are located in Texas. What is the highest point in the state?
12. Explain why so many Texas rivers flow in a generally southeastern direction.
13. How were most Texas lakes formed?
14. What three natural vegetation regions are found in Texas?
15. List the main minerals found in Texas. Of those listed, which are the most important?
16. Describe the effects of a norther.

Critical Thinking

17. **Locating** Describe your town or community in terms of absolute and relative location.
18. **Analyzing** Describe your town or community in terms of place. What are specific characteristics that make it a unique place?
19. **Making Generalizations** What are some of the ways in which people in your area interact with the environment? Think in terms of work or recreation.
20. **Determining Cause and Effect** How does Texas's great size contribute to its varied climate?
21. **Making Generalizations** How have the rivers of Texas affected the lives of Texans?
22. **Evaluating** Do you think the Ogallala Aquifer is a renewable water source? Explain your answer.

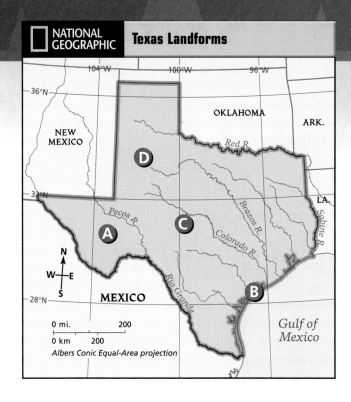
Texas Landforms map

Geography and History Activity

Identify the physical features found in Texas by matching the terms below with the letters on the map.

23. plateau
24. mountains
25. barrier island
26. plains

Economics and History Activity

27. **Cities** In what part of the state of Texas are most large cities located? How did the location affect the cities' growth?

Cooperative Learning Activity

28. **Creating a Model** Working in groups, create a model of an ideal community. The plans for your community should include a map of the area, indicating the important geographical features and where the major industries and commercial areas will be developed. Then write a brief description of what your ideal community would be like.

Practicing Skills

29. **Understanding a Map Key** Draw a street map of an area near your school or home. Include such things as highways, railroad tracks, bridges, or other landmarks. Be sure to add a map key. For an added challenge, create a scale that reflects the actual distances you have mapped.

TEXAS HISTORY *Online*

Self-Check Quiz

Visit the texans.glencoe.com Web site and click on **Chapter 1—Self-Check Quizzes** to prepare for the chapter test.

Building Technology Skills

30. **Using the Internet** Search online to find a picture or photograph of either Palo Duro or Tule Canyon that you can print. Write a caption describing the physical characteristics of the image.

The Princeton Review

TAKS PRACTICE

Use the graph to answer the following question.

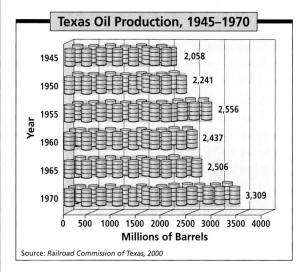

Texas Oil Production, 1945–1970

Year	Millions of Barrels
1945	2,058
1950	2,241
1955	2,556
1960	2,437
1965	2,506
1970	3,309

Source: *Railroad Commission of Texas, 2000*

Which of the following statements can be determined from the information in this graph?

A The Civil War created an enormous demand for oil.

B An increase in the number of cars contributed to higher demand for fuel.

C The greatest increase in oil production occurred between 1965 and 1970.

D Oil refineries were more efficient between 1945 and 1970.

Test-Taking Tip:

Look for a statement that is supported by the graph. For example, answer A is not supported by the data.

Economics & History

Migrant Workers Provided Needed Labor

Did you know that cotton is Texas's number one crop? Or that one out of every five bales of cotton produced in the United States is grown in Texas? The production of cotton is vital to the state's economy.

Texas Has What Cotton Farmers Need

What you may not have thought much about was why so much cotton is planted in Texas. The answer is that the geography of Texas favors the growth of cotton. Texas has the climate, the soil, and the labor needed to make cotton growing profitable. Texas is so large north to south that it takes a while for the warm temperatures needed to begin the planting season to work their way up the state. This was very important for cotton farmers because it meant that the farm workers needed to pick the cotton could start in the southern part of the state and move northward as the cotton plants grew ready for harvesting.

Migrant Families

Farmers during the 1920s through the 1950s needed thousands of temporary workers, or "hands," to harvest the cotton. The demand for labor was filled by poor people who needed work to survive. By joining the **Big Swing**—migrating work that took them from southern Texas to the High Plains—these people could earn a living.

Entire families made up the force of cotton pickers. Most were of Mexican descent, either having been born in Texas, having lived in the United States for many years, or having recently arrived from their home country. They traveled to farms in their own cars, or with individuals who drove them from farm to farm on a platform truck. In Spanish, this driver was called *el troquero.* The bed of the truck became "home" for families as they moved from farm to farm. The *troquero* was responsible for finding work for his "crew" on the route north.

The Big Swing

Migrant workers began their yearly migration in southern Texas. The weather was warm enough in the Lower Rio Grande Valley for farmers to plant their cotton crop in late February and early March.

Mexican workers board the train for transport to U.S. farms.

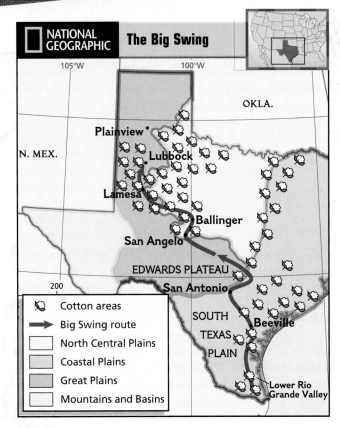

NATIONAL GEOGRAPHIC

The Big Swing

105°W   100°W

OKLA.

Plainview

Lubbock

N. MEX.

Lamesa

Ballinger

San Angelo

EDWARDS PLATEAU

200   San Antonio

SOUTH
TEXAS
PLAIN   Beeville

Lower Rio
Grande Valley

Cotton areas
Big Swing route
North Central Plains
Coastal Plains
Great Plains
Mountains and Basins

From the 1920s to the early 1960s the route for picking cotton was known as the Big Swing. The route took migrant workers from the warmer climates of southern Texas to the cooler dry climates of northern Texas.

By April or May, workers started the process of thinning the young plants. During late June and continuing into the next few weeks, the cotton-picking season began.

From southern Texas, the migrants drove to central Texas. In farms surrounding San Marcos,

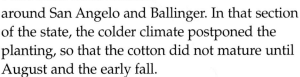

New Braunfels, and Lock-hart, men, women, and children toiled in temperatures of more than 100 degrees to make an average of $1.75 per day. By late August, the migrant laborers prepared to move again, this time to West Texas farms located around San Angelo and Ballinger. In that section of the state, the colder climate postponed the planting, so that the cotton did not mature until August and the early fall.

The final stopping point for the cotton pickers was the High Plains. When the crews arrived around September and October, the late-planted cotton was ripe for picking. By November, many migrant families were on their way home.

Settling Down

Many of the migrants, however, did not travel back to their places of origin in Mexico or South Texas. They began new Spanish-speaking communities in towns such as Lamesa, Lubbock, and Plainview. They found jobs, married, and raised families. In this way, Mexican American culture was transplanted to new geographical areas, where it remains today.

TAKS PRACTICE

1. **Drawing Conclusions** How does the geography of Texas help to support migratory work?
2. **Analyzing** What were some benefits and drawbacks for migrant workers during cotton-picking season?
3. **Writing About Economics** Write a paragraph that develops one of the themes listed below. Use standard grammar, spelling, sentence structure, and punctuation. Include information and examples from the feature as details to support your argument.
   a. People rely on a variety of jobs to earn a living.
   b. Family members make contributions in different ways.
   c. People make sacrifices to earn a living.

Regions of Texas

Why It Matters

The regions of Texas have different natural resources. These differences are one reason why Texas has many economic activities. The large and varied population of Texas depends upon the diversity of its regions.

The Impact Today

Geographic factors continue to influence where Texans live today. For example:
- *The majority of Texans live in the eastern regions where there is abundant rainfall and large cities with job opportunities.*
- *The boundary area with Mexico is one of the fastest growing parts of Texas.*
- *Cities such as Austin, San Antonio, Dallas, and Houston are located along important transportation routes.*

c. 65 million B.C.
★ *Earthquakes and volcanoes formed Coastal Plains*

c. 140 million B.C.
★ *Big Bend and Edwards Plateau created from limestone*

Texas

United States   *c. 140 million B.C.*   *c. 65 million B.C.*   *c. 53 million B.C.*

World

c. 65 million B.C.
• *Great Plains formed*

c. 53 million B.C.
• *First horses appeared*

A field of bluebonnets dots the Texas landscape.

FOLDABLES™ TAKS
Study Organizer PRACTICE

Categorizing Information Study Foldable
Make and use this foldable to organize what you learn about the four natural regions of Texas.

Step 1 Mark the midpoint of a side edge of one sheet of paper. Then fold the outside edges in to touch the midpoint.

Step 2 Fold in half from side to side.

Step 3 Open and cut along the inside fold lines to form four tabs. Label your foldable as shown.

Cut along the fold lines on both sides.

Reading and Writing As you read the chapter, write information under each tab of your foldable about the geographic features, population, economy, natural resources, and people of each region of Texas. Use what you learn to compare and contrast the regions.

c. 2 million B.C.
★ Ice Age advance affected Texas climates

c. 9,500 B.C.
★ Ancient people reached Texas

| c. 2 million B.C. | c. 1.5 million B.C. | | c. 9,500 B.C. |

c. 1.5 million B.C.
• Grand Canyon forms

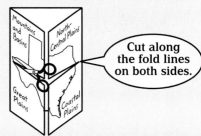

TEXAS HISTORY *Online*

Chapter Overview
Visit the texans.glencoe.com Web site and click on **Chapter 2—Chapter Overviews** to preview chapter information.

The Coastal Plains

Guide to Reading

Main Idea
The Coastal Plains region contains five diverse geographic sections, all affected by their nearness to the Gulf of Mexico.

Key Terms
petrochemical
alluvial soil

Reading Strategy
Organizing Information Complete a table like the one shown here as you read.

Geographic Section	Principal Landforms	Major Urban Centers

Read to Learn
• about the Coastal Plains sections.
• about differences in each geographic subsection within a natural region.
• about the movement of resources.

Section Theme
Economic Factors The Coastal Plains include the state's major cities where manufacturing, trade, and education are centered.

Preview of Events

♦ *c. 65 million B.C.* ──────────── ♦ *c. 35 million years B.C.*

└─ Coastal Plains region takes shape

└─ Mammoths and giant armadillos roam plains and woodlands

George S. Perry

A
Texas Story

Texas can be divided into four natural regions. They are the Coastal Plains, the North Central Plains, the Great Plains, and the Mountains and Basins. George S. Perry, a Rockdale writer, traveled the entire state in 1942 and collected humorous tales from the different regions. He found that Texas seemed too big for a single description. "Yes, it's that big—too big, actually, to visualize in one hunk. It's better to think of it, for the moment, as a group of federated realms."

The Most Populated Region

The largest natural region in Texas is the Coastal Plains. This region extends from the eastern and southern United States through Texas and continues south far into Mexico. As its name implies, this region lies along the coast—the area where the land meets the water. The Coastal Plains vary from being completely flat to having rolling hills. The height above sea level is generally low—from a few feet to about 1,000 feet (305 m).

The Coastal Plains are home to more Texans than any other natural region. About two out of three Texans live and work here. The nearby Gulf of Mexico provides the region with a mild climate. Winds blowing across the Gulf pick up moisture and drop it on the land. A plentiful water supply, coupled with its flat land, make the Coastal Plains ideal for farming and ranching. It is easier to build cities on this level surface, too. Major cities in the Coastal Plains include Dallas, Austin, Pasadena, San Antonio,

Houston, Corpus Christi, Galveston, Victoria, Brownsville, and Laredo. These cities are centers of manufacturing, trade, and services such as banking, tourism, trade, and education.

The Coastal Plains have many rich natural resources. The pine forests of East Texas produce large amounts of lumber and other wood products. Other parts of the Coastal Plains have rich soil for growing cotton, rice, vegetables, and grains. Grasses in the drier areas feed most of the cattle raised in Texas.

Great oil fields are also found in this region. The first large oil discovery, the **Spindletop Field,** was discovered near Beaumont in 1901. The greatest oil field ever discovered in Texas, the **East Texas Oil Field,** was found near Henderson in 1930.

NATIONAL GEOGRAPHIC **Natural Regions of Texas**

Mountains and Basins
Great Plains
North Central Plains
Coastal Plains

Fort Davis, at 5,050 feet (1,539 m), is the highest town of any size in Texas.

The geographic center of the state is in the northern part of McCulloch County, about 9 miles (14.5 km) southwest of Mercury.

There is no place in Texas below sea level. The coastal counties have the lowest elevations.

TAKS PRACTICE

The Coastal Plains, the North Central Plains, the Great Plains, and the Mountains and Basins regions of North America extend into Texas.
Identifying Regions For each natural region in Texas, name a nearby state that most likely shares physical characteristics of that region.

COLORADO · KANSAS · MISSOURI · ARIZONA · NEW MEXICO · OKLAHOMA · ARK. · TEXAS · LA. · CHIHUAHUA · MEXICO · COAHUILA · NUEVO LEÓN · DURANGO · ZACATECAS · TAMAULIPAS

Amarillo · Lubbock · Wichita Falls · Fort Worth · Dallas · El Paso · Midland · San Angelo · Mercury · Fort Davis · Austin · Bastrop · Beaumont · Houston · Pasadena · Galveston · San Antonio · Victoria · Corpus Christi · Laredo · Brownsville

Gulf of Mexico

108°W · 104°W · 100°W · 96°W · 34°N · 30°N · 26°N

0 mi. 200
0 km 200
Albers Equal-Area projection

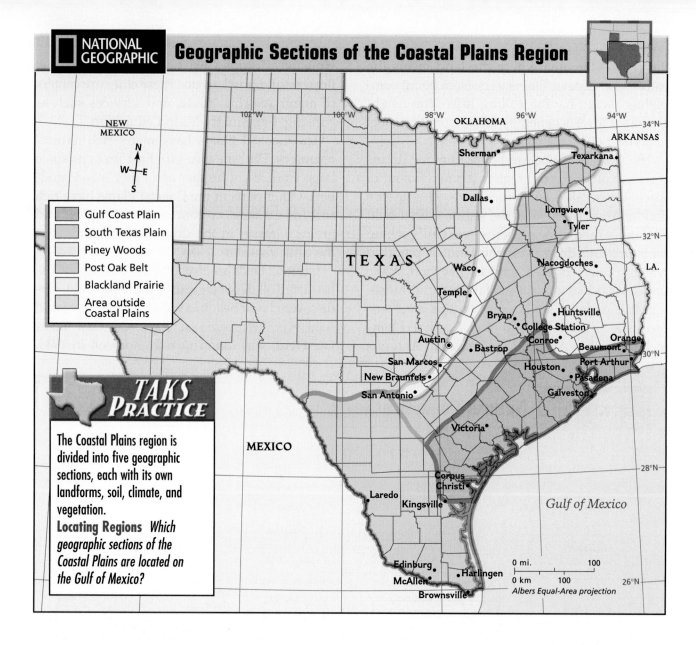

NATIONAL GEOGRAPHIC

Geographic Sections of the Coastal Plains Region

Legend:
- Gulf Coast Plain
- South Texas Plain
- Piney Woods
- Post Oak Belt
- Blackland Prairie
- Area outside Coastal Plains

TAKS PRACTICE

The Coastal Plains region is divided into five geographic sections, each with its own landforms, soil, climate, and vegetation.
Locating Regions Which geographic sections of the Coastal Plains are located on the Gulf of Mexico?

Map labels: NEW MEXICO, OKLAHOMA, ARKANSAS, TEXAS, MEXICO, LA., Gulf of Mexico

Sherman, Texarkana, Dallas, Longview, Tyler, Waco, Nacogdoches, Temple, Bryan, Huntsville, College Station, Austin, Bastrop, Conroe, Orange, Beaumont, San Marcos, Houston, Port Arthur, New Braunfels, Pasadena, San Antonio, Galveston, Victoria, Corpus Christi, Laredo, Kingsville, Edinburg, Harlingen, McAllen, Brownsville

0 mi. 100 / 0 km 100
Albers Equal-Area projection

Later discoveries close to Kilgore and Longview proved to be part of the same field. Historically, this field made Texas the leading producer of oil in the United States. Processing oil and oil products is a major industry in the region, especially along the coast. Related industries, such as shipping and warehousing, have also developed.

The level land of the plain allows free movement of goods and people. The state's seaports are connected by roads, railroads, and pipelines to the rest of the state and the nation. Goods from the other natural regions in Texas funnel into the seaports such as Houston, Galveston, and Corpus Christi for shipment to the rest of the world. Likewise, goods arriving from other nations enter Texas for further distribution. The **Gulf Intracoastal Waterway,** a

protected shipping channel, extends along the coast from Brownsville to Apalachee Bay, Florida. This important waterway links Texas to the southeastern United States and the world.

Three of the natural regions of Texas are divided into geographic subsections that have different types of vegetation. The Coastal Plains region has five different geographic subsections. These are the Piney Woods, the Gulf Coast Plain, the Post Oak Belt, the Blackland Prairie, and the South Texas Plain. All five sections lie on the plain near the Gulf of Mexico. There are many differences in the vegetation, wildlife, and other natural resources of each section.

Reading Check **Explaining** What features of the Coastal Plains make it a popular region?

The Piney Woods

The Piney Woods area gets its name from the pine trees that cover much of the land. (See the map on page 50.) Four national forests can be found in this part of Texas—Angelina, Sabine, Sam Houston, and Davy Crockett. The southeastern part of the Piney Woods is made up of the Big Thicket National Preserve, an area with dense growths of pines, other trees, and shrubs. Much of the Big Thicket, however, is swamp.

Economic growth in the Piney Woods region occurred thanks to the presence of two vital natural resources—wood and oil. Lumbering is a particularly important economic activity in this part of Texas, and lumber-related businesses are the most important industries here. Much population growth occurred in the 1930s as a result of an enormous oil field discovered in Gregg, Rusk, and Smith Counties.

Farming is an important economic activity. The long growing season in the Piney Woods allows a variety of fruits and vegetables to be grown. Also located here are several major garden industries, such as growing roses and bedding plants. The Piney Woods area has been settled for hundreds of years. Native Americans, Spaniards, African Americans, and Anglo Americans all were attracted to this rich area. Texarkana, a manufacturing and medical center, straddles the Texas–Arkansas boundary. Longview is an industrial, recreational, and convention center. Nacogdoches is the home of Stephen F. Austin State University, while Huntsville is the home of Sam Houston State University and the headquarters of the Texas Department of Criminal Justice (the state prison system). Conroe has many residents who commute to Houston and its suburbs. Many of the northern suburbs of Houston are in the Piney Woods.

The Gulf Coast Plain

Heavy stands of grasses grow in many parts of the Gulf Coast Plain. This grass provides excellent feed for cattle. Cattle raising is the most important agricultural activity in this part of Texas. There are more cattle per square mile here than in any other geographic region in the state.

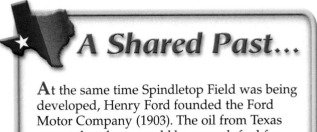

A Shared Past...

At the same time Spindletop Field was being developed, Henry Ford founded the Ford Motor Company (1903). The oil from Texas meant that there would be enough fuel for hundreds of thousands of automobiles. Oil from Texas made it possible to put "America on wheels."

The Gulf Coast Plain benefits from a long growing season that allows farmers to grow many kinds of crops, including rice, cotton, and grain sorghum (for livestock feed). Rice is an important crop in this geographic region. (Texas rice is sold to more than 100 countries around the world.) Wharton County produces more rice than any other county.

Some parts of the Gulf Coast Plain are heavily industrialized. Many of the industries turn oil or natural gas into products such as gasoline, plastics, fertilizer, antifreeze, and synthetic rubber. Petrochemical industries—businesses related to oil and gas products—stretch in a line from Corpus Christi through Houston and Beaumont, ending at Port Arthur and Orange on the Louisiana border. Some petroleum fields are found off the Texas coast in the Gulf of Mexico.

Two large cities—Houston and Corpus Christi—were built in the Gulf Coast Plain. Houston, in Harris County, is Texas's largest city. It is home to more than 3 million people.

Houston supports a wide variety of businesses and services. The **Johnson Space Center,** which trains America's astronauts, has spurred the development of many scientific industries. Houston's largest economic role, however, is as the center of the state's petrochemical industry.

Houston is the third-largest seaport in the United States and is a

TEXAS HISTORY Online

Student Web Activity Visit the texans.glencoe.com Web site and click on **Chapter 2—Student Web Activity** to learn more about the Johnson Space Center in Houston.

Exploring **Geography**

This oil tanker is moored in a loading bay of an oil refinery in Houston, Texas. How is it possible for ships to reach Houston from the Gulf of Mexico?

major center for international shipping. Ships from around the world arrive from the Gulf of Mexico through an artificial waterway called the **Houston Ship Channel.** Many foreign banks and financial institutions have offices in Houston. The city has one of the finest medical research complexes in the United States. Suburban Houston has attracted a large computer manufacturing industry.

A large petrochemical industry also thrives in Corpus Christi, another major port on the Gulf of Mexico. An important center for fishing and shrimping, Corpus Christi is a home port city for the United States Navy. Tourists come to the city in large numbers, and many of them visit the Texas State Aquarium and the World War II aircraft carrier *Lexington.*

Other cities in the Gulf Coast Plain include Beaumont, an important site for petroleum refining. Located southeast of Houston, Galveston is a popular spot for tourism, fishing, and shipping. Victoria, southwest of Houston, is a hub for agricultural and petrochemical production.

Reading Check **Identifying** List four important economic activities in the Gulf Coastal Plain.

The Post Oak Belt

As its name suggests, the Post Oak Belt contains many oak trees. Intermixed with these are other hardwood trees, such as hickories. Running through the Bastrop area is an extensive, isolated band of pine trees. Because this pine covered terrain does not connect to the Piney Woods, this area is sometimes called the Lost Pines.

Many crops grow well in the Post Oak Belt, including corn, grains, cotton, peanuts, pecans, hay, watermelons, peaches, and Christmas trees. Livestock graze and fatten in the area, too.

Although this section contains no large cities, education and light industry have thrived. The Bryan and College Station area—with a combined population of approximately 150,000 people—is the home of Texas A&M University. It is also an important center for medicine, agriculture, and service industries. Tyler, the largest city in the Post Oak Belt, produces thousands of rosebushes and calls itself the "Rose Capital of the World."

The Blackland Prairie

This region includes more of the state's larger cities and towns than does any other geographic section. It has excellent transportation systems and a large work force. Much of Texas's manufacturing takes place here.

Nowhere in this section is the growing season less than seven and one-half months, and early settlers found the soil fertile. As a result, this area is one of the most important agricultural regions in the state. Cotton, once dominant, remains an important crop here.

Dallas, the largest city in the Blackland Prairie, is the second largest city in Texas. An important transportation, commercial, and financial center, it serves as headquarters for more national insurance companies than any other city in the United States. Service groups such as the Boy Scouts of America also have their headquarters in Dallas. Also located in Dallas is The Women's Museum. The mission of this organization is to educate, enrich, and inspire all visitors by celebrating the history of women.

Dallas is an important merchandising center. Store owners from all over the country travel here to preview items before deciding what to buy for their stores. Dallas is also a center for Texas's high technology industry. This industry produces electronic products designed to make life more pleasant and efficient.

Dallas owes much of its growth to its centralized location. National highways and rail lines meet in Dallas. The Dallas–Fort Worth International Airport—one of the busiest airports in the nation—provides an important central pathway to other national and international airports.

The third largest city in Texas, San Antonio, lies at the edge of the Blackland Prairie and the Balcones Escarpment. San Antonio is the major metropolitan area in the southern part of Texas and plays a particularly important role as a distribution center. The federal government has located important military installations in San Antonio.

San Antonio is the number one tourist destination in Texas, attracting visitors to the **Alamo,** Fiesta Texas, River Walk, and the Institute of Texan Cultures. The city has a large and popular convention center. One of the most Hispanic of Texas's largest cities, San Antonio is a hub of Mexican American culture. Its special Tejano flavor is a major factor in attracting tourists to the city and surrounding area.

Austin, the capital of Texas, lies mostly within the Blackland Prairie. Travis County, which includes Austin, has experienced rapid growth and today has more than 800,000 people. In addition to being the center of state government, the city is also home to the University of Texas at Austin. Many high technology firms have moved to Austin, and it has become an important computer research center. Austin is often referred to as the live music capital of the world because of its large number of bands and dance halls.

Smaller cities also dot this geographic section. Sherman is the home of one of the state's best-known private colleges—Austin College. Waco, with key industries including agribusiness, general manufacturing, and health, is home to Baylor University, the state's largest Baptist university. San Marcos residents take pride in Southwest Texas State University, which houses the largest geography department in the nation.

✓ **Reading Check** **Analyzing** How did Dallas's location contribute to its rapid growth?

✵ *Exploring* **Geography**

The city of Dallas is located in the Blackland Prairie. How does the city skyline contrast with the natural landscape?

The South Texas Plain

The South Texas Plain tends to be much drier than the Gulf Coast Plain. Natural vegetation in much of this area includes plants that require little water such as prickly pear cactus, mesquite, blackbrush, and other small shrubs.

Many people in the South Texas Plain earn their living in agriculture and farming-related industries. Because of its southern location, the growing season here is more than 10 months. In the "Winter Garden" area in Dimmit and Zavala Counties, farming depends on water from wells and small streams. Cotton, vegetables, peanuts, and beef cattle are important agricultural products.

The southernmost part of this geographic section is called the Lower Rio Grande Valley. Rich **alluvial soils** have been deposited here by the Rio Grande over many years. These rich soils and Rio Grande water support an important citrus fruit industry. Texas is one of the nation's four largest producers of oranges, grapefruit, and lemons. Freezes strike the Lower Rio Grande Valley every few years, however, killing many trees.

Cities in the South Texas Plain include Laredo, which is located on the Rio Grande and is a gateway to Mexico. Laredo has varied manufacturing and meat-packing businesses and is also an important rail center. It is the chief entry point for Mexican and American trucks carrying products entering under the **North**

Exploring Geography

Many ranches in Texas have become corporations or multinational companies. What skills would be needed today to run a Texas ranch successfully?

American Free Trade Agreement (NAFTA). Kingsville, home of Texas A&M–Kingsville University and headquarters for the famous **King Ranch,** is a center for oil, gas, and ranching and farming. Brownsville, located at the southern tip of Texas, is a focus for farming and tourism and is another gateway to Mexico. Other large communities in the South Texas Plain are McAllen, Edinburg, and Harlingen.

✓ **Reading Check** **Explaining** Why do many people in the South Texas Plain work in farming-related industries?

SECTION 1 ASSESSMENT

Checking for Understanding

1. **Using Key Terms** Define petrochemical and alluvial soil and write a sentence using each word.
2. **Reviewing Facts** What is the largest natural region in Texas?

Reviewing Themes

3. **Economic Factors** What discovery made Texas the leading producer of oil in the United States?

Organizing to Learn

4. **Identifying** Create a chart like the one shown here. List what each city in the Piney Woods is known for.

City	Known for
Texarkana	
Longview	
Nacogdoches	
Huntsville	

Critical Thinking

5. **Making Comparisons** How are the Piney Woods and the Post Oak Belt similar?

TAKS PRACTICE

Determining Supporting Details
Dallas is an important marketing and transportation center. Write three supporting details that help prove this fact.

Texas LITERATURE

Randolph Barnes Marcy

R.B. Marcy spent much of his career on the frontier. After completing the U.S. Military Academy, he served a distinguished career in the U.S. Army. He fought in the Mexican War and later was assigned to duty in the western wilderness. His expertise led to his writing a guidebook for emigrants heading west. *The Prairie Traveler: A Handbook for Overland Expeditions,* published in 1859, became a bestseller.

Reading to Discover

As you read, imagine how you would feel if you were to chart and map an unknown area. What hopes and fears might you experience?

Reader's Dictionary

interspersed: distributed among other things

glade: an open space in a forest

summit: highest point or part

quarry: pit from which stone is taken

meanders: twists and turns

excursion: short journey

Explorations of the Big Wichita, etc.

by R.B. MARCY

In 1854, Captain R.B. Marcy explored and mapped the Big Wichita and Brazos Rivers. This excerpt from Marcy's report reveals an explorer's eye view of the uncharted Little Wichita River.

Our march this morning led us along a gradual slope of beautiful and picturesque country, **interspersed** with mesquite **glades** and prairie lawns, for about eight miles . . . when we found ourselves . . . upon the **summit** level of three streams, the "Brazos," "Trinity," and the "Little Witchita" . . . Were it not for the scarcity of timber . . . this would undoubtedly prove a desirable farming locality.

In previous communications to the War Department, I have spoken of the great deficiency of building timber where I have traveled west of the "Cross Timbers." It may be added here, that the same facts are observed in this section; and although mesquite is found sufficient for fuel, yet there is a great scarcity of timber, suitable for building purposes. There are, however, many **quarries** of stone, which might answer as a substitute . . .

After noon, we continued on for about eight miles over mesquite glades, when we arrived in a broad lowland valley, through which **meanders** a stream about twenty feet wide and two feet deep. This proved to be the main trunk of the Little Witchita. Its banks are about ten feet high . . . and skirted with elm and cotton wood.

We remained in camp on the 20th, making preparations to leave . . . while Major Neighbors and myself proposed to make an **excursion** towards Red River.

ANALYZING LITERATURE

Evaluate and Connect Why was it important for Texas to be explored and mapped?

Interdisciplinary Activity

Writing Create a travel brochure to promote the land Marcy describes.

The North Central Plains

Main Idea
The North Central Plains region includes the Cross Timbers, the Grand Prairie, and the Rolling Plains. Ranching and farming are important activities.

Key Terms
butte
agribusiness

Reading Strategy
Organizing Information As you read this section, complete a chart like the one shown here.

Geographic Section	Climate	Vegetation	Minerals

Read to Learn
• about the North Central Plains.
• about principal landforms and urban centers in each section.
• about the economy in each section.

Section Theme
Continuity and Change The North Central Plains region is mainly rural and agricultural with a relatively small population base.

Preview of Events

♦ *c. 140 million B.C.–c. 65 million B.C.*

└─ North Central Plains take shape

Mesquite tree

A
Texas Story

The North Central Plains are traditionally known as "where the West begins." Settlers moving into this area adapted to the new drier environment. Perry summed up the practice of early settlers who dug mesquite tree roots for firewood and climbed up to the springs of water running out of canyon walls—"The Texan will tell you that in West Texas you have to dig for wood and climb for water."

A Ranching and Farming Region

The North Central Plains actually start in Canada and extend across the midsection of the United States before ending in Texas. The Balcones Escarpment and the Caprock Escarpment separate the region from the rest of Texas.

The North Central Plains are higher in elevation than are the Coastal Plains. In many places, rivers making their way to the Gulf of Mexico have carved the North Central Plains into hills and valleys.

Relatively far from the Gulf of Mexico with its moderating winds, the North Central Plains have a continental climate that is colder in winter and hotter in summer than the lands near the Gulf. This region also receives less rainfall than the East. Much of the land is covered with grasses and brush instead of trees. Many of the large cattle ranches of the state are located here. In addition, because the region still receives good rainfall, flatter parts are used for farming row crops.

The small population of the North Central Plains reflects the mainly rural, agricultural nature of the area. The largest city, Fort Worth, began as a marketing center for cattle raised in the region. Today Fort Worth is a manufacturing center for airplanes, computers, and clothing. Other cities in the region include Abilene and San Angelo, which are marketing centers for ranch products such as wool and mohair.

The North Central Plains may be divided into three geographic subsections. They are the Cross Timbers, the Grand Prairie, and the Rolling Plains.

Reading Check **Examining** Why are many large cattle ranches located in the North Central Plains?

The Cross Timbers

Common trees in the wooded areas include post oaks, blackjack oaks, hickories, pecans, and elms. Today the Cross Timbers area is mostly agricultural. Peanuts, fruit, and vegetables are the main crops grown here. Most peanut farmers in the region grow Spanish peanuts, which can better tolerate dry spells than other varieties. Dairying and raising livestock are other important agricultural activities.

The Cross Timbers area contains several important cities. Arlington, located in the East Cross Timbers, is a leader in manufacturing, recreation, and tourism. Students are attracted to the city of Denton, also in the East Cross Timbers, because the University of North Texas and Texas Woman's University are located here. Brownwood, located in the West Cross Timbers, is an important center of regional trade and distribution.

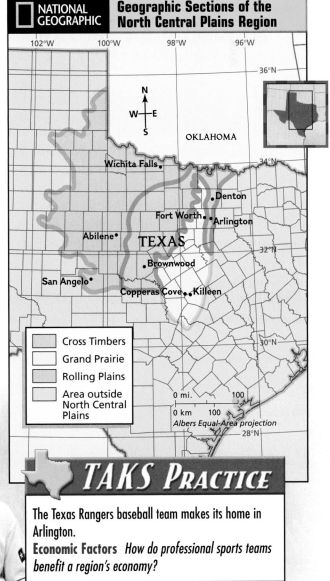

NATIONAL GEOGRAPHIC

Geographic Sections of the North Central Plains Region

Legend:
- Cross Timbers
- Grand Prairie
- Rolling Plains
- Area outside North Central Plains

0 mi. 100
0 km 100
Albers Equal-Area projection

TAKS PRACTICE

The Texas Rangers baseball team makes its home in Arlington.
Economic Factors *How do professional sports teams benefit a region's economy?*

The Grand Prairie

Limestone lies under the soil of the Grand Prairie, causing rain to soak through quickly. Because the soil fails to hold moisture for very long, trees are scarce throughout much of this area. Grasses and shrubs cover much of the terrain here, while trees are usually found along the banks of the numerous streams.

Agriculture is the most important economic activity in the Grand Prairie. Cattle are numerous and crops grown here include wheat, peanuts, corn, grain sorghum, and cotton.

Most towns in the Grand Prairie are rather small, but this section does have one of the state's largest cities, Fort Worth. Fort Worth and Dallas are the main cities of a 20-county area known as the **Metroplex.** The Metroplex is a major manufacturing and trade center. Whereas Dallas is a trade center that serves people who live mainly in the cities, Fort Worth likes to refer to itself as "the place where the West begins." Grain elevators, feed mills, and many other businesses serve the agricultural needs of rural people living farther west. Fort Worth is also an important financial hub. In addition, large-scale aircraft manufacturing brings in employees from across the state.

Two smaller communities located in the southern part of the Grand Prairie are Killeen and Copperas Cove. Both are located close to **Fort Hood,** one of the nation's largest military installations. They draw economic support from the army personnel and others who are employed at Fort Hood.

✓**Reading Check** **Analyzing** Why do you suppose Fort Worth describes itself as "the place where the West begins"?

The Rolling Plains

Lying west of the Cross Timbers, the Rolling Plains is the largest geographic section within the North Central Plains region. It is sometimes called the Lower Plains because of the higher Great Plains to the west. The Rolling Plains stretch for about 300 miles (483 km) from the northernmost to the southernmost point. At its widest point, this geographic section is just under 200 miles (322 km) across.

In most of the Rolling Plains, the landscape is slightly rolling. In some places, however, there are distinct hills, mesas, and **buttes,** or small flat-topped hills.

Large cattle ranches sprawl over many parts of the Rolling Plains. Sheep and goats graze in the drier western parts of this section. They can survive on the sparse vegetation better than cattle can. In the wetter area to the east, field crops of various kinds are grown. These include cotton, grain sorghum, and wheat. Specialty crops, including pecans and peaches, are also grown. Texas is one of the nation's leading producers of these two crops.

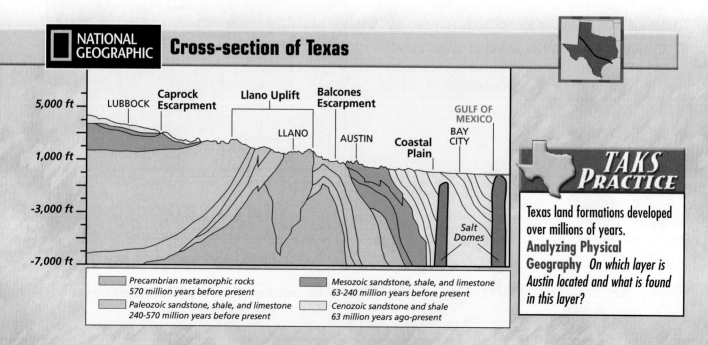

NATIONAL GEOGRAPHIC **Cross-section of Texas**

5,000 ft —
LUBBOCK | **Caprock Escarpment** | **Llano Uplift** | **Balcones Escarpment** | GULF OF MEXICO
LLANO | AUSTIN | **Coastal Plain** | BAY CITY

1,000 ft —

-3,000 ft —
Salt Domes

-7,000 ft —

Precambrian metamorphic rocks
570 million years before present

Paleozoic sandstone, shale, and limestone
240-570 million years before present

Mesozoic sandstone, shale, and limestone
63-240 million years before present

Cenozoic sandstone and shale
63 million years ago-present

TAKS PRACTICE

Texas land formations developed over millions of years.
Analyzing Physical Geography On which layer is Austin located and what is found in this layer?

Exploring **Geography**

Caprock Canyons State Park is the state's third largest park and contains part of the Caprock Escarpment. It is located in the Rolling Plains. How does the escarpment affect the landscape?

Only a few settlements dot the Rolling Plains. One of the larger communities is Wichita Falls, a city in the northeastern part of the section. Armed forces personnel work at the large United States Air Force base, and students move here to attend Midwestern State University. Distribution and marketing are important activities in Wichita Falls. Because Wichita Falls is located near the Texas–Oklahoma border, the city serves the people of both states.

Abilene, in the south-central part of the Rolling Plains, is an important oil services and marketing center. It is home to three church-related institutions of higher learning: Abilene Christian University, Hardin–Simmons University, and McMurry University. San Angelo, in the extreme southwestern part of the region, is a major center for agribusiness (large-scale commercial farming) and the home of Angelo State University. It is also the largest wool-producing market in the United States.

✓**Reading Check** **Explaining** Why is the Rolling Plains area less populated than other parts of Texas?

SECTION 2 ASSESSMENT

Checking for Understanding

1. **Using Key Terms** How is a butte similar to a hill and a plateau?
2. **Reviewing Facts** According to the text, in what country do the North Central Plains begin?

Reviewing Themes

3. **Continuity and Change** How has Fort Worth changed its commercial activities over time? Identify some specific products.

Organizing to Learn

4. **Identifying** Use the information in this section to create a chart like the one shown. List the major crops grown in each region in the chart.

Area	Crops
Cross Timbers	
Grand Prairie	
Rolling Plains	

Critical Thinking

5. **Analyzing Information** How does the amount and frequency of rainfall affect agriculture in the Rolling Plains area?

TAKS Practice

Drawing Inferences Peaches and pecans are specialty crops grown on the Rolling Plains. What can you infer about the economic activities of this area?

Reading an Economic Map

Why Learn This Skill?

Maps are designed to help people learn information about geographic areas. An economic map is a type of thematic, or special purpose, map. This economic map shows how people earn their living, but many economic maps show the distribution of products in a particular area. The Texas Economic Resources Map on this page illustrates what and where farm products are produced in Texas. It also shows where principal natural gas and oil production occurs. The map key explains what each symbol stands for. These symbols are placed on the map wherever the products are raised or produced in the state.

Learning the Skill

To read an economic map, follow these steps:

- Read the title of the map to identify the geographic area and the kind of information shown on the map.

- Read the map key to see what symbols (or sometimes colors) are used to represent this information.

- Use the symbols shown in the key to interpret the information on the map.

Practicing the Skill

Study the economic map on this page and then answer the following questions:

❶ Besides cattle, what other kinds of livestock are raised in Texas?

❷ Where are most sheep raised in Texas?

❸ What crop is grown only in the Coastal Plains region?

❹ Are cattle raised in East Texas, West Texas, or both?

❺ What farm products are raised in South Texas?

❻ Which mineral resource—natural gas or oil— occurs most often in the state?

NATIONAL GEOGRAPHIC — Texas Economic Resources

Map key:
Corn	Cattle
Cotton	Sheep
Rice	Natural gas
Wheat	Petroleum

0 mi. 200
0 km 200
Albers Equal-Area projection

TAKS PRACTICE

Creating a Thematic Map   Sketch a map of your school. Create a map key based on common school-day activities. Place the map key symbols on your map.

Glencoe's **Skillbuilder Interactive Workbook, Level 1,** provides instruction and practice in key social studies skills.

GO TO

The Great Plains

Texas farmstead during 1938 drought

★ A
Texas Story

In 1942, memories of Great Plains dust storms of the 1930s were fresh in the minds of Texans. The Great Plains could be beautiful and productive because they possessed great natural resources. They could also be harsh. Perry tells of a farmer on the Panhandle who was asked how he liked the weather. He said he did not like it. He explained, "The rain was all wind, and the wind was all sand."

The Real "Old West"

The Great Plains begin in Canada and run along the east side of the Rocky Mountains through Texas and into Mexico. The Caprock Escarpment divides the Great Plains from the North Central Plains to the east.

The Great Plains are at a higher elevation than are lands to the east. They reach their highest point in the northwestern corner of the Panhandle. Generally level, the Great Plains—often called a "sea of grass"—were once home to immense herds of buffalo and to nomadic Native Americans. Later, cattle raisers divided the land into giant ranches. Today much of the land is used to grow cotton and wheat.

Located far from the moist Gulf winds, the Great Plains region is a dry area. Long periods of less than normal precipitation, called **droughts,** are often problems. Only irrigation from underground water sources such as the Ogallala Aquifer and new techniques make farming possible. Because of its high elevation, the Great Plains often have cooler summers than other parts of Texas, and the winters are cold.

Many non-Texans picture Texas as it appears in movies about the Old West—as a land of sprawling ranches and isolated farms. Much of the Great Plains fulfill this image. Three geological subsections lie within the Great Plains region: the Edwards Plateau, the Llano Basin, and the High Plains.

✓ **Reading Check** **Explaining** How do farmers survive periods of drought in the Great Plains?

The Edwards Plateau

The Edwards Plateau lies farthest south of the three sections of the Great Plains. It is bordered on the east by the Blackland Prairie and on the south by the South Texas Plain and the Rio Grande. The Edwards Plateau occupies a large area of Texas. Its maximum east-to-west extent is nearly 300 miles (482 km). Its north-to-south depth varies from 50 to 175 miles (80 to 282 km).

Most of the Edwards Plateau ranges between 2,000 and 3,000 feet (610 and 914 m) above sea level. Throughout much of its area, the landscape is level to gently rolling. The landscape changes along its eastern borders, however. The boundary between the Edwards Plateau and the much lower Blackland Prairie is the Balcones Escarpment. As the Edwards Plateau nears this escarpment, it becomes a hilly area of eroded limestone called the Hill Country.

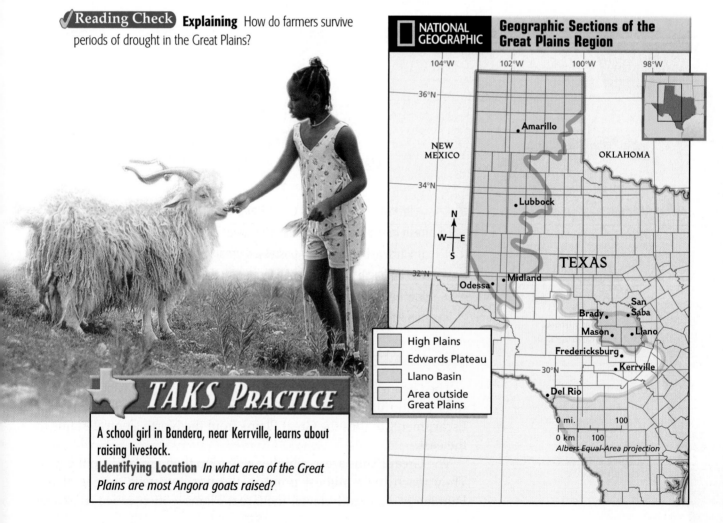

TAKS PRACTICE

A school girl in Bandera, near Kerrville, learns about raising livestock.
Identifying Location *In what area of the Great Plains are most Angora goats raised?*

NATIONAL GEOGRAPHIC
Geographic Sections of the Great Plains Region

High Plains
Edwards Plateau
Llano Basin
Area outside Great Plains

NEW MEXICO
OKLAHOMA
TEXAS

Amarillo
Lubbock
Odessa • Midland
Brady • San Saba
Mason • Llano
Fredericksburg
Kerrville
Del Rio

0 mi. 100
0 km 100
Albers Equal-Area projection

The Edwards Plateau has only a thin layer of soil, making most of the area ill-suited for farming. Almost the entire region is covered with a growth of cedar, small oak, and mesquite. Weeds and tree foliage provide food for sheep. The economy of the area depends largely on cattle, goat, and sheep raising. Most of the Angora goats in the entire United States can be found within 100 miles (161 km) of the center of the Edwards Plateau. This section is among the nation's most important wool-producing areas. The long hair of Angora goats is sheared and sold worldwide as mohair.

Parts of the San Antonio and Austin urban areas spill west onto the fringes of the Edwards Plateau. Towns such as San Marcos and New Braunfels also sit on its eastern boundary. Relatively few cities and towns, however, lie entirely on the Edwards Plateau. **Del Rio,** the area's largest city, is on the Rio Grande. It was founded by Paula Losoya Taylor and her sister, Refugia Losoya, around 1860. It is a center for trade with Mexico and a popular point for tourists to cross into that country. Two other cities—**Kerrville** and **Fredericksburg**—lie in the eastern Hill Country. Kerrville is a tourist center, a retirement community, and the location of several exotic game ranches. Fredericksburg is famous for its peaches and its German heritage.

The Hill Country itself attracts many visitors to its dude ranches. The famous LBJ Ranch, the Texas home of former **President Lyndon Johnson,** is here as well. The Hill Country also supports the greatest concentration of white-tailed deer in the world. Deer hunting attracts nearly 200,000 hunters to the Edwards Plateau each year. In the most recent year with the complete figures reported, Texas had the second-largest number of paid hunting license holders in the country. Only Pennsylvania issued more licenses.

Reading Check **Describing** What mineral lies under most of the Hill Country?

The Llano Basin

The Llano Basin is the smallest geographic section in Texas. It averages about 75 miles (121 km) east to west and about 60 miles (97 km)

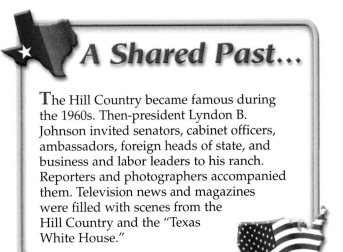

north to south. Elevations here are as much as 1,000 feet (305 m) lower than in the Edwards Plateau. The land is lower here because of erosion. The land has been worn away by the flowing waters of the Llano (LAH•no), San Saba (san SAH•ba), Pedernales (pur•duh•NAL•his), and Colorado Rivers. The terrain consists of rolling plains broken up by hills.

Part of the area is occupied by large lakes and reservoirs on the Colorado River. Lake Buchanan is the largest of these. The combination of lakes and hills has given this section the name Highland Lakes Country.

The Llano Basin has few towns. The main towns are seats of county government. Llano is a center for tourism, hunting, and livestock production. **San Saba,** in the northern part of the section, is a small town known for pecan-growing and processing. **Brady** has some industry—mainly the cleaning of wool and mohair. Scenic **Mason** is a market and supply center for area ranches. It also supports a growing tourism and guidebook publishing industry.

The High Plains

The High Plains occupy most of the Texas Panhandle, from the Oklahoma border southward about 350 miles (563 km). Elevations in this region reach more than 4,000 feet (1,219 m) above sea level in the northwestern part of the Panhandle. Visitors to the High Plains are often struck by the flatness of the land.

Longhorn Cavern Few places have had such an exciting and varied history as this large cavern located near Burnet. Comanches once met here in councils of war *(below right)*. Gunpowder was made and storehoused here during the Civil War. The cavern was even rumored to be the hideout of the outlaw Sam Bass. During Prohibition—when the sale of alcohol was banned—the cavern became a dancehall, nightclub, and restaurant *(bottom left)*. The park was officially opened in 1932.

When the first Spanish explorers crossed the High Plains, they were awed by what they saw. Pedro de Castañeda described the plains:

> 66The country is spacious and level … In traversing 250 leagues, the other mountain range was not seen, nor a hill nor a hillock which was three times as high as a man … The country is like a bowl, so that when a man sits down, the horizon surrounds him all around at the distance of a musket shot … [A]nd even if a man only lay down on his back he lost sight of the ground.99

Two areas have characteristics that are quite different from the general flat aspect of the High Plains. These are the Canadian Breaks and Palo Duro Canyon. The Canadian Breaks is a rugged area that follows the course of the Canadian River across the Panhandle. Because it is not well suited for farming, it is used mainly for grazing cattle. Palo Duro Canyon is a very rugged area that has been carved by the Red River. Palo Duro Canyon has long been home to wildlife and people alike. Native Americans used the canyon as a campsite and refuge from northers. Buffalo still grazed there when ranchers began moving to the area in 1876. Today, wild turkeys, deer, and many other kinds of wildlife share the Palo Duro Canyon State Park with visitors. The exciting musical drama "Texas" is performed every summer in the Pioneer Amphitheater in the canyon.

The High Plains section is divided into two major parts. The North Plains extends from the northern border of the Panhandle to about 50 miles (80 km) north of Lubbock. Wheat and grain sorghum (a major feed grain for cattle) are the most important crops. Cattle ranching and petroleum also contribute to this area's economy.

The South Plains occupies the southern part of the High Plains section. Cotton is the most important crop here. More cotton is raised in the

South Plains than in any other part of Texas. Lubbock has the world's largest cottonseed processing industry. Most of the crop is irrigated with water from the Ogallala Aquifer.

Several important urban centers can be found in the High Plains section. Amarillo, the largest city of the North Plains, is the most northern of Texas's major cities. It is a transportation and commercial center serving parts of Texas, New Mexico, Kansas, and Oklahoma. It also plays an important role in wheat distribution and as a major cattle market. Oil field equipment is manufactured here. Lubbock, the largest city in the South Plains, is the hub of a rich cotton-producing area. Lubbock serves as the commercial and cultural center for a large area of the Texas Panhandle and western Texas. Texas Tech University, one of the state's larger public universities, is located in Lubbock.

Midland and Odessa are located a few miles apart in the Permian Basin in the extreme southern part of the High Plains. The Permian Basin is an important petroleum-producing area. Life in Midland and Odessa centers around the oil industry. These cities also serve the needs of farmers and ranchers in the surrounding countryside. The University of Texas of the Permian Basin is located in Odessa.

✓ Reading Check **Identifying** Name one striking characteristic that visitors to the High Plains often notice.

Exploring Geography

Lubbock is the wholesale trade center for most of the Panhandle and eastern New Mexico. It is also the world leader of the cottonseed industry. What products from this area would be on these trains in the Lubbock railroad yards?

SECTION 3 ASSESSMENT

Checking for Understanding

1. **Using Key Terms** Sketch an illustration that shows you understand the meanings of the terms drought and erosion.
2. **Reviewing Facts** How is Amarillo's location important?

Reviewing Themes

3. **Economic Factors** How have people used Palo Duro Canyon both in the past and in the present?

Organizing to Learn

4. Complete a chart like the one shown here and list the major industries for each city in the Great Plains region.

City	Industries
Amarillo	
Lubbock	
Midland/Odessa	

Critical Thinking

5. **Analyzing Information** Based on the description of the High Plains given by Pedro de Castañeda, what two areas of the High Plains were *not* being described?

★ TAKS PRACTICE

Drawing Conclusions What did Spanish explorers find to be so awe-inspiring about the High Plains?

The Mountains and Basins

Guide to Reading

Main Idea

The Mountains and Basins region is an area of majestic peaks and stark deserts.

Key Terms

basin
maquiladoras

Reading Strategy

Organizing Information As you read this section, complete a chart like the one shown here.

Natural Vegetation	Minerals	Crops

Read to Learn

• about landforms and urban centers.
• about climate and resources.
• about human/environment interactions.

Section Theme

Geography and History The Mountains and Basins region maintains close economic and cultural ties to Mexico.

Preview of Events

♦ c. 140 million B.C.–65 million B.C.

└─ Mountains and Basins take shape

Yucca plants

A Texas Story

Much of the Mountains and Basins region gets only seven inches of rainfall per year. The other natural regions already discussed in this chapter contain several smaller sections. The entire Mountains and Basins region, however, is usually considered to be a single geographic section. Perry describes this region in his book: "Here is where Texas travels farthest west and dies of thirst. A citizen of this section, when asked how much it rained here, replied simply, 'Mister, it don't.'"

The Dry Environment

The Mountains and Basins region is part of the Rocky Mountain system that begins in Canada and extends into Mexico. It is the westernmost natural region in Texas. It is also the highest and driest of the regions.

Water—or lack of it—is the single most important factor affecting life in this region. It is mostly a desert area, and so little rain falls here that trees will grow only along the few scattered streams. The region's natural vegetation includes desert plants such as cactus, yucca, and creosote bush. Harsh extremes of climate are softened by its great natural beauty. Canyons and mountain plateaus contrast with saucer-shaped depressions called **basins.**

Of the few people who live in the region, nearly two-thirds live in El Paso. Farming is done mainly along the Rio Grande and in a few areas where springs or wells irrigate the land. Cotton is the main crop, but many farmers have pecan trees as well. Pecos, in Reeves County, is an area famous for its cantaloupes.

Many people in the Mountains and Basins region live near the Rio Grande where industries provide work. Towns have grown here around the trade with Mexico. The region has strong economic and cultural ties to Mexico, partly because the area is so far from the rest of Texas. The landforms, climate, and culture that make this area quite different from any other region in Texas also make it a favorite with tourists from other parts of the state and nation.

Mountain Ranges

All of Texas's true mountains are found in the Mountains and Basins region. The highest range, the Guadalupe Range, extends into New Mexico. The highest mountain in Texas, Guadalupe Peak at 8,749 feet (2,667 m), stands tall in this range. El Capitán, at 8,085 feet (2,464 m), is another Texas mountain in this range.

The Davis Mountains are located close to the center of the Mountains and Basins region. The highest peak here, Mount Livermore, stands at 8,206 feet (2,501 m). South of the Davis Mountains is a part of Texas called the Big Bend Country, which gets its name from a sharp bend in the Rio Grande. The Chisos Mountains make up the most important

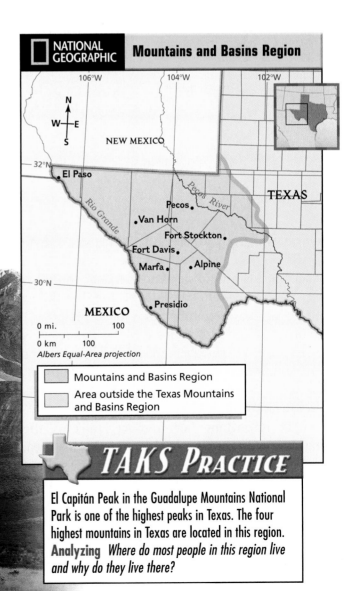

NATIONAL GEOGRAPHIC

Mountains and Basins Region

Mountains and Basins Region

Area outside the Texas Mountains and Basins Region

0 mi. 100
0 km 100
Albers Equal-Area projection

TAKS PRACTICE

El Capitán Peak in the Guadalupe Mountains National Park is one of the highest peaks in Texas. The four highest mountains in Texas are located in this region. **Analyzing** Where do most people in this region live and why do they live there?

Exploring **Geography**

Border crossings between cities like El Paso in Texas and Ciudad Juárez in Mexico offer opportunities as well as difficulties for many people. What opportunities and difficulties exist for Americans and Mexicans who live near the United States–Mexico border?

El Paso

mountain group in the Big Bend area. Steep canyons with spectacular scenery can be seen along the Rio Grande. The extreme southern part of this area consists of the Big Bend National Park, a popular area for tourists.

Much of the Mountains and Basins region is very dry. Cacti, yucca, and small desert shrubs are common in this region. Yet, a few mountain areas catch enough rainfall to support forests and meadowlands.

One important farming area lies in the extreme western part of this region. This area, the Upper Rio Grande Valley, is a narrow strip of irrigated land that runs east of El Paso for 75 miles (121 km) and north into New Mexico. Cotton is the most important crop grown here.

Petroleum and natural gas resources lie in the Mountains and Basins region. Other minerals include limestone, shale rock, and clay used in the production of cement. Copper, sulphur, salt, and talc also can be found here. Talc is used in the production of ceramics, paint, and artificial rubber.

Reading Check **Identifying** What are some of the desert plants of the Mountains and Basins region?

El Paso

Most of the Mountains and Basins region is very sparsely settled. The region, however, does have one of the state's largest cities—El Paso. El Paso is located at the far western tip of Texas. It is situated where the boundaries of Texas, Mexico, and New Mexico join. El Paso is far from Texas's other large cities. Many of the city's commercial ties are with New Mexico, Arizona, California, and Mexico.

El Paso has a strong Hispanic tradition. A popular tourist spot, it is located just across the Rio Grande from the large Mexican city of **Ciudad Juárez.** The combined population of El Paso and Ciudad Juárez is larger than that of any other urban center on the United States–Mexico border.

El Paso is the commercial center of the Upper Rio Grande Valley. Increased manufacturing has followed the establishment of the North American Free Trade Agreement (NAFTA). Many *maquiladoras,* which are often called "twin factories," have been built in Juárez and El Paso. These factories in Mexico serve as sources of labor for piecework contracts with large corporations from the United States, Japan, Germany, and other industrialized nations. El Paso also has oil refining facilities, diverse factories and businesses, and important military installations. The University of Texas at El Paso is located here as well.

NAFTA took effect in 1994. The goal of this agreement is to stimulate economic growth between Canada, the United States, and Mexico. Because of Texas's relative location, El Paso and other border cities are greatly affected. Since 1994, increased trade has helped companies along the United States–Mexico border grow. As a result, millions of new jobs were created in all three NAFTA countries, but especially in Mexico. On the negative side, some U.S. and Canadian

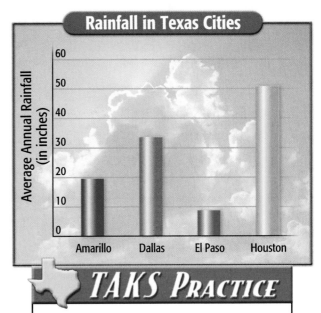

Rainfall in Texas Cities

Average Annual Rainfall (in inches)

Amarillo   Dallas   El Paso   Houston

TAKS PRACTICE

Comparing   The graph compares the average precipitation received by four Texas cities.
Why must many years of data be averaged to arrive at an accurate figure?

companies moved their factories to Mexico, where wages are lower. As a result, hundreds of U.S. and Canadian workers lost their jobs. The economic futures of border cities are closely related, and the effect of NAFTA on Texas cities such as El Paso is already being seen.

✓**Reading Check** **Examining** What is the purpose of the *maquiladoras?*

SECTION 4 ASSESSMENT

Checking for Understanding

1. **Using Key Terms** Define the terms basin and *maquiladoras* by using them in sentences.
2. **Reviewing Facts** Why does this region in Texas maintain ties with Mexico?

Reviewing Themes

3. **Geography and History** What is the single most important factor affecting life in the Mountains and Basins region?

Organizing to Learn

4. **Identifying Key Characteristics** Create a chart like the one shown here. Using the information in the section, identify the key characteristics of the Mountains and Basins region.

Largest city	
Highest mountain	
Main crop	
Major river	

Critical Thinking

5. **Making Comparisons** How is El Paso different from many other large Texas cities?
6. **Making Inferences** An "open" border is one that is fairly easily crossed. What are some advantages and disadvantages of open borders?

TAKS PRACTICE

Determining Cause and Effect   How has Mexico affected El Paso's economy?

Chapter Summary

Regions of Texas

Main Idea
The Coastal Plains region is the most populated and includes:

- Piney Woods
- Gulf Coast Plain
- Post Oak Belt
- Blackland Prairie
- South Texas Plain

Main Idea
The North Central Plains region is largely rural and includes:

- Cross Timbers
- Grand Prairie
- Rolling Plains

Main Idea
The Great Plains region is dry and high and includes:

- Edwards Plateau
- Llano Basin
- High Plains

Main Idea
The Mountains and Basins region is part of the Rocky Mountain system.

Reviewing Key Terms

Match each term with the correct definition.

a. *maquiladoras*
b. petrochemical
c. butte
d. erosion
e. basin
f. drought
g. alluvial soil

1. Product made from petroleum or natural gas
2. Soil that has been deposited from river water
3. A flat-topped hill, smaller than a mesa
4. Dry period in which less than the normal precipitation falls, often causing extensive damage to crops
5. The wearing away of the earth's surface by the movement of water, wind, ice, and gravity
6. A sunken area in a plateau found between mountain ranges
7. Factories in Mexico that assemble parts made in the United States

Reviewing Key Facts

8. Explain why the Coastal Plains region has a variety of agricultural activities.
9. What is the most important agricultural crop grown in the Lower Rio Grande Valley?
10. Explain why businesses are attracted to Houston, Dallas, and San Antonio.
11. List the important economic activities in the Cross Timbers.
12. What city is known as "the place where the West begins"?
13. What section is among the nation's most important wool-producing areas?
14. Name four urban centers—large cities—in the High Plains and their major industries.
15. Describe the climate of the Mountains and Basins region.

Critical Thinking

16. **Synthesizing Information** Why do you think five of the six most populous counties in Texas are located in the Coastal Plains?
17. **Making Comparisons** Choose two urban areas found in Texas. Compare their locations, industries, and other features.
18. **Making Conclusions** Do you think the people of Texas would benefit if the state were divided into several smaller states? Why or why not?

Geography and History

19. Create a chart like the one below. Place a check mark in the column in which the city is located.

City	Coastal Plains	North Central Plains	Great Plains	Mountains and Basins
Amarillo				
Austin				
Corpus Christi				
Dallas				
El Paso				
Fort Worth				
Houston				
San Antonio				

Cooperative Learning Activity

20. **Creating Models** After the class has been organized into four groups, have each group choose one of the four natural regions of Texas. Each group will make a physical model, or diorama, of a natural region. Use clay or a mixture of flour and water to indicate land features and rivers. Paint your diorama and exhibit it in your classroom.

Practicing Skills

Reading an Economic Map *Study the economic map on page 60 and then answer the following questions.*

21. According to the title, what kinds of resources are shown on this map?

22. How many different products are shown on this map?

23. Where are petroleum-producing regions found?

Economics and History Activity

24. **Local Economy** What are the major industrial and agricultural products of your community? Write a paragraph explaining what effects these industrial and agricultural products have on your daily life. Save your work for your portfolio.

Citizenship and History Activity

25. **Community Pride** Choose a town in Texas. Imagine you have been hired by the Chamber of Commerce to attract businesses or tourists to the region. Design a poster that would persuade businesses that this region would be a good place to locate.

 ## Portfolio/TAKS Writing Activity

26. **Generalizing and Supporting** Write a paragraph starting with this opening sentence: "The people living in Texas are fortunate because . . ." Use at least four facts in the chapter to support your conclusion. Consider geographic, economic, and social factors. After you have completed your paragraph, review it for possible spelling, capitalization, punctuation, or grammatical errors. Then exchange your paper with a student in your class to check again for possible errors. Make corrections and save the final draft for your writing portfolio.

 ## Building Technology Skills

27. **Creating a Database** Choose a city in Texas from the chapter. Using the Internet, find the official government Web site for the city that you chose, if possible. From the Web site, make a database of interesting facts about the city. Hint: Many Texas cities with an official Web site have the following URL: www.ci.[name of city].tx.us.

Use your knowledge of Texas geography to answer the following question.

Which of the following statements does not apply to the Great Plains region of Texas?

F Abilene is an important center in the Great Plains.

G The Great Plains frequently suffer from droughts.

H The Great Plains region is well-suited to cattle ranches and farms.

J Few people live in the Great Plains area of the state.

Test-Taking Tip:

Information of a general nature is often more likely to be true in a response than detailed information.

THE STORY OF TEXAS

THE BOB BULLOCK Texas State History Museum

Symbols of Texas

*T*exas is called the Lone Star State because of the single star on the state flag. Some symbols, like the flag, are visual. Others, including the pledge to the flag and the state motto, are expressed in words. No matter what form they take, symbols represent the values of the people of Texas and serve to keep alive the state's unique history.

Scenic Texas The bluebonnet became the state flower in 1901. The legislature declared the pecan the state tree in 1919. The mockingbird is the official state bird of Texas. ▶

Visit The Bob Bullock Texas State History Museum in Austin to see artifacts and exhibits such as these about Texas history and heritage.

"Honor the Texas flag: I pledge allegiance to thee, Texas, one and indivisible."

▲ Pledge to the Texas Flag

▲ **Texas State Seal**
By law, the Texas state seal is required to appear on official documents of the state.

The Six Flags of Texas

Spain The Spanish flag was ▶ the first to fly over Texas. During the 300 years of Spanish rule, Texas had several flags.

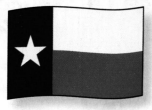

◀ **France** France was the second nation to claim Texas. The flag of royalist France showed golden lilies on a field of white.

▼ **The State Motto**

Mexico The Mexican flag ▶ was the official flag of Texas from 1821 until Texas independence in 1836.

◀ **Republic of Texas** The Lone Star flag, the state flag today, was also the flag of the Republic of Texas. It was approved in 1839.

The motto of the state of Texas is "friendship."

*The motto comes from the greeting "Tejas," with which the Native Americans of East Texas first met the early Spanish explorers. The word **tejas** means friends.*

Confederate States of America ▶
When Texas joined the confederacy in 1861, the "Stars and Stripes" was replaced by the Confederate flag.

◀ **United States of America**
Texas is symbolized by the 28th star in the American Flag.

UNIT ★
2 Explorers and Settlers

Beginnings to 1821

Why It Matters

As you study Unit 2, you will learn how Spain's three hundred years in Texas left a permanent impression that is expressed in law, language, religion, place names, and culture. Millions of Texans look proudly upon their own Spanish heritage.

Primary Sources Library

See pages 686–687 for primary source readings to accompany Unit 2.

Camp of the Lipans by Texas artist Theodore Gentilz (San Antonio Museum Association). The Lipans were an independent Apache group who lived near the Hill Country of central Texas.

"Long live America for which we are going to fight."

—Father Miguel Hidalgo,
"Cry of Dolores," September 16, 1810

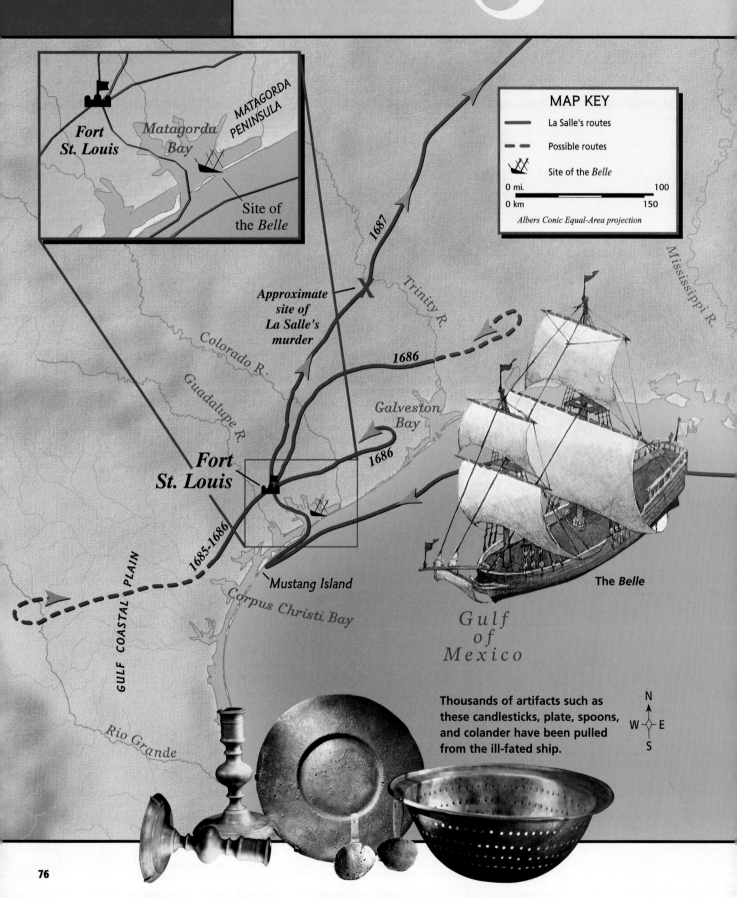

Fort St. Louis

Matagorda Bay

MATAGORDA PENINSULA

Site of the *Belle*

MAP KEY

— La Salle's routes

--- Possible routes

Site of the *Belle*

0 mi. 100
0 km 150

Albers Conic Equal-Area projection

1687

Trinity R.

Mississippi R.

Approximate site of La Salle's murder

Colorado R.

1686

Guadalupe R.

Galveston Bay

1686

Fort St. Louis

GULF COASTAL PLAIN

1685-1686

Mustang Island

Corpus Christi Bay

The *Belle*

Gulf of Mexico

Rio Grande

Thousands of artifacts such as these candlesticks, plate, spoons, and colander have been pulled from the ill-fated ship.

N
W E
S

Years of searching for the exact location of Fort St. Louis ended successfully in 1996 with the discovery of eight cannons.

Mississippi River Delta

Scientists were afraid that trying to raise the ship would destroy it. Instead of raising the ship, a watertight enclosure was built around the *Belle* and the water pumped out. Then the ship and artifacts could be safely brought up.

LA SALLE'S DOOMED EXPEDITION

In 1995 excited archaeologists discovered a shipwreck in Matagorda Bay. Three decorated bronze cannons assured them it was the *Belle,* one of four ships on an expedition led by La Salle. Sifting through artifacts, archaeologists are filling in the details of the four-year expedition whose aim was to establish a French colony at the mouth of the Mississippi.

From survivors' journals we know the explorers missed their destination and lost all four of their supply-laden ships. The diaries also described the hardships the colonists endured while La Salle scouted the area and searched for the main branch of the Mississippi.

The following discoveries are some examples of how the shipwreck findings support the survivors' accounts.

- A skeleton reveals death by drowning or thirst. Survivors said most of the settlers drowned, starved, got sick, died of thirst, or were killed by Native Americans.

- More than 500,000 glass beads and brass rings intended for trade with Native Americans were found. La Salle hoped the trinkets would persuade the Native Americans to help them capture Spanish silver mines.

- Fancy dishes, jewelry, candlesticks, and chess games on the *Belle* indicate some settlers intended to live in style.

- Muskets, cannons, and ammunition show that colonists were prepared to fight Native Americans or Spaniards.

Another discovery in 1996 excited Texas historians. Archaeologists located the site of La Salle's camp, Fort St. Louis. At that site, eight cannons were found. Bones of deer, bison, fish, turtles, snakes, and pigs verified that colonists had brought livestock from Europe and also hunted for food.

LEARNING *from* GEOGRAPHY

1. If you had been planning La Salle's expedition, what would you have taken to establish the colony?

2. Where was the wreck of the *Belle* found? About how far was it from La Salle's intended destination? (Hint: Use the scale on the map to find out.)

Native Texans

Why It Matters

The Native Americans who inhabited Texas led varied lives. Some were farmers and some were hunters. Some lived in skin tepees, and others in brush huts. The diversity of Texas's land and climate that you read about in Unit I was reflected in the lifestyles of the Native Americans.

The Impact Today

- Native Americans in Texas live both upon reservations and in the cities and small towns of the state.
- Pride in Native American culture is demonstrated at frequent festivals and tribal gatherings.
- All people—not just Texans—benefit from crops and customs developed by Native Americans.

c. 11,500–9500 B.C.
★ Ancient peoples arrived in Texas

c. 100 B.C.
★ Farming began in Texas

Texas

United States   c. 35,000 B.C.   c. 8,000 B.C.   c. A.D. 100

World

c. 35,000 B.C.
• People crossed to the Americas

c. 8,000 B.C.
• Last Ice Age ended

c. 2500 B.C.
• Egyptians made a type of paper from papyrus plant

Buffalo Hunt, Chase *by George Catlin. Catlin was one of the few artists to paint Native Americans in the 1830s and 1840s.*

FOLDABLES™ TAKS
Study Organizer PRACTICE

Sequencing Data Study Foldable Make this foldable and use it to sequence note cards with information about the original inhabitants of Texas—the native Texans.

Step 1 Fold a 2-inch tab along the long edge of a sheet of paper.

> Fold the left edge over 2 inches.

Step 2 Fold the paper in half so the tab is on the inside.

> The tab can't be seen when the paper is folded.

Step 3 Open the paper pocket foldable and glue the edges of the pockets as shown.

> Glue here.   Glue here.

Step 4 Follow steps 1 to 3 using another sheet of paper and label the pockets as shown.

| Ancient Texans | 1500–1699 | | 1700–1899 | 1900–2000 |

Reading and Writing As you read the chapter, record key facts about the first Texans on note cards or on quarter sheets of notebook paper. Organize your notes by placing them in your pocket foldable inside the appropriate pockets.

1875
★ Comanches were forced onto reservations

1850
★ 20 million buffalo lived on the plains

A.D. **1200**   **1400**   **1600**   **1800**

1271
• Italian Marco Polo traveled to China

1609
• Henry Hudson sailed up the Hudson River

1349
• Black Death killed one-third of the population of Europe

TEXAS HISTORY Online

Chapter Overview
Visit the texans.glencoe.com Web site and click on **Chapter 3—Chapter Overviews** to preview chapter information

The Ancient Texans

Guide to Reading

Main Idea
The first people to live in the Americas came from Asia in a series of migrations. Their patterns of living reflected a remarkable adaptation to their environment.

Key Terms
archaeologist, artifact, culture, anthropologist, nomad

Reading Strategy
Classifying Information As you read this section, complete a chart like the one shown here identifying how the different people in Texas adapted to their environment.

Native Americans	Gulf Peoples	Europeans

Read to Learn
• why people migrated to the Americas.
• how early people obtained food.
• about physical environment and early Native Americans.

Section Theme
Culture and Traditions Life in Texas has changed significantly since the first people arrived in Texas.

Preview of Events

c. 11,500 to 8500 B.C. — First humans reach regions of Texas

c. A.D. 100 — Farming begins in Texas

Women pounding corn

A
Texas Story

A woman put corn into a hollow log and pounded it into meal with a pole. As she pounded the corn, it disappeared, and she got no meal. Another woman came to pound corn in the log. Just as before, even though she put corn in, she got no meal out. The first woman got an axe and split the log. Out rolled a coyote. The coyote had turned himself into a hollow log so that he could eat the corn.

—From a Caddo folktale

The First Texans Arrive

The story of the people of Texas really begins before written records. Instead of writing knowledge down on paper, people passed it down by telling stories. Because corn was the most important crop for the farming

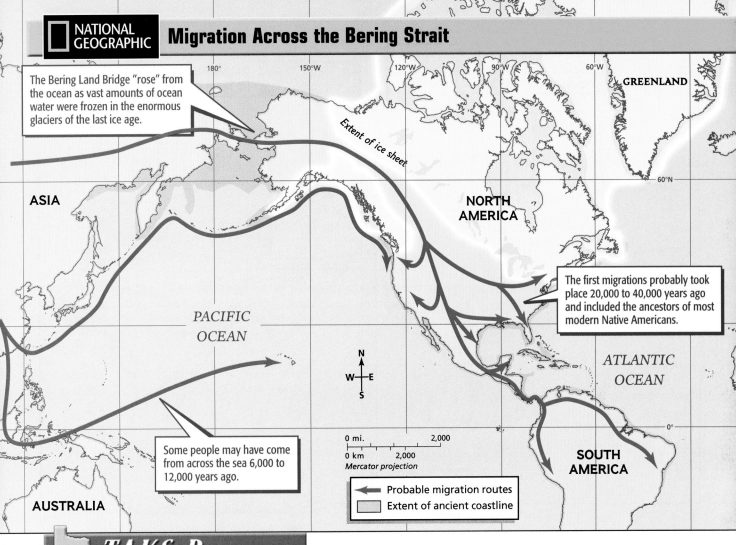

Migration Across the Bering Strait

The Bering Land Bridge "rose" from the ocean as vast amounts of ocean water were frozen in the enormous glaciers of the last ice age.

The first migrations probably took place 20,000 to 40,000 years ago and included the ancestors of most modern Native Americans.

Some people may have come from across the sea 6,000 to 12,000 years ago.

ASIA

NORTH AMERICA

GREENLAND

PACIFIC OCEAN

ATLANTIC OCEAN

SOUTH AMERICA

AUSTRALIA

Extent of ice sheet

0 mi. 2,000
0 km 2,000
Mercator projection

⟵ Probable migration routes
Extent of ancient coastline

TAKS PRACTICE

During an Ice Age approximately 35,000 years ago, people began to cross a land bridge at the Bering Strait from Siberia into the Americas.

Making Inferences *What reasons would cause people to migrate from Siberia to the Americas and move southward?*

people, many of those tales were about corn. Thousands of years before Europeans arrived in the Americas, people lived in Texas and learned about their early history from storytellers.

People migrated to the Western Hemisphere as early as 35,000 years ago. They migrated from Asia over a land bridge connecting Siberia and Alaska. Today Siberia and Alaska are separated by a narrow body of water, the **Bering Strait.** During the last Ice Age, however, water did not always cover this area, and people simply walked across the land.

Why did these people migrate? These early people were hunters. They followed herds of animals to modern-day Alaska. Throughout the centuries, the newcomers ventured farther and farther into the interior of North America, while new waves of immigrants crossed the Bering Strait. Evidence indicates that humans first reached regions of Texas approximately 11,500 years ago.

Artifacts Are Historical Clues

Much of what is known about ancient people comes from studies by **archaeologists.** These scientists study evidence of past human activity. They search the earth for **artifacts,** such as tools, artwork, human and animal bones, pottery, baskets, and shells. Paintings on rocks and in caves and canyons of Southwest Texas provide glimpses of how ancient people viewed

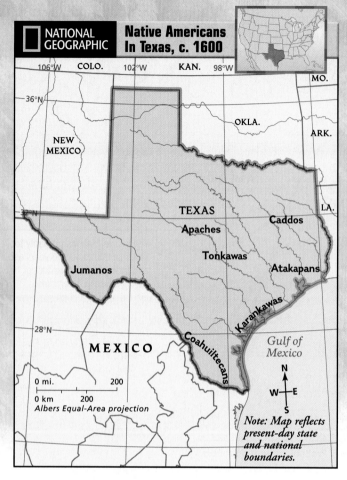

Native Americans In Texas, c. 1600

106°W COLO. 102°W KAN. 98°W
MO.
36°N
OKLA.
ARK.
NEW MEXICO
TEXAS
Caddos
LA.
Apaches
Tonkawas
Atakapans
Jumanos
Karankawas
28°N
Coahuiltecans
MEXICO
Gulf of Mexico

0 mi. 200
0 km 200
Albers Equal-Area projection

N
W E
S

Note: Map reflects present-day state and national boundaries.

Native Americans Settled In Texas By 1800

106°W COLO. 102°W KAN. 98°W 94°W
MO.
36°N
Kiowas
Kiowa Apaches
OKLA.
ARK.
NEW MEXICO
Cherokees
Comanches Wichitas
Alabama-Coushatta
Tiguas Mescalero Apaches
Caddos
LA.
TEXAS
Tonkawas
Lipan Apaches
Atakapans
Kickapoos
Karankawas
28°N
Coahuiltecans
MEXICO
Gulf of Mexico

0 mi. 200
0 km 200
Albers Equal-Area projection

N
W E
S

TAKS PRACTICE

By 1800, there were more Native American groups living in Texas than in 1600.
Analyzing Population Changes *What reasons might account for the presence of more Native American groups in Texas by 1800?*

themselves and how they lived. Changes in pottery or tool styles may be evidence of people moving into an area. Human bones, like those found near the Texas cities of Midland and Leander, provide information about how ancient people looked and what diseases they endured.

✓ **Reading Check** **Summarizing** What are some items archaeologists study to learn how people once lived?

Early People Hunt for Food

The first inhabitants of Texas arrived during the Paleolithic period, or the **Stone Age** (about 8,500 to 11,500 years ago). These people obtained their food by hunting large animals, such as the mastodon, mammoth, and giant bison. The people lived in small groups and stayed in one place only temporarily. More often they followed the herds of animals. They also hunted small animals such as rabbits, squirrels, and birds.

These people had several advantages, even though they were smaller, and slower than many of the animals they hunted. The people had tools and developed a notched throwing stick called an *atlatl* (AT•lat•el). They used flint-tipped spears and darts to make a kill. Strategy was another advantage. One strategy was the "surround," in which the hunters encircled a herd of animals and then moved in and killed the animals as they tried to escape.

During the **Archaic Age,** about 8,000 years ago, life in early Texas changed. The climate became warmer and drier, and large game animals disappeared. People still hunted, but now they pursued smaller game. To help them find and prepare their food, they developed a variety of tools made of stone or bone. These included axes, picks, drills, choppers, scrapers, and grinding tools, such as mortars and pestles. They did not depend on meat alone, but gathered berries, nuts, and roots. The hunter-foragers stayed in one area longer than the earlier hunters but did not settle permanently because they were always searching for food.

Hunters Become Farmers

While wandering bands of hunters and gatherers searched for food in Texas, people in central Mexico were growing their own food. Sometime around A.D. 100, several groups of people in Texas began to adopt this settled way of life. Among the first crops to be grown were peanuts, corn, tomatoes, various beans, pumpkins, squash, and cotton.

How did the rise of farming change the way people lived? First, farming meant a more dependable source of food. More available food resulted in an increase in the population. Now, however, people could not leave their gardens and farms untended. People no longer roamed in search of food. Instead they began to settle in one area for years at a time, building and living in villages. Living in one place meant that there was other work to do. This led to more complex societies that included craft workers, warriors, and political and religious leaders, as well as farmers.

Different Cultures Emerge

The early people of Texas developed into distinct cultures—all the ways groups of people express and conduct themselves. Culture includes language, customs, clothing, shelter, ways of working and playing, and beliefs.

At the time the first Europeans arrived in what they called the Americas, there were four separate culture groups living in the area that became Texas. Anthropologists have named these the **Southeastern, Gulf, Pueblo** (pweh•BLOH), and **Plains cultures.**

Each of these cultures developed differently as they adapted to the physical surroundings. Some Indians of the Southeastern United States lived in the fertile and well-watered land of East Texas. They raised crops and settled in permanent villages. The land of the Gulf people, on the other hand, was unsuitable for farming. The Gulf people did not stay in one place but were nomads who hunted and foraged. These Native American cultures influenced Europeans who migrated to the area later. Europeans learned to prepare new foods, cultivate plants that would grow well in the region, and hunt native animals. New arrivals often adopted Native American names for places, foods, and animals. For example, the Native American word "cotoyl" became "coyote" and "tamalli" became "tamale."

✓ Reading Check **Defining** What is culture?

SECTION 1 ASSESSMENT

Checking for Understanding

1. **Using Key Terms** Write a sentence using the words archaeologist, artifact, and culture.
2. **Reviewing Facts** How did early people first reach the American continent from Asia?

Reviewing Themes

3. **Culture and Traditions** How do scientists learn how ancient people viewed themselves?

Organizing to Learn

4. **Sequencing** Create a time line like the one shown here. Place the following events in the proper sequence.

   ┼────┼────┼────┼────┼

   a. Europeans arrive in Texas.
   b. People obtain food by hunting.
   c. People migrate from Asia to present-day Alaska.
   d. People grow food.

Critical Thinking

5. **Explaining** How did farming change the way native people in Texas lived?

TAKS PRACTICE

Determining Cause and Effect
What was one reason why cultures in Texas developed differently? Consider geography and economics in your answer.

Identifying Primary and Secondary Sources

Why Learn This Skill?

Knowing the source of information is one way to evaluate how accurate it is.

Historical information comes from primary and secondary sources. Primary sources are documents created at the time the event occurred. Letters, speeches, journals, newspaper articles, and photographs are examples of primary sources. Secondary sources are documents created after an event occurred by someone who was not an eyewitness. A secondary source uses primary sources for information.

Not all sources of information are written. Historians also rely on artifacts and pictures. Artifacts are objects that humans made and used.

Learning the Skill

Follow these steps to help you analyze information:
- Identify the kind of information, who created it, and when.
- Examine the information and try to answer the "five W" questions: Who is it about? What is it about? When, where and why did it happen?
- Summarize the key ideas.

Practicing the Skill

Read the following primary source passage. Use the steps to help you analyze the information.

"You white men often forget your promises . . . You want to settle us on a reservation near the mountains . . . I don't want to settle. I love to roam over the prairies. There I feel free and happy . . . A long time ago this land belonged to our fathers; but when I go up the river I see camps of soldiers . . . These soldiers cut my timber, they kill my buffalo, and when I see that it feels as if my heart would burst with sorrow."

Satanta, Kiowa chief, 1867

Chief Satanta

❶ Is this a primary or secondary source? How can you tell?

❷ Who is the author?

❸ When was it written?

❹ What is the passage about?

❺ What emotions does the Kiowa chief express about the situation?

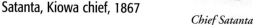
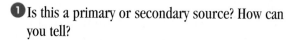

TAKS Practice

Identifying Primary and Secondary Sources
Imagine that historians in the distant future are analyzing primary sources to find out more about your life. What written or visual sources might they analyze? List as many specific examples as you can.

Glencoe's **Skillbuilder Interactive Workbook,** Level 1, provides instruction and practice in key social studies skills.

Southeastern and Gulf Cultures

Guide to Reading

Main Idea
Native American people of Southeastern and Gulf cultures developed different ways of life based on their environment and needs.

Key Terms
confederacy, matrilineal, shaman

Reading Strategy
Organizing Information As you read this section, complete a chart like the one shown here, identifying different aspects of each tribe's way of life.

	Food	Settlements
Caddos		
Coahuiltecans		
Karankawas		
Wichitas		

Read to Learn
• how the environment shaped the Southeastern and Gulf cultures.
• how European settlements affected Native Americans.

Section Theme
Culture and Traditions The people who lived in Texas before the Europeans arrived shared many similarities, but also differed from each other.

Preview of Events

♦1500	♦1600	♦1700	♦1800

Many Native American people occupy Texas

late 1780s
Alabama and Coushatta nations settle in East Texas

1820
Cherokees settle in Texas

Bear on hind legs

A
Texas Story

Bear owned Fire and carried it with him. One day Bear put Fire down so that he could eat acorns. Bear forgot about Fire. Fire grew weak and cried, "Feed me." People heard Fire and asked, "What do you eat?" Fire replied, "I eat wood." The People brought sticks and Fire grew stronger. Bear came back. Fire said, "You forgot me, so I no longer know you." Fire then said to People, "If you will take care of me, I will take care of you." That is how People got Fire.

—From an Alabama–Coushatta legend

Early People

People who lived in Texas before Europeans arrived shared many similarities. Most lived in small groups and shared responsibility for decision making. Early people believed spirits caused rain, fire, the change of seasons, and the existence of streams and rivers. According to Native American beliefs, these spirit beings walked the earth and interacted with human beings. Sometimes they helped, but they were also known to cause harm. The cultures of early people in Texas also believed that animals, plants, and humans once understood each other's languages. People were connected with the earth in a special relationship. Each of these cultures had a creation story, or explanation of how the earth and people were created. But these Native Americans also were different from one another. They did not speak the same language. Some were peaceful, but some were warlike. While many lived in communities, others moved frequently.

Southeastern Farmers and Gatherers

The Native American people of the Southeastern culture—among them the Caddos (KAD•ohz), Karankawas (kah•RAHNK•ah•wahz), and Coahuiltecans (koh•ah•weel•TAY•kahnz)—also were not alike. Some of these Southeastern people, like the Caddos, farmed. When people had a steady source of food, they did not have to move constantly searching for wild berries and roots. They were able to build permanent settlements and more permanent housing. Many villages became trade centers for the surrounding areas. (See the Economics and History feature on pages 98–99 for an explanation of how trade developed between the eastern and western regions of Texas.) Others, like the Karankawas and Coahuiltecans of the Gulf cultures, used the coastal waters for fishing, and many groups gathered foods that grew in the wild such as roots and berries. During the 1600s, as new Native American groups joined the Caddos, these groups turned to raising crops.

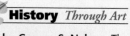

History *Through Art*

Mural by George S. Nelson. The Caddo people were farmers who lived in the Piney Woods region of East Texas. They built domed structures for living quarters. What natural resources did they use to build their homes?

Caddo land

The Caddos

More than 24 groups made up the Caddo people. These groups were part of larger associations called **confederacies.** Two of the confederacies that lived within the boundaries of present-day Texas were **matrilineal,** tracing descent through their mothers.

Each Caddo group had its own government, headed by two leaders. One leader handled matters of war and peace, and the other directed religious affairs. A Caddo leader usually had many helpers, and both women and men could hold powerful positions in government. The Caddos were the most numerous and agriculturally productive of all the native Texas nations. From 1520 to 1690, because of the introduction of European diseases, their numbers decreased from around 200,000 to only about 12,000.

For hundreds of years, the Caddos lived and farmed in the East Texas timberlands. They cultivated fields of squash, beans, pumpkins, melons, sunflowers, plums, and two crops of corn each year. The men cleared the fields, and Caddo women planted and tended the crops.

Although they grew much of their food, the Caddos also gathered wild fruit and berries. They also excelled at fishing. Across a stream Caddos often strung a trotline, a long, heavy fishing line to which they attached several baited hooks. This practice is used in fishing today. Caddo men also hunted for turkeys, deer, and bears.

Most Caddos lived in permanent villages. They built dome-shaped houses of mud, poles, and straw, sometimes 50 feet (15 m) in diameter.

The Caddos often engaged in warfare. They fought other Native American nations, sometimes other members of the confederacies, and occasionally European settlers who arrived near their settlements after the 1600s. They were usually on friendly terms with the French, who were more interested in trade than in taking Caddo land. When there was trouble between Spain and France, the Caddos were likely to support the French.

The Caddos were part of a vast trade network that stretched from the Great Lakes to the Gulf of Mexico and from the Rocky Mountains to the

It is fiction that large herds of buffalo roamed the Great Plains. Zoologists do not consider the "American buffalo" to be a true buffalo. They call it a *bison.* Unlike the true buffalo of India, Asia, and Africa, bison have a large head and neck and humped shoulders. They also have 14 pairs of ribs, instead of the 13 pairs like true buffalo. The use of the term *buffalo* is still commonly accepted, however.

Appalachians. Shells, stones, and other trade goods from hundreds of miles away have been found in eastern Texas. The center of the trade network was Cahokia, located near present-day St. Louis, Missouri. In 1859, the Caddos were relocated to reservations in present-day Oklahoma, where their descendants live today.

Reading Check **Describing** Briefly describe the Caddo system of government.

The Search for Food

While the Caddos were building farming communities, the Native American people along the Gulf of Mexico led a nomadic life. The environment left them little choice. The marshy lands along the Texas coast made farming difficult for Gulf people, like the Coahuiltecans and the Karankawas. They lived by hunting small game and gathering nuts, cacti, and other plants.

The Coahuiltecans

The Coahuiltecans seldom strayed from the dry and brushy land called the South Texas Plain. With bows and arrows, the Coahuiltecans hunted deer, bison, and javelina. The javelina is a small animal that looks something like a wild boar without tusks. The Coahuiltecans gathered cacti, mesquite, agave, and other plants, dried them, and ground them into flour. When game was scarce, they ate worms, lizards, and plants. Constantly on the move to find food, Coahuiltecans seldom spent more than a few weeks at each campsite.

Picturing **History**

The shaman led religious ceremonies, gathered herbs, and made medicines to heal the sick in Native American cultures. What are some elements of this shaman's costume?

All members of Coahuiltecan society enjoyed equal status and shared the available food and water. In camp, everyone had to work. Women took care of the camp, and men hunted. Those who were unable or too old to do heavy labor still worked at other tasks. **Shamans,** people believed to have the power to summon spirits and to cure the sick, were important to Coahuiltecan life, just as they were to other Native American people. Shamans led the religious ceremonies, made medicine from plants, and cared for the sick.

By the time Texas became a part of the United States, the Coahuiltecans had almost disappeared from the Gulf region. Many had been killed in battle. Others had moved into Mexico or into other areas. A great many Coahuiltecans had died from diseases that the Europeans brought to the region.

Reading Check **Identifying** What was the role of the shaman in Native American culture?

The Karankawas

The Karankawas lived along the Gulf Coast and on the small islands between Galveston and Corpus Christi Bays. The people roamed in search of food. From about March to September, the Karankawas built camps near the forests. This allowed them to gather nuts and berries and hunt deer, bears, and stray buffalo that occasionally wandered onto the coastal prairie. In the fall and winter, the Karankawas moved their camp to near the sea. Karankawans in dugout canoes—their most treasured possessions—caught fish, porpoises, and turtles. They also gathered clams, oysters, and underwater plants.

Members of the Karankawa family worked together to make tools necessary for their existence. They made pottery jars and bowls and wove baskets. The pottery and baskets were coated with tar to make them waterproof. When North American settlers moved onto the Coastal Plains in the 1820s, fighting broke out between settlers and Karankawas. By the mid-1800s, almost all Karankawas were displaced or killed.

Other Southeastern Cultures

After the Europeans explored Texas during the early 1500s, other Native American people arrived in the area just west of Caddo country. Many of these newcomers came from areas north of Texas. Technology introduced by the Europeans, such as guns and horses, had changed tribal relationships. Some were trying to escape warring neighbors. Others were looking for a place where living would be easier. Many began to trade with local Native American groups, the French, or the Spaniards.

The Wichitas

The prairies and oak timberlands that today surround the cities of Dallas, Fort Worth, Waco, and Wichita Falls were once the home of the Wichitas. Several tribes were collectively known as Wichitas. During the 1600s, they moved from a region in present-day Kansas into lands along the Trinity, Red, and Brazos Rivers.

The Wichitas built villages, grew crops, and hunted game. Wichita villages and houses resembled Caddo villages and houses. Wichita women held positions of leadership and shared work with the men.

Because they lived in lands sought by others, the Wichitas often were at war. Like the Caddos, they got along well with French traders. They often fought Spanish settlers, who tried to force them into the Spanish settlements. When the Spaniards began trading with them instead, the fighting would stop. Like the Caddos, the Wichitas were forced by the Anglo American settlers to give up their land. Today several hundred descendants of the Wichitas live in Oklahoma.

More Native American Groups Arrive

Several groups called the Atakapans lived along the coast between Galveston Bay and the Sabine River. They are classed as part of the Southeastern culture, but in many ways they followed the practices of other cultures. Their culture was much simpler than that of the Caddos.

About 1820, some Cherokees voluntarily moved from the Allegeny Mountains in the eastern United States and settled in Texas. They built homes in the woodlands north of

A Shared Past...

Although ancient North Americans domesticated many plants, they had only two domesticated animals—the dog and the turkey. Meanwhile European, African, and Asian people were domesticating many animals including cattle, horses, sheep, goats, chickens, camels, and pigs. The first Native Americans to see Europeans on horseback were amazed by the sight.

Nacogdoches. In 1839 Anglo settlers forced the Cherokees to move to present-day Oklahoma.

Between 1780 and 1816, the Alabama and the Coushatta nations—two Native American groups from east of the Mississippi River—migrated to Texas and established a village by the Trinity River. They left the region during the Texas war for independence. In 1854, after years of nomadic life, the Alabamas and the Coushattas agreed to live on a reservation near present-day Livingston.

✓ **Reading Check** **Explaining** Why did the Wichitas and Caddos exist peacefully with the French?

SECTION 2 ASSESSMENT

Checking for Understanding

1. **Using Key Terms** Write a paragraph about early Native American tribes in Texas. Use the terms confederacy, shaman, and matrilineal.
2. **Reviewing Facts** What tasks did Caddo government leaders take charge of?

Reviewing Themes

3. **Culture and Traditions** Describe the importance of the role played by the shaman in Native American cultures.

Organizing to Learn

4. **Categorizing** Create a chart like the one shown here. Decide which groups of Native Americans still live in Texas today. Place a check in the appropriate column.

Native American Group	In Texas	Out of Texas
Caddos		
Wichitas		
Alabamas		
Karankawas		

Critical Thinking

5. **Explaining** Both the Coahuiltecans and the Karankawas migrated. What were their reasons for doing so?
6. **Analyzing** How were the Caddos involved in trade with other groups of the time?

TAKS PRACTICE

Drawing Conclusions How did the French and the Spanish affect the lives of Native Americans in Texas?

Pueblo and Plains Cultures

Guide to Reading

Main Idea
Native American people of the Pueblo and Plains cultures developed different ways of life based on their environment and needs.

Key Term
middlemen
adobe
tepee

Reading Strategy
Organizing Information As you read this section, complete a web like the one shown here. List the Native American people of the Pueblo and Plains cultures.

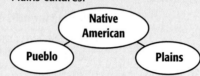

Native American
Pueblo
Plains

Read to Learn
• how the environment shaped the Pueblo and Plains cultures.
• about the buffalo's importance.

Section Theme
Groups and Institutions Native American people fought to protect their way of life from other Native Americans and from the Europeans who came to Texas.

Preview of Events

1500	1600	1700	1800
The Spaniards introduce the modern horse	Tonkawas arrive in Texas	Apaches and Comanches settle in Texas	20 million buffalo live on the Plains

Desert plant

A
Texas Story

Wind was talking to Thunder, "I do all the work. I make the grasses and trees bow down." "No," Thunder said, "I do all the work. I bring the Rain, which washes away everything in its path." Wind said, "My power is greater." Thunder became angry and left. Wind thought, "I don't need him. I can make the plants grow." Wind blew and the earth became dry. He blew even harder, but the harder he blew, the more the plants withered. Wind learned that the earth needs Wind and Rain.
                                                    —From an Apache legend

The Jumanos and the Tiguas

One group of Pueblo people were the **Jumanos** (hoo•MAH•nohz). They lived by trading and hunting buffalo throughout present-day Texas, New Mexico, and northern Mexico. Jumanos acted as middlemen, or go-betweens, for the eastern farming tribes, such as the Caddos, and the western Pueblo people who lived in cities built on the sides of cliffs. The Plains Jumanos traded animal skins and meat for agricultural products—such as corn, squash, and beans. They also traded for decorative items such as paint pigments, turquoise, and feathers. Their arrows were so well made that the eastern tribes were eager to trade for them.

Jumanos had distinctive striped tattoos on their faces. These markings made it easy for a member of another tribe to recognize the individual as a peaceful trader. Men cut their hair short except for one long lock to which they tied colorful feathers. Women wore their hair in long braids.

Other Jumanos lived a more settled life along the Rio Grande where it flows from present-day El Paso to Big Bend National Park. They were farmers who used natural irrigation methods long before the arrival of the Spanish. The settled, or Pueblo, Jumanos raised corn, squash, beans, and other vegetables for food. When there was no rain and the crops failed, the Jumanos gathered and ate mesquite beans, prickly pear tunas, and other edible cacti. They also hunted small animals, deer, and buffalo.

The farmhouses of the Pueblo Jumanos were unlike the houses of the Gulf and Southeastern cultures. A typical Jumano house was large, perhaps 28 by 30 feet (8 by 9 m), and made of sun-dried earth and straw called **adobe.** The flat roof, made of poles and branches, was covered with adobe. Adobe houses stayed cool in summer and warm in winter. Because the climate was very dry, these houses lasted for years.

About the time that the Spanish were exploring the Plains homes of the Jumanos, the Apaches were moving south onto the Plains. The Jumanos fought to maintain their territory and their trade relationships, but the Apaches prevailed. Long before Texas became part of the United States, the Jumanos almost disappeared. Some moved into Mexico, and others joined other Native American bands.

Another Pueblo people, the Tiguas (TEE•wahs), moved to **Ysleta** (ihs•LEHT•uh) near present-day El Paso after a revolt by Pueblo tribes in New Mexico in 1680. Their descendants live in the same area today. The state of Texas recognized the Tigua people as Texas Native Americans in May of 1967 and set up a reservation for them. Traditional Tigua kinship was matrilineal, meaning that the home and land belonged to the mother's clan group. Today, however, the Tigua custom is to trace descent through the father. Ownership is transferred through the male members of the family. The Tiguas' principal public celebration is Fiesta de San Antonio, held on June 13. The men dress in calico-fringed jackets and the women wear colorful dresses from the days when Spain ruled them.

✓ **Reading Check** **Contrasting** How were the Pueblo Jumano homes unique?

Picturing **History**

The Tigua homes were often pueblos made of adobe (dried mud) bricks. The dome-shaped structure was an oven for baking. What were the benefits of an adobe house?

Buffalo Chase, Bulls Making Battle With Men and Horses by George Catlin, 1832 to 1833 This image illustrates Native Americans among the buffalo. How was hunting buffalo a risky venture?

The Plains Cultures

The way of life of the Plains culture changed with the arrival of horses. Horses crossed the Bering land bridge from Asia at the same time humans did, but many animals became extinct on this continent at the end of the last Ice Age. Spaniards reintroduced horses to the Americas beginning around A.D. 1500. There was no animal more suited for life on the plains. Spanish horses were swift and strong and could eat any available grass. Although most people of the Plains culture did not have horses until the late 1600s, they soon learned to use horses to their best advantage. With horses, the people of the Plains culture became outstanding hunters in peace and dangerous foes in war.

Buffalo, actually a type of bison, had roamed the plains for centuries. They were found nearly everywhere in Texas, except in the Piney Woods region. In 1850 about 20 million buffalo lived on the plains. By the late 1800s, however, white hunters had slaughtered millions of the animals. Plains people depended on the buffalo for food, and the destruction of the great herds meant the end of the Plains people's way of life.

The Tonkawas

The Tonkawas (TAHN•kah•wahz) of the Plains culture arrived in Texas in the 1600s. They lived on the southeastern edge of the Edwards Plateau near present-day Austin. Some Tonkawas also lived on the coastal plains to the south or along the eastern rivers.

Although the Tonkawas depended on buffalo for food and shelter, few herds roamed through Tonkawa hunting grounds. Buffalo were plentiful in the open plains to the west, but hunting there was risky. Fierce Apaches and Comanches (koh•MAN•cheez) resented other groups hunting in their territories. Forced to look for other food, the Tonkawas hunted deer, rabbits, turtles, and snakes.

Never large in number, the Tonkawas lost many people because of almost constant conflict with other Native Americans and European settlers. However, the Tonkawas survived despite hardships, war, and removal from what is now Texas.

✓ **Reading Check** **Summarizing** What were two ways that Plains people used the horse?

The Apaches

Apaches speak an Athapaskan language similar to the languages of Native Americans in northwest Canada and Alaska. Because of this, anthropologists believe the ancestors of Apaches came from the far north and migrated south along the Rocky Mountains. By 1700 several independent Apache groups had entered Texas. The Mescaleros made their homes in the mountains ranging from New Mexico through West Texas into northern Mexico. The Lipans lived in the Hill Country of central Texas north to the Red River.

The Lipans spent most of their final years in Texas in desperate warfare. The Spanish threatened from the south, but even more dangerous were the Comanches from the north.

Outnumbered, the Lipans abandoned their hunting grounds in central Texas and moved westward to the mountains where the Mescaleros lived. A few lived there until the late 1800s. Today most Apaches live on reservations in New Mexico.

Reading Check **Explaining** How does language study help determine a group's origins?

The Comanches

From the early 1700s until the late 1800s, the Comanches lived on the prairies, plateaus, and plains of western Texas. Their territory, the **Comanchería,** was a vast land. It covered parts of Mexico, Texas, Kansas, Oklahoma, Colorado, and New Mexico.

Comanchería
c. 1750

History *Through Art*

***Comanche War Dance* by Herrera.** The Comanches gained a reputation in Texas as fierce warriors. What might have been one purpose of a war dance?

The Comanches spoke a language related to the languages of Native American groups in the northern Rockies and of the Aztecs in Mexico. The Aztecs claimed an ancestral home called Aztlán, which some scholars believe may have been located in the southwestern United States.

The Comanches were divided into many groups, with each group having its own leaders and a council of older men who made important decisions. No leader or council of one group could make a decision or reach an agreement for the members of another group. No person or group council had the right to speak for all the Comanche people.

Comanche life centered on two activities—hunting and war. Hunters stalked bear, elk, antelope, and buffalo. A buffalo hunt was an important event involving most of the group. Working under an elected leader, hunters on horses surrounded the buffalo and forced the herd to move in a circle. Then the hunters, armed with bows and arrows and spears, made the kill as the buffalo passed. After a successful hunt, the Comanches ate some of the meat and always dried and saved the rest for another time.

Because Apaches, Wichitas, Tonkawas, and white settlers threatened from all sides, the Comanches fought fiercely to keep control of the **Comanchería.** This territory grew gradually in size, until most of the lands that had once belonged to the Apaches were now controlled by the Comanches. In this vast territory, the Comanches could live according to their customs and traditions, hunting buffalo, foraging for fruits, berries, and nuts, and finding shelter in the steep canyon walls. In addition, Comanche warriors often fought to take their enemies' horses. Although the Comanches gathered some wild mustangs from the plentiful herds on the southern plains, they especially prized horses taken from their enemies.

Until 1875, the Comanches fought desperately to keep their lands and way of life. The destruction of the buffalo herds and a loss of many horses forced them to accept reservation life in present-day Oklahoma.

✓ **Reading Check** **Identifying** Comanche life centered on what two activities?

Painted tepee

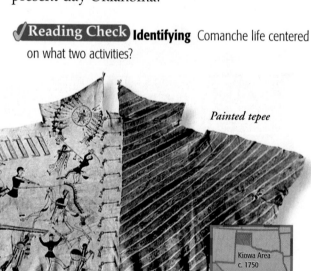

📷 *Picturing* **History**

The Kiowa way of life was designed for easy packing and quick movement. How does this image of a Kiowa woman and papoose reflect these ideas?

The Kiowas

The Comanches shared the Plains of Texas with their allies, the Kiowas (KY•oh•wahz). Like the other nomadic people of the Plains, the Kiowas were prepared to move quickly and often. In times of danger, whole camps could be packed up and moved in 30 minutes. Families lived in tepees of tanned hides that were easy to move. Up to 20 tanned hides were fastened around a framework of 20 to 24 poles. The hides were sewn together and usually were decorated with beautiful paintings. The entrance—an opening 3 or 4 feet (about 1 meter) high—faced the east, so that the sun could warm the interior in the early morning. A fire burned in the center of the tepee, and beds of willow branches and animals skins lined the sides.

Like the other Plains Indians, the horse, the buffalo, and the tepee were very important elements of the culture. The horse provided freedom of movement and speed for hunting game. The buffalo provided almost everything the group would need to survive including food, hides, robes, and horns for making spoons and needles. Even the buffalo hoof could be turned into glue.

The Kiowas, like the Apaches and Comanches, fought to maintain their way of life but finally were forced onto reservations. (See the TAKS Skillbuilder activity on page 84 that analyzes a primary source excerpt from Kiowa chief White Bear, or Satanta. In this excerpt he describes the basic conflict between the life styles of the nomadic Kiowa hunters and the white settlers moving onto territory that was the Kiowa's by tradition.)

The Kiowas had always prized tradition and ceremony. They kept histories of their travels and painted pictures on buffalo hides to record important events in their lives. Every season, the Kiowas held ceremonies and festivals. The most important event was the annual sun dance in June. The Kiowas believed that honoring the sun would bring happiness, plentiful buffalo, and victory in war. All males were expected to become warriors.

The Native American influence lived on after the people moved to reservations. When immigrants from Mexico settled in Texas, they were familiar with some Native American customs. Some of these settlers intermarried with the Native Americans and adopted some of their ways of life. With the coming of the Europeans, however, the traditional Native American cultures began to disappear.

TEXAS HISTORY Online

Student Web Activity Visit the texans.glencoe.com Web site and click on **Chapter 3—Student Web Activity** to learn more about Kiowa settlements in Texas.

✓ **Reading Check** **Explaining** How did the Kiowas "record" their history?

SECTION 3 ASSESSMENT

Checking for Understanding

1. **Using Key Terms** Why do you think adobe is still used today in construction?
2. **Reviewing Facts** Where did the Comanches live?

Reviewing Themes

3. **Groups and Institutions** What were some reasons Native American tribes fought other Native Americans and European settlers?

Organizing to Learn

4. **Describing** Create a chart like the one shown here and write an interesting fact about each group.

Group	Fact
Jumanos	
Tiguas	
Tonkawas	
Apaches	
Comanches	
Kiowas	

Critical Thinking

5. **Analyzing Information** How did buffalo bring prosperity and change the way of life of the Native American people?

TAKS PRACTICE

Determining Supporting Details
Draw a picture of a Jumano house using specific details mentioned in the text. Use labels on your drawing.

Chapter Summary

Native Texans

Main Idea

- First settlers arrive in Texas during Stone Age.
- Early humans survive by hunting and gathering.

Supporting Detail

- Early people settle in permanent locations when they learn to farm and no longer have to move in search of food.

Supporting Detail

- Four Native American cultural groups live in Texas: Southeastern, Pueblo, Plains, and Gulf cultures.

Supporting Detail

- Southeastern and Pueblo cultures live in permanent villages and depend on farming.

Supporting Detail

- Plains and Gulf cultures live a nomadic life based on hunting and foraging.

Reviewing Key Terms

Next to each number, write the letter of the term it defines.

a. artifact   e. anthropologist
b. shaman   f. adobe
c. culture   g. nomad
d. confederacy   h. archaeologist

1. a person who studies evidence of past human activity
2. a league for mutual support and common action
3. a person who is believed to have the power to cure the sick
4. a way of life; the pattern of people's knowledge, skills, and beliefs
5. group member who wanders from place to place

Reviewing Key Facts

6. Name one of the most important discoveries made by early humans.
7. Name three Native American peoples of southeastern Texas.
8. Describe the Caddo system of government.
9. What markings did the Jumanos put on their faces? What did this mean?
10. Why are the Apaches remembered mostly as warriors?
11. Identify the Comanchería.
12. How did the Kiowas keep records of their lives?

Critical Thinking

13. **Determining Cause and Effect** How did the geography of Texas affect the patterns of Native American settlement?
14. **Making Comparisons** Compare the lifestyles of the prehistoric hunters, the hunter-foragers, and the farmers.
15. **Identifying Alternatives** How would the Plains culture have been different without horses and buffalo? To answer this question, first consider how the horse and buffalo were used. Use the graph below to organize your thoughts.

Uses	
Horse	**Buffalo**

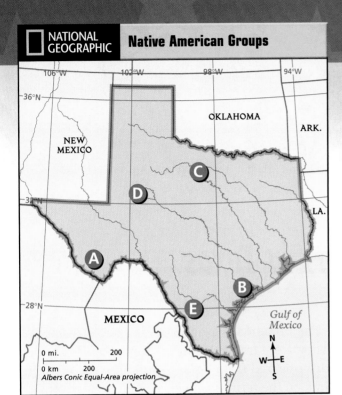

Geography and History Activity

On a separate sheet of paper, write which Native American groups lived near the location indicated by each of the letters on the map above. Use the maps on page 82.

16. A

17. B

18. C

19. D

20. E

Cooperative Learning Activity

21. **Researching Cultures** Working in groups, research the history of one of the four Native American cultures of Texas: the Southeastern, the Pueblo, the Gulf, and the Plains. Describe the location of the culture; the way the people obtained food; their weapons, tools, clothing, and form of government and social structure. Present your combined research in the form of a chart or visual aid.

Building Technology Skills

22. **Review the Cooperative Learning Activity** Use an electronic database such as a computerized library catalog or the Internet to find additional information about the Native American culture that you have chosen to research.

TEXAS HISTORY *Online*

Self-Check Quiz
Visit the texans.glencoe.com Web site and click on **Chapter 3—Self-Check Quizzes** to prepare for the chapter test.

Portfolio/TAKS Writing Activity

23. **Comparing and Contrasting** Ancient people adapted to their environment in order to survive. Identify some of the ways we have to adapt today. Then identify some ways we can modify, or change, our environment. Finally, compare and contrast the way we adapt today to the way the ancient people had to adapt. Combine your thoughts into an essay and save your work for your portfolio.

Practicing Skills

24. **Identifying Primary Sources** Archaeologists—people who study materials from the past—and historians use artifacts to understand history. An artifact is another type of primary source. Review the chapter and make a list of some artifacts that an archaeologist or historian would use to study Native Americans. Write a paragraph in which you explain how the various tribes might have used the artifacts.

Use the information in this chapter to answer the following question.

Which of the following is one way that the Spaniards influenced the Americas?

A They introduced modern horses to the continent.

B They helped Texas become the largest oil-producing state.

C They taught Native Americans how to grow corn.

D They destroyed missions in the American Southwest.

Test-Taking Tip:

You will need to recall information you read earlier to answer this question. You can eliminate some answers immediately by using common-sense reasoning skills. For example, B must be wrong because the Spanish did not drill for oil in Texas—the time period is wrong.

Economics & History

Jumano Traders in Texas

How often have you been traveling on one of Texas's many highways and been passed by an "eighteen-wheeler"? Have you ever wondered where these vehicles are going or what they are carrying? Most big highway trucks are part of the **intrastate** or **interstate commerce system.** Intrastate means from place to place within a state. Interstate means from one state to another state. Long ago, the work of the inter-state truckers was done by the Jumano Indians.

The Jumanos belonged to the Pueblo culture. They were traders until the time that their tribe disappeared from Texas around the early 1700s. In fact, the term *Jumano* is a Spanish word that means a type of trader.

Using Natural Resources

The Jumanos of the South Plains built villages in a region spreading from present-day San Angelo on the east, then south towards Del Rio, from there west along the Rio Grande to beyond Presidio/Terlingua. From that location on the border, the Jumano territory covered all the way up towards what became Lubbock, on the High Plains. In West Texas, the nomadic Plains Jumanos found natural resources that they knew to be valuable to them and to people living in other parts of Texas. Wild game, such as deer, rabbits, doves, quail, fish, and buffalo were plentiful in this region. It was also ideal for raising horses. The Jumanos captured and raised wild horses as early as the 1600s. Vegetation suitable for eating, such as wild berries and pecans, also grew abundantly in West Texas. During that time, the Concho Rivers were a source of pearls, and the Jumanos fished the waters for the mussel shells that housed the pearls. Today, most people regard activities such as hunting and diving as a form of recreation, but to the Jumanos, it was just work.

Jumano trader

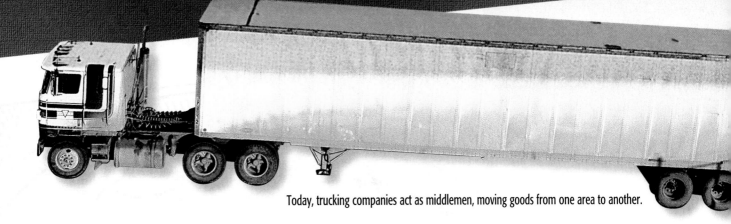

Today, trucking companies act as middlemen, moving goods from one area to another.

The Barter System

While the Plains Jumanos gathered various products that other tribes wanted, such as pearls, game, and berries, neighboring people also had articles that the Jumanos wanted. The Caddos of eastern and southeastern Texas, for instance, were farmers. They raised corn, beans, and a variety of vegetables. The Spaniards possessed many manufactured products, such as guns, hoes, needles, clothes, cooking pans, and axes. The Native Americans of New Mexico traded with the Spanish for these items.

The Plains Jumanos used the **barter system.** They traded one product for another without using money. Seasonally, they traveled to East Texas to acquire Caddo goods, traveling along primitive routes far different from today's highways.

At the same time, they acted as intermediaries, bringing woolen materials and other products to Caddo country from as far away as modern-day New Mexico. On the return trip to New Mexico, they carried pottery and other hand-made utensils obtained from Native American groups living in the Mississippi Valley.

Trading Posts

The Plains Jumanos also established trading posts on the South Plains to bring all those involved in this long-distance commerce together. At these annual fairs, people traded not only goods with other merchants, but they also exchanged ideas and customs.

The next time you are traveling on a highway or on the Interstate, remember that the Jumanos also used roads (actually, more like paths) to carry items of value from one destination to another, just as truckers do today.

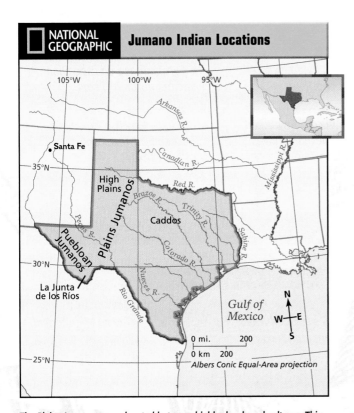

NATIONAL GEOGRAPHIC **Jumano Indian Locations**

105°W 100°W 95°W

Arkansas R.

Santa Fe

35°N

Canadian R.

Mississippi R.

High Plains

Red R.

Brazos R.

Trinity R.

Plains Jumanos

Caddos

Pecos R.

Sabine R.

Colorado R.

Puebloan Jumanos

30°N

Nueces R.

La Junta de los Ríos

Rio Grande

Gulf of Mexico

N
W—E
S

0 mi.   200

0 km   200

Albers Conic Equal-Area projection

25°N

The Plains Jumanos were located between highly developed cultures. This put them in a good position to act as traders.

TAKS PRACTICE

1. **Making Generalizations** What things of value does nature produce in your part of the state?
2. **Drawing Conclusions** What finished products must your community import from another part of Texas?
3. **Writing About Economics** Write a paragraph on one of the themes listed below. Use standard grammar, spelling, sentence structure, and punctuation. Include information and examples from the feature as details to support your argument.
   a. People turn their environments into a livelihood.
   b. For some people, their work is also recreation.
   c. Many careers today are not limited by location.

Early Explorers

Why It Matters

The Spanish explorers found neither precious metals nor large numbers of Native Americans in Texas. Losing interest, Spain turned instead to present-day Mexico. It was not until the French appeared in Texas that the Spanish looked again at its northern possession.

The Impact Today

The Spanish were the first Europeans to explore Texas. Their writings about the great distances and natural beauty of Texas were printed in Europe. What they said about Texas influences the way many people think about the state today.

1519
★ *Álvarez de Pineda explored the Texas coastline*

1528
★ *Cabeza de Vaca shipwrecked on what is believed to have been Galveston Bay*

1541
★ *Coronado led an expedition across northern Texas*

1542
★ *De Soto–Moscoso expedition reached East Texas across northern Texas*

Texas

United States   1490   1510   1530   1550   1570

World

1492
• *Columbus reached the Americas*

1519
• *Cortés invaded Aztec empire in Mexico*

1576
• *The first permanent theater opened in London*

This painting, *La Salle Discovering Louisiana, by Theodore Gudin (1844) portrays La Salle's arrival in Matagorda Bay in 1685.*

Cause-Effect Study Foldable Make this foldable to help you explain the causes and effects of Spain's interest or lack of interest in Texas.

Step 1 Fold a sheet of paper in half from side to side.

Fold it so the left edge lays about $\frac{1}{2}$ inch from the right edge.

Step 2 Turn the paper and fold it into thirds.

Step 3 Unfold and cut the top layer only along both folds.

This will make three tabs.

Step 4 Turn and label the foldable as shown.

Spain Interested in Texas

Spain Loses Interest in Texas

Spain Regains Interest in Texas

Reading and Writing As you read, write what you learn about the first Europeans to explore Texas. Write key facts under the appropriate tabs of your foldable.

1685
★ *La Salle established the first French settlement in Texas*

TEXAS HISTORY
Online

Chapter Overview
Visit the texans.glencoe.com
Web site and click on
Chapter 4—Chapter Overviews to preview chapter information.

1630   *1650*   *1670*   *1690*

1607
• *Jamestown colony in Virginia founded*

1608
• *Samuel de Champlain founded Quebec*

1620
• *Pilgrims landed at Plymouth Rock*

1643
• *Taj Mahal completed in India*

1676
• *Influenza epidemic in England*

1690
• *New England Primer, first elementary book published*

CHAPTER 4   Early Explorers   **101**

First Steps in a New Land

Guide to Reading

Main Idea
Spain desired to establish an empire in the Americas in the 1500s. Explorers began to map out the region.

Key Terms
conquistador
friar
mission

Reading Strategy
Organizing Information As you read this section, complete a chart like the one shown here, noting the areas of exploration of each explorer.

Explorer	Areas of Exploration
Columbus	
Cortés	
de Pineda	
Cabeza de Vaca	

Read to Learn
• why the Spanish conquistadores and friars explored Texas.
• whether the expeditions succeeded or failed.

Section Theme
Global Connections The Spanish came to Texas to seek wealth and adventure, to expand Spain's empire, and to build missions.

Preview of Events

♦1519 — Pineda maps the Texas coast

♦1528 — Cabeza de Vaca becomes first European to live in present-day Texas

A
Texas Story

Some of the earliest Europeans to visit Texas were from the Coronado expedition. Pedro de Castañeda found a huge land, full of strange animals and wonderful sights. "Some make it an uninhabitable country, others have it bordering on Florida, and still others on Greater India . . . They [cannot] give any basis upon which to found these statements. There are those who tell about very peculiar animals, who are contradicted by others who were on the expedition."
—*Journal of Pedro de Castañeda*

Armadillo

Columbus Sights a New World

After sailing west across the Atlantic Ocean for 33 days straight, **Christopher Columbus** and the crews of his three small ships sighted land in October 1492. They saw several islands in the Caribbean Sea.

While searching for a new route to the riches of Asia, Columbus had reached a continent unknown in Europe.

Columbus was Italian, sailing under the flag of Spain. In the years following this first voyage, Spain established an empire in what the Europeans came to call the Americas. Most of South America, many islands in the Caribbean, Mexico, all of Central America, and part of the land that makes up the United States were claimed by Spain.

Columbus returned to the Americas three times after his first voyage. On his second visit, he established a permanent colony on one of the islands of the West Indies. From there, Spaniards sailed forth to explore the American mainland.

New Spain

Spanish soldiers, called conquistadores, sought riches and power for themselves and wealth and glory for Spain. With superior weapons, they made their way through the Americas. Where they defeated Native Americans, they strengthened Spanish claims. The conquistadores made it possible for others to follow after them and build towns, lay out roads, open mines, and develop farms and ranches.

Friars, members of Catholic religious orders, also helped Spain gain a foothold in the Americas.

Spain was a Catholic nation, and its rulers wanted to convert the Native Americans to the Catholic faith. As friars entered lands in the north, they established religious outposts called missions. Often the mission was the first Spanish settlement in an area.

✔ Reading Check Explaining What motivated Spanish soldiers to sail to the Americas?

Cortés Lands in Mexico

In the spring of 1519, **Hernán Cortés** sailed from Cuba and landed his army of about 600 soldiers on the eastern coast of Mexico. Learning that the powerful Aztec people ruled a large empire, he led his army inland toward **Tenochtitlán** (teh•noch•tee•TLAHN), their capital. Along the way, Cortés persuaded thousands of Native Americans who had suffered under Aztec military rule to rebel.

At first the Aztecs welcomed Cortés to Tenochtitlán. They believed he was their legendary god Quetzalcoatl (kets•ahl•KWAHT•ahl), who had sailed east many years earlier with a promise to return. Tenochtitlán was perhaps the most spectacular city in the world at that time. The Spanish marveled at the palaces, zoos, and

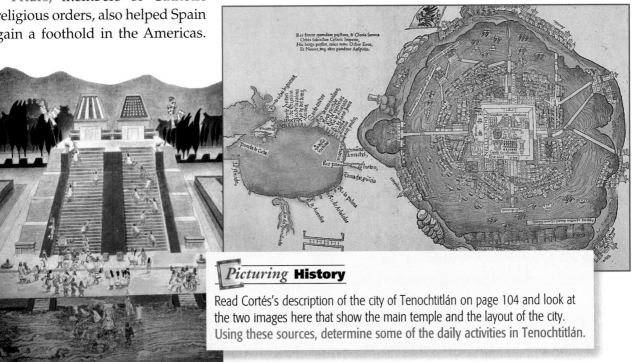

Picturing **History**

Read Cortés's description of the city of Tenochtitlán on page 104 and look at the two images here that show the main temple and the layout of the city. Using these sources, determine some of the daily activities in Tenochtitlán.

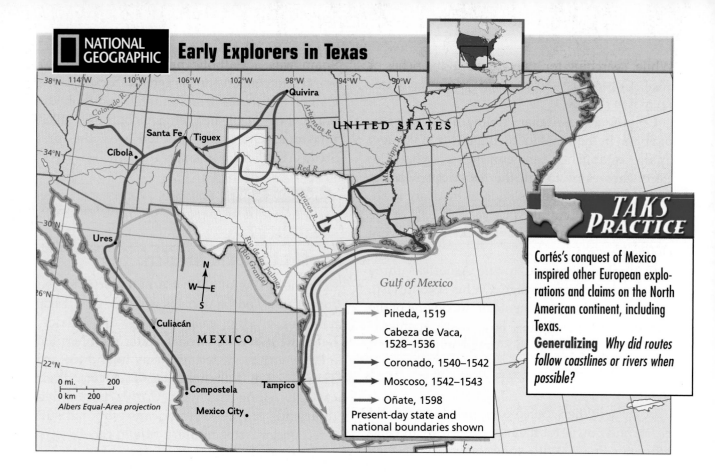

UNITED STATES

Quivira

Santa Fe · Tiguex

Cíbola ·

Ures ·

Culiacán ·

MEXICO

Compostela ·

Tampico ·

Mexico City ·

Gulf of Mexico

Colorado R.
Arkansas R.
Mississippi R.
Red R.
Brazos R.
Rio de las Palmas (Rio Grande)

N
W — E
S

0 mi.   200
0 km   200
Albers Equal-Area projection

→ Pineda, 1519
→ Cabeza de Vaca, 1528–1536
→ Coronado, 1540–1542
→ Moscoso, 1542–1543
→ Oñate, 1598
Present-day state and national boundaries shown

TAKS PRACTICE

Cortés's conquest of Mexico inspired other European explorations and claims on the North American continent, including Texas.
Generalizing *Why did routes follow coastlines or rivers when possible?*

complex art. In his own words, Cortés described the wonders of Tenochtitlán:

66The city has many open squares in which markets are continuously held and the general business of buying and selling proceeds . . . [T]here are daily more than sixty thousand folk buying and selling. Every kind of merchandise such as may be met with in every land is for sale there, whether of food and victuals [supplies], or ornaments of gold and silver, or lead, brass, copper, tin, precious stones, bones, shells, snails and feathers; limestone for building is likewise sold there, stone both rough and polished, bricks burnt and unburnt, wood of all kinds and in all stages of preparation . . .

Finally, . . . I will simply say that the manner of living among the people is very similar to that in Spain, and considering that this is a barbarous nation shut off from a knowledge of the true God or communication with enlightened nations, one may well marvel at the orderliness and good government which is everywhere maintained.99

In spite of his admiration of Aztec culture, Cortés and his forces imprisoned and killed the emperor, **Moctezuma.** They also tore down Tenochtitlán and plundered the city's treasure. Upon the ruins they built a new city and named it Mexico, after the Aztec name for themselves. Mexico City became the capital of New Spain.

The success of Cortés inspired other Spaniards to come to the Americas. Many journeyed into the uncharted lands in search of treasure. Some joined expeditions for adventure and out of curiosity. Other Spaniards explored for possibilities of settlement. Still others hoped to spread the Catholic faith among the Native Americans.

✓**Reading Check** **Examining** Why did the Aztecs first welcome Cortés?

Pineda Explores the Texas Coast

In 1519, the same year Cortés landed in Mexico, **Alonso Álvarez de Pineda** (ah•LOHN•soh AHL•vah•rays day pee•NEH•dah) became the first European to explore the Texas coast. As he sailed along the uncharted coastline from Florida to Mexico, he observed and mapped the land. He stopped for 40 days at the mouth of a river, which he called the Río de las Palmas. Although he did not go into the interior, Álvarez de Pineda wrote enthusiastically about the new land and called for the establishment of settlements there.

Shipwrecked in Texas

The first Europeans and Africans who came to Texas did not think they would stay. Chance and misfortune brought **Alvar Núñez Cabeza de Vaca** (AHL•vahr NOO•nyays kah•BAY•sah day VAH•kah) and his companions to Texas. Cabeza de Vaca was a member of a large expedition sent to conquer the area between Florida and Mexico in 1527. The expedition, led by the conquistador **Pánfilo de Narváez** (PAHN•fee•loh day nar•VAH•ays), failed. Moreover, the ships that were to pick up the explorers never arrived. Stranded, de Narváez and his followers built five boats and sailed along the coast toward Mexico. However, in early November 1528, the boats were tossed in a terrible storm and driven aground near present-day Galveston. Cabeza de Vaca called the island *Malhado,* the isle of misfortune.

These survivors were the first Europeans to enter what is now Texas. The Karankawas, who lived on the coast, were kind and generous to their cold and starving visitors. The Native Americans built fires and brought fish and roots for food. Within a few months, however, all but a handful of the shipwrecked explorers died from disease and exposure. Disease took a heavy toll among the Karankawas, too. In time, Native Americans would associate Europeans with disease and find both unwelcome.

Cabeza de Vaca and his companions survived by adopting the ways of the Karankawas. Cabeza de Vaca and **Estevanico** (ehs•TEH•vahn•nee•koh) from Morocco, who was the first known black man to enter Texas, became highly regarded shamans, or healers. Cabeza de Vaca was also a trader. As he made his way along the coast and into the interior, he learned much about the geography and the people of what would later be called Texas.

After spending nearly six years among the Native American people of South Texas, Cabeza de Vaca and his companions journeyed west toward Mexico. They traveled for many months, possibly passing through present-day South and West Texas and northern Mexico. Finally, in early 1536, they reached Culiacán (koo•lee•ah•KAHN), Mexico.

✓ **Reading Check** **Explaining** How did Cabeza de Vaca and his men survive in Texas?

SECTION 1 ASSESSMENT

Checking for Understanding

1. **Using Key Terms** Write one or two sentences describing the different goals of the conquistadores and the friars.
2. **Reviewing Facts** How did the aims of Spanish explorers in Mexico and Texas differ?

Reviewing Themes

3. **Global Connections** Why was Cortés interested in conquering the Aztecs?

Organizing to Learn

4. **Sequencing** Create a time line like the one shown here. Place the following explorers on the time line in their proper sequence.

1490 1500 1510 1520 1530 1540 1550

- Cortés
- Columbus
- Cabeza de Vaca and Estevanico
- Cabeza de Vaca and Narváez
- de Pineda

Critical Thinking

5. **Analyzing** What did the treatment of Cabeza de Vaca and his companions reveal about the Karankawas?

TAKS PRACTICE

Identifying Points of View
Although Cortés compared Tenochtitlán to Spain in some ways, he also described it as a "barbarous nation." In Cortes's opinion, why was Tenochtitlán barbaric?

Analyzing a Topic

Why Learn This Skill?

Analytical questions help you find accurate information about your research topic. The two main purposes for asking questions are to make the topic more specific and to make it easier to find specific information.

Learning the Skill

There are three steps involved in writing useful questions:

• Brainstorm several questions about the topic.

• Decide if each question is related to the topic.

• Rewrite them as simpler questions.

Suppose you want to learn more about Cabeza de Vaca's experiences in Texas in the 1500s. Questions to make the topic more specific are:

• What were his experiences with the Karankawas?

• What happened after leaving the Karankawas?

Using the first question as your research topic, decide which questions below would help you find the right information.

A What food and shelter did the Karankawas have?

B How many ships landed in Texas?

C Where did Cabeza de Vaca grow up?

D Why did Cabeza de Vaca come to the Americas?

Question **A** is directly related to the chosen topic. Questions **B**, **C**, and **D** will not give you information about the chosen topic.

Practicing the Skill

Read below and decide which questions would be useful in researching this topic.

Topic: The life of a foot soldier exploring the Southwest with Coronado.

1 How far did soldiers travel in an average day?

2 Who put up the money for the expedition?

3 What were the greatest dangers of the trip?

4 Who chose Coronado to lead the expedition?

5 What type of food did the soldiers eat?

Estevanico (center) *and Cabeza de Vaca* (right)

TAKS PRACTICE

Analyzing a Topic Select a topic you would like to know more about. Then write five questions about this topic that would help you research it.

GO TO Glencoe's **Skillbuilder Interactive Workbook,** Level 1, provides instruction and practice in key social studies skills.

The Spanish Explore Texas

Guide to Reading

Main Idea
Tales of gold, gems, minerals, and fabulous cities lured the Spanish into further exploration of Texas.

Key Terms
viceroy
pueblo

Reading Strategy
Organizing Information As you read the section, complete a chart like the one shown here.

Explorer	Goals	Native Americans Encountered
Fray Marcos		
Estevanico		
Coronado		
Moscoso		

Read to Learn
• about early Spanish expeditions.
• what the explorers hoped to find.

Section Theme
Geography and History Spain was willing to fund the costly exploration of Texas in the hope of finding the vast wealth that was rumored to be there.

Preview of Events

♦1541 ♦1542   ♦1609

Coronado journeys across Texas

Luis de Moscoso leads expedition into East Texas

Spaniards set up colony on upper Rio Grande

Spanish soldier, circa 1530–1540

A
Texas Story

Exploring was dangerous, as Pedro de Castañeda describes in his journal. "The army spent [2 weeks] here, preparing jerked beef to take with them. It was estimated that during this time they killed 500 buffalo. Many fellows were lost . . . Every night they took account of who was missing, fired guns and blew trumpets and beat drums, and built great fires, but some of them were so far off that all this did not give them any help."
—Journal of Pedro de Castañeda

The Quest for Texas Gold

Cabeza de Vaca's arrival in Culiacán and Mexico City astonished the Spanish. What he said excited them even more. He recounted tales of herds of huge "cows" with small horns. What he had seen were buffalo, the first reported sighting of the animal by a European. He described Texas as "vast and handsome" and "very fertile."

Cabeza de Vaca announced that he saw no gold. However, he passed on tales he had heard about cities with magnificent houses and lands rich with copper, emeralds, and turquoise. He suggested that an expedition be sent north to search for these treasures. Inspired by visions of gold and glory, would-be conquistadores throughout New Spain volunteered for the expedition to Texas.

Spain's highest ranking official in New Spain was a **viceroy,** an official who represents the monarch. Viceroy **Antonio de Mendoza** heard Cabeza de Vaca's report with interest. After the unexpected discovery of a new continent and of the rich Aztec empire, anything seemed possible to Mendoza. He had heard tales about mysterious lands to the north. Somewhere in those regions, he had heard, were seven fabulous cities containing vast treasures. Cabeza de Vaca's report made Mendoza eager to investigate these stories. Because Cabeza de Vaca wanted to return to Spain, Mendoza had to find others to lead the search.

Fray Marcos Leads a New Expedition

Viceroy Mendoza wanted to organize a large expedition at once, but he decided to move cautiously. He selected a priest, **Fray Marcos de Niza,** to head an advance party to check on the stories. Estevanico accompanied Fray Marcos's party as a guide and to ensure the friendship of Native Americans along the way.

In March 1539 Fray Marcos and the advance party began moving northward from Culiacán. Shortly after, Estevanico, who rode ahead, sent back exciting news: a land called **Cíbola** was 30 days away. Within Cíbola were seven cities, rich in gold, silver, and precious gems. Beyond Cíbola, according to Estevanico, were even richer lands.

Estevanico pressed on, but the Zuñi Indians killed him when he ventured onto their land, near present-day Gallup, New Mexico. Shaken by Estevanico's death, Fray Marcos nevertheless continued northward until he saw Cíbola from a distance. Then he hastily returned to Mexico to report. Cíbola was actually a **pueblo,** a series of connected flat-roofed buildings. It was built near the present-day boundary of Arizona and

History *Through Art*

Francisco Vázquez de Coronado Making His Way Across New Mexico by Frederic Remington, 1905 Coronado's expedition was made up of young soldiers from Spain, Portugal, Italy, France, Germany, and Scotland. Why would men from other countries join a Spanish expedition?

People of Texas

Cabeza de Vaca c.1490–c.1557

Alvar Nuñez Cabeza de Vaca's journey remains one of the most amazing feats of exploration in the Americas. In 1527 he left Spain as part of an expedition. After failing to find treasure and becoming shipwrecked near what is now Galveston, Cabeza de Vaca and the other survivors were the first non-Native Americans to set foot on Texas soil.

Facing starvation, Cabeza de Vaca soon realized he needed the Native Americans. Although at first he fought them, by the end of his six-year journey, he sympathized with and respected Native Americans, often trading with and relying on them. Cabeza de Vaca was one of the first Spaniards to live among the coastal Native Americans of Texas and survive to write about them.

New Mexico. However, Fray Marcos, who may have seen Cíbola at sunset, claimed he got a glimpse of a golden city filled with treasures. It was, he said, "a land rich in gold, silver, and other wealth . . . great cities . . . and civilized people wearing woolen clothes."

✓ **Reading Check** **Inferring** Why did Fray Marcos believe Cíbola had great riches?

Coronado Is Disappointed

Viceroy Mendoza organized a full-scale expedition at once, assembling more than 300 soldiers and several hundred Native Americans. He chose **Francisco Vázquez de Coronado,** a young, rich, and trusted noble, as leader of the expedition. Fray Marcos accompanied the troops.

On July 7, 1540, after five months of travel, Coronado found Cíbola —and disappointment. Instead of golden treasures, the expedition found only mud, stone, and angry Zuñi warriors ready to defend their village. In disgrace, Fray Marcos hurriedly bid good-bye to Coronado and returned to Mexico City.

Rather than go back to New Spain empty-handed, Coronado, believing that treasure must lie somewhere in the vast wilderness, decided to stay and explore. He divided his forces. A small group traveled west across present-day New Mexico and Arizona and reached the Grand Canyon before returning to the main camp. Coronado's group traveled east, setting up camp at the village of Tiguex (TEE•gehs), near present-day Albuquerque, New Mexico. There Coronado and his troops met a Native American whom they called the Turk. The Turk told of a fabulous place called Quivira (kee•VEE•rah), said to be located farther east and filled with riches. A member of the expedition recorded the Turk's description:

❝A river . . . [stretched] two leagues wide, in which there were fishes as big as horses . . . [T]he lord of the country took his afternoon nap under a great tree on which were hung a great number of little gold bells, which put him to sleep as they swung in the air. [The lord] also said that . . . jugs and bowls were of gold.❞

TEXAS HISTORY *Online*

Student Web Activity Visit the texans.glencoe.com Web site and click on **Chapter 4—Student Web Activity** to learn more about early Spanish explorers in Texas.

Don Juan de Oñate 1550–1626

Don Juan de Oñate founded the first European settlement in the upper Rio Grande. In 1598 Oñate led a 4-mile-long expedition group that included 600 people, 83 wagons, and 7,000 animals.

After 3 months, Oñate's group celebrated their safe arrival at the Rio Grande. They performed the ceremony "La Toma" (the Taking), which means that they were taking the new land for Spain. They also held a mass and a feast which could have been the first Thanksgiving in the nation, an event usually credited to the Puritans.

Oñate is responsible for naming El Paso del Norte, the Path of the North. In his honor, the largest equestrian bronze sculpture in the nation (over three stories high) is on display in downtown El Paso.

Some of the Spanish soldiers were skeptical. Coronado, however, decided to investigate the Turk's story. In the spring of 1541, the expedition set out, marching east.

The trek to Quivira brought Coronado's expedition to the plains of Texas. Several members kept records of the journey. The plains were so level that the sky appeared "like a bowl" over them. The horizon surrounded them on all sides. There were no trees "except at rivers," and the lakes were "round as plates."

Coronado's troops were always in danger of losing their way. The grass "never failed to become erect after it had been trodden down." Although Coronado's hunters and scouts left signs so they could find their way back, they got lost frequently, "wandering about . . . as if they were crazy."

The Spaniards were amazed by the "cows" of the plains. The cows they saw were buffalo, "in such numbers that nobody could have counted them." They also viewed with amazement the way the Plains people hunted and used the buffalo.

With the Turk leading the way, the Spaniards reached a great ravine, probably the Palo Duro Canyon, located near present-day Amarillo. Then the expedition continued northward to Quivira, near present-day Wichita, Kansas.

They found a Native American settlement built of sticks and skins, but they found no treasure. Angry and frustrated, Coronado put the Turk to death. After claiming the entire Wichita country for the King of Spain, Coronado began the long journey back. Led by Wichita guides, he returned to the Rio Grande. There, the expedition spent a terrible winter in Pueblo country with little food. Finally, Coronado issued the order to return to New Spain. In a report to the Spanish king, Coronado noted that Texas was "a country of fine appearance" and its soil promised good farming. Coronado also reported that "there is not any gold nor any other metal—nothing but little villages." No doubt, the viceroy was disappointed with this report.

Reading Check **Summarizing** What did Coronado regretfully report to the Spanish king?

Moscoso Explores East Texas

As Coronado's expedition was traveling across the Great Plains, another Spanish expedition was marching west from Florida toward Texas. The expedition's leader, Hernán de Soto, had landed in Florida in 1539 with several hundred troops. After moving slowly westward, de Soto reached the Mississippi River in 1541. This marked the first time a European expedition had reached the Mississippi. De Soto died there in the spring of 1542.

Luis de Moscoso then led the expedition as far west as the lower Brazos River. They met many Native Americans but found no riches. Finally, Moscoso led the expedition back to the Mississippi River. There they built boats and set off down river, eventually sailing along the coast to Mexico.

New Mexico Is Founded

Between 1528 and 1543, Spaniards had seen much of the land that is now Texas. No one had found treasures like those that had been found in Mexico City. For this reason Spain's interest in Texas decreased. Spanish officials made few attempts to build settlements in Texas at this time, preferring to build towns in other areas.

In 1609 a group of Spaniards set up a permanent colony on the upper waters of the Rio Grande where Native American tribes had settled. They named the colony New Mexico and established its capital at Santa Fe. Over the years, several expeditions set out from New Mexico and explored the area around present-day San Angelo.

Spaniards visited and traded with the Jumano people and set up a temporary outpost on the San Sabá River. One of the legends that arose during this time involves the story of María de Jesús de Agreda, known as the Lady in Blue. She was a Spanish nun who claimed that her spirit made 500 trips from 1620 to 1631, all without physically leaving Spain. The Jumanos in eastern New Mexico and West Texas, as well as the Caddos in East Texas, told numerous stories of having been taught by the legendary Lady in Blue.

In spite of the large number of Jumanos who accepted Christianity, the Spaniards abandoned the outpost and did not return to the land of the Jumanos for many years.

✓ **Reading Check** **Explaining** Why did Spain's interest in Texas diminish?

SECTION 2 ASSESSMENT

Checking for Understanding

1. **Using Key Terms** Write a short paragraph explaining why the viceroy was a powerful figure.
2. **Reviewing Facts** Why did Spanish explorers search for Cíbola and Quivira, and what did they find?

Reviewing Themes

3. **Geography and History** Select one explorer and estimate his travels in terms of miles.

Organizing to Learn

4. **Comparing** Create a chart like the one below to identify discoveries that encouraged the explorers and the setbacks that disappointed them.

Explorers	Discoveries	Setbacks
Cabeza de Vaca		
Coronado		
Moscoso		

Critical Thinking

5. **Analyzing** What motivated the Spanish explorers to leave home for these daring expeditions to the Americas?

TAKS PRACTICE

Distinguishing Fact From Fiction In their search for cities of gold and wealth throughout Texas, what other resources did Spanish explorers fail to recognize and appreciate?

La Salle Awakens Spanish Interest

Guide to Reading

Main Idea
When the French established a presence in Texas, it forced Spain to renew its interest in the area.

Key Terms
stockade
sandbar

Reading Strategy
Organizing Information As you read this section, complete a chart like the one shown here.

European Nation	Location of Colonies in North America
England	
France	
Spain	

Read to Learn
• how France challenged Spain's claim to Texas.
• about La Salle's expeditions.

Section Theme
Geography and History La Salle claimed vast territories for France, but his plans for colonization failed.

Preview of Events

♦1685 — French flag flies over Texas

♦1700 — late 1600s Spain decides to settle Texas

Monument of La Salle near present-day Fort St. Louis

A Texas Story

When the French tried to settle along the Texas coast after Coronado's expedition, Spain renewed its interest in this area. "I always notice that when we have something valuable in our hands . . . we do not value it or prize it as highly as if we understood how much we would miss it . . . After we have lost . . . we have a great pain in the heart and we are all the time trying to find ways and means by which to get it back again."

—*Journal of Pedro de Castañeda*

France Challenges Spanish Claims

In the early 1600s, other countries began to conquer land in the Americas. England founded colonies along the Atlantic coast of North America, while France established the colony of Quebec in Canada.

Some years later, France tried to challenge Spain's claim to Texas.

The leader of the French quest for an empire in Texas was **René Robert Cavelier, Sieur de La Salle** (reh•NAY roh•BEAR kah•vel•YAY soor duh lah SAHL). In 1682 La Salle led the first European expedition that navigated the Mississippi River south to the Gulf of Mexico. He claimed the entire inland region surrounding the Mississippi and named the land Louisiana in honor of the French king, Louis XIV.

When La Salle returned to France, he proposed that a French colony be founded at the mouth of the Mississippi River. Possibly La Salle hoped that from there he could capture some of the rich silver mines in northern New Spain. The king agreed, and La Salle organized the expedi-tion. On August 1, 1684, four ships carrying about 280 colonists set sail for Louisiana on what would become a very difficult journey.

La Salle, not an easy person to get along with, quarreled with the ship captains. Spanish pirates captured one of the vessels. The other three ships were separated in a storm. Worst of all, the expedition missed the mouth of the Mississippi and sailed 400 miles to the west, along the coast of Texas.

After sailing west and south along the coast of Texas, searching in vain for the Mississippi in early 1685, La Salle decided the expedition must go ashore. He chose a spot on the shore of **Matagorda Bay.** During the landing, one of the ships wrecked, losing badly needed supplies.

✔ **Reading Check** **Evaluating** Why did La Salle propose an expedition to the New World?

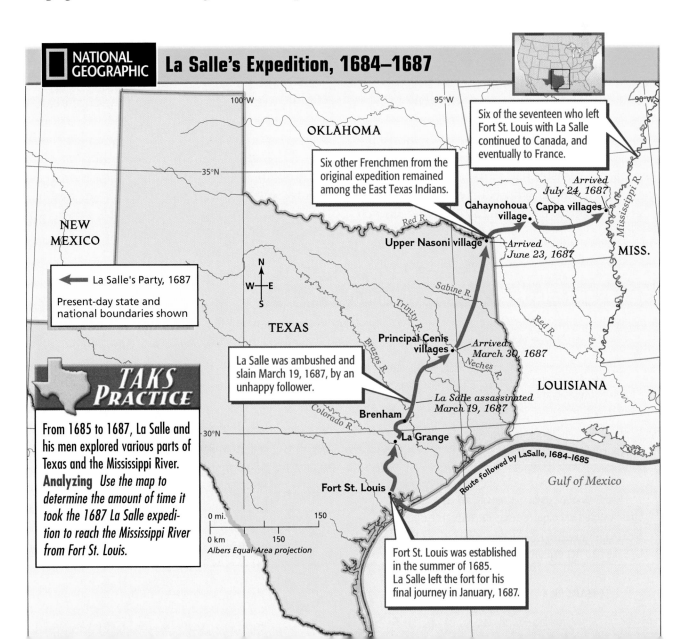

NATIONAL GEOGRAPHIC

La Salle's Expedition, 1684–1687

Six of the seventeen who left Fort St. Louis with La Salle continued to Canada, and eventually to France.

Six other Frenchmen from the original expedition remained among the East Texas Indians.

OKLAHOMA

Arrived July 24, 1687

Cahaynohoua village • Cappa villages

Upper Nasoni village • Arrived June 23, 1687

MISS.

NEW MEXICO

Red R.

Sabine R.

Trinity R.

←— La Salle's Party, 1687

Present-day state and national boundaries shown

TEXAS

Principal Cenis villages • Arrived March 30, 1687

Neches R.

Red R.

LOUISIANA

La Salle was ambushed and slain March 19, 1687, by an unhappy follower.

Brazos R.

La Salle assassinated March 19, 1687

Colorado R.

Brenham

La Grange

TAKS PRACTICE

From 1685 to 1687, La Salle and his men explored various parts of Texas and the Mississippi River. **Analyzing** Use the map to determine the amount of time it took the 1687 La Salle expedition to reach the Mississippi River from Fort St. Louis.

Fort St. Louis

Route followed by LaSalle, 1684–1685

Gulf of Mexico

0 mi. 150
0 km 150
Albers Equal-Area projection

Fort St. Louis was established in the summer of 1685. La Salle left the fort for his final journey in January, 1687.

The French Flag Flies Over Texas

La Salle and the colonists built a crude stockade, or an enclosure of posts made to form a defense, on the banks of a small river. They named this outpost Fort St. Louis. Overhead they flew the flag of France, which displayed golden lilies on a field of white. Later the settlers built huts and a small chapel.

La Salle then ordered some of the colonists to stay and defend Fort St. Louis while he explored the area. Finding no European settlements to the west, La Salle returned to discover that during his absence disaster had struck. Overwork, poor food, and conflicts with Native Americans had claimed the lives of many of the French colonists. One of the ships from the expedition had sailed back to France. The other had wrecked on a sandbar, a ridge of sand built up by currents in a river or coastal waters. The colonists were effectively stranded in the wilderness. Crops failed. Disease struck one colonist after another. Others died fighting with Karankawas. By the summer of 1686, only 45 of the original 280 settlers remained alive.

La Salle then decided to head east to try to find the Mississippi. On a third expedition, he ventured into East Texas, perhaps in present-day Grimes County. There members of the expedition refused to continue the search and murdered La Salle on March 19, 1687.

Without La Salle's leadership, the French colony was lost. Some of the colonists were taken into Karankawa camps.

Historians believe there were about 20 people left behind. These included individuals that La Salle, for whatever reason, did not want with him on the expedition—women, children, and the disabled. An eyewitness account remains, written by Jean Baptiste Talon. He recorded that the Karankawas staged a surprise attack on the outpost sometime around Christmas of 1688. Among those captured were Talon's three younger brothers and one younger sister. Six children were adopted by the Karankawas, but most of the colony was killed. (These children were later rescued by Alonso de León and raised as servants in the house of the viceroy of Mexico.)

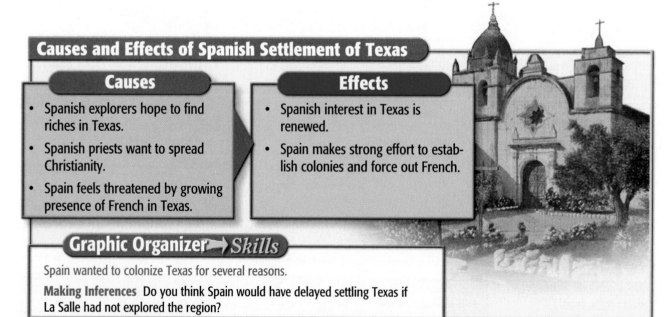

Causes and Effects of Spanish Settlement of Texas

Causes
- Spanish explorers hope to find riches in Texas.
- Spanish priests want to spread Christianity.
- Spain feels threatened by growing presence of French in Texas.

Effects
- Spanish interest in Texas is renewed.
- Spain makes strong effort to establish colonies and force out French.

Graphic Organizer → Skills

Spain wanted to colonize Texas for several reasons.

Making Inferences Do you think Spain would have delayed settling Texas if La Salle had not explored the region?

Six of the 17 colonists who had left Fort St. Louis with La Salle enlisted the aid of a Tejas guide to help them find their way to the French settlement of Quebec in Canada. They eventually made it safely to Canada, and some in the party decided to travel onward to France. Another small group remained behind in East Texas. For many years afterward, rumors were heard that some members of La Salle's ill-fated colony who had been spared in the Fort St. Louis massacre were still living among the Native Americans.

Although Fort St. Louis failed as a permanent settlement, La Salle's efforts bore many results. For France, it led to establishing trade with Native Americans of the Mississippi Valley and, although the French never did any real settling in Texas, they kept the claim to Texas alive in the French imagination. The most direct result for Texas was that it shifted the focus of Spanish interest from western Texas to eastern Texas. The Spanish began an extensive exploration of the northern Gulf shore. For many years after, every Spanish move in Texas and the borderlands came as a reaction to a French threat, real or imagined.

La Salle's journeys in Texas also provided the United States with a reason to claim Texas as part of the 1803 Louisiana Purchase. Some of the

A Shared Past...

In 1685 the nations of Europe operated their economies according to an economic idea called *mercantilism*. Under mercantilism, governments believed that a nation's strength lay in its wealth and in its strong military. Colonies were created to increase the wealth of European countries. Spain, France, Holland, Sweden, Britain, and Russia established colonies in North America.

Americans argued that France had considered Texas part of the Louisiana Purchase. It was not a claim with much merit, and it provided more emotional than legal support to the Americans. Because of this claim, however, for many years the United States and Spain argued about the location of the border between American and Spanish territories.

✓ **Reading Check** **Analyzing** Would you consider La Salle's expedition successful?

SECTION 3 ASSESSMENT

Checking for Understanding

1. **Using Key Terms** Use the following words in a sentence that demonstrates your understanding of the terms: sandbar, stockade.

2. **Reviewing Facts** When the French colonists established Fort St. Louis in 1685, they expected to make it a permanent settlement. Why did Fort St. Louis fail?

Reviewing Themes

3. **Geography and History** Although Fort St. Louis failed as a permanent settlement, the French efforts in Texas had a number of important results. Describe some.

Organizing to Learn

4. **Relative Chronology** Place the events of La Salle's Texas expedition on the time line in their proper sequence.

1680   1690

a. La Salle's ship sails too far west and south.
b. La Salle is murdered.
c. La Salle searches for other settlements.
d. Fort St. Louis is built.
e. La Salle intends to establish a Mississippi River colony.

Critical Thinking

5. **Analyzing** What are some of the reasons why King Louis XIV was willing to approve and finance La Salle's expedition to the Americas? Make a poster or visual aid that summarizes some possible motives for exploration and colonization.

TAKS PRACTICE

Finding and Summarizing the Main Idea La Salle established a French settlement in Texas. Why did Spain view a French Texas as a threat?

Chapter Summary

Early Explorers

Spanish

1492
- Christopher Columbus sights the new world.

1519
- ★ Cortés lands in Veracruz, Mexico.
- Álvarez de Pineda is the first European to map the Texas coast.

1528
- ★ Cabeza de Vaca becomes first European to set foot in Texas.

1540
- Coronado reaches Cíbola but finds no gold.

1541
- ★ Coronado reaches Quivira but finds no gold.
- De Soto explores the Mississippi River.

1609
- Spanish establish a colony at Santa Fe, New Mexico.

French

1685
- ★ La Salle establishes Fort St. Louis near Matagorda Bay.
- The French flag flies over Texas.

1687
- Spain is concerned by French presence in Texas.
- Fort St. Louis settlement fails.

Reviewing Key Terms

Examine each group of terms below. Explain the similarities and differences among the terms in each group.

1. conquistador, friar, viceroy
2. pueblo, mission, stockade

Reviewing Key Facts

3. Why did Spain fund the expensive expeditions to the New World?
4. Why was Texas a disappointment to the early Spanish explorers?
5. What were the settlements of the friars called, and how did they differ from other settlements?
6. Who were the first Europeans to enter Texas? Who helped them survive, and what did the Europeans learn from these Native Americans?
7. Name two of the fabled cities of gold and tell why the explorers were so willing to believe the rumors about them?
8. Was Coronado's expedition a success?
9. Where did Moscoso lead his expedition?
10. Why was 1519 a significant year in the history of Mexico and Texas?
11. Who led the French into Texas, and what settlement did he try to establish?
12. Why did the French presence motivate the Spanish to return to Texas?

Critical Thinking

13. **Drawing Conclusions** La Salle was a difficult man to get along with, yet without his leadership the French colony struggled. Why do you think this happened?
14. **Analyzing** What did Pedro de Castañeda mean when he wrote in his journal, "[W]hen we have something valuable in our hands . . . we do not value it or prize it as highly as if we understood how much we would miss it . . . after we have lost it."
15. **Making Inferences** Why were European countries attempting to establish colonies in the New World at similar times?
16. **Understanding Cause and Effect** What effect did La Salle's expedition have on Spain?

Cause		Effect
La Salle's Expedition	→	

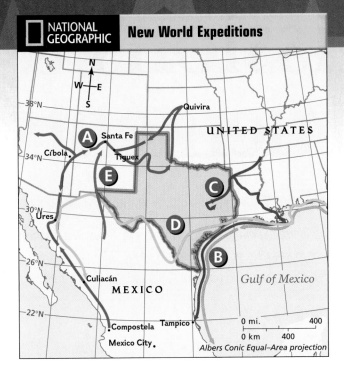

NATIONAL GEOGRAPHIC New World Expeditions

Geography and History Activity

The paths of the explorers have been drawn on the map above. Write the letter of the path that each explorer followed on a separate piece of paper.

17. _____Alonso Álvarez de Pineda 1519

18. _____Alvar Núñez Cabeza de Vaca 1528–1536

19. _____Francisco Vázquez de Coronado 1540–1542

20. _____Luis de Moscoso 1542–1543

21. _____Juan de Oñate 1598

Cooperative Learning Activity

22. **Writing a Report** Working in groups, write a report about one of the expeditions in Texas. Include a map tracing the expedition's path and how the expedition affected the settlement of the Americas. Each member of the group should present a part of the report to the class.

Practicing Skills

23. **Analyzing a Topic** Suppose you want to learn why early French settlements in Texas were unsuccessful. Explain why each of the following sentences does or does not relate to the research topic.

   a. In what year was the colony of Quebec established?

   b. Were Native Americans friendly to French settlers?

   c. Over what route did the French travel to Texas?

   d. Who was the first European to travel through Texas?

   e. What kinds of conditions did the French settlers experience?

TEXAS HISTORY *Online*

Self-Check Quiz
Visit the texans.glencoe.com Web site and click on **Chapter 4—Self-Check Quizzes** to prepare for the chapter test.

Portfolio/TAKS Writing Activity

24. **Making Generalizations** Use proper punctuation and full sentences in answering the following question. *How did the success of Cortés inspire other Spaniards to travel to Texas?*

Building Technology Skills

25. **Using the Internet for Research** Use an electronic encyclopedia or the Internet to find a picture of one of the following: Moctezuma, Hernán Cortés, Cabeza de Vaca, Estevanico, Francisco Vázquez de Coronado, or La Salle. Print the picture. Describe the person's attire, his expression, any activity in the picture, and whether you think it is a positive or negative image. If time permits, present your picture and summary to the class.

The Princeton Review

TAKS PRACTICE

Use the passage *and* your knowledge of Texas history and culture to answer the following question.

"Their horns are small . . . [and] the hair is very long . . . Of the small hides the Indians make blankets to cover themselves with, and of the taller ones they make shoes and targets. These cows . . . are found all over the land for over four hundred leagues."

—Alvar Núñez Cabeza de Vaca

Cabeza de Vaca was one of the first Spaniards to see Texas. In this passage, he describes —

F cattle farmers   **H** how native people made shoes

G herds of buffalo   **J** the mouth of the Rio Grande

Test-Taking Tip:
Sometimes passages use *figurative language,* language that does not mean literally what it says. Always check each answer choice within its context to make sure it is consistent with the passage.

Missions & Settlements

Why It Matters

The La Salle expedition alerted Spain to France's interest in Texas. The Spanish decided that if they were to keep Texas, they must occupy it. Spanish missions and settlements provided a stronger hold on Texas than did the French traders.

The Impact Today

Early Spaniards originally named some of Texas's settlements—San Antonio, Nacogdoches, and La Bahía. Many cities in Texas have the names of Catholic saints. These include San Marcos, San Augustine, Santa Elena, and many more.

Texas

1690
★ First Spanish mission dedicated in East Texas

1718
★ Mission San Antonio de Valero, the Alamo, was established

1722
★ Los Adaes became the unofficial capital of Texas

United States   1690   1718   1765

World

1718
• French founded city of New Orleans

1719
• France declared war on Spain

1756
• Seven Years' War began in Europe

1765
• The British Parliament passed the Stamp Act

This painting of the San José Mission *by W. A. Aiken is typical of missions built in Texas in the late 1600s and early 1700s.*

FOLDABLES™ Study Organizer

TAKS PRACTICE

Categorizing Information Study Foldable
Make this foldable to help you organize information from the chapter.

Step 1 Fold the paper from the top right corner down so the edges line up. Cut off the leftover piece.

Fold a triangle. Cut off the extra edge.

Step 2 Fold the triangle in half. Unfold.

The folds will form an X dividing four equal sections.

Step 3 Cut up one fold line and stop at the middle. Draw an X on one tab and label the other three.

Step 4 Fold the X flap under the other flap and glue together.

This makes a three-sided pyramid.

Reading and Writing As you read, write what you learn about the missions, settlements, and communities in Texas under each appropriate pyramid wall.

TEXAS HISTORY Online

Chapter Overview
Visit the texans.glencoe.com Web site and click on **Chapter 5—Chapter Overviews** to preview chapter information

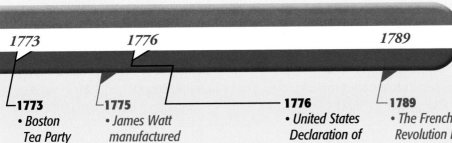

1773   1776   1789

1773
• Boston Tea Party

1775
• James Watt manufactured the steam engine

1776
• United States Declaration of Independence was signed

1789
• The French Revolution began

First Missions Are Built

Guide to Reading

Main Idea
Fearing a French presence, Spain renewed efforts to settle eastern Texas during the 1600s and 1700s.

Key Terms
presidio
council

Reading Strategy
Organizing Information As you read this section, complete a table like the one shown here by filling in the dates of the first Spanish missions in Texas.

Location	Mission	Date
Near El Paso		
East Texas		

Read to Learn
• about Spanish and French settlers in Texas.
• why East Texas missions failed.
• about Spanish reaction to the French.

Section Theme
Continuity and Change The Spanish attempted to establish missions in Texas but faced difficulties.

Preview of Events

♦1682   ♦1690   ♦1714

Ysleta is the first permanent European settlement in Texas

Father Damián Massanet establishes first mission in East Texas

Louis de St. Denis meets with Spanish officials

Texas seashore

A
Texas Story

Many soldiers sent to Texas to establish missions and presidios had never seen the sea. Father Damián Massanet (dah•mee•AHN mah•sah•NAY), a priest who worked in Texas, wrote about the sea. "And after we arrived, some of the soldiers said that they wished to bathe in the sea, [this] being esteemed so remarkable a thing that they carried away flasks of seawater . . . later it [seawater] was held a great favor to try to taste because it was seawater."

Spain Looks to Texas

As part of the settlement of New Spain, friars in 1682 founded the first permanent settlement of Europeans in Texas—the **mission of Corpus Christi de la Ysleta**, located near present-day El Paso. Most Spanish activity during the 1690s, though, was in the eastern part of Texas, near French Louisiana. Fearing the arrival of La Salle in 1685 would produce French settlements, Spanish officials made a stronger effort to establish colonies. In the next several decades, Spain built missions, military outposts called **presidios,** and towns in lands occupied by Native Americans.

Spanish officials learned of La Salle's fort in Texas soon after it was built. They immediately sent troops to destroy it. An expedition led by **Alonso de León** (ah•LOHN•soh day lay•OHN), the governor of Coahuila, reached the site on April 22, 1689, only to find the fort deserted and in ruins.

A Tejas Mission

De León then led his troops northeast. Near the Colorado River, they met a large group of Hasinai people, whom they called the *Tejas,* (TAY•hahs) a word meaning "friend." **Angelina,** a Caddo woman, served as guide and interpreter. **Father**

Damián Massanet, a Catholic church official on the expedition, promised he would come back. When the expedition returned to Mexico, Massanet asked the viceroy for permission to found a mission among the Tejas.

The viceroy agreed, and in the spring of 1690 Father Massanet, three other friars, and about 100 soldiers set out for East Texas. When the expedition arrived at the Tejas villages in late May, the Tejas greeted the Spanish visitors with a feast.

The first Spanish mission in East Texas was dedicated on June 1, 1690. It was a crude log building and contained only a few simple furnishings. Named **San Francisco de los Tejas** (sahn frahn•SEES•koh day lohs TAY•hahs), the mission was located a few miles west of the Neches River near the present-day town of Weches.

Mission Corpus Christi de la Ysleta

Mission San Francisco de los Tejas

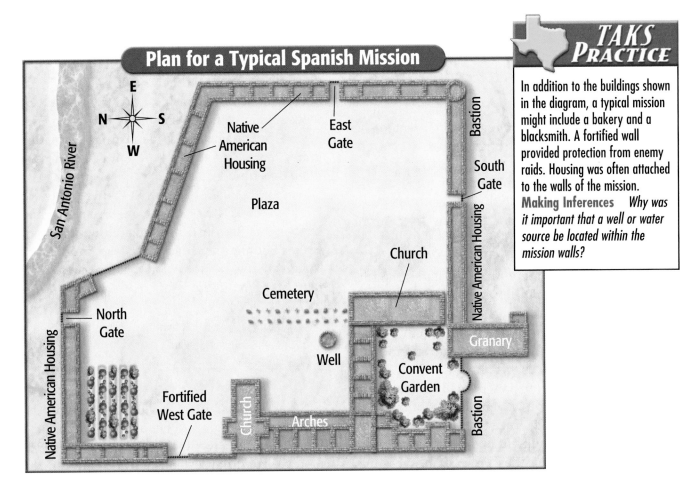

Plan for a Typical Spanish Mission

San Antonio River

N E S W

Native American Housing

East Gate

Bastion

South Gate

Plaza

Native American Housing

Church

Cemetery

North Gate

Well

Granary

Convent Garden

Fortified West Gate

Church

Arches

Native American Housing

Bastion

TAKS PRACTICE

In addition to the buildings shown in the diagram, a typical mission might include a bakery and a blacksmith. A fortified wall provided protection from enemy raids. Housing was often attached to the walls of the mission. **Making Inferences** *Why was it important that a well or water source be located within the mission walls?*

The original location of the Presidio La Bahía in 1721 was on Matagorda Bay, but after many moves it is now located in Goliad, near the San Antonio River. Why would a mission chapel be part of the presidio?

Goliad

A Mission Abandoned

Despite the promising beginning, troubles soon struck San Francisco de los Tejas. Drought ruined the Tejas's crops, and disease killed many of the Native Americans and one of the friars. The Tejas rejected the Catholic religion and resented the Spaniards' attempts to change the way they lived.

Meanwhile, officials in Mexico City decided that the mission must be abandoned. Realizing France was not a threat, there was no reason to spend money supporting missions so far from Spanish settlements.

Although the failure of the mission was a disappointment, its mere presence had strengthened Spain's claim to Texas. The Spaniards now realized that a colony needed presidios and Spanish families who would settle on the land.

From 1693 to 1714, Spain made no effort to settle Texas, but settlements along the Rio Grande flourished. **Mission San Juan Bautista** (sahn hwan bah•TEES•tah) was built west of the river near the present-day town of Eagle Pass in 1699. The mission, five miles from the Rio Grande, was strategically located near a series of crossings

providing access to Texas. Here the outpost eventually grew into a complex of three missions, a presidio, and a town. The mission earned the title of the "Mother of Texas Missions" because it was the base for many expeditions whose aims were to establish missions in East Texas. The mission at San Juan Bautista provided grain, cattle, and horses to the missionaries on these expeditions.

One of its missionaries was **Father Francisco Hidalgo** (ee•DAHL•go), a gentle friar who had known the Tejas of San Francisco de los Tejas. Father Hidalgo repeatedly asked permission to return there to start another mission. His requests were ignored.

Reading Check **Explaining** Why was the first Spanish mission unsuccessful?

France Threatens Again

Several years after La Salle's venture in the 1680s, France made another attempt to claim the lands drained by the Mississippi. In 1699 a French expedition established a colony on the

Gulf Coast at Biloxi in present-day Mississippi. Soon other French trading posts were scattered throughout the Mississippi Valley.

The French were not interested in taking territory or converting the Native Americans to Catholicism. French traders won the friendship of many Native American groups, and the French made large profits exchanging blankets, guns, and wine for furs and skins. The French also hoped to trade with Spanish merchants in Mexico, but Spanish law prohibited foreigners from trading in the colonies of New Spain.

Without the knowledge of Spanish officials, Father Hidalgo wrote a letter to the French governor in Louisiana, asking that the French establish a mission among the Tejas. The French governor listened to Hidalgo's proposal because it offered an opportunity to open trade.

The French governor appointed **Louis de St. Denis** (loo•EE dahs sahn deh•NEE) to negotiate with the Spanish officials on the Rio Grande. St. Denis had traded successfully with Native Americans in Louisiana. On the way to the Rio Grande, he built a trading post, Natchitoches, on the Red River. Then St. Denis and a small party left for San Juan Bautista, arriving in July 1714.

The unexpected arrival of the French party alarmed **Captain Diego Ramón,** the presidio's commander. He arrested St. Denis and sent him to Mexico City to be examined by the viceroy. St.

A Shared Past...

While Spain's colonies were ruled by a strong, unified government, Britain often neglected its North American colonies to concentrate on problems at home. English colonists often had to fend for themselves. This experience at self-rule later fueled their fight for independence.

Denis insisted that France had no plans to occupy East Texas.

The Spanish viceroy and his council, or advisers, did not believe St. Denis. They ordered new missions to be built in East Texas with Spanish soldiers to protect them. Trade between the Spanish and French was stopped. Curiously, the viceroy appointed St. Denis to guide the Spaniards into East Texas. The Spaniards could benefit from his knowledge of Texas trails and his good relations with Native Americans. St. Denis was also given permission to marry Manuela, the step-granddaughter of Captain Ramón.

✓**Reading Check** **Explaining** Why did Captain Ramón arrest St. Denis?

SECTION 1 ASSESSMENT

Checking for Understanding

1. **Using Key Terms** Identify the difference between a presidio and a mission. In your definition, include the purpose of each of these.
2. **Reviewing Facts** What was the name of the first Spanish mission in East Texas?

Reviewing Themes

3. **Continuity and Change** Explain how politics, religion, and climate all played a role in the failure of Mission San Francisco de los Tejas.

Organizing to Learn

4. **Identifying** Create a chart like the one shown below. Explain how each person played a role in the establishment of the early missions in Texas.

Person	Role
de León	
Angelina	
Massanet	
Hidalgo	
St. Denis	
Ramón	

Critical Thinking

5. **Comparing and Contrasting** How did the French and the Spanish differ in their relationships with Native Americans in Texas?

TAKS PRACTICE

Drawing Inferences What were Father Massanet's motives when he asked the viceroy for permission to found a mission among the Tejas? What do you think his reaction would be to the failure of the mission?

Spanish Settlements

Guide to Reading

Main Idea
Spain expanded efforts to colonize Texas during the first half of the 1700s, but many of the settlements failed.

Key Term
province

Reading Strategy
Classifying Information Complete a chart like the one shown here, recognizing how Native Americans in the Plains felt about the Spanish in Texas.

Native Americans	Attitudes Toward Spanish
Apaches	
Comanches	
Tonkawas	

Read to Learn
• what settlements Spain built in East Texas.
• what missionary efforts the Spanish first made among the Plains people.

Section Theme
Culture and Traditions The Spanish and French established settlements in Texas and interacted with Native Americans.

Preview of Events

◆1716	◆1718	◆1722
Six missions are established in East Texas	Mission San Antonio de Valero, the Alamo, is founded	Los Adaes becomes the unofficial capital of Texas

A
Texas Story

Native American stake-house

Father Massanet was well educated and had a keen eye. His observations provide information about the Native Americans he knew. "The house is built of stakes thatched over with grass . . . is round, and has no windows, daylight entering through the door only. In the middle of the house is the fire, which is never extinguished, day or night . . . Ranged around one-half of the house are ten beds, which consist of a rug made of reeds, laid on four forked sticks. Over the rug they spread buffalo skins, on which they sleep."

Missions Are Established in East Texas

Guided by St. Denis, with Angelina as interpreter, a large Spanish force arrived in June, 1716 at the site of San Francisco de los Tejas. For the first time, Spanish families came to live in the forests of East Texas. The Native

Americans were friendly and did not resist the Spanish effort. Within a year, the Spanish had established six missions and a small fort, a presidio they named Nuestra Señora de los Dolores. The presidio, located on the Neches River, was built to protect the missions from attacks by the Native Americans or the French.

San Antonio Is Founded

Spanish officials again saw the need for a settlement midway between New Spain and the new missions. The 500-mile (805-km) journey from the Rio Grande to East Texas was dangerous. Supplies arrived slowly, if at all. At times the people of East Texas had no choice but to trade with the French in Louisiana or starve.

Spanish officials chose a site on the San Antonio River as the best place for the new settlement. A friar described it as follows:

> 66The best site in the world, with good and abundant irrigation water, rich lands for pasture, plentiful building stone, and excellent timber.99

Presidio San Antonio de Béxar, on one side of the San Antonio River, was built in 1718 under the leadership of Martín de Alarcón (day ah•lar•KOHN). Many of the soldiers brought families, began digging irrigation canals for farming, and settled permanently. The women tilled the land, cooked, cleaned, and cared for the children. Across the river Father Antonio de San

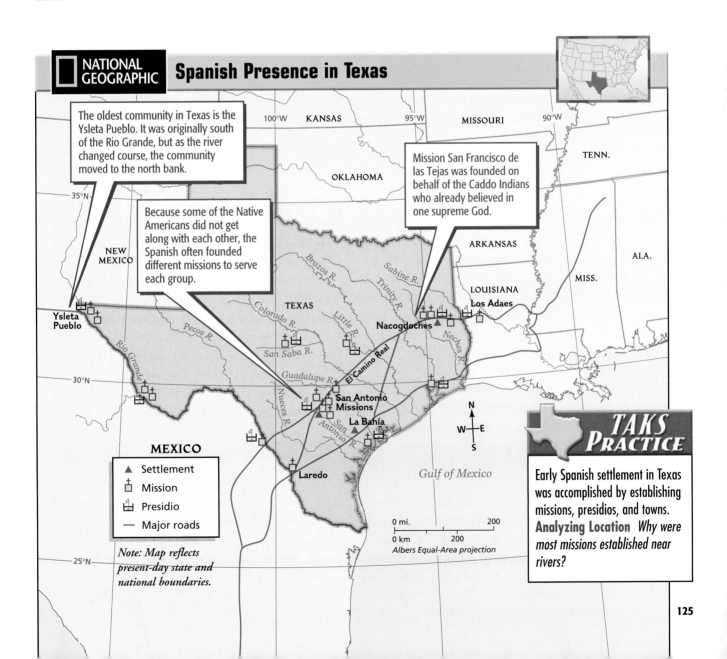

NATIONAL GEOGRAPHIC Spanish Presence in Texas

The oldest community in Texas is the Ysleta Pueblo. It was originally south of the Rio Grande, but as the river changed course, the community moved to the north bank.

Because some of the Native Americans did not get along with each other, the Spanish often founded different missions to serve each group.

Mission San Francisco de las Tejas was founded on behalf of the Caddo Indians who already believed in one supreme God.

Ysleta Pueblo

Nacogdoches

San Antonio Missions

La Bahía

Laredo

MEXICO

▲ Settlement
✝ Mission
Presidio
— Major roads

Note: Map reflects present-day state and national boundaries.

Gulf of Mexico

0 mi. 200
0 km 200
Albers Equal-Area projection

TAKS PRACTICE

Early Spanish settlement in Texas was accomplished by establishing missions, presidios, and towns. **Analyzing Location** *Why were most missions established near rivers?*

125

A Shared Past...

In 1739, Spanish and French streams of settlement and exploration met in Santa Fe. French Canadian brothers Paul and Pierre Mallet arrived from the Missouri country. Their route later became the Santa Fe Trail, which opened trade between Missouri and New Mexico. When they left Santa Fe, they crossed the Panhandle of Texas and journeyed to New Orleans.

Buenaventura Olivares founded **Mission San Antonio de Valero.** The mission chapel, which was built a few years later, is now known as the **Alamo.** Throughout its history, San Fernando de Béxar (later called San Antonio) has been the site of many battles. With Texas's independence, the town found itself a distance from the bulk of the new republic's population.

✓**Reading Check** Evaluating Why did the Spanish settle along the San Antonio River?

Aguayo Defends the Missions

The settling of East Texas halted when war broke out between Spain and France in 1719. A small unit of French soldiers from Louisiana seized the Spanish mission near Nacogdoches. An escaped mission brother exaggerated the size of the invading French army. Panic-stricken missionaries, soldiers, and families in East Texas fled to San Antonio later that year.

Angry and determined, the viceroy of New Spain immediately planned to retake East Texas. He ordered the **Marqués de San Miguel de Aguayo** (mar•KAYS day sahn mee•GEL day ah•GWY•oh) to organize a force to meet the French threat. Aguayo was the governor of the **provinces** of Coahuila and Texas. In the spring of 1721, Aguayo marched to Texas with more than 500 soldier-settlers, thousands of horses and mules, and large herds of sheep and cattle. He again established the abandoned missions

there and moved Presidio Nuestra Señora de los Dolores from the Neches River to the banks of the Angelina River.

Aguayo Founds Two Cities

Near the French post of Natchitoches, not far from present-day Robeline, Louisiana, Aguayo built a large presidio, **Nuestra Señora del Pilar de los Adaes** (noo•WEHS•trah seh•NYO•rah dehl pee•LAHR deh lohs ah•DAH•ehs). A force of 100 soldiers and their families started a village nearby. Six brass cannons guarded the fort. St. Denis, now the French commander at Natchitoches, protested that the presidio was in French territory. However, he made no effort to drive the Spanish soldiers and settlers away.

Years before, in 1691, Spanish authorities had recognized Texas as a province and had appointed the first governor. For many years officials governed the province from settlements in other areas of northern Mexico. The threat from the French, however, suggested the need for closer supervision. Soon after Aguayo established Los Adaes, it became the unofficial capital of Texas in 1722. It remained the capital for almost 50 years.

From Los Adaes, Aguayo traveled southwest to Garcitas Creek Bay where his expedition established a mission and a presidio near the ruins of La Salle's fort. The mission and presidio were later moved to the San Antonio River, near the present-day town of Goliad (GOH•lee•ad). The Spaniards named the settlement La Bahía del Espíritu Santo (lah bah•EE•ah dehl ehs•PEER•ee•too SAHN•toh), or, simply, **La Bahía.**

✓**Reading Check** Analyzing Why did the Spanish designate Los Adaes as the unofficial capital of Texas?

An Uneasy Peace

When Aguayo returned to his home in Coahuila, he left Texas's 9 missions, 2 villages, and 4 presidios protected by 300 soldiers. Spanish rule in Texas seemed secure. Then, in 1727, Spanish officials concluded that expenses were too high. To reduce spending, the Spaniards soon abandoned the presidio on the Angelina River, reduced the number of soldiers at Los Adaes, and moved 3 of the East Texas missions to San Antonio.

The French continued to be active in East Texas. Although their trading with Native Americans there irritated the Spaniards, France did not occupy any territory west of the Arroyo Hondo (ah•ROH•yoh HOHN•doh), a small stream located between Los Adaes and Natchitoches that flows into the Red River. With this boundary generally accepted by both Spanish and French officials, relations between the two countries usually were peaceful.

Plains People Resent Missions

The first Spanish missionaries in Texas traveled among the Native American people of East Texas. The people there were not very interested in Catholicism, but they rarely threatened the lives of the Spanish friars or settlers. Many other Native Americans, those living along the coast and along the Rio Grande, joined the friars in the mission towns.

Native American people of the Plains, on the other hand, resented the intruders who had come to their hunting grounds. Apaches regularly raided San Antonio, making life dangerous for the European settlers. The Comanches fiercely fought the invaders and greatly valued the prized Spanish horses they were able to capture. Despite the obvious dangers, Spanish friars were eager to spread the Catholic religion and teach the Plains people the Spanish way of life. To do so, they established missions in central and western Texas.

TWO VIEWPOINTS

Colonizing Texas

Early Spaniards were not in agreement about the benefits of Spain's efforts to colonize Texas. Read the two views below and then answer the question.

Explorer Has a Favorable Response

The Tejas are a very well governed people and plant large quantities of maize, beans, calabashes, cantaloupes and watermelons. They are very familiar with the fact that there is only one true God, that He is in Heaven . . . And certainly it is a pity that people so rational, who plant crops and know there is a God, have no one to teach them the Gospel, especially when the province of Texas is so large and so fertile and has so fine a climate.
—Report of explorer Alonso de León, May 1689

A Spanish Official Visiting Texas Is Not Impressed by the Province

A villa without order, two presidios, seven missions, and an errant population of scarcely 4,000 persons of both sexes and all ages that occupies an immense desert country stretching from the abandoned presidio of Los Adaes to San Antonio does not deserve the name of the Province of Texas . . . nor the concern entailed in its preservation.
—Commandant-General Teodoro de Croix to José de Gálvez, October 30, 1781

Learning From History

Why do you think an explorer and a military officer would have such different points of view?

Between 1748 and 1751, three San Xavier (sahn sah•VEE•her) missions were founded along the San Gabriel River (then known as the San Xavier), near present-day Rockdale. Intending to serve the Tonkawa people, the missionaries suffered many misfortunes. Apaches raided the settlement, smallpox and measles struck the settlers, drought ruined the crops, and the Tonkawas left. After a short time, the Spanish friars abandoned one of the missions and moved the other two closer to San Antonio.

San Sabá Mission Fails

In 1757 missionaries founded **Mission Santa Cruz de San Sabá** (sahn•tah CROOZ day sahn sah•BAH), near present-day Menard in central Texas. Soldiers built a presidio a few miles away. The founding of the mission was a bold step. More than 100 miles (161 km) filled with danger separated San Sabá from the nearest Spanish settlement. Both Apaches and Comanches roamed the area.

Why did the Spaniards take such a risk? Spanish missionaries wanted an opportunity to convert the Apaches into Christians. The Apaches had, in fact, asked for the mission, hoping to use the Spaniards as protection from their fierce Comanche enemies. Apaches visited the mission from time to time to receive food and gifts but never stayed very long.

Comanche attacks on the mission in 1758 and 1759 took nearly 30 lives. Although the Spanish maintained a presidio on the San Sabá River until 1769, they moved missionary efforts for the Apaches to the Nueces River.

The Texas missions, including San Sabá, failed in their efforts to Christianize the Plains people. Isolated missions lacked the supplies and people to survive in the remote region, far from administrative help. The Apaches and Comanches were too fiercely independent to give up their nomadic lifestyle. In the San Antonio area, however, missions succeeded in persuading some Native Americans to settle, farm, and practice Catholicism. Even there, the mission towns changed. They came to resemble Spanish towns and attracted Spaniards as well as Native Americans.

TEXAS HISTORY Online

Student Web Activity Visit the texans.glencoe.com Web site and click on **Chapter 5—Student Web Activity** to learn more about early Spanish missions in Texas.

✓**Reading Check** **Evaluating** Were the friars successful in converting the Apaches to Christianity?

SECTION 2 ASSESSMENT

Checking for Understanding
1. **Using Key Terms** Define province. What word in United States government correlates to province?
2. **Reviewing Facts** List the main points of conflict between the Plains people and the Spanish missionaries.

Reviewing Themes
3. **Culture and Traditions** Why did Spanish missionaries continue their work in East Texas and on the Plains when many people there resented them?

Organizing to Learn
4. **Listing** Create a chart listing the major missions that were founded in East Texas. Write why each mission was significant.

Mission	Significance
San Francisco de los Tejas	
San Antonio de Valero	
La Bahía del Espíritu Santo	
Santa Cruz de San Sabá	

Critical Thinking
5. **Synthesizing Information** Relations were usually peaceful between the Spanish and the French because they recognized a common boundary. Explain the need for a commonly recognized boundary between cultures in conflict today.

TAKS PRACTICE

Cause and Effect Explain some of the reasons that caused the mission at San Sabá to fail.

Making Comparisons

Why Learn This Skill?

When you examine two or more groups, situations, events, or documents, you are making comparisons. This skill helps you identify *similarities* (the ways things are alike) and *differences* (the ways things are different).

Learning the Skill

Follow these steps to make comparisons:
- Read or study each item to be compared.
- Ask yourself the same questions about each of them.
- Analyze how the answers to these questions are similar or different.

Native Americans gather at a mission.

Practicing the Skill

Refer back to page 124 and reread "A Texas Story," which describes a Caddo chief's house. Then read the following passage describing Native American homes in Mission San José. Answer the questions that follow.

"Arranged along this [wall], . . . were the stone quarters where the [Indians] lived. They had flat roofs . . . Each house had a bedroom and a kitchen, and each family was supplied with a cooking flatiron, a grindstone for corn, a water jar, a bed, a chest of drawers, and a clothes closet . . . near the houses were several baking ovens."

❶ Describe the building style used for each type of house. Were they similar or different?

❷ How were the insides of the houses, including furniture and tools, alike? Different?

❸ What tools and materials available at the Spanish mission did the Caddo people not appear to have?

❹ What advantage is there in sharing baking ovens among the families?

TAKS PRACTICE

Making Comparisons What advantages and disadvantages might the Native Americans experience by living in a house at a Spanish mission? Make lists under the headings "advantages" and "disadvantages."

Glencoe's **Skillbuilder Interactive Workbook**, Level 1, provides instruction and practice in key social studies skills.

Building Communities

Guide to Reading

Main Idea
Farmers and ranchers adapted to life in Texas missions, presidios, and settlements.

Key Terms
ayuntamiento
alcalde
mestizos
Tejano

Reading Strategy
As you read this section, create a chart like the one shown here on how the settlers improved life in the missions.

School	Health	Recreation

Read to Learn
• how settlers lived daily life.
• about mission life.
• what factors drew Native Americans into Spanish settlements.

Section Theme
Groups and Institutions Spanish missions were busy centers of activity, but many Native Americans disliked them.

Preview of Events

♦ Mid to Late 1700s	♦ 1772	♦ 1790
More civilian settlers move to Texas	San Antonio, largest settlement, becomes the capital	Women make up 45 percent of population

Presidio la Bahía

A
Texas Story

Massanet spent many years building churches among the Native Americans in East Texas. "I told the governor [Native American Leader] . . . that I heartily appreciated his desire to have the priests in his household, but that . . . it might be well to build a dwelling for the priests." Despite the friendliness of the natives, the churches did not last. In 1693, Massanet set fire to the last church and returned to Mexico.

Life in the Missions

Spanish missions were busy centers of activity. The friars worked hard to persuade Native American people to live close to the missions. They hoped to teach the Native Americans the Spanish way of life. Gifts were sometimes offered to make this life seem more attractive.

Sometimes the Spaniards used force to get the Native Americans to settle near the missions.

The Native Americans who accepted mission life were kept busy from dawn to dusk. Each day started with prayers. After breakfast, the children attended school, including classes in religion. The women wove cloth, molded pottery, or cooked. The men worked in the fields or learned carpentry or blacksmithing. After supper came more religion classes for adults, followed by prayers.

The friars generally were strict, and in most missions, the food was plentiful. Large herds of cattle, sheep, and goats guaranteed a regular meat and milk supply. Mission farms, especially those at San Antonio and Goliad, produced rich harvests of corn, beans, cantaloupes, cucumbers, watermelons, chiles, pimientos, peaches, and sweet potatoes. Father Morfi described the activity of the Native American people at Mission San José in San Antonio from his—the European—viewpoint:

> ❝These Indians are today well instructed and civilized and know how to work very well at their mechanical trades and are proficient in some of the arts. They speak Spanish perfectly, with the exception of those who are daily brought in . . . They go about well dressed, are abundantly fed.❞

The following report on San José de Aguayo, dated 1785, describes the construction and organization of a Spanish mission in Texas.

> ❝Situated on a broad plain, rather sparsely wooded, its grounds and buildings . . . offer an attractive sight . . . [H]ouses are built next to each other and have ample room, with [a] kitchen for each family. They are sufficiently protected against rain, wind, and other inclemencies of the weather . . . [S]eparated from the habitations of the Indians by a street, stand the missionary's house, the church, and the sacristy. The first contains not only rooms for housing the missionaries, but also a kitchen, and the offices of the community. It is all of stone and lime and flat-roofed; the quarters for the missionary form a second story, and every part is in good taste.❞

Although some Native Americans adapted to mission life, most refused to stay at the missions. They were not accustomed to the strictly regulated lifestyle. Many did not want to become farmers or blacksmiths or carpenters. Moreover, Native Americans found it difficult to leave behind a way of life that had served them well for centuries.

✓ **Reading Check** **Describing** What was life like for Native Americans in the missions?

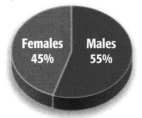

Picturing **History**

Settlers in Texas and Mexico enjoyed dancing the fandango in their leisure time. Families tried to live as they had in Spain. **Were there more men or women in Spanish settlements during this period?**

Population of Spanish Settlements, 1790

Females 45%
Males 55%

Soldiers Face Hardships

The life of the Spanish soldier on an isolated frontier outpost was difficult and dangerous. The soldiers' duties included protecting the mission and nearby settlements, maintaining control over the Native Americans in the missions, and scouting the countryside for intruders. Most of the soldiers were also settlers. They brought their families to the military towns and farmed and soldiered for a living.

Military men were often poorly equipped and lived under difficult conditions. Father Morfi described the conditions at the San Antonio presidio:

> 66The soldiers' quarters, originally built of stone and adobe, are almost in ruins . . . The presidio is surrounded by a poor stockade on which are mounted a few swivel guns, without shelter or defense, that can be used only for firing a [round of shots]. There is no other trade than that required to supply the needs of the . . . garrison and . . . of the wretched settlers.99

The soldier-settlers sometimes traded with the Native Americans living in the missions. According to the friars, the soldier-settlers took advantage of the Native Americans, who did not know Spanish ways. By the same token, the soldiers accused the friars of taking away the Native Americans' freedoms.

Important Settlements in Spanish Texas

San Antonio, Goliad, Los Adaes, and Nacogdoches were the most important civilian settlements in Spanish Texas. San Antonio was the largest settlement and by 1772 served as the capital. It was the only authorized settlement in Texas where the people had some voice in their government. Landowners elected a city council called an *ayuntamiento* and a chief official with the title of *alcalde*.

The Spanish authorities had wanted to increase the population of San Antonio. They tried to bring in 200 families from the Spanish colony of the Canary Islands, off the African coast, but only 15 families came to Texas in 1731. Some of the oldest families of modern San Antonio trace their ancestors from the Canary Islanders. Several were wealthy women like María Betancour. At the time of her death, her will noted that she owned a 26-acre (11-hectare) ranch, a stone house with various household furnishings, and cattle marked with her brand. In 1776, María Josefa Granados owned the largest general store in San Fernando de Béxar (San Antonio). In 1814, María Pérez Cassiano, a Canary Islands descendant, ran the affairs of state while her husband, the Spanish governor, was out of town. Spanish troops called her La Brigadiera (the Brigadier–General).

Reading Check **Identifying** Name the major civilian settlements in Texas in the late 1700s.

Living in Spanish Texas

People in Texas made their living in several ways. Some were farmers who irrigated their fields with water brought in through an elaborate system of canals. Male and female ranchers raised thousands of cattle. There were also shopkeepers, shoemakers, fishers, barbers, blacksmiths, tax collectors, oxen drivers, seamstresses and tailors, healers, and servants.

The population in Spanish Texas was not limited to Spaniards and Native Americans. Mestizos, people of mixed Spanish and Native

American heritage, also lived in Spanish Texas. Some mestizos were the children of soldier-settlers and Canary Islanders. A few African Americans living in Texas at this time were free, although some were enslaved. Felipe Ulua, for example, a Louisiana creole and slave, purchased his freedom and that of his wife, Mary Ortero. They and their children settled in San Antonio in 1807. Free African Americans also worked as domestics, farmers, ranchers, merchants, carpenters, and miners.

Most men and women were married, but widows and widowers made up 10 percent of the population. Doña Rosa María Hinojosa de Ballí was one of the earliest ranchers and landowners. A widow who inherited her husband's and father's land grants, she owned about one-third of the present lower Rio Grande Valley in 1798. Her ranch headquarters were near present-day La Feria, Texas, but she lived on the other side of the river in Reynosa, Mexico.

A Tejano Heritage Takes Shape

By this time a Tejano character was becoming part of the Texas cultural landscape. The term *Tejano* describes people of Mexican heritage who consider Texas their home. This Tejano heritage is reflected in the population, religion, language, institutions, and customs of Texas today.

Mission San José at San Antonio

The settlers tried to improve community life. No school system existed, but some communities hired teachers. Tejano settlers started the first community school in San Antonio. Medical doctors were practically unknown, but officials tried to guard public health by forbidding practices such as dumping trash and washing clothes in the drinking water supply. Although life often was difficult for the new settlers, there were opportunities for different kinds of recreation. Communities sponsored dances, horse races, and holiday fairs in the village plazas.

Reading Check **Identifying** What were two ways the settlers tried to improve their lives in San Antonio?

SECTION 3 ASSESSMENT

Checking for Understanding

1. **Using Key Terms** What is the relationship between an *alcalde* and an *ayuntamiento*?
2. **Reviewing Facts** How did officials guard public health?

Reviewing Themes

3. **Groups and Institutions** Identify the disagreements between the friars and soldier-settlers over the Native Americans.

Organizing to Learn

4. **Categorizing** Create a web like the one shown here, identifying occupations in Spanish Texas. Fill the ovals with information from the section.

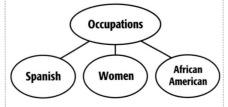

Critical Thinking

5. **Making Comparisons** How did Native Americans' way of life at the missions differ from their traditional way of life?

TAKS PRACTICE

Drawing Conclusions What must the environmental conditions have been like at San Antonio and Goliad for the missions to have produced rich harvests of fruits and vegetables?

Chapter Summary

Missions and Settlements

1682
- Corpus Christi de la Ysleta becomes the first permanent European settlement in Texas.

1690
★ Father Damián Massanet sets up the first Spanish Mission in East Texas. Drought and disease force its closure.

1693–1714
- Spanish interest in Texas declines until the French reappear.

1699
- French establish a colony in Biloxi in present-day Mississippi.

1716
- Spanish establish six missions and one fort in East Texas.

1718
- Villa San Fernando de Béxar is settled; it later becomes San Antonio.
★ Mission San Antonio de Valero, the Alamo, is founded.

1722
- Several settlements are established, including Los Adaes, which becomes the first unofficial capital of Texas.

1772
- Efforts to Christianize the Plains Indians fail.
- San Antonio, the largest settlement, becomes the capital.

1790
★ Women make up 45 percent of population of Spanish settlements.

Reviewing Key Terms

1. *Write a letter to the viceroy of Spain explaining what has happened with the Spanish missions in Texas. Use these words in your letter:* **presidio, council, province,** *alcalde, ayuntamiento,* **mestizo,** *and* **Tejano.**

Reviewing Key Facts

2. What did Spanish officials do when they learned of La Salle's fort in Texas?
3. What was the name of the first permanent settlement, and where was it built?
4. How did French traders make profits in Texas?
5. Why did Spanish officials choose a site on the San Antonio River for a new settlement?
6. What consequences occurred when a brother escaped from French soldiers at the mission near Nacogdoches?
7. Who was made governor of the province that included Texas?
8. How long did Los Adaes remain the capital of Texas?
9. Why did Spain risk building a settlement at San Sabá?
10. What were conditions like at the San Antonio presidio?
11. How did Spanish authorities try to increase the population of San Antonio?

Critical Thinking

12. **Summarizing** What problems did Spanish friars and soldier-settlers face in early Texas? Use the chart below to help organize your thoughts.

Group	Problems
Friars	
Soldier-Settlers	

13. **Making Generalizations** Which seemed to influence the Spanish more in their establishment of Texas—a desire to teach Native Americans or a desire to keep out the French? Support your answer with examples from the text.

14. **Making Inferences** Why would the war between Spain and France in Europe stop Spanish missionary efforts in Texas?

15. **Drawing Conclusions** The growth of trade between Europe and the Americas changed the world. Do you think trade today is just as important? Why or why not?

Geography and History Activity

Use the following clues to determine the answer.

16. I am located west of the Neches River and was dedicated on June 1, 1690. What am I?

17. I played an important role in Texas history and was founded in 1718. What am I?

18. I stood near the ruins of LaSalle's fort and was later moved to the San Antonio River. What am I?

Cooperative Learning Activity

19. **Architecture** Form a research team to consider some of the various types of settlements during this period. Research the architecture of this period in Texas. Prepare a presentation for a classroom discussion about your topic. If possible, provide illustrations with captions.

Practicing Skills

20. **Making Comparisons** Create a chart like the one shown here. Then reread Section 3. Complete the chart and pose three questions that can be answered by comparing the places from the chart.

	Missions	Presidios	Settlements
What was the purpose?	to convert Native Americans		
Who lived there?		Spanish soldiers	
What were the daily activities?			Ranching, farming, community events
What were the main problems?			

 ## Portfolio/TAKS Writing Activity

21. **Evaluating** In what ways would life in Texas be different today if the French had more vigorously pursued establishing settlements? Write a paragraph explaining your answer. Save your work for your portfolio.

 ## Building Technology Skills

22. **Building a Database** Conduct a search to gather information about daily life in the missions, presidios, and settlements in early Texas. Organize the information by categories of your choosing. Then write a report based on the information about life in one of these communities. Include photos, maps, or diagrams to illustrate life in the community you chose. If you have access to the technology, scan the images into a Power Point or other authoring software presentation.

Use the information you have read in the chapter to answer the question below.

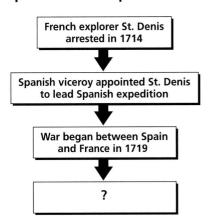

Which of the following correctly completes the flowchart?

A France gained control of the Mississippi River Valley.

B The French settled San Antonio.

C France lost most of its land in North America.

D The Spanish settled west of Arroyo Hondo.

Test-Taking Tip:

When deciding where to place events in a flowchart, first read the list of events. Do not always assume that you can correctly identify the order of events from reading the list. Make sure to refer back to the text.

CHAPTER 6

End of Spanish Rule

Why It Matters

Europeans had ruled the New World for centuries. In the late 1700s people in the Americas began to throw off European rule. The thirteen English colonies were first. The French colony of Haiti was next. Texas was one part of the grand story of the independence of the Spanish colonies. For the people living in Texas, though, the transition from Spanish province to a territory in the independent nation of Mexico was tremendously important.

The Impact Today

- *Texas was the region of North America in which Spanish, French, English, and Native Americans met.*
- *Contact among people encourages new ways of thinking. Later the number of groups in Texas increased as African and Asian people, as well as others from all over the world, brought their cultures.*

Texas

1760
★ Atascosito Road used for military purposes

1773
★ Spanish abandon East Texas missions

1779
• Nacogdoches founded

United States 1760   1770   1780   1790

World

1763
• Treaty of Paris ended Seven Years' War

1773
• Captain James Cook crossed the Antarctic Circle

1783
• Great Britain and United States signed peace treaty

1789
• George Washington became first president

1793
• Eli Whitney invented the cotton gin

Although painted in 1849 after Texas became part of the United States, this image of San Antonio's Main Plaza shows the influence of Spain and Mexico.

1819
★ Adams–Onís Treaty signed

1821
★ Mexico gained independence from Spain

1800   1810   1820

1803
• United States bought Louisiana from France

1804
• Napoleon Bonaparte became emperor of France

TEXAS HISTORY Online

Chapter Overview
Visit the texans.glencoe.com Web site and click on **Chapter 6—Chapter Overviews** to preview chapter information.

Spanish Texas 1763–1819

Guide to Reading

Main Idea
Alliances among several countries changed the boundary and settlement of Texas.

Key Terms
alliance
filibuster

Reading Strategy
Identifying Cause and Effect Write an "effect" for each "cause."

Cause	Effect
Spain entered Revolutionary War	
Treaty of Paris	
Purchase of Louisiana Territory	

Read to Learn
• how the balance of power changed between Spain and France.
• why Spain closed missions.
• about the Louisiana Purchase.

Section Theme
Geography and History Changes in boundaries and land possession changed Texas history.

Preview of Events

1773	1779	1783		1819
Four missions close in East Texas	Town of Nacogdoches is founded	American Revolution ends in British defeat		Adams–Onís Treaty is signed

Catching mustangs

A Texas Story

Seventeen-year-old Peter Ellis Bean illegally entered Texas in 1800 to catch mustangs. Captured by Spanish soldiers, he became a prisoner, a Mexican soldier, and an Indian agent. He wrote of his capture: "In about six day's journey we came to the Trinity River . . . In the vast prairie there was no wood, or any other fuel than buffalo-dung, which lay dry in great quantities . . . and we were forced to eat the flesh of wild horses."
—*Memoir of Peter Ellis Bean,* 1816

Spain Acquires Louisiana

Great Britain's victory over France in the Seven Years' War (1756–1763) suddenly changed the balance of power in the Americas. Under the Treaty of Paris of 1763, Great Britain gained Canada and all French land east of the Mississippi River, except New Orleans. Spain received New Orleans and all French land west of the Mississippi. With Spain controlling Louisiana, the boundary between Spanish and foreign territory became the Mississippi River. France was no longer a colonial power in North America. Spanish officials questioned whether the East Texas missions and presidios were still needed.

Spain Closes East Texas Missions

The Spanish government sent the **Marqués de Rubí,** a Spanish officer, to investigate the need for missions. After a 7,000-mile (11,263 km) tour of New Spain, Rubí realized that there was a great difference between what Spain claimed and what it controlled. Spain had neither the wealth nor the power to defend its missions.

Rubí suggested that Spain abandon all its missions in Texas except those at San Antonio and Goliad (La Bahía). Then Spain could concentrate on forming alliances, or working agreements, with the Comanches. Both would fight the Apaches. He also recommended that Spanish settlers in East Texas should move closer to San Antonio for protection. Rubí also called for a line of 15 forts stretching across northern Mexico from near Laredo to the Gulf of California. His plan was adopted in 1772.

In 1773, the new Spanish governor of Texas, the **Barón de Ripperdá** (reep•pehr•DAH), closed the four missions in East Texas and ordered the 500 settlers in the area to move to San Antonio. The East Texans did so, but reluctantly. San Antonio was hotter and drier than East Texas and required irrigation for farming. The best land had already been taken by earlier settlers, leaving the newcomers only rocky soil to farm.

Nacogdoches Founded

The leader of the East Texans, **Gil Ybarbo** (HEEL ee•BAHR•boh), pleaded for permission for the families to return to their former homes. Governor de Ripperdá refused, but he did allow some of them to settle along the Trinity River. In 1774 these East Texans settled near present-day Madisonville. They named their town **Bucareli** (boo•kah•RAY•lee) after a Spanish lieutenant general and viceroy.

During the next four years, the colony did well. Then crop failure, a smallpox epidemic, and conflict with the Comanches forced the colonists to move. In early 1779, Ybarbo, without government approval, led the settlers back into the East Texas timberlands. They built the town of **Nacogdoches** near the abandoned Mission Guadalupe.

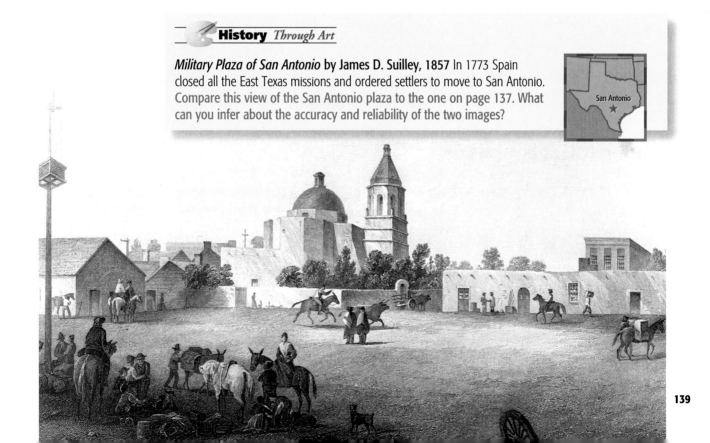

History *Through Art*

***Military Plaza of San Antonio* by James D. Suilley, 1857** In 1773 Spain closed all the East Texas missions and ordered settlers to move to San Antonio. Compare this view of the San Antonio plaza to the one on page 137. What can you infer about the accuracy and reliability of the two images?

San Antonio

Nacogdoches was deep in the Piney Woods. Some of its early settlers had once lived in French Louisiana. Because they were isolated, the French colonists in Texas developed a more independent way of life. Spain had little control over what the settlers did.

Reading Check **Explaining** Why did the Spanish decide to abandon most of their missions in Texas?

Settlers Face Many Dangers

Spain tried to colonize Texas throughout the late 1700s, but conflict with Apaches and Comanches interfered. Governor de Ripperdá was anxious to make the province safe for settlers but did not have the troops to do this. Spain was losing its hold on Texas, and by 1778, many people agreed with Governor **Domingo Cabello** when he said:

❝There is not an instant by day or night when reports do not arrive from all these ranches of barbarities and disorders falling on us. Totally unprotected as we are, they will result in the absolute destruction and loss of this province.❞

In the 1790s, Spain stopped funding the Texas missions. The Spanish government insisted that the churches support themselves. In the government's view, the missions had already succeeded in transforming the mission-based Native Americans into "good citizens."

Spain Helps the American Colonists

While the Spanish were wrestling with problems in Texas, Americans east of the Mississippi River were fighting for independence from Great Britain. During the American Revolution, both France and Spain supported the colonists. **Bernardo de Gálvez,** the governor of Spanish-held Louisiana, opened the port of New Orleans to American ships and supplied weapons, clothing, money, and medical supplies to American troops.

When Spain entered the war against Great Britain in 1779, Gálvez raised an army of soldiers from Spain, Mexico, and Cuba. He also recruited African and Native American volunteers. The Spanish efforts kept New Orleans and the lower Mississippi Valley out of British hands.

After the American Revolution, British and American leaders signed a peace treaty in 1783. Great Britain recognized the United States as an

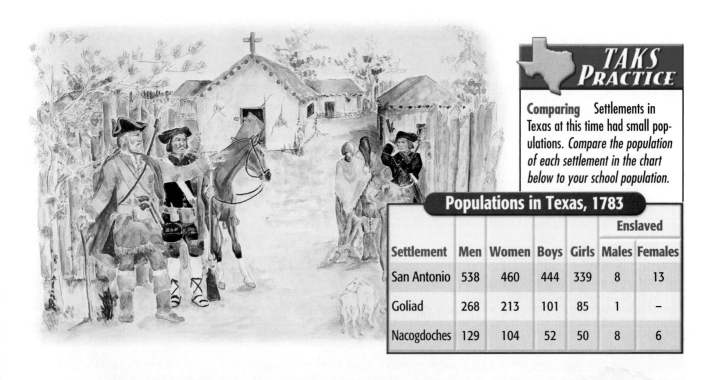

TAKS PRACTICE

Comparing Settlements in Texas at this time had small populations. *Compare the population of each settlement in the chart below to your school population.*

Populations in Texas, 1783

Settlement	Men	Women	Boys	Girls	Enslaved Males	Enslaved Females
San Antonio	538	460	444	339	8	13
Goliad	268	213	101	85	1	–
Nacogdoches	129	104	52	50	8	6

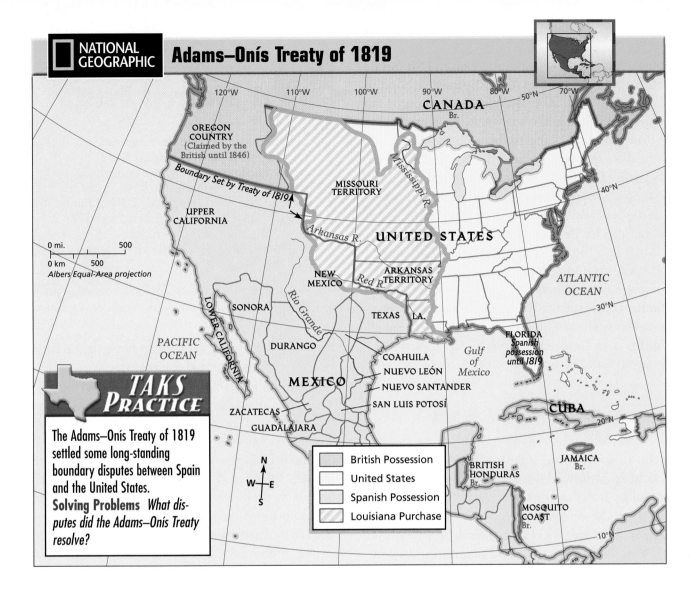

NATIONAL GEOGRAPHIC — Adams–Onís Treaty of 1819

OREGON COUNTRY (Claimed by the British until 1846)

Boundary Set by Treaty of 1819

CANADA Br.

MISSOURI TERRITORY

Mississippi R.

UPPER CALIFORNIA

Arkansas R.

UNITED STATES

NEW MEXICO

ARKANSAS TERRITORY

Red R.

SONORA

Rio Grande

TEXAS   LA.

ATLANTIC OCEAN

PACIFIC OCEAN

LOWER CALIFORNIA

DURANGO

MEXICO

COAHUILA

NUEVO LEÓN

NUEVO SANTANDER

SAN LUIS POTOSÍ

Gulf of Mexico

FLORIDA Spanish possession until 1819

CUBA

ZACATECAS

GUADALAJARA

BRITISH HONDURAS Br.

JAMAICA Br.

MOSQUITO COAST Br.

0 mi. 500
0 km 500
Albers Equal-Area projection

Legend
- British Possession
- United States
- Spanish Possession
- Louisiana Purchase

TAKS PRACTICE

The Adams–Onís Treaty of 1819 settled some long-standing boundary disputes between Spain and the United States.
Solving Problems What disputes did the Adams–Onís Treaty resolve?

---

independent nation. The new nation's boundaries were set at Canada in the North, the Mississippi River in the West, and Florida in the South. Spain's claim to Florida was reconfirmed, and both the United States and Great Britain were granted trading rights on the Mississippi.

The United States Buys Louisiana

In 1800, Spain was forced to give Louisiana back to France. Three years later, the United States purchased the Louisiana Territory from France for about $15 million. The territory doubled the size of the United States.

From the first settlements at Jamestown in Virginia, and Plymouth in Massachusetts, settlers in the English colonies had been moving westward. By the 1760s, they occupied all the area from the Atlantic Ocean to the Appalachian Mountains. During the Revolution they migrated

over the mountains into Tennessee and Kentucky. With the purchase of Louisiana, Anglos pushed across the Mississippi toward Spanish-held Texas.

✓ **Reading Check** **Identifying** Whose interest did France and Spain support during the American Revolution?

Disputes About Boundaries

There was a controversy between the United States and Spain about the boundary between Spanish Texas and Louisiana. The United States insisted that the American territory extend at least to the Sabine River and possibly include Texas. Spain claimed that the eastern boundary was a line from the Arroyo Hondo to the Calcasieu (KAL•kuh•shoo) River in Louisiana.

For several years, Spanish and American authorities argued about the boundary. Finally **James Wilkinson,** the commander of United

States forces in Louisiana, and **Colonel Simón de Herrera,** the commander of Spanish troops in East Texas, compromised. Neither Spain nor the United States would occupy the area between the Sabine River and the Arroyo Hondo–Calcasieu line. This territory became the **Neutral Ground.** Between 1806 and 1819, no nation governed the Neutral Ground. It soon became a haven where smugglers and fugitives from both Spanish and American territories could escape the law.

In 1819, the United States and Spain signed the **Adams–Onís Treaty,** settling the boundary dispute. Spain transferred Florida to the United States and agreed to the Sabine River as the eastern boundary of Texas. In return, the United States surrendered all claims to Texas. The Neutral Ground was now in U.S. territory.

Americans Migrate to Texas

Peter Bean was only one of many Americans who migrated into Spanish Texas. Some were farmers and traders. Other Americans who came to Texas were adventurers, or **filibusters.** Some of these plotted to seize control of Texas.

One filibuster was Philip Nolan, an adventurer who had come to the United States from Ireland. Nolan made his money as a mustanger—capturing and selling wild horses—often in Texas. The Spaniards, however, suspected that Nolan was a spy, working for General Wilkinson, the American military commander in Louisiana.

A Shared Past...

Texas's contribution to the American Revolutionary War was small but still significant. Texas did not have enough population to supply men to serve under Spanish governor Bernardo de Gálvez, but it provided meat to feed the forces. From 1779 to 1782, Texans from San Antonio and La Bahía supplied cattle for Gálvez's army.

Spanish officials warned Nolan not to come back to Texas, but he ignored the warning.

In the fall of 1800, Nolan and a party of 27, including an enslaved black man named Caesar, again entered Texas. They spent the winter in Central Texas trapping horses. In March 1801, Spanish soldiers surrounded their camp on the Brazos River and demanded their surrender. Nolan refused. Fighting broke out, and Nolan and another man were killed. Upon surrendering, Nolan's men were marched to a Mexican prison. Peter Ellis Bean is the only member of the Nolan party known to have survived and gained freedom.

✓ **Reading Check** **Analyzing** What were some reasons that Americans migrated to Texas?

SECTION 1 ASSESSMENT

Checking for Understanding

1. **Using Key Terms** Use the word alliance in a sentence.
2. **Reviewing Facts** What change in the period 1763–1819 had the greatest impact on Texas?

Reviewing Themes

3. **Geography and History** How did the Neutral Ground become a haven for smugglers and fugitives?

Organizing to Learn

4. **Sequencing** Create a time line for the following events.

1770 —————————— 1780

   a. Barón de Ripperdá closes four missions.
   b. Fifteen forts are built from Mexico to Gulf of California.
   c. Nacogdoches is founded.
   d. Bucareli is founded.

Critical Thinking

5. **Making Predictions** If France had not sold the Louisiana Territory to the United States in 1803, how might Texas be different today?

TAKS PRACTICE

Analyzing Outcomes The Treaty of Paris of 1763 ended the Seven Years' War. How did the treaty benefit Spain?

Determining Cause and Effect

Why Learn This Skill?

History is the analysis of events. Usually one event produces, or causes, another event to happen. Historians look for cause-and-effect relationships to explain why things happen.

Learning the Skill

The diagram below illustrates a simple cause-and-effect relationship from Chapter 6.

> **France loses Louisiana to Spain**
> (Cause)
>
> ▼
>
> **Spain closes East Texas missions**
> (Effect)

This diagram shows that when France lost Louisiana to Spain, Spain no longer needed the missions in East Texas to protect its eastern boundary, so the missions were closed.

Often the effect of one action may in turn cause other events to occur. This is called a **cause-and-effect chain.** This relationship is often illustrated in a flowchart like the one below.

> **France loses Louisiana to Spain**
> (Cause)
>
> ▼
>
> **Spain closes East Texas missions**
> (Effect)
>
> ▼
>
> **Settlers move to San Antonio**
> (Effect)

Because so many historical events are related, cause-and-effect chains can be very long and can include events that happen over a long period of time. One effect may be produced by various causes. One event can produce several different effects.

When you are reading history, look for words and phrases such as *because, as a result, for this reason, led to, produced, therefore, brought about, since,* and *caused* that indicate cause-and-effect relationships.

Practicing the Skill

Below is another link in our continuing cause-and-effect chain.

- Spain gives Louisiana back to France, which then sells it to the United States.

Place the following events in chronological order to complete the cause-and-effect flowchart.

- Adams–Onís Treaty gives the Neutral Ground to the U.S., which can then enforce laws there.
- Spain and the U.S. agree to create the Neutral Ground, which neither government rules.
- Spain and the U.S. dispute the boundary between Texas and Louisiana.

TAKS PRACTICE

Determining Cause and Effect Bernardo Gutiérrez de Lara was not the only person to seek Texas independence. James Long of Natchez, Mississippi, did the same in 1819. Create a cause-and-effect flowchart that shows Long's attempt to establish independence.

 GO TO

Glencoe's **Skillbuilder Interactive Workbook,** Level 1, provides instruction and practice in key social studies skills.

Unrest Grows in Texas

Guide to Reading

Main Idea

As the call for freedom from Spain was proclaimed in Mexico, many patriots also called for the freedom of Texas.

Key Terms

liberation
republic

Reading Strategy

Classifying Information Complete a chart like the one shown here.

People	Significant Action
Bernardo Gutiérrez and Augustus Magee	
Michel Aury and Jean Laffite	
James Long	

Read to Learn

• why Father Miguel Hidalgo y Costilla called for freedom from Spain.
• how the Republican Army of the North received its name.

Section Theme

Government and Democracy Father Hidalgo's call for the independence of Mexico from Spain resulted in many attempts to seize control of Texas.

Preview of Events

♦1810	♦1813	♦1819
Mexican independence movement begins	The end of the Republican army	James Long tries to free Texas

José María Morelos y Pavón

A
Texas Story

When rebellion broke out in Mexico, prisoners were offered freedom to fight against the Mexican rebels. Peter Ellis Bean took the offer, then switched sides to fight for the rebel army of José María Morelos y Pavón.

Bean remembered ". . . the king's order that every fifth man was to be hung for firing on the king's troops. This was to be decided by throwing dice . . . Whoever threw lowest, was to be executed . . . All my companions, except one, threw high; he threw four. I gained the prize of my life, for I threw five."

Hidalgo Calls for Independence

Many Mexicans became unhappy with Spanish rule. The best jobs in Mexico were reserved for men sent from Spain as administrators. Spain increased Mexican taxes to help pay for wars in Europe. This and other acts

greatly increased Mexican unhappiness with foreign rulers. On September 16, 1810, **Father Miguel Hidalgo y Costilla** issued a call for freedom from Spain. Hidalgo and his followers believed that the people of Mexico should govern themselves. In his call, or *grito,* for independence, Father Hidalgo appealed to the people:

> 66My children: a new dispensation [order of things] comes to us today. Will you receive it? Will you free yourselves? Will you recover the land stolen 300 years ago from your forefathers? . . . We must act at once . . . Will you not defend your religion and your rights as true patriots?99

For a time, Hidalgo's forces did well in battle. Their failure to capture Mexico City doomed Hidalgo's cause. He was captured in 1811 and executed.

One of Hidalgo's followers, Juan Bautista de las Casas, seized San Antonio and other Texas towns. Forces loyal to the Spanish government, led by Juan Zambrano, fought de las Casas. On March 2, 1811, they again established Spanish control over Texas.

✓Reading Check **Explaining** Why did Mexico seek independence from Spanish rule?

Gutiérrez–Magee Expedition

Hidalgo's death did not stop the movement for independence. Rebels sent one of Father Hidalgo's supporters, **Bernardo Gutiérrez de Lara** (goo•TYEH•rehs day LAH•rah), to the

United States for money and supplies. After Hidalgo was defeated, Gutiérrez de Lara decided to invade Texas to free it from Spanish rule. Gutiérrez de Lara began recruiting soldiers to help in the **liberation,** or freeing, of Texas. A young lieutenant, **Augustus Magee,** resigned from the American army and joined Gutiérrez de Lara. Together, they planned to establish a government in which voters would choose people to represent them. Because such a government is called a **republic,** their forces were called the **Republican Army of the North.**

In August 1812 the Gutiérrez–Magee army, including Tejanos, Native Americans, and Anglo Americans, crossed the Sabine River and easily captured Nacogdoches. Soon other recruits joined, and the army—now 800 strong—moved toward **Goliad** (La Bahía).

📌Picturing History

Father Miguel Hidalgo y Costilla has been called the "Father of Mexican Independence" because he was one of the first to call for Mexico to free itself from Spanish control. Knowing that failure was possible, was it worthwhile for Father Miguel to defend his cause?

People of Texas

Jane Long 1798-1880

Jane Long was one of the first Anglo women to settle in Texas. Long was married to adventurer James Long, who was captured near San Antonio and "accidentally" killed in Mexico City.

Unaware of her husband's death, Jane continued to wait for him at Point Bolivar even though food supplies were running out. The Karankawa were a threat, so Jane fired a cannon to convince them that the fort was still protected by soldiers. She left Texas upon learning of her husband's death.

Jane returned in 1832 and opened a hotel in Brazoria, which became a center for social and political activities. She never remarried. Kian Long, an enslaved woman, stayed with Long and her family for most of her life.

The Republican army captured Goliad in early November. A larger Spanish force laid siege to Goliad for four months. Magee died in February 1813. His place as commander of the troops was taken by another American, **Samuel Kemper.**

In March the Spanish troops, suffering heavy losses, retreated from Goliad toward San Antonio. Kemper's forces chased the retreating Spanish troops and defeated them in battle on March 29. Spanish officials surrendered San Antonio to the jubilant Republican forces. The leaders of the Republican army issued a declaration of independence for Texas.

Disagreements and Defeats

Soon, however, trouble swelled within the Republican army. The Americans and Mexicans quarreled over the nature of the new government for Texas. The Americans favored a government with elected officials, like that of the United States. The Mexicans preferred a government with appointed officials, much like New Spain's. Gutiérrez de Lara also wanted Texas to remain a part of Mexico. American leaders pushed for Texas either to become independent or become a part of the United States.

In August 1813 the troubled Republican army fought its last battle near the Medina River, about 15 miles (24 km) south of San Antonio. Spanish forces commanded by **General Joaquín de Arredondo** (hwah•KEEN day ah•ray•DOHN•doh) won a resounding victory. Most of the Republican army troops were killed on the battlefield. Others surrendered and then were executed. A few survivors made their way back to the United States.

Arredondo executed settlers in San Antonio and East Texas whom he suspected of helping Gutiérrez de Lara. Other settlers were forced to leave Texas. As a result, the towns of Goliad and Nacogdoches were virtually deserted.

✓ **Reading Check** **Contrasting** What type of government did the Americans want?

Revolutionaries and Pirates

Even though the movement to free Texas from Spanish rule had failed, revolutionaries continued their activities in Louisiana and along the Gulf Coast. A few of the survivors of the Gutiérrez–Magee expedition found safety on Galveston Island. The island was an ideal base for operations against the Spanish fleet sailing the Gulf of Mexico.

The revolutionaries secured the aid of the French pirate **Louis Michel Aury** (OH•ree), who sailed the Gulf waters. Mexicans who

TEXAS HISTORY Online

Student Web Activity Visit the texans.glencoe.com Web site and click on **Chapter 6—Student Web Activity** to learn more about the Gutiérrez–Magee expedition in Texas.

favored independence from Spain appointed Aury as commissioner of Galveston. For several months Aury captured Spanish vessels along the coast of Texas. Then in April 1817, he transported an expedition of rebel troops along the Mexican coast under the command of Francisco Mina.

Aury returned to Galveston Island only to find that another pirate, **Jean Laffite,** now controlled it. Aury sailed on to Florida where he joined British adventurers trying to seize that area from the Spanish.

Jean Laffite had aided the American army against the British during the War of 1812. For this service President James Madison pardoned Laffite for previous crimes, and the pirate moved his base to Galveston Island. Laffite said he was fighting for Mexican independence, but he was really more interested in capturing Spanish vessels for their valuable cargoes. When some of Laffite's pirates attacked American ships, the United States Navy stopped them. Laffite abandoned Galveston Island and sailed southward into the Caribbean. According to legend, Laffite buried a treasure of gold and silver on one of the islands along the Gulf Coast, but the treasure has never been found.

Spain Exiles French Colonists

While Laffite occupied Galveston Island, a group of French colonists tried to settle on the Trinity River near present-day Liberty. The leader, **Charles François Lallemand**

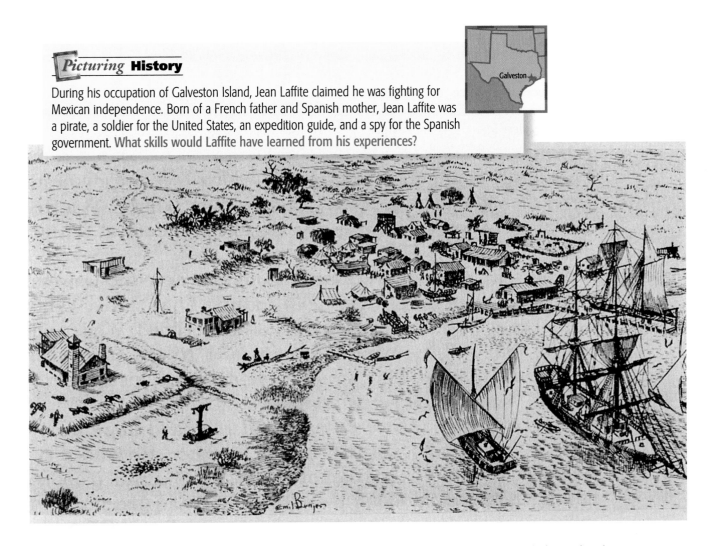

Picturing **History**

During his occupation of Galveston Island, Jean Laffite claimed he was fighting for Mexican independence. Born of a French father and Spanish mother, Jean Laffite was a pirate, a soldier for the United States, an expedition guide, and a spy for the Spanish government. **What skills would Laffite have learned from his experiences?**

(frahn• SWAH lahl•leh•MAHN), had been a general in the French army before coming to America. With 120 men and women, Lallemand built a fort and settlement. The Spanish governor in Texas sent troops and ordered the colonists to leave. In July 1818, the colony was abandoned.

James Long Invades Texas

James Long of Natchez, Mississippi, was another filibuster who tried to free Texas from Spain. The Adams–Onís Treaty of 1819 had angered Long. He objected to the United States surrendering its claim to Texas.

Long led a force into Texas in the summer of 1819. The 300 rebels easily captured the nearly deserted town of Nacogdoches. Long and his followers declared that Texas was a free and independent republic, and Long was elected president.

After setting up a government, Long journeyed to Galveston Island to ask Jean Laffite for help. Laffite refused, saying the revolutionaries had no chance without a large, disciplined army. While Long was in Galveston, Spanish troops attacked and defeated Long's forces in East Texas.

Long returned to New Orleans for more recruits. Again he invaded Texas, this time by sea.

A Shared Past...

In 1812 President James Madison asked the U.S. Congress for a declaration of war with Great Britain. Augustus Magee, leader of the Gutiérrez–Magee Expedition, had graduated from the U.S. Military Academy at West Point, New York. He resigned from the U.S. Army because he did not get the promotions he expected. Had he waited a little longer to resign, Texas history might have been different. The War of 1812 meant that the U.S. Army needed more officers, which increased the chances that Magee would have been promoted.

He landed at Point Bolivar on Galveston Bay. After several months, Long's troops moved along the coast to the San Jacinto River and inland. They captured Goliad but were surrounded by Spanish troops and forced to surrender. Long was taken to Mexico City, where he was killed by a guard.

Reading Check **Analyzing** What was Jean Laffite's primary purpose in capturing Spanish vessels?

SECTION 2 ASSESSMENT

Checking for Understanding

1. **Using Key Terms** Write a short paragraph explaining how liberation and republic are connected to the Republican Army's 1813 declaration of independence.

2. **Reviewing Facts** Why did James Long disagree with the Adams–Onís Treaty?

Reviewing Themes

3. **Government and Democracy** Give examples from this section of instances when the Americans cooperated with the Mexicans.

Organizing to Learn

4. **Identifying Outcomes** Many events contributed to changes for Texas. Make a chart like this one, and for each event, write the outcome.

Event	Outcome
Hidalgo calls for independence	
Americans and Mexicans quarrel over new government	
James Long invades Texas	

Critical Thinking

5. **Using Judgment** If Long had convinced Laffite to help fight for independence, how might Texas history be different?

TAKS PRACTICE

Making Inferences Charles François Lallemand brought 120 men and women and started a settlement near present-day Liberty. Shortly thereafter the Spanish governor sent troops who ordered the colonists to leave. Since there is no indication that they were breaking laws, why were they forced to leave?

Texas LITERATURE

Robert Carter

Robert Carter is a native Texan and descendant of a pioneer family. He is a retired lawyer and naval captain. His interest in the founding of the first missions in Texas led him to write the novel, *The Tarnished Halo.* During his research his "interest grew, but . . . so did my amazement that such a character and . . . story had received such casual treatment by historians." He has published many articles and another novel, *Sugar for the Roan.* Carter lives in Houston.

Reading to Discover

As you read this selection, imagine how you would feel if you were forced to move away from new friends against your choice. How would you tell them goodbye?

Reader's Dictionary

dialect: a regional variety of a language

venison: meat of a deer used as food

crucifix: an image or figure of Jesus on the cross

The Tarnished Halo
by ROBERT CARTER

In this excerpt, Father Hidalgo tries to explain his departure to his friend, Chief Totonac.

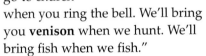

Hidalgo hurried across the clearing toward the small knot of [Indians]. As he neared them, the solemn, dignified chief continued to watch with an indifferent air, which Hidalgo knew, was only a mask to hide his true feelings. The friar . . . blurted out awkwardly in the mixture of Indian **dialect** and Spanish that both of them understood, "Totonac, the whiteskins are leaving."

"My eyes have told me so. Why you leave?"

"We have no food for the winter. We do not even have candles to burn on the altar."

"Has Totonac angered his whiteskin friends?"

"No, no! Totonac has been a faithful friend. So have these others here with you. But you are so few!" Despite his effort to suppress it, Hidalgo knew that his voice must carry a note of bitterness.

Totonac drew himself up, and seemed even taller as he replied. "You know, father, that all Indians are not the same. Bernardino is evil. His braves are evil. But we are your friends."

"I know that well, Totonac."

"If you want a bigger hogan,

we'll build it for you. We'll go to church when you ring the bell. We'll bring you **venison** when we hunt. We'll bring fish when we fish."

"God bless you, my son. I do not want to leave. Please believe me. But the other whiteskins will it. They will not let me stay here alone" . . . [He faced the old chief.] "Totonac, I'm sorry. I cannot sway my brethren. But I give you my word—I promise," he lifted the **crucifix** that hung from his neck and held it out, "I shall return. Some day, I'll return! I go to plead with my chiefs to send me back with more men and supplies. But my thoughts—my heart—my prayers—will be here with you, always."

ANALYZING LITERATURE

1. **Recall and Interpret** How did Totonac encourage Father Hidalgo and his people?
2. **Evaluate and Connect** Why did Father Hidalgo leave?

Interdisciplinary Activity

Persuasive Writing Write a letter to the viceroy pleading for more supplies.

Spanish Rule Ends in Texas

Peter Ellis Bean

A
Texas Story

During the 1820s and 1830s, Peter Ellis Bean worked for the Mexican government in East Texas. "I received a letter from General Morelos relating all his misfortunes, and requesting me, if I could pass to the United States, to do so as soon as possible; . . . and, if I could, to make some provision for a supply of arms."

After Texas independence, Bean returned to Mexico, where he died in 1846.
—*Memoir of Peter Ellis Bean,* 1816

Texas at the End of Spain's Rule

In September 1821 Mexico became independent from Spain. The province of Texas was part of this new country. Although Spain had claimed Texas for 300 years, there had been little growth. Only three settlements—San Antonio, Goliad, and Nacogdoches—stood in Texas's interior. San Antonio, the capital and the largest town, had more than 2,000 people. Goliad, about 60 miles (97 km) from the Gulf of Mexico, once had more than 1,200 people, but many had left following the Gutiérrez–Magee expedition. Something similar had occurred at Nacogdoches in East Texas. At one time more than 500 people lived there, but the town was almost abandoned after the Gutiérrez–Magee expedition.

A few settlements existed along Texas's several borders. Laredo, on the lower Rio Grande, grew to be a center of ranching, but the Spaniards did not consider Laredo part of the province of Texas. Some settlers lived at Ysleta in West Texas near El Paso, but they were governed by Spanish authorities in New Mexico. Anglo Americans from Arkansas had settled at Pecan Point and Jonesborough, along the Red River in northeastern Texas. The settlers there considered themselves part of the Arkansas Territory, which belonged to the United States. Vast stretches of northern and western Texas lay unoccupied or were controlled by nomadic Native American people who did not recognize Spanish authority.

Reading Check **Identifying** Name the three settlements located in Texas's interior by 1821.

Spanish Neglect

Spain had been unable to attract many Spanish settlers to Texas for several reasons. There was not gold or silver to lure fortune hunters and adventurers to Texas. From as early as the 1500s, Mexico City developed into a sophisticated city with universities, artists, physicians, and all the comforts of civilized societies. Ambitious men knew that to get ahead in law, politics, the church, or the military, they had to be in Mexico City instead of a remote province like Texas.

Farmers and cattle ranchers preferred more fertile areas of Mexico and the Pacific slopes of California. One common reason for migration was the pressure to find new land—this pressure did not exist in Mexico. The established regions of Mexico were not yet crowded and there was still open land in these more preferred settings. These areas had good soil and peaceful Native Americans willing to work the fields and tend the livestock. In Texas, most Native Americans remained unfriendly or showed little interest in Spanish culture and religion.

Spanish authorities had historically neglected the province of Texas. The region was not high

History *Through Art*

Vaqueros in a Horse Corral by James Walker, 1877
The Spanish vaqueros contributed many skills and tools to Texas, some of which are still in use today.
What influences can you identify in this image?

ONLY in TEXAS

Justin Boot Company The cowboy, or *vaquero*, is a legacy of Spanish Texas *(below right)*. H. J. Justin, newly arrived from Indiana, began a boot repair business in his home at Spanish Fort in 1879 *(top right)*. Soon he was making boots for cowboys using the Chisholm Trail. By 1959, the Justin Boot Company was sponsoring the National Rodeo Finals in Dallas *(below left)*. The Centennial Edition boots *(center)* celebrate the history of the great state of Texas.

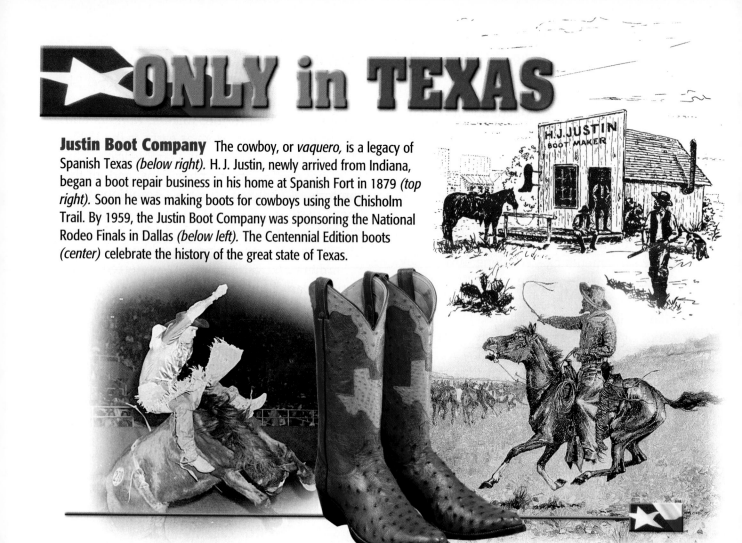

on their list of priorities. **Antonio Martínez** had become governor in 1817 after winning military honors in Europe. In this letter, as the last Spanish governor of Texas, he describes the poor conditions in San Antonio as late as 1817:

> ❝I have found this province in a very sad state, as much in the matter of subsistence for the troops and civilians, as in the matter of its defense . . . My troops had been living entirely on roots of the field for several days. The amount of money that the paymaster has sent has not been enough to pay the debts that my predecessor had contracted for the temporary maintenance of the troops. For this reason, I have not been able and I shall not be able to give any help whatever to either officers or troops . . . The storehouse is entirely unprepared for any emergency that may arise.❞

In another letter to the government officials in Mexico City, Martínez expressed the need for more soldiers.

> ❝There are no quarters where a dozen soldiers could be placed and, as soon as the powder house is finished, I think I will try to build a room near the main guard house . . .
>
> But to do all this I need help, which I do not have, particularly troops, for, having reinforced Bahía with fifty-five men, the troops that are left have not even the absolute necessities for making frequent raids against the infamous Lipans who constantly trouble us . . . Therefore, I must have the number of troops I asked of you.❞

Martínez went on to explain that without these additional troops, he could not defend Spain's interests in Mexico and Texas.

Spanish Legacy

Despite not populating the region, Spain left its mark on Texas. Spaniards mapped and explored this vast land. Many places in Texas have Spanish names. Most river and bay names remind modern Texans of the Spanish legacy of their state. Dozens of cities, such as Amarillo, El Paso, San Antonio, Llano, Del Rio, and Ganado, bear names derived from the Spanish language.

Spaniards laid out the first roads, often over old trails used by Native Americans. The best known of these roads was **El Camino Real,** or the King's Highway. Known later as the Old San Antonio Road, this route ran through Nacogdoches and San Antonio where it branched to San Juan Bautista and Lare do before meeting up in Saltillo. Another early road was the Atascocita Road, which was used for military purposes by 1760. Its eastward extension, called the Opelousas Trail, connected Texas to Louisiana. This trail went through the area where the cities of Beaumont, Liberty, and Houston are located. Today, Highway 90 follows a similar route.

Settlers brought horses, cattle, sheep, and pigs into Texas. Texans used the Spanish ranching system, with its practices, methods, and equipment, such as lariat and chaps. In addition, *vaqueros* made the first long cattle drives from South Texas to markets in Louisiana.

In Texas, settlers adapted Spanish customs to frontier conditions. Their adjustments formed the beginning of a distinct Tejano culture that has continued in the state to the present day.

The story of the Spanish settlers did not end when Mexico gained its independence. Many remained in Texas. Others from Mexico immigrated later. Nearly six million Texans today have Spanish names. Many more speak, read, and write Spanish.

Reading Check **Summarizing** How did Antonio Martínez describe San Antonio in 1817?

A Shared Past...

Even though Spain lost title to Texas, many important elements of Spanish law are found in the U.S. today. One is the community property law. That law requires that married couples share equally in property they acquire while married. Another Spanish law still in effect protects debtors. A person's tools cannot be taken from him when he cannot pay his debts. His home is also protected from creditors.

SECTION 3 ASSESSMENT

Checking for Understanding

1. **Using Key Terms** Write a short paragraph explaining how the *vaquero* has influenced Texas today.
2. **Reviewing Facts** Name five places in Texas, such as cities or rivers, that have Spanish names.

Reviewing Themes

3. **Culture and Traditions** Describe two cultures other than Spanish that have influenced Texas.

Organizing to Learn

4. **Identifying Spanish Influences** Draw a chart like the one below and give specific examples of Spanish influences on Texas culture.

	Spanish Influences
Place names	
Roads	
Animals	
Ranching	

Critical Thinking

5. **Drawing Inferences** In what region and what aspects of life in Texas would you expect the "Spanish influence to be greatest"?

TAKS PRACTICE

Using Judgment If Spain had been more successful in populating Texas with Spanish citizens, what might have been the outcome?

Chapter Summary

End of Spanish Rule

1763
• Spain acquires Louisiana after the Seven Years' War.

1773
★ East Texas missions are closed.

1776
★ U.S. Declaration of Independence written.

1779
• Spain enters the war against Great Britain.

1783
• The American Revolution ends.

1790s
• Spain secularizes the missions.

1800
• France acquires Louisiana.

1803
• The U.S. purchases Louisiana.

1810
★ Father Hidalgo calls for Mexican independence in Spain.

1812–1813
• The Republican army fights for Texan independence but is unsuccessful.

1819
• U.S. and Spain sign the Adams–Onís Treaty.
• James Long declares Texas a republic. It is short-lived.

1821
• Mexico gains independence from Spain.

Reviewing Key Terms

Using the thesaurus or a dictionary, find a synonym (word that means the same) for each of these vocabulary words.

1. alliance
2. filibuster
3. liberation
4. republic
5. *vaquero*
6. lariat

Reviewing Key Facts

7. How did Great Britain's victory over France in the Seven Years' War change the balance of power in the Americas?
8. What did Marqués de Rubí recommend after he completed his 7,000-mile tour of New Spain?
9. What happened to the Texas missions in the 1790s?
10. What was the significance of the Adams–Onís Treaty of 1819?
11. Give two reasons why Mexicans became unhappy with Spanish rule.
12. What was the important event that took place in September 1821? What happened to the province of Texas as a result?

Critical Thinking

13. **Identifying Cause and Effect** What was the effect of Marqués de Rubí's tour of New Spain on the missions (with the exception of San Antonio and Goliad)? Use the diagram below to help organize your thoughts.

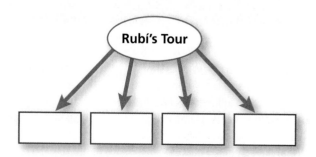

14. **Analyzing Information** Why did the Americans and Mexicans in the Republican army quarrel over the type of government for Texas?
15. **Evaluating** Why was Mexico's independence from Spain important for Texas?

Geography and History Activity

Review the section about the Neutral Ground. Pretend you are giving a TV news report about the Adams–Onís Treaty of 1819 and the Neutral Ground. Make sure to consider the following questions when giving your report.

16. What formed the western boundary of the Neutral Ground?

17. What formed the eastern boundary of the Neutral Ground?

18. After the Adams–Onís Treaty was signed, what became the eastern boundary of Texas? What did the United States surrender?

Building Technology Skills

19. **Using the Internet for Research** Using the Internet and a search engine such as Yahoo!, enter the name James Long in the search box. Write down how many "hits" you received. Now, enter the name "James Long" (with quotations at either end of the name). Compare the number of "hits" you received. When searching for a person, it is usually wise to put quotation marks around the name; otherwise, you will get all the people with James in their name, all the people with Long in their name, and finally James Long.

Portfolio/TAKS Writing Activity

20. **Writing a Paragraph** Write a paragraph explaining how the location and geography of Texas affected its development while under Spanish rule. Consider its distance from Mexico City, the type of land available for farmers and ranchers, and relations with Native Americans.

Cooperative Learning Activity

21. **Finding Spanish Influences** Form a research team of 4–5 students to find and record evidence of Spanish influence on your town. After each member has recorded their findings, the group should compare their results. Each group should then determine categories in which these items would logically fit. For example, a category of "architecture" might include house, fast food building, and school. After the list is completed and categorized, the teams should present their findings to the class.

Self-Check Quiz
Visit the texans.glencoe.com Web site and click on **Chapter 6—Self-Check Quizzes** to prepare for the chapter test.

Practicing Skills

22. **Determining Cause and Effect**

Read the statement below taken from the letter by the last Spanish governor of Texas, Antonio Martínez. Write the word or phrase that points out a cause-and-effect relationship. Then draw a diagram that illustrates that relationship.

> "Your Excellency can not count upon the [790 bushels] set aside for these troops, as a large part of it is being consumed by the muleteers since there is not enough money with which to pay the freight, and it is necessary to give them corn that they may have something to eat."

Use the primary source passage to answer the following question.

The Treaty of Córdoba, 1821

This kingdom of America shall be recognized as a sovereign and independent nation; and shall, in future, be called the Mexican Empire.

The government of the empire shall be monarchical, limited by a constitution.

Which of the following is the main idea of these paragraphs from the Treaty of Córdoba?

F Mexico became an independent monarchy from Spain.

G The Treaty of Córdoba awarded lands to Native Americans.

H The Mexican Empire claimed all of America as its territory and formed its own government.

J Texas won its freedom from Mexico.

Test-Taking Tip:

The *main idea* is the most important idea that a paragraph or passage makes. Make sure the answer choice you select explains the text from the treaty.

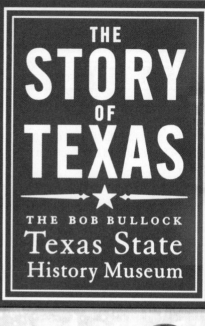

THE STORY OF TEXAS

THE BOB BULLOCK Texas State History Museum

Museum Tour **2**

Encounters on the Land
Cultures Collide

Texas culture is the sum of interactions among different groups. As native peoples moved across the land, they traded with neighbors, made treaties, and competed for resources. The Europeans—first the Spanish, later the French and English—would become new players in these constantly shifting encounters.

◀ **Exploration** Beginning in the early 1500s, Spanish explorers began to chart the region now known as Texas. They brought horses to use in their search for fortune. The horse became an important item of trade.

Visit The Bob Bullock Texas State History Museum in Austin to see artifacts and exhibits such as these about Texas history and heritage.

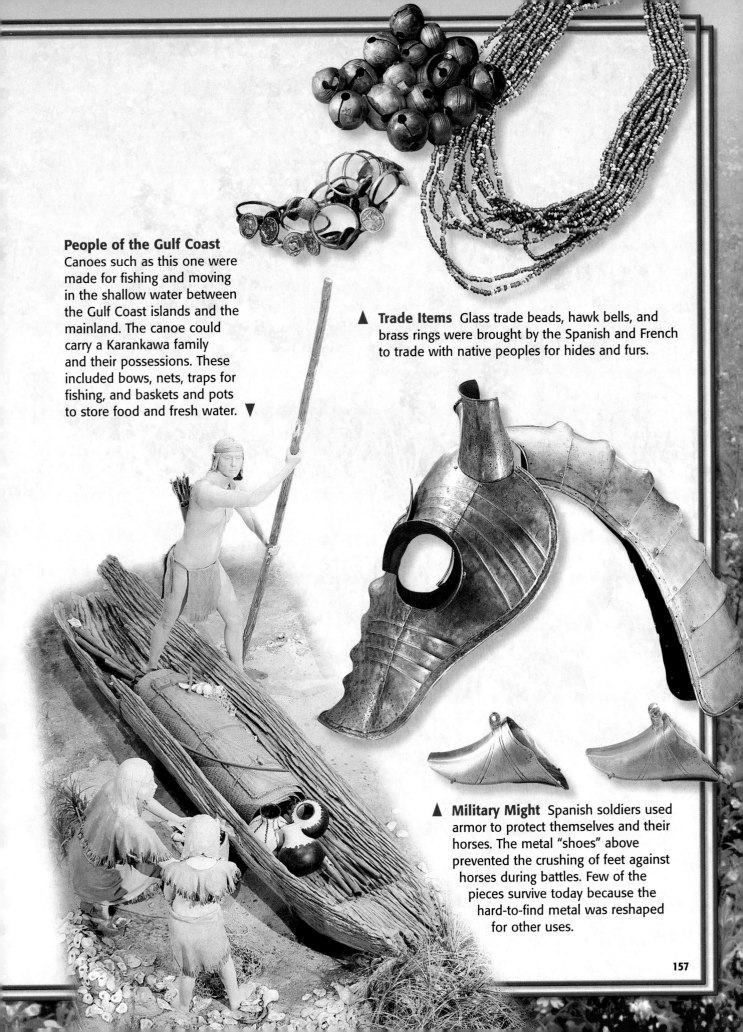

People of the Gulf Coast
Canoes such as this one were made for fishing and moving in the shallow water between the Gulf Coast islands and the mainland. The canoe could carry a Karankawa family and their possessions. These included bows, nets, traps for fishing, and baskets and pots to store food and fresh water. ▼

▲ **Trade Items** Glass trade beads, hawk bells, and brass rings were brought by the Spanish and French to trade with native peoples for hides and furs.

▲ **Military Might** Spanish soldiers used armor to protect themselves and their horses. The metal "shoes" above prevented the crushing of feet against horses during battles. Few of the pieces survive today because the hard-to-find metal was reshaped for other uses.

157

3 Mexican Texas

1821–1836

Why It Matters

As you study Unit 3, *you will learn that in the early to mid-1800s, Texas was pulled in a tug-of-war between Anglos—from the U.S. and Europe—and Mexico. Texas was torn between the conflicts of the past and the promises of the future.*

Primary Sources Library

See pages 688–689 for primary source readings to accompany Unit 3.

William Travis and David Crockett are foremost among the Texas heroes honored by this memorial at Alamo Park in San Antonio.

"*Public concerns are valued in honor, reputation, and good name.*"

—José Antonio Navarro (1795–1871)

TRAVIS   CROCKETT

NATURE'S SUPERMARKET

In an era before hardware and grocery stores, Native Americans and pioneers depended on a wide variety of local plants and animals to survive.

Early settlers found many uses for plants. They chopped down walnut, pecan, pine, and other trees to make houses and furniture. Native Americans bent willow branches and covered them with hides to create dome-like shelters. Early settlers wove flexible willow branches to create baskets, cradles, and other furniture. They made dyes from walnut hulls, agarita bark and roots, and also tiny cochineal insects that live on prickly pears. Wild plums, blackberries, prickly pears, pecans, and other fruits and nuts made tasty treats. Early settlers sometimes planted bois d'arc (BO•dark) trees as natural barriers to keep animals off their property.

Plants provided many medicines. Tea brewed from willow bark relieved headaches, fevers, and rheumatism. Walnut leaves were used to eliminate fungal infections, dogwood bark helped malaria victims, blackberry tea helped to treat diarrhea, pulp from prickly pear cactus soothed wounds and snake bites, and citronella oil from horse mint was used to keep fleas away.

People also relied heavily on native animals. They fished, and they hunted deer, black bear, javelina (also know as peccary), and other animals. They made clothing from the soft skin of the deer and warm blankets or robes from bearskins. Animal fat was used for cooking and making soap. Native Americans and pioneers made clever use of the plants and animals around them—and very little went to waste.

Pioneers used the green hull of the black walnut to make dye. They made furniture from the wood.

Cochineal insects live on the prickly pear cactus. To hide, and avoid drying out, they cover themselves with a white waxy substance they produce.

Settlers dried the cochineal and crushed them to make dye.

LEARNING from GEOGRAPHY

1. What are three ways people used the willow tree?

2. List the Texas plants and animals that you have seen in your neighborhood or around the state.

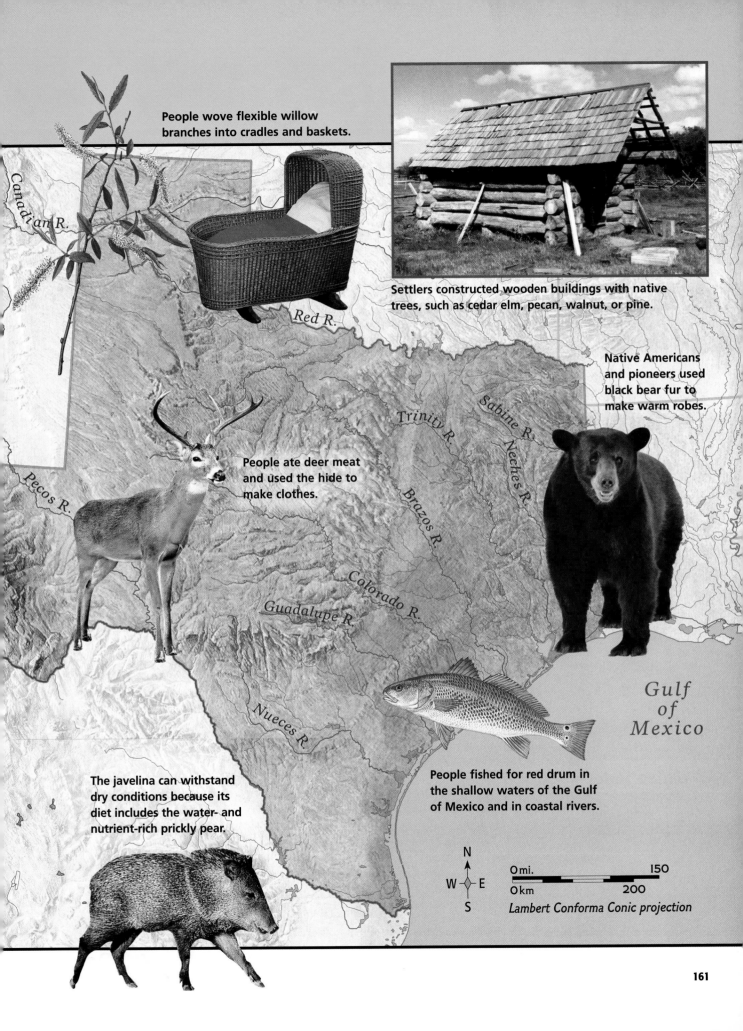

People wove flexible willow branches into cradles and baskets.

Settlers constructed wooden buildings with native trees, such as cedar elm, pecan, walnut, or pine.

Native Americans and pioneers used black bear fur to make warm robes.

People ate deer meat and used the hide to make clothes.

The javelina can withstand dry conditions because its diet includes the water- and nutrient-rich prickly pear.

People fished for red drum in the shallow waters of the Gulf of Mexico and in coastal rivers.

Canadian R.

Red R.

Pecos R.

Trinity R.

Sabine R.

Neches R.

Brazos R.

Colorado R.

Guadalupe R.

Nueces R.

Gulf of Mexico

N
W E
S

0 mi. 150
0 km 200

Lambert Conforma Conic projection

Age of Empresarios

Why It Matters

By inviting English-speaking settlers from the United States into Texas, Mexico changed Texas more in 15 years than Spain had changed it in hundreds of years.

The Impact Today

- *The land survey (measurement) system used during the time Mexico ruled Texas is in effect in much of the state today.*
- *Some of today's landowners can trace the titles of their properties back to Mexican land grants.*

1825
★ Green DeWitt authorized to bring 400 families to Texas

1821
★ Stephen F. Austin brought first colonists to Texas

1824
★ San Felipe de Austin became the unofficial capital of Austin's colony

 Texas

United States   1819   1821   1823   1825

World

1820
• Missouri Compromise passed

1822
• Liberia founded in West Africa

1823
• Monroe Doctrine issued

1825
• First public railroad opened in Britain

The View of Austin *by Ida W. Hadra captured the natural beauty of the future state's capital.*

FOLDABLES™ **TAKS**
Study Organizer **PRACTICE**

Summarizing Study Foldable
Make this foldable and use it as a journal to help you take notes about Mexican Texas.

Step 1 Stack four sheets of paper, one on top of the other. On the top sheet of paper, trace a large circle.

Step 2 With the papers still stacked, cut out all four circles at the same time.

Step 3 Staple the paper circles together at one point around the edge.

Staple here. → This makes a circular booklet.

Step 4 Label the front cover as shown and take notes on the pages that open to the right.

The Age of Empresarios

Reading and Writing As you read the chapter, write what you learn about Mexican Texas in your foldable.

1831
★ *Mary Austin Holley described everyday life in Texas*

1833
★ *Population of Texas was estimated at around 20,000*

1827   1829   1831   1833

1827
• *Freedom Journal, first African American newspaper, published*

1829
• *Mexico passed law ending slavery*

1830
• *Congress passed the Indian Removal Act*

TEXAS HISTORY Online

Chapter Overview
Visit the texans.glencoe.com Web site and click on **Chapter 7—Chapter Overviews** to preview chapter information.

Austin Establishes a Colony

Guide to Reading

Main Idea
Stephen F. Austin faced challenges and opportunities while establishing his colony in Texas.

Key Terms
depression
survey
empresario
militia

Reading Strategy
Classifying Create a chart similar to the one below and list the events that were advantages or disadvantages in the settlement of Stephen F. Austin's colony.

Advantages	Disadvantages

Read to Learn
- who brought the first Anglo settlers to Texas.
- why Anglo settlers wanted to come to Texas and the challenges they faced.

Section Theme
Groups and Institutions Anglo Americans came to Texas with the assistance of an empresario.

Preview of Events

♦1821	♦1824	♦1825
Stephen F. Austin starts a colony in Texas	San Felipe de Austin becomes unofficial capital of Austin's colony	DeWitt is authorized to bring 400 families to Texas

Sailing vessel

A Texas Story

Thomas Jefferson Pilgrim was an immigrant who heard about opportunities in Texas. In New Orleans, he bought a ticket to Texas and a new life. "We were now on the Gulf . . . Soon all on board were seasick except the crew and me, and many wished they had not started . . . [After landing at Matagorda Bay] the others went eastward to the Brazos, I on foot and alone, made my way north to San Felipe, about 60 miles distant."

—*Diary of Thomas J. Pilgrim*

Moses Austin Paves the Way

In 1821, **Moses Austin** paved the way for Anglo American colonization of Texas. He was the first Anglo American to secure permission from Spain to bring American settlers into Texas.

Born in Connecticut, Moses Austin moved to present-day Missouri in 1798, when that area of Louisiana still belonged to Spain. As a result, he was familiar with Spanish laws and regulations.

At first, Moses Austin prospered. By 1819, however, this changed dramatically. A **depression,** a time in which businesses suffer and people lose jobs, swept the United States that year, and Austin's business was ruined. He looked for a way to regain his fortune. Austin knew that the Spanish government was now anxious to populate Texas. He also thought that there were many Americans who were eager to obtain cheap land.

In the fall of 1820, Austin and an enslaved African American named Richmond set out on an 800-mile journey to Texas to meet with **Governor Antonio Martínez.** Austin hoped to get a contract from Spanish authorities, allowing him to bring 300 American families to Texas. At first, Austin was turned down.

As Austin left Governor Antonio Martínez's office, he happened to meet an old friend, a man known to the Spanish as the **Baron de Bastrop.** The baron, whose real name was Philip Hendrik Nering Bögel, was Dutch. He had lived in Spanish Missouri and had known Austin there.

Bastrop was now a man of some importance in San Antonio and was a personal friend of Governor Martínez.

Bastrop helped Austin convince the governor that his plan was not an excuse for the United States to grab land. After returning to Missouri, Austin received word that the Spanish had approved his request. Before he could carry out his plans, however, he became seriously ill with pneumonia. The long, difficult journey to San Antonio and his work in preparing for colonization had exhausted him. On June 10, 1821, Moses Austin died. His last request was that his son, Stephen, carry out the plans for settling Texas.

Stephen F. Austin Continues His Father's Work

At the time of his father's illness, Stephen was living in New Orleans, studying law and working for a newspaper. When he learned that the colonization contract had been approved, he left for San Antonio to help his father explore the country and set up the colony. He was near Natchitoches, Louisiana, when he learned his father had died.

People of Texas

Stephen F. Austin 1793-1836

Often referred to as "The Father of Texas," Stephen F. Austin founded the first Anglo American colony in the state.

After Mexico banned immigration of United States colonists into Texas, Austin went to Mexico City to consult with President Santa Anna. Santa Anna agreed to change the law, but refused Austin's other request for statehood. Austin left to return home, but was arrested en route and returned to Mexico City. He was imprisoned for one year for suspicion of encouraging revolt against the Mexican government.

After his release from prison, Austin supported independence. In 1836 the Texas War for Independence was won at San Jacinto. Austin served as secretary of state of the new Republic of Texas until his death.

Born in Virginia, **Stephen Fuller Austin** had grown up on the frontier. He attended Transylvania University in Kentucky, served in the Missouri territorial legislature, and had been a circuit judge in Arkansas. Although he was only 27 years old when his father died, Austin possessed the strength of character that allowed him to carry on through difficulties.

Stephen F. Austin was determined to carry out his father's colonization plan. He decided to go to San Antonio to see Governor Martínez. **Erasmo Seguín** (eh•RAHS•moh seh•GEEN), a leading citizen of San Antonio, traveled with him. When Austin arrived in August 1821, Governor Martínez warmly greeted him, then discussed Austin's plans for settlement.

✓ **Reading Check** **Identifying** Who was Stephen F. Austin?

Austin Sets Colony Boundaries

Austin spent most of September exploring Texas. He decided that the region between the Colorado and the Brazos Rivers was a good place for a colony. It had fertile soil, abundant water, natural resources, a mild climate, and no other settlements. As he toured the land, Austin wrote in his journal of September 19, 1821:

❝One of our group went hunting and killed the fattest deer I ever saw in my life. We started about nine o'clock, continued a north course along the large body of timber which lay to our right. Prairies of the richest kind of black sandy land, intersected by branches and creeks of excellent water—heavily timbered, beautifully rolling.❞

After returning to the United States, Austin wrote a full report of his journey to Governor Martínez. In it, he outlined the boundaries that he wanted for his colony. Although he expected to establish most of the settlements in the Colorado and Brazos Valleys, he made a request for additional land along the coast. In order to be successful, Austin knew he would need a port for landing the groups of settlers and needed supplies.

Picturing **History**

Stephen F. Austin had his land surveyed and also drew a map of the colony. Why did Austin need to survey his land?

Austin's Colony

Advertising for Colonists

Austin began advertising for settlers to come to his colony. Because of the similarities of climate, economy, and culture, the advertisements appeared mainly in newspapers in the southern states. One ad said that "no drunkard, no gambler, no profane swearer, no idler" would be allowed in the colony.

The land policy proposed by Austin was very generous. Every man would receive 640 acres (259 hectares) for himself, 320 acres (129 hectares) for his wife, 160 acres (65 hectares) for each child, and 80 acres (32 hectares) for each slave. People of special value to the community, such as merchants, doctors, mill operators, and ferry operators, would receive additional grants of land.

Austin himself took the responsibility for having the land surveyed, or measured, to determine grant sizes and boundaries. After a survey, settlers could obtain legal rights to the property. In return, the settlers would pay Austin 12.5 cents per acre. Austin could then use this money to cover the considerable expense of conducting the surveys, purchasing advertisements to attract new settlers, preparing titles and records, registering new grants, and traveling to conduct business with government officials. Austin was willing to extend credit to the new settlers, however, allowing individuals time to pay.

Settlers coming to Texas were required to become citizens of their new country and to take an oath of allegiance to the Spanish—and later Mexican—government. They also had to become Catholic and be of good moral character. Austin wanted settlers who were willing to work hard and who would be loyal to the government.

Good Land and Low Prices Attract Settlers

Austin had no trouble finding colonists. The prospect of obtaining good farmland at a low price attracted many people. When Austin returned home from his first trip to Texas, nearly 100 letters from families who wanted to settle in Texas were waiting for him. In November 1821, Austin purchased a ship, the *Lively*, to take people and supplies to the new colony. It made

A Shared Past...

New Orleans was the most important U.S. city for Austin's colonizing efforts. Supplies for the colony were purchased there and put on ships for Texas. Travelers to Texas very often passed through New Orleans. Some went by boat across the Gulf of Mexico. Others steamed up the Mississippi River to the Red River to Natchitoches, Louisiana. They traveled by road from there.

its first voyage from New Orleans to Texas. Austin found that several families had already made their way to the new colony.

The first settler to enter the land claimed by Austin was Andrew Robinson. He set up a ferry across the Brazos River. That site later became the town of **Washington-on-the-Brazos.** Robinson would later open a hotel and saloon in town.

Most of the early colonists owned small farms and a few cows or horses. Some early settlers, however, brought slaves to Texas. The wealthiest of the new colonists was Jared E. Groce, a planter and lumberman from Alabama. He brought 50 wagons and 90 slaves with him.

Austin himself helped the colonists to find the land they wanted, but everything did not go as planned. In February of 1822 the *Lively*, loaded with additional settlers and supplies, wrecked on the western shore of Galveston Island. The loss of the colonists and the badly needed seed and supplies was a grave disappointment to Austin. Still more trouble lay ahead.

In March 1822, Austin went to San Antonio to report to Governor Martínez on the progress of the colony. There he learned that Mexico had won its independence from Spain in September of the previous year. He also found out that the new government did not recognize Austin's right to colonize Texas. Governor Martínez suggested that Austin travel to Mexico City to seek the new government's approval of his colonization contract.

✓ **Reading Check** **Evaluating** What major setbacks did Austin encounter in 1822?

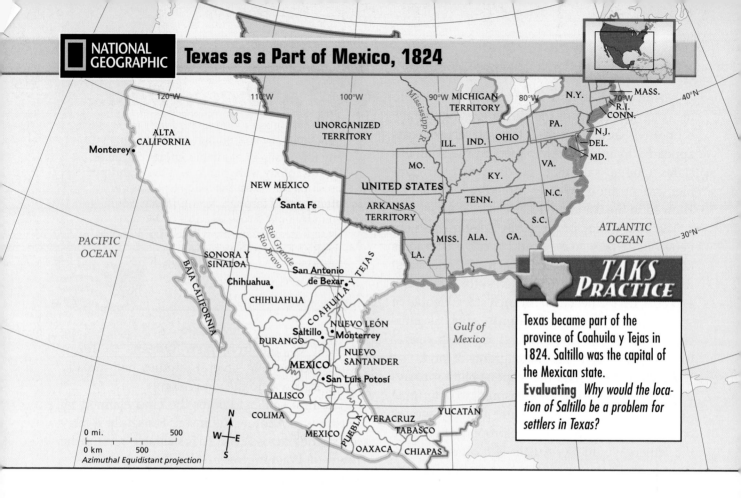

TAKS PRACTICE

Texas became part of the province of Coahuila y Tejas in 1824. Saltillo was the capital of the Mexican state.
Evaluating Why would the location of Saltillo be a problem for settlers in Texas?

Austin Impresses Mexican Leaders

Austin appointed an old friend, Josiah Bell, as land agent in his absence. Then he set out on the 1,000-mile journey to Mexico City. He did not know then that he would be gone from his colony for more than a year.

In Mexico City, Austin found much confusion. The new government had many problems and could give only limited attention to Texas. Other Americans in Mexico City were also seeking land contracts. This made the government reluctant to approve Austin's contract.

In 1823 the Mexican congress passed a general colonization law, and Austin was given a contract under its terms. Under the Mexican law of 1823, the amount of land each settler received was increased. Families who raised livestock and farmed could receive a total of 4,605 acres. Austin himself would earn about 100,000 acres of land for his services as empresario (a land agent whose job it was to bring in new settlers to an area). As under his original contract, Austin would be permitted to settle 300 families. Shortly after, a new government took power in Mexico and suspended the colonization law of 1823. As a result, only Austin could go ahead with his settlement. Others seeking land grants would have to wait until the government worked out a new law.

During his long stay in Mexico, Austin accomplished a great deal. He gained approval from Mexico's government. He learned much about Mexican customs and institutions. He learned Spanish and met many important Mexican leaders. Austin impressed these leaders with his honesty and sincerity. They became convinced that he wanted to be a loyal Mexican citizen and had no desire to cause trouble for the Mexican government.

Problems Develop in the Colony

Many problems faced Austin when he returned to the colony. Some of the colonists had left Texas because of a serious drought that had affected the area while Austin was away in Mexico. Many others were waiting for their land to be surveyed. Disagreements arose over ownership of certain lands. For the next several months, Austin and Baron de Bastrop, who had been appointed land commissioner, settled claims and recorded deeds to the land.

During Austin's trip to Mexico City, the Karankawas along the coast and the Tonkawas in Central Texas raided settlements and stole horses and cattle. Native Americans did not like the settlers intruding on their territory. Austin tried to negotiate with the Native Americans to establish peace. When they continued to raid, Austin raised a *militia*, a temporary army unit, to protect the colony. By the end of 1824, relations between the Native Americans and the settlers quieted.

Reading Check **Summarizing** List some of the problems faced by the early colony.

Men and Women of the Old Three Hundred

By the spring of 1825, Austin had almost completed the terms of his contract. He had issued titles to nearly 300 families. The settlers in his colony became known as the Old Three Hundred. Most of them had come from Louisiana, Alabama, Arkansas, Tennessee, and Missouri. Being among the very first people to settle in the new area, these early colonists had an opportunity to select the very best land available on which to build their new homes and farms. Many of the families chose plots along the Brazos, Colorado, and San Jacinto Rivers or beside smaller streams such as Oyster Creek and Buffalo Bayou.

Several members of the Old Three Hundred had been in Texas even before Austin arrived. Jane Long, who secured a land title on the lower Brazos, had been on her husband's expedition. Aylett C. Buckner, who built the first house on the Colorado River, had been a member of both the Gutiérrez–Magee expedition and the Long expedition. In 1826, Buckner was named by Austin as commander of the colony's militia.

Another member of the Old Three Hundred was R.M. Williamson. Although disabled, he

TEXAS HISTORY Online

Student Web Activity Visit the texans.glencoe.com Web site and click on **Chapter 7—Student Web Activity** to learn more about the settlers called the "Old Three Hundred" in Texas.

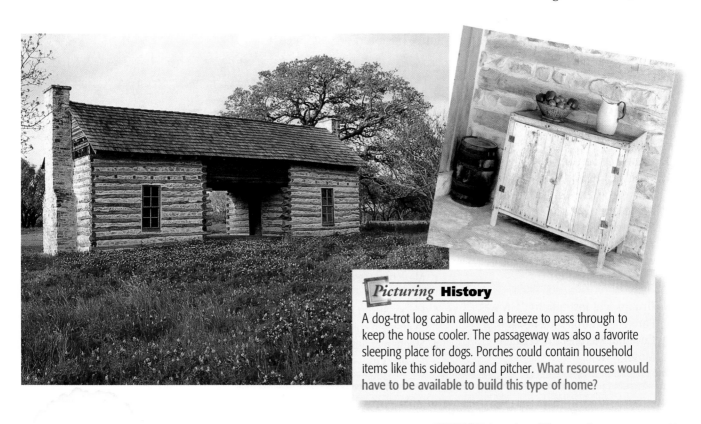

Picturing **History**

A dog-trot log cabin allowed a breeze to pass through to keep the house cooler. The passageway was also a favorite sleeping place for dogs. Porches could contain household items like this sideboard and pitcher. What resources would have to be available to build this type of home?

devised a wooden leg to support his weight. He was an outstanding lawyer who later became a leader in the Texas independence movement.

Mary Crownover Rabb, one of Austin's Old Three Hundred, recalled what her first home in Texas was like.

❝❝The house was made of logs. They made a chimney to it. The door shutter was made of thick slabs split out of thick pieces of timber, and [to fasten the door] we had a large pin or peg that was drove in hard and fast [at night], and then the Indians could not get in.❞❞

Rebekah Cumings came to Texas with three sons. Her daughter, Rebecca, was later engaged to William B. Travis. Soon after their arrival in Texas, Nancy Spencer's and Elizabeth Tumlinson's husbands were killed by Native Americans. Both women stayed to become members of the Old Three Hundred.

The Colony Gets a Capital

Austin decided that the west bank of the Brazos, where the Atascocita Road crosses the river, would be a good location for the new colony's capital. In July 1824, a town was officially organized. The name of the town, **San Felipe de Austin,** honored

TEXAS FACT

Surveyors used standard length measuring chains, a compass, a transit to measure angles, and a level with a telescope, called a peep sight. They spent weeks working up one side of a river dividing the land into tracts. They ran the lines from trees which they marked with letters and numbers and made notes like: "100 feet from the pin oak marked 'S' to a pecan on the edge of the prairie marked 'W'. "

both Austin and San Felipe, the patron saint of Texas **Governor Luciano García.** In 1827, San Felipe, with a population of about 200, became the capital. Austin lived one-half mile back from the river, on the west bank of a little creek. Noah Smithwick, an early settler and writer, described Austin's dog-trot home.

❝❝[It was] a double log cabin with a wide 'passage' through the center, a porch with a dirt floor on the front, with windows opening upon it, and a chimney at each end of the building.❞❞

✓**Reading Check** **Identifying** Who were the Old Three Hundred?

SECTION 1 ASSESSMENT

Checking for Understanding

1. **Using Key Terms** Define the key terms depression, survey, and empresario, and use each term in a sentence.
2. **Reviewing Facts** Why did Moses Austin and, later, Stephen F. Austin, want to bring colonists to Texas?

Reviewing Themes

3. **Groups and Institutions** Why was Baron de Bastrop's friendship with Governor Martínez important to Moses Austin?

Organizing to Learn

4. **Sequencing** Place the letters of the following events in correct order.

1820	1825

   a. San Felipe de Austin becomes capital of the colony.
   b. The *Lively* sinks.
   c. Mexico passes a general colonization law.
   d. Moses Austin receives approval to create a colony.
   e. Stephen F. Austin goes to Mexico City.

Critical Thinking

5. **Making Predictions** If Moses Austin had lived longer, do you think he would have been a successful empresario? What qualities did he possess that may have been important to a person with his goals?

TAKS PRACTICE

Analyzing What political and economic advantages would be available for members of the Old Three Hundred?

TAKS Skillbuilder

Making a Time Line

Why Learn This Skill?

A time line is a concise way to show the order of historical events within a certain time period. Most time lines are drawn horizontally. They represent different amounts of time, or time spans. Look at the two time lines shown below.

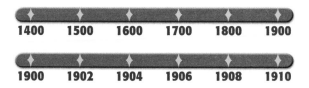

| 1400 | 1500 | 1600 | 1700 | 1800 | 1900 |

| 1900 | 1902 | 1904 | 1906 | 1908 | 1910 |

Both time lines are the same size. The first one, however, represents a time span of 500 years while the second one represents 10 years. On the first, the spaces between the dates represent 100 years, or a century. The spaces on the second line represent only two-year periods and add up to 10 years, or a decade.

Learning the Skill

The four steps to make a time line are:

- Identify the total time span it will represent.
- Break the total time into equal periods.
- Write the dates either horizontally or vertically.
- Fill in the events in the proper places on the time line.

Practicing the Skill

Key events from this chapter are listed in the next column. Find the dates on which these key events occurred and put them in correct chronological (date) sequence.

Ⓐ Stephen F. Austin nearly completes the terms of his first contract.

Ⓑ Mary Austin Holley writes about life in Texas.

Ⓒ Stephen F. Austin visits Mexico City.

Ⓓ Moses Austin visits Texas for the first time.

Ⓔ San Felipe de Austin becomes the capital of Austin's colony.

Ⓕ Nancy Tevis becomes a founder of the city of Beaumont.

Answer the questions that follow to make a time line of the previous events. After you answer the questions, draw a time line and label the events.

❶ What is the time span represented by the time line?

❷ How many years are in each equal time period?

TAKS PRACTICE

Time Line Find the key dates and events from this chapter that relate to the colonization of Texas. After you make the time line, answer the following questions:

1. In what decade do most of the events occur?

2. What types of settlements did you include on the time line?

3. Does your time line show that settlement followed the passage of colonization laws, or did the passage of colonization laws follow settlement?

GO TO Glencoe's **Skillbuilder Interactive Workbook,** Level 1, provides instruction and practice in key social studies skills.

The Colonies Grow

Guide to Reading

Main Idea

As Stephen F. Austin and other empresarios encouraged settlement in Texas, many groups made important contributions.

Key Terms

Federalist, Centralist, dowry, department

Reading Strategy

Classifying Information As you read this section, complete a web like the one shown here. List actions taken by the government and name the successful empresarios during the early colonization of Texas.

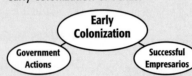

Early Colonization

Government Actions

Successful Empresarios

Read to Learn

• what actions the government took.
• about the successful empresarios.
• what groups came to Texas.
• what roles women played.

Section Theme

Groups and Institutions Empresarios brought more settlers into Texas as more favorable immigration laws were passed.

Preview of Events

♦1824	♦1825	♦1827	♦1831
Mexican Congress passes new colonization law	Legislature of Coahuila y Tejas passes Colonization Law of 1825	Austin is granted third contract	Austin receives final contract to settle 800 families

NOTICE.—The Subscriber respectfully informs his friends, and the Public, that he has lately removed his SCHOOL, for its better accommodation, to the Settlement of McNeil, and Westall, in Gulph Prairie. A commodious House, has been erected, very eligibly situated being surrounded by beautiful shades, and but ten miles distant from the Gulph shore, with no timber between to prevent a free circulation of the Sea Breeze, and no stagnant waters near, to render it deleterious to health Scholars wishing to attend from a distance, can be accommodate with board and washing, in a number of respectable families, from six to ten dollars per month. Terms of Tuition.—Reading and Writing, $2, per month; English Grammar, Geography, Rhetoric, History, Composition, Aritomatic, Natural Philosophy, $2.50 cents, per month; Moral Philosophy, Languages, and Mathematics, $4, per month. A strict attention to the interests of the School is faithfully promised, and public patronage humbly solicited by   THOMAS J. PILGRIM.
Jan. 15, 1830.—3t.

TO RENT, for the Term of one year, THE PLANTATION, belonging to the estate of the late Alexander Jackson, on Peach Creek. For terms apply to James Whitesides, Esq.

Advertisement for Austin Academy

A

Texas Story

Most immigrants to Austin's colony came for land grants. Thomas Pilgrim was different. He wanted to open a school. Encouraged by Stephen F. Austin, Pilgrim advertised for students for a new school he named Austin Academy. A bill found among Pilgrim's records shows that Austin paid for two students.

To one scholar (student) 9 months ending Dec. 13th at $2.50 per month $22.50

To one scholar 3 months ending Dec. 13th at $3 per month $ 9.00

The Constitution of 1824

On March 19, 1823, Mexican emperor **Agustín de Iturbide** was overthrown. The people who formed the new government were called Federalists because they believed in sharing power between the states and the national government. Their opponents, called **Centralists**, believed that power should be concentrated in the national, or central, government of Mexico City.

In 1824 the Federalists wrote a constitution for Mexico that divided the nation into 19 states and 4 territories. The former Spanish provinces of **Coahuila** (koh•ah•WEE•lah) and Texas were united as one Mexican state—Coahuila y Tejas. The constitution provided that Texas might become a single Mexican state, but only after its population grew large enough.

Texas was entitled to select only 1 of 12 members of the state legislature that met in **Saltillo** (sahl•TEE•yoh) in Coahuila. Baron de Bastrop was chosen as the first representative from Texas.

Mexico Passes Colonization Law

In 1824 the congress in Mexico City passed a new colonization law, in which the Mexican states would be responsible for working out their own detailed plans for settlement. The federal government set up certain restrictions for colonization. The most important were:

1) no one could receive more than 48,708 acres of land;
2) no colony could be established within 10 leagues (about 30 miles) of the coast nor within 20 leagues (about 60 miles) of an international boundary without permission of the Mexican government; and
3) only those who intended to live permanently in Texas could receive land contracts.

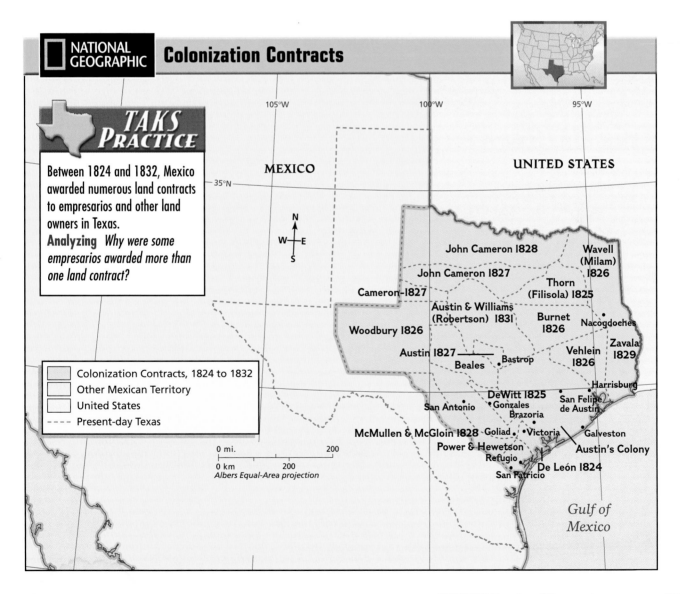

NATIONAL GEOGRAPHIC **Colonization Contracts**

TAKS PRACTICE

Between 1824 and 1832, Mexico awarded numerous land contracts to empresarios and other land owners in Texas.

Analyzing *Why were some empresarios awarded more than one land contract?*

MEXICO

UNITED STATES

35°N

105°W   100°W   95°W

John Cameron 1828

John Cameron 1827

Cameron–1827

Austin & Williams (Robertson) 1831

Woodbury 1826

Austin 1827

Beales

Wavell (Milam) 1826

Thorn (Filisola) 1825

Burnet 1826

Nacogdoches

Zavala 1829

Vehlein 1826

Bastrop

Harrisburg

DeWitt 1825

San Antonio   Gonzales

Brazoria

San Felipe de Austin

McMullen & McGloin 1828   Goliad   Victoria   Galveston

Power & Hewetson

Refugio

De León 1824

San Patricio

Austin's Colony

Gulf of Mexico

Colonization Contracts, 1824 to 1832
Other Mexican Territory
United States
- - - - Present-day Texas

0 mi.   200
0 km   200
Albers Equal-Area projection

At the time this act was passed, many people were in Mexico City seeking contracts to set up colonies in Texas. When they learned that contracts were to be granted by the individual states, many people left for Saltillo, the capital of the state of Coahuila y Tejas.

Reading Check **Summarizing** What were some new colonization restrictions of the Mexican government?

How State Colonization Laws Worked

In 1825 the legislature at Saltillo passed a new state law providing for colonization. Under this law, foreigners were invited to immigrate to

Texas. They could receive title to land as individuals or through an empresario.

After a payment of $30, a family could receive as much as 4,428 acres (1,792 hectares) of land (one league). Colonists would not have to pay general taxes for a set number of years. Single men usually would receive only 1,107 acres (448 hectares) of land (one-fourth of a league). They would be given another 3,321 acres (1,345 hectares) (three-fourths of a league) when they married. If a man married a Mexican woman, he would receive a bonus of an additional 1,107 acres (448 hectares).

Colonists had to show evidence of good moral character. They also had to be Roman Catholics. However, the Mexican authorities did not bother settlers who practiced other religions

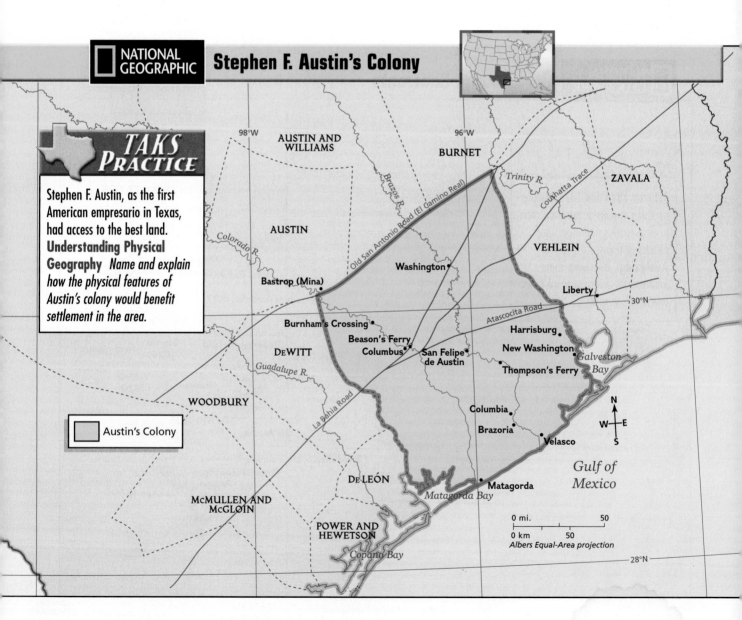

NATIONAL GEOGRAPHIC **Stephen F. Austin's Colony**

TAKS PRACTICE

Stephen F. Austin, as the first American empresario in Texas, had access to the best land. **Understanding Physical Geography** *Name and explain how the physical features of Austin's colony would benefit settlement in the area.*

AUSTIN AND WILLIAMS
BURNET
98°W
96°W
Trinity R.
Coushatta Trace
ZAVALA
Brazos R.
AUSTIN
Old San Antonio Road (El Camino Real)
Colorado R.
VEHLEIN
Washington
Liberty
Bastrop (Mina)
30°N
Burnham's Crossing
Atascocita Road
Harrisburg
Beason's Ferry
New Washington
Columbus
San Felipe de Austin
Galveston Bay
DeWITT
Thompson's Ferry
Guadalupe R.
WOODBURY
La Bahía Road
N
Columbia
W—E
Austin's Colony
Brazoria
S
Velasco
DE LEÓN
Gulf of Mexico
McMULLEN AND McGLOIN
Matagorda
Matagorda Bay
POWER AND HEWETSON
0 mi. 50
0 km 50
Albers Equal-Area projection
28°N
Copano Bay

because there was a shortage of Catholic priests to oversee church matters.

While the new laws made it possible for individual families to settle on their own, most settlers came into Texas as part of an empresario contract. There were two main reasons for this system. Most settlers could not speak Spanish and therefore had trouble getting title to their land without an empresario's help. In addition, most of the desirable lands were held by an empresario.

Each empresario would receive about 23,000 acres of land for every 100 colonists he brought to Texas. Empresario contracts ran for 6 years. If the empresario was not able to get at least 100 families settled on the land within those 6 years, the empresario's contract would be canceled by the Mexican government. In the years that followed, other federal and state colonization laws were passed, including the granting of 25 new empresario contracts.

The Most Successful Empresario

Stephen F. Austin continued to be the most successful empresario. He received four additional contracts under the new laws in 1825. The first of these provided for the settlement of an additional 500 families within the boundaries of his first colony.

Another contract was granted in 1827. This provided for the settlement of 100 families east of the Colorado River and north of the San Antonio Road. In his application for this contract, Austin pointed out that such a colony would provide protection for travelers on the way to San Antonio. The town of **Bastrop** became the headquarters for the "Little Colony," the name given to the land covered by the new contract.

Bastrop and the Little Colony

In 1828 Austin received special permission for the settlement of 300 families in a 10-league zone along the coast. Austin's last contract was obtained in 1831. It provided that Austin and his partner, Samuel M. Williams, could settle 800 families in a large area north and northwest of his

Stephen F. Austin issued land contracts to eager settlers who were determined to make a new life in a vast land. What problems did Austin encounter with his last colonization contract of 1831?

first colony. This contract, however, included land that had been granted to another group of settlers from Tennessee, led by **Sterling C. Robertson.** For many years, disagreements flared over the ownership of this land. In 1847 Texas courts awarded the grant to Robertson and the Nashville Company. More than 800 families settled there, establishing the towns of Salado, Viesca (later Milam), and Nashville.

✓ **Reading Check** **Comparing** How much land would single male colonists receive as compared to families?

Why Austin's Colonies Succeeded

Several reasons contributed to Stephen F. Austin's success as a colonizer. He demonstrated from the beginning his ability to deal successfully with Mexican authorities. His colonists had little difficulty getting title to their land and making improvements. Native Americans became less of a threat.

In addition, Austin's contracts included lands with some of the most fertile soil in Texas. Of the many motives for immigrating, the search for fresh land was the most common. Like the southern United States, Texas mainly produced cotton.

Cotton farmers rarely used wise soil conservation practices. They repeatedly planted cotton crops in the same fields. They did not protect against erosion. The fields became less productive. The decline in soil fertility forced them to search for new lands that had never been farmed. Texas offered what they needed.

In Texas the land was well watered, contained enough timber for homes and fuel, and was crossed by roads and rivers that provided a means of transportation.

Green DeWitt's Success

Next to Austin, the most successful empresario was **Green DeWitt** of Missouri. In 1825 he was authorized to bring 400 families into Texas. His colony was situated west of Austin's first colony and south of the San Antonio Road. The town of **Gonzales** was established as headquarters for the colony.

Native Americans began a series of raids, which slowed the early growth of DeWitt's colony. Nevertheless, by 1831, he had issued 166 titles to land.

Martín de León, Empresario

Another successful empresario was **Martín de León.** De León, a native of Mexico, was an expert horseman and rancher. In 1805 he had established a ranch on the Aransas River in Texas. Later he received permission to bring Mexican settlers into Texas. He settled about 200 families along the Guadalupe River near the coast. **Patricia de la Garza de León** helped her husband, Martín, found the town of Victoria in 1824, which they named for the first president of the Republic of Mexico. Their fortune had its beginnings in the dowry, or valuable goods, Patricia brought to the marriage. She also gave gold, land, and furnishings to establish the first church in Victoria. Later, she sided with the Texans during their war with Mexico and contributed large amounts of money to the war effort. Despite her support, she and her family, along with other Mexican Texan supporters of the war for independence, would become the victims of anti-Mexican sentiments and would be forced to flee.

Picturing History

Mexican empresario Martín de León brought Mexican settlers into Texas. In what other ways did he and his wife, Patricia de la Garza de León, contribute to the development of Texas?

Native American raids also troubled de León's colony, which was southeast of the DeWitt settlement. The colonists prospered, however, by farming and ranching. By the 1830s, thousands of cattle were grazing on the rich grasses of this area. Victoria became an important center for trade between Texas and Mexico.

Other Contracts

James Power and James Hewetson, both natives of Ireland, settled Irish immigrants along the Gulf Coast. Their central town, Refugio, was established on the site of an old Spanish mission by that name. John McMullen and James McGloin established a second colony of Irish immigrants at San Patricio.

Many other empresarios held contracts to bring settlers into Texas. Among these, Haden Edwards, David G. Burnet, Joseph Vehlein, Arthur Wavell, and Lorenzo de Zavala are the best known. Some empresarios, such as David

Burnet and Lorenzo de Zavala, later became active in the Texas independence movement. Their land holdings encouraged their participation in government and politics.

Many families came into Texas without help from empresarios. One such family was that of Noah and Nancy Tevis, who with seven children came to southeast Texas from Tennessee in 1824. Several years later they received a land grant from de Zavala. They settled along the Neches River and began farming. Noah died in 1835, but Nancy continued to live on the farm. In 1836 she became one of the founders of Beaumont, which was established on her land.

Various Nationalities Settle in Texas

The total number of Tejanos living in Texas during Mexican rule did not change much. There was, however, an overall increase in population during the colonial period. This was due to the generous land policies of the Mexican government. The policies attracted thousands of settlers from the United States and other parts of the world.

By and large these newcomers were farmers and people of some means, although in coming to Texas, some may have left behind them debts they could not pay. Since documents from that time show that only a small number of crimes were reported, it is thought that the immigrants were generally honest and law abiding.

Although travel was often dangerous in those days, people risked the journey to Texas for many reasons. They might be joining relatives or friends, or looking for a promising new place to raise a family. When the economy was bad, many families looked for new starts in distant lands. Some pioneers were simply motivated by a sense of adventure and plain curiosity. Most, of course, came for the cheap land in the hopes of creating productive farms and homesteads.

Many of the immigrants were women. Some came with husbands and families, but others bravely faced the journey alone. Most of the Anglo settlers came from the Southern states, especially Louisiana, Alabama, and Arkansas.

There were more than 3,000 people of Mexican ancestry, most of whom lived in the Department of Béxar. A **department** is a large administrative unit, similar to a territory. Several pioneer families of Spanish or Mexican ancestry still lived in East Texas. Most of the settlers in the Refugio and San Patricio colonies were of Irish descent.

The **Imperial Colonization Law** recognized slavery but outlawed slave trading. Other laws or acts, though, were broad enough that slavery was a fact of life in colonial Texas. Slavery did not exist, however, to the extent that it did in other Southern states, possibly because of the uncertainty of the laws.

More than 2,000 enslaved African Americans lived in Texas. Many of them worked on farms or plantations in the rich valleys along the Brazos, Colorado, and Trinity Rivers. Although the Mexican government opposed slavery, the Anglo American colonists argued that slave labor was necessary to clear the land; to cultivate cotton, corn, and sugarcane; and to make a profit.

Not all African Americans living in early Texas were slaves. Greenbury Logan, Samuel H. Hardin, Lewis B. Jones, William Goyens, and Hendrick Arnold were free African Americans, to name a few. It is estimated that by the time of the Texas Declaration of Independence, 150 free African Americans lived in Texas. Some fought for independence from Mexico.

Reading Check **Identifying Locations** In which areas did many of the slaves work?

Estimated Population in Texas, 1834

Department	Population	Main Towns
Nacogdoches	9,000	Anahuac, Bevilport, Liberty, Nacogdoches
Brazos	8,000	Bastrop, Brazoria, Columbia, Gonzales, Harrisburg, Matagorda, San Felipe de Austin
Béxar	4,000	Goliad, San Antonio, San Patricio, Victoria

TAKS PRACTICE

Summarizing Study the chart and write a sentence about the Texas population in 1834.

Women Play Important Roles

Colonists in Texas endured great hardships. Early settlers had to bring most of their household articles with them. **Mary Austin Holley,** a cousin of Stephen F. Austin, visited Texas in 1831 and wrote a series of letters in which she described everyday life in Austin's colony.

❝Housekeepers should bring with them all indispensable articles for household use . . . together with as much common clothing (other clothing is not wanted) for themselves and their children, as they, conveniently can . . . Where the population increases beyond the increase of supplies, articles of necessity, as well of luxury, are dear. If, on arrival, they find a surplus on hand, it can be readily disposed of to advantage; for trade, by barter, is much practiced, and you buy provisions with coffee, calico, tea-kettles, and saucepans, instead of cash.❞

Life was difficult for women in early Texas. They worked alongside the men, building houses, tending livestock, and defending their land. Despite their contributions, women held few rights under law. They could not vote, hold public office, or serve on a jury. Slave women suffered worse conditions. They labored long hours without pay, with no prospect of freedom. Their families often were split up because of slave sales.

Despite these obstacles, women made important contributions. Mary Austin Holley's books about Texas helped attract settlers from the United States. María Calvillo was both the daughter and the wife of ranchers. She eventually became the sole owner of her father's ranch. Drawing on her courage, organizational skills, and talents, she improved and expanded her holdings.

Jane McManus arrived in Texas in 1832, and she and her brother became empresarios. They succeeded in bringing a few German colonists to Texas in 1833. Tamar Morgan came to Texas as a slave in 1832. She purchased her freedom with the proceeds of her own labor and contributed to the Texas economy by becoming a successful landowner in Brazoria County, along with her husband, Emanuel J. Hardin.

Picturing History

Mary Austin Holley and other early settlers to Texas valued their household goods to such an extent that they could be used for barter. Why would household items be scarce in early Texas?

Lorenzo de Zavala 1788-1836

Of all the men who signed the Texas Declaration of Independence, few matched Lorenzo de Zavala in education, political experience, or diplomacy. He spoke Spanish, French, English, and Latin. When he was imprisoned for his political views he studied medical texts in jail.

When released, he was elected to public office. He served in the Mexican congress and senate in the new Republic of Mexico, and as minister of the treasury. President Santa Anna appointed him minister to France, but he resigned when Santa Anna assumed dictatorial powers.

He moved his family to Texas where he became a strong supporter of the independence movement. He was the ad interim vice president of Texas in 1836.

Education in the Colonies

A lack of funds prevented the Mexican government from ever providing public education for the children in the new colonies. As a result, the job of educating children was left to the colonists themselves.

Wealthy colonists hired private teachers to instruct their children. Others chose to send their children to schools in the United States. Most new settlers, however, joined together to establish private schools in the new communities.

In 1829, **Thomas J. Pilgrim** opened the first school in the new town of San Felipe de Austin. In the mid-1830s, **Frances Trask** opened one of the first schools for girls in Texas, in present-day Independence. By the 1830s almost every town in the new settlements had at least one teacher providing children with the basics in reading, writing, and arithmetic.

✓ **Reading Check** **Explaining** What were some rights not granted to women?

SECTION 2 ASSESSMENT

Checking for Understanding

1. **Using Key Terms** Write an imaginary newspaper headline for each of the following words: Federalist, Centralist, dowry, department.

2. **Reviewing Facts** What restrictions on colonization did the Mexican government set in 1824?

Reviewing Themes

3. **Groups and Institutions** Why was Stephen F. Austin a successful empresario?

Organizing to Learn

4. **Summarizing** Complete a web like the one shown below. List the different groups who came to Texas and the various roles of women.

Growth of Texas

Women's Roles

Groups

5. **Analyzing** According to Mexican land grants, when a man married he received 3,321 acres. If he married a Mexican woman, he received a bonus of an additional 1,107 acres of land. Why do you think the government offered this bonus?

TAKS PRACTICE

Contrasting How did the Mexican government feel about slavery in contrast to most Anglo American colonists in Texas?

Chapter Summary

Age of Empresarios

1820
- Moses Austin travels to Texas after his business is ruined.

1821
- Spain approves Moses Austin's request to bring American settlers to Texas.
- Moses Austin dies.
- Stephen F. Austin takes up his father's cause.
- ★ American settlers begin arriving in Texas.

1822
- ★ Stephen F. Austin travels to Mexico City.

1823
- The Mexican congress passes a general colonization law.
- ★ Stephen F. Austin is given a contract to settle 300 families.

1824
- Mexico adopts a constitution and becomes a republic.
- Texas and Coahuila become one state.
- San Felipe de Austin becomes the capital of Austin's colony.

1825
- Stephen F. Austin largely completes his contract to bring 300 settlers to Texas.
- A new state colonization law allows foreigners to settle in Texas.
- ★ Green DeWitt receives permission to settle 400 families in Texas.

1827
- Stephen F. Austin is granted a third contract.

Reviewing Key Terms

Write a paragraph in which you properly use the key terms listed below:

1. depression
2. survey
3. empresario
4. Federalist
5. Centralist
6. department
7. dowry

Reviewing Key Facts

8. Name the friend of Moses Austin who provided needed assistance in San Antonio.
9. How did Stephen F. Austin become involved in the colonization of Texas?
10. List three requirements for new settlers of Texas.
11. What two qualities about Texas were particularly attractive to prospective settlers?
12. Describe some of the problems that new settlers faced.
13. Besides Stephen F. Austin, who was the most successful empresario?

Critical Thinking

14. **Synthesizing Information** Describe the population of Texas in the early 1800s.
15. **Comparing and Contrasting** Compare the 1824 colonization law by Mexico to the 1825 colonization law of Coahuila y Tejas. Complete a chart like the one below to list the major parts of each law. Consider the similarities and differences. Compare the impact of each law.

Colonization Law of 1824	Colonization Law of 1825

16. **Identifying Assumptions** How do you think the Native Americans must have reacted when hundreds of settlers came to the lands they had first inhabited?
17. **Making Inferences** Why was it important for Austin to have settlers loyal to the Spanish and, later, to Mexico?
18. **Analyzing** Explain how obtaining land without the help of an empresario would be difficult for settlers.

Geography and History Activity

19. According to Mexico's Colonization Law of 1824, "There cannot be colonized any lands . . . within twenty leagues of the limits of any foreign nation, nor within ten leagues of the coasts." Why do you think the Mexican government included such a provision in the law?

 Building Technology Skills

20. Creating Graphs Using the population statistics in the table entitled "Estimated Population of Texas, 1834" on page 177, create a circle graph or a bar graph. Draw the graph by hand or use a computer spreadsheet program such as *Microsoft Excel* if you are familiar with such a program.

 Portfolio/TAKS Writing Activity

21. Writing a Letter When Stephen F. Austin arrived in Texas and surveyed the area which he wished to colonize, he wrote in his journal about the abundant resources and the beauty of the land. Write a persuasive letter that Stephen F. Austin might have written to a friend in Missouri urging the friend to immigrate to Texas.

Cooperative Learning Activity

22. Creating a Map Working in groups of four, draw a large map of Texas. Begin by adding the major rivers that were so important to the colonization process in the early 1800s. Include the San Antonio, Guadalupe, Colorado, Brazos, Nueces, and Aransas Rivers. Draw the boundaries of Stephen F. Austin's first settlement. Locate and label San Antonio, Goliad, Nacogdoches, San Felipe, Gonzales, Victoria, Refugio, San Patricio, and Galveston Island. (Refer to other maps to help find some of these rivers and towns.)

Practicing Skills

Making a Time Line *Use information that you have studied in prior chapters to determine when the following events occurred. On a separate sheet of paper, place the events in their correct chronological order. Then draw a time line beginning with the year 1760 and ending with 1830.*

23. Mexico wins independence from Spain.

24. The United States acquires Louisiana.

25. Spain surrenders San Antonio to the Republican Army.

26. Gálvez aids colonies in the American Revolution.

27. Spain acquires Louisiana from France.

 TEXAS HISTORY *Online*

Self-Check Quiz
Visit the texans.glencoe.com Web site and click on **Chapter 7—Self-Check Quizzes** to prepare for the chapter test.

Economics and History Activity

28. Environment Although cotton was a major crop in the early 1800s, cotton farmers did not practice soil conservation. Describe the social, economic, and environmental effects of not using conservation methods.

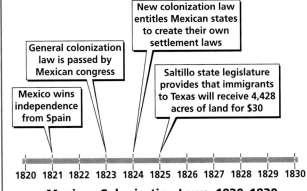

TAKS PRACTICE

Use the time line and your knowledge of Texas history to answer the following question.

Mexican Colonization Laws, 1820–1830

During the 1820s, immigration to Texas

A was an orderly and smooth process.

B decreased because of conflicts with Native Americans.

C was encouraged by the Saltillo state legislature after 1825.

D grew slowly because many immigrants could not meet the residency conditions.

Test-Taking Tip:

If you do not recognize a word or term in a test question, read the test question carefully for context clues. The word *conflict* is a negative condition, whereas the word *encouraged* is a positive condition. These clues might help you guess.

Economics & History

Learning to Succeed

While talking with your classmates, you have probably discovered that their parents work at many different sorts of jobs. They may work in a factory or for a construction firm, on a ranch or farm, or for the city's public works departments. Or, they may work with computers or in stores or banks. Today, the majority of people in the state work in a service industry. Instead of producing goods, these businesses provide services to people, such as repairing computers or shipping important packages.

Many factors determine what kind of career or job a person holds. Education is important but so are personal skills, attributes, and traits. In the past, when formal education was not available to many people, personal characteristics were even more important.

One of the most successful Texans in the 1820s and 1830s was Stephen F. Austin. As an empresario, he earned his livelihood by bringing Anglo American settlers into Texas and granting them land.

Austin Studies Hard

Austin attended college at Transylvania University in Kentucky (though he did not receive his degree). He also studied law. But for him to be successful in Mexican Texas (1821–1836), he had to possess more than just schooling. He had to be good at promoting his business interests. For this he needed to be an effective communicator. That meant he needed to learn Spanish, the language spoken in Texas and Mexico at that time.

Austin arrived in Texas in 1821 without

Stephen F. Austin

knowing Spanish. Soon after, he began studying and practicing the language daily, stopping only to exercise and work. By 1822, he was speaking and writing Spanish fluently.

Representing Different Interests

Between 1822 and 1836, Austin's ability to speak English and Spanish proved valuable to him over and over. It allowed him to develop high-level contacts in Mexico with persons of influence and government officials who could ensure the success of his Texas enterprise. Between 1821 and 1831, he entered into five contracts with the Mexican government to settle families in Texas. Mexico paid Austin very well for fulfilling those contracts. In exchange for bringing a stated number of families to Texas, he stood to acquire thousands of acres of land, which he could then sell. In addition, Austin charged settlers a small price for surveying their lands and registering their titles to the property. When families could not afford to pay with money, Austin accepted slaves or farm animals, or he gave them time to pay on credit.

Protesting Laws

Austin's Spanish-speaking abilities benefited him in still other ways. His understanding of Mexican laws written in Spanish inspired confidence in his abilities to govern and helped him attract many new people to the area. Because of his fluency, he was able to protest those laws that slowed or prevented the colonization of Texas. In 1830, he protested the Law of April 6, which ended immigration from the U.S., and later Austin helped convince Santa Anna to repeal it. This again opened Texas up to settlement by prosperous immigrants from the United States and Europe.

Austin also lobbied against efforts in Mexico to abolish slavery, for he believed enslaved African Americans were needed to work the new land. In 1835, he wrote and sent a pamphlet to the Mexican government explaining why many Texans wanted to be a separate state and not part of Coahuila. When disturbances in Texas increased, Austin continued to abide by his agreement with the Mexican government for as long as possible.

Successful Businessman

Because of his education—both formal and informal—and his willingness to learn about other people and other cultures, Stephen F. Austin became a skillful and successful businessman. When he passed away in 1836, the value of his land holdings was estimated at over $500,000. Additionally, he had been able to pay off debts he owed before his arrival in Texas. Hard work, personal integrity, and his knowledge of the Spanish language and customs had been instrumental to his economic success.

Bilingual sign at Brownsville car dealership

TAKS PRACTICE

1. **Making Generalizations** What qualities do you think are needed to be successful in business?
2. **Drawing Conclusions** What are some benefits of acquiring new skills?
3. **Writing About Economics** Write a paragraph that describes a time when knowledge of another language would have helped you. Use standard grammar, spelling, sentence structure, and punctuation. Include information and examples from the feature as details to support your argument.

CHAPTER 8

Growing Tensions

Why It Matters

Tensions increased between Texans and the Mexican government in the 1820s and 1830s. Some Texans believed that separation from Mexico—even if it meant war—was the only solution to their grievances. Other Texans believed it was possible to remain a part of Mexico. Stephen F. Austin's imprisonment in Mexico City pushed many Texans into believing that war was necessary.

The Impact Today

Almost all conflicts have two results that last longer than the wars themselves. First, hatred and suspicion often remain on both sides. Second, acts of courage are remembered long after the war. The Texas Revolution had both results.

1823
★ Santa Anna rebels against Mexico's Emperor Augustín de Iturbide

1826
★ The Fredonian Revolt

Texas

United States   1823   1825   1826   1828

World

1825
• World's first public railroad opened in Great Britain

1828
• Noah Webster published an American dictionary

The many buildings in this view of Mexico City in the 1830s indicate the city's wealth and importance.

FOLDABLES™
Study Organizer

TAKS
PRACTICE

Cause-Effect Study Foldable
Make this foldable to organize information and describe the events that led to growing tensions in Texas during the 1820s and the 1830s.

Step 1 Fold one sheet of paper in half from side to side.

Fold the sheet vertically.

Step 2 Fold again, 1 inch from the top. (Tip: The middle knuckle of your index finger is about 1 inch long.)

Step 3 Open and label as shown.

ACTIONS by Texas or Mexico   REACTIONS

Draw lines along the fold lines.

Reading and Writing As you read this chapter, record information that you learn about the actions and reactions of Texans and the Mexican government. Underline the actions and events you have listed that led to war.

1830
★ The Law of April 6 stopped immigration from U.S.

1833
★ Convention of 1833 prepared constitution

1830   *1831*   *1833*

1830
• Baltimore & Ohio Railroad opened first stretch of track

1831
• Cholera epidemic spread to central Europe
• London Bridge opened

1833
• American Anti-Slavery Society formed

TEXAS HISTORY
Online

Chapter Overview
Visit the texans.glencoe.com Web site and click on **Chapter 8—Chapter Overviews** to preview chapter information.

The Difficulties Begin

Guide to Reading

Main Idea
While the Anglo American colonists were concerned about Mexican rule, the Mexican government was concerned about the growing American influence in Texas.

Key Terms
decree, exempt, customs duty

Reading Strategy
Analyzing Results As you read this section, make a web like the one below, identifying ways the Law of April 6, 1830, changed colonists' lives.

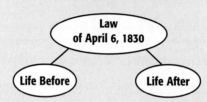

Law of April 6, 1830

Life Before   Life After

Read to Learn
• about the Republic of Fredonia.
• what Mier y Terán reported.
• why the Law of April 6 was alarming to the settlers.

Section Theme
Groups and Institutions The Mexican government issued the Law of April 6 to offset the growing influence of Anglo American settlers.

Preview of Events

♦1826 — The Fredonian Revolt collapses

♦1829 — Mexican government issues decree abolishing slavery

♦1830 — Mexican government issues Law of April 6, 1830

General Manuel de Mier y Terán

A
Texas Story

The Mexican government, concerned about the growing American influence in East Texas, sent General Manuel de Mier y Terán (myehr ee teh•RAHN) on an inspection trip. "It is incredible," he wrote in 1828, "that the export of deerskins in less than a year has risen to 40 thousand in number. The export of bearskins amounts to 1,500. Otter and beaver have almost been [wiped out] because of the relentless pursuit of American trappers."

Differences Create Tension

The opening of Texas to settlement in the early 1820s resulted in major changes. Trade expanded and the population grew. Farms and plantations produced corn, cotton, and sugarcane. At the same time,

Some of the immigrants looking for new homes in Texas had been expelled from the United States. During the 1820s and 1830s, the United States removed many Native Americans from their homelands. South-eastern Native American people, such as the Cherokees, settled in Texas. Native Americans from as far away as the Great Lakes came to Mexican Texas, looking for a new home.

differences arose between Mexican officials and the Anglo American settlers.

During most of the 1820s, when the **Federalists** held power in Mexico, the colonists were left alone. Anglo American settlers received land titles, cleared fields, and built their homes. They began to establish their own schools and newspapers. The colonists even brought in slaves, an action the Mexican government opposed.

When the **Centralist Party** came to power in 1829, it put an end to these independent acts. It issued regulations to bring the states and provinces of Mexico more under the authority of the national government. Most of the Anglo American colonists considered these regulations to be unnecessary and unfair. A series of clashes eventually resulted in a revolution.

✓Reading Check **Analyzing** When the Centralist Party came to power, what changed for the colonists?

Trouble Begins in East Texas

The first clash between colonists and Mexican authorities came in 1826. The state government had awarded a vast tract of land in East Texas to an empresario named **Haden Edwards.** Edwards was permitted to settle 800 families in the **Nacogdoches** area.

Edwards arrived in Nacogdoches in October 1825. He discovered that there were already many people living on his lands. His contract required him to recognize the rights of those settlers who already held legal titles. Many of the early settlers, however, did not have clear titles to their property.

Edwards announced that all settlers must show their titles to him. All others would have to move or acquire a title from him. This angered many of the settlers, who included families from Louisiana. Also living in the area were Cherokees and Mexicans whose ancestors had lived there for decades. Political Chief **José Antonio Saucedo** (sow•SAY•doh) sympathized with the settlers and told Edwards that he could not charge them for new land titles.

The Republic of Fredonia

Benjamin Edwards, Haden's brother, believed that his only hope for solving the problem was to declare the colony independent from Mexico. He made an alliance with **Richard Fields,** a Cherokee chief, and prepared for action.

Picturing **History**

Haden Edwards and his wife show determination in their faces. Paintings from this period often showed people with their hands in their coats because it was easier for the painter not to paint the hands. Why would Haden Edwards need to be a determined person?

Causes and Effects of Mexican/Anglo Conflict

Causes

- The State Colonization Law of 1825 encourages immigration.
- New Anglo American settlers far outnumber Mexican residents.
- Mier y Terán's report warns of possible loss of Texas.

Effects

- In the Law of April 6, 1830, Mexico forbids immigration from the U.S.
- New limits on trade with U.S. spark Anglo protests.
- Additional Mexican troops arrive in San Antonio.

Graphic Organizer → Skills

The Law of April 6, 1830, was the turning point in relations between the Mexican government and colonists.

Analyzing Information Why did this law ultimately have a negative effect?

On December 16, 1826, Edwards led a small group of 15 to 30 armed settlers in taking the Old Stone Fort in Nacogdoches. They raised a red and white flag bearing the words "Independence, Liberty, and Justice" and proclaimed the creation of the **Republic of Fredonia.**

Republic of Fredonia

The Edwards brothers appealed for help from Austin's colony and from the United States, but they received no assistance. Austin even offered to help the Mexican government put down the revolt. When Mexican troops from San Antonio approached Nacogdoches in late December, the **Fredonian Revolt** collapsed. Some of the Fredonians were captured, but most of them fled across the Sabine River into the United States.

Mier y Terán Investigates

Although the Fredonian Revolt was a minor event and most colonists had refused to support Edwards, Mexican officials became worried. They thought the Fredonian Revolt was part of an American scheme to acquire Texas. Two hundred Mexican soldiers, commanded by **Colonel José de las Piedras** (PYAY•drahs), were sent to Nacogdoches to prevent new uprisings.

Mexican fears about Texas continued to grow. The U.S. ambassador to Mexico, **Anthony Butler,** proposed that Mexico sell Texas to the United States. This only reinforced Mexican suspicions that the United States wanted Texas. The Mexican government sent an inspection party to investigate, led by the soldier and scientist **General Manuel de Mier y Terán.**

Mier y Terán observed that the Anglo American influence was strong in East Texas since Anglo American settlers outnumbered the Mexican settlers by at least five to one.

In his report to the Mexican president, Mier y Terán expressed concern about the growing American influence in Texas. He made recommendations to the government concerning the future of the area. Mier y Terán made it clear that if the Mexican government did not act at once, Texas would be "lost forever."

Meanwhile, the Anglo American colonists were also becoming concerned. Those colonists who held slaves were worried about government efforts to abolish slavery. In 1829 the president of Mexico issued a **decree,** or order, abolishing slavery. He was persuaded to **exempt,** or excuse, Texas from the decree, but his actions caused fear among many of the Anglo American slaveholders. They believed that it was only a matter of time before the decree would apply to them, too.

TEXAS HISTORY *Online*

Student Web Activity Visit the texans.glencoe.com Web site and click on **Chapter 8—Student Web Activity** to learn more about the Fredonian Revolt in Texas.

✓ **Reading Check** **Analyzing** Why was Anglo American influence so strong in East Texas at this time?

The Law of April 6, 1830

On April 6, 1830, the Centralist government in Mexico issued a law based on many of Mier y Terán's recommendations. It stopped immigration from the United States. It also suspended most empresario contracts that had not been completed. Instead, the government encouraged the immigration of Mexican and European families to Texas with generous land grants and financial assistance. The law read in part:

The introduction of foreigners across the northern frontier is prohibited under any pretext whatsoever, unless the said foreigners are provided with a passport issued by the agents of this Republic . . . [I]t is prohibited that emigrants from nations bordering on this Republic shall settle in the states or territories adjacent to their own nation. Consequently, all contracts not already completed and not in harmony with this law are suspended.

—*Texas Gazette,* July 3, 1830

The law also set up new forts. Soldiers in the forts would prevent smuggling, the introduction of slaves, and illegal land speculation. Mexico discouraged trade between foreign nations and Texas by placing taxes called **customs duties** on goods made in foreign nations. Most Anglo American colonists considered these actions unfair.

A Shared Past...

Mier y Terán was in Nacogdoches during the U.S. presidential election of 1828. He commented on it in his diary. The election was won by Andrew Jackson of Tennessee. All previous presidents had been from the Atlantic coastal states. Jackson's election made it clear that the U.S. was looking westward.

Settlers in Texas were alarmed by the **Law of April 6, 1830.** The prosperity of many citizens depended upon continued growth and trade with the United States. Many colonists had friends and relatives who wanted to come to Texas. The Law of April 6, 1830, was an early turning point in relations between the colonists and the Mexican government. Each side began to distrust the other. Stephen F. Austin was concerned and tried to negotiate with Mexican leaders. He soon realized, however, that serious damage had already occurred in relations between Texas and the Mexican government.

✓ **Reading Check** **Examining** Why did the Mexican government issue the Law of April 6, 1830?

SECTION 1 ASSESSMENT

Checking for Understanding

1. **Using Key Terms** Write a sentence using the words exempt and customs duty(ies).
2. **Reviewing Facts** What was a difference between the Centralist Party and the Federalist Party?

Reviewing Themes

3. **Groups and Institutions** Why was it so difficult for Anglo colonists to adjust to the Mexican government's restrictions?

Organizing to Learn

4. **Sequencing** Create a chart like the one below and number these statements about the Fredonian Revolt in chronological order.

	Red and white flag was raised at the Old Stone Fort
	Haden Edwards arrived at Nacogdoches
	Fredonians fled across the Sabine River

Critical Thinking

5. **Analyzing** What was the major significance, or impact, of the Fredonian Revolt? Consider the relationship between Texas and Mexico in your answer.

TAKS PRACTICE

Making Judgments The Law of April 6, 1830, introduced many changes. What parts of the Law of April 6 might an Anglo American farmer object to?

Rebellions, 1831–1832

Main Idea
Although conflicts continued in Texas, the colonists maintained their loyalty to the Mexican government.

Key Terms
commerce
import
skirmish
resolution

Reading Strategy
Understanding Cause and Effect Create a chart like the one below and list the effect of each event.

Event	Effect
Attempts to collect customs duties	
Turtle Bayou Resolutions adopted	
Conventions of 1832 and 1833	

Read to Learn
• about the Anahuac protest.
• about the Turtle Bayou Resolutions.
• about the Conventions of 1832 and 1833.

Section Theme
Government and Democracy The colonists and Mexico tried to resolve their differences.

Preview of Events

♦1832   ♦1833

June 12
Turtle Bayou Resolutions are adopted

June 26
The Battle of Velasco

October 1
Austin is elected president of Convention of 1832

April 1
Convention of 1833 proposes Mexican state of Texas

A
Texas Story

A covered wagon, c. 1820

In 1828, General Mier y Terán reported to his government his views on some of the Texas colonists. "Foreigners . . . have this frontier of our federation open to them to enter without fulfilling the requirements of the law. This country is the asylum for fugitives from the neighboring republic [the United States] . . . [Farmers] settle where it suits them, and they take over whatever land they desire without the *alcalde's* approval and in defiance of the laws."

Settlers Protest at Anahuac

The first serious conflict over Mexico's actions occurred at the port town of **Anahuac**. Anahuac was the site of a small Mexican garrison established to control commerce, or the movement of goods, into Mexico.

It was commanded by **John (Juan) Davis Bradburn.** A native of Kentucky, Bradburn had fought against Spain for Mexican independence and was rewarded with the rank of colonel in the Mexican army.

Bradburn quarreled with the colonists living at Anahuac about several matters. The colonists accused him of taking supplies and refusing to give up runaway slaves. As commander of the garrison, Bradburn believed in the strict enforcement of all Mexican laws.

The tax collector at Anahuac attempted to collect customs duties on goods imported into Mexico from the United States. This angered the merchants because they would have to travel long distances to process the paperwork giving permission for such goods to cross the border into Mexico.

The final blow occurred in May 1832. Bradburn arrested and imprisoned two lawyers, **William B. Travis** and **Patrick C. Jack,** for interfering in his efforts to enforce the laws. About 160 settlers in two groups marched to Anahuac, demanding Travis's and Jack's release. **Frank W. Johnson** led one group from San Felipe. **John Austin** and **William H. Jack,** the brother of one of the prisoners, led the other party from Brazoria.

A small skirmish, or fight, occurred between the colonists and Bradburn. Bradburn agreed to release the prisoners if the colonists retreated from Anahuac. Not all the settlers withdrew, however. Bradburn refused to release the prisoners and called in extra forces to strengthen his position.

After another skirmish, the colonists realized that they needed more firepower. While the colonists made camp at Turtle Bayou, between Anahuac and Liberty, John Austin went to **Brazoria** to bring back a cannon.

Colonists Adopt the Turtle Bayou Resolutions

While the colonists waited for John Austin's return, they adopted a number of statements known as the **Turtle Bayou Resolutions** on June 12, 1832. In the formal statements, called resolutions, the colonists declared their loyalty to Mexico. They denied that they were rebelling against Mexican authority. Instead, the colonists insisted that they were supporting **Antonio López de Santa Anna.** Santa Anna was leading a revolt in Mexico against Centralist President **Anastasio Bustamante** (boos•tah•MAHN•tay). Bustamante was unpopular with the colonists because he was ignoring the federal Mexican

***Picturing* History**

This cannon, an "eight pounder," was used in various military skirmishes by Texas colonists against Mexican troops. This same cannon was very likely used at the Battle of the Alamo. Today, it is on public view in San Antonio. Why did the Texas colonists need to get the cannon from Brazoria?

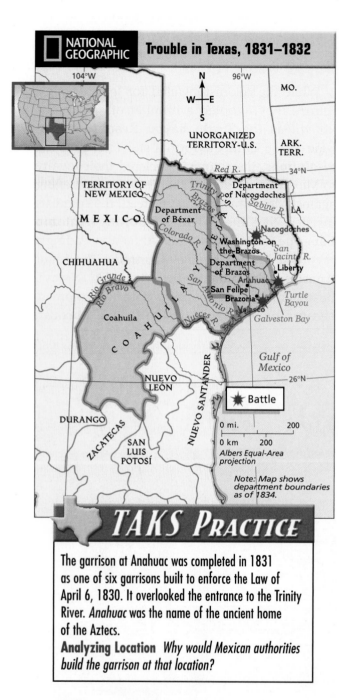

104°W

N
W—E
S

96°W

MO.

UNORGANIZED
TERRITORY-U.S.

ARK.
TERR.

Red R.

34°N

TERRITORY OF
NEW MEXICO

Trinity R.

Department
of Nacogdoches

Sabine R.

LA.

MEXICO

Department
of Béxar

Brazos R.

Nacogdoches

Colorado R.

Washington-
on-the-Brazos

San
Jacinto R.

CHIHUAHUA

Department
of Brazos

Liberty

Rio Grande

San Felipe

Anahuac

Turtle
Bayou

Rio Bravo

San Antonio R.

Brazoria

Velasco

Coahuila

Nueces R.

Galveston Bay

C O A H U I L A

Gulf of
Mexico

26°N

NUEVO
LEÓN

★ Battle

DURANGO

ZACATECAS

SAN
LUIS
POTOSÍ

NUEVO SANTANDER

0 mi.   200

0 km   200

Albers Equal-Area
projection

Note: Map shows
department boundaries
as of 1834.

TAKS PRACTICE

The garrison at Anahuac was completed in 1831
as one of six garrisons built to enforce the Law of
April 6, 1830. It overlooked the entrance to the Trinity
River. *Anahuac* was the name of the ancient home
of the Aztecs.

Analyzing Location *Why would Mexican authorities
build the garrison at that location?*

Constitution of 1824. Santa Anna, on the other
hand, had promised to support this Texan-
favored constitution.

Before John Austin and his group returned
with the cannon, Colonel José de las Piedras, commander of the Mexican garrison at Nacogdoches,
arrived at Anahuac. Colonel Piedras promised the
Texans that Bradburn would be removed from
command. Piedras then released Travis and Jack.
Bradburn resigned and left Texas. Soldiers at
Anahuac declared support for Santa Anna and
joined his growing forces in Mexico.

Clash at Velasco

Although peace and order were restored
at Anahuac, a clash did occur at Velasco on
June 26, 1832, near the mouth of the Brazos
River. John Austin's group had picked up a
cannon at Brazoria and loaded it onto a
ship. Judging them rebels, the Mexican commander, **Colonel Domingo de Ugartechea**
(oo•gahr•teh•CHAY•ah), would not let them
pass when they reached Velasco. Fighting erupted
between the Texans and the Mexican troops.

The fighting at the **Battle of Velasco** was bitter,
with loss of life on both sides. When the Mexican
garrison exhausted its ammunition, Ugartechea
surrendered. Austin's group then sailed on to
Anahuac with the cannon, only to discover that
Travis and Jack had already been freed.

Meanwhile, those supporting Santa Anna
were winning battles elsewhere, including one at
Nacogdoches. In late summer 1832, Bustamante
resigned as president of Mexico, and Santa Anna
began serving as president in 1833. Most Texas
colonists were pleased. They thought Santa
Anna would support Texas because he had
declared himself to be a Federalist.

✓Reading Check **Analyzing** Why did the colonists
support Santa Anna in Mexico?

Conventions of 1832 and 1833

Texans called a convention to discuss
changes needed in Texas. Fifty-eight delegates
to the convention assembled in **San Felipe** on
October 1, 1832. Stephen F. Austin was elected
president of the convention. The convention
resolved that Texas be made a separate
Mexican state and that immigration from the
United States be permitted again. Also, the delegates asked for an exemption from certain
import taxes, improved educational facilities,
better protection from Native Americans, and
land titles for settlers in East Texas. The convention selected **William H. Wharton** and
Rafael Manchola to present their resolutions to
officials in Mexico City. For various reasons,
these resolutions were never presented to officials in Mexico.

Sam Houston 1793–1863

Though he was born in Virginia and elected to several offices in the state of Tennessee, Sam Houston played a significant role in Texas history. After several years as Tennessee's governor, he moved to Texas where he became commander in chief of the Texas armies in 1836. His army defeated Santa Anna on April 21, 1836, securing Texas's independence. The new Lone Star Republic elected Houston its first president in 1836 and reelected him in 1841.

When Texas became a state in 1845, Houston was elected senator and later became governor in 1859. He strongly opposed the secession of Texas from the Union and, when Texas voted to separate, Houston was removed from office. He retired to Huntsville, Texas, where he lived until his death in 1863.

A few months later, another group of Anglo American colonists concerned with the situation in Texas called a convention at **San Felipe** on April 1, 1833. Most of the delegates had not attended the previous convention. Among the new delegates was Sam Houston, representing Nacogdoches.

The **Convention of 1833** adopted resolutions like those adopted in 1832. However, the convention also prepared a constitution for the proposed Mexican state of Texas. Stephen F. Austin, **Dr. James B. Miller,** and **Erasmo Seguín** were chosen to carry the resolutions to Mexico City. Miller and Seguín were unable to make the trip at the time, so Austin made the journey alone.

☑ **Reading Check** **Analyzing** Why was Stephen F. Austin elected president of the 1832 convention?

SECTION 2 ASSESSMENT

Checking for Understanding

1. **Using Key Terms** Write in your own words the definitions for the terms resolution, commerce, import, and skirmish.
2. **Reviewing Facts** Why were the merchants upset by the customs duties collected at Anahuac?

Reviewing Themes

3. **Government and Democracy** What did the colonists hope to explain to the Mexican authorities by adopting the Turtle Bayou Resolutions?

Organizing to Learn

4. **Comparing and Contrasting** Create a chart like the one below to compare the Conventions of 1832 and 1833. *Three* issues are discussed at *both*, *one* is exclusive to the Convention of 1833. Place a star next to this one.

Texas as a separate Mexican state
A constitution for the proposed Mexican state of Texas
Import taxes
Removal of the restrictions on immigration

Critical Thinking

5. **Predicting Consequences** The text explains that the delegates to the 1833 convention wrote a constitution for the proposed new state of Texas. Do you think this would help or hurt the case for an independent Mexican state? Give reasons for your answer.

★ **TAKS PRACTICE**

Map Study What river formed the southern boundary of the Department of Béxar?

Increased Tensions, 1833–1835

Guide to Reading

Main Idea
Conflicts increased as Santa Anna switched to the Centralist Party.

Key Terms
cholera
repeal
malaria
dictator

Reading Strategy
Analyzing As you read this section, draw a chart like the one below and insert important events in either the "peace" or "war" category.

Events Leading to Peace	Events Leading to War

Read to Learn
• why Stephen F. Austin was imprisoned.
• what action William B. Travis took.
• about the Consultation.

Section Theme
Groups and Institutions As tensions increased, Texans aligned with either the War Party or the Peace Party.

Preview of Events

♦1833	♦1834	♦1835

1833
Cholera epidemic strikes coastal towns

January
Austin is arrested in Mexico

December
Austin is released from prison

June
Conflict at Anahuac

November
Consultation meets

A
Texas Story

Mexican creole landowner, c. 1820

General Mier y Terán warned his government to take immediate action if Mexico wanted to keep Texas. "From the state of affairs a [hatred] has emerged between Mexicans and foreigners . . . [I] tell you that, if timely measures are not taken, Tejas will pull down the entire [Mexican] federation."

Austin's Mission Is Stalled

In April 1833, Stephen F. Austin left San Felipe and began the long trip to Mexico City. He arrived in the Mexican capital three months later, but Santa Anna was out of town. When Austin arrived, Santa Anna's government was not yet well organized. No plans had been made for dealing with the question of Texas. A cholera epidemic raged in the capital, and thousands of people were dying from the deadly bacteria. Austin waited impatiently through October. After becoming discouraged by his lack of accomplishments, Austin wrote a letter to authorities in San Antonio describing the difficulties he faced and encouraging Texans to form their own government.

Austin Is Imprisoned and Released

By November 1833, the situation in Mexico City seemed more hopeful. Santa Anna finally had returned to the capital and agreed to some of the reforms Austin requested. The president did not grant Texas separate statehood. He was willing, however, to **repeal,** or do away with, the law restricting immigration from the United States. Santa Anna also agreed to improve the court and postal systems. Pleased with the work that he had done in Mexico City, Austin left the capital on December 10 to return home.

In January 1834, Austin reached the city of **Saltillo** in northern Mexico. Because of a letter he had written to authorities in San Antonio, he was arrested. Austin was taken to Mexico City under guard. He remained in prison for one year. While in prison, Austin wrote several letters to his family and friends in Texas:

> ❝I have no idea when I shall be at liberty . . . It is much in my favor that all remains quiet in Texas. I was confident that no friend of mine would try to get up an excitement but I feared that my enemies would. Such a thing would have increased my difficulty, for I would have been blamed for it all. My confinement has been very rigid but I am in good health, and have borne it with tolerable patience. I had no books the first month, and it was solitary enough— after that I prevailed on the sergeant to go to D. Victor Blanco who sent them—he and Padre Muldoon have been firm and unwavering in their friendship to me in all this business.❞

Local officials at various Texas towns began to press for Austin's freedom. **Ramón Músquiz** (MOOS•kees), a political leader in San Antonio and a trusted friend, wrote to Mexican officials requesting that Austin be released. Lawyers Peter W. Grayson and Spencer H. Jack went to Mexico City to help.

Picturing **History**

Mexico City's imposing cathedrals and monuments were just a few of the sights Stephen F. Austin might have seen on his journey to and from the city. How might what he saw in Mexico City influence his thoughts of Texas?

Stephen F. Austin's diary

On Christmas Day 1834, Mexican authorities agreed to release the prisoner on bail. Austin was required to stay in Mexico City and wait for the final decision on his case.

On July 11, 1835, Austin was given his complete freedom. He traveled to Vera Cruz, where he took passage on a ship returning to Texas. Austin landed in Texas on September 1, 1835. He had been away from his colony for two years and four months.

Reading Check Questioning Was Austin successful at convincing Santa Anna to approve the reforms?

Reforms Begin in Texas

While Austin was in Mexico, changes occurred in Texas. The cholera epidemic of 1833 struck New Orleans, San Antonio, Matamoros, Monclova, and Mexico City, as well as the Brazoria area. There, over 80 people died, including eight members of the Austin family. Heavy rains in the autumn of 1833 and many cases of malaria, a disease carried by mosquitoes, added to the suffering.

Unfortunately, the practice of medicine was not very sophisticated at this time. Training was poor, and most Texas doctors had to work as farmers or merchants in addition to treating patients. They set bones, extracted bullets, amputated limbs to prevent gangrene, and prescribed drugs to reduce fever or relieve pain. The most common diseases of the time were malaria, yellow fever, and cholera. Many of the medicines used to treat these diseases, however, proved to be highly dangerous. For example, mercury, a common "cure," destroyed the patient's gums and intestines.

The year 1834 was better in Texas. The cholera epidemic ended, and the weather improved. The reforms Santa Anna had promised began. These included recognizing English as an official language for transactions, allowing immigration from the United States, improving the court system, and increasing the number of Texas representatives in the state legislature of Coahuila from one to three. In addition, religious tolerance was granted.

Although Texans had continued to be concerned about Austin's imprisonment during 1834, they were hopeful about their own situation. They believed that relations with the national government were improving. Mexico had sent **Colonel Juan Almonte** (ahl•MOHN•tay) on an inspection tour of Texas in 1834. Almonte had reported that all was quiet in Texas and urged that reforms be continued. He had also recommended that Austin be released from prison. The plea was ignored at that time.

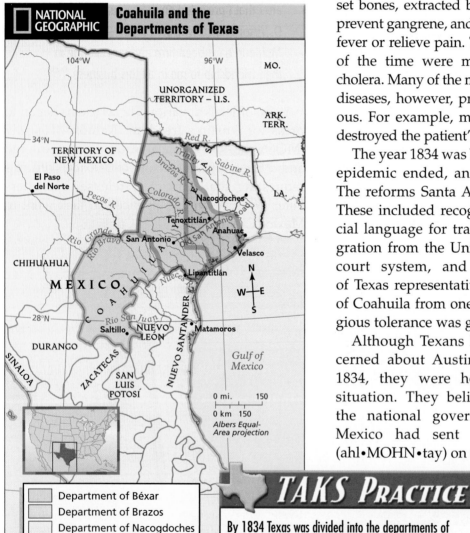

NATIONAL GEOGRAPHIC
Coahuila and the Departments of Texas

- Department of Béxar
- Department of Brazos
- Department of Nacogdoches
- Coahuila

TAKS PRACTICE

By 1834 Texas was divided into the departments of Béxar, Brazos, and Nacogdoches. As part of Santa Anna's reforms of 1834, a representative from each department of Texas would sit in the legislature.
Identifying *Through what departments does the Trinity River flow?*

Trouble Erupts Again

In early 1835, the troubles between Mexico and the Texas colonists broke out once again around Anahuac. Captain **Antonio Tenorio** was the commander of the garrison there.

Local residents at Anahuac, led by a merchant named **Andrew Briscoe,** quarreled with Tenorio about customs duties. They argued that these taxes were not being collected in other ports in Texas, and they refused to pay the duties until the law was enforced equally. This angered Tenorio, who arrested Briscoe.

Briscoe's arrest caused resentment among the colonists. In late June, a group in San Felipe, led by William B. Travis, decided to take action. They marched to Anahuac and forced Tenorio to surrender. In addition, Tenorio and his soldiers agreed to leave Texas.

Some Texans did not approve of the actions taken by Travis. Several towns adopted resolutions assuring the Mexican government of their loyalty. Local leaders at San Felipe wrote a letter of apology to **General Martín Perfecto de Cós,** Santa Anna's brother-in-law and commander of the Mexican forces in Coahuila.

✓ Reading Check **Describing** What reforms did Santa Anna make in 1834?

General Cós Rejects the Apology

General Cós was in no mood for an apology. He was upset by the fiery words of the Texans. He demanded that Texas officials arrest those involved in the disturbances, including William B. Travis, Frank W. Johnson, and Samuel M. Williams. General Cós wanted them turned over to the military for trial. In doing so, he was acting on Santa Anna's orders. Santa Anna was no longer a Federalist; he had become a Centralist.

Cós also ordered the arrest of **Lorenzo de Zavala,** a distinguished Mexican politician. Zavala had helped to frame the Mexican Constitution of 1824. He had been critical of recent actions of Santa Anna in Mexico and had moved to Texas for safety. Cós announced that he was taking many soldiers to Texas to arrest those he considered disloyal.

Picturing **History**

Samuel M. Williams *(left)* and Frank W. Johnson *(right)* followed the leadership of William B. Travis in driving Captain Tenorio from Anahuac. **What was General Cós's reaction to this disturbance?**

Texans Call for a Consultation

Cós's actions caused great concern in Texas. Texans were not willing to turn their friends over to a Mexican military court. On August 20, 1835, leaders in the town of Columbia issued a call for a convention so the people could discuss the situation. This convention was to

be known as the **Consultation** and was to meet at Washington-on-the-Brazos on October 15.

The colonists had mixed reactions. One group of colonists, known as the **Peace Party,** feared that the Consultation might cause trouble.

Another group, known as the **War Party,** favored the Consultation. This party was led by settlers who had been disappointed when the Mexican government stopped issuing contracts for lands in Texas. Leaders like William H. Wharton and William B. Travis favored an immediate declaration of independence from Mexico, even if this meant war.

When Stephen F. Austin arrived from Mexico, the call for the Consultation had already gone out. The invitation noted that the delegates should work for a peaceful solution if it could be secured on agreeable terms. The invitation also

People of Texas

Santa Anna 1794–1876

Antonio López de Santa Anna was born in Vera Cruz. At age 16 he began his long military career. During his life, he served as a president of Mexico 11 times.

He refused to accept the Mexican Constitution of 1824 and, when Anglos and Mexicans in Texas revolted against the Mexican government in 1836, Santa Anna led the attack on the Texans defending the Alamo. Later, he fought against Sam Houston at the Battle of San Jacinto where Santa Anna's capture was a great victory for the Texans. Houston spared the life of Santa Anna, who later returned to Mexico, where he continued in politics and eventually came to power as president again. Overthrown in 1855, Santa Anna died in poverty in Mexico City on June 21, 1876.

urged the delegates to "prepare for war—if war is inevitable."

Leaders of the Peace Party were hopeful that Austin would oppose the Consultation and that the meeting would not be held. Austin, however, gave his approval to the Consultation. Austin had become convinced that Santa Anna was becoming a **dictator** (a ruler with absolute power). He worried about the decision to send large numbers of troops to Texas. After long consideration, Austin believed the time had come to act. He urged the people to unite:

> **66**War is our only resource. There is no other remedy. We must defend our rights, ourselves, and our country by force of arms.**99**

✓ **Reading Check** **Analyzing** What brought about the Consultation meeting?

SECTION 3 ASSESSMENT

Checking for Understanding

1. **Using Key Terms** Write one sentence each for the following three terms: repeal, malaria, dictator.
2. **Reviewing Facts** Why was Stephen F. Austin stopped at Saltillo and returned to Mexico City?

Reviewing Themes

3. **Groups and Institutions** Who were the colonists who favored holding the Consultation? Were they members of the Peace Party or the War Party?

Organizing to Learn

4. **Sequencing** Place the letters representing the following events in the proper chronological order on the time line to show what Stephen F. Austin encountered between 1833 and 1835.

    ┼──────┼──────┼──────┼

    a. Began trip to Mexico City
    b. Returned to Texas
    c. Arrested and imprisoned
    d. Wrote a letter to local authorities
    e. Traveled to Vera Cruz

Critical Thinking

5. **Identifying Cause and Effect** While he was in Mexico City, what did Stephen F. Austin write in his letter to the authorities in San Antonio that caused him to be arrested and imprisoned?

TAKS PRACTICE

Analyzing Compare the statements by Stephen F. Austin on page 195 ("Austin Is Imprisoned and Released") with the remarks he made in the quoted passage above. Why did Stephen F. Austin's attitude change between those times?

Recognizing Bias

Why Learn This Skill?

Most people have a point of view, or *bias*, which influences the way they understand and write about events. Recognizing bias helps you judge the accuracy of what you hear or read.

Learning the Skill

To recognize bias, follow these steps:
- Examine the author's identity and how his or her views and particular interests could show a bias.
- Identify statements of fact.
- Identify expressions of opinion or emotion.
- Determine the author's point of view and how it is reflected in the work.

Practicing the Skill

Mary Helm was an Anglo New York schoolteacher. Read her account of life among Native Americans after she moved to Texas. Use the steps given above to answer the questions that follow.

"It was amusing to see [Native Americans] parade the streets of Matagorda with their . . . garments, which I had made for them, the tails tipped with ornamental feathers. One of the young women learned to speak very good English . . . and one day [I] thought to have some fun with her, [so I] invited her to take tea with me. But the joke turned to my own expense, for she not only used her knife and fork properly but her cup, saucer and plate . . ."

—*Scraps of Early Texas History*, 1884

❶ To what ethnic group did Mary Helm belong?

❷ Why did she invite a Native American woman to have tea, and how did the woman act?

❸ Analyze Mary Helm's attitude about Native Americans based on this account.

Texas schoolteacher with students

TAKS PRACTICE

Recognizing Bias In "A Texas Story" in Section 2 (page 190), General Manuel de Mier y Terán wrote a letter on July 7, 1828, about foreign settlers in Texas. Review the passage and answer the following questions.

1. What country does Mier y Terán represent?
2. How might his background reflect his views?
3. Does any information appear to be inaccurate? If so, which information?

 Glencoe's **Skillbuilder Interactive Workbook,** Level 1, provides instruction and practice in key social studies skills.

Chapter Summary

Growing Tensions

1826

★ Haden Edwards and his family declare independence from Mexico in the unsuccessful Fredonian Revolt.

1829

• The Centralist Party comes to power in Mexico.

1830

• Mexico issues the Law of April 6 to stop immigration from the U.S.

1832

• American colonists adopt the Turtle Bayou Resolutions in support of Santa Anna.

★ The Battle at Velasco between Texans and Mexican troops is caused by Ugartechea's refusal to let the Texans' ship pass by Velasco.

• The Convention of 1832 calls for reforms in Texas.

1833

★ Santa Anna becomes president of Mexico.

• The Convention of 1833 calls for a new state of Texas separate from Coahuila.

1834

★ Stephen F. Austin is imprisoned in Mexico City when his letter urging Texans to form their own government is discovered.

1835

• Troubles erupt in Anahuac between Texans and Mexicans over taxes.

• Texans form the Consultation to discuss Mexican actions.

• Stephen F. Austin returns to Texas and calls for war.

Reviewing Key Terms

With a partner, make 16 flash cards. Write one term from the list below on each of the first eight cards. On the eight cards that remain, write the definitions, one per card. Quiz one another by matching the words with the correct definitions.

1. decree
2. exempt
3. repeal
4. malaria
5. resolution
6. skirmish
7. customs duty
8. dictator

Reviewing Key Facts

9. What was the source of conflict between the Edwards brothers and the Mexican government?

10. Name two groups that declined to help the Edwards brothers in the Fredonian Revolt.

11. What recommendation was made by Mier y Terán concerning the control of Texas?

12. In the Law of April 6, 1830, what specific actions did the Mexican government take?

13. What was the purpose of the Turtle Bayou Resolutions?

14. When Stephen F. Austin arrived in Mexico City, what problems were present?

Critical Thinking

15. **Predicting Consequences** What was the attitude of the Mexican authorities toward Texas during the early colonial years? What effect did this have on the colonists?

16. **Identifying Cause and Effect** The Law of April 6, 1830, was described as "an early turning point in relations between the colonists and the Mexican government." Why do you think this law had such an effect?

17. **Comparing** Compare the views of the Mexican government and the Anglo American colonists after the Fredonian Revolt. Use a chart like the one below to organize your responses.

Views After the Fredonian Revolt	
Mexican government	Anglo American colonists

18. **Generalizing** Why was it so difficult for Anglo American colonists to adjust to the restrictions placed on them by the Mexican government?

19. **Making Predictions** How did William B. Travis's actions at Anahuac in 1835 cause problems?

Geography and History Activity

20. Draw a chart that gives examples of Anglo influence in Texas. Then use information from the chapter to create a map that shows where Anglo influences would be strongest in Texas. Include a key or legend.

Portfolio/TAKS Writing Activity

21. Writing a Newspaper Article Imagine you are a reporter covering events in Texas in 1834 and 1835. Write an article about the trouble between Texas and Mexico in which you present the point of view of each side. You may want to directly quote from your "personal interviews" with colonists and Mexican officials. Use standard grammar, spelling, sentence structure, and punctuation.

Building Technology Skills

22. Using a Word Processor Use a word processing program (such as Microsoft Word) to type your "Portfolio Writing Activity." Be sure to check your spelling with the spellchecker, and you may want to use the thesaurus (either online or on your toolbar) to help locate alternative words for your article.

Practicing Skills

23. Recognizing Bias To determine the accuracy of what you hear or read, it is important to recognize the bias, or point of view, of the author. Read the statement below by John Holland Jenkins, an Anglo American settler who was 13 years old in 1835. Then answer the questions that follow.

> "We come now to the fall of 1835, when without reservation or mercy Mexico threw aside all obligation involved in the treaty of 1824 and became so [unjust] in her dealings with Texas, as to venture to seal her authority even by force of arms . . . This unwarrantable piece of tyranny and oppression of course aroused every loyal Texan, and there was a general rallying to arms and preparation for war."
>
> —From *Recollections of Early Texas,* 1885

a. How does the writer describe Mexico's treatment of Texas at that time?

b. Why does the writer hold these opinions about Mexico?

c. What information in this statement is likely to be accurate?

d. What information in this statement constitutes an expression of emotion?

TEXAS HISTORY *Online*

Self-Check Quiz
Visit the texans.glencoe.com Web site and click on **Chapter 8—Self-Check Quizzes** to prepare for the chapter test.

TAKS PRACTICE

Use the graph to answer the following question.

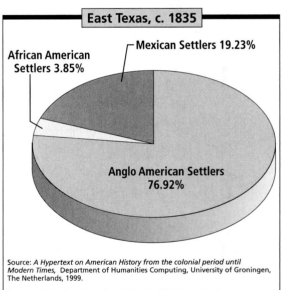

East Texas, c. 1835

- African American Settlers 3.85%
- Mexican Settlers 19.23%
- Anglo American Settlers 76.92%

Source: *A Hypertext on American History from the colonial period until Modern Times,* Department of Humanities Computing, University of Groningen, The Netherlands, 1999.

Based on *An Outline of American History*, the U.S. Information Agency.

In East Texas, most early settlers

F strongly supported their Mexican heritage.

G fled hardships or persecution in Europe.

H supported Anglo American schools and newspapers.

J supported the Mexican government's decision to abolish slavery.

Test-Taking Tip:

In this question you are being asked to make an inference based on the type of data presented. According to the graph, most of the settlers were Anglo American. What logical inference can you make about how they would act or feel? Can you infer anything about their personal beliefs or histories?

9

Road to Independence

Why It Matters

The Mexican president Antonio López de Santa Anna responded harshly to tensions in Texas. Delegates to a convention held at Washington-on-the-Brazos believed freedom from Mexico was the only answer to their problems. They wrote a declaration of independence and a constitution for a new government.

The Impact Today

Texans trace the origins of the current constitution back to the one written in 1836. That basic law of the land continues to provide for stable government and protection of the rights of the people.

CONSTITUTION
OF THE
REPUBLIC OF TEXAS.

1835
★ The Battle of Gonzales was fought between Mexican troops and Texas colonists
★ The Consultation set up a provisional government

Texas

United States   1832   1833   1834   1835

World

1832
• July 4, "America" sung publicly for the first time

1834
• National Republicans changed their name to Whigs

Austin artist Bert Rees completed a mosaic of the Battle of Gonzales in 1959, part of which is shown here. It appears on the front of the Gonzales City Hall.

FOLDABLES™ Study Organizer
TAKS PRACTICE

Identifying Main Ideas Study Foldable
Make this foldable and use it as a journal to help you record information as well as questions and thoughts you have about Texas's journey to independence.

Step 1 Fold a sheet of paper in half from top to bottom.

Step 2 Then fold the paper in half from side to side.

Step 3 Label the foldable as shown.

Reading and Writing As you read the chapter, write journal entries in your foldable from the viewpoint of someone who is personally experiencing the political tensions in Texas at this time. Write descriptive entries about your life as a Texan while Texas struggled for independence.

1836
★ The Declaration of Independence from Mexico adopted on March 2
★ The Texas Constitution approved on March 16

| 1836 | 1837 | 1838 | 1839 |

1838
• Cherokees driven from their homelands onto the Trail of Tears

1839
• Opium War began in China

TEXAS HISTORY Online

Chapter Overview
Visit the texans.glencoe.com Web site and click on **Chapter 9—Chapter Overviews** to preview chapter information.

Revolution Begins

Guide to Reading

Main Idea
The first shots of the Texas Revolution were fired, and Texans took steps to govern themselves.

Key Terms
committees of correspondence, siege, provisional government, municipality, regular army

Reading Strategy
Organizing Information As you read this section, complete a table like the one shown by filling in the significance of the persons listed.

Person	Significant Actions
General Cós	
Colonel Ugartechea	
Stephen F. Austin	
Sam Houston	

Read to Learn
- which battles began the Texas Revolution.
- what decisions were made at the Consultation of 1835.

Section Theme
Civic Rights and Responsibilities Texans turned a struggle for state self-government into a war for independence.

Preview of Events

♦1835

October 2	November 3	November 7
Battle of Gonzales	Consultation begins at San Felipe	Consultation adopts "Declaration of the People"

Steamboat, c. 1835

A Texas Story

In a letter to his wife Martha, dated December 7, 1835, Micajah Autry wrote: "I have taken passage on the Steam Boat *Pacific* and . . . have met on the same boat a number of acquaintances from Nashville and the District bound for Texas among whom are George C. Childress and his brother. Childress thinks the fighting will be over before we get there and speaks cheeringly of the prospects."

Within three months of Micajah Autry's journey, George Childress would write the Texas Declaration of Independence.

A Mexican Army Arrives in Texas

Tension continued to build in Texas. It seemed to officials both back in the Mexican capital and in Texas that radicals like William B. Travis were becoming disloyal. The small number of soldiers at the forts had been unable to control the tense situation. More soldiers were needed. The arrival of **General Cós** with additional troops brought the number of Mexican soldiers in San Antonio to 650. Their presence in Texas caused much concern among the settlers. Towns formed committees of safety in case of threat by federal soldiers. Patrols watched the roads to give warnings of approaching troops. Rumors spread through the countryside that General Cós was planning to arrest all Texan leaders and march them back to Mexico in chains. Committees of correspondence—local groups sharing political and military information, much like those that were formed during the American Revolution—sprang up to keep the colonists informed.

Gonzales—The Lexington of Texas

The first conflict between Mexican troops and Texan colonists came at **Gonzales** on October 2, 1835, two weeks before the scheduled start of the Consultation at **Washington-on-the-Brazos.** The first battle of the American Revolution had taken place at Lexington, Massachusetts, when British soldiers had attempted to take arms and ammunition away from the people. Because of this similarity in the circumstances that touched off the two revolutions, Gonzales is known as the "Lexington of Texas."

A Shared Past...

The Texan independence fighters must have learned at least one important lesson from the patriots of the American Revolution. Before the days of e-mail and the Internet, getting information from one place to another was a slow process. Setting up a communication network was the first step toward any kind of united political action. The committees of correspondence in both the American and the Texas Revolutions directed much of the early activity of the revolutionaries.

Colonel Ugartechea (oo•gahr•teh•CHAY•ah), the Mexican commander at San Antonio, ordered the people of Gonzales to surrender their small brass cannon. The local official refused and sent runners to the surrounding areas to gather armed men. Colonel Ugartechea then ordered about 100 soldiers to take the cannon by force.

The people buried the cannon in a peach orchard until reinforcements arrived from the countryside. The Texan forces dug up the cannon and mounted it on a wagon. A local blacksmith quickly forged some ammunition out of iron scraps and pieces of chain. The Texans decorated

History *Through Art*

Battle of Gonzales by Bruce Marshall James Tumlinson acquires the cannon from the Mexican government in 1831 (*center back*); after the Battle of Gonzales in 1835, it is buried at Sandies Creek (*center right*); it is unearthed by a flood in 1936 (*bottom right*). Do you think the artist was successful in his effort to tell the story of the Gonzales cannon? Why or why not?

the front of the cannon with a white flag that bore the words "Come and Take It."

When the Mexican troops arrived at Gonzales, they faced 160 armed Texans command-ed by **Colonel John H. Moore.** The fighting at Gonzales lasted only a few minutes. After the brief struggle, the Mexican leaders ordered their troops to withdraw toward San Antonio. One Mexican soldier was killed. No Texans died in the confrontation.

Although the Battle of Gonzales was brief and casualties were light, news of the clash quickly spread throughout Texas. Many colonists who previously had been indifferent about the prospect of fighting were now enthusiastic. At San Antonio, General Cós regarded the actions at Gonzales as the outbreak of war.

On to San Antonio

On October 9th—one week after the fight-ing at Gonzales—a force of about 100 Texans took the garrison at Goliad by surprise. They battled for about thirty minutes before captur-ing the presidio. The surrender of the Mexican troops and the victories at Gonzales and Goliad convinced many Texans that Mexican troops could be defeated easily. The only large Mex-ican force remaining in Texas was the army commanded by General Cós at San Antonio. Texans began gathering around Gonzales for the march against Cós. The cry was now "On to San Antonio!"

Stephen F. Austin was called upon to take com-mand of the 300 Texans assembled at Gonzales. Known as the **Army of the People,** Austin's troops started their march. On their way toward San Antonio, more and more volunteers joined, until nearly 600 made up the ranks. After some brief fighting around San Antonio, the Texans decided to make camp and lay siege to (set up a military blockade around) the city. They had no heavy artillery and wished to avoid an all-out attack on the Mexican defensive positions. The Texans hoped Cós would run out of supplies and quickly be forced to surrender.

✓ **Reading Check** **Describing** Which two battles made the colonists believe the Mexicans could be easily defeated?

People of Texas

Juan Nepomuceno Seguín 1806–1890

Juan Seguín fought in the Texas Revolution and became a captain in the army. He survived the Battle of the Alamo because he was away searching for reinforcements. He made his way to East Texas where Sam Houston was putting together an army, but it was too late—the Alamo had fallen. He fought with Houston at the Battle of San Jacinto and helped defeat Santa Anna's army.

Seguín served in the Texas Senate and as a high official in San Antonio. He helped defeat a Mexican expedition against San Antonio but was later accused of treason. Born and raised in San Antonio, he was finally forced to leave Texas because he felt like a "foreigner" in his native land.

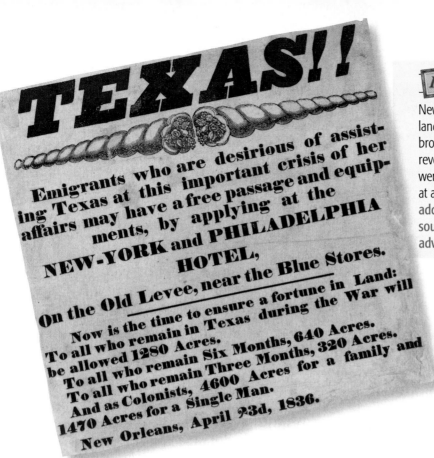

TEXAS!!

Emigrants who are desirious of assisting Texas at this important crisis of her affairs may have a free passage and equipments, by applying at the NEW-YORK and PHILADELPHIA HOTEL,

On the Old Levee, near the Blue Stores.

Now is the time to ensure a fortune in Land: To all who remain in Texas during the War will be allowed 1280 Acres. To all who remain Six Months, 640 Acres. To all who remain Three Months, 320 Acres. And as Colonists, 4600 Acres for a family and 1470 Acres for a Single Man.

New Orleans, April 23d, 1836.

Peace Party Prevails at the Consultation

While the Texan troops camped near San Antonio, other Texans met in **San Felipe** at a **Consultation** on November 3, 1835. Originally, the meeting had been scheduled to take place in Washington-on-the-Brazos on October 15, but it was delayed because of the events at Gonzales and Goliad. The meeting was moved to San Felipe because the town had a printing press.

Fifty-eight delegates representing 14 towns or districts attended the Consultation. **War Party** delegates favored an immediate declaration of independence from Mexico. They believed that the fighting had shown that Texas could no longer live peaceably under Mexico's rule. **Peace Party** delegates also agreed that Texans should oppose Santa Anna, but they objected to an immediate declaration of independence. They wanted the Consultation to declare that Texas was fighting for the Mexican Constitution of 1824, which Santa Anna had overthrown. The Peace Party hoped to win Mexican support with this argument.

On November 6, delegates of the Consultation voted. A motion calling for immediate independence was defeated. Fifteen delegates voted for independence, while 33 members voted against the proposal.

On the following day, the Consultation adopted a statement known as the "Declaration of the People of Texas in General Convention Assembled." In this declaration, printed in both Spanish and English, the Texans declared themselves to be loyal citizens of Mexico. They pledged to support the Mexican Constitution of 1824 and declared that they had taken up arms only to defend themselves and to oppose the rule of Santa Anna. The declaration stated that Texas was no longer bound by the compact of union but that Texans offered their support to such members of the Mexican confederacy as would take up arms against military dictatorship. They urged all Mexican citizens, both in Texas and elsewhere, to join their struggle for democratic government. They also offered land to volunteers who would help them.

✓ **Reading Check** **Summarizing** What was stated in the Declaration of the People drafted at the Consultation?

TEXAS TODAY

Since 1957 the citizens of Gonzales have gathered to celebrate their Texas heritage in a three-day "Come and Take It" festival each October. It is here that the first Texas Army of Volunteers gathered, fired the first shot of the Texas Revolution, and became the Alamo's only reinforcements.

A Provisional Government Begins

After adopting the Declaration of the People, the Consultation created a **provisional government,** or temporary government, for Texas. It consisted of a governor, a lieutenant governor, and a general council with one representative from each of the locally governed areas known as **municipalities.** The powers of the governor and council were defined only vaguely, however. That vagueness would eventually lead to conflict.

The Consultation chose **Henry Smith** of Brazoria as governor and **James W. Robinson** of Nacogdoches as lieutenant governor. Smith and Robinson both were members of the War Party and supported Texas independence, but most of the members chosen for the council supported the Peace Party. Quarrels continued between the two sides because of their different beliefs.

The Consultation adopted a plan for the creation of a **regular army** of full-time, paid soldiers. **Sam Houston** was chosen to be the commander of the regular army, but he was not given authority over the volunteer army still camped at San Antonio. Born in Virginia, Sam Houston had moved to Tennessee while a young man. He lived with nearby Cherokees for three years, learning their language and customs. After serving in the War of 1812, Houston entered politics as a district attorney and was later a United States congressman and governor of Tennessee. He moved westward in 1829 and lived for several years among the Cherokees again, this time in Arkansas Territory. He began visiting Texas in 1832, and by 1835 had permanently moved to Texas.

The Consultation named Stephen F. Austin, William H. Wharton, and Branch T. Archer as commissioners to represent Texas in the United States. They were told to obtain troops, supplies, and money to finance the expected war and to aid in the struggle against Santa Anna.

Reading Check **Identifying** Who was chosen as governor of the new provisional government?

SECTION 1 ASSESSMENT

Checking for Understanding

1. **Using Key Terms** Pretend you are a soldier in Texas. Write a letter to your family using these words: siege, provisional government, municipalities, and regular army.
2. **Reviewing Facts** What were the political goals of the Peace Party and War Party?

Reviewing Themes

3. **Civic Rights and Responsibilities** Why is Gonzales known as the "Lexington of Texas"?

Organizing to Learn

4. **Searching for Facts** Draw a chart like the one shown below. Use the information in this section to answer the following questions about the Consultation of November 1835.

Where was the Consultation held?	
Who attended?	
Why did they meet?	
What did they decide?	

Critical Thinking

5. **Making Comparisons** Name advantages and disadvantages of the provisional government's structure.
6. **Identifying Leadership Qualities** How would Sam Houston's background help him as a leader?

TAKS Practice

Summarizing Describe the steps leading up to the Battle of Gonzales. What effect did the battle have on the fight for independence?

Evaluating a Web Site

Why Learn This Skill?

The Internet has become a valuable research tool. It is convenient to use, and the information contained on the Internet is plentiful. However, it is up to the user to distinguish between quality information and inaccurate or incomplete information, just as you would with printed material.

Learning the Skill

On a reliable Web site, the author and publisher or sponsor should be clearly indicated. The information on the site should be current, and the site should be easy to navigate.

To evaluate a Web site, ask yourself the following questions:

- Is more than one source used for background information within the site?
- Does the site contain a bibliography?
- Are the links within the site up to date?
- Is the author clearly identified?
- Does the site explore the topic in depth?
- Does the site contain links to other useful resources?
- Is the information easy to access?
- Is the design appealing?

Practicing the Skill

Visit the Web site featured on this page and answer the following questions.

Lone Star Junction (**www.lsjunction.com**)

❶ Who is the author and sponsor of the Web site?

❷ What links does the site contain?

❸ What sources were used for the information contained on the site?

❹ Does the site explore the topic in depth? Why or why not?

❺ Is the design of the site appealing? Why or why not?

TAKS PRACTICE

Evaluating a Web Site   Go to a Web site that you visit regularly or choose a Web site that you want to learn more about. Answer the following questions about the Web site.

1. Name each of the links.

2. Choose one of the links and describe its contents.

3. Is the information from that link reliable? Why or why not?

4. Is the information from that link detailed? Why or why not?

The Capture of San Antonio

Guide to Reading

Main Idea
Texans won a victory at San Antonio, but the provisional government failed.

Key Terms
veto
override

Reading Strategy
Classifying Information As you read this section, complete a chart like the one shown here outlining the importance of the following dates.

Date	Importance
December 5, 1835	
December 9, 1835	
March 1836	

Read to Learn
• what military events occurred in the winter of 1835–1836.
• what problems were caused by the provisional government.

Section Theme
Culture and Traditions People of many ethnicities joined together in the fight for Texas independence.

Preview of Events

♦ 1835   ♦ 1836

November 25 — Austin leaves for U.S. to seek aid

November 26 — Grass Fight outside San Antonio

December 5 — Attack on San Antonio begins

A
Texas Story

Adventurous Americans had a lively interest in Texan affairs and searched for news of the latest events. In 1835, Micajah Autry wrote, "Major Arnold from Tennessee and myself left the rest of the company . . . and went down to Orleans for the purpose of learning the true state of things in Texas . . . The result was that the war is still going favourably . . . It is thought that Santa Anna will make [an invasion] . . . in the Spring but there will be soldiers enough of the real grit in Texas by that time to overrun all Mexico."

New Orleans dock

The Grass Fight

Stephen F. Austin left his command at San Antonio for the United States on November 25, 1835, to plead for aid. **Edward Burleson** of Mina (MEE•nah), present-day Bastrop, was chosen to command the volunteer army.

Soon after Burleson became commander of the volunteers, one of the army scouts, **Erastus "Deaf" Smith,** reported that a Mexican mule train was heading toward San Antonio. The Texans believed that the mules were carrying bags of silver to pay Cós's soldiers at San Antonio. A group of Texans went to intercept the "silver train." The troops fought with the Mexican mule handlers and captured some of the mules. The Texans were disappointed to discover that the mules were carrying only grass for Cós's cavalry horses. This skirmish came to be known as the **"Grass Fight."**

Except for the Grass Fight, there was little military activity around San Antonio in October and November 1835. The Texan volunteers grew restless, discouraged, and hungry. Winter was approaching, and most of the soldiers had no coats. Many of the original volunteers returned to their homes in late November. In early December, the siege was called off and the baggage wagons were loaded.

The Assault on San Antonio

As Burleson prepared to leave the camp near San Antonio, he received information that Cós's army was weak and could not win against a major attack. By this time, news of the war had spread, and hundreds of volunteers were arriving in Texas from the United States.

Ben Milam, an empresario, had helped in the capture of Goliad and marched with the army towards San Antonio. When he learned that a majority of the army had decided not to attack, Milam was convinced that this would be disastrous for the cause of independence. He knew a

victory would encourage Texans to continue the fight. He then made his famous plea: "Who will go with old Ben Milam into San Antonio?" The 47-year-old leader gathered about 300 volunteers to follow him to the old Spanish capital. Milam divided his force into two columns, leading one himself and designating **Frank W. Johnson** to lead the other. Johnson, a close friend of Stephen F. Austin, was in favor of going to war with Mexico and complete independence for Texas.

NATIONAL GEOGRAPHIC

Gonzales to San Antonio

98°W 97°W

Gonzales (October 2, 1835)

San Antonio (October 28, 1835 November 26, 1835 December 5–9, 1835)

29°N

Goliad (October 9, 1835)

San Antonio R.

Guadalupe R.

Lavaca R.

Colorado R.

Nueces R.

Gulf of Mexico

0 mi. 50
0 km 50
Albers Equal-Area projection

★ Battle

N W E S

TAKS PRACTICE

November 26, 1835, was the occasion of the Grass Fight between Mexican and Texan forces outside San Antonio.
Predicting Consequences *What is the approximate distance between San Antonio and Gonzales?*

Picturing **History**

Ben Milam (*left*) was killed when the Texas forces laid siege to the Mexican troops at the Battle of San Antonio. Who assumed command after Milam's death?

The assault began on December 5 and lasted for four days. Milam's troops had the advantage because the Mexican army was equipped for fighting only on open battlefields. On the third day of the battle (also called the **Siege of Béxar**), Milam was killed, and Johnson took full command. During the fighting, the Mexican forces were driven toward the center of town and took refuge in the abandoned mission known as the **Alamo**. Cós asked for surrender terms on December 9 and promised he would never again fight against the colonists or the Constitution of 1824. He and his soldiers were allowed to return to Mexico on Christmas Day, 1835.

The capture of San Antonio was a significant victory. A volunteer army of about 500 Texans had defeated a force of nearly 1,000 Mexican troops.

Two Texans were killed, and 26 were wounded. About 150 Mexican soldiers were killed, wounded, or captured.

The Texas army now held both Goliad and the Alamo. Texas soil was cleared of Mexican troops. Believing that the war was over, the Texan volunteers began returning to their homes.

✓ Reading Check **Explaining** What did Cós promise according to the surrender terms?

Tejanos and African Americans Join the Fight

The Siege of Béxar had divided the Tejanos of San Antonio. Most stayed neutral, but some helped Cós. The Texas army at San Antonio included more than 100 Tejanos. Many of them served in a scouting company, commanded by **Captain Juan N. Seguín.** Born in San Antonio, Seguín was a supporter of the Texas movement for independence. As Cós began his invasion of Texas, Seguín recruited volunteers from Mexican ranches along the San Antonio River. Plácido Benavides of Victoria brought 30 Mexican ranchers to join the fight. Manuel Flores of San Antonio volunteered to serve under Seguín, his brother-in-law.

Hendrick Arnold, a free African American, guided Milam's column in the battle. As did Flores, Arnold later served in the Battle of San Jacinto. Another free African American, Greenbury Logan, was the third Texan wounded at San Antonio, suffering a wound to his right arm that crippled him for life.

NATIONAL GEOGRAPHIC **San Antonio in the 1830s**

irrigation canal

The Alamo

N
W—E
S

San Antonio R.

San Fernando Cathedral

Spanish Governor's Palace

Main Plaza

Military Plaza

irrigation canal

La Villita

irrigation canal

irrigation canal

San Antonio R.

San Antonio

David G. Burnet 1788–1870

Born in New Jersey, Burnet was raised by a brother after his parents died. A lawyer, he moved to Galveston in 1831.

His political career began in 1833 as a member of the convention that drafted a proposed constitution for Texas as a state. At the Convention of 1836, which declared Texas's independence, Burnet was elected ad interim (temporary) president of the Republic of Texas. In spite of angering many Texans during his term, he was later elected vice president under Mirabeau Lamar.

When Texas became a state, Burnet was appointed its first secretary of state. After the Civil War, he was chosen to represent Texas in the U.S. Senate, but because Texas did not meet Republican Reconstruction requirements, he was unable to serve.

The Provisional Government

While the fighting was raging at San Antonio, the provisional government carried on the work of the Permanent Council, a group formed before the Consultation met. The Permanent Council had created a post office and had made plans for a navy and an army. It also appealed to U.S. citizens for more men, money, and supplies.

Governor Henry Smith of the provisional government and members of the general council quarreled frequently. In December the council voted to hold a convention of the people in March 1836. Governor Smith vetoed, or rejected, the proposal. The general council then overrode, or passed the proposal over, his veto.

Another disagreement concerned a proposed expedition to capture the Mexican town of Matamoros (mah•tah•MOH•rohs). The council approved the plan, but again the governor opposed it. Neither side would cooperate with the other. The result was a near breakdown of government. In early 1836, when Texas should have been making preparations to fight Santa Anna, little was being accomplished.

✓ **Reading Check** **Examining** Why was there a near complete breakdown in Texas government?

SECTION 2 ASSESSMENT

Checking for Understanding

1. **Using Key Terms** What is a synonym for **veto**? What is a synonym for **override**?
2. **Reviewing Facts** What did Texans find on the Mexican silver train?

Reviewing Themes

3. **Culture and Traditions** How many Tejanos were in the Texas army at San Antonio?

Organizing to Learn

4. **Categorizing** Draw a chart and describe the actions each individual took during the siege of San Antonio in 1835.

Person	Action
Milam	
Johnson	
Cós	
Seguín	

Critical Thinking

5. **Contrasting** In 2 or 3 sentences, compare how the volunteers probably felt after the Grass Fight and after the capture of San Antonio.

TAKS PRACTICE

Determining Cause and Effect
What were some of the reasons that caused the near breakdown of the provisional government?

The Convention of 1836

Guide to Reading

Main Idea
Texans declared their independence and set up their government as Santa Anna's forces defeated Texans at the Alamo and in South Texas.

Key Terms
petition, executive, legislative, judicial, civil rights, ad interim

Reading Strategy
Organizing Information As you read, complete a chart like the one shown here listing three grievances that led to Texas's Declaration of Independence from Mexico.

Grievances
1.
2.
3.

Read to Learn
• what the Texas Declaration of Independence from Mexico stated.
• what provisions the Texas Constitution included.

Section Theme
Civic Rights and Responsibilities The Texas constitution provided for representative government.

Preview of Events

♦1836 ——————————————————————————————————————— ♦1837

March 2
Texas Declaration of Independence adopted

March 16
Texas constitution approved

Texas cannon

A
Texas Story

Texas immigrant and new patriot Micajah Autry wrote to his wife in the spring of 1835. "I have little doubt but that the army will receive ample supplies . . . as the people of Texas have formed themselves into something like a government which will give them credit in Orleans . . . I am determined to provide a home . . . or perish." Autry died at the Alamo defending the land he had lived in for only two months.

Santa Anna Crosses Into Texas

In December 1835, the council—over the veto of Governor Smith—called for a new convention, to be held in March 1836. Texans hoped that Santa Anna would make no real movements toward Texas until after the convention. They were disappointed to learn that the Mexican president was marching toward Texas with a large army. In early February, Santa Anna crossed the Rio Grande. His army arrived in San Antonio on February 23. The Texans still remaining in San Antonio moved into the Alamo. As they were making the Alamo stronger, other Texans were traveling to Washington-on-the-Brazos.

The Convention Declares Independence

Many Texans were looking forward to the new convention. During the last week of February, elected delegates began arriving at Washington-on-the-Brazos. The town consisted of a few poorly constructed cabins, and tree stumps were still standing in the main street. There was no library, no printing press, and no convention hall. The delegates, who were all male, met in near-freezing weather, in an unfinished house. They hung cloth over the open windows in an attempt to keep out the biting north winds.

The Convention of 1836 began its work on March 1, 1836, with 59 delegates. Only 2 of the members, **José Antonio Navarro** and **José Francisco Ruíz,** were native Texans. At least 3 other native-born Texans—Gaspar Flores, Juan N. Seguín, and José María Carbajal—were elected as delegates but did not attend. Forty-five of the delegates were natives of southern states of the United States. Seven had been born in northern states. There was one member from Mexico, one from England, one from Scotland, one from Ireland, and one from Canada.

The first work of the convention was to elect Richard Ellis as chairman and H.S. Kimble as secretary of the meeting. A motion was then passed that a committee be created to write a declaration of independence from Mexico. It is generally agreed that the declaration presented the next morning was written by **George C. Childress,** a recent arrival from Tennessee.

TEXAS HISTORY Online

Student Web Activity Visit the texans.glencoe.com Web site and click on **Chapter 9—Student Web Activity** to learn more about the Texas Convention of 1836.

A Shared Past...

Sections of the Constitution of 1836 of the Republic of Texas were copied word for word from the United States Constitution. One difference, however, was that the Texas Bill of Rights, which had been added as amendments to the U.S. Constitution, was put in the main body of the Texas constitution. Neither of the original constitutions addressed the treatment of enslaved African Americans.

The Texas Declaration of Independence was similar to the U.S. Declaration of Independence written 60 years earlier. The Texas Declaration stated that the government of Santa Anna had violated the liberties guaranteed under the Mexican Constitution of 1824. The declaration charged that Texans had been deprived of freedom of religion, the right to trial by jury, the right to bear arms, and the right to **petition,** or request something from, the government. It stated that Mexico had failed to provide a system of public education. Because the Mexican government had sent a large army, the declaration also noted that the Texans' protests against these policies were met with force. Because of these grievances, the declaration proclaimed the following:

❝The people of Texas, in solemn convention assembled, appealing to a candid world for the necessities of our condition, do hereby resolve and declare that our political connection with the Mexican nation has forever ended; and that the people of Texas do now constitute a free, sovereign, and independent republic.❞

The Declaration of Independence was adopted by unanimous vote of the Convention on March 2, 1836. The signing of the document began the next day. March 2 is celebrated as Texas Independence Day.

✓ **Reading Check** **Summarizing** What grievances did the Texas Declaration of Independence address?

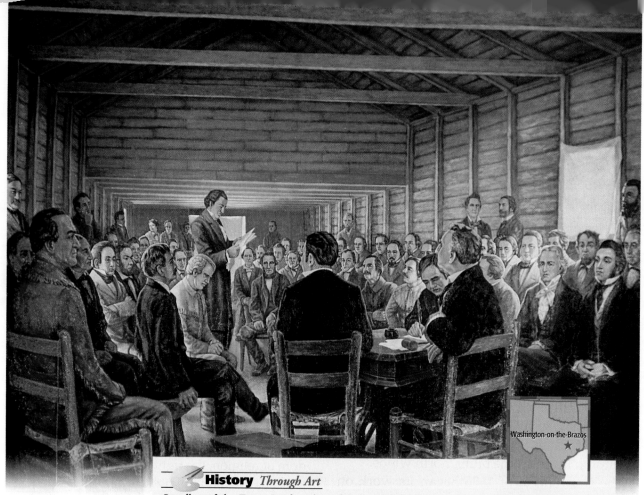

Reading of the Texas Declaration of Independence by Charles and Fanny Normann This document was adopted unanimously by the delegates of the Convention of 1836. Who are some of the individuals who would have been present at the reading?

Washington-on-the-Brazos

The Delegates Write a Constitution

After the adoption of the Declaration of Independence, the convention turned to writing a constitution for the new republic. For two weeks, the delegates debated and discussed various provisions of this document. The delegates were anxious to finish the Texas constitution quickly. Santa Anna's presence in Texas meant a possible attack by Mexican troops. On March 16, the document was completed and approved.

There were similarities between the Constitution of Texas and that of the United States. Provisions were made for three branches of government: the executive (chief governing officer), legislative (lawmaking), and judicial (court) branches. The chief executive, or president, was given a great amount of power to carry out the duties of the office entrusted to him.

The Texas constitution contained a Bill of Rights, guaranteeing freedom of speech, freedom of the press, freedom of religion, trial by jury, and other basic civil rights, or guaranteed freedoms. Some of the parts of the constitution were based on practices common in Spanish-Mexican law courts. These included recognizing that property was jointly owned by husbands and wives and measures to help people in debt. Some provisions were unique to Texas at the time. Ministers and priests were barred from holding public office—a strict interpretation of the principle of the separation of church and state.

The Texas constitution made slavery legal. The legislature was forbidden to free slaves in Texas or to prevent their importation from the United States. Free African Americans were not permitted to live in the Republic of Texas without congressional permission. African

Americans who fought for Texas independence found themselves in a strange position. They were unable to live freely in the state that they, as free people, had helped liberate.

The Ad Interim Government Takes Control

With Mexican troops in Texas, it was impossible to hold general elections to approve the constitution and to vote for a leader of the new republic. It became necessary to set up a government. The convention's last act was to select officers for an ad interim, or temporary, government. (See table on page 218.) These officers were to serve until regular elections could be held. **David G. Burnet,** an early pioneer in Texas and formerly an empresario, was chosen as the ad interim president. Sam Houston was elected by unanimous vote as commander in chief of the army. The convention did not repeat the mistake of the Consultation—Houston was put in charge of both the volunteers and the regular army.

✔ **Reading Check** **Identifying** Who was the president of the ad interim government?

A Convention Diary

Colonel William F. Gray, a visitor at the convention, kept a diary of the proceedings. Entries from Gray's diary provide a vivid picture of the delegates, their work, and their feelings.

Sunday, February 28, 1836
This evening a number of members arrived, among them Lorenzo de Zavala, the most interesting man in Texas. He is a native of Yucatán; was Governor of the State of Mexico five years, minister of the fiscal department, and ambassador to France from the Republic of Mexico, which post he renounced when Santa Anna proved [disloyal] to the liberal cause . . . He now lives on his estate on Buffalo Bayou, near Galveston Bay. He is a fine writer and a Republican; a fine statesman . . . [He] has published a volume of travels in the United States, printed in Paris in the Spanish language.

Monday, February 29, 1836
A warm day, threatening rain from the south. Many other members are coming in and it is

History *Through Art*

Delegates Voting on the 1836 Constitution **by Bruce Marshall**
News of the fall of the Alamo reached Washington-on-the-Brazos shortly before the convention adjourned. As Santa Anna was rumored to be on the way, delegates left quickly. The new government moved to Harrisburg, near present-day Houston. **What mood does the artist convey in this painting of the adjournment of the Convention of 1836?**

now evident that a quorum will be formed tomorrow. Gen'l Houston's arrival has created more sensation than that of any other man. He is evidently the people's man, and seems to take pains to ingratiate himself with everybody . . .

Wednesday, March 2, 1836

The morning clear cold, but the cold somewhat moderated . . .

Mr. Childress from the committee reported a Declaration of Independence, which he read. It was received by the house . . . and unanimously adopted in less than one hour from its first and only reading. It underwent no [changes] . . . The only speech made upon it was a [short address] . . . by General Sam Houston . . .

A committee of one member from each municipality was appointed to draft a constitution. They subdivided themselves into three committees, on the executive, legislative, and judicial branches; Zavala chairman on the executive.

An express was this evening received from Col. Travis, stating that on the 25th a

demonstration was made on the Alamo by a party of Mexicans of about 300 . . . It is believed the Alamo is safe.

Sunday, March 6, 1836

This morning, while at breakfast, a dispatch was received from Travis, dated Alamo, March 3, 1836. The members of the Convention and the citizens all crowded into the Convention room to hear it read . . .

A great many persons are . . . preparing to start to the [scenes of fighting]. In the afternoon Houston left, accompanied by his staff . . . The town has been [in a bustle all day], but is now quiet enough.

Wednesday, March 16, 1836

. . . [After supper the delegates met again and] proceeded to business. The constitution not being quite ready, they adjourned until 10 o'clock. They met at that hour and went to work. At 12 [a.m.] the constitution was finally adopted. A [law] organizing a provisional government was then adopted, consisting of president and vice-president . . . with most of the powers conferred by the Constitution on the president and congress.

. . . an election was held [immediately]. David G. Burnet and Samuel P. Carson were nominated for president. Burnet was elected by a majority of seven. Lorenzo de Zavala was then nominated for vice president by Robert Potter; no opposition. He was elected by a unanimous vote . . .

Frequent alarms were brought in during the night. Spies and patrols were ordered out; much excitement.

Ad Interim Government Officers

President	David G. Burnet
Vice President	Lorenzo de Zavala
Secretary of State	Samuel P. Carson
Secretary of Treasury	Bailey Hardeman
Secretary of War	Thomas J. Rusk
Secretary of Navy	Robert Potter
Attorney General	David Thomas
Commander of the Army	Sam Houston

TAKS PRACTICE

Making Inferences With the threat of Mexican troops in Texas making elections impossible, the first officials to serve under the new constitution were elected by the members of the Convention of 1836, rather than by the general public. *How does the list of government offices reflect the fact that Texans believed their new state to be in danger?*

Santa Anna Advances

On March 17 the convention adjourned. Two days earlier, reports had been received that the Alamo had fallen. A messenger arrived on March 17 and reported that Santa Anna's army

People of Texas

George C. Childress 1804-1841

Childress was born in Nashville, Tennessee, where he also practiced law and edited the *Nashville Banner.* He made his first trip to Texas in 1834 to visit his uncle, but after raising money and volunteers in Tennessee for the Texas army, he decided to move to Texas permanently.

Childress was an elected representative of Milam Municipality at the Convention of 1836. He introduced a resolution authorizing a committee of five members to draft a declaration of independence. He was appointed chairman of the committee and is recognized as the primary author of the declaration. Following the convention, Childress was sent to Washington, D.C., as a diplomatic agent of the Republic of Texas.

was marching toward Washington-on-the-Brazos. William F. Gray wrote in his diary that, after the convention adjourned, the members scattered "in all directions, with haste and in confusion." General panic seemed to spread throughout central Texas.

President Burnet and his cabinet immediately left Washington-on-the-Brazos and headed southeast. They established a government at Harrisburg, a small town that today is part of Houston. A few weeks later, as Santa Anna's army approached, the Texas government again was forced to flee, this time to Galveston. The war was underway, and the future looked bleak for the new Republic of Texas.

✓ Reading Check **Explaining** Why was the ad interim government forced to flee so many times?

SECTION 3 ASSESSMENT

Checking for Understanding

1. **Using Key Terms** Define petition, executive, legislative, judicial, civil rights, and ad interim.
2. **Reviewing Facts** Who were the two native Texans that attended the Convention of 1836?

Reviewing Themes

3. **Civic Rights and Responsibilities** What were some of the key points of the Texas Declaration of Independence adopted by the Convention of 1836?

Organizing to Learn

4. **Sequencing** Create a time line and arrange the following events in the correct sequence.

├────┼────┼────┼────┤

a. Declaration of Independence was unanimously adopted.
b. Lorenzo de Zavala was elected vice president.
c. Convention receives a dispatch about the Alamo from Travis.
d. General Houston arrived at the convention.

Critical Thinking

5. **Making Comparisons** Use the information in this section to name and describe some of the similarities between the Texas Constitution of 1836 and the United States Constitution.

TAKS PRACTICE

Drawing Inferences What did the Texas constitution say about African Americans? Knowing this information, how do you think the African Americans felt about their position in the area?

Chapter Summary

Road to Independence

1835

★ Texas colonists and Mexican troops fight at Gonzales on October 2.

• Texans form the Consultation in San Felipe on November 3 to discuss Santa Anna's rule.

• The Consultation discusses independence, adopts the Declaration of the People, forms a provisional government, and establishes a regular army.

★ Texans capture the Alamo from Mexican forces on December 9.

• The general council of the provisional government calls for a new convention to be held in March 1836.

1836

★ Santa Anna arrives with Mexican troops in San Antonio on February 23.

• The convention begins in Washington-on-the-Brazos on March 1.

★ The convention adopts a Declaration of Independence from Mexico on March 2.

★ The convention approves the Texas Constitution on March 16 and selects temporary officers for the government.

• The convention adjourns on March 17.

• Santa Anna's army advances toward Harrisburg.

Reviewing Key Terms

Number your paper from 1 to 8. Next to each number, write the term from the list below that best completes the sentence.

siege	regular army	petition
executive	municipality	legislative
ad interim	veto	

1. The president decided to _____ the new land bill.

2. The _____ branch of government made new laws.

3. The Texans chose to lay _____ to the city of San Antonio.

4. The new constitution established a strong _____ branch, with a president elected to a two-year term of office.

5. The citizens of the _____ voted to elect a new city council.

6. Sam Houston was chosen as commander of the _____.

7. Texans wanted the right to _____ their government if they believed they had a grievance against it.

8. Officers of the government were appointed on an _____ basis until elections could be held.

Reviewing Key Facts

9. List three ways in which Texans tried to protect themselves against the arrival of General Cós and his troops in 1835.

10. Name two African Americans and two Tejanos who fought for Texas independence.

11. Explain why the capture of San Antonio was an important victory for Texas.

12. Cite reasons why Texas was almost without a government during the early months of 1836.

13. Describe the document read and adopted by the Convention of 1836 on March 2.

14. Identify the author of the Texas Declaration of Independence.

Critical Thinking

15. **Making Inferences** What did the Battle of Gonzales demonstrate about Texas colonists?

16. **Analyzing Information** Why could it be said that during 1835 Texans were talking peacefully but acting warlike?

Old San Antonio Road

0 mi. 100
0 km 100
Albers Conic Equal—Area projection

 Geography and History Activity

17. Study the map above. In two or three sentences describe the relative location of San Antonio. Why were so many battles fought near this important city?

Practicing Skills

Evaluating a Web Site *A Web site can provide information about a variety of topics. However, it is important to consider the accuracy of the source and content. Visit the official Web site of the State of Texas (www.state.tx.us) and answer the following questions.*

18. Are the links up to date and current?

19. Do the links provide useful and accurate information?

20. Is the design appealing?

21. Is the information easy to access? Is it properly labeled?

You might also want to compare the State of Texas Web site with another state's Web site.

 Building Technology Skills

22. **Recognizing People** Visit the Web site **www.lsjunction.com** and click on **"People"** under the **Archives** section. Examine the list that appears. How many of the individuals do you know something about? Record what you know, and then click on each individual's name to learn more.

TEXAS HISTORY *Online*

Self-Check Quiz
Visit the texans.glencoe.com Web site and click on **Chapter 9—Self-Check Quizzes** to prepare for the chapter test.

 Portfolio/TAKS Writing Activity

23. **Writing Letters With a Point of View** Imagine that you are a delegate to the Convention of 1836. Write a letter describing the actions at the Convention. Explain how you would have voted on key issues.

Cooperative Learning Activity

24. **Debating Issues** Read the following debate position statement: *The Texas Revolution could not have been avoided.* Form two teams of two members each. Team A will argue for the statement; Team B will argue against the statement. The first speaker on Team A will make a three-minute speech for the statement. A speaker from Team B will make a three-minute speech against it. The second speaker from Team A will answer the arguments of Team B. The second speaker from Team B will answer the arguments of Team A.

The Princeton Review
TAKS PRACTICE

Use information from this chapter to answer the question below.

The Texas Constitution stated that

A San Antonio would become the temporary capital of the Republic of Texas.

B Sam Houston was to be the first president of the Republic of Texas.

C free African Americans had to petition the legislature to remain in Texas.

D all citizens of Texas became citizens of the United States.

Test-Taking Tip:

A statement can be incorrect because just one or two words make it incorrect. In order to spot the details that make the statement incorrect, read slowly and then ask yourself if the statement is true.

The Alamo and Goliad

Why It Matters

The Texans' courageous defense of the Alamo cost Santa Anna high casualties and upset his plans. The Texas forces used the opportunity to enlist volunteers and gather supplies. The loss of friends and relatives at the Alamo and Goliad filled the Texans with determination.

The Impact Today

The site of the Alamo is now a shrine in honor of the defenders. People from all over the world visit the site to honor the memory of those who fought and died for the cause of Texan independence. The Alamo has become a symbol of courage in the face of overwhelming difficulties.

1836
- ★ February 23, Santa Anna bombarded the Alamo
- ★ March 6, the Alamo fell
- ★ March 20, Fannin's army surrendered to General Urrea
- ★ March 27, 350 Texas troops executed at Goliad

Texas

United States   1835   1836

World

1835
- • Halley's Comet reappeared
- • Hans Christian Andersen published first of 168 stories

1836
- • Betsy Ross—at one time given credit by some for making the first American flag—died

Remember the Alamo *by F.C. Yohn. The Battle of the Alamo has been a popular theme with painters.*

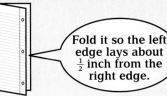

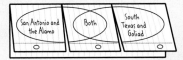
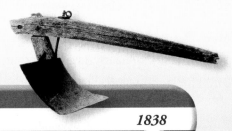

1837   *1838*

1837
• *Revolts took place in upper and lower Canada over constitution*

• *First Canadian railroad opened*

1837
• *Gag Rule prohibited discussion of abolitionist petitions in Congress*

1838
• *John Deere developed first steel plow*

TEXAS HISTORY Online

Chapter Overview
Visit the texans.glencoe.com Web site and click on **Chapter 10—Chapter Overviews** to preview chapter information

A Clash of Armies

Guide to Reading

Main Idea
The Texas army scattered and divided as Santa Anna moved into Texas in early 1836.

Key Term
recruit

Reading Strategy
Organizing Information Complete a chart like the one shown here by filling in the information about volunteers in the Texas army.

Reasons for Volunteering	
Occupations	
Nationalities	

Read to Learn
• what strengths and weaknesses existed in the Texas army.
• which individuals played key roles in defending the Alamo.

Section Theme
Geography and History Some Texans began to gather at the Alamo to face Santa Anna's army.

Preview of Events

♦1836 ——————————————————————————————————————— ♦1837

January 17
Houston sends Bowie to the Alamo

February 3
William Travis joins the Alamo volunteers

February 8
David Crockett arrives at the Alamo

Volunteer Texan soldier

A
Texas Story

Andrew Boyle, an Irish immigrant, volunteered for service at Goliad. "Colonels Bowie and Crockett, then in command of the Alamo, sent a courier to Colonel Fannin . . . asking for reinforcements. A hundred men were at once detailed, and had crossed the San Antonio River, . . . when they were recalled on account of a report of the advance of the Mexican army under General Urrea, toward San Patricio."
—*I Survived the Goliad Massacre,* by Andrew A. Boyle

A Missed Opportunity

When General Cós surrendered San Antonio to the Texans in December 1835, Santa Anna was furious. Santa Anna was determined to punish the Anglo rebels in Texas and those Tejanos who had defied his government. Because of the distance between Texas and Mexico City, however, it would be some time before Santa Anna would be able to get to Texas. The Texans did not use the time

wisely, however. During the first two months of 1836, Texas drifted without strong leadership toward an extremely critical period. Instead of organizing and training, most of the volunteer soldiers who had captured San Antonio returned home. The Texas army became smaller and smaller.

Most of those who remained in the army were new arrivals from the United States. They came to Texas for a variety of reasons. Some arrived to obtain the land promised by the Texas government. Some came because of their strong belief in liberty. Others were drawn by the spirit of adventure.

Some of the volunteers, such as former U.S. Congressman **David Crockett** of Tennessee, were already well-known public figures. Many others who joined the struggle were unknown farmers, hunters, and clerks who were part of the westward movement. They represented various nations, including England, Wales, Ireland, Scotland, and Germany.

Texas Forces Are Divided

The Texan forces were badly divided at the end of 1835. No single leader was in control. General Sam Houston, who was made commander of the regular Texas army and the volunteers, attempted to bring the various military units together but met with little success. Many volunteers refused to recognize General Houston's

authority. Some volunteers were used to electing their own commanding officers. In addition, the provisional government headed by Governor Smith gave the same special assignment to several commanders. As an example, three men—**Colonel Frank W. Johnson, Dr. James Grant,** and **Colonel James W. Fannin**—were authorized to attack the Mexican city of **Matamoros,** near the mouth of the Rio Grande.

The Texan forces remained scattered. About 100 men were still in San Antonio under the command of **Colonel James C. Neill.** Johnson and Grant each had 50 men near **San Patricio.** Fannin had 400 men at **Goliad.** Another force was slowly being assembled at Gonzales. Little communication or coordination existed among these scattered units.

Picturing History

David Crockett became famous for a saying that he adopted and made popular: "Be always sure you're right—then go a-head!" How did Crockett follow his own advice? Do you agree with this saying?

People of Texas

James Fannin 1804–1836

James Walker Fannin arrived in Texas in 1834 and very soon became involved with the Texas cause for independence. He participated in the Battle of Gonzales and, along with Jim Bowie, led Texas forces in the Battle of Concepción.

In 1836 he was put in charge of 400 troops at Goliad. Used to the discipline of a regular army, he disliked leading volunteers and was seen as arrogant by many of his men.

General Houston ordered Fannin to retreat to Victoria, but Fannin delayed and found himself surrounded by Mexican forces at the Battle of Coleto. He and his men surrendered and were imprisoned inside the presidio at Goliad.

On March 27, 1836, by order of Santa Anna, he and his men were put to death. "Remember Goliad" became a Texas battle cry.

Santa Anna Moves North

While the Texans remained scattered and divided, General Santa Anna moved his army of some 6,000 soldiers northward. Part of the Mexican army had been **recruited,** or enlisted, quickly. Most of the new troops were untrained and undisciplined. Many of them were poorly clothed and fed. Many had to fight with old muskets and poor equipment and were forced to fight against their will.

Most Texans expected that Santa Anna would wait until the spring of 1836 to move northward so there would be grass for his horses and mules. Santa Anna, however, raised an army and marched it several hundred miles in the winter. He received information about the movement of the Texan troops from some of the Mexican ranchers in South Texas. He hoped to surprise the Texans and end the rebellion against his authority. As Santa Anna marched northward, he divided his 6,000 troops into two main columns. Under his personal command, the larger column crossed the Rio Grande at Paso de Francia (near modern-day Eagle Pass) and headed toward San Antonio. The other column, commanded by **General José Urrea** (oo•REE•ah), crossed the Rio Grande at Matamoros and moved along the Gulf Coast toward Goliad.

TEXAS HISTORY Online

Student Web Activity Visit the texans.glencoe.com Web site and click on **Chapter 10—Student Web Activity** to learn more about the defenders of the Alamo.

✓**Reading Check** **Identifying** What were three major reasons Texas troops were not well prepared for Santa Anna?

Texans Occupy the Alamo

Meanwhile, the Texan troops at San Antonio occupied the abandoned Mission San Antonio de Valero. Built in 1718, the old mission had once housed a Spanish colonial company from Alamo de Parras in Mexico. As a result, most people referred to the building as the Alamo.

Colonel Neill had 104 soldiers in the Alamo. In January, he complained to the General Council that he needed guns and troops. On January 17, 1836, General Houston ordered **Colonel James Bowie** and about 25 Texans in Goliad to go to the Alamo. Bowie was to inspect the situation there and decide whether or not to abandon the post.

Bowie was already a well-known figure in the Southwest. He had gained a reputation as a formidable fighter after winning a struggle using an "overly-large" knife. The blade was actually the creation of his brother, but it was made famous by Jim Bowie. Blacksmiths received many orders to copy the famous Bowie Knife.

Bowie came to Texas in 1828 where he searched for a Spanish mine on the San Sabá River. He met Stephen F. Austin and began buying and selling land. It is reported that his activities in this business eventually irritated Austin, however. Like many adventurers of the time, Bowie took chances, skirted the law, and made as many enemies as he did friends. After the Battle of Concepción, diarist Noah Smithwick wrote:

> ❝His voice is still ringing in my old deaf ears as he repeatedly admonished us. Keep under cover boys and reserve your fire; we haven't a man to spare.❞

In 1831, Bowie gained property and position with his marriage to Ursula María de Veramendi, the daughter of the vice governor of Coahuila y Tejas.

Travis Arrives at the Alamo

On February 3, **Lieutenant Colonel William B. Travis** of the regular Texas army and about 30 soldiers from San Felipe joined the Alamo garrison. Although Travis had been a volunteer at other skirmishes in Texas, he missed the action at Gonzales. In 1835 Travis joined the regular army as a lieutenant colonel of the cavalry. He had been ordered by Governor Henry Smith to reinforce Colonel Neill and his men. Several days later

Lt. Colonel William B. Travis

David Crockett and 12 more volunteers arrived. Crockett was a frontier legend. A skilled sharpshooter, hunter, and storyteller, David Crockett claimed to have killed more than 100 bears in less than a year. He often dressed in colorful frontier clothing that included a coonskin cap. He served as a colonel in the Tennessee militia and as a representative in the Tennessee legislature and the United States Congress. He was 50 years old when he came to Texas. "I would rather be in my present situation than to be elected to a seat in Congress for life," he wrote his daughter in January 1836. Although offered a command in the regular army by Travis, Crockett preferred to serve as a private among the Alamo volunteers.

Some Tejanos played an active part in the uprisings—first against Spain and then Mexico. These Tejanos risked more than just their lives. They fought for freedom at the price of their lands, their homes, and their families. They had, at times, more to lose than did the Anglo Americans or Europeans seeking adventure,

Picturing **History**

William B. Travis (*left*) and Jim Bowie (*right*) both commanded troops at the Alamo, Travis as a lieutenant colonel. What impressions does the engraving at right convey about Bowie?

land, or liberty. Many Tejanos considered Santa Anna a dictator, especially because he did not follow the Constitution of 1824 that guaranteed a more democratic government for Mexico.

At least nine Tejanos helped defend the Alamo. They were Brigido Guerrero (geh•REH•roh), Juan Abamillo (ah•bah•MEE•yoh), Juan Antonio Badillo (bah•DEE•yoh), Carlos Espalier (ehs•pahl•YEHR), Gregorio Esparza, Toribio Domingo Losoya, Antonio Fuentes (FWEN•tehs), Damasio Jiménez (hee•MEN•ehs), and Andrés Nava. Captain Juan Seguín was at the Alamo when Santa Anna's army arrived, but he was sent out to raise more volunteers.

In early February, Colonel Neill left the Alamo because of family illness. Bowie was chosen commander of the volunteers in San Antonio. Travis became commander of the regular army soldiers. The election of Bowie to lead the volunteers did not mean that the men did not like or respect Travis. For many years there had been an ongoing dispute between regular and volunteer soldiers. The volunteers simply did not want to take orders from a regular officer. For a while, the two men served as joint commanders of the garrison. On February 23, however, Bowie became ill and passed command of the Alamo to Travis.

A Shared Past...

"This is the kind of mess I like to have my spoon in," was David Crockett's explanation of why he was in Texas. Crockett's reason for being in Texas also had a great deal to do with politics in the United States. President Andrew Jackson's supporters had formed the Democratic Party. Others formed the Whig Party to oppose Jackson. Crockett first supported Jackson and then switched to the Whig Party. Jackson used his influence to defeat Crockett when he ran for reelection to Congress. Crockett looked upon Texas as a place to get a fresh start after his congressional defeat.

Travis accepted the theory that Santa Anna would not enter Texas until late March, April, or May. In early February, Juan Seguín, who commanded a party of scouts for the Texan army, reported that Santa Anna's army had crossed the Rio Grande. Despite this report, Travis continued to believe that he would have more time.

✔ **Reading Check** **Explaining** Why did some Tejanos join the colonists' fight against Santa Anna?

SECTION 1 ASSESSMENT

Checking for Understanding

1. **Using Key Terms** Use the word recruit in a sentence about the Mexican army.
2. **Reviewing Facts** How did the Alamo get its name?

Reviewing Themes

3. **Geography and History** Why did many Texans, including Lieutenant Colonel William B. Travis, believe Santa Anna would wait until spring to move northward?

Organizing to Learn

4. **Creating Charts** Create a chart like the one shown here and mark an X in the appropriate column for either James Bowie or David Crockett.

	James Bowie	David Crockett
Famous for his knife		
Member of the Tennessee legislature		
Wore a coonskin cap		
Ordered from Goliad to the Alamo		

Critical Thinking

5. **Analyzing Information** While at the Alamo, David Crockett wrote in a letter, "I would rather be in my present situation than to be elected to a seat in Congress for life." What does this say about Crockett's heroism and sense of adventure?

TAKS PRACTICE

Drawing Inferences How did the lack of communication and coordination among Texas army units affect their preparations for Santa Anna's advance?

Texas LITERATURE

Gary Clifton Wisler

Gary Clifton Wisler's writing career began with the encouragement of his students. His first novel, *My Brother, the Wind,* was nominated for the 1980 American Book Award. Since then he has published 72 books, and his work has been translated into five foreign languages. Wisler currently lives in Plano, Texas.

Reading to Discover

As you read this excerpt, imagine how you would feel knowing that enemy forces of a thousand or more were on their way to the area where you live.

Reader's Dictionary

resolution: a formal statement of a decision or expression of opinion put before or adopted by a governmental assembly

Tejanos: those of Mexican descent living in Texas

cavalry: troops trained to fight on horseback

All for Texas
by GARY CLIFTON WISLER

Jefferson and Miguel worry about the impact of war on their families.

. . . "Yes, I know it seems odd," he said, laughing. "Do you know that, here in Goliad, a **resolution** was passed for an independent Texas? This happened, but then some of the old people said we should not break away. Many **Tejanos** would not join a rebellion against their mother country. Some continued to feel that way. My father is a man of the law—a judge, you would call him. Because he is not a supporter of Santa Anna he is no longer."

"Where [is he]?" I asked.

"It's difficult to know," Miguel said, staring southward. "In January he left to purchase a bull. We have no letters from him. Maybe he is arrested. Who can say?"

"My pa's supposed to be at the fort," I said, sighing. "I guess we both wonder, huh?"

"I don't think this will be a good time for either of us, amigo. A thousand **cavalry**? These are the best soldiers in all of Mexico. Too many, I think, for Fannin. Too many, perhaps, for all of Texas to fight.". . .

I finally faded off into a light sleep, but a thousand Mexican horsemen rode through my dreams, and I found no peace. Not long after dawn, . . . [a] handful of riders

dressed in every kind of outfit imaginable galloped toward us, led by a young girl.

Among the other riders was a trio of red-haired fellows—and Pa!

"Jefferson, you've gone and grown old on me," he declared.

"I'm not so old," I said, handing over Ma's letters. "We've missed you past measuring."

"As I have you, son," he declared as he opened the first letter.

ANALYZING LITERATURE

Recall and Interpret Why are Jefferson and Miguel worried about their fathers?

Interdisciplinary Activity

Writing Letters Jefferson was carrying letters from his mother to his father. Write a letter from Jefferson's mother explaining what life is like at home while her husband is at war.

Texans Defend the Alamo

Guide to Reading

Main Idea
The Texans at the Alamo fought bravely but were ultimately defeated by Santa Anna's army.

Key Terms
fortify
bombard

Reading Strategy
Classifying Information As you read this section, complete a chart like the one shown here listing the strengths and weaknesses of the Alamo.

Strengths	Weaknesses

Read to Learn
- what events occurred at the Alamo.
- how events at the Alamo helped to unite Texans in their struggle for independence.

Section Theme
Individual Action The sacrifices of those at the Alamo helped the fight for independence.

Preview of Events

♦1836 — ♦1837

February 23
Santa Anna's army arrives in San Antonio

February 24
Travis sends urgent plea for help

March 6
Battle of the Alamo; almost all defenders are killed

Mexican officer

A
Texas Story

Most of Colonel Fannin's men were captured as they withdrew from Goliad. Andrew Boyle wrote, "[A]t the hospital, the Mexican officers seemed kindly disposed to me . . . Mr. Brooks, aide to Colonel Fannin, was there. I found him completely ignorant of what was going on. Upon being informed, he said, 'I suppose it will be our turn next.' In less than five minutes [he was] carried out, cot and all, placed in the street, and there shot."

In Defense of the Alamo

When Bowie arrived at the Alamo, he knew there were too few soldiers. He and Travis, however, believed that holding the Alamo was vital to the fate of Texas. They began to strengthen its defenses.

Travis was surprised on February 23, when the advance wing of Santa Anna's army arrived at San Antonio. The Texans barely made it inside the walls of the Alamo before the Mexican cavalry roared into the town.

In some ways, the Texans had a good defensive position. The walls of the old mission were 2 to 3 feet thick and 12 feet high. Twenty-one cannons fortified, or strengthened, the mission, including one powerful 18-pounder. Travis placed it at a southwest angle so his troops could command movements in the town. Supplies of beef and corn were high, and sufficient water was available. The Texans were well provisioned.

Serious weaknesses, however, hurt the Alamo's defense. The wall surrounding the main plaza of the old mission was incomplete—there was a gap between the south wall and the old chapel on the southeast. Although a fence of sticks and dirt was built to close this gap, it remained the weakest point in the defense. Also, the mission was too large for Travis to defend with the few troops he had. The walls enclosed nearly three acres of land, and Travis had fewer than 200 men. To defend the Alamo successfully, a much larger army was necessary.

Travis Declares "Victory or Death"

Travis was determined to hold the Alamo. The mission had come to symbolize to many of the defenders the achievements that had been so dearly won in the struggle for independence. Travis wrote several messages to the people of Texas and the United States, asking them to answer his call for assistance. His letter of

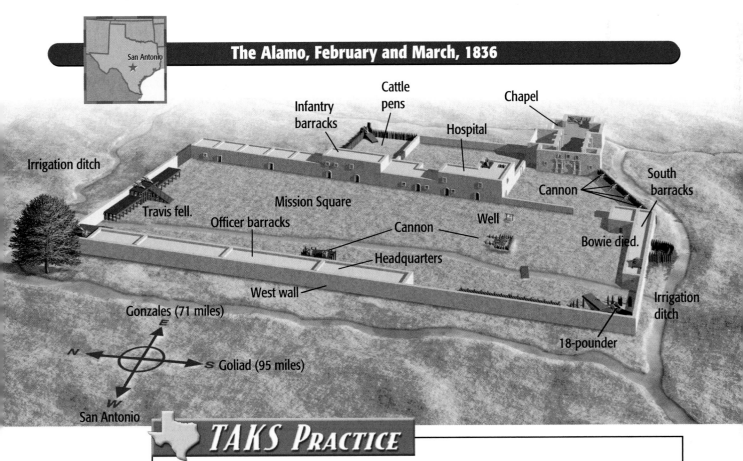

The Alamo, February and March, 1836

San Antonio

Irrigation ditch

Infantry barracks

Cattle pens

Hospital

Chapel

Cannon

South barracks

Mission Square

Travis fell.

Officer barracks

Cannon

Well

Headquarters

Bowie died.

West wall

Irrigation ditch

Gonzales (71 miles)

Goliad (95 miles)

18-pounder

San Antonio

TAKS PRACTICE

This model details the layout of the Alamo as it existed during the Battle of the Alamo in 1836. Note where some of the cannons were placed and which areas seemed most heavily defended. Models are often used by present-day military commanders in order to consider areas of strength and weakness and to develop strategy. **Analyzing** Review the text and study this model carefully. In your opinion, what areas of the Alamo were easiest to attack and which were easiest to defend?

February 24, 1836, is one of the finest statements of courage in American history. He knew the odds were clearly against him. He wrote:

Commandancy of the Alamo
Béxar, Feby. 24th, 1836

To the People of Texas & all
Americans in the world—Fellow
Citizens & compatriots—

I am besieged by a thousand or more
of the Mexicans under Santa Anna—
I have sustained a continual
Bombardment & cannonade for 24
hours & have not lost a man—The
enemy has demanded a surrender at
discretion, otherwise, the garrison are
to be put to the sword, if the fort is
taken—I have answered the demand
with a cannon shot, & our flag still
waves proudly from the walls—I shall
never surrender or retreat. Then, I
call on you in the name of Liberty, of
patriotism & everything dear to the
American character, to come to our
aid, with all dispatch—The enemy is
receiving reinforcements daily & will
no doubt increase to three or four
thousand in four or five days. If this
call is neglected, I am determined to
sustain myself as long as possible &
die like a soldier who never forgets
what is due to his own honor & that
of his country—Victory or Death!

William Barret Travis
Lt. Col. comdt.

P.S. The Lord is on our side—When
the enemy appeared in sight we had
not three bushels of corn—We have
since found in deserted houses 80 or
90 bushels, & got into the walls 20 or
30 head of Beeves [cattle]—

The outside help brought by the letters did not arrive in time. Meanwhile, Texan military forces were still poorly organized and spread out. Travis hoped that Fannin would move with his army from Goliad, but Fannin lacked enough wagons to move all of his supplies. On March 1, Travis received 32 volunteer reinforcements from Gonzales. Led by **Albert Martin** and **George C. Kimball,** they made their way into the Alamo while it was still dark.

Santa Anna made his headquarters at the San Fernando church, which faced eastward toward the Alamo. He ordered the red flag of "no quarter" to be flown, meaning that he did not intend to take any prisoners in the coming battle.

On March 3, Travis wrote his last appeal for help at the Alamo. It was sent by messenger to the president of the Convention of 1836, which was meeting at **Washington-on-the-Brazos.** Travis described the fighting that had already taken place and repeated his request for assistance. He warned that "the power of Santa Anna is to be met here, or in the colonies; we had better meet them here than to suffer a war of devastation to rage in our settlements." He ended with the statement that he and his troops were determined to hold the Alamo. Although no troops were sent, James Bonham, the messenger, returned knowing he would face his death.

Reading Check **Evaluating** Why didn't Travis receive much response from his letters?

A Shared Past...

Some Whigs (a national political party) in the United States thought the Texas Revolution was a conspiracy of slaveowners to extend slavery. They disapproved of Americans volunteering to fight in the revolution. They wondered whether the volunteers were violating the Neutrality Act of 1818, which did not allow Americans to invade a country with which the United States was at peace. In December 1835, a federal judge in New York said that the volunteers going to Texas were not violating the Neutrality Act.

History *Through Art*

Dawn at the Alamo by H.A. McArdle, 1876–1883
Although Texans fought bravely, the Alamo fell to Santa
Anna and his forces on March 6, 1836. How accurate
does the artist's representation seem?

Facing Certain Death

As Mexican armies encircled the Alamo, it became apparent to Travis that he had no chance for victory. On the afternoon of March 3, Travis explained to his troops that remaining in the Alamo meant certain death. According to legend, Travis took his sword and drew a line on the ground. All those who wished to stay and defend the Alamo were asked to cross over the line. According to the story, all but one of the men crossed over the line.

The one man who supposedly did not cross the line was Louis "Moses" Rose, a native of France who had come to Texas in 1826. He was a veteran of the Napoleonic wars and saw no need to sacrifice his life for a hopeless cause. It is not important whether or not Travis drew the line on the ground. It is not important whether or not one man chose to leave the Alamo. Nearly 200 men—mostly volunteers—were free to leave the Alamo, but they decided to stay and fight for a cause in which they believed.

The defenders of the Alamo held the garrison against heavy odds. Since February 23, Mexican cannons had **bombarded,** or fired upon, the Alamo daily. The Texans, with their long-range Kentucky rifles, were able to shoot Mexican troops at great distance. Despite this, it was clear Santa Anna had most of the advantages.

Texan Troops Give Ground

On the night of March 5, 1836, Santa Anna's troops were in place for battle. Santa Anna ordered the attack on the Alamo to begin at dawn. At 5:30 on the morning of March 6, the battle began. Some sources estimate that 1,800 Mexican troops took part in this final assault. Three columns of infantry moved forward to attack at three different points. Mexican buglers played the notes of "El Degüello" (ehl deh•GWAY•yoh), an ancient chant indicating that no mercy would be shown.

The Texans were ready, and the first wave of Mexican attackers was riddled by cannon and rifle fire. A second wave met the same fate. The Texan defenders put up a stubborn fight, but the third assault of Mexican troops successfully pushed back the Texans and allowed Santa Anna's men to storm over the walls. The fighting within the compound was especially fierce as rifles gave way to knives and clubs. Although the Mexican forces suffered heavy casualties scaling the walls, they continued to attack until the whole garrison was overpowered. By 7:00 on the morning of March 6, the battle for the Alamo was over.

TWO VIEWPOINTS

The Death of Davy Crockett

Historians today are still debating details about the death of legendary hero, Davy Crockett. Read the two views below and then answer the question.

A Newspaper Article Describes a Hero's Death

From the [beginning] to its close, the storming lasted less than an hour. Major Evans, master of ordnance, was killed when in the act of setting fire to the powder magazine, agreeably to the previous orders from Travis. The end of David Crocket [sic] . . . was as glorious as his career through life had been useful . . . The countenance of Crockett was unchanged: he had in death that freshness of hue, which his exercise of pursuing the beasts of the forest and the prairie imparted to him. Texas places him, exultingly, amongst the martyrs of the cause.
—A newspaper account from after the Alamo's fall

A Mexican Army Officer Claims Crockett Surrendered

Seven men survived . . . and . . . were brought [by General Castrillón] before Santa Anna. Among them was . . . the naturalist David Crockett . . . who had undertaken to explore the country and who, finding himself in Béxar at the very moment of surprise, had taken refuge in the Alamo, fearing that his status as a foreigner might not be respected. Santa Anna answered Castrillón's intervention [on] Crockett's behalf with . . . indignation and, addressing himself to the [troops closest to him], ordered his execution.
—From the de la Peña diary, published 1975

Learning From History

What are the strengths and weaknesses of eyewitness testimony?

It is difficult to determine exactly how many people were killed at the Alamo—after the fighting ended, the bodies of the defenders were burned. Santa Anna reported that 600 Texans were killed in the battle. Historians believe that about 200 defenders died. Bowie, Travis, and Crockett were among those killed. A Mexican officer, **Colonel Enrique de la Peña** (ehn•REE•kay day lah PEH•nyah), wrote that Crockett survived the battle. According to de la Peña, Santa Anna ordered the immediate execution of Crockett and six others.

Mexican losses in the battle also are difficult to determine. Santa Anna originally claimed that he lost only 70 men. Many Texans believe that more than 1,000 Mexicans were either killed or wounded. Most historians believe this figure is too high. They estimate 600. Even so, Santa Anna paid heavily for the capture of the Alamo.

✓**Reading Check** **Examining** Why were Travis's troops unsuccessful at the Alamo?

A Battle Cry for Victory

Although Santa Anna ordered that all defenders of the Alamo be put to death, several people did survive. Santa Anna released the women and children who had been in the Alamo during the battle. Among these were the wives of three soldiers—Ana Salazar de Esparza, wife of Gregorio Esparza; Juana Navarro de Alsbury, whose husband was with Houston's army; and Susanna Dickinson, wife of an officer in the Alamo. She, her daughter Angelina, and Joe Travis, an enslaved person held by William Travis, were allowed to leave San Antonio and carry word of the disaster to the Texans at Gonzales. Andrea Castañon Villanueva (Señora Candelaria), another Tejano woman, had nursed James Bowie.

People of Texas

Andrea C. Villanueva 1785–1899

Andrea Castañon Villanueva (Señora Candelaria) survived the Alamo along with 12 other women and children.

When she was about 25, she moved to San Antonio and married Candelario Villanueva. Señora Candelaria was a caring woman who often nursed the sick, helped the poor, and gave money to strangers. Over a lifetime, she adopted 22 orphans and raised them along with her 4 children.

Historians are in disagreement over her claim that she was actually at the Alamo, but most believe her. In spite of the difference of opinion, the Texas legislature gave Señora Candelaria a pension for being an Alamo survivor. She lived to be 113.

At least one member of the garrison itself, Brigido Guerrero of San Antonio, survived the battle. He convinced Santa Anna that he had been a prisoner of the Texans and had been forced to fight against his will.

Some historians believe that Texas would not have won its independence without the Battle of the Alamo. Santa Anna lost many professional soldiers in the fighting and may have been delayed because of it. In addition, the courage of Travis and his forces made Texans more determined than ever to win their independence. The battle also encouraged citizens of the U.S. to help Texans in their struggle for freedom. Santa Anna hoped the fall of the Alamo would convince other Texans that it was useless to resist his armies. Instead, the heroism of those in the Alamo inspired other Texans to carry on the struggle. "Remember the Alamo!" became the battle cry of Houston's army.

 Reading Check **Examining** How did the battle at the Alamo aid the ultimate independence of Texas?

SECTION 2 ASSESSMENT

Checking for Understanding

1. **Using Key Terms** What is a synonym for fortified? What is a synonym for bombard?
2. **Reviewing Facts** What did Santa Anna's red flag of "no quarter" mean?

Reviewing Themes

3. **Individual Action** Why did most volunteers stay to defend the Alamo when they knew it meant almost certain death?

Organizing to Learn

4. **Identifying Points of View** Reread the text about the battle at the Alamo. Then create a chart like the one shown, listing the losses at the Alamo.

According to...	Mexico's Losses	Texas's Losses
Santa Anna		
Historians		
Texans		Not given

Critical Thinking

5. **Explaining** Santa Anna hoped that the fall of the Alamo would convince Texans that it was useless to resist his armies. What happened instead?

TAKS PRACTICE

Determining the Main Idea Reread and summarize the advantages and disadvantages of the Mexican army at the Battle of the Alamo.

Identifying Central Issues

Why Learn This Skill?

Historical dates, events, and names are easier to understand and remember when they are connected to the main idea in the material. Identifying central issues allows you to grasp the whole picture.

Learning the Skill

To identify central issues, follow these steps:

❶ Read the material and ask, "What is the purpose of this material?"

❷ Ask, "What are the most forceful statements in the material?"

❸ Identify any details that support a larger idea or issue.

❹ Identify the central issue, or main idea.

Practicing the Skill

Read again the following excerpt from William B. Travis's letter asking for reinforcements at the Alamo. Use the questions listed under **Learning the Skill** to identify the central issue.

I am besieged by a thousand or more of the Mexicans under Santa Anna—I have sustained a continual Bombardment & cannonade for 24 hours & have not lost a man—The enemy has demanded a surrender at discretion, otherwise, the garrison are to be put to the sword, if the fort is taken—I have answered the demand with a cannon shot, & our flag still waves proudly from the walls—I shall never surrender or retreat. Then, I call on you in the name of Liberty, of patriotism & everything dear to the

Courtyard of the Alamo

American character, to come to our aid, with all dispatch—The enemy is receiving reinforcements daily & will no doubt increase to three or four thousand in four or five days. If this call is neglected, I am determined to sustain myself as long as possible & die like a soldier who never forgets what is due to his own honor & that of his country—Victory or Death!

TAKS PRACTICE

Identifying Central Issues Read the excerpt entitled "Marriage Bond" in the Primary Source Library on page 689. Use the questions listed under **Learning the Skill** to identify the central issue.

Glencoe's **Skillbuilder Interactive Workbook,** Level 1, provides instruction and practice in key social studies skills.

Defeat in South Texas

Guide to Reading

Main Idea
After Fannin delayed his withdrawal from Goliad, General Urrea's forces overpowered and destroyed the Texas armies.

Key Term
dispatch

Reading Strategy
Organizing Information As you read this section, complete a chart like the one shown here, outlining what happened on each of the following dates.

Date	What Happened
March 13	
March 19	
March 20	
March 27	

Read to Learn
• what factors caused the Texan defeats at the Battle of Coleto and in South Texas.
• about the massacre at Goliad.

Section Theme
Groups and Institutions The Mexican army defeated the Texans at Goliad.

Preview of Events
♦1836   ♦1837

March 19
Fannin withdraws troops from Goliad

March 20
Mexican troops capture Fannin's soldiers

March 27
Mexican troops execute Texas prisoners

Mexican officers

A
Texas Story

Andrew Boyle was captured during the withdrawl from Goliad. "[A]fter the murder of Mr. Brooks, an officer addressed me. He said, 'Make your mind easy, sir, your life is spared.' He had taken my name and description from my sister, Mary, at whose house he had been quartered while [he] occupied San Patricio. She refused all [money] from him, only asked that if I should fall into his hands I be treated kindly." Andrew escaped death because of his sister's kindness.

Urrea Sweeps Northward to Refugio

While the fighting at the Alamo raged, the other unit of the Mexican army under General José Urrea was advancing from Matamoros up through South Texas. Urrea had about 600 soldiers under his command as he moved northward. At San Patricio on February 27, 1836, he destroyed a force of 50 Texans under Frank W. Johnson's command. Only Johnson and 4 others escaped. On March 2, part of Urrea's army defeated about 30 of Dr. James Grant's men at Agua Dulce.

As Urrea advanced, civilians in his path fled. Some of the people at **Refugio** asked Colonel Fannin at Goliad to send  them help. Fannin **dispatched** Captain Amon B. King and 30 soldiers to help them, but just as King arrived at Refugio, part of Urrea's army surrounded the town. King and his men took refuge in the Mission Señora del Refugio and asked Fannin to send more forces.

Fannin sent Colonel William Ward and more than 100 Texans to help King. Ward reached Refugio on March 12. The Texans, however, divided their forces. While Ward and his troops remained in the mission, King led his men on a scouting expedition. His party was stopped by Urrea's forces and most of the men were either killed or captured. Colonel Ward was able to withdraw his troops from Refugio but suffered heavy losses while retreating. The remainder of the force was captured by Urrea's army near **Victoria.** The loss of lives at San Patricio, Refugio, and Victoria was a severe blow to the Texan efforts to halt the Mexican army's drive northward.

Fannin Delays His Departure

The inability of Fannin, the commander of the Texan troops at Goliad, to make a decision and stick to it also hurt the Texas cause. In late February, Fannin had decided to help Travis at the Alamo. However, a shortage of wagons for transporting supplies caused him to return to Goliad. On March 13 Fannin received orders from General Houston to retreat toward Victoria. Houston did not think the Texans were ready to fight the Mexican army. Fannin waited several days hoping to hear the fate of King and Ward. Fannin then lost a skirmish with an advance force of Mexican troops. He finally began his withdrawal on March 19.

Fannin's withdrawal from Goliad was slowed by oxen pulling the heavy cannon. On the afternoon of March 19, he allowed his soldiers to rest and eat. They were about three miles from **Coleto Creek** in an open field. Suddenly, Fannin and the Texans were surrounded by Urrea's troops. Fannin had about 300 men, and Urrea had 450 to 600 men. Fannin assembled his soldiers in a square to meet Urrea's attack. Mexican troops charged three times, but each time they were driven back. During the fighting, 7 Texans were killed and 60 were wounded. Colonel Fannin himself was wounded in the leg.

Both sides spent the night strengthening their positions. The Mexicans had the advantage of being in the nearby woods. The Texans had little cover and no water. Even so, their spirits remained high. Some of them believed that help would arrive from Victoria. When morning came, however, it was Urrea who received reinforcements. At daybreak on March 20, Mexican cannons opened fire on Fannin's army. After a brief exchange of gunfire, Fannin asked General Urrea for the terms of surrender. The officers held a brief discussion, and Fannin signed an agreement of surrender. The **Battle of Coleto** was over.

✓ **Reading Check** **Analyzing** What factors led to Fannin's surrender?

A Shared Past...

Support for the Texas Revolution was strongest in the Southern United States. On November 10, 1835, a meeting was held in Macon, Georgia, to show support for the Texans. The people raised $3,141 to help the cause, and 29 men volunteered to fight in Texas. As they were marching away, Johanna Troutman gave the soldiers a flag she had made. It featured one blue star (the lone star) on a white background with the words "Liberty or Death" below the star. For this, Troutman became known as the Betsy Ross of Texas.

The presidio at Goliad was renamed Fort Defiance by James Fannin in February of 1836 in preparation for the Mexican attack. Do you think the name helped or hurt the Texas cause?

Texans Surrender

There has been much confusion about the terms of surrender. Many Texans believed they were prisoners of war and would be treated fairly by their captors. However, the surrender agreement, now in the Mexican archives, contains no such promise. The document states that the Texans surrendered unconditionally, placing themselves at the mercy of the Mexican commander.

Evidence shows that Urrea assured Fannin that the Texans would be treated fairly, no matter what document was signed. According to several Texan survivors, Mexican officers said that the Texans would soon be released. After the surrender was signed, Fannin and his troops were marched back to Goliad, where they were imprisoned in the old presidio. Other Texans captured in the area were taken to Goliad within the next several days.

Santa Anna's "Cruel Necessity"

Most of the prisoners waited for their release. General Urrea wrote to President Santa Anna, requesting that the lives of the prisoners be spared. In his reply, Santa Anna ordered the immediate execution of the Texans. He feared that if he let the Texans go, they would join others in the rebellion. He also relied on the Mexican law that required the execution of those who took up arms against the government.

On Palm Sunday, March 27, the able-bodied prisoners were divided into three columns and marched out onto the prairie. They believed they were to perform a work detail. Upon a signal, the Mexican soldiers fired at them. Other prisoners who had been wounded and were unable to march were executed later in the morning. A few who pretended to be dead escaped. According to most accounts, Colonel Fannin was the last prisoner to be shot. It is believed that about 350 Texans were executed. General Urrea deeply regretted President Santa Anna's decision. He wrote the following in his diary:

> 66It was painful to me, also, that so many brave men should thus be sacrificed, particularly the much esteemed and fearless Fannin. They doubtlessly surrendered confident that Mexican generosity would not make their surrender useless . . . I used my influence with the general-in-chief to save them, if possible, from being butchered, particularly Fannin. I obtained from His Excellency only a severe reply, repeating his previous order, doubtlessly dictated by cruel necessity.99

Several prisoners, including two physicians and some workers, were not executed because the Mexicans needed their skills. Many of the Mexicans living in Goliad opposed the execution. Some of the Mexican soldiers shot over the heads of the Texans and allowed several to escape. **Señora Francita Alavez,** the wife of a Mexican army officer, helped care for the Texans during their imprisonment. She also helped several Texans avoid execution. The survivors later referred to her as the "Angel of Goliad."

The Lessons of the Alamo and Goliad

By the beginning of April 1836, Santa Anna seemed to have everything going his way. His forces had crushed the defenders of the Alamo and overwhelmed the Texas troops withdrawing from Goliad. Santa Anna concluded from these battles that driving the rest of the rebels out of Texas would be an easy task.

In fact, however, Texans may never have won their independence without the Battle of the Alamo. The battle cost Santa Anna the lives of a considerable number of professional soldiers, and the Mexican general and his troops were delayed for more than two weeks by the fighting. This delay was of great value to the Texan cause.

News of the battle also inspired U.S. citizens to aid the Texans in their fight for freedom. People and money flowed into Texas. Santa Anna had hoped that the fall of the

History *Through Art*

The March to the Massacre by Andrew Houston Although Fannin and his troops expected to be released, Mexican forces executed almost all of the Texans who were imprisoned at Goliad. How did this massacre influence Texas history?

★ Goliad

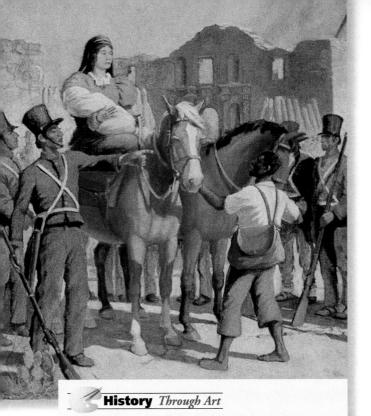

History *Through Art*

Untitled painting by Harry Anthony DeYonng Susanna Dickinson was allowed by Santa Anna to leave the Alamo. She helped to spread news of the Alamo defeat to the other Texas forces. What is the significance of the Battle of the Alamo to the people of Texas?

historian wrote that never did Americans fight more bravely than in Texas, and never did they manage their affairs more poorly. Dividing authority between volunteer groups and a regular army and the ill-fated attempt to capture Matamoros had produced nothing but disaster for the Texans. The fighting in South Texas revealed the lack of cooperation among Texas forces. The defeats at the Alamo and Coleto convinced General Sam Houston that he must not allow his forces to be separated into small groups. The disasters at Coleto, San Patricio, and Agua Dulce showed the folly of trying to fight the Mexican Army on the open plains of South Texas. On those plains the Mexican cavalry had a huge advantage over the Texans due to the superiority of cavalry on open terrain.

News of the defeat at the Alamo and the executions at Goliad spread rapidly throughout the eastern settlements of Texas. Some of the fallen soldiers were Tejanos who had lived all their lives in Texas. Others were recent arrivals who had been in Texas only a few weeks. The news of their deaths angered Texans. "Remember Goliad" now joined "Remember the Alamo" as the rallying cries of the Texas soldiers.

Alamo would convince the Texans to give up. The defeat had just the opposite effect.

Sam Houston and his Texan army drew other lessons from these same battles. One

✓**Reading Check** **Explaining** Why were Santa Anna's execution orders called a "cruel necessity"?

SECTION 3 ASSESSMENT

Checking for Understanding

1. **Using Key Terms** Use the key term dispatch in a sentence.
2. **Reviewing Facts** Why was Señora Francita Alavez called the "Angel of Goliad"?

Reviewing Themes

3. **Groups and Institutions** Although Santa Anna ordered the immediate execution of the Texans being held at Goliad, why were some prisoners not executed?

Organizing to Learn

4. **Creating Charts** Fill in a chart like the one shown here to answer the question, "What happened to each of the Texas commanders' troops as they encountered General Urrea?"

Texas Commander	What Happened
Frank Johnson	
Dr. James Grant	
Amon King	
William Ward	

Critical Thinking

5. **Evaluating** Reread "Fannin Delays His Departure." Do you agree with the actions of Colonel Fannin? If you were in the same situation, what choices would you have made?

TAKS PRACTICE

Determining Supporting Details General Urrea and Santa Anna were on the same side, yet they disagreed on some decisions. What evidence from the text supports this?

Chapter Summary

The Alamo and Goliad

1836

After Cós's defeat in 1835, Santa Anna vows to crush Texan resistance. ★

On January 17, Gen. Houston orders Col. Bowie and 25 other Texans to the Alamo.

Santa Anna's army arrives at the Alamo on February 23. ★

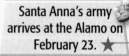

★ Colonel Travis sends out message for assistance on February 24.

The Alamo falls to Santa Anna's army on March 6. Nearly all Texans at the Alamo are killed. ★

Gen. Fannin surrenders to ★ General Urrea at Coleto on March 20. Prisoners are taken to Goliad where, on orders of Santa Anna, they are executed.

The courage and tragedy at the Alamo and Goliad help unite Texans against Santa Anna.

Reviewing Key Terms

Number your paper from 1 to 3. Next to each number, write the letter that correctly defines each vocabulary word.

1. fortify
2. recruit
3. bombard

a. to enlist in an armed service
b. to make strong by forts or batteries
c. to attack with artillery

Reviewing Key Facts

4. Why were the Texas forces badly divided in late 1835?
5. Name the Texas leaders at the Alamo.
6. Why did Travis write several letters to the people of Texas and the United States?
7. Indicate how the Texans at the Alamo knew that Santa Anna did not intend to take any prisoners.
8. In which city is the Alamo located?
9. Describe the significance of the Battle of the Alamo to Texas history.
10. What military disadvantages did Fannin and his troops face when they encountered the Mexican troops at Coleto Creek?
11. Why did Santa Anna order that the Texas prisoners taken at Coleto be executed?

Critical Thinking

12. **Drawing Conclusions** Explain what the fighting in South Texas demonstrated about Texas military forces and the lessons that Sam Houston learned from these important battles.
13. **Making Generalizations** Describe the troops who remained to defend Texas after December 1835. Explain who they were, their reasons for coming, and how well organized and trained they were.
14. **Making Inferences** What do you think was the most important factor in the Texans' defeat at the Alamo, Coleto, and South Texas? Explain your answer.
15. **Determining Cause and Effect** How did Colonel Fannin's indecision hurt the Texans' cause?
16. **Evaluating Leadership Qualities** Compare Santa Anna's style of leadership with that of the Texas leaders. Create a chart like the one below to organize your ideas.

Leaders	Examples of Leadership
Santa Anna	
Travis	
Fannin	

Geography and History Activity

17. Create a model of the Alamo as it existed in 1836. Your model can be 3-D, a diorama, or a design on paper. Review the diagram on page 231 for ideas.

Cooperative Learning Activity

18. Creating a Display With other members of your class, design a bulletin board or 3-D display about the events at the Alamo. Include reports on the men and women who were there, a diagram and pictures of the Alamo, and daily bulletins describing the events that took place.

Practicing Skills

Identifying Central Issues Identifying central issues, or main ideas, in historical materials leads to a clearer understanding of the events being studied. Read the excerpt below, then answer the questions that follow.

> *While at Gonzales awaiting recruits, tidings came to us of the fall of the Alamo on the 6th of March, and of the terrible loss of 180 men, . . . [including] the band of 27 Texans who during the siege made their way into the fort and were all slain. Many of the citizens of Gonzales perished in this wholesale slaughter of Texans, and I remembered most distinctly the shrieks of despair with which the soldiers' wives received news of the death of their husbands. I now could understand that there is woe in warfare, as well as glory and labor . . . A heavy gloom seemed to settle upon our men after the fall of the Alamo . . .*

—John Holland Jenkins
Recollections of Early Texas, 1885

19. What is the purpose of the passage?

20. What points are stated most forcefully?

21. What details are provided that support a larger issue or idea?

22. What is the central issue of the passage?

 Portfolio/TAKS Writing Activity

23. Writing a Paragraph According to this chapter, "one historian wrote that never did Americans fight more bravely than in Texas, and never did they manage their affairs more poorly." This is one historian's opinion based on an interpretation of historical fact. Write a paragraph either supporting this opinion or opposing it. Save your work for your portfolio.

 **TEXAS HISTORY** *Online*

Self-Check Quiz
Visit the texans.glencoe.com Web site and click on **Chapter 10—Self-Check Quizzes** to prepare for the chapter test.

 Building Technology Skills

24. Creating a Computer Slide Show Create a computer presentation of 4 to 6 slides about the Battle of the Alamo or other events discussed in this chapter. A popular tool for computer slide shows is PowerPoint, although there are other programs as well. Refer to the TAKS Skillbuilder in Chapter 28 for more instructions if necessary.

Culture and History Activity

25. Locating Places of Importance in Texas Visit the official Alamo Web site (http://www.thealamo.org) and take one of the virtual walking tours.

Use the diagram to answer the following question.

Some Early Events in 1836

| Colonels Neill and Travis occupy the Alamo in San Antonio | → | Colonel Travis sends his letter "To the People of Texas" appealing for more troops | → | After the Battle of the Alamo, Mexican troops win control of the Alamo | → | ? |

Which of the following events completes the flowchart?

F Texans were captured at Coleto then executed at Goliad.

G The Mexican army lost its commander, Santa Anna.

H Heavy spring rains posed a problem for the Mexican forces.

J Travis's letter mobilized troops and supplies.

Test-Taking Tip:

A flowchart shows a cause-and-effect relationship between events. To determine the missing event in a flowchart, establish the cause-and-effect relationship between the events.

CHAPTER 11

Independence Won

Why It Matters

The Battle of San Jacinto, on April 21, 1836, was a decisive battle in Texas history. By defeating the Mexican forces and capturing Santa Anna, the Texans won their independence from Mexico. Everyone in Texas—Mexicans, Anglo settlers, African Americans, and Native Americans—was affected by the 18-minute battle.

The Impact Today

Texans still celebrate April 21 as San Jacinto Day. There are speeches, parades, and reenactments of the Battle of San Jacinto. The San Jacinto Monument near Houston, built in the 1930s, rises 570 feet over the field of battle. Many of the celebrations take place there.

1836
- ★ March 4, Sam Houston named commander in chief
- ★ March 13, Houston's army began retreat to the Colorado River
- ★ April 18, the Texas army reached Buffalo Bayou
- ★ April 21, Texans defeated Santa Anna at the Battle of San Jacinto

Texas

United States   *1836*   *1838*

World

1837
• Charles Dickens began to write Oliver Twist

1839
• Charles Goodyear found commercial use for rubber

A defeated Santa Anna surrenders to Sam Houston after the Battle of San Jacinto in this painting by William Henry Huddle.

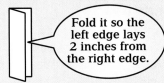

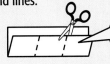

1840   1842

1841
• William Henry Harrison, ninth president, died one month after taking office
• First university degrees granted to women

1841
• Britain gained control of Hong Kong

1842
• Riots and strikes occurred in northern England

The Road to San Jacinto

Guide to Reading

Main Idea
Sam Houston ordered the Texas army to retreat, and panic spread as the Mexican troops moved deeper into Texas.

Key Term
massacre

Reading Strategy
Classifying Information Complete a chart like the one shown here, identifying the actions of Houston.

Houston's Location	Action
Gonzales	
Colorado River	
Brazos River	
Groce's Plantation	
Buffalo Bayou	

Read to Learn
- why Santa Anna stayed in Texas.
- about the Battle of San Jacinto.

Section Theme
Geography and History Houston's decision to retreat gave him valuable time before he met Santa Anna's forces.

Preview of Events
♦1836

March 4	March 28	April 7	April 18
Houston is appointed commander in chief of Texas army	Houston retreats with army to the Brazos River	Santa Anna's troops reach Brazos River	Houston and Santa Anna arrive at Buffalo Bayou

Settlers fleeing from Santa Anna's army

A
Texas Story

In 1836, General Santa Anna was marching eastward from San Antonio, and settlers were fleeing to safety in Louisiana in what was called the Runaway Scrape. Only such a great danger would have forced Dilue Rose Harris's family to try a difficult river crossing. "The horrors of crossing the Trinity are beyond my power to describe," she wrote. "When the party got to the boat the water broke over the banks and ran around us. We were surrounded by water."

Santa Anna Remains in Texas

The Texas cause seemed hopeless in March of 1836. The fall of the Alamo and the losses in South Texas opened the way for the Mexican army to move farther into Texas.

Santa Anna ordered his troops to burn every town and settlement in their path. The general was anxious to return to Mexico to take care of other matters. He believed that the Texas rebellion was crushed. His armies, which were now commanded by **General Vicente Filisola** (fee•lee•SOH•lah), could finish the task by occupying the towns in central and East Texas and by arresting **David G. Burnet** and the temporary government. Santa Anna thought this would be simple, and he prepared to return to Mexico.

Not everyone agreed that the campaign was over, however. General Filisola, an Italian with a long record of service in the Mexican army, believed that the Texans would fight more stubbornly as the Mexicans advanced against their homes and land. Santa Anna was persuaded to delay his return to Mexico until after central and East Texas were occupied by Mexican troops.

Houston Builds the Texas Army

Sam Houston also knew that the Texas campaign was not over. Houston attended the Convention of 1836 at Washington-on-the-Brazos. On March 4, the delegates named him commander in chief. He left the convention that same day to join the army at Gonzales.

When Sam Houston arrived at Gonzales on March 11, he found more than 370 volunteers. They had gathered mainly in answer to the appeals sent out from the Alamo by William B. Travis. Some of them, such as Edward Burleson, were long-time Texas residents. Others, such as the Kentucky and Ohio volunteers, commanded by Captain Sidney Sherman, were new arrivals. All were anxious to fight Santa Anna at San Antonio.

Two days after his arrival at Gonzales, Houston learned that the Alamo had fallen. He faced a difficult decision—fight or flee. His troops numbered fewer than 400, and they were untrained. Houston ordered a retreat eastward toward the Colorado River, hoping to pick up more soldiers. At the same time, he sent orders for Fannin to retreat from Goliad, blow up the garrison there, and join him. Houston needed Fannin's 300 soldiers.

Houston's Army Retreats

Houston's army began its withdrawal from Gonzales on Sunday, March 13, 1836. A rear guard commanded by Juan Seguín destroyed those provisions that could not be carried. Seguín's unit also helped civilians in the area to escape.

The army crossed the Colorado River at **Burnham's Crossing,** which was flooded by heavy rains. Houston waited there for nine days, drilling his troops while civilians living west of the river crossed over to safety. Houston's forces grew in number as volunteers arrived from the United States. Houston now had nearly 1,000 soldiers under his command, although many of them were untrained and poorly equipped.

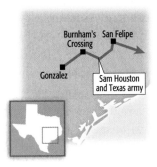

Picturing **History**

Edward Burleson served in many military and political capacities in Texas before joining the volunteers at the Alamo. Why would volunteers come from outside of Texas to help Texans in their fight for independence?

Houston was greatly concerned about the fate of Fannin and his unit at Goliad. He sent scouts to find out what had happened to Fannin's army. On March 25, Houston learned that Fannin and his soldiers had been captured and that Santa Anna's army was moving toward the Colorado River. Houston again ordered a retreat, this time to the **Brazos River.** Anger and resentment rose among many of Houston's officers and soldiers. They wanted to fight now. Their homes were being destroyed, and their families were fleeing from Mexican troops. Houston, however, believed his forces were still too weak to oppose the Mexican army. He also knew that as the Mexican army was drawn farther east, its supply lines became stretched. In East Texas, the Texans might get help from the United States.

✓**Reading Check** **Evaluating** With more than 1,000 troops, why did Houston retreat to the Brazos River?

Panic Causes the Runaway Scrape

Houston's decision to continue the retreat panicked the families living between the Colorado and Brazos Rivers. They had heard of the Alamo disaster and soon learned of the massacre (to kill many at one time) of Fannin's unit. They feared that the Mexican army would harm them, too, after it moved into their area.

Hundreds of families gathered their belongings and headed east toward the **Sabine River.** Many carried everything that could be moved. Women, children, slaves, horses, cattle, and creaking wagons trudged along the muddy roads. Heavy spring rains, lack of food, and sickness made their journey miserable. This event was known as the **Runaway Scrape.**

Noah Smithwick later included an account of farms deserted by frightened Texans in his book *The Evolution of a State, or Recollections of Old Texas Days:*

❝Houses were standing open, the beds unmade, the breakfast things still on the tables, pans of milk moulding in the dairies. There were cribs full of corn, smoke houses full of bacon, yards full of chickens that ran after us for food, nests of eggs in every fence corner, young corn and garden truck rejoicing in the rain, cattle cropping the luxuriant grass, hogs, fat and lazy, wallowing in the mud, all abandoned. Forlorn dogs roamed around the deserted homes, their doleful howls adding to the general sense of desolation. Hungry cats ran mewing to meet us, rubbing their sides against our legs in token of welcome.❞

✓**Reading Check** **Analyzing** What event began the Runaway Scrape?

Picturing **History**

Fearing for their lives, many Texas families headed east toward Louisiana. What were some of the difficulties of moving household goods at that time?

The Texas Revolution: The Alamo to San Jacinto

Susanna Dickinson informs Sam Houston of the fate of the Alamo defenders and of Santa Anna's intention toward Texas.

In March General Filisola moved north to occupy the towns of east and central Texas and to arrest David G. Burnet and the ad interim government. His retreat after San Jacinto assured Texan independence.

The Texans overwhelm the Mexican forces at San Jacinto on April 21, 1836.

San Antonio
(The Alamo, February 23 – March 6, 1836)

Bastrop
Burnham's Crossing
Gonzales
Beason's Ferry
Groce's Plantation
San Felipe
Harrisburg
San Jacinto (April 21, 1836)
Fort Bend
Columbia
Brazoria

Coleto Creek (March 19 – 20, 1836)
Victoria
Goliad
Matagorda

Refugio (March 14, 1836)
San Patricio (February 27, 1836)

Presidio del Rio Grande
To Monclova
Laredo

Gulf of Mexico

To Saltillo
Rio Grande
Rio Bravo

Matamoros

| Mexican Army |
| Texas Army |
| Battle |

N W E S

0 mi. 100
0 km 100
Albers Equal-Area projection

TAKS PRACTICE

The Mexican army traveled greater distances than the Texas army to reach the battle sites, and the battles took place in Texas.
Explaining Why would this be an advantage for the Texas army?

Houston Trains His Army

On March 28, 1836, Houston's army reached the Brazos River at San Felipe de Austin. Two companies refused to retreat farther, so Houston posted them to guard the river crossing. Then he turned the main body of his army northward along the Brazos River to the plantation of Jared Groce, near present-day Hempstead.

Houston used the two weeks spent at **Groce's Plantation** to train the army in the fundamentals of warfare. Long hours were devoted to drilling and marching. The troops complained. The rain and mud fueled their bad tempers. Some left the army to find their families and help get them to safety. Many began to talk about choosing a new general. President David G. Burnet, who had moved the government to Harrisburg, sent Houston a letter urging him to attack Santa Anna. Burnet wrote:

> **❝**The enemy are laughing you to scorn. You must fight them. You must retreat no farther. The country expects you to fight. The salvation of the country depends on you doing so.**❞**

Despite the pleas of President Burnet, Houston refused to discuss his plans or to move the troops

A Shared Past...

When Sam Houston needed to get his army across the Brazos, a large steamboat at Groce's Landing made the task possible. The *Yellow Stone* had been built in Louisville, Kentucky, in 1831 and was initially used on the upper Missouri River. Its owners sent it to Texas in late 1835. It had an American crew and flew the flag of the United States. It took seven trips, but the Texan army made it safely across the Brazos.

before he was ready. **Hendrick Arnold,** an African American scout under Deaf Smith's command, kept Houston informed about Santa Anna's army. Posing as a runaway slave, Arnold moved through the Mexican army's camps and gathered information.

The Mexican Army Moves East

Meanwhile, the Mexican forces advanced toward the Brazos River. On April 5, 1836, Santa Anna crossed the Colorado River trying to overtake the Texans. He left some slower units behind and reached the Brazos River at San Felipe on April 7. After failing to overcome the two Texas companies defending the river crossing, Santa Anna moved 30 miles down river.

There, Santa Anna learned that President Burnet and his advisers were only 30 miles away at **Harrisburg.** The Mexican leader moved one column of his army toward Harrisburg. He arrived there on April 15, 1836, only to learn that the Texan officials had moved to New Washington on Galveston Bay. Santa Anna's troops set fire to Harrisburg and went to New Washington. The Texas government, however, had fled again, this time to Galveston Island.

As Santa Anna moved to Harrisburg, Houston moved his army toward the San Jacinto River. At Groce's Landing, Houston received two six-pound cannons—named "The Twin Sisters"—a gift from the people of Cincinnati, Ohio.

Many of Houston's troops believed that his strategy was to lead the Mexican army east to the Sabine River. There, Houston might receive aid from **General Edmund P. Gaines** and his American troops. On April 17, however, Houston took the road south to Harrisburg instead of the road east to Louisiana. His soldiers now knew that he meant to fight.

The Texas army reached **Buffalo Bayou** on April 18. Houston learned that the Mexican army was nearby. Santa Anna was moving toward the San Jacinto River. Houston moved his army along the banks of Buffalo Bayou to meet the Mexican troops.

Reading Check **Analyzing** Why did the Texas government move so often?

SECTION 1 ASSESSMENT

Checking for Understanding

1. **Using Key Terms** Use the word massacre in a sentence about the Alamo or Goliad.
2. **Reviewing Facts** Describe the events of the Runaway Scrape.

Reviewing Themes

3. **Geography and History** What gift did Houston receive from the people of Ohio?

Organizing to Learn

4. **Sequencing** Place the following key events in their proper sequence.

   ———+———+———+———

   a. Sam Houston is made commander of Texas army.
   b. Harrisburg is set on fire.
   c. Houston's army arrives at Buffalo Bayou.
   d. Houston begins army's retreat.

Critical Thinking

5. **Analyzing** How did Hendrick Arnold help Sam Houston's army? In what other ways are spies valuable and necessary during wartime?

TAKS PRACTICE

Making Predictions Had Sam Houston not taken the time to train his army, what might the consequences have been upon meeting Santa Anna's army?

Reading a Diagram

Why Learn This Skill?

A diagram is a drawing that shows how something works or how its parts fit together. Diagrams are often used to make complicated information easier to understand.

Learning the Skill

To read a diagram, follow these steps:

- Read the title or caption of the diagram to determine what it represents.
- Read all the labels on the diagram.
- Read the legend and identify the symbols or colors on the diagram.
- Look for numbers, which may show a sequence of steps.
- Look for arrows, which may show the direction of movement.

Practicing the Skill

The diagram at right shows the Battle of San Jacinto. Study this diagram, then answer the questions that follow.

1. What is the title of this diagram?

2. What bodies of water are shown?

3. Where were the Texas soldiers camped?

4. How is the town of Lynchburg represented in this diagram?

5. What do the blue arrows represent?

6. What three types of military units were in Houston's army?

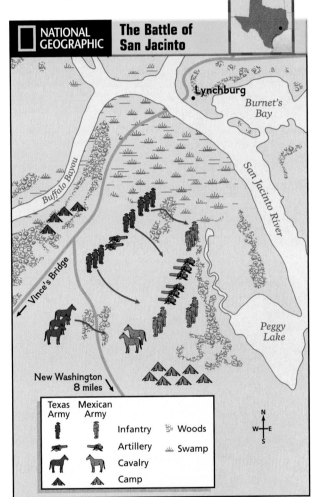

NATIONAL GEOGRAPHIC — **The Battle of San Jacinto**

Lynchburg
Burnet's Bay
Buffalo Bayou
San Jacinto River
Vince's Bridge
Peggy Lake
New Washington 8 miles

Texas Army	Mexican Army		
		Infantry	Woods
		Artillery	Swamp
		Cavalry	
		Camp	

N W E S

Victory at San Jacinto

Guide to Reading

Main Idea
The Texas army defeated Santa Anna at the Battle of San Jacinto.

Key Terms
cavalry
flank
infantry

Reading Strategy
Classifying Information Complete a chart summarizing the advantages and disadvantages of the Texan and Mexican armies.

Situation of	Advantages	Disadvantages
Texans	1. 2.	1. 2.
Mexicans	1. 2.	1. 2.

Read to Learn
- about the Mexican and the Texan armies at Buffalo Bayou.
- about the Battle of San Jacinto.
- about the Treaties of Velasco.

Section Theme
Geography and History After the victory at San Jacinto, the Treaties of Velasco removed the threat of Mexican invasion.

Preview of Events

♦ 1836

April 20	April 21	May 14
Skirmish between Texas cavalry and Mexican army	Battle of San Jacinto	Treaties of Velasco signed

Spreading the word

A
Texas Story

After Sam Houston's victory at San Jacinto, settlers were free to return home. Dilue Rose Harris gave this account: "We had been at Liberty three weeks . . . One Thursday evening we heard a sound like distant thunder. The [shelling of the cannons] lasted only a few minutes, and Father said that the Texans must have been defeated. We left Liberty in half an hour . . . We could see a man on horseback . . . he said 'Turn back! The Texas army has whipped the Mexican army. No danger! No danger! Turn back.'"

The Eve of Battle

On April 20, 1836, the Texan troops camped in a grove of oak trees along the banks of the Buffalo Bayou where it joins the **San Jacinto River.** Buffalo Bayou was at their backs, and the San Jacinto River was on their left. A wide prairie extended in front of the camp toward **Vince's Bayou** on their right.

On that same day, Santa Anna's army moved to a campsite on the edge of the prairie along the San Jacinto River. The Mexican site was about three-quarters of a mile from Houston's camp. Marshland and swamps extended to the right and rear of the Mexican army. Some of the Mexican officers complained that Santa Anna was in a poor location to fend off a major enemy attack. Nevertheless, Santa Anna was confident that the Texans would not attack but would fight on the defensive, as they had at San Antonio and during their withdrawal from Goliad.

On the afternoon of April 20, a small skirmish occurred between the Texan cavalry and the Mexican army. A private from Georgia named **Mirabeau B. Lamar** so distinguished himself in the fighting that the next day he was placed in command of the entire Texan cavalry—the mounted horse soldiers.

San Jacinto Soldiers From Varied Backgrounds

Only one company in General Houston's army was made up entirely of native Texans. Juan Seguín commanded these 20 to 30 Tejanos. Houston was concerned that Seguín and his troops might be shot by mistake in the coming battle. To protect them, he gave the Tejanos the job of guarding the Texan camp, but Seguín and his men were insulted. **José Antonio Menchaca,** speaking for the soldiers who could not speak English, told Houston they had joined the army to fight and wanted to face the enemy. Houston admired the courage of the Tejanos and made the decision to change his order. Seguín's men wore pieces of cardboard in their hatbands so the Texans would not mistake them for Mexican troops.

Only 171 soldiers owned land in Texas. Many had come to Texas in the weeks just before the battle. A recruit from the United States, who arrived on the morning of the battle, recorded the nature of Houston's army:

❝We found the Texian force under Gen'l S. Houston encamped in the timber near Lynch's ferry over the San Jacinto River. A scene singularly wild and picturesque presented itself to our view. Around 20 or 30 campfires stood as many groups of men: English, Irish, Scots, Mexicans, French, Germans, Italians, Poles, Yankees, all unwashed and unshaved, their long hair and beards and mustaches matted, their clothes in tatters and plastered with mud. A more savage looking band could scarcely have been assembled. Yet many were gentlemen, owners of large estates. Some were distinguished for oratory, some in science, some in medicine . . . Their guns were of every size and shape. They numbered less than 800.❞

✓**Reading Check** **Describing** Where did the Texan troops camp on April 20, 1836?

Causes and Effects of the Battle of San Jacinto

Causes

- Santa Anna believes Texans are weak and becomes overconfident.
- Houston takes time to train his army so that they are prepared.
- Memory of defeat at Alamo and Goliad inspires Texans.

Effects

- Houston's army is victorious, ensuring Texan independence.
- Santa Anna is captured.
- The Treaties of Velasco are signed. Santa Anna promises not to fight Texans again.

Graphic Organizer ➔ *Skills*

Despite Santa Anna's promise, the Mexican government did not recognize Texas as an independent nation.

Comparing and Contrasting What were the major advantages of Texas gaining independence from Mexico?

Houston Calls a Council of War

The sun shone brightly on the morning of April 21, 1836, as Houston's soldiers began their daily activities. The Mexican army's flags fluttered in the breeze across the prairie. Santa Anna had about 850 troops with him on April 20. On the morning of April 21, General Martín Perfecto de Cós and 540 more soldiers joined Santa Anna. Fortunately for the Texans, most recruits in Cós's unit were inexperienced. Santa Anna did not post enough guards around the Mexican camp. Because Cós's men had marched much of the night, Santa Anna allowed them time to eat and rest. At midday, Santa Anna himself retired to his tent.

Meanwhile, in the late morning, Houston ordered his scouts **Erastus "Deaf" Smith** and **Henry Karnes** to destroy the bridge across Vince's Bayou to the southwest. Destruction of the bridge would cut off a path of retreat for both the Texan and Mexican armies.

At noon, General Houston called a council of war with his officers to determine whether to fight that day or to wait until dawn. All favored fighting, but disagreement arose over whether to attack directly or to set up a defensive position and wait for the enemy to attack. Houston dismissed his officers without announcing a decision.

"Remember the Alamo"

At 3:30 that afternoon, General Houston ordered his officers to assemble the troops for an immediate attack. The battle line was formed

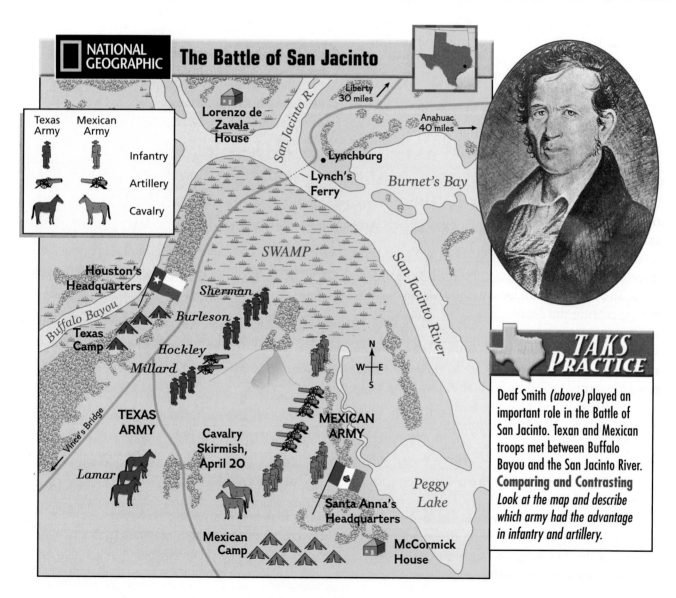

NATIONAL GEOGRAPHIC

The Battle of San Jacinto

Texas Army	Mexican Army	
		Infantry
		Artillery
		Cavalry

Liberty 30 miles

Anahuac 40 miles

Lorenzo de Zavala House

San Jacinto R.

Lynchburg

Lynch's Ferry

Burnet's Bay

San Jacinto River

SWAMP

Houston's Headquarters

Sherman

Burleson

Buffalo Bayou

Texas Camp

Hockley

Millard

Vince's Bridge

TEXAS ARMY

Cavalry Skirmish, April 20

MEXICAN ARMY

N W E S

Lamar

Santa Anna's Headquarters

Peggy Lake

Mexican Camp

McCormick House

TAKS PRACTICE

Deaf Smith (*above*) played an important role in the Battle of San Jacinto. Texan and Mexican troops met between Buffalo Bayou and the San Jacinto River. **Comparing and Contrasting** *Look at the map and describe which army had the advantage in infantry and artillery.*

San Jacinto battle site

The Battle of San Jacinto by Henry Arthur McArdle, 1898 This painting hangs in the Senate Chamber in the Texas Capitol. The artist paid great attention to the details of the uniforms, equipment, and likenesses of the people. Does the painting support the physical description of the battle site given in the text?

with Sidney Sherman's regiment on the far left side, or flank, and Edward Burleson's regiment to the immediate right of Sherman. The Twin Sisters were in the center, pulled by 30 men under **George W. Hockley's** command. Four infantry units (companies of foot soldiers), led by Henry Millard were to the right of Hockley. The cavalry unit commanded by Mirabeau B. Lamar was on the extreme right. His duty was to keep Mexican soldiers from escaping across the prairie.

Houston drew his sword and ordered the troops to advance. With this signal, the Texans moved out of the woods and across the open prairie that separated the two armies. Three fife players and Dick the Drummer, an African American, played a popular tune of the day, "Will You Come to the Bower?" Deaf Smith rode up and announced, "Vince's Bridge is down!" Santa Anna and the Texans were cut off without support.

As the Texans moved across the open prairie, the Mexican camp remained quiet. While many of Santa Anna's soldiers were resting, others were watering their horses in a nearby stream.

Incredibly, the Texans were upon the enemy camp before the Mexicans knew an attack was upon them.

"Remember the Alamo! Remember Goliad!" was the battle cry as the Texans opened fire with rifles and cannons. The Twin Sisters blew a hole in the Mexican fortifications. The Texans stormed through the enemy's lines, seized the Mexican artillery, and engaged in hand-to-hand combat.

The Mexican officers tried to rally their forces. The effort, however, was of little use. Total confusion resulted, and many of the Mexican soldiers attempted to flee from the battle. Some of the Mexican cavalry tried to escape across Vince's Bayou, but they found that the bridge had been destroyed. Others fled onto the prairie but were cut down by Lamar's cavalry. The organized Mexican resistance lasted 18 minutes. The killing continued until dark, however, as the Texans cut down the Mexican soldiers who had fled to the swamps behind Santa Anna's camp.

Reading Check **Examining** Why was Santa Anna not prepared for the Texans?

Mexicans Suffer Heavy Losses

The losses in Houston's army at the **Battle of San Jacinto** were light. Fewer than 10 Texans were killed or fatally wounded in the fighting. Thirty others, including General Houston, were injured. A musket ball had shattered Houston's ankle. The Lorenzo de Zavala home just across Buffalo Bayou was made into a temporary hospital to care for the Texan and Mexican troops.

The Mexican army, missing the experienced soldiers that had fallen at the Alamo, suffered heavy losses at San Jacinto. In his battle report to President Burnet, General Houston listed 630 Mexicans killed and 730 taken prisoner. Santa Anna was among the prisoners.

Santa Anna had disappeared during the fighting. The next day he was found in the tall grass. Because he was dressed as a common soldier, the Texans did not recognize him at first. On the way to camp, however, his own men singled him out. He was taken to General Houston, who rested under a large oak tree. Through an interpreter, the Mexican president introduced himself as "General Antonio López de Santa Anna . . . a prisoner of war at your disposition."

Picturing **History**

The image at right shows Santa Anna *(standing)* after the Battle of San Jacinto. Below, he is surrendering to Sam Houston. Why was Santa Anna's capture an important achievement for the Texans?

Comparing Reports

After the Battle of San Jacinto, both Houston and Santa Anna described the encounter to their superiors. Houston's description of the battle was in a report to President David G. Burnet.

❝The conflict lasted about eighteen minutes from the time of close action until we were in possession of the enemy's encampment, taking one piece of cannon (loaded), four stands of colours, all their camp equipage, stores, and baggage. Our cavalry had charged and routed that of the enemy upon the right, and given pursuit to the fugitives, which did not cease until they arrived at the bridge . . .

[A]s to the conduct of those who commanded in the action, . . . our success in the action is conclusive proof of their daring intrepidity and courage; every officer and man proved himself worthy of the cause in which he battled while the triumph received a lustre from the humanity which characterized their conduct after victory.❞

Santa Anna's explanation is translated below.

❝What was the cause of the fateful defeat of San Jacinto? It was the excessive number of raw recruits in the five hundred men under command of General Cós . . . A cargo of supplies I had ordered not to be brought, . . . capture of an order that was sent to me from Thompson's as well as that of the officer bringing it, . . . fatigue and lack of food . . . [all were] cause[s]. The disdain with which a constantly fleeing enemy was generally viewed by our troops was another cause, for without a close vigilance such as I had emphatically ordered, it permitted the enemy to occupy successfully the woods to the right, as it did in an act of desperation. None of these causes was the result of neglect on my part or of acts immediately emanating from me.❞

The capture of Santa Anna was a great achievement for the Texans. It prevented him from rejoining his other troops in Texas, thus leaving them without a high commander. Had he escaped, Santa Anna might have continued the war for some time, which would have resulted in many more deaths. At Houston's request, Santa Anna signed an order instructing General Filisola to withdraw all Mexican troops to south of the Rio Grande.

The Texan Navy Controls the Coast

The small Texan navy played an important role in the final days of the revolution. The navy had only four ships, but they were able to control the coastal waters of Texas. The navy brought necessary supplies to the Texan armies, while cutting off supplies to the Mexican divisions. Several thousand Mexican troops remained

TEXAS HISTORY Online

Student Web Activity Visit the texans.glencoe.com Web site and click on **Chapter 11—Student Web Activity** to learn more about the Battle of San Jacinto.

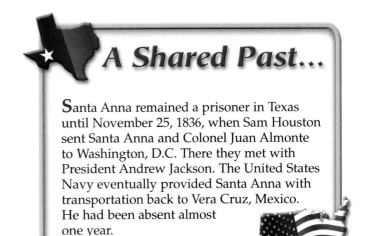

A Shared Past...

Santa Anna remained a prisoner in Texas until November 25, 1836, when Sam Houston sent Santa Anna and Colonel Juan Almonte to Washington, D.C. There they met with President Andrew Jackson. The United States Navy eventually provided Santa Anna with transportation back to Vera Cruz, Mexico. He had been absent almost one year.

in Texas after the Battle of San Jacinto. Due to the navy's effectiveness, they were forced to withdraw because of their shortage of food and ammunition.

Treaties of Velasco

After President Burnet visited San Jacinto, he moved the government from Galveston Island to the town of Velasco at the mouth of the Brazos River. The capital of Texas was located at Velasco for several months. Santa Anna was taken there to sign two treaties with the Texas government. Both were signed on May 14, 1836. One treaty was made public. The other was kept secret.

In the public treaty, the Mexican ruler promised to never again fight against the Texans. He also agreed to order all Mexican forces out of Texas immediately. The treaty also provided for an exchange of Texan and Mexican prisoners captured in the fighting. In addition, all property taken by the Mexican forces during the war was to be returned to the rightful owners.

In return for his freedom, Santa Anna privately agreed in the secret treaty to work for Mexican recognition of Texas independence. The secret terms called for the Texas government to release Santa Anna immediately and give him an escort back to Mexico. In return, Santa Anna would also agree to work inside Mexico to get the Texas boundary set at the Rio Grande.

✓ **Reading Check** Identifying Location Where did President Burnet move the capital after leaving Galveston Island?

ONLY in TEXAS

Mineral Wells Is Home to "Crazy Water" *(bottom left)*. The town of Mineral Wells was founded by J.A. Lynch in 1887. Its waters first gained fame as a cure for rheumatism. Mineral Wells became a popular resort with visitors once the Crazy Well was dug in 1885. People would "take the waters" by visiting springs and wells *(right)*, drinking the water, or bathing in it. Bathhouses *(bottom center)*, hotels, drinking fountains, and pavilions throughout the town catered to the bathers and health-seekers.

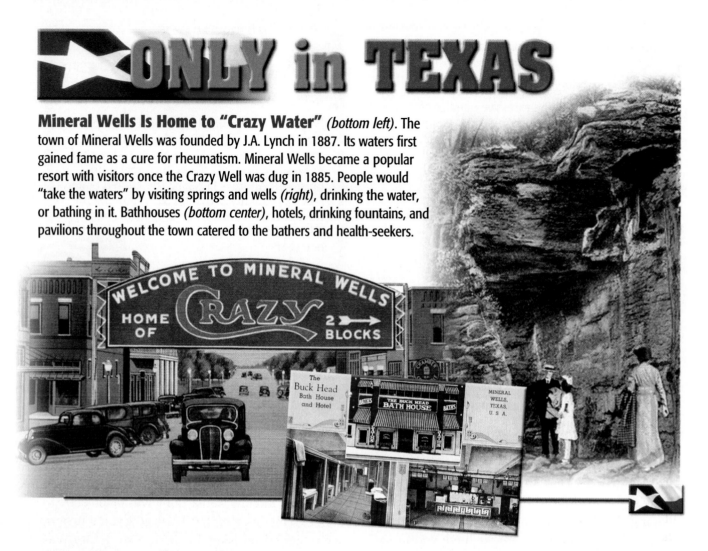

Many Texans Wanted Revenge

Immediately following the Battle of San Jacinto, many Texans wanted to hang Santa Anna for the deaths at the Alamo and Goliad. But Houston refused to let the soldiers kill the general. Houston explained his reasons later:

> ❝My motive in sparing the life of Santa Anna was to relieve the country of all hostile enemies without further bloodshed, and to secure his acknowledgment of our independence.❞

Later, President Burnet also spared the life of Santa Anna. Burnet was determined to carry out the terms of the **Treaties of Velasco.** When Santa Anna, with his secretary and military aide, boarded the ship *Invincible* in June 1836 to return to Mexico, a group of angry Texan army officers prevented the ship from sailing. They demanded that Santa Anna be turned over to the army for execution.

Burnet stopped the officers from executing Santa Anna, but they prevented Santa Anna from returning home. He was taken from the *Invincible* and held captive. He was finally allowed to leave Texas several months later.

Victory's Consequences

The Battle of San Jacinto was one of the most decisive battles in history. By defeating the Mexican forces and capturing General Santa Anna, the Texans had won their independence from Mexico.

News of the amazing victory soon spread throughout Texas. Houston sent word to those who had fled in the Runaway Scrape that it was now safe to return home. Many found their homes burned and possessions gone. On their way home, the family of Dilue Rose Harris passed by the battlefield. It was a scene of death and destruction, but Dilue wanted to maintain appearances, as she wrote in the following account two days before her eleventh birthday:

❝We crossed the San Jacinto the next morning and stayed until late in the evening on the battle field. Both armies were camped near . . . I had lost my bonnet crossing Trinity Bay and was compelled to wear a table cloth again. It was six weeks since we had left home, and our homes were very much dilapidated. I could not go to see the Mexican prisoners with a table cloth tied on my head for I knew several of the young men.❞

Following the battle, Houston went to New Orleans to seek medical treatment for his wounded ankle. Santa Anna's second in command, Vicente Filisola, led the defeated Mexican army home. Volunteers from the United States arrived to discover that they were too late. The Texans had already won the war.

President David Burnet and **Vice President Lorenzo de Zavala** now faced numerous challenges. The Texans had won the war. They returned to their farms and towns not as Mexican citizens but as citizens of the new Republic of Texas.

✓ **Reading Check** **Identifying** Who was president of Texas's interim government at this time?

Picturing **History**

The San Jacinto monument is listed in the *Guinness Book of World Records* as the world's tallest stone column memorial. Why would some historians rank the Battle of San Jacinto in the top 15 most decisive battles in world history?

SECTION 2 ASSESSMENT

Checking for Understanding

1. **Using Key Terms** Use the words cavalry and infantry to describe a military situation.
2. **Reviewing Facts** Who made up Houston's army? Were they all Texans?

Reviewing Themes

3. **Geography and History** List four reasons that the smaller Texas army defeated Santa Anna's forces.

Organizing to Learn

4. **Summarizing** Create a chart like the one shown here. List the key terms of the public and secret Treaties of Velasco signed after the Battle of San Jacinto.

Public Treaty	Secret Treaty

Critical Thinking

5. **Evaluating** After the Battle of San Jacinto, Santa Anna was captured. What were some reasons why President Burnet did not want to see Santa Anna executed?

Describing List the reasons that Santa Anna gave for his defeat at the Battle of San Jacinto.

Chapter Summary

Independence Won

March 1836

- Santa Anna moves his troops through central Texas toward East Texas.
- ★ Sam Houston is appointed commander in chief at the Convention of 1836.
- Houston goes to Gonzales and begins his retreat toward the Colorado River.
- ★ Runaway Scrape begins on a large scale.
- Houston retreats toward the Brazos River.
- Runaway Scrape intensifies.

April 1836

- Houston trains his army at Groce's Plantation.
- Santa Anna crosses the Brazos River and sets fire to Harrisburg.
- The Texas army and the Mexican army reach Buffalo Bayou.
- ★ The Texas army defeats the Mexican army at the Battle of San Jacinto on April 21.

Reviewing Key Terms

Number your paper from 1 to 4. Write four sentences using the vocabulary words listed below.

1. cavalry
2. massacre
3. infantry
4. flank

Reviewing Key Facts

5. Why did General Filisola believe Santa Anna should delay his return to Mexico?
6. After being named to what position did Houston immediately leave the Convention of 1836?
7. Where did Houston's volunteers come from?
8. Why did Houston order a retreat from the Brazos River?
9. What was the Runaway Scrape?
10. What prevented Santa Anna's army from crossing the Brazos River at San Felipe de Austin?
11. What name did the Texas soldiers give to the cannons used at the Battle of San Jacinto?
12. Why did Houston decide to take the road south to Harrisburg instead of the road east to Louisiana?
13. Why was the Battle of San Jacinto important?
14. What happened to Santa Anna on the ship *Invincible?*
15. Why did Houston retreat twice from the Mexican army and how did his troops benefit?
16. Why did Houston's troops spend almost two weeks at Groce's Plantation? How did the troops react when Houston ordered this delay?

Critical Thinking

17. **Drawing Conclusions** Explain why 1836 was a significant year in Texas history.
18. **Determining Cause and Effect** Explain the effect of the destruction of the bridge across Vince's Bayou.
19. **Making Comparisons** Draw a chart like the one below. Compare the losses of the Mexican army to those of the Texas army at San Jacinto.

Mexican Losses	Texan Losses

Geography and History Activity

20. Refer back to the map on page 249. For each of the following locations, create a symbol that represents an event or activity at the location. Next to the symbol, describe the meaning of the symbol.

> Gonzales
>
> Burnham's Crossing
>
> Groce's Plantation
>
> San Jacinto

Cooperative Learning Activity

21. **Writing a Newspaper** Organize into five groups and make a newspaper covering the events of the Texas Revolution. The first group will act as journalists, writing about the military and political events. The second group will write an opinion page. The third group will write classified advertisements of the period. The fourth group will create the society page. The fifth group will draw illustrations for the articles.

The Alamo, February and March 1836

Infantry barracks
Cattle pens
Hospital
Chapel
Irrigation ditch
Mission Square
Well
South barracks
Travis fell.
Cannon
Bowie died.
Officer barracks
Headquarters
Gonzales (71 miles)
West wall
18-pounder
Irrigation ditch
Goliad (95 miles)

Practicing Skills

Reading a Diagram *Diagrams often make complicated information easier to understand. Study the diagram of the Alamo above, then answer the questions that follow.*

22. What does the color blue represent in this diagram?
23. Where was the 18-pounder placed?
24. Where did the officers sleep and eat?
25. How far did reinforcements from Gonzales have to come?

TEXAS HISTORY Online

Self-Check Quiz

Visit the texans.glencoe.com Web site and click on **Chapter 11—Self-Check Quizzes** to prepare for the chapter test.

26. Why would the Alamo have its own cattle pens?
27. What is significant about the barrier between the south wall and the chapel?

Portfolio/TAKS Writing Activity

28. **Supporting a Point of View** Pretend you are an individual who left during the Runaway Scrape but just heard about Houston's victory at the Battle of San Jacinto. Write a letter to Sam Houston in which you evaluate his decisions. Explain how you felt about moving out of your home and how you feel about the victory.

Which of the following is an *opinion* stated in this quote about the Battle of San Jacinto?

Robert Hancock Hunter, a soldier who fought with Sam Houston at the Battle of San Jacinto, later recalled, "Santa Anna said that it was not a battle, [instead] he called it a massacre. Plague on him. What did he call the Alamo?"

A Santa Anna believed that the Battle of San Jacinto was a turning point.

B Robert Hancock Hunter believed that Texans had been massacred at Goliad.

C Robert Hancock Hunter believed that Mexican and Texan prisoners of war should be exchanged.

D Santa Anna believed that his troops had been cornered and unfairly cut down.

Test-Taking Tip:

Read test questions and answer choices carefully. This question asks you to identify an opinion *stated in the quotation* about the Battle of San Jacinto. Read the quotation carefully to find a personal judgment about the fight at San Jacinto.

THE STORY OF TEXAS

THE BOB BULLOCK
Texas State
History Museum

Museum Tour 3

Building the
Lone Star Identity
Independence

*T*he first shots of the Revolution were heard at Gonzales as the war began over one small cannon. Mexican soldiers had arrived in 1835 to reclaim the cannon that had earlier been loaned to the settlers. They were met with a defiant "Come and Take It."

◄ Citizen Soldiers The Texan defenders were not professional soldiers like those in the Mexican army. Here, John Henry Moore and neighbors fire on Mexican troops sent to bring back the cannon.

Visit The Bob Bullock Texas State History Museum in Austin to see artifacts and exhibits such as these about Texas history and heritage.

Military Dress This coat belonged to an officer in Santa ▶ Anna's army. He wore it during the storming of the Alamo. Spurs, like the one shown below, were worn by Mexican officers who rode horses into battle. ▼

▲ **Flags and Standards** This is one of the flags carried by the Mexican cavalry. Armies often carried personal standards, or banners, for identification. This one is quite different from the "homemade" flag of the Texas volunteers from Gonzales.

▲ **Artifacts** Officers in the Mexican army were allowed some luxuries. Shown is one of General Santa Anna's sleeping caps and a glass bottle for serving beverages. The contents of Santa Anna's personal chest were divided among the victorious Texas officers after the Battle of San Jacinto.

UNIT ★

4 The Republic of Texas

1836–1845

Why It Matters

As you study Unit 4, *you will learn about Texas as a republic. After the creation of the United States from the original 13 colonies, other territories were granted statehood. Only Texas entered the union as a separate and independent nation. The distinctive nature of Texas owes much to its having been a republic before it was a state and to the influence of its settlers.*

Primary Sources Library

See pages 690–691 for primary source readings to accompany Unit 4.

Going Visiting by Friedrich Richard Petri (c. 1853) from the Texas Memorial Museum, Austin, Texas. Socializing with neighbors was an important part of community life during the years of the republic. Not all Texas settlers wore buckskin and moccasins as this well-dressed family shows.

RICH HERITAGE

There are many reasons why people take the big step of leaving their homes and moving to an unknown land—and Texas, during the years 1820 to 1860, witnessed all of them. The newly arriving immigrant groups tended to settle in one particular area, since it was easier to work with and live around people who spoke the same language and practiced the same customs.

Many Mexicans came north while Texas was still a Spanish territory to set up farms on the fertile Coastal Plains. As the United States grew, more Native Americans, who had been forced off their lands east of the Mississippi, also moved into Texas. After Texas independence, thousands of Anglo Americans, mostly from the southern states, were drawn by the lure of cheap, plentiful land. Many came from slave-holding states and brought enslaved African Americans. Finally, immigrants from Germany and almost every other country in Europe arrived by ship to escape famine, political unrest, or religious persecution.

Texas's wide-open spaces seemed to offer endless possibilities to anyone with dreams or a keen sense of adventure. Unfortunately, not all immigrant groups shared in the political freedom and economic opportunities Texas had to offer. Native Americans were pushed farther west or north into Oklahoma. Many African Americans—who made up one-third of Texas's population in 1860—still lived in slavery, and Mexican residents faced continued prejudice.

Nevertheless, each immigrant group made its own unique contribution to Texas's history and culture. Today Texans celebrate their ethnic heritage in festivals and competitions all across the state. Many of Texas's place names, as well as the listings in local phone directories, still reflect those original patterns of settlement from the early nineteenth century.

A traditional band plays lively German music at the Texas Folklife Festival.

A Hispanic woman dances joyfully at a fiesta.

LEARNING *from* GEOGRAPHY

1. **Where did your immigrant ancestors settle? Do you live close to where they originally settled?**

2. **Describe a festival you have attended. What are your most vivid memories?**

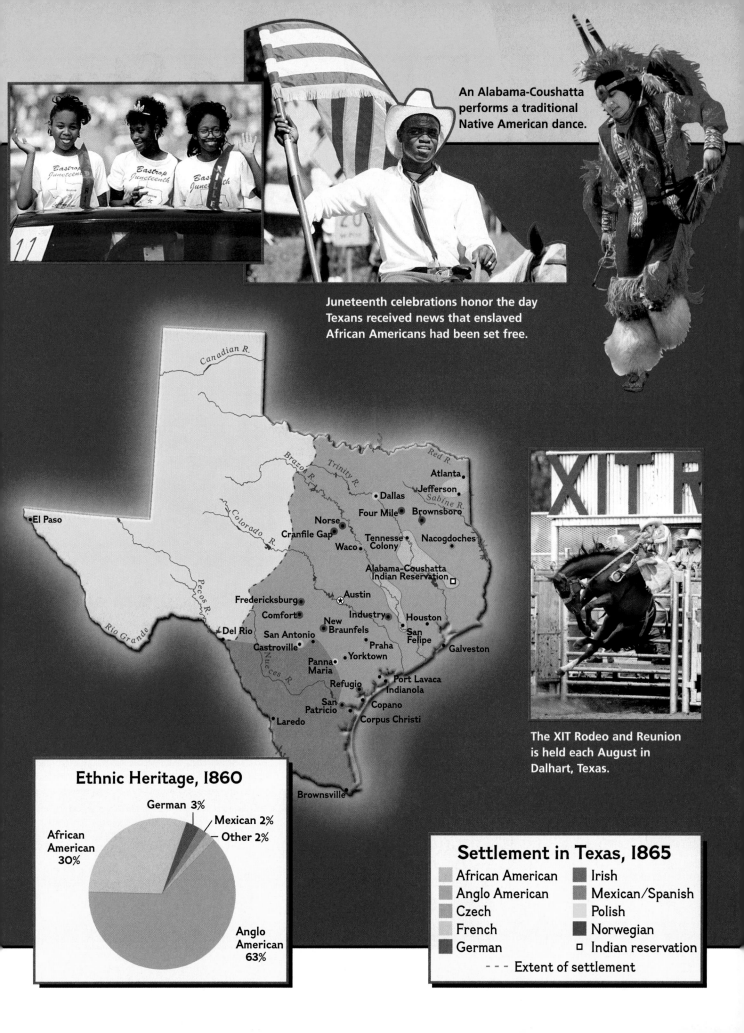

An Alabama-Coushatta performs a traditional Native American dance.

Juneteenth celebrations honor the day Texans received news that enslaved African Americans had been set free.

Map labels

Canadian R.
Red R.
Brazos R.
Trinity R.
Sabine R.
Colorado R.
Pecos R.
Rio Grande
Nueces R.

El Paso
Atlanta
Jefferson
Dallas
Four Mile
Brownsboro
Norse
Cranfile Gap
Tennessee Colony
Nacogdoches
Waco
Alabama-Coushatta Indian Reservation
Fredericksburg
Austin
Comfort
Industry
Houston
New Braunfels
San Felipe
Del Rio
San Antonio
Praha
Castroville
Yorktown
Galveston
Panna Maria
Refugio
Port Lavaca
Indianola
San Patricio
Copano
Laredo
Corpus Christi
Brownsville

The XIT Rodeo and Reunion is held each August in Dalhart, Texas.

Ethnic Heritage, 1860

German 3%
Mexican 2%
Other 2%
African American 30%
Anglo American 63%

Settlement in Texas, 1865

- African American
- Anglo American
- Czech
- French
- German
- Irish
- Mexican/Spanish
- Polish
- Norwegian
- □ Indian reservation
- - - - Extent of settlement

The Lone Star Republic

Why It Matters

The victory at San Jacinto began a 10-year period in which Texas was an independent nation. Those 10 years brought both challenges and achievements. Eventually Texas voluntarily gave up its independent status and became a part of the United States.

The Impact Today

• *The existence of Texas as an independent republic continues to be a source of great pride to Texans. Several organizations such as the Daughters of the Republic of Texas and the Sons of the Republic of Texas were formed to honor the people who lived in Texas at that time and to preserve Texas history.*

• *The United States itself would have a vastly different character if Texas had chosen to remain a separate republic.*

1836
★ Sam Houston elected first president of the Republic of Texas
★ Houston became capital of Texas

1838
★ Mirabeau Lamar elected president

1839
★ Austin became new capital of Texas

Texas

United States   *1835*   *1837*   *1839*

World

1837
• Queen Victoria began her reign in Great Britain

1841
• New Zealand became a British colony

This image, titled View of Houston, *shows the city in its earliest days. For a brief time, Houston was a capital of the Republic of Texas.*

Sequencing Events Study Foldable Time lines are used to list important dates in chronological order. Use this foldable to sequence key events that occurred in the first several years after Texas became a republic, or an independent nation.

Step 1 Fold two sheets of paper in half from top to bottom.

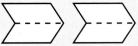

Step 2 Turn the papers and cut each in half.

Cut along fold lines.

Step 3 Fold the four pieces in half from top to bottom.

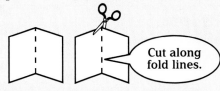

Step 4 Tape the ends of the pieces together (overlapping the edges very slightly) to make an accordion time line and label it as shown.

1836 1837 1838 1839 1840 1841 1842 1844

Pieces of tape

Reading and Writing As you read the chapter, record key events that occurred each year during the important years of the Lone Star Republic.

1845
★ Texas became the 28th state in the United States of America

1867
★ The Houston "Stonewalls" beat the Galveston "Robert E. Lees" in first recorded baseball game in Texas.

1844   1845   1870

1844
• Samuel Morse sent first long-distance telegraph message between Baltimore and Washington
• James K. Polk elected president of the United States

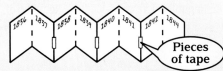

TEXAS HISTORY *Online*

Chapter Overview
Visit the texans.glencoe.com Web site and click on **Chapter 12—Chapter Overviews** to preview chapter information.

Sam Houston's Government

Guide to Reading

Main Idea
After gaining independence, Texans faced the challenge of building a new nation.

Key Terms
capitol, annexation, expenditure, revenue, tariff

Reading Strategy
Organizing Information As you read this section, complete a chart like the one shown here by filling in the significance of each person listed.

Person	Significance
Henry Morfit	
William Wharton	
Memucan Hunt	
J. Pinckney Henderson	

Read to Learn
• what problems faced the Republic of Texas during its first years.
• why Texans wanted the United States to annex Texas.

Section Theme
Government and Democracy Texas leaders worked to build a successful government that would be recognized and annexed by the United States.

Preview of Events

♦1836	♦1837	♦1838	♦1839	♦1840

September
Sam Houston is elected first president of Republic of Texas

December
Houston designated as first capital of Republic of Texas

March 3
United States grants recognition to Republic of Texas

September 25
France recognizes Republic of Texas

Sam Houston

A Texas Story

In his inaugural speech after taking the oath of office for president, Sam Houston said: "I am perfectly aware of the difficulties that surround me . . . Had it been my destiny, I would infinitely have preferred the toils, privations, and perils of a soldier, to the duties of my present station."

Later, President Mirabeau Lamar called himself a *Texian* during this period to foster a sense of pride and nationalism. Texians or Texans, the pioneers of the republic faced many dangers in securing the safety of their nation.

Houston Forms a Government

In September 1836, Texans elected Sam Houston as the first president of Texas and Mirabeau B. Lamar as the first vice president. Texans also approved the Constitution of 1836 and the proposal that Texas join the

United States. Houston and the Texas Congress met at **Columbia** in Brazoria County in October 1836 to organize the new government.

Houston named Stephen F. Austin as secretary of state, but he served only a few weeks. Austin died of pneumonia on December 27, 1836, at the age of 43. President Houston declared that "the Father of Texas is no more. The first pioneer of the wilderness has departed."

Selecting a new capital was one of the first decisions of the new government. Columbia was too small. John K. Allen and his brother Augustus had founded **Houston,** on Buffalo Bayou. The Allens promised to build a handsome city if the congress would locate the capital there. In December 1836, congress designated Houston as the capital for three years. The decision on a permanent site was delayed.

Early visitors to the new capital often commented on the muddy streets, crudely built houses, and swarms of mosquitoes. Eventually, the government moved to the large, two-story capitol at the corner of Main Street and Texas Avenue.

Picturing **History**

This building served as the first capitol in Houston from 1837 to 1839, and again in 1842. The historic Rice Hotel was later built on the same ground as the old capitol. How does this building compare to modern government buildings?

Houston Faces Trouble With the Army

Houston also faced serious problems with the military. Many adventurers and soldiers had arrived in Texas too late to fight in the revolution but they wanted action. Army commander Felix Huston called for an invasion of Mexico.

President Houston wanted no part of such a plan. He realized that a war would be costly and could mean a quick end for the new republic. The president sent all but 600 of the soldiers home on leave and never recalled them to duty. The threat from the army disappeared.

The United States Delays Annexation

In the September 1836 elections, Texans had indicated their strong desire to join the United States. Most Texans had emigrated from the United States and wanted U.S. protection. Texas and the United States had strong cultural ties.

Annexation, or becoming a part of the United States, did not come easily. Mexico refused to recognize Texas's independence. The United States government did not want to annex Texas if it meant damaging relations with Mexico.

Another problem was slavery. Many anti-slavery groups in the United States were against

annexation because Texas would join the Union and tip the balance of power in the U.S. Senate towards the slave states. These groups were strong enough to block annexation and to delay official recognition of Texas as a republic.

✓ **Reading Check** **Examining** Why was annexation a difficult process for Texas?

Recognition as a Nation

The United States did not officially recognize Texas as a nation for several months. In 1836, **President Jackson** sent **Henry Morfit** of Virginia to Texas on a fact-finding mission. Morfit recommended that the United States delay recognition of Texas. Morfit doubted that Texas could keep its independence against a Mexican invasion.

President Jackson accepted Morfit's recommendation, but President Houston did not give up. He sent **William H. Wharton** and **Memucan Hunt** to Washington, D.C., to work for both recognition and annexation.

Wharton and Hunt convinced Congress that Texas had a responsible government. On March 3, 1837, President Jackson granted official recognition of Texas.

President Houston now moved to open diplomatic negotiations with European powers. He sent **J. Pinckney Henderson** to obtain recognition and negotiate commercial treaties with France and Great Britain. At first these countries hesitated to recognize Texas because they did not want to offend Mexico. They also believed that Texas would be annexed quickly by the United States.

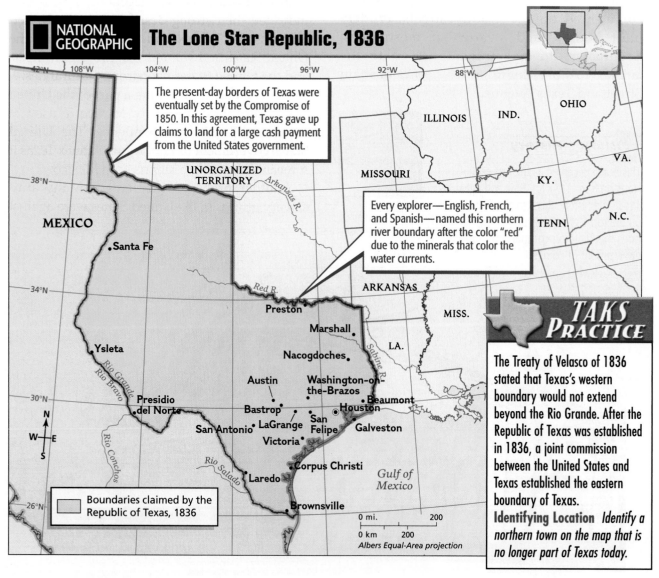

NATIONAL GEOGRAPHIC

The Lone Star Republic, 1836

The present-day borders of Texas were eventually set by the Compromise of 1850. In this agreement, Texas gave up claims to land for a large cash payment from the United States government.

Every explorer—English, French, and Spanish—named this northern river boundary after the color "red" due to the minerals that color the water currents.

OHIO

ILLINOIS   IND.

UNORGANIZED TERRITORY   Arkansas R.   MISSOURI   VA.

KY.

MEXICO

Santa Fe   Red R.   ARKANSAS   TENN.   N.C.

Preston   MISS.

Marshall

Ysleta   Nacogdoches

Austin   Washington-on-the-Brazos   LA.   Sabine R.

Rio Grande   Rio Bravo   Presidio del Norte   Bastrop   Beaumont   Houston

San Antonio   LaGrange   San Felipe   Galveston

Victoria

Rio Conchos   Corpus Christi   Gulf of Mexico

Rio Salado   Laredo

Boundaries claimed by the Republic of Texas, 1836

Brownsville

0 mi.   200
0 km   200
Albers Equal-Area projection

N W E S

TAKS PRACTICE

The Treaty of Velasco of 1836 stated that Texas's western boundary would not extend beyond the Rio Grande. After the Republic of Texas was established in 1836, a joint commission between the United States and Texas established the eastern boundary of Texas.

Identifying Location *Identify a northern town on the map that is no longer part of Texas today.*

Picturing **History**

During the Republic of Texas, the Texas Rangers were used in part for patrolling the frontier. **How did President Houston use the Texas Rangers?**

Henderson continued to press for recognition of the Republic of Texas. France extended recognition on September 25, 1839, and a commercial treaty was negotiated between the two countries. A year later Great Britain and the Netherlands recognized Texas.

Houston hoped that if these countries, especially Great Britain, showed interest in Texas, the United States would move quickly to annex Texas. European countries were looking for ways to limit United States expansion. By the same token, the United States did not want European countries to have a foothold on the continent.

Reading Check **Identifying** What countries recognized Texas as a nation during Houston's presidency?

Native American and Texan Conflicts

As more and more Anglo Americans settled in central Texas, the Wichitas, Comanches, Kiowas, and other Native Americans resented the newcomers. They began a series of raids that lasted from 1836 through 1837. In one attack, Comanches and Kiowas killed several settlers and kidnapped two women and several children, including **Cynthia Ann Parker,** from Parker's Fort near present-day Groesbeck.

The frequency of the raids decreased after President Houston called on the Texas Rangers to patrol central Texas. In a letter to Major Thomas I. Smith, the president wrote:

❝I have been informed that there are some persons on the frontier who have a disposition to molest the . . . Lipan Indians. They cannot be good citizens, or they would wish to preserve peace with them.

Should any property be stolen from the Indians, or injury done them, I hope you will have active measures taken for its restoration and for the preservation of their friendship.❞

During this time Houston also tried to improve relations between Texans and the Cherokees in East Texas. Cherokees had moved into Texas under Mexican rule in the 1820s after being forced from their homes in Georgia. The provisional government sent Houston and others to reach an agreement with the Cherokees during the Texas Revolution.

In the February 1836 treaty, the Cherokees promised to remain peaceful during the Texas fight for independence. In return, the Texan negotiators promised the Cherokees title to their land. Later, however, the Senate of the Republic of Texas refused to accept this treaty. The Cherokees did not receive title to their land, and each day more settlers moved into land in East Texas claimed by Native Americans.

Texas Debt Soars

Like many developing nations, the Republic of Texas constantly had money problems. Expenditures, or money paid out, were much greater than revenue, or money received. In addition, Texas had unpaid bills for the supplies and equipment of the revolution. When Houston became president, the debt was $1.25 million.

Congress took steps to raise money. It placed a tariff, or tax, on various goods imported into Texas. Congress also imposed property taxes, business taxes, and land title fees. These taxes were difficult to collect, and the government continued to spend more money than it collected. By the end of Houston's first term as president, the public debt of Texas had climbed to $2 million.

The Release of Santa Anna

Some Texans hoped that the release of Santa Anna in November 1836 would lead to better relations with Mexico. After he was freed, Santa Anna briefly visited the United States. He returned to Mexico in March 1837. On his arrival, he renounced all promises he had made in Texas and declared that he had left politics forever. His retirement was brief. Within a few years, Santa Anna was back in power. Little had changed. Santa Anna's release had not improved Texas–Mexico relations. The Mexican government still refused to recognize the independence of Texas.

Reading Check **Explaining** How did Texas attempt to reduce its debt?

SECTION 1 ASSESSMENT

Checking for Understanding

1. **Using Key Terms** Define expenditure, annexation, revenue, capitol, and tariff.
2. **Reviewing Facts** Who were the first president, vice president, and secretary of state of the Republic of Texas?

Reviewing Themes

3. **Government and Democracy** On what date did the United States recognize the government of Texas?

Organizing to Learn

4. **Identifying Solutions** Create a chart and indicate how each conflict was resolved during Houston's presidency.

Conflict	Solution
U.S. delays recognition of Texas	
Raids by Comanches and Kiowas	
F. Huston's desire to invade Mexico	

Critical Thinking

5. **Explaining** Why did the Texas Congress designate Houston as the first capital?
6. **Summarizing** Why did the public debt of Texas continue to increase through the years of the Republic?

TAKS PRACTICE

Identifying Problems Give two reasons why some people in the United States opposed the annexation of Texas.

Lamar Becomes President

Guide to Reading

Main Idea
President Lamar's policies differed sharply from Houston's policies.

Key Terms
endowment fund
cabinet
redback

Reading Strategy
Classifying Information As you read this section, complete a table like the one shown here with the key issues, goals of Lamar's administration, and what actions were taken.

Issue	Goals	Actions Taken
Education		
Native Americans		
Military		

Read to Learn
• what policies Lamar's administration used toward Native Americans.
• how the programs of the Lamar and Houston administrations were different.

Section Theme
Government and Democracy Government policy promoted public education.

Preview of Events

```
     ♦1838                          ♦1839                               ♦1840
```

Mirabeau Lamar is elected president

Lamar orders removal of Cherokees

October Austin becomes new capital

Council House Fight between Texans and Comanches

Native American holding peace pipe

A Texas Story

In his 1836 inaugural address, Sam Houston had expressed his desire to have peaceful relations with Native Americans. "Treaties of peace . . . and the maintenance of good faith with the Indians, present themselves . . . as the most rational grounds on which to obtain their friendship."

Mirabeau Lamar Becomes President

The Constitution of 1836 stated that the president could not serve consecutive terms; therefore, Houston could not be reelected when his term ended in 1838. Texans elected Mirabeau B. Lamar, who had served as vice president under Houston. Lamar, who had great hopes for Texas, opposed annexation. He believed that one day Texas would be a powerful, independent nation that would extend all the way to the Pacific Ocean.

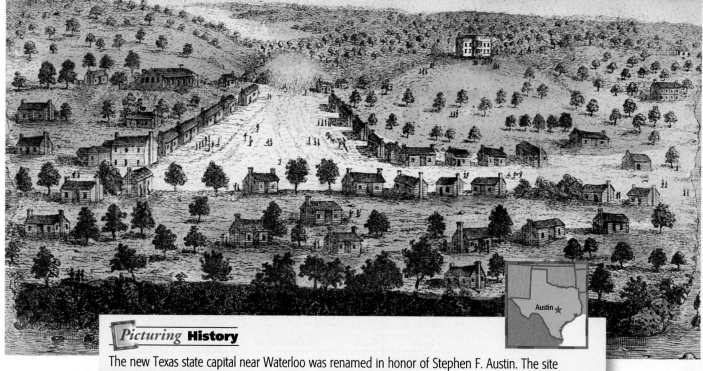

Improving education was one of the new president's goals. As did Thomas Jefferson, Lamar believed that citizens of a republic must be educated so they could make intelligent decisions. In his inaugural address, he said:

> ❝A cultivated mind is the guardian genius of Democracy, and while guided and controlled by virtue, the noblest attribute to man.❞

Stirred by Lamar's ideas, congress set aside nearly 18,000 acres of land in each Texas county for the support of public schools. Congress reserved an additional 231,400 acres (93,717 hectares) of public land in central Texas as a source of income for two universities. Later governments of Texas substituted land in West Texas. The value of the endowment fund multiplied when oil was discovered on these lands in the 1900s. Because of Lamar's efforts, he is sometimes called the "Father of Education in Texas."

The Capital Is Moved to Austin

It had been agreed that Houston would serve as the capital only until another site was chosen. In 1839 a commission and congress approved a site on the Colorado River near the village of Waterloo. Lamar was delighted with the decision. He wanted to expand Texas settlement westward.

The government appointed **Edwin Waller** to lay out streets and construct a capitol on the site. In October 1839, President Lamar and his cabinet arrived in the new capital, named Austin in honor of Stephen F. Austin. Austin joined Columbia, South Carolina, and Raleigh, North Carolina, as cities founded specifically to be capitals.

Lamar's Policy Toward Native Americans

Lamar reversed Sam Houston's policy toward Native Americans. Many Cherokees had settled on farms and in villages in northeastern Texas in what is today Smith and Cherokee Counties, and Lamar believed the Cherokees had no fair claim to the Texas lands they occupied.

In addition, President Lamar had heard rumors that Mexican agents were attempting to stir up the Cherokees against Texas. In the summer of 1839, President Lamar ordered the removal of the Cherokees from Texas. On July 16 the Texas army attacked the Cherokees near the

Neches River not far from present-day Tyler. Several Texans and nearly 100 Cherokees were killed. Among the dead was the leader of the Cherokees, **Duwali,** also known as **Chief Bowles.** The army burned Cherokee villages and farms. The surviving Cherokees were forced from their land and moved across the Red River, out of Texas.

✓ **Reading Check** **Explaining** How did President Lamar view Cherokee ownership of land?

Raids Lead to Council House Fight

The government also tried to deal with the Comanche presence. During 1838 and 1839, Comanches raided several outlying settlements. After a series of battles with Texans along the upper Colorado River, however, the Comanches agreed to meet with Texas authorities. In the meeting held in San Antonio in 1840, hopes for peace quickly vanished. The Comanches had promised to bring their Anglo captives, but they produced only one, a girl named **Matilda Lockhart.** According to an eyewitness, "her head, arms, and face were full of bruises and sores." Matilda told the Texans that 13 others

Picturing **History**

Chief Bowles attempted to save Cherokee land in Texas but was unable to do so. He was killed near Tyler fighting the Texas army. **Given President Lamar's policies toward the Native Americans, what options did Chief Bowles have?**

were being held captive in the hills west of San Antonio. Angry Texan troops attempted to take the Comanche negotiators as hostages until the Comanches freed their captives. The Comanches resisted, and in the struggle—known as the

People of Texas

Mirabeau Lamar 1798-1859

Mirabeau Lamar was born in Georgia and moved to Texas in 1835. After the battle of San Jacinto, David Burnet appointed him secretary of war. He also served as major general and commander of the Texas army.

When Houston was elected president, Lamar became his vice president. Two years later he became the second president of the republic. Lamar was popular with Texans and was thought of as an eloquent speaker.

Lamar is responsible for choosing Austin as the capital of Texas. He earned the nickname "Father of Education in Texas" for urging congress to set aside land for public education, including two colleges or universities.

Council House Fight—7 Texans and 35 Comanches died. The Comanches killed many of their white captives and set out to avenge the Comanche deaths. One historian called the Council House Fight "the greatest blunder in the history of Texan–Native American relations," because after the incident the Comanches refused to make treaties with Texans. They would talk peace with American soldiers, but not with Texans. Years of bitter warfare resulted and many lives were lost.

News of daring raids by the Kiowas and Comanches under the command of **Buffalo Hump** spread quickly throughout Texas. Volunteers gathered, commanded by **Edward Burleson**. **Ben McCulloch** led a group of Texas Rangers. At Plum Creek, the Texans encountered a Comanche party. Texans killed nearly 100 Comanches and lost only one of their own men.

The Texans invaded Comanche country in revenge for earlier attacks on Victoria and Linnville. In October 1840, **Colonel John H. Moore** led a surprise attack on a large Comanche village on the upper Colorado River. Nearly 130 Comanches died in the attack. Most of the southern Comanches withdrew toward the area of the Red River.

Texas Rebuilds Its Navy

Lamar thought that having a strong military would force Mexico to recognize the Republic of Texas. Lamar ordered the newly restored navy into Mexican waters. The navy aided rebels who were fighting for independence from Mexico in the province of Yucatán. Lamar hoped, in vain, that the Mexican government would recognize Texas in exchange for the promise that the Texan navy would not harass Mexican ships. When Sam Houston regained the presidency in 1841, he recalled the navy.

The Santa Fe Expedition

Although the **Nueces River** traditionally had been the boundary between Texas and Mexico, Texans claimed the Rio Grande as the border after the revolution. Texans were interested in controlling Santa Fe, the trading center on the upper Rio Grande. Santa Fe was the destination of traders from St. Louis, Missouri.

Lamar sent an expedition to Santa Fe to control the region and open trade with New Mexico. The **Santa Fe expedition** (consisting of soldiers, merchants, wagon drivers, and adventurers) began its trek on June 20, 1841, from a camp near Austin. Misfortune and hardship plagued the members every step of the way. Heat, lack of water and food, and attacks by Native Americans led to suffering.

As the expedition neared Santa Fe, the exhausted members encountered a Mexican army detachment that forced the Texans to surrender. The prisoners were marched more than 1,000 miles (1,609 km) from Santa Fe to Mexico City. Many died on the way, and others

Causes and Effects of Western Conflict

Causes

- Settlers immigrate to Texas.
- Cherokees move to Texas but do not hold title to land.
- Comanches raid Texas settlements.

Effects

- Lamar orders Cherokees to leave.
- Texas Rangers retaliate against raids.
- Comanches withdraw to the High Plains, leaving more land to the Anglo settlers.

Graphic Organizer → *Skills*

President Lamar took a different approach to relations with Native Americans than Houston.

Identifying Points of View Which president's approach would the Native Americans have preferred and why?

perished in a Mexican prison. Most of those who survived were released in April 1842, after British and American diplomats worked for their release. The Santa Fe expedition was a failure in many ways. It angered the Mexicans, resulted in the loss of many lives, and failed to take control of Santa Fe.

Financial Difficulties

Lamar's campaigns were costly, both in terms of colonists and Native Americans killed and in money. The Indian wars cost the Republic of Texas nearly $2.5 million during his three years in office. Lamar was just as extravagant in other matters, such as outfitting expeditions and reorganizing the Texas navy. He bought several ships, and kept the navy on active duty in the Gulf of Mexico.

TEXAS HISTORY Online

Student Web Activity Visit the texans.glencoe.com Web site and click on **Chapter 12—Student Web Activity** to learn more about the Texas navy.

Lamar failed in attempts to borrow money from the United States and European nations. Additional paper money, known as redbacks, was issued but quickly shrank in value. By the end of Lamar's term, a paper dollar in

Picturing **History**

Three hundred twenty-one people and twenty-one ox-drawn wagons carried supplies and merchandise of the traders on the ill-fated Santa Fe expedition. **Why were people willing to participate in such an expedition?**

Texas was worth about 15 cents. The public debt rose to $7 million. Many in Texas were becoming concerned about the increasing national debt.

✓ **Reading Check** **Analyzing** Why did Lamar face financial difficulties?

SECTION 2 ASSESSMENT

Checking for Understanding

1. **Using Key Terms** Use the word cabinet in a sentence that pertains to President Lamar and the government of Texas.
2. **Reviewing Facts** Why was Houston not reelected when his first term ended in 1838?

Reviewing Themes

3. **Government and Democracy** Why did the Texas Congress reserve 231,400 acres of public land?

Organizing to Learn

4. **Listing** Create a web like the one shown below. List the problems that the Texans encountered during the Santa Fe expedition. Include details about what led to the expedition and what the results were. (The results would include any lessons learned.)

Critical Thinking

5. **Explaining** Why did President Lamar want to have a strong military?
6. **Evaluating Solutions** How effective were President Lamar's solutions to financial difficulties?

TAKS PRACTICE

Determining Cause and Effect What was the effect of the Council House meeting in San Antonio between Texas authorities and the Comanches?

Texas LITERATURE

John R. Knaggs

John Knaggs' interest in Texas history began as a child. Knaggs grew up near one of the Nueces River crossings used by Mexican forces during the Texas Revolution. While researching the revolution, he found several "gaps" in information from the records of crucial events. In *The Bugles Are Silent,* Knaggs uses his own imagination to fill in the "gaps."

Reading to Discover

Imagine that you are present when this fictional conversation is taking place. How would you know that Houston valued Chief Bowle's advice?

Reader's Dictionary

aspiration: a great ambition or ultimate goal

annexation: an addition to something larger or more significant

obtain: succeed in gaining possession of; to acquire

reap: to harvest; to win or obtain

The Bugles Are Silent

by John R. Knaggs

In this chapter, General Houston talks about annexation and the presidency.

. . . When [Houston] returned, [Elizabeth] was leaning against a column . . . "Samuel, I want you to know how much I appreciate the admirable manner in which your men conducted themselves tonight . . . I'm confident your army will be successful. You should become a man of means following the war . . . But you will need some property to fulfill your political **aspirations.** I assume you will become president of the Republic of Texas."

"I intend to seek that office."

"And beyond?"

"I would steer toward **annexation** into the United States."

"After which you will become . . . perhaps even president of the United States."

"I must admit, I would seek the office, if I had the opportunity."

"I hope you will indeed become president . . . fulfilling your highest aspiration."

"I have never said that was my highest aspiration."

"What could be more important?"

". . . I turned my back on my Anglo society rejoining the Cherokees as a member of the tribe . . . One night . . . Chief Bowles sat me down for a talk. He said that I had run

away to find myself, but that I had remained lost. 'You must return to your people,' he said. 'You are blessed with a rare opportunity to **obtain** the most valuable of all possessions, wisdom. You must sow carefully the fields of knowledge and understanding. Then, my brother, you will **reap** wisdom, which is more precious than wealth or power. Your destiny is to lead your people; but without wisdom, the sun of life, you will remain in despair.'"

ANALYZING LITERATURE

Evaluate and Connect

What do you believe Chief Bowles was trying to tell General Houston when he spoke with him about wisdom and leading his people?

Interdisciplinary Activity

Journalism Prepare a CNN-style interview with Elizabeth after the election of General Houston as the president of Texas. What information might she have to share with the citizens of the Republic of Texas?

Houston Regains Presidency

Guide to Reading

Main Idea
Sam Houston's return to the presidency signaled a change in the government's economic and Native American policies.

Key Term
archives

Reading Strategy
Organizing Information As you read this section, complete a chart like the one shown here, outlining important events and their outcomes.

Event	Outcome
Archives War	
Woll Invasion	
Mier Expedition	
Regulator–Moderator War	

Read to Learn
- what ways President Houston tried to reduce government spending.
- about conflicts with Mexico.
- how Houston attempted to resolve the Texan–Native American conflicts.

Section Theme
Economic Factors Texas attempted to balance the budget, yet the debt increased.

Preview of Events

♦1842

March
Mexican army invades southern Texas and retreats

September
Mexican army occupies San Antonio and retreats

December
Texas army attacks Mexican town of Mier and then surrenders

President Sam Houston

A
Texas Story

In a bitter campaign filled with gossip and scandal, Sam Houston defeated Lamar's chosen successor—David G. Burnet—for the presidency. Houston had disliked Lamar's policies and programs and wanted to undo the damage he felt Lamar's administration had done to Texas. The major issues during Houston's second term were the budget, the threat of invasion from Mexico, and annexation by the United States.

A Policy of Economy

When Houston regained the presidency in 1841, he eliminated dozens of government positions and cut the size of the army. He sold navy ships to citizens of Galveston and accepted them back as gifts.

Despite these cost-cutting steps, the debt of the republic increased, largely because of the high interest that had to be paid.

Angelina Eberly played a decisive role in preventing Sam Houston from moving the government archives from Austin to Houston in 1842. Why is it important to protect government archives?

A Temporary Peace

Houston also tried to renew peaceful and fair dealings with Native Americans. His letter of October 9, 1842, to Indian commissioners expressed his views concerning Native American rights:

> ❝Neither the Indians nor the whites shall pass into the territory of the other without lawful permission . . . Should a white man kill an Indian or commit any crime upon an Indian on his property . . . he shall be punished by laws of the republic.❞

Treaties signed with various Native American groups at Bird's Fort and at Torrey's Trading House ensured a period of calm for several years.

Invasion Triggers the Archives War

The Santa Fe expedition produced a response from Mexico. In March 1842 a Mexican army of about 500 soldiers, commanded by **General Rafael Vásquez,** invaded Texas and occupied San Antonio, Goliad, and Refugio.

Although Vásquez withdrew after several days, many Texans panicked. President Houston declared a public emergency and tried to save the government archives, or official documents, by moving them from Austin to Houston. Many Austin residents suspected that Houston intended to move the capital from Austin permanently. When government officials tried to move the archives, some Austin residents, led by **Angelina Eberly,** fired on them. This skirmish, called the **Archives War,** ended with the archives—and the capital—remaining in Austin.

✓ Reading Check **Explaining** What caused the Archives War?

Woll Invades Texas

In September 1842, Mexican forces invaded Texas again. This time a larger Mexican army, numbering 1,400 and commanded by **General Adrián Woll,** occupied San Antonio. The Texas militia and the Texas Rangers rushed to San Antonio. After some heavy fighting, Woll's army was driven out of Texas.

The Texans suffered losses in the fighting. The Mexican army trapped **Captain Nicholas Dawson** and a company of volunteers from Fayette County. Dawson and about 35 of the volunteers were killed. Dawson and his fallen soldiers were later buried on Monument Hill near La Grange, Texas.

The Mier Expedition

The Woll invasion angered Texans. Many citizens demanded that President Houston take action to protect the republic. Houston tried to settle the problems peaceably. Houston hoped that the U.S., France, and Great Britain would pressure Mexico to leave Texas alone.

In November 1842, Houston ordered **General Alexander Somervell** and a militia of 750 to patrol the area from San Antonio to Laredo. When Somervell's forces reached Laredo, they found no signs of the Mexican army, so Somervell ordered his soldiers back to Gonzales. About 300 of the soldiers balked at the decision. Under the leadership

of **Colonel William S. Fisher,** these Texans moved down the Rio Grande and attacked the Mexican town of **Mier** (MEE•ehr). The Texans expected an easy victory. Early in the battle, however, **General Pedro Ampudía** and 900 Mexican soldiers arrived to reinforce the troops defending Mier. After two days of fighting, the Texans, outnumbered and low on supplies, surrendered on December 26, 1842.

The Drawing of the Black Beans

The Mexican army began to march their captives to Mexico City, but the Texans overpowered their guards and escaped on February 11, 1843. The Texans lost their way in the mountains and some died of starvation and exposure. Mexican troops recaptured the survivors about a week later.

Santa Anna, now back in power in Mexico, ordered every tenth Texan executed as punishment for their escape attempt. Of the 176 men recaptured, 17 were to die. To determine which men would be executed, the prisoners were ordered to draw beans from a jar. Those who drew black beans were shot; those who drew white beans were marched to prison in Mexico City.

Thomas J. Green described the drawing of the black beans:

❝The decimation [selection of every tenth prisoner to die] took place by the drawing of black and white beans from a small earthen mug. The white ones signified exemption, and the black death. One hundred and fifty-nine white beans were placed in the bottom of the mug, and seventeen black ones placed upon the top of them. The beans were not stirred, and had so light a shake that it was perfectly clear they had not been mixed together. Such was their anxiety to execute Captain Cameron, and perhaps the balance of the officers, that first Cameron, and afterward they, were made to draw a bean each from the mug in this condition.❞

History Through Art

Mier Expedition: The Drawing of the Black Bean by Frederic Remington, 1896 This image captures the tension and anxiety of the prisoners whose fate will be decided by the bean they draw. **Does this image support Thomas Green's description in the text? Explain.**

The remaining prisoners were transferred to Vera Cruz, where they joined the San Antonio prisoners Woll had taken. A few of the Texas captives were pardoned, eight prisoners managed to escape, and others died of disease or starvation. On September 16, 1844, those who remained in prison were released.

Feuds Lead to Unrest in East Texas

Late in his second term, Houston also had to deal with trouble that developed in East Texas from 1839 to 1844 near the old Neutral Ground Territory. The feud between old settlers and more recent arrivals began over land titles. Two groups of settlers—the **Regulators** and the **Moderators**—had been fighting for several years. Each group had formed to keep law and order because there were few local officials available to do so. As a result of the conflict, property was burned and several people were murdered. A general state of unrest and lawlessness prevailed in Shelby and neighboring counties. Local law enforcement tried but could not stop the feud. Some of the lawmen were even personally involved on one side or the other.

In August 1844, the situation worsened and spread to surrounding counties in Texas and

A Shared Past...

Many historians believe the election of 1840 (William Henry Harrison vs. Martin Van Buren) was the first "modern" presidential campaign in the U.S. Two parties, the Whigs and the Democrats, conducted parades, mass meetings, and bonfires to draw attention to their candidates. Personal attacks and accusations of scandal were common. Texas politicians followed this trend in the election of 1841.

Louisiana. Houses were burned, people were driven out of their homes, and violence seemed to be everywhere. Houston sent 600 soldiers into the area to bring about peace. Houston himself traveled there and reminded the settlers that they were all Texans and should not fight each other. He persuaded both sides to end the Regulator–Moderator War.

✓ **Reading Check** **Summarizing** What occurred as a result of the Mier expedition?

SECTION 3 ASSESSMENT

Checking for Understanding

1. **Using Key Terms** Use the word archives in a sentence describing what kinds of documents these might be.
2. **Reviewing Facts** Why did the capital remain in Austin instead of moving to Houston in 1842?

Reviewing Themes

3. **Economic Factors** Public debt refers to money owed by a government. Why did the public debt of Texas continue to increase despite attempts by Houston to balance the budget?

Organizing to Learn

4. **Sequencing** Create a time line like the one shown here. Place the letters of the following events in the proper order.

   <del>───┼───┼───┼───┼───</del>

   a. Fisher and his militia attack Mier.
   b. Mexican army commanded by Vásquez occupies San Antonio, Goliad, and Refugio.
   c. Escaped prisoners from the Mier expedition are recaptured.
   d. Houston tries to move archives from Austin.

Critical Thinking

5. **Explaining** What happened to those who drew a black bean as compared to a white bean? Why were the officers more likely to draw the black beans?
6. **Analyzing** How did Houston make temporary peace with the Native Americans?

TAKS PRACTICE

Drawing Conclusions What had the Regulators and the Moderators been fighting over for several years? What could have prevented this conflict?

Distinguishing Fact From Opinion

Why Learn This Skill?

When studying past or current events, it is important to distinguish between fact and opinion. Facts relate exactly what happened, when and where it happened, and who was involved. An opinion expresses a feeling or belief about the event. You should know how to distinguish a fact from an opinion so that you will have accurate information and not confuse the two.

Learning the Skill

Here are some ways to distinguish facts from opinions:

- Check facts for accuracy by comparing them to other sources.
- Can you ask questions beginning with *who, what, when,* or *where?* If so, you are dealing with facts.
- Identify opinions by looking for statements of feelings or beliefs.
- Opinions often begin with "I believe" or "In my view."
- Opinions often contain words like *should, would, could, best, greatest, all, every,* or *always.*

Practicing the Skill

Read each statement below. Then, on a separate piece of paper, write *F* if the statement is a fact or *O* if it is an opinion.

❶ Houston is the most wonderful place in the world.

❷ Comanches and Kiowas killed several settlers and kidnapped two women and several children from Parker's Fort.

❸ There was a cowardly tribe among us, the Tonkawas . . . hated by all other Indians of every tribe.

❹ In the Council House Fight, 12 Comanche chiefs, 20 warriors, and several women and children were killed.

❺ Congress passed acts in 1839 and 1840 that set aside nearly 18,000 acres (7,290 hectares) of land in each Texas county for public education.

Early Texas schoolhouse

❻ She is a noble woman, wife, mother, and patriot—a woman of great thought and heart—yet the most modest and unpretentious of women—Texas is proud of her.

TAKS PRACTICE

Distinguishing Fact From Opinion Read an article from your local newspaper. Determine whether you can distinguish fact from opinion in the article. Write down some examples of opinions and facts from the article. Refer back to the questions under **Learning the Skill** if necessary. Share this with your class.

Glencoe's **Skillbuilder Interactive Workbook,** Level 1, provides instruction and practice in key social studies skills.

Texas Becomes a State

Guide to Reading

Main Idea

Efforts for Texas annexation were given a boost by the changing political atmosphere in the United States.

Key Terms

manifest destiny
joint resolution

Reading Strategy

Organizing Information Complete a table like the one shown here by filling in the roles that these people played in the annexation of Texas.

Person	Role
James Polk	
John Tyler	
Anson Jones	
J. Pinckney Henderson	

Read to Learn

• about the "Texas Question."
• about the annexation of Texas.

Section Theme

Government and Democracy With the approval of the United States Congress, Texas became a state as soon as its people approved annexation and adopted a state constitution.

Preview of Events

♦1845   ♦1846

February 28
U.S. Congress passes joint resolution on annexation

July 4
Texas approves annexation

December 29
President Polk signs resolution making Texas a state

February 19
Ceremony recognizes Texas as the 28th U.S. state

Sam Houston's sword and scabbard

A
Texas Story

A strange thing happened during Houston's inaugural address. He was to give up his sword to symbolize the transition from war to peace. When the time came, Houston could not let go of it. He stood silent on the speaker's platform, staring at the sword in his hands. He finally spoke: "I have worn it with some humble pretensions in defence [sic] of my country; and should the danger of my country again call for my services, I expect to resume it, and respond to that call, if needful, with my blood and life."

The Texas Question

Throughout the years of the republic, most Texans still wanted Texas to join the United States. In 1836, they had voted overwhelmingly for annexation. Sam Houston had worked for this outcome throughout his first term as president of the republic. However, the push for annexation stopped when Mirabeau B. Lamar, who did not favor becoming part of the U.S., succeeded Houston.

By Houston's second term, the "Texas Question" had become important in United States politics. Those against annexation believed that it would benefit southern slaveholders. They also argued that annexation would mean war with Mexico. Annexation was more popular than it had been in 1836. Thousands of Americans had immigrated to Texas, strengthening ties to the United States.

In April 1844, representatives from the United States and Texas signed a treaty that would make Texas a territory of the United States. The treaty also provided that Texas would give its public lands to the United States. In return for this, the United States agreed to pay all the debts of the Republic of Texas.

Some Texans were disappointed with the terms of the treaty. They had hoped for immediate statehood, but the treaty only made Texas a territory. Others fought the treaty, arguing that Texas should keep its very valuable public lands. Even under these terms, however, the majority of Texans favored the treaty of annexation.

Texans confidently expected the United States to accept the treaty. They were surprised when the United States Senate rejected it by a vote of 35 to 16. Many senators opposed the treaty because Texas would ultimately enter the U.S. as a slave state. This would give the South an advantage in the United States Senate. Other senators voted against the treaty because they did not want to anger Mexico. Still others voted against it because 1844 was an election year and they wished to avoid controversy. Yet, the Texas question soon became the center of controversy throughout the United States.

History *Through Art*

Emigrants to the West **by W.M. Cary, 1880** Many settlers immigrated to Texas. What dangers would be met along the road to the West?

Anson Jones 1798–1858

Anson Jones settled in Texas in 1833 and established a successful medical practice. As tension increased between Texas and Mexico, Jones joined the army. Later, he was appointed Texas's minister to the United States, and secretary of state.

In 1844, he was elected the last president of the Republic of Texas and held this office until Texas's annexation, which he opposed. Jones resigned his presidency and turned over the government to Governor Henderson, the first governor of the state of Texas.

After Texas became a state, Jones hoped to be elected to the U.S. Senate, but Sam Houston and Thomas Jefferson Rusk were chosen. Jones's stand on statehood had cost him his political career. He never got over his defeat, and he died a bitter man.

Polk Wins Election

Annexation became an issue during the United States presidential election of 1844. The Democratic Party candidate was **James K. Polk** of Tennessee. Polk, as well as his supporters, wanted Texas to become part of the United States. **Henry Clay** of Kentucky, the Whig Party candidate, was against immediate annexation. He feared the country would split over the issue of slavery. Polk's victory in a very close election showed that most of the voters favored annexation.

Annexation gained momentum from growing support for expansion. Settlers wanted to live in the fertile lands in Oregon, California, and Texas. Merchants wanted ports on the Pacific coast where American ships could stop on their way to trade with Asia. Most Americans believed the United States was destined to expand coast to coast. This belief was called manifest destiny.

Even before Polk took office, **President John Tyler** asked Congress to reconsider annexation. Tyler argued that Congress could no longer delay its decision. The voters had expressed their wishes, and it was time for Congress to act.

✓ **Reading Check** **Identifying** Who were the two U.S. presidential candidates in 1844?

Congress and Texas Approve Annexation

Congressional leaders who wanted annexation proposed that Texas be annexed by a joint resolution. This resolution, passed by both houses of Congress, would have the force of law and would require only a simple majority of votes in each house. Approving a treaty, on the other hand, required a two-thirds majority in the Senate.

On February 28, 1845, Congress passed a joint resolution for annexation. It contained terms more favorable to Texas than those of the treaty of 1844. Texas could enter the Union as soon as its people approved annexation and adopted a state constitution. Texas could keep its public lands but could sell some of these lands to pay its debts. The resolution also stated that Texas could be divided into as many as five states with the approval of Texas and the United States. President Tyler signed the resolution on March 1 and submitted the offer to the Texas government. Most Texans were pleased with the terms. The joint resolution provided for immediate statehood, bypassing the time Texas would be a territory.

Anson Jones, elected president of Texas in 1844, called a special session of the Texas Congress to consider the terms of annexation, which were quickly accepted. The people would have to endorse annexation and draft a new state constitution. The convention, meeting in Austin on July 4, 1845, overwhelmingly backed annexation. The convention then wrote a new state constitution.

On October 13, Texas approved annexation by a vote of 4,254 to 257 and ratified the constitution by 4,174 to 312. The Congress of the United States consented to the Texas Constitution of 1845 in December. On December 29, 1845, President Polk signed the resolution that made Texas a state.

Mexico Offers Recognition

Mexico refused to recognize Texas independence until 1845, when the United States and Texas finally agreed on annexation. Great Britain and France both preferred that Texas remain an independent nation rather than become a part of the United States. For this reason, British and French diplomats tried to convince Mexico that it should recognize Texas independence. In May 1845, Mexico agreed to acknowledge an independent Texas on one condition—Texas must reject annexation by the United States.

Though accepting the offer would ensure that Texas and Mexico would enjoy improved relations, Texas was not interested. The Texas Congress quickly rejected the Mexican proposal and voted to accept annexation by the United States.

A Shared Past...

The United States Congress tried to admit states in pairs—one slave state and one free state—so the U.S. Senate would be equally balanced between slave and free states. The admission of Florida as the 27th state tipped the balance toward slave states. Texas became the 28th state and tipped the balance even more. Iowa and Wisconsin soon were added to the Union to restore the balance in the Senate.

"The Republic of Texas Is No More"

On February 19, 1846, at a ceremony in front of the Texas capitol, Anson Jones, the last president of the republic, turned over the government to J. Pinckney Henderson of San Augustine, the first governor of the state. President Jones closed his farewell address by declaring that "the final act in this great drama is now performed: the Republic of Texas is no more." The Lone Star flag was lowered, and the Stars and Stripes was raised. Texas officially became the 28th state in the United States of America.

✓ **Reading Check** **Analyzing** Why did the U.S. Congress favor annexation by joint resolution?

SECTION 4 ASSESSMENT

Checking for Understanding

1. **Using Key Terms** Define manifest destiny and joint resolution.
2. **Reviewing Facts** Why were some people in the United States against annexing Texas?

Reviewing Themes

3. **Government and Democracy** Why (to the surprise of many Texans) did the United States Senate reject the treaty of 1844 to annex Texas?

Organizing to Learn

4. **Creating Charts** Create a chart like the one shown here, outlining the important dates in the annexation of Texas.

Date	Event
February 28, 1845	
March 1, 1845	
July 4, 1845	
October 13, 1845	
December 29, 1845	
February 19, 1846	

Critical Thinking

5. **Identifying Viewpoints** The annexation of Texas to the U.S. caused different opinions among Texans. Why did some Texans favor annexation in 1845? Why did some Texans oppose annexation?

TAKS PRACTICE

Drawing Inferences Why do you suppose Sam Houston would not give up his sword during his inauguration ceremony?

Chapter Summary

The Lone Star Republic

Key Issues During the Republic of Texas

President	Issues and Events
Sam Houston 1836–1838	• New capital is Houston. • U.S. grants Texas official recognition. • Houston attempts to improve relations with Native Americans. • Debt of Texas increases.
Mirabeau Lamar 1838–1841	• Lamar sets aside land for public education. • Comanches raid Texas settlements. • Austin becomes the capital. • Comanches withdraw to the High Plains. • Santa Fe expedition fails.
Sam Houston 1841–1844	• Texas signs peace treaties with some Native American tribes. • Houston settles civilian disputes. • Mexican and Texan troops engage in military skirmishes.
Anson Jones 1844–1846	• U.S. Congress votes to annex Texas. • Texas approves of annexation with the U.S. • Texas joins the U.S. on December 29, 1845.

Reviewing Key Terms

1. For each term in the left-hand column, choose a word from the right-hand column that relates to it and write a sentence including the two terms.

joint resolution	tariff
expenditure	annexation
cabinet	capitol
endowment fund	revenue

Reviewing Key Facts

2. List two reasons why annexation of Texas to the United States was delayed.

3. Describe the actions of the Native Americans in central Texas during 1836 and 1837.

4. Why did the government debt of Texas grow during the beginning of the republic?

5. Examine what Lamar hoped to accomplish by sending the Texas navy into Mexican waters. What happened to the navy when Sam Houston became president?

6. Describe the results of the Texas attack on the Mexican town of Mier.

7. What did selecting a black bean mean for those Texans who were taken prisoner after the Mier expedition?

8. List three terms of the joint resolution for annexation.

Critical Thinking

9. **Synthesizing Information** Why was President Houston concerned about the treatment of Native Americans?

10. **Making Comparisons** Compare the presidencies of Houston and Lamar. Make a chart like the one below.

Issue	Houston	Lamar
Education		
Native Americans		
Military		
Debt		

11. **Determining Cause and Effect** How did Santa Anna's release affect Texas's relations with Mexico?

12. **Analyzing Information** The Texas voters approved both annexation and the constitution by a great majority. Why do you think so many Texans wanted to be annexed by the United States? What do you think they hoped to gain?

Geography and History Activity

Draw the following on a blank map of Texas. Refer to the map titled The Lone Star Republic on page 272 to complete the following directions.

13. Label and draw stars next to the republic's first and second capitals.

14. In the area of East Texas, draw three arrows pointing toward the Red River. Label the area "Cherokees."

15. In the area of central Texas, write the names of the following tribes: Wichitas, Comanches, and Kiowas.

Cooperative Learning Activity

16. **Evaluating the Presidents** As presidents of the Republic of Texas, Sam Houston (who served twice), Mirabeau Lamar, and Anson Jones had many problems to solve. Divide into groups of three or four students. As a group, decide what grade (A to F scale) you would give each president of the republic. Give Sam Houston a grade for each term. Consider the following issues: foreign relations, relations with Native Americans, establishing a government, reducing the debt, education, and conflicts among Texans. The group should write a report card for each president.

Practicing Skills

17. **Distinguishing Fact From Opinion** To get accurate information about past and current events, you must be able to distinguish between facts and opinions. Read the following account of the Council House Fight. Then write two examples of fact and two examples of opinion.

> *On Tuesday, 19th of March, 1840, 65 Comanches came to town to make a treaty. They brought with them, and reluctantly gave up, Matilda Lockhart, whom they captured in December 1838 . . .*
>
> *This was the third time these Indians had come for a talk, pretending to seek peace, and trying to get ransom money for their . . . captives. Their proposition now was that they should be paid a great price for Matilda . . . Now the Americans, mindful of the treachery of the Comanches, answered . . .*
>
> *"We will . . . keep four or five of your chiefs, whilst the others of your people go to your nation and bring all the captives, and then we will pay all you ask for them . . . This we have determined, and, if you try to fight, our soldiers will shoot you down."*
>
> —From *Memoirs of Mary Maverick*, 1921

Self-Check Quiz

Visit the texans.glencoe.com Web site and click on **Chapter 12—Self-Check Quizzes** to prepare for the chapter test.

 ## Portfolio/TAKS Writing Activity

18. **Persuasive Writing** Imagine you are a Texan in 1840 who favors annexation. Write a letter to a friend who does not want Texas in the United States. Try to persuade your friend to support your position. Save your work for your portfolio.

Use the graph to answer the following question.

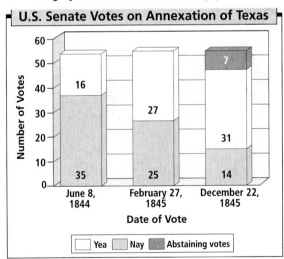

In February of 1845, about how many more U.S. senators supported the annexation of Texas than in June of 1844?

F 5   **G** 10   **H** 15   **J** 20

Test-Taking Tip:

Decide what information you require and disregard any information that you do not need. The two numbers that you need to answer the problem are the number of senators who supported annexation in June and the number who supported it in February.

Economics & History

To Protect and to Serve

All societies try to find ways to guard their citizens from threats posed by those who do not obey laws. During the 1820s and early 1830s, the people of Texas formed volunteer companies for self-protection. These companies patrolled the frontier regions looking for danger and, when their work was completed, returned home to care for their families and tend to their fields.

The ad interim, or temporary, government created three companies of citizen-soldiers in 1836 and charged them with protecting Anglo settlers from attacks by Native Americans. They were also to serve as an army in the event of an invasion by Mexico. In this way, the Texas congress was fulfilling one of the major duties of any government—to guarantee the safety of its citizens.

Texas Rangers

Unfortunately, the ad interim Texas government could ill afford a military force of any kind. It paid volunteers little or nothing at all. The men had to provide their own horses and bring their own firearms. Often, the Rangers, as these men eventually came to be called, had to live off the land. About all the government could do was pledge to pay them $25 a month, provide them with land, and supply them with ammunition. Many Rangers served their terms out of dedication and civic duty. Some, however, used their authority for personal gain. Occasionally, innocent people suffered from the rough system of frontier justice.

Jack Hays

Sam Houston became the republic's first president in September 1836, but his election did not bring the Rangers better conditions or wages. There were limits to how much the Rangers would endure in the name of patriotism. Once finished with their scouting assignments, they generally returned home.

Jack Hays

Rangers like Jack Hays added to their small government income by working as surveyors. Ranger duties called for protecting surveyors while they

Jack Hays *(above right)* was a member of the Texan Mounted Militia *(above)*.

worked near Native American hunting grounds. Since Hays was out on the frontier anyway, he accepted jobs from private individuals who wished to have their land marked and measured. In this manner, Hays was able to supplement his government salary.

Hays went on to become one of the most famous of the Texas Rangers during the 1840s. President Mirabeau B. Lamar adopted a "get-tough" policy against those who opposed the goals of the new republic. Congress issued legislation in 1841 creating new Ranger companies to resolve conflicts with the Native Americans and protect the republic from Mexico. Jack Hays won an appointment to head one of the Ranger forces.

This time the congress did better for the Rangers, paying them $30 monthly. Hays's pay was $150. However, it was still not easy for the Rangers to support themselves. Some even had to borrow money to pay for their expenses while on duty, as there were few government benefits.

Patrolling the Plains

Fearing for his own safety, Hays purchased a Colt revolver. This handgun had just been manufactured and it seemed ideal for protecting settlers on the frontier. Because it could shoot five

rounds without reloading, most of the Rangers wanted the handgun. Since the government had limited finances, Hays may have bought his own Colt from a Waco merchant. Other Rangers acquired their revolvers secondhand from the Texas navy, which had procured the weapons for its sailors in 1839.

Hays and his fellow Rangers spent much of their time during the Lamar administration as employees of the government, safeguarding Texas immigrants and handling issues with Native American tribes angered over Anglo movement westward. Rangers also patrolled the frontier looking for raiding expeditions from south of the Rio Grande. When war broke out with Mexico in 1846, companies of Rangers fought beside U.S. Army troops. Jack Hays was among them.

Texas Rangers continue to serve Texans today.

TAKS Practice

1. **Making Generalizations** What reasons other than pay may exist to attract a person to a job?
2. **Making Inferences** How might working for the government differ from working for a business?
3. **Writing About Economics** Write a paragraph that develops one of the themes listed below. Use standard grammar, spelling, sentence structure, and punctuation. Include information and examples from the feature as details to support your argument.
   a. Careers in law enforcement or the military provide opportunities to serve one's country.
   b. Government workers deserve generous job benefits.
   c. Individuals can show patriotism or civic-mindedness.

CHAPTER
13

Pioneer Life

Why It Matters

Texans had won their independence from Mexico; they now felt its influence less and were open to other cultural and social forces. Much of the distinctiveness of Texas culture comes from actions taken and decisions made during the Republic of Texas period.

The Impact Today

Settlement patterns begun in the days of the republic and early statehood period can be seen today in the regions of Texas. The German influence in the Hill Country and the "Old South" culture of East Texas both emerged during this period.

1841
★ Sam Houston returned to the Texas presidency

1840
★ Rutersville College opened

1842
★ Galveston Daily News *first published*

Texas

United States

1838   1840   1842   1844   184

World

1839
• Slave rebellion on the Amistad

1846
• Large numbers of Irish immigrants arrived in the U.S.
• Mormons settled in Utah

1846
• Irish potato famine began

The painting above, by an unknown artist, is titled Moving West. Texas was an important destination in the westward movement of settlers.

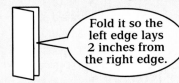
Summarizing Information Study Foldable
Make this foldable and use it to record information about the people and places and about the growth and development of Texas during its years as a republic.

Step 1 Fold a sheet of paper from side to side, leaving a 2-inch tab uncovered along the side.

> Fold it so the left edge lays 2 inches from the right edge.

Step 2 Turn the paper and fold it into thirds.

Step 3 Unfold and cut along the two inside fold lines.

> Cut along the two folds on the front flap to make 3 tabs.

Step 4 Label the foldable as shown.

PIONEERS

| Texas and Immigrants | Farming and Ranching | Commerce and Transportation |

Reading and Writing As you read the chapter, use what you learn to summarize how the early influences and developments of each group of pioneers affects Texas today.

1847
★ German Emigration Company had brought in 7,000 German immigrants

1854
★ Texas set aside $2 million for public education
★ First telegraph line strung in Texas

1848   1850   1852   1854

1848
• Zachary Taylor elected president of the U.S.

1848
• Revolutions broke out in Germany and France

1851
• Gold discovered in Australia

TEXAS HISTORY Online

Chapter Overview
Visit the texans.glencoe.com Web site and click on **Chapter 13—Chapter Overviews** to preview chapter information.

Population Growth

Guide to Reading

Main Idea

Immigrants from the United States, Europe, and Mexico came to Texas during the days of the republic.

Key Term

immigrant agent

Reading Strategy

Comparing and Contrasting As you read this section, complete the chart by listing population statistics in 1836 and 1846.

Group	1836 Population	1846 Population
Anglos and Tejanos		
Slaves		

Read to Learn

- why immigrants chose to move to Texas.
- how African Americans were treated.
- why Mexican Texans faced tensions.

Section Theme

Culture and Traditions African Americans and Mexican Americans faced challenges to their cultures.

Preview of Events

♦1839   ♦1840   ♦1842

Texas Congress passes Homestead Act

Free African Americans are allowed to petition to stay in Texas

German Emigration Company is formed

A
Texas Story

Early settler's home

Mathilda Wagner was born to hard-working German immigrants who settled near Fredericksburg. "The house my father made for us had only two rooms, the kitchen and the room where we slept. There was no stove in the kitchen, only the chimney. We made bread and everything in the chimney fire . . ." Mathilda and her family were determined to succeed in making a new life in a new land.

—from Mathilda Wagner's memoirs

The Republic Attracts Immigrants

The Republic of Texas grew rapidly. Thousands of colonists from the United States crossed the Sabine and Red Rivers into Texas each year. In the decade between the Battle of San Jacinto and statehood, the population more than tripled. In 1836 approximately 35,000 Anglos and Tejanos lived in Texas; by 1846 the population had grown to more than 125,000. The enslaved population increased at an even faster rate—from an estimated 5,000 in 1836 to 38,000 in 1846.

The chart on page 300 shows how the constitution awarded land to settlers. Settlers were not required to live on the land and sometimes sold it to speculators. In 1839 the Texas Congress passed an act, sometimes known as the **Homestead Act.** This law protected a family's home, tools, and 50 acres (20 hectares) of land from seizure for nonpayment of debts.

William Bollaert, a Texas resident in the early 1840s, identified what land meant to new settlers:

> ❝It is their own and their children's with no proud landowner to look up to, no rents or taxes to pay. To use an American expression, 'One feels freed and one is free.' They enjoy life and their families, certain that poverty cannot threaten them.❞

Immigrant Agents Bring Settlers

Congress also granted contracts to immigrant agents—people paid in land or money to relocate settlers to an area—to bring colonists to Texas. An agent received 10 sections of land (6,400 acres; 2,592 hectares) for every 100 families. Often the agent also charged the colonists for services rendered. **W.S. Peters and Associates, Henri Castro,** and the **German Emigration Company** were three of the most successful agents.

W.S. Peters obtained a contract to settle colonists in an area from the Red River to slightly south of present-day Dallas. Despite many legal complications and some mismanagement, Peters's company settled more than 2,000 families in this area between 1841 and 1848. Most of these settlers came from Missouri, Tennessee, and Illinois.

Other agents brought colonists from Europe. Henri Castro, a French Jew, received two grants in southwestern Texas. Like Stephen F. Austin, Castro spent most of his life, fortune, and energy working for the welfare of his colonists. In September 1844, he established the town of **Castroville** on the Medina River, about 20 miles (32 km) west of San Antonio. Castro brought more than 2,000 colonists to Texas between 1844 and 1847, mostly from France, Germany, and Switzerland.

German nobles organized the German Emigration Company, or *Adelsverein* (ah•DEHLS•vehr•ine), in 1842 to promote German immigration to Texas. The company obtained permission to set up colonies in an area north of San Antonio. Overpopulation, poverty, heavy taxes, and political problems in Germany influenced many to leave their homeland. Under the leadership of **Prince Carl of Solms-Braunfels** and **John O. Meusebach,** German settlers

Picturing **History**

Prince Carl of Solms-Braunfels chose lands north of San Antonio for the German immigrants. Name the two largest towns in Texas settled by German immigrants.

established several towns. The largest towns were New Braunfels and Fredericksburg, near San Antonio. In the 1850s, an American architect named Frederick Law Olmsted visited New Braunfels and described it the following way:

❝The main street of town . . . was very wide—three times as wide as . . . Broadway in New York. The houses [that] thickly lined [the main street] on each side for a mile were small, low cottages . . . generally looking neat and comfortable. Many [had] verandas and gardens and [most] were either stuccoed or painted . . .

There are four gristmills . . . A weekly newspaper is published—the *Neu Braunfels Zeitung*. There are 10 or 12 stores and small tradesmen's shops, two or three drugstores, and as many doctors, lawyers, and clergymen.

There are several organizations among the people which show an excellent spirit for social improvement . . . In New Braunfels and the surrounding German towns, there are five free schools for elementary education, one exclusive Roman Catholic school, and a private school. In all of these schools English is taught with German.❞

By 1847 the German Emigration Company had helped about 7,000 Germans immigrate to Texas. Citizens in Boerne, Comfort, Sisterdale and similar towns organized clubs to study German writings and musical groups to play their favorite German tunes.

✓ **Reading Check** **Identifying** What was the immigrant agent's job?

Slavery Continues in Texas

Not all who arrived in Texas came freely. The Mexican government had discouraged slavery but did little to stop its spread. After independence the government of the Republic of Texas made no efforts to limit slavery. Therefore, slavery increased during the early days of the republic. People established plantations in East and central Texas. The planters brought slaves, sometimes in chains, to work their fields.

Farmers also used enslaved people, although in fewer numbers. One of every four families in Texas had at least one slave at this time. Even people who did not own slaves, such as merchants, depended upon the success of the cotton crop that slaves produced.

Although most slaves worked on farms and plantations, some labored in towns. There were

People of Texas

William Goyens 1794–1856

William Goyens was a free African American born in North Carolina. He moved to Nacogdoches in 1820 and lived there the rest of his life. He could not write, but was a wise and successful businessman, in spite of the fact that the Texas laws at that time made it very difficult for African Americans to own property. He made his fortune as a blacksmith, wagon maker, and freight hauler.

Goyens was appointed as an agent to deal with the Cherokees and negotiate treaties. Over the course of the Texas Revolution, he acted as an interpreter with Sam Houston during treaty negotiations with the Cherokees.

In 1936 the Texas Centennial Commission erected a marker at Goyens' grave to honor his memory.

significant numbers of skilled slaves who worked as blacksmiths, carpenters, bricklayers, and in other crafts. Other slaves worked on ranches, tending cattle and breaking horses.

By the mid-1840s, African Americans made up almost 30 percent of Texas's population. Tax rolls from 1845 show that Harrison, Brazoria, Montgomery, Bowie, Nacogdoches, San Augustine, Washington, and Red River Counties had the largest number of enslaved people.

The treatment of slaves varied from one slaveholder to another. Some cared for their slaves and provided them with adequate food, clothing, and shelter. Other slaveholders overworked their slaves; failed to provide adequate food, clothing, and shelter; and whipped them as punishment.

Even under the gentlest slaveholders, slavery was inhumane. Slaves were denied the most basic human rights. They were subject to physical and emotional abuse. Sometimes, families were broken up by the sale of family members.

Slaveholders justified slavery using different reasons. Some quoted parts of the Bible, while others cited "scientific" articles that "proved" the superiority of the white race. The underlying reason, however, was economic.

Slaveholders believed that cotton production depended upon slave labor.

Despite the harsh conditions, slaves were able to sustain a rich culture through family, artistic expression, and religion. Slaves also found ways to resist their owners and rebel against the institution of slavery. Some slaves would withhold cooperation, break their tools, or pretend to be ill. A common form of protest was running away. Although most runaways were captured, some did make their way to freedom.

✓ **Reading Check** **Explaining** How did slaveholders justify their actions?

Free African Americans Build Lives

Several hundred free African Americans lived in Texas before the Civil War. Some had served with Texas armies during the revolution and were granted land for their service. Most free African Americans lived as farmers in rural areas. **William Goyens** of Nacogdoches, who served as an interpreter of Native American languages during the revolution, started a freight line, bought and sold land, and operated an inn, a sawmill, and a gristmill. In 1840 the Congress of the Republic of Texas passed a law allowing free African Americans to petition for the right to remain in Texas. **Mary Madison,** a nurse and free African American, submitted a petition around 1850 signed by 80 of her white Galveston friends and patients, praising her as a valuable citizen and attesting to her kind and tender care of the sick. Her request was one of the few granted. Though most petitions were denied, free people stayed anyway.

Mexican Texans Face Tensions

Mexican Texans, even those who fought for Texas independence, also suffered hardships in the new republic. Many new Anglo settlers after the revolution assumed that all Tejanos had opposed the war for independence. Anglo settlers often held racial and religious prejudices against Tejanos. Some Anglo settlers used force to take the land from Mexican settlers. Some Tejanos, such as Patricia de León and her family, of Victoria, were forced to flee. Juan Seguín, who had led troops at San Jacinto and was mayor of San Antonio, sought refuge in Mexico for several years. He felt as if he was "a foreigner in my native land." Nonetheless, the opportunity to own land and start a new life attracted other Mexicans to Texas. Between 1838 and 1841, more than 500 Mexicans obtained land under Texas's land policy.

✓**Reading Check** **Describing** How were Tejanos treated after the war?

Land Provisions of the Constitution of 1836

Category	Amount of Land Received
Head of family living in Texas before March 2, 1836	4,605 acres
Head of family coming to Texas between 1836 and October 1837	1,208 acres
Head of family coming to Texas between November 1837 and 1842	640 acres
Veterans (people with experience in the armed forces) arriving in Texas before August 1836	4,605 acres
Additional bequests to disabled veterans; veterans of San Jacinto; heirs (those who inherit) of soldiers killed at the Alamo and other battles, and at Goliad.	Various amounts
African Americans	None
Native Americans	None
Married women	None

TAKS PRACTICE

Interpreting Information The Constitution of 1836 specified the amount of land that Texans received from the republic. This varied according to whether a person had served in the military, was male or female, or was single or married. *What other criteria were used to determine land grants?*

SECTION 1 ASSESSMENT

Checking for Understanding

1. **Using Key Terms** The immigrant agent is similar to what modern-day profession? Explain.
2. **Reviewing Facts** Most immigrants came to Texas for what purpose?

Reviewing Themes

3. **Culture and Traditions** In what ways did immigrant agents contribute to various cultural groups influencing areas of Texas?

Organizing to Learn

4. **Classifying** Create a chart like the one below and fill in information about the three most successful immigrant agents.

Agent	Number of Settlers	Area Settled
W.S. Peters		
Henri Castro		
Adelsverein		

Critical Thinking

5. **Determining Cause and Effect** The enslaved population in Texas increased rapidly from 1836 to 1846. Create a circle graph that represents the enslaved population of Texas in the mid 1840s.

TAKS PRACTICE

Analyzing What was the single most important factor leading to the fast rise in the population of Texas? Explain.

Determining Relevance

Why Learn This Skill?

When you do research, it can be confusing to sort through many pieces of information. If you can determine the relevance of each piece of information, you will be able to select only the most important information that you need.

Learning the Skill

Here are three important steps for determining relevant information:

• State your research topic as a question.
• Read various pieces of information.
• Decide which pieces of information help to answer the research question.

Example:

The topic "Occupations in the Early Republic of Texas" can be turned into the question "What did most people do in the Republic of Texas?" One of the following statements would be relevant: a) Many German settlers did not get the best farmland, or b) Most early Texans were farmers and ranchers. Statement b would be relevant.

Practicing the Skill

Read each topic below. Then restate each one as a question.

Ⓐ education in the Republic of Texas

Ⓑ land policy in the Republic of Texas

Ⓒ German settlement in Texas

Now read the topic question and the quotations that follow. Decide whether each quotation is relevant to the topic question. Then explain your answer.

Topic: How were German and Anglo American settlements in Texas different?

❶ "While most American Texans seemed satisfied with their drafty lean-tos and dog-trot log cabins, the Germans . . . were busily building snug homes."

❷ "There are four gristmills . . . A weekly newspaper is published—the *Neu Braunfels Zeitung.*"

❸ "There was no orphanage in [the German settlement of] Fredericksburg, although there was one at New Braunfels [another German settlement] at the time."

❹ "The one big difference between Anglo and German farmers was that the [Germans] were less mobile. When Germans put down roots, they did not leave."

❺ "Unlike some Southerners, who sought fortunes, many Germans came for political freedom."

TAKS PRACTICE

Determining Relevance Create a topic research question about your family's history. Then ask questions of your parents or other family members. Identify and list three points that relate to your topic.

GO TO

Glencoe's **Skillbuilder Interactive Workbook,** Level 1, provides instruction and practice in key social studies skills.

Texans on Farms and Ranches

Main Idea
Although most Texans lived on farms and ranches, new towns began to develop throughout the state.

Key Term
subsistence crop

Reading Strategy
Analyzing Create a chart similar to the one below. Explain why these towns were settled.

Towns	Reasons for Settling
Marshall	
Grand Saline	
Preston	
Liberty	

Read to Learn
• what cash crops were grown.
• what subsistence crops were grown.
• why new towns were built.

Section Theme
Economic Factors The fertile soil, abundant and nourishing grasslands, climate, and rivers contributed to the growth of Texas.

Preview of Events

♦1841		♦1856

└ Dallas settlement begins

└ Kerrville is established

Picking cotton

A
Texas Story

Immigrant parents often found it hard to earn enough money to feed a large family. When Mathilda Wagner was about nine, she was sent to work for a family in San Antonio. She wrote in her memoirs, "While I stayed at the Longrapers I had to go to New Braunfels each summer to pick cotton. I had to bring [home] every nickel I made . . . We were fed one thick piece of corn bread and a glass of buttermilk. We got twenty-five cents for one hundred pounds of cotton. Sometimes I didn't have a quilt to lie on at night."

Texas Life Centers Around Farming

At this time, most Texans farmed or raised livestock. Most farms in Texas grew both cash crops and subsistence crops. Cash crops were sold to raise money so that Texans could buy things that they could not make for

TEXAS HISTORY *Online*

Student Web Activity Visit the texans.glencoe.com Web site and click on **Chapter 13—Student Web Activity** to learn more about cotton farming before the Civil War.

themselves. Food products that are eaten on the farm where they are grown are called **subsistence crops.** Corn was the main subsistence crop, eaten in the form of cornbread, tortillas, and hominy. Farmers also fed corn to their horses, mules, and oxen that pulled plows and wagons.

Sugarcane was an important cash crop along the Brazos and Colorado Rivers in Matagorda, Brazoria, and Fort Bend Counties. The most important cash crop, though, was cotton. It was grown on the fertile bottomlands of Texas's rivers and on the less fertile sandy soil of the hills of East Texas. By the eve of the Civil War, cotton farming had moved to the rich, productive soils of the Blackland Prairie. By 1845, Texas was selling 30,000 bales of cotton per year. Most of it went by boat to Europe and the northeastern

United States. By 1860, cotton production had soared to 400,000 bales per year.

Other crops were sweet potatoes, white potatoes, and other vegetables. Pork was the most common meat. A typical Texas farm also would have a milk cow and chickens.

Both men and women worked hard on Texas farms. Women usually took care of the animals and gardens. They also worked long hours preparing the food and making clothes. Alongside the men, women cleared the land, cut wood, built fences, and picked cotton, in addition to cooking, weaving, and sewing. Native American women worked hard, too, although not in farming. It was their work to butcher the buffalo, cure the hides, and turn them into tepee coverings and clothing.

Ranches Flourish

While some of the Mexican ranchers in the Goliad–Victoria area lost their enormous holdings after independence, many Tejanos kept their property and continued to raise cattle. One of the most successful was Doña María del Carmen Calvillo of Floresville. She inherited a ranch from her father and increased the ranch's livestock to 1,500 cattle and 500 goats, sheep, and horses.

It was relatively easy for new settlers to get into the cattle business. Herds of

History *Through Art*

Just Married by Velox Ward Farm families would be called in from the fields to eat meals of cornbread, sweet potatoes, and fresh or salt pork. What subsistence crop did farmers most often use at mealtime?

wild cattle roamed much of South and East Texas. The region's climate was well suited for livestock, and the nourishing and abundant grass helped the cattle population multiply.

While most of the planters and ranchers were men, women also owned and managed plantations. Mildred Satterwhite Littlefield owned a large plantation along the Guadalupe River in Gonzales County. Sarah Mims and Rebecca Hagerty also owned and managed their own plantations. The writer Amelia Barr of Austin remarked:

66 The real Texas women were . . . brave and resourceful . . . They were then nearly without exception fine riders and crack shots, and quite able, when the men of the household were away, to manage their ranches or plantations, and keep such faithful guard over their families and household[s], that I never once in ten years, heard of any Indian, or other tragedy occurring. 99

✓ **Reading Check** **Examining** Why did so many ranches flourish?

Settlers Establish New Towns

More settlers came to Texas from the United States after independence. Some of the older settlements declined in importance as new towns were established. San Felipe and Harrisburg, which were burned during the revolution, never regained their former importance.

At the time of the revolution, only Clarksville, Jonesborough, and Pecan Point existed in northeastern Texas. Settlers, especially from Tennessee, Arkansas, and Missouri, established new towns. Some towns, like Marshall and Jefferson, were built along transportation routes. Before railroad lines, **Jefferson** was the outlet for cotton grown in northeastern Texas. Steamboats went from Jefferson to Louisiana by way of Cypress Bayou, Caddo Lake, and the Red River.

Other towns were created to serve as seats of government for newly created counties. A few

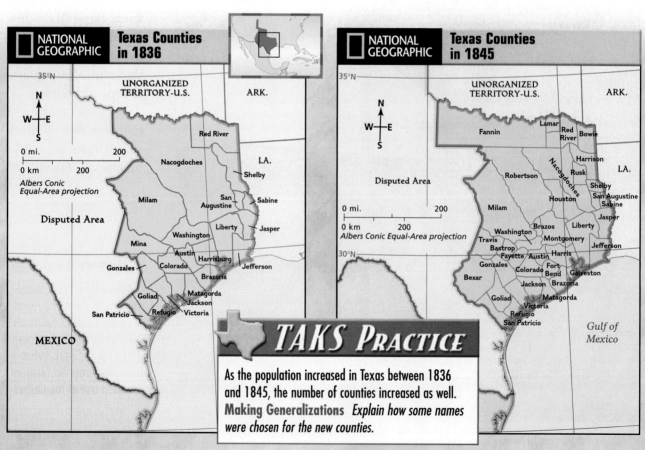

TAKS PRACTICE

As the population increased in Texas between 1836 and 1845, the number of counties increased as well.
Making Generalizations *Explain how some names were chosen for the new counties.*

settlements were founded to take advantage of some natural resource. In the case of **Grand Saline,** it was salt mines. Preston, in Grayson County, soon became the gateway for immigrants moving into North Texas. **John Neely Bryan** started a settlement near the fork of the Trinity River in 1841. This settlement was the beginning of the town of Dallas.

In southeastern Texas, towns were often located along rivers. Liberty and Beaumont both increased in population during the days of the republic. Houston's site was chosen because the Allen brothers thought that steamboats could go up Buffalo Bayou no farther than Houston. The boats would have to unload cargo there.

Conflicts with Native Americans kept Anglos from settling in the Brazos Valley north of the Old San Antonio Road until the early 1840s. In 1845 an immigrant from Scotland, **Neal McLennan,** settled on the South Bosque River north of an old Waco settlement. Four years later **George Erath,** an immigrant from Vienna, Austria, and **Jacob de Cordova** surveyed the town of Waco.

The Hill Country was more rugged than lands farther to the east, but settlers pushed up the valleys of the Blanco, Guadalupe, and Pedernales Rivers. Kerrville was organized by a group of cypress shingle makers in 1856.

South Texas grew slowly as the region was exposed to raids by Native Americans, Mexicans, and Anglo desperadoes. New towns, however, sprang up. Indianola, called Karlshaven by the

Raising cattle, such as this Texas longhorn, was a major economic activity of the new settlements.

Germans, was established on the west bank of Matagorda Bay. **H.L. Kinney** built a trading post at the mouth of the Nueces River. Other traders settled in this area, and the town of Corpus Christi was established.

Developments in other parts of Texas had little effect on the area south of Corpus Christi and the Nueces River. The economy of the area was linked more to Mexico than to the United States.

Along the Rio Grande the oldest settlement was Laredo, founded by **Tomás Sánchez** in 1755. Upstream from Laredo were crossings of the Rio Grande near San Juan Bautista. The settlements of Eagle Pass, Texas, and Piedras Negras, Mexico, developed near these crossings.

✓ Reading Check **Analyzing** Why did Texas towns often develop along rivers?

SECTION 2 ASSESSMENT

Checking for Understanding

1. **Using Key Terms** Describe what you might find on a farm in Texas growing subsistence crops.
2. **Reviewing Facts** Why did new settlers often choose to become cattle ranchers?

Reviewing Themes

3. **Economic Factors** Cotton was the main cash crop in Texas. In what areas of the state was cotton grown?

Organizing to Learn

4. **Analyzing** Draw a chart like the one below. List the common uses for cotton and corn. Keep in mind the definitions of subsistence and cash crops.

Uses for Cotton (cash crop)	Uses for Corn (subsistence crop)

Critical Thinking

5. **Decision Making** What would be the determining factors as to whether a farmer concentrated on growing cash crops or subsistence crops?

TAKS PRACTICE

Analyzing If most Texans farmed or raised livestock, why was it an advantage to have towns located nearby?

Commerce and Transportation

Guide to Reading

Main Idea
As the population increased, there were advances in commerce, transportation, and education.

Key Terms
raft
charter
fiesta

Reading Strategy
Classifying Information As you read the section, draw a chart like the one below. Next to each title, list as many specific examples of occupations as you can find.

General Occupation	Examples
Tradesmen	
Professions	
Industry	

Read to Learn
• about trades and professions.
• about types of transportation.
• about social functions.
• about types of education.

Section Theme
Economic Factors Growth of commerce and transportation relied heavily upon rivers and existing roads.

Preview of Events

1842	1845		1854	1857

- 1842 — *Galveston Daily News* begins
- 1845 — Baylor University is established
- Texas and Red River Telegraph Company starts service
- 1854 — Mail service is established between San Antonio and San Diego, California

A
Texas Story

A Christmas present

As an immigrant child, Mathilda Wagner worked long hours in the fields. "I couldn't spend a nickel of the money I earned for candy or something I would have liked . . . I couldn't play. I never had anything at Christmas time. I remember I was given a big red apple one year, and I thought it was so beautiful that I put it in my trunk . . . When the lady who had given it to me asked once, 'Did you eat your apple?' I told her I was saving it, but went to see it and it had rotted."

Trades and Professions

Some Texans made their living in trades, including brick masons, blacksmiths, carpenters, and wheelwrights. Others entered professions such as law, medicine, the ministry, and teaching.

The increase in Texas population meant more people with specific skills settled in the republic. Doctors, ministers, and lawyers arrived but often divided their time between their professions and farming. **Ashbel Smith** was a diplomat, soldier, educator, planter, and scientist, as well as a doctor. **John S. "Rip" Ford,** the famous Texas Ranger and frontiersman, was a physician. He was also a newspaper editor, lawyer, politician, and playwright. **Frances Cox Henderson** ran her husband's law office while Mr. Henderson and his partner were out of town.

Some physicians increased their incomes by selling medicines, hair tonics, and perfumes. A doctor in New Braunfels was also a baker and druggist. Another Houston physician formed a partnership with a local barber. Together they offered shaves, haircuts, tooth pulling, and surgery. Midwives—women who helped deliver babies—also performed valuable services.

Industry and Commerce Fuel Growth

The few industries in early Texas were located in towns or along major roads or rivers. Most communities already had a sawmill for cutting lumber and a gristmill for grinding grain. Over time Texans built brickyards, tanneries, iron foundries, cotton gins, soap factories, carriage factories, and textile mills.

Able and creative leaders promoted the growth of business. **Gail Borden, Jr.,** an early resident of San Felipe de Austin, moved to Galveston in 1837 as a customs collector and inventor. Among his early inventions was a meat biscuit that won a gold medal at the 1851 Crystal Palace Exhibition in London. He also developed a process for making condensed milk. He moved his factory to New York State so he could sell Borden products to a larger market.

Better Transportation Is Needed

Even local travel in Texas was difficult. Some of the roads had been Native American trails, while others were originally built in the Spanish and Mexican eras. Almost all the roads were unpaved, and rains often turned them into mud. Crossing streams was especially dangerous, and travelers had to be prepared to swim to safety.

Almost all of the goods transported in early Texas were carried by freight wagons drawn by oxen or mule teams. In San Antonio and other towns of South Texas, Mexican Americans played an important role in moving goods from one part of Texas to another.

Stagecoaches and Steamboats

The stagecoach was a popular but expensive means of travel. The Butterfield Overland Line crossed Texas from near Preston on the Red River to El Paso. This line provided

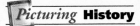

Picturing **History**

What farmers and ranchers could not grow or produce for themselves they came to shop for in town. In 1857, Walter and Eduard Tip established a hardware store on Congress Avenue in Austin, with tin, ironware, pig iron, leather goods, and general merchandise for sale. What other types of goods and services could be found only in the towns?

transportation and all mail service to St. Louis and Memphis to the east and San Francisco to the west. In 1857 mail and passenger service opened between San Antonio and San Diego, California. The scheduled trip took 30 days and cost $200 for a one-way ticket. For most Texans this amounted to about a year's wages.

Stagecoach lines connected towns and cities within Texas. Stagecoaches traveled at five to eight miles per hour in good weather. In wet weather, travel was much slower. Passengers frequently had to get out and push the stage-coach out of mud holes.

Steamboats carrying passengers and freight operated on Texas's major rivers. While steam-boat travel was comfortable and cheap, it was not free of problems. Driftwood tangles, or **rafts**, and sandbars blocked parts of the twisting waterways. The Colorado River, for example, could not carry heavy traffic for a time because of a large raft near its mouth.

Buffalo Bayou, which connected Houston with the port of Galveston, was the most heavily trav-eled waterway in Texas. The bayou was narrow and surrounded by overhanging limbs. Still, it was an effective passageway for steamboats that car-ried cotton from the interior of Texas to Galveston.

✓ **Reading Check** **Identifying** What was the most heavily traveled waterway in Texas at this time?

Railroads Aid Business

The first Texas railroads were built shortly after statehood and into the early 1850s. In 1852 work began on the Buffalo Bayou, Brazos, and

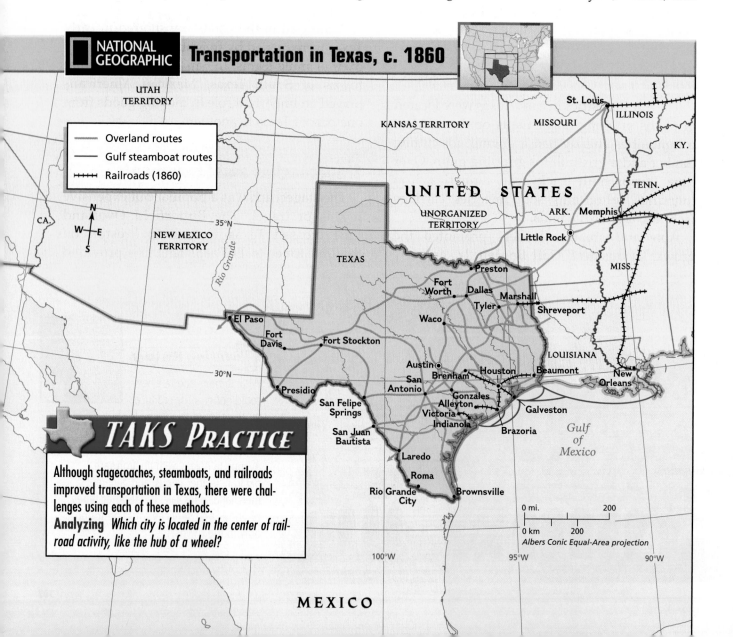

NATIONAL GEOGRAPHIC **Transportation in Texas, c. 1860**

Overland routes
Gulf steamboat routes
Railroads (1860)

UTAH TERRITORY
KANSAS TERRITORY
MISSOURI
St. Louis
ILLINOIS
KY.
UNITED STATES
ARK. Memphis
TENN.
CA.
NEW MEXICO TERRITORY
35°N
Rio Grande
UNORGANIZED TERRITORY
Little Rock
TEXAS
MISS.
Preston
Fort Worth
Dallas
Marshall
Tyler
Shreveport
Waco
30°N
El Paso
Fort Davis
Fort Stockton
LOUISIANA
Austin
San Antonio
Brenham
Houston
Beaumont
New Orleans
Presidio
Gonzales
San Felipe Springs
Alleyton
Victoria
Galveston
Indianola
San Juan Bautista
Brazoria
Gulf of Mexico
Laredo
Roma
Rio Grande City
Brownsville

0 mi.   200
0 km   200
Albers Conic Equal-Area projection

100°W   95°W   90°W

TAKS PRACTICE

Although stagecoaches, steamboats, and railroads improved transportation in Texas, there were chal-lenges using each of these methods.
Analyzing Which city is located in the center of rail-road activity, like the hub of a wheel?

MEXICO

Colorado Railroad, commonly called the Harrisburg Railroad. Sidney Sherman, a veteran of San Jacinto and a business leader in early Harrisburg and Houston, organized the railroad.

To encourage the extensions of the rail lines, the state gave bounties of land and loaned money from the school fund to railroad companies. Some local communities and counties also supported railroad development. The citizens of Houston strongly encouraged railroad building. By 1860 several railroads connected Houston with neighboring communities. These railroads brought many kinds of products in and out of Houston and helped to make it one of the state's most vital cities.

Telegraph and Newspapers

One of the first telegraph lines in Texas connected Houston with Galveston. A telegraph firm called the Texas and Red River Telegraph Company had been chartered, or established by a state contract, in January 1854. The company opened the first telegraph office in Marshall in 1854 and began extending lines to Shreveport, Henderson, Rusk, Crockett, Montgomery, Houston, and Galveston. In 1856 another company began constructing lines from Galveston to San Antonio and Austin.

In early Texas, newspapers were an important source of information. The *Telegraph and Texas Register,* published originally in San Felipe and later in Houston, was the most influential of the early newspapers. Another widely read paper, the *Galveston Daily News,* published its first issue in 1842. In 1848 **Simon Mussina,** a Jewish attorney in Brownsville, began publishing the *American Flag.*

Many newspapers began publishing after Texas became a state. By 1860 there were more than 70 newspapers

TWO VIEWPOINTS

Frontier Women

Adjusting to life on the Texas frontier was easier for women whose families were prosperous. Compare the two views below and then answer the questions.

A Southern Belle in San Antonio in 1839

This year our [slaves] plowed and planted above the Alamo and were attacked by Indians. In November, a party of ladies and gentlemen from Houston came to visit San Antonio—they rode on horseback. They were, ladies and all, armed with pistols and bowie knives. I rode with this party around the head of the San Antonio River. We galloped home, and doubted not that Indians watched us from the heavy timber of the river bottom. The gentlemen of the party numbered six, and we were all mounted on fine animals.
—from *Memoirs of Mary A. Maverick,* published in 1921

A German Immigrant in the 1840s

My years in San Antonio were hard, lonesome years. It seems to me that I stayed there a long time, working and longing all the time. The cholera hit San Antonio just after I came here. The people died by the scores. The graveyards filled in a hurry and many, many little orphans were made. There were few houses where death didn't come.
—from Mathilda Wagner's memoirs

Learning From History

1. Why do you think these women's memories are so different?
2. Do you think men and women might remember the same experiences in different ways?

ONLY in TEXAS

Pioneer Flour In 1851 Carl Hilmer Guenther, a young German immigrant, founded his first flour mill on Live Oak Creek near Fredericksburg *(below).* Relocated a few years later to San Antonio, C.H. Guenther & Son, Inc., is now more than 150 years old. Today, the 20-story Pioneer grain elevator rises above the mill in San Antonio *(right).* The maker of Pioneer Brand flour and other baking products is believed to be the oldest family-owned business in Texas and the oldest continuously operated family-owned milling company in the United States. The Pioneer Flour Mills logo *(below right)* is still used today.

in publication. Most were printed only once a week, but there were several daily newspapers as well.

Texans Gather for Social Life

During the 1850s most Texans lived on isolated farms and had few occasions to visit with their neighbors. Texans combined many social activities with work. Log rollings, shooting matches, husking bees, quilting parties, house-raisings, church dinners, and cotton choppings were practical activities that made work more enjoyable. Hunting and fishing were sports that provided food for the family table.

Dancing was one of the most popular forms of recreation. According to most accounts, the dancing was lively and the music was loud. Among the more popular tunes were "Molly Cotton-Tail," "Money Musk," "Leather Breeches," and "Piney Woods." The fandango, a spirited Spanish dance, was a favorite with

some Hispanic residents. The *baile,* held in a hall or in the open air, was a popular dancing occasion with Mexican Americans. On more formal occasions, such as the San Jacinto Ball held in Houston each year, Texans wearing their finest clothes danced graceful waltzes and reels. In the slave quarters, people sometimes enjoyed "ring" dances.

The fiesta, a festival or religious celebration, was a part of the Hispanic culture and an important part of life for everyone. Dancing, games, exhibitions of art and culture, and refreshments such as chocolate, coffee, lemonade, and pastry were part of this celebration.

Formal Education Advances Slowly

Although the Texas Congress set aside land for public education during the Lamar administration, no state public school system was established. There were many private schools, but only Houston had a public school. In 1839 the Houston city council hired the first public school teacher in the republic, the Reverend Richard Salmon of New York. In rural areas, mothers often taught their children the basics of reading, writing, and arithmetic. Some rural area families hired teachers, who were usually paid in produce, not money. Nearly every town had a private elementary school.

Under the leadership of **Governor Elisha M. Pease,** the legislature in 1854 set aside $2 million as a permanent school fund. Interest earned by the permanent fund was distributed according to the number of school-age children living in each county. Even with the school fund, Texas established few public schools.

Colleges were also founded by churches. Methodist leaders established Rutersville College near La Grange in 1840. Baylor University, a Baptist school, was chartered at Independence in 1845. In 1849, Presbyterian leaders established Austin College in Huntsville. It was later moved to Sherman. Other early colleges were founded at Galveston, San Augustine, Clarksville, and Chappell Hill.

Religious Diversity Flourishes

Before the Texas Revolution, the Mexican government recognized only the Roman Catholic faith. It did little, however, to stop Anglo settlers

A Shared Past...

While Texas took small steps to provide education for some children, a revolution in schooling occurred in Massachusetts. There, former teacher and government secretary Horace Mann led a reform movement that would result in free public schools for all children. Eventually all states would adopt the Massachusetts reforms.

from worshipping in their own way. Many immigrant towns built various places to worship.

After independence, the Constitution of 1836 guaranteed freedom of religion, and Protestant churches grew in popularity. The Methodist Church had the biggest gains, and the Baptist and Presbyterian faiths also were successful. In 1856 the first Jewish services were held in Galveston thanks to the efforts of Rosanna Osterman, an early resident. The Roman Catholic Church remained a strong force, however. Besides religious services, churches were also social centers.

✓ **Reading Check** **Identifying** Where was the first public school?

SECTION 3 ASSESSMENT

Checking for Understanding

1. **Using Key Terms** Write three sentences in which you use the terms raft, charter, and fiesta to show that you understand their meanings.
2. **Reviewing Facts** Why were social activities combined with work?

Reviewing Themes

3. **Economic Factors** Why was it important to locate industries in towns or along major roads or rivers?

Organizing to Learn

4. **Considering Options** Draw a chart like the one below. List the positive and negative aspects of transportation in Texas at this time.

Type of Transportation	Positive Aspects	Negative Aspects
Freight wagon		
Stagecoach		
River transportation		
Railroad		

Critical Thinking

5. **Analyzing** On page 307 the statement is made that "doctors, ministers, and lawyers arrived but often divided their time between their professions and farming." Why do you think it was necessary for these individuals to do both?

TAKS PRACTICE

Making Judgments Why was the growth of commerce directly dependent upon better transportation in Texas?

Chapter Summary
Pioneer Life

1839
- First public school teacher is hired in Houston.
- ★ Texas Congress passes the Homestead Act.

1840
- ★ Rutersville College is established.

1842
- Galveston Daily News publishes its first issue.
- ★ German immigrants begin to arrive in Texas.

1845
- Baylor University is established.
- ★ Slaves account for almost 30 percent of Texas population.

1852
- Work begins on Buffalo Bayou, Brazos, and Colorado Railroad.

1854
- First telegraph lines are built in Texas.
- $2 million is set aside as permanent school fund by the legislature and Governor Pease.

1857
- Stagecoach service begins between San Antonio and San Diego, California.

1860
- Several railroads connect Houston with neighboring communities.
- ★ More than 70 newspapers are in print.

Reviewing Key Terms

Use a dictionary or thesaurus to find synonyms (words that mean the same) for these terms. On a separate sheet of paper, write these synonyms beside the terms.

1. immigrant agents
2. raft
3. fiesta
4. subsistence crop
5. charter

Reviewing Key Facts

6. List three of the most important immigrant agents.
7. Name a free African American who was an important businessman during this period.
8. What is the difference between a cash crop and a subsistence crop?
9. What two industries were usually the first to be established in early Texas towns?
10. When rural families hired teachers for their children, what did they often use for payment?

Critical Thinking

11. **Making Judgments** Was life in Texas more difficult for men or women?
12. **Making Inferences** What do you think would have happened if slavery had been abolished in Texas at this time?
13. **Analyzing Geographic Factors** Why were most settlements near major rivers and how would this affect social and economic development?
14. **Comparing** Compare the education available to children during the days of the republic with that which is available now.
15. **Evaluating** What would be some effects on Texas resources such as land and water as a result of steamboats and railroads?
16. **Taking Action** Slaves were able to resist their owners in protest against their conditions. What were some methods slaves used to resist?
17. **Analyzing** What reasons caused Germans to leave Germany and where did they tend to settle in Texas?
18. **Analyzing** In what ways did German immigrants maintain their culture?

Geography and History Activity

Refer to the Transportation in 1860 map on page 308.

19. If you lived in Houston in 1860, explain how you might travel to Memphis, Tennessee.

20. What area of Texas had the most railroads in 1860?

21. Name one town or city that was connected by roads, steamboats, and the railroad.

Building Technology Skills

22. **Using Calculators** Fill out the population chart below and write two questions relating to the statistics. Use your own calculator or one on a computer to do the calculations. Provide the answers to your questions.

Group	1836 Population	1846 Population
Anglos and Tejanos		
Slaves		

Portfolio/TAKS Writing Activity

23. **Writing a Letter** You are a new immigrant to Texas. Write a letter to a friend or relative (who lives in the country from which you came) in which you describe the good and bad aspects of your life in Texas during the republic. Use standard grammar, spelling, sentence structure, and punctuation.

Cooperative Learning Activity

24. **Creating a Newspaper** In small groups, create a newspaper that could have been published in one of the settlements founded in the early days of the republic. Assign various tasks such as editor, illustrator, reporter, and typist. Possible articles would include political events, social life, and economic activities. Create or include advertisements, cartoons, and an opinion column. Refer to Chapters 12 and 13 for material and consult encyclopedias and the Internet if necessary.

Practicing Skills

25. **Determining Relevance** Read the following question and statements. Decide which statements provide relevant information.

    What was life like for Mexicans in the Republic of Texas?

    a. Many Mexicans in Texas lost their land.

TEXAS HISTORY Online

Self-Check Quiz
Visit the texans.glencoe.com Web site and click on **Chapter 13—Self-Check Quizzes** to prepare for the chapter test.

b. Many Mexicans were small farmers or ranchers who often faced many hardships.

c. Immigrant agents brought many Germans to Texas.

d. Some free African Americans started their own businesses.

TAKS PRACTICE

Use the graph to answer the following question.

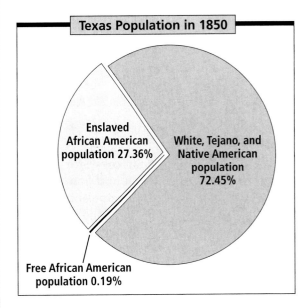

Texas Population in 1850

Enslaved African American population 27.36%

White, Tejano, and Native American population 72.45%

Free African American population 0.19%

About what portion of Texas's total population was enslaved in 1850?

A 1/4   C 3/4

B 1/2   D 1/10

Test-Taking Tip:
You will have to approximate to answer this question. In real life, figures rarely come out to an even number. Rounding off to the nearest 5 percent will lead you to the correct answer.

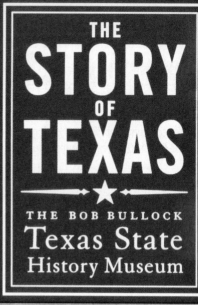

THE STORY OF TEXAS

THE BOB BULLOCK
Texas State
History Museum

Building the Lone Star Identity
The Republic

*O*ne of the few points of agreement between presidents Sam Houston and Mirabeau Lamar was that citizenship in the Republic of Texas should be granted to male Anglos and Tejanos—about 60 percent of the population. Overall, the population of Texas grew quickly during the years of the republic.

◄ **Success Story** Despite support from prominent Houstonians, Fanny McFarland's petition to stay in Texas as a free African American was denied. She stayed anyway and from humble beginnings as a laundress, she became one of Houston's first real estate developers.

▲
Traveling Trunk Immigrants brought with them personal items needed to begin a new life in Texas.

◄ Comanche War Bonnet
The Comanches were fierce
and skilled warriors. At first,
relations with the Anglos were
friendly, but the advance of
settlers into the Comanchéria
dashed hopes for peace.
Below is a Comanche tepee,
decorated with drawings of
a successful buffalo hunt.
▼

▲ Tejano Statesman José
Antonio Navarro stayed
in the Republic but faced
increasing prejudice from
some Anglo Texans.

*Visit The Bob Bullock Texas State History
Museum in Austin to see artifacts and exhibits
such as these about Texas history and heritage.*

315

UNIT ★

5 The Lone Star State

1845–1876

Why It Matters

As you study Unit 5, you will learn that the time from when Texas became a state until it left the Union and was later readmitted was an eventful period. Long-standing problems, such as the public debt and relations with Mexico, were settled. The tragedy of the Civil War and the events of Reconstruction shaped Texas politics for many years.

Primary Sources Library

See pages 692–693 for primary source readings to accompany Unit 5.

Cowboy Dance by Jenne Magafan (1939) was commissioned for the Anson, Texas, post office to honor the day Texas was admitted to the Union as the twenty-eighth state. Today it can be seen at the Smithsonian American Art Museum in Washington, D.C.

"I love Texas too well to bring strife and bloodshed upon her."

—Sam Houston,
"Address to the People," 1861

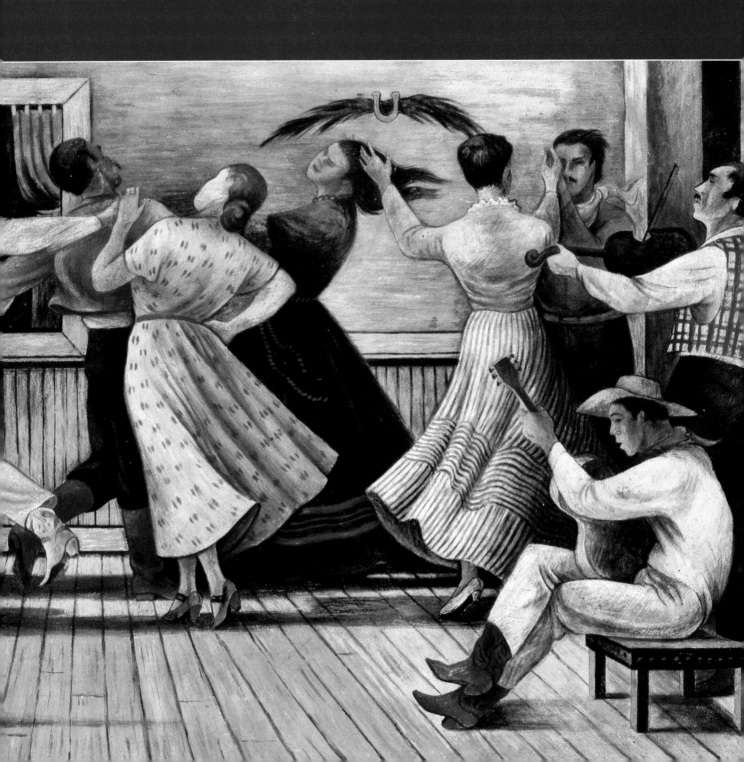

KING COTTON

1880

1910

**Cotton Production
1880–1974
Bales of Cotton
(Per County)**

25,000 to more
than 100,000

1,000 to
24,999

999 or less

Looking at the 1880 map, you can see that cotton farming only took place in East Texas during this time. Why do you think this was so?

By 1910, cotton farming had spread into central and West Texas. Where was production highest?

Cotton has been "king" throughout most of Texas history. Before the Civil War it was the mainstay of the economy. To be profitable, cotton farming relied on the labor of enslaved people who worked the fields of large plantations. Dependence on slavery helped persuade Texas to join the Confederate cause and to secede from the Union during the Civil War.

The defeat of the Confederacy put an end to slavery, but the cultivation of cotton continued. Many formerly enslaved people stayed on as tenant farmers, renting plots of land from the former plantation owners or working for them as sharecroppers. In the late

1800s, the cotton belt spread westward as new technologies emerged. Better, stronger plows made it easier for farmers to break up the dry but fertile prairie sod, and new irrigation techniques allowed them to bring water to the thirsty plants. Improvements to the cotton gin increased the yield per acre, while the growing network of railroads provided ready access to faraway markets for the crop.

The boll weevil, an insect that destroys cotton, devastated crops during the early 1900s. Many tenant farmers went broke, abandoning their small plots to work in towns or cities. Pesticides, improved methods of

A sign advertises the cotton market in Taylor in 1903. When cotton production suffered, the entire community felt the negative effects.

1949

1974

By 1949, cotton was grown almost all over the state. Why do you think the center of production shifted north and west?

Twenty-five years later, cotton was still concentrated in the same general regions, but production had increased. What factors could account for this?

cultivation, and crop rotation finally brought the weevils under control. As you can see from the last two maps, cotton farming continued to spread into new areas right up through the 1970s. Today, Texas cotton is sold throughout the United States and in other parts of the world.

Cotton remains important, but the addition of other profitable crops such as rice, citrus fruits, and peanuts ensures that Texas and its farmers will never again be entirely dependent on one crop.

LEARNING from GEOGRAPHY

1. Describe what life might have been like for a cotton farmer in post–Civil War Texas.

2. Cotton is one of the most versatile materials ever developed, having many uses and applications. Look around you and make a list of things that are made of cotton.

The Young State

Why It Matters

Very soon after Texas entered the Union, the United States and Mexico clashed in all-out war. The major dispute between the two countries was the annexation of Texas by the United States. The main result of the war was the acquisition of much of the American Southwest by the United States.

The Impact Today

Portions of Texas, Arizona, Colorado, New Mexico, and Wyoming, and all of California, Nevada, and Utah are part of the United States today as a result of the Mexican–American War of 1846–1848.

1845
★ José Antonio Navarro served as a delegate to Convention of 1845

1846
★ Mexican and American troops clashed at the Rio Grande

★ Fredericksburg founded by German immigrants

Texas

United States   *1845*   *1846*   *1847*

World

1846
• Mexican–American War began

• United States divided Oregon Country with Great Britain

1847
• Charlotte Brontë wrote Jane Eyre

Guenther's Mill *by Hermann Lungkwitz (1885). The artist portrayed the primarily rural nature of the new young state.*

1850
★ Texas surrendered all claims to New Mexico territory in Compromise of 1850
★ Texas constitution amended

1848   **1849**   **1850**

1848
• Mexican–American War ended with Treaty of Guadalupe Hidalgo
• First women's rights convention met in Seneca Falls, New York

1849
• French physicist measured speed of light

1850
• World Exhibit in London

A New State Government

Guide to Reading

Main Idea

Many problems needed to be studied and solved as Texas entered the era of statehood.

Key Terms

legislature
amend
convention

Reading Strategy

Making Comparisons As you read this section, complete a chart like the one shown below to differentiate among major political parties.

Party	Main Ideas
Democrat	
Whig	
American	

Read to Learn

• about the new state constitution.
• about the first elected Texas officials.
• about the major political parties.

Section Theme

Civic Rights and Responsibilities As most Texans aligned themselves with political parties that protected their interests, free African Americans fought to protect their freedoms.

Preview of Events

♦1845 — The first state government officials are elected

Texas constitution is amended

♦1850 — First U.S. Census count in Texas

Arabian camel

★★★★★★★★
A
Texas Story

On May 13, 1856, the residents of Indianola abandoned their activities and headed for the docks. A ship was unloading an extraordinary cargo— 33 camels! At Camp Verde, near Kerrville, the U.S. Army was experimenting to see if the animals could be used in warfare or to haul supplies. Edward Fitzgerald Beale wrote in the *Outwest* newspaper: "The harder the test [the camels] are put to, the more fully they seem to justify all that can be said of them. They pack water for days under a hot sun and never get a drop."

A New Constitution

The delegates attending the convention in July of 1845 worked hard at writing a new constitution. The new constitution was well organized and well written. Texans patterned their basic governing document after the constitutions of other states. The Texas constitution was similar to Louisiana's constitution.

The **Constitution of 1845** provided for a governor to be elected for a two-year term. It also provided for a legislature made up of two houses. The members of the House of Representatives were elected for two years, and members of the Senate were elected for four years. The constitution also created a supreme court and district and county courts. Originally, the governor appointed the judges of the state courts. Then in 1850 the constitution was amended, or changed, to provide for the election of all judges. This shifted some power from political leaders to the voters. The new constitution protected the system of slavery and barred women from voting.

Reading Check **Summarizing** What terms of office were designated by the Constitution of 1845?

Texas Legislators at Work

The governor's term was two years, and no governor was allowed to serve more than two terms in a row. Governors had to be citizens and residents of Texas for at least three years before their election and be at least thirty years of age.

J. Pinckney Henderson of San Augustine was elected as the first governor. He served only one term. His wife, Frances Cox Henderson, was the first woman to practice law in Texas. Sam Houston and Thomas J. Rusk were the first Texans elected to the U.S. Senate. David Kaufman and Timothy Pillsbury were elected to the U.S. House of Representatives.

Members of the early Texas legislature kept busy trying to solve the problems of the young state. Landscape architect Frederick L. Olmsted,

TAKS PRACTICE

Analyzing Many settlers came to Texas in covered wagons. Addressing the needs of these new settlers became an important responsibility for the first elected officials. *What were some of the needs of the growing population?*

First Government Officials	
Governor of Texas	J. Pinckney Henderson
U.S. Senators	Sam Houston Thomas J. Rusk
U.S. Representatives	David Kaufman Timothy Pillsbury

People of Texas

Frances Cox Henderson 1820–1897

Frances Cox Henderson has been called the "First Lady of Texas." She spoke 18 languages, was skilled in math, was a talented musician, and wrote and translated short stories.

She married James Pinckney Henderson, and they settled in the town of San Augustine where he opened a law practice. When he was elected governor, she remained in San Augustine. She became active in helping to found churches in many East Texas cities, often contributing her own money for this purpose. She was also a supporter of woman suffrage.

Frances kept learning her whole life. While in her 50s, she wrote a book about an African American woman and life on a plantation—*Priscilla Baker: Freed Woman.*

---

who visited the state in the 1850s, admired how well the legislators went about their work. He described his impressions in *A Journey Through Texas,* published in 1857:

66 We visited, several times, the Texas Legislature in session, and have seldom been more impressed with respect for the working of Democratic institutions.

I have seen several similar bodies . . . the Federal Congress; and the Parliament of Great Britain, in both its branches, on occasions of great moment [importance]; but none of them commanded my involuntary respect for their simple manly dignity and trustworthiness for the duties that engaged them, more than the General Assembly of Texas. There was honest eloquency [fine speaking] displayed at every opportunity for its use, and business was carried on with great rapidity. 99

Political Parties

For the most part, Texas politics revolved around strong leaders like Sam Houston. By the 1850s, however, political parties became organized. Most of the leaders of early Texas joined the Democratic Party. The Democratic Party was very strong in the South, and Democrats had favored Texas annexation.

The Democratic Party generally represented farmers and laborers. The **Whig Party**—the other major party in the United States in the 1830s to the 1850s—represented mostly business and commercial interests. The Whig Party lacked support in Texas. Voters had not liked the party's opposition to annexation. Also, many Whigs opposed expanding slavery to the nation's new territories.

In 1854 and 1855, some Texans joined the **American,** or **Know-Nothing, Party.** Its members tried to keep new immigrants from voting or holding public office. They were called Know-Nothings because, when asked about their organization or activities, they replied, "I know nothing." The American Party remained a force in Texas politics for only a few years, but it had an influence on the Texas Democratic Party. In fact, Texas Democrats patterned their own party organization after that of the American Party. They also adopted a practice that the American Party in Texas had used—nominating candidates at political meetings called conventions.

None of the major political parties during this period represented African Americans. Free African Americans were not eligible to vote or join political parties. They engaged in political activity by filing petitions with the legislature to remain as free people in the state. Others went to court to protect their freedom. In 1850, Mary Madison, a Galveston nurse, filed her petition to stay in Texas. It was one of the few granted by the legislature. Another African American woman, known as Emeline FWC (Free Woman of Color), hired attorneys and went to court in Harris County. She claimed she had been sold as a slave in a case of mistaken identity. She and her children were freed by the jury, which awarded her $1 in damages.

Federal Aid for Reservations

The federal government stationed troops in western Texas to prevent clashes between settlers and Native Americans. By 1851, however, the line of settlements had moved beyond the line of newly built forts. The federal government built a new string of seven forts about 100 miles to the west.

As settlers pushed westward, clashes between the newcomers and Native Americans increased. The United States government made plans to relocate Native Americans to reservations. The Wacos and Tonkawas were moved to a reservation near present-day Graham. Another reservation, located on the Clear Fork of the Brazos, was established for the nomadic Comanches.

The Texas reservation system never was a success. The Native Americans were not given enough land. Others simply refused to adopt the restricted way of life.

Early Governors of Texas

Governor	Term of Office
James P. Henderson	1846–1847
George T. Wood	1847–1849
Peter H. Bell	1849–1853
James W. Henderson	Nov.–Dec. 1853
Elisha M. Pease	1853–1857
Hardin R. Runnels	1857–1859
Sam Houston	1859–1861

TAKS PRACTICE

Identifying Most of the early governors of Texas had distinguished backgrounds in the military or politics. *What do you think would be an important leadership quality for an early governor of Texas?*

Many settlers in Texas opposed the reservation system. They believed that raids in northern and central Texas were made by Native Americans from the reservations. To try to stop the conflict, the government decided in 1859 to move Native Americans into the Indian Territory, north of the Red River. The Comanches and Kiowas continued to attack the settlements.

✓ Reading Check **Explaining** Why did the U.S. government place Native Americans on reservations?

SECTION 1 ASSESSMENT

Checking for Understanding

1. **Using Key Terms** Write one sentence that includes the words *legislature* and *amend*.
2. **Reviewing Facts** Why did few Texans support the Whig Party?

Reviewing Themes

3. **Civic Rights and Responsibilities** How did free African Americans engage in political activity if not through political parties?

Organizing to Learn

4. **Categorizing** Draw a cluster like the one below illustrating the main provisions of the Texas constitution.

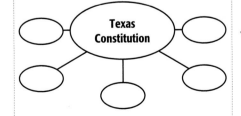

Texas Constitution

Critical Thinking

5. **Analyzing** What were some of the reasons why the U.S. government's reservation system was not successful?

TAKS PRACTICE

Drawing Conclusions Why would the American, or Know-Nothing, Party try to keep new immigrants from voting or holding public office?

War With Mexico

Guide to Reading

Main Idea
Conflict between the United States and Mexico led to war.

Key Terms
cede
abolitionist

Reading Strategy
Identifying Key Elements Complete a chart like the one below. Identify how the Treaty of Guadalupe Hidalgo met the concerns of the United States.

Concern	Treaty Resolution
Texas boundary	
Pacific port	
Damages from Mexican wars	

Read to Learn
• about the war with Mexico.
• about Texas's role in the war.
• where the new Texas boundaries were after the war.

Section Theme
Global Connections Mexico abandoned all claims to Texas, confirming Texas's annexation to the United States.

Preview of Events

◆1846	◆1847	◆1848
The U.S. Congress declares war on Mexico	American troops capture Mexico City	Peace treaty is signed at Guadalupe Hidalgo

Pack mule

A
Texas Story

The U.S. army's experiments with camels showed that the animals could haul much heavier loads than could horses or mules. Camels could also travel much greater distances without food or water. As E.F. Beale wrote in *Outwest,* "They pack heavy bundles of corn and oats for months and never get a grain, and on the bitter greasewood and other worthless shrubs, not only subsist, but keep fat." The Camp Verde soldiers in charge of transport did not like the camels, though, because they scared the horses and mules.

Causes of the War

The government of Mexico never recognized the Republic of Texas and considered the annexation of Texas by the United States an insult to Mexico. Even those Mexicans who had accepted Texas independence could not accept the Rio Grande as the boundary between Texas and Mexico. Mexico insisted that the Nueces River separated the two countries. It did not appear that this issue could be settled through talking.

Another problem was the commerce created by continued American westward expansion. American merchants in Texas had expanded trade into Mexico. By the 1840s, they were engaged in brisk business both in Santa Fe and Brazos Santiago. American merchants also were trading with China and other countries in the Pacific and East Asia. To help this trade expand further, the United States wanted to acquire the Pacific port of **San Francisco,** then in Mexican California. **President James K. Polk** was determined to accomplish this goal.

Yet another argument was that Mexico's army had destroyed much American property during the Texas Revolution. Earlier, the United States had demanded that the Mexican government pay the victims of this damage. Now, the U.S. was prepared to pay all of the debts owed to its citizens and give $30 million to Mexico. In return, Mexico would accept the Rio Grande as the Mexico–Texas boundary and cede, or give up, California and the western half of New Mexico to the United States. President Polk sent **John Slidell** to Mexico to negotiate. Slidell was to try to settle the damage claims of U.S. citizens. In addition, he was to try to negotiate the

Picturing **History**

General Zachary Taylor commanded U.S. troops during the Mexican–American War. He was a soldier for 40 years before he became president of the United States. Which Texas politicians fought in the Mexican–American War?

boundary dispute and offer to buy California. Slidell arrived in the fall of 1845, but neither the old nor the new president of Mexico wanted to make concessions to the United States. They were afraid that if they were to do so, their enemies would denounce them as weaklings. No representative of the Mexican government

Causes and Effects of the Mexican–American War

Causes

- Disputes over the United States' annexation of Texas
- Boundary disputes between U.S. and Mexico
- Mexico's refusal to negotiate with the U.S.

Effects

- Santa Anna flees to Jamaica.
- Mexico cedes almost 50 percent of its land to the U.S. in the Treaty of Guadalupe Hidalgo.

Graphic Organizer → *Skills*

President Polk wanted to gain the port of San Francisco either through negotiations or by war to assist American trade in the Pacific and East Asia.

Analyzing Information What prompted the U.S. to declare war on Mexico?

NATIONAL GEOGRAPHIC
Battles of Mexican–American War

The transfer of California and New Mexico to the United States was of major importance to the nation's future.

The dispute over who owned the land between the Nueces River and the Rio Grande was a major reason for the war.

United States
Claimed by Mexico
Mexico
— American troops
— Mexican troops
--- Present-day Texas
✳ Battle

The battle near Palo Alto was fought on May 8, 1846. This was 5 days before the official declaration of war by the U.S. Congress.

It was not until five months after Mexico City was captured that Mexico agreed to the peace treaty ending the war.

PACIFIC OCEAN

0 mi. 200
0 km 200
Albers Conic Equal-Area projection

MEXICO

UNITED STATES

TEXAS

Sacramento, San Francisco, Monterey, Los Angeles, San Diego, San Pascual, El Brazito, Doña Ana, El Paso, Sacramento, Chihuahua, Mazatlán, San Luis Potosí, Mexico City, Cerro Gordo, Veracruz, Tampico, Buena Vista, Saltillo, Parras, Monterrey, Monclova, Matamoros, Palo Alto, Corpus Christi, San Antonio, Nueces R., New Orleans, Bent's Fort, Santa Fe, Fort Leavenworth

would speak to Slidell. As a result, diplomatic relations completely broke down. In March 1846, President Polk ordered **General Zachary Taylor** to move his troops across the Nueces River to the Rio Grande.

War Declared

In late April and early May 1846, American and Mexican soldiers clashed just north of the Rio Grande. When President Polk learned of the fighting between Americans and Mexicans, he declared that "Mexico . . . shed American blood upon

TEXAS HISTORY *Online*

Student Web Activity Visit the texans.glencoe.com Web site and click on **Chapter 14—Student Web Activity** to learn more about the Mexican–American War.

TAKS PRACTICE

American forces traveled overland through Texas and also by sea to invade Mexico.
Drawing Conclusions Why would American troops want to attack Mexico City in particular?

American soil." Because this spot was in the disputed land, Mexican president **Mariano Paredes** could have claimed that Mexican blood had been shed on Mexican soil. However, on May 13, the U.S. Congress declared war. Some members of Congress questioned the American motives. Abolitionists, the people who worked to end slavery, considered it a scheme to steal "bigger pens to cram in slaves."

More than 5,000 Texans quickly answered the call to arms. Texans who served as officers in the United States Army included Edward Burleson,

Albert Sidney Johnston, and Mirabeau B. Lamar—former president of the republic. J. Pinckney Henderson took a leave of absence from his duties as governor to take command of Texas troops. Several companies of Texas Rangers served as scouts for the American army as it marched into Mexico. Tragically, because of their anti-Mexican feelings, some of the Texans took out their anger against Mexican civilians.

✓ **Reading Check** **Identifying** What were three points of disagreement between Mexico and the United States?

United States Victory

The United States forces were better equipped and better led than were their opponents. After General Zachary Taylor's army occupied northern Mexico, it moved south. In late September his forces captured Monterrey. In February 1847 Taylor defeated a large Mexican army under the command of Santa Anna at **Buena Vista.** Troops led by **General Winfield Scott** landed at Vera Cruz and captured Mexico City in September 1847. Other American forces moved from Fort Leavenworth, Kansas—by way of Santa Fe—to occupy California.

Women also took an active part in the war. For example, Sarah Borginnis traveled with General Taylor's army— cooking, washing, loading cartridges, and dressing wounds. Teresa Vielé, the wife of an army officer, recalled that Mexican women nursed the American army's sick and wounded.

On February 2, 1848, representatives of both governments signed a peace treaty at Guadalupe Hidalgo (gwad•ah• LOO•pay ee•DAHL•goh), a small town located near Mexico City. Mexico abandoned all claims to Texas and accepted the Rio Grande as the boundary. Mexico

TWO VIEWPOINTS

The Mexican–American War (1846–1848)

Views about the Mexican–American War, more than many other events, were challenged by historians as time passed. Read the two views below and then answer the questions.

You Can't Stop Progress

People in the United States had a reputation that they were in awe of nothing and nothing could stand in their way. The word was boundlessness— there were no bounds, no limits, to what an individual, society, and the nation itself could achieve . . . The United States was often times referred to as a "go-ahead nation," a "go-ahead people" with the locomotive almost as a symbol . . . The Mexican–American War was an example of this boundlessness and reform spirit—a quest for a better place for the nation, a test of the model republic and the ability of a democracy to respond to a crisis . . .
—Robert W. Johanssen, historian

U.S. Mobilization Was an Outright Attack

In the eyes of the [Mexican] government, the mobilization of the U.S. army was an outright attack on Mexico's territorial integrity and clearly demonstrated that the United States had no intention of subjecting itself to the terms of the 1828 border treaty. As a consequence, the Mexican government [acted to] protect the border, meaning the territory located between the Río Grande and the Nueces River.
—Jesus Velasco-Márquez, historian

Learning From History

1. According to Velasco-Márquez, why did the Mexican government go to war?

2. What is meant by "go-ahead nation"?

also surrendered to the United States all territory between western Texas and the Pacific Ocean. This vast area of transferred land, known historically as the **Mexican Cession,** included all of California, Nevada, and Utah, and parts of Arizona, Colorado, New Mexico, and Wyoming. In return for this land, the United States paid Mexico $15 million and agreed to pay claims of American citizens against Mexico up to $3.25 million. Mexicans living in the lost territory were guaranteed all rights of United States citizenship, including political rights and the right to keep their lands. They had a year to decide if they wished to become American citizens.

The New Mexico Boundary Dispute

The **Treaty of Guadalupe Hidalgo** ended the dispute between the United States and Mexico concerning Texas. However, the question of whether Santa Fe would become part of Texas became a political issue in the United States.

During its period as a republic, Texas claimed the Rio Grande as its southern and western boundaries. Such a claim gave Texas control of about one-half of New Mexico, including Santa Fe. Many of the people of Santa Fe did not want to be part of Texas. They preferred to become a separate territory or state. Also, many people in the northern United States feared that the

A Shared Past...

President Polk asked Congress for a declaration of war against Mexico, saying, "Mexico . . . shed American blood upon American soil." Serving in Congress at the time was a member from Illinois named Abraham Lincoln. Lincoln was not in favor of war with Mexico, and he introduced his famous "Spot Resolutions" to oppose Polk. The "Spot Resolutions" asked Polk to point out the "spot on the map" where American blood had been shed. Lincoln was less sure it was American soil.

Texans would introduce slavery into this area. They argued that Texas should give up the disputed territory. Members of Congress, led by Henry Clay, worked out a solution. In the **Pearce Act,** a part of the **Compromise of 1850,** Texas agreed to surrender its claims to a portion of the disputed area. The United States agreed to give Texas $10 million. At long last, Texas could pay its debt and get its finances in order.

Reading Check **Examining** What areas did the United States secure after the peace treaty?

SECTION 2 ASSESSMENT

Checking for Understanding

1. **Using Key Terms** Write two sentences in your own words to demonstrate your understanding of the key terms abolitionist and cede.

2. **Reviewing Facts** How were Texas's borders changed after the war?

Reviewing Themes

3. **Global Connections** Texas joined the Union in 1845. How did the United States' war with Mexico validate this union?

Organizing to Learn

4. **Identifying Points of View** Complete a chart like the one below and describe the view of each person or group toward the Mexican–American War.

Individual/ Group	View on War
Polk	
Abolitionists	
5000 Texans	
Some members of Congress	

Critical Thinking

5. **Resolving Conflicts** What are some of the steps the United States tried to take to resolve many of its conflicts with the government of Mexico? Do you think the U.S. government should have tried harder to resolve the conflict peacefully?

TAKS PRACTICE

Drawing Conclusions How did President Polk justify declaring war on Mexico on May 13, 1846?

Drawing Conclusions

Why Learn This Skill?

"Elementary, my dear Watson!" Fictional detective Sherlock Holmes often said this to his assistant after he examined all the available facts and solved the case.

Drawing conclusions can help you to form ideas that are not stated directly by using the available facts and your own knowledge and experience to form a judgment or opinion about the material.

Learning the Skill

Some steps in learning to draw conclusions are:

- Review the facts that are stated directly.
- Develop some conclusions about these facts, using what you already know.
- Look for information to check the accuracy of your conclusions.

Practicing the Skill

Read the excerpt below about the Mexican–American War and then answer the questions.

There is no evidence that [President] Polk wanted a war with Mexico for its own sake. He did want Texas and California and was willing to fight, if necessary, to get them . . . [T]he Rio Grande . . . gave the United States a clearly defined southern boundary, which the Nueces could not do. The expansion to the western ocean . . . left the United States as the dominant power upon the North American continent.

Polk honestly tried to buy the Mexican claims to Texas and California. But a power struggle was . . . inevitable . . . The Mexicans were not just stubborn; they were [unmovable] . . . Mexico also began preparations for a larger war . . .

The South and Southwest, as always, were ready

Mexican–American War battle scene

for war . . . But the rest of the nation was not, and a majority in Congress stood opposed to a war with Mexico, over Texas or anything else.

1 What steps did President Polk take to avoid war with Mexico?

2 What does the author say about Mexico's role?

3 What conclusion can you draw about why Polk went to war with Mexico?

4 How could you check the accuracy of your conclusions?

TAKS PRACTICE

Drawing Conclusions Re-read **A Texas Story** on page 326. What conclusion can you reach as to which animal the army should have used to haul supplies?

GO TO

Glencoe's **Skillbuilder Interactive Workbook,** Level 1, provides instruction and practice in key social studies skills.

Immigrants Come to Texas

Guide to Reading

Main Idea
As a young state, Texas continued to attract immigrants of many national and cultural origins.

Key Terms
census
teamster
descendant

Reading Strategy
Evaluating Results Complete a web like the one shown here. Identify positive and negative results of the population explosion of the 1850s.

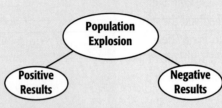

Population Explosion

Positive Results

Negative Results

Read to Learn
- about immigrants in Texas.
- about increased migration to Texas.
- about policies toward Native Americans.

Section Theme
Culture and Traditions As Europeans came to Texas, Mexican Americans and Native Americans experienced tension from Anglos.

Preview of Events

♦1859	♦1860
Texas Native Americans are moved into Indian Territory	The population in Texas is three times larger than in 1850

Tombstone of Hadji Ali

****
A
Texas Story

★

When the U.S. Army bought camels to test in the desert, they also brought three Arab and two Turkish men to care for them. One Arab was named Hadji Ali. When experiments showed that the animals could adapt to Texas's climate, plans were made to develop a route to California. Hadji Ali was appointed to lead the caravan. The Civil War disrupted plans and the camels were sold or turned loose. Hadji Ali stayed in the U.S. After his death, a tombstone with a camel on it was erected in Arizona in his honor.

Texas Population Booms

The population of Texas grew rapidly during the early years of statehood. The United States Census Bureau of 1850 counted 212,592 Texans. This was almost a 50 percent increase over the state census (a count of the population) figure in 1847. In the next 10 years, the population nearly tripled to 604,215.

Annexation, the lure of inexpensive land, and legalized slavery attracted thousands to Texas during the 1840s and 1850s. Under the Homestead Act, settlers obtained land merely by living on it and improving it. Additional land could be purchased at low cost.

Most of the new arrivals came from the southern United States. In 1860 more than 42,000 residents were Tennessee natives. Travelers visiting southern states in the pre-Civil War years reported seeing abandoned cabins marked with the initials "GTT"—Gone To Texas.

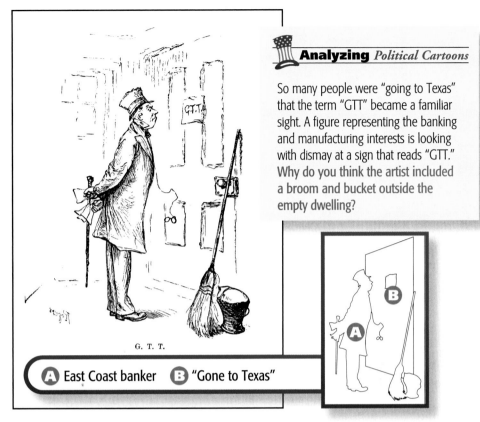

G. T. T.

Ⓐ East Coast banker   Ⓑ "Gone to Texas"

The large increase in population created a need for new counties to be formed to take care of administrative and governmental concerns, such as collecting taxes and arranging for elections. When Texas entered the Union in 1845, there were 36 counties (see maps on page 304). By 1860, that number had grown to 122. One of the first actions of the first session of the state legislature was creating 26 new counties. Some of them, such as Dallas, Tyler, Upshur, and Polk, were named for United States government officials. Competition among towns to become county seats was often fierce. Those towns that won that competition could expect to enjoy increased employment opportunities, as well as great prestige.

Mexican Texans

In addition to the thousands crossing the Red and Sabine Rivers from other parts of the United States, Mexicans moved north into Texas. The United States Census of 1860 lists 12,443 people of Mexican descent living in Texas. This figure might be low, however. One study indicates that 25,000 Mexican Americans resided in Texas at the time.

Most Mexican Americans lived in one of three areas of Texas: in the wedge-shaped region between the Nueces River and Rio Grande, in the San Antonio–Goliad area, and along the Rio Grande from Del Rio to El Paso. After the Mexican–American War, South Texas towns like Laredo, Corpus Christi, Eagle Pass, Brownsville, Edinburg, and Rio Grande City grew rapidly. While most of the people living in South Texas were Tejanos, most of the political leaders were Anglos.

Farming and ranching provided the main occupations for Mexican Americans. Some owned ranches, but most worked as cowhands, sheepherders, and ranch laborers. Mexican Americans living in the towns were business owners, teamsters (animal drivers), domestic servants, day laborers, and craftworkers. After the Civil War, José Policarpo Rodríguez became a surveyor, army and Texas Ranger guide, and a minister. Luis Sánchez served Texas as an interpreter during the republic and statehood periods.

✓ Reading Check **Summarizing** What were some of the most common occupations of Mexican Americans?

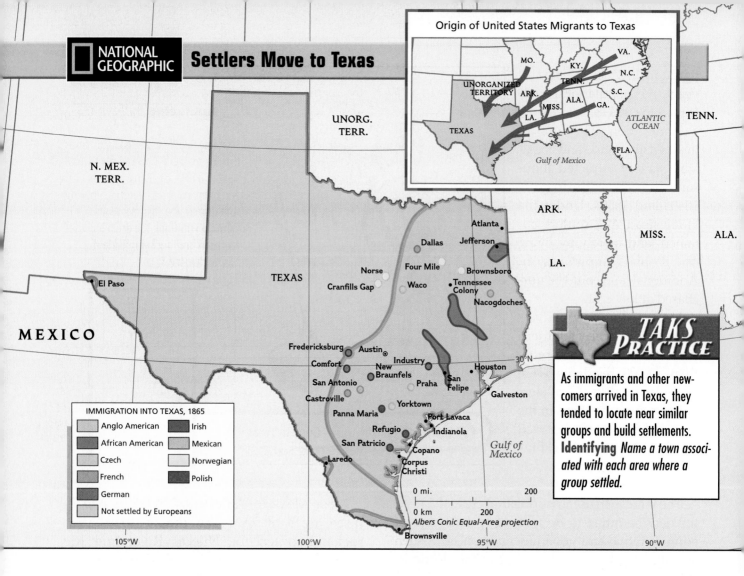

Settlers Move to Texas

Origin of United States Migrants to Texas

IMMIGRATION INTO TEXAS, 1865

- Anglo American
- African American
- Czech
- French
- German
- Not settled by Europeans
- Irish
- Mexican
- Norwegian
- Polish

TAKS PRACTICE

As immigrants and other newcomers arrived in Texas, they tended to locate near similar groups and build settlements. **Identifying** *Name a town associated with each area where a group settled.*

Politics and Bias

Some Mexican Americans were active in political life. **José Antonio Navarro** and **Santos Benavides** (SAHN•tohs beh•nah•VEE•days) made worthwhile contributions to Texas history. Navarro, a native of San Antonio, signed the Texas Declaration of Independence and was a member of the congress during the republic, a delegate to the Constitutional Convention of 1845, and a state senator. Navarro County, created in April 1846, was named for him. Santos Benavides was a prosperous merchant who became mayor of Laredo and later chief justice of Webb County. He also served three times in the Texas legislature.

Despite the contributions of Navarro, Benavides, and others, too many Mexican Americans faced hostility and prejudice. **Juan Cortina** came to be seen as a protector of the rights of Mexicans and Tejanos, and he was a hero to many families along the border. Government

authorities in both Texas and Mexico during the late 1850s generally looked upon him as an outlaw, however. Although he was accused of many crimes, the extent of his activities is uncertain. The Texas Rangers were never able to capture Juan Cortina. Eventually, the Mexican army captured him and removed him from the valley.

The Texas Rangers' constant patrolling of the countryside north of the Rio Grande and the Mexican army's patrolling south of it helped reduce lawlessness. This peace did not come easily, however, and many Mexican Americans would remember these years with bitterness.

In part, the negative feelings against Mexican Americans were a result of the battles fought at the Alamo and Goliad and the entire Texas struggle for independence. That Tejanos held lands wanted by Anglos was another reason for the bitterness toward them. Despite the prejudice and discrimination, Mexican Texans retained their cultural heritage—their religion, language, and traditions. As time passed, an important Mexican culture mixed with Anglo American culture and tradition. Today, most Mexican Americans are bicultural and many are bilingual.

✓ **Reading Check** **Examining** Why were some Anglos biased against Mexican Americans?

German Texans

Thousands of people immigrated to Texas from Europe. In 1860 the foreign-born citizens of Texas numbered 43,422 and represented almost every country of western Europe. The German migration that began during the period of the republic continued. New Braunfels, Fredericksburg, and other German communities in central and South Texas expanded further. Some Germans settled in the larger cities of the state. By 1860 one-fifth of the residents of Houston, Galveston, and San Antonio were Germans, and more than 20,000 Germans were living in Texas.

Many people migrated to Texas to escape the hardships in Germany. The potato blight that struck Ireland in the mid-1840s also hit Germany and northwestern Europe. Political and economic difficulties led more and more Germans to seek a fresh start in America.

Germans contributed to the social and intellectual life of the young state. Dr. Ferdinand Herff became one of the most famous surgeons in Texas

and received national recognition for his services to the medical profession. Dr. Ferdinand Jacob Lindheimer, the editor of a German newspaper published in New Braunfels, gained a national reputation as a scientist.

Other European Arrivals

Immigrants from other European countries came to Texas during its early years of statehood. Natives of Ireland, England, and France settled in major Texas cities and became merchants, artisans, and laborers. In 1855 a group of about 350 French immigrants founded the colony of La Réunion (la ray•oo•NYAW) near Dallas. Although the colony failed, most of the settlers remained in Texas.

Several hundred Polish families migrated to Texas during the 1850s. Polish settlers started the town of Panna Maria (Virgin Mary) in Karnes County. Father Leopold Moczygemba (LEE•oh•pohld moh•chee•GEHM•bah), a young priest who lived in Castroville and New Braunfels, influenced many Poles to settle in Texas.

Many Czechs came to Texas to escape the fighting in Europe during the late 1840s. Anthony Michael Dignowity, who visited Texas in 1836, is believed to have been the first Czech in the state. Dignowity originally came to San Antonio with a group of volunteers to fight in the Mexican–American War. Afterwards, he settled

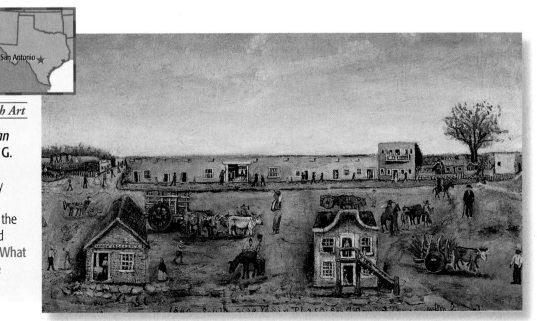

San Antonio ★

History *Through Art*

South Side Main Plaza, San Antonio Texas **by William G. Samuel, 1849**
San Antonio provided many services for settlers moving farther west. In 1860 it was the largest city in Texas and had many German inhabitants. **What other cities attracted large immigrant populations?**

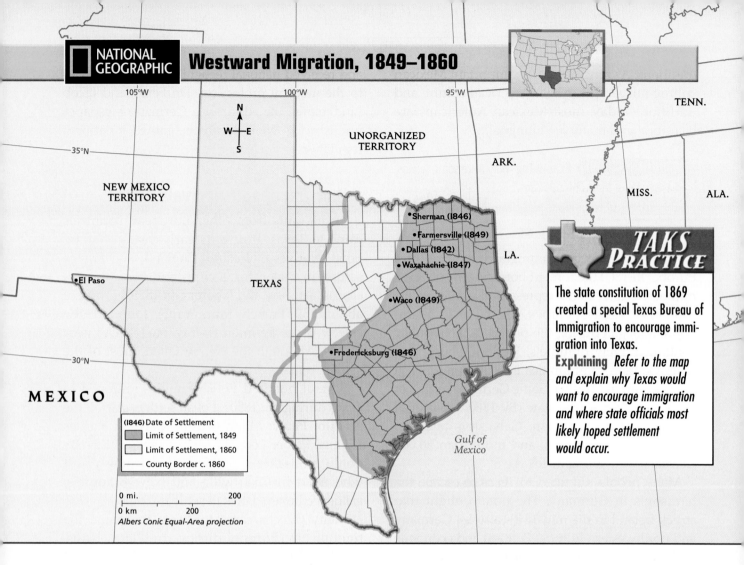

35°N

105°W 100°W 95°W TENN.

N
W—E
S

UNORGANIZED
TERRITORY

ARK.

NEW MEXICO
TERRITORY

MISS. ALA.

•Sherman (1846)

•Farmersville (1849)

•Dallas (1842)

•Waxahachie (1847)

LA.

•El Paso

TEXAS

•Waco (1849)

30°N

•Fredericksburg (1846)

MEXICO

Gulf of
Mexico

(1846) Date of Settlement

Limit of Settlement, 1849

Limit of Settlement, 1860

County Border c. 1860

0 mi. 200
0 km 200
Albers Conic Equal-Area projection

TAKS PRACTICE

The state constitution of 1869
created a special Texas Bureau of
Immigration to encourage immigration into Texas.
Explaining *Refer to the map
and explain why Texas would
want to encourage immigration
and where state officials most
likely hoped settlement
would occur.*

in San Antonio in 1846 and practiced medicine. His wife, Amanda McCann Dignowity, had studied to be a doctor. Her knowledge of medicine enabled her to work with her husband conducting research.

Ernst Bergmann led some Czechs who settled at Cat Spring. Josef Lesikar guided others to a settlement near New Ulm. New Bremen, Fayetteville, Hostyn, Dubina, and Praha were early communities with sizable Czech populations.

Several hundred Norwegians migrated to Texas during the early years of statehood. Johan Reinert Reiersen, a Norwegian traveler who visited Texas in 1844, was very impressed by its economic and social conditions. Two years later he and his father returned to establish a Norwegian settlement in Henderson County. This settlement, first called Normandy, later became Brownsboro. A second Norwegian settlement was made on the Kaufman and Van Zandt County line in 1848. By

1860 more than 300 Norwegians lived in Texas. **Elise Waerenskjold** (a•LEES VAY•ren•shold) was a pioneer writer and community leader from Norway. She became known as the "walking newspaper."

In 1850 **Lewis Levy,** a Houston Jew, wrote a letter to the *Asmonean,* a New York newspaper, urging persecuted European Jews to move to Texas.

66 Thousands of acres of land can be bought, within the settled portions of the State, for the small sum of 25 cents to $1 per acre . . . where a man can make his living to his liking, and [be] more independent than the Autocrat of Russia, or the Emperor of Austria. 99

Jewish immigrants were active in Texas since the early days of colonization. Moses Albert Levy was the surgeon general of the volunteer army and a defender of San Antonio. Henri Castro helped bring many French families to Texas. Adolphus Sterne was a prominent Nacogdoches merchant and political leader. Jacob de Cordova, a reporter and writer, was a founder of Waco.

The new arrivals to Texas brought their music, arts, languages, literature, and traditions. They also brought their intellectual pursuits, industrial crafts, and agricultural skills. All of these elements contributed to the development of a diverse Texas culture—one that is a unique product of people from many lands.

The Alabama–Coushattas

Only a few Native Americans continued to live peaceably in Texas. Before the revolution, the Alabama–Coushattas had settled along the lower Trinity River in East Texas. In 1854 the Texas legislature purchased 1,280 acres (518 hectares) of land in Polk County for the Alabama tribe, but no specific grant was ever made for the Coushattas. Some Coushattas, through marriage or by special permission from the Alabama people, came to live on the reservation where they continued to hunt and trade. By 1855 more than 300 Alabama–Coushattas lived on the reservation.

The Tiguas and the Kickapoos

Texas has recognized two other Native American groups: the Tiguas and the Kickapoos. The Tiguas have lived near El Paso for 300 years. They are believed to be descendants, or offspring,

Kickapoo warrior

of the Pueblos of New Mexico. The Kickapoos originally lived in Illinois but migrated to East Texas and other areas of the Southwest United States in the 1820s. They were eventually forced to leave East Texas. Some went to Oklahoma, while others moved to northern Mexico. The Kickapoos were recognized as a sovereign nation in 1989 and are now officially known as the Kickapoo Traditional Tribe of Texas. The Kickapoos have two settlements, one in Nacimiento, Mexico, and the other on 125 acres (51 hectares) of land near Eagle Pass, Texas.

✓ **Reading Check** **Identifying:** List five groups of immigrants who settled Texas in the 1840s and 1850s.

SECTION 3 ASSESSMENT

Checking for Understanding

1. **Using Key Terms** Define teamster, census, and descendant.
2. **Reviewing Facts** Identify three factors that attracted new settlers to Texas.

Reviewing Themes

3. **Culture and Traditions** Which Native Americans are considered descendants of Pueblos?

Organizing to Learn

4. **Categorizing Population Data** Fill in the population figures for each census listed. Calculate the approximate population for the 1847 census. (See pp. 332–333.)

Census	Population
1847	
1850	
1860	

Critical Thinking

5. **Explaining** Why did Mexican Americans face hostility and prejudice during the early years of Texas's statehood?

TAKS PRACTICE

Making Comparisons In what ways were many of the immigrants to the new state similar?

Chapter Summary

The Young State

1845
- Texas drafts a new constitution.

1846
★ The Mexican–American War begins.

1848
★ The Treaty of Guadalupe Hidalgo ends the Mexican–American war.

- Mexico accepts the Rio Grande as Texas's southern boundry.

- Mexico cedes the New Mexico and California territories to the United States.

1846–1860
- Texas has resources to pay off debt because of the Compromise of 1850.

★ Texas's population explodes as many immigrants arrive.

★ Clashes between settlers and Native Americans become more frequent as settlers push westward.

- The U.S. government places many Native Americans onto reservations.

Reviewing Key Terms

Number your paper 1 to 8. Next to each number, write the letter of the group of words that correctly defines each key term.

1. legislature
2. amend
3. convention
4. cede
5. abolitionist
6. teamster
7. census
8. descendant

   a. an organized body of people having the power to make laws

   b. a complete count of the population by the government

   c. to change or to add to a document

   d. a person who works to end slavery

   e. a meeting of delegates of a political party

   f. proceeding from an ancestor

   g. a person who drives or directs a team of animals

   h. to give up, especially by treaty

Reviewing Key Facts

9. List some problems faced by the new state of Texas.
10. Describe the Constitution of 1845.
11. Describe the boundary dispute between the United States and Mexico.
12. List two reasons why American forces overwhelmed their Mexican opponents.
13. What treaty ended the war between the United States and Mexico?
14. List two reasons for the rapid increase in population in Texas by 1860.
15. What Native American tribes have been recognized by the State of Texas?

Critical Thinking

16. **Making Generalizations** Why did the Whig Party have little or no support in Texas before the Civil War?
17. **Determining Cause and Effect** What was the effect of the Homestead Act on the settlement of Texas?
18. **Identifying Motives** What were some reasons that Europeans came to Texas during its early years of statehood?
19. **Analyzing Immigration Issues** What were some ways that immigrants influenced Texas?

Geography and History Activity

20. Population Forecast Draw a graph like the one shown. Project Texas's population growth for the years 2005 and 2010 based on the trends you observed on the chart for the years 1990 to 2000.

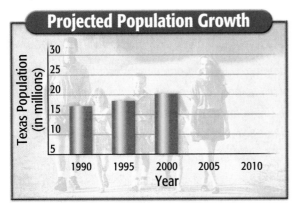

Projected Population Growth

Texas Population (in millions)

Year

Cooperative Learning Activity

21. Role Playing Working in groups of four, formulate one question you would ask of (1) a Democratic Party representative, (2) a Kickapoo chief, (3) Juan Cortina, and (4) Mexican president Mariano Paredes. Have each student represent one of the above individuals and try to answer the question. Then discuss questions and answers to gain a greater understanding of these individuals' perspectives.

Practicing Skills

22. Drawing Conclusions Read the following excerpt from a speech by Sam Houston during the Mexican–American War. Then answer the question that follows.

> "[T]here is an instinct in the American people which impels them onward, which will lead them to pervade [dominate] this continent, to develop its resources, to civilize its people and receive [its] rich bounties . . . The Americans regard this continent as their birth-right."

What reason does Houston give for Anglo Americans to keep moving westward?

Portfolio/TAKS Writing Activity

23. Writing Critically Read the following description of a Texas Ranger by former Ranger captain Bob Crowder:

> "A Ranger is an officer who is able to handle any given situation without definite instructions from his commanding officer or higher authority."

TEXAS HISTORY Online

Self-Check Quiz

Visit the texans.glencoe.com Web site and click on **Chapter 14—Self-Check Quizzes** to prepare for the chapter test.

Write a paragraph explaining why you think leadership qualities were especially necessary for early Rangers stationed in central or West Texas to protect settlements.

Government and History Activity

24. Foreign Relations Research the current relationship between the U.S. and Mexico. In a brief essay, discuss one aspect of how relations have improved.

TAKS PRACTICE

The Princeton Review

Use the graph to answer the following question.

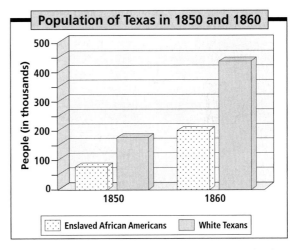

Population of Texas in 1850 and 1860

People (in thousands)

Enslaved African Americans   White Texans

About how many more enslaved African Americans lived in Texas in 1860 than in 1850?

F 150,000   **H** 125,000

G 200,000   **J** 250,000

Test-Taking Tip:

When a question involves reading a graph, do not skip over the title and labels. Instead, read them carefully. They contain important information, such as the purpose of the graph and the units of measurement used in the graph.

CHAPTER 15

The Civil War

Why It Matters

Most Texans did not support the Union. They felt isolated from decision makers in faraway Washington, D.C. The Confederacy promised to preserve their way of life. This way of life, however, meant that slavery would continue. In order for slavery to end, Union forces had to triumph. Texas did not suffer as much damage as other Southern states, but both Union and Confederate supporters in Texas made sacrifices.

The Impact Today

Key events that happened during this time still shape our lives today. For example,
- *the institution of slavery has been abolished.*
- *laws made by the federal government override state laws.*
- *Texas has many customs and traditions that it shares with Southern states.*

Texas

1861
★ Texans voted to join the Confederate States of America

1862
★ Galveston taken by Union forces

United States   *1860*   *1861*   *1862*

World

1860
• Guiseppe Garibaldi and the "Red Shirts" conquered Sicily and Naples

1861
• The Civil War began

1862
• R.J. Gatling invented the 10-barrel Gatling gun

General David Twiggs commanded the Union forces in Texas at the start of the Civil War.

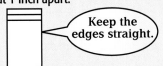

FOLDABLES™ TAKS PRACTICE
Study Organizer

Sequencing Events Study Foldable
Make this foldable to organize information and sequence events that took place in Texas during the Civil War.

Step 1 Collect three sheets of paper and place them about 1 inch apart.

Keep the edges straight.

Step 2 Fold up the bottom edges of the paper to form 6 tabs.

This makes all tabs the same size.

Step 3 When all the tabs are the same size, crease the paper to hold the tabs in place and staple the sheets together. Turn the paper and label each tab as shown.

The Civil War in Texas
1861
1862
1863
1864
1865

Staple together along the fold.

Reading and Writing As you read, use your foldable to describe significant events that occurred in Texas during each year of the Civil War. Be sure to write the information under the correct tab.

1863
★ Galveston recaptured by the Confederacy
★ Battle of Sabine Pass

1865
★ Last battle of the Civil War fought at Palmito Ranch
★ Slavery was abolished in Texas

1863   *1864*   *1865*

1863
• Emancipation Proclamation
• Confederate forces surrendered at Vicksburg

1864
• Maximilian became emperor of Mexico

1865
• General Lee surrendered
• Abraham Lincoln assassinated

1863
• International Red Cross founded in Switzerland

TEXAS HISTORY Online

Chapter Overview
Visit the texans.glencoe.com Web site and click on **Chapter 15—Chapter Overviews** to preview chapter information.

Texas Secession

Main Idea

Abraham Lincoln was elected president in 1860. In 1861, Southern states, including Texas, formed the Confederate States of America.

Key Terms

states' rights, secede, sovereignty, ordinance, perpetual

Reading Strategy

Classifying Information As you read this section, complete a chart like the one shown here, comparing the views of the North and South on the following issues:

Issue	Union	Confederacy
Slavery		
States' Rights		
Tariffs		

Read to Learn

- what issues divided the North and the South.
- about events leading to the Civil War.

Section Theme

Economic Factors The two main issues that divided the Union and the Confederacy were states' rights and slavery.

Preview of Events

♦1860 ♦1861

November
Abraham Lincoln is elected president

December
Southern states begin to secede

January
Texas Secession Convention meets in Austin

February
Confederate States of America is formed

March
Governor Houston is removed from office

A
Texas Story

Civil War diary

Lucy Pier Stevens, a young, unmarried woman from Ohio, arrived at her aunt and uncle's home in Austin County on Christmas Day, 1859, for a long visit. When the Civil War broke out, she could not safely return to her home in Ohio. Her Texas relatives supported the Confederacy. Her Ohio family supported the North. Lucy had learned how to look at two sides of a question. In her diary, she had written, "[H]ow strange that some people can only look on one side of a question." Lucy, like millions of other Americans, was torn between two loyalties.

Many Issues Divide the Country

In 1861 Texas joined 10 other Southern states that withdrew from the United States to form the **Confederate States of America.** This action followed years of long-standing differences between the North and the South. The two sections disagreed on many issues—tariffs, distribution of public lands, and **states' rights.** States' rights was the belief that the federal government should not have too much power over the affairs of individual states. Above all, the North and the South clashed over slavery. Every attempt to solve the question of slavery seemed only to further divide both sides.

The Republican Party Opposes Slavery

At one time, slavery existed in many Northern states, but leaders had taken steps over the years to stop it. The abolitionists wanted to end slavery everywhere. Not all Northern whites shared their view. Many, perhaps even the majority, were prejudiced against African Americans—both free African Americans in the North and slaves in the South. But even those who were not completely opposed to slavery did not want it to spread into new territories.

Many Northerners who were against slavery joined the new **Republican Party.** Slavery was not the party's only issue, however. Many Northern business leaders and farmers believed that **Southern Democrats**—who supported slavery—were responsible for the economic depression of the late 1850s and that prosperity could be brought back by a high tariff, a homestead act, and internal improvements. Southerners were against these measures. They thought such policies would only benefit the North. For these reasons, most Southerners believed that victory for the Republican Party would mean the end of slavery and the Southern way of life.

Reading Check **Explaining** Why did Southerners believe the Republican Party was the party of the North?

Southern States Vow to Secede

During the 1860 presidential campaign, some Southern leaders had threatened that if the Republicans won the election, the South would **secede,** or withdraw, from the Union. They argued that **sovereignty,** or supreme power,

History *Through Art*

***Slave Auction of African Family* by Taylor, 1852** Slave auctions were a common part of life in the South before the Civil War. Slaves often had to wear identification badges. **How did these auctions affect African American families?**

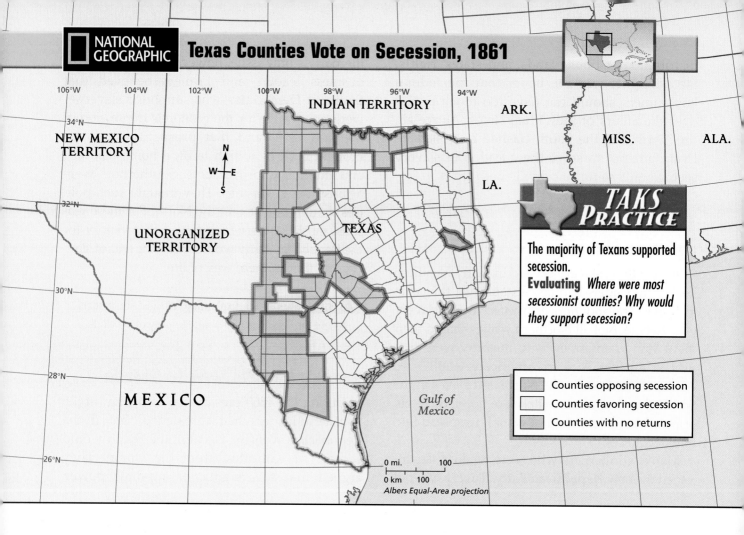

Texas Counties Vote on Secession, 1861

INDIAN TERRITORY

ARK.

NEW MEXICO
TERRITORY

MISS.

ALA.

LA.

N
W E
S

UNORGANIZED
TERRITORY

TEXAS

TAKS PRACTICE

The majority of Texans supported secession.
Evaluating Where were most secessionist counties? Why would they support secession?

MEXICO

Gulf of
Mexico

Counties opposing secession
Counties favoring secession
Counties with no returns

0 mi. 100
0 km 100
Albers Equal-Area projection

rested in the states. The sovereign states had entered the Union voluntarily, and they should be able to leave it voluntarily. When Republican candidate **Abraham Lincoln** won the 1860 presidential election, Southern leaders carried out their threat to secede. In December 1860 and January 1861, six states—**South Carolina, Mississippi, Florida, Alabama, Georgia,** and **Louisiana**— voted to withdraw from the Union. Many Texans urged Governor Houston to issue a call for a convention to consider the secession of Texas.

The Convention Votes on Secession

Sam Houston opposed secession. He argued that Texas could better protect its interests by staying in the Union. Houston did not believe the South could win the war. He said:

❝Let me tell you what is coming. After the sacrifice of countless millions of treasure and hundreds of thousands of lives you may win

Southern independence, but I doubt it. The North is determined to preserve this Union. They are not a fiery, impulsive people as you are, for they live in colder climates. But when they begin to move in a given direction, they move with the steady momentum and perseverance of a mighty avalanche.❞

He refused to call a special session of the legislature so it, in turn, could recommend a secession convention. Without Houston's approval, several Texans who favored secession called a convention. They argued that the citizens should decide whether Texas would remain with the Union or secede from it. They urged Texans to take part in electing delegates to the convention. Texans who were against secession argued that the convention was illegal. Many who wanted no part of secession refused to take part in the election. As a result, most delegates chosen to the convention favored secession.

When Governor Houston realized that the convention was going to meet with or without his backing, he called a special session of the legislature. He hoped the legislature would declare the convention illegal. Instead, the legislature supported the convention and gave it the authority to act for the people.

The **Texas Secession Convention** met in Austin on January 28, 1861. The delegates quickly adopted a decree called the **Ordinance of Secession.** This ordinance, or local law, declared that the United States government had abused its power in order to "strike down the interest and prosperity of the people of Texas." Another part of this ordinance read, "Texas is a separate sovereign state, and . . . her citizens . . . are absolved [freed] from all allegiance to the United States." Delegates also called for a vote by the people on the question of secession. On February 23, 1861, the people of Texas approved secession from the Union by a vote of 46,153 to 14,747. Texas became the seventh state to withdraw from the Union. During the next three months, **Virginia, Arkansas, Tennessee,** and **North Carolina** also seceded.

✔ **Reading Check** **Analyzing** Why did Sam Houston believe the North would win the war?

The Confederacy Is Formed

The states that withdrew from the Union took steps to form a new nation at a convention in Montgomery, Alabama, on February 8, 1861. Confident that Texans would vote for secession, Texas sent seven delegates to the convention.

Members of the **Montgomery convention** formed the new nation, which was to be called the Confederate States of America, and drew up a constitution. This constitution was much like the Constitution of the United States, but there were important differences. Under the **Confederate constitution,** the states were given more power, and the federal government was given less. One section guaranteed the protection of slavery.

Delegates to the Montgomery convention also selected officers for the new government. **Jefferson Davis** of Mississippi was elected as president of the Confederacy. **Alexander H.**

Stephens of Georgia was chosen as vice president. A Texan, **John H. Reagan,** became postmaster general in President Davis's cabinet. The Texas Secession Convention held a second session and quickly approved the Confederate constitution. It also prepared the Texas Constitution of 1861. This document replaced references to the United States with references to the Confederacy.

Houston Is Removed and War Begins

The Texas Secession Convention then ordered all state officials to take an oath of allegiance to the Confederacy. The oath taker promised to "serve [the Confederacy] honestly and faithfully against all enemies or opposers whatsoever." When Governor Houston refused to take the oath, the convention declared the office of governor vacant. President Lincoln offered to send federal troops

Confederate President Jefferson Davis

Picturing **History**

This joint resolution by the Texas legislature on February 1, 1861, supported the right of the states to secede. What alliance was formed by the Southern states?

Lieutenant Governor Edward Clark, who had taken the oath to the Confederacy, replaced Sam Houston as governor. Houston retired to his home in Huntsville, where he lived quietly until his death two years later in 1863.

The federal system, under which the U.S. government was formed, allowed for the sharing of power between the central government in Washington, D.C., and the various states. Problems arose when there was disagreement between the central government and the states, such as in the case of placing taxes on imported or exported goods. The Southern states believed they had the right to leave, or secede, from the United States, but President Lincoln noted that the Union was perpetual, or continuing forever. The Southern states, he said, had no right to leave it. He said he would carry out the law of the land in all states. Lincoln vowed that he would preserve the nation at all costs. Early in 1861, the Confederate states seized United States arsenals, forts, and navy yards within their borders. When, on April 12, 1861, United States troops refused to evacuate **Fort Sumter** in Charleston, South Carolina, Confederate forces opened fire. The firing on Fort Sumter marked the beginning of the Civil War.

to Texas to keep Houston in office if he would head a government loyal to the Union. When some Texans urged him to accept Lincoln's offer, Houston declined:

❝Would you be willing to deluge [flood] the capital of Texas with the blood of Texans, merely to keep one poor old man in a position for a few days longer, in a position that belongs to the people? No! . . . Go tell my deluded friends that I am proud of their friendship, of their love and loyalty, . . . [but] to go to their homes and to conceal from the world that they would have been guilty of such an act.❞

Reading Check **Comparing** What was the main difference between the U.S. and Confederate constitutions?

SECTION 1 ASSESSMENT

Checking for Understanding

1. **Using Key Terms** Write a short paragraph explaining how sovereignty relates to the issue of states' rights.
2. **Reviewing Facts** Why did some Southern states secede from the Union when Lincoln was elected president?

Reviewing Themes

3. **Economic Factors** How did the South's economic dependence on cotton affect politics with the North?

Organizing to Learn

4. **Sequencing** Create a time line like the one shown. Place letters of the the key events in their proper sequence.

   ——+———+———+———+——

   a. Texas joins the Confederacy
   b. Attack on Fort Sumter
   c. Abraham Lincoln elected president
   d. Texas Secession Convention meets
   e. Sam Houston removed as governor
   f. South threatens secession during presidential campaign

Critical Thinking

5. **Evaluating** Do you think there is any situation in which a state or group of states should be allowed to secede from the United States? Explain your answer and provide two reasons why or why not.

TAKS PRACTICE

Distinguishing Fact From Opinion Explain whether you think the quotation by Sam Houston on page 344 is an example of fact or of opinion. List key words that helped you decide.

Texans Go to War

Guide to Reading

Main Idea
Defending Texas and its trade routes to international ports was vital for the Confederate economy.

Key Terms
conscription, Unionist, vigilante, preventive strike, blockade

Reading Strategy
Classifying Information As you read, describe the importance of each of these battles on a chart like the one shown.

Battle	Importance
Galveston	
Sabine Pass	
Laredo	
Red River	

Read to Learn
• Union supporters' role in Texas.
• about Texans' economic contributions.
• about Texas battles against Union forces.

Section Theme
Economic Factors Union forces tried to invade and blockade Texas to stop the flow of exports and supplies.

Preview of Events

1861	1862	1863	1864
February Volunteers take Union post at San Antonio	**April** Civil War begins	**April** Confederate Conscription Act is passed	**September** Confederate forces win Battle of Sabine Pass

Texas Brigade soldier

A
Texas Story

Lucy Pier Stevens, a Northerner, was visiting relatives in Texas when war was declared. Her cousin Sammy enlisted on his 17th birthday. Her uncle James was exempt from the draft because he was postmaster at Travis. He enlisted in the militia anyway and went to guard Union prisoners at the Hempstead prison camp. By 1863, Lucy had written sadly in her diary, "We are tired of war." Like many Texas families, Lucy's family had to deal with the pain of loss and separation from loved ones during the Civil War.

Many Texans Become Soldiers

When fighting began, Confederate President Jefferson Davis called for volunteers. Although thousands of Texans immediately joined the army, more soldiers were needed by the end of the first year of the war. To meet

Disease was the first enemy new recruits faced. Healthy soldiers fell victim to illnesses that were spread by the large number of people in the camps, the unsanitary conditions, and the poor diet. Childhood diseases such as measles could devastate regiments, and many men succumbed to diarrhea and dysentery. Of the nearly 620,000 soldiers who died during the Civil War, two-thirds died not of bullets and bayonets but of disease and infection.

this need, the Confederate Congress passed the **Conscription Act** on April 16, 1862. Conscription is the forced enrollment of people into military service. This act required all men between the ages of 18 and 35 to serve in the armed forces of the Confederacy. However, the act excused some people and allowed the hiring of substitutes. In most areas of Texas, the Conscription Act met little resistance. In counties of central Texas, however, some German American settlers objected to fighting against the Union. Later, when more soldiers were needed, conscription acts extended age limits to men between the ages of 17 and 50.

Most Texans Support the South

Before the Civil War began, nearly one-fourth of all Texans were against secession. After the fighting began, however, most people supported the Confederacy. **James W. Throckmorton** of Collin County was one of eight delegates at the Texas Secession Convention of 1861 who voted against secession. After the war began, however, he knew he could not fight against Texas and took an oath to support the Confederacy. Before the war ended, Throckmorton had risen to the rank of brigadier general in the Texas state troops. Texans elected Throckmorton governor in 1866.

About 60,000 Texans joined the armed forces of the Confederacy. Nearly one-third fought in armies east of the Mississippi River. The others served along the coast and on Texas's borders, and in Louisiana, Arkansas, New Mexico, Missouri, and Indian Territory. Some slaveholders brought along their slaves to serve as orderlies. Theophilus Perry of Harrison County took his slave Norfleet Perry. Norfleet's wife Fannie wrote, "I hope it will not be long before you can come home." Slaves also were forced to build fortifications.

Many distinguished Civil War officers came from Texas. **Albert Sidney Johnston** commanded the army of the Republic of Texas. He was the second-highest-ranking general in the Confederate army and commanded Confederate troops in Tennessee. Johnston was killed at the **Battle of Shiloh** in April 1862. His death was a severe blow to Texas and to the Confederacy.

For most Texas soldiers, this was the first time they had fought in battle. Many were teenagers. Private Dunbar Affleck was an 18-year-old serving with Terry's Texas Rangers. In a letter to his parents, Affleck described the Battle of Murfreesboro, or Stones River, which took place south of Nashville on December 31, 1862, and again on January 2, 1863.

Dear Mother & Father:
   I take this opportunity of writing you to let you know that I came out safe, and unhurt from the battle which has been going on here for several days and in which we are again victorious, having driven the enemy back with heavy loss. So far we have taken about 7500 prisoners, killed about four thousand, and wounded about twenty thousand . . . Our killed and wounded is about half their number. We had a great many more wounded than killed. The rangers suffered more in this fight than they ever have yet, having had some fifteen or twenty killed and a great number wounded amongst whom were several of our best Lieutenants. Co. B. had six wounded, and our 2nd Lieut, who was mortally wounded . . . all the Washington Co. boys are safe.

✓ **Reading Check** **Explaining** Why did the Confederate Congress pass the Conscription Act?

Some Texans Aid the Union

Slightly more than 2,000 Texas Unionists, or people who supported the Union cause, joined the Union army. Approximately 50 of the Unionists were African American soldiers. One African American Texan, **Milton Holland,** won the Medal of Honor, the highest American award for valor in action against an enemy force. Holland was cited for his bravery and valor on the battlefields of Virginia.

While some Mexican Americans fought under the command of **Colonel Santos Benavides** and in other units for the Confederate cause, others fought on the Union side. Often these Mexican Americans fought against the Confederacy to strike back at the Anglo society they blamed for taking away their lands.

Some Texas Unionists did not want to fight for one side or the other. For many, this meant leaving Texas. Many managed to leave Texas early in the war. Still, the risk of getting caught trying to flee was great. In August 1862, a large group of German settlers attempting to flee to

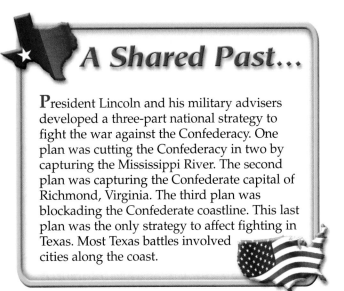

A Shared Past...

President Lincoln and his military advisers developed a three-part national strategy to fight the war against the Confederacy. One plan was cutting the Confederacy in two by capturing the Mississippi River. The second plan was capturing the Confederate capital of Richmond, Virginia. The third plan was blockading the Confederate coastline. This last plan was the only strategy to affect fighting in Texas. Most Texas battles involved cities along the coast.

Mexico was killed by Confederate cavalry near the Nueces River.

Some Texas Unionists remained in the state. Many hid to escape conscription officers. Some were captured and arrested. Others were forced into the Confederate army. Still others were killed. **Vigilantes,** citizens who act as the

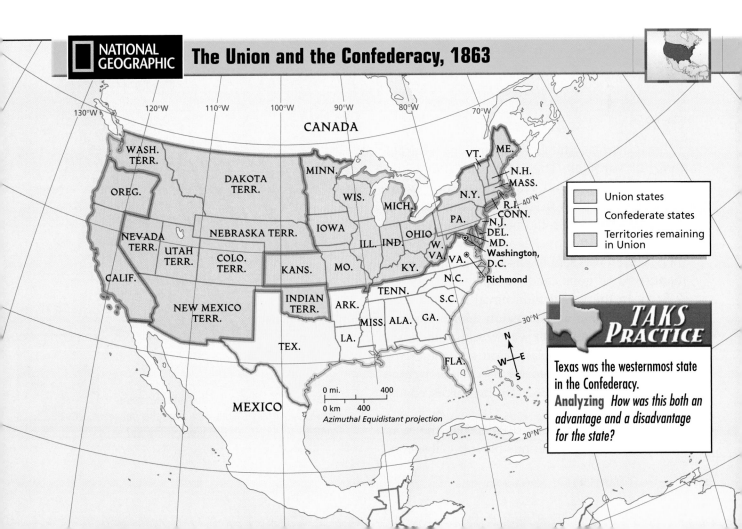

The Union and the Confederacy, 1863

NATIONAL GEOGRAPHIC

Union states
Confederate states
Territories remaining in Union

TAKS PRACTICE

Texas was the westernmost state in the Confederacy. **Analyzing** *How was this both an advantage and a disadvantage for the state?*

0 mi. 400
0 km 400
Azimuthal Equidistant projection

unauthorized police power for an area, hanged about 40 suspected Unionists at Gainesville in 1862. Sometimes the vigilantes even had the approval of the authorities.

Texans on the Attack

The first task of the newly organized army under the Confederacy was to take over Union garrisons and capture their supplies and equipment. A company of volunteers took the federal post in San Antonio in February 1861. Other forts in the west surrendered within the next month. United States army troops were permitted to leave Texas unharmed until the opening shots of the Civil War on April 12, 1861. After that, about 600 were held as prisoners of war.

At the end of the year, Texans launched an offensive against United States forces in New Mexico. This was a preventive strike, undertaken to prevent a possible future attack by Union forces. It was also an attempt to capture Santa Fe and New Mexico. **Brigadier General Henry H. Sibley** led the New Mexico campaign. Although he captured Santa Fe, he made some crucial mistakes, and by late spring 1862, the Confederacy abandoned the campaign.

Fighting for Galveston

Texas was a vital link in the Confederate chain of supplies. The Union navy used its ships to blockade all Texas ports to prevent goods and supplies from leaving and entering by water. The navy could not, however, control the flow of cotton over land to Mexico. From there, cotton was sent to Europe in exchange for manufactured goods and war materials.

Early in the war, Union naval commanders stationed ships near **Galveston.** Union leaders realized that Galveston was weakly defended because many of the large guns in the city's forts had been removed for use in other campaigns. In October 1862, Union forces easily captured the city.

Confederate leaders realized that the war effort would suffer a serious blow if Galveston,

the state's busiest seaport, remained in Union hands. **General John B. Magruder,** a new Confederate commander for Texas, assumed his duties in November and immediately made plans to retake Galveston. Two river steamers, the *Bayou City* and the *Neptune,* were refitted as gunboats. Soldiers placed bales of cotton on the decks to protect the gunners from enemy fire. The two ships moved down Buffalo Bayou from Houston and attacked the Union vessels in **Galveston Harbor.** At the same time, over 500 Confederate soldiers crossed the railroad bridge from the mainland to the island and attacked the Union soldiers.

The daring Confederate attack, made during the early morning of January 1, 1863, was a complete success. Several hundred Union soldiers and a Union vessel surrendered. Another

Picturing **History**

This image from *Harper's Weekly* in 1863 illustrates the battle at Galveston Harbor in January of 1863 where the Confederates were victorious over the Union. How does this image contrast with modern day images of wars?

ship was blown up by its own crew after it ran aground. The Union forces made no other tries at retaking Galveston, although they imposed a blockade around its port. By 1864, Galveston was one of the few open ports still available to the Confederacy. Slipping through Union blockades became increasingly significant as these vessels brought much-needed supplies to Texas. These ships were known as blockade runners and played a very important role in the war effort. The *Denbigh* was one of the most successful of the blockade runners of the war until it was destroyed by Union naval vessels in 1865. The arrivals and departures of blockade runners always caused great excitement at the port.

✓ **Reading Check** **Interpreting** Why was recapturing Galveston important to the Confederacy?

Texans Defend Sabine Pass

Later in 1863, Union forces made another try at invading Texas—this time by sailing up the Sabine River. Twenty-two Union transport vessels carrying 4,000 soldiers and 4 gunboats sailed from New Orleans, by now under Union control, to the southeastern coast of Texas. **Major General William B. Franklin,** the Union commander, planned to land his troops near Sabine Pass at the mouth of the river and march overland to capture Beaumont and Houston.

Any vessels sailing up Sabine Pass had to travel past **Fort Griffin.** A company of 47 soldiers, commanded by **Dick Dowling** and called the **Davis Guards,** was stationed at the fort. When the Union gunboats tried to sail past Fort Griffin, the Confederates opened fire. In a brief battle, the Guards took about 350 Union soldiers prisoner and captured 2 Union ships. General Franklin gave up the attempt to land, and the Union fleet returned to New Orleans.

TEXAS HISTORY *Online*

Student Web Activity Visit the texans.glencoe.com Web site and click on **Chapter 15—Student Web Activity** to learn more about blockade runners.

Picturing **History**
The Battle of Sabine Pass was an important victory for the Confederacy. How was this battle significant?

The **Battle of Sabine Pass** was an important victory for the Confederacy. Union plans to launch a major campaign against Texas were dashed. Both General Magruder and Confederate President Davis praised the courage of the Davis Guards and awarded them medals.

Forces Battle Near Brownsville

Although Union forces continued the blockade of Texas cotton by patrolling the Gulf of Mexico, traders could ship cotton out of Matamoros on foreign ships, which could not be stopped by the Union. Wagon trains also carried supplies and goods across South Texas from Brownsville near the mouth of the Rio Grande. Hoping to cut off this overland supply line, Union strategists focused on capturing the supply center of Brownsville.

In November 1863, a Union force took the city and then moved up the Rio Grande, until it was stopped near Laredo by Colonel Santos Benavides. Confederate troops, commanded by **Colonel John S. Ford,** drove the Union army back and recaptured Brownsville in July 1864. The Union troops were limited to occupying the port of Brazos Santiago on Brazos Island at the mouth of the Rio Grande.

Picturing **History**

The Taylor brothers were teenage members of Hood's Texas Brigade. What might have motivated these young brothers to join Hood's Texas Brigade?

(40 km) from the Texas border. In some of the heaviest fighting of the western campaigns, the smaller Confederate army routed the Union forces, taking more than 1,000 prisoners. Among Texans who fought was Tom Green, a former member of the congress of the Republic and a veteran of the Battle of San Jacinto and the Mexican–American War.

Many Texas military units also fought in battles far from the boundaries of their state. Between 15,000 and 20,000 Texans served in armies east of the Mississippi—in Virginia, Tennessee, and Georgia.

Hood's Texas Brigade and **Terry's Texas Rangers** were among the better-known Texas units serving east of the Mississippi. Both units were cited for their bravery and courage. Hood's Brigade fought in many of the great battles in Virginia. General Robert E. Lee, who commanded Confederate troops in Virginia, called Hood's men his "finest soldiers." Terry's Texas Rangers, officially the Eighth Texas Cavalry Regiment, fought in more battles than did any other cavalry regiment in the Civil War.

Red River and Beyond

Early in the war, Union forces captured New Orleans and occupied southern Louisiana. From there they launched an invasion of northeastern Texas in the spring of 1864. An army of 25,000 Union soldiers moved up the **Red River** in Louisiana and marched overland toward East Texas. Confederate leaders hastily called in troops from Texas, Louisiana, Missouri, and Arkansas. The troops, commanded by **Richard Taylor,** son of former U.S. President Zachary Taylor, set out to block the incoming Union forces. The two armies met near **Mansfield, Louisiana,** only 25 miles

✓ **Reading Check** **Analyzing** Why did Union forces need to control Texas ports?

SECTION 2 ASSESSMENT

Checking for Understanding

1. **Using Key Terms** Use the vocabulary terms that follow to write a short paragraph about a Civil War battle: preventive strike, blockade.

2. **Reviewing Facts** Why was the Battle of Sabine Pass an important victory for the Confederacy?

Reviewing Themes

3. **Economic Factors** Why were Union forces determined to blockade the export of Texas cotton?

Organizing to Learn

4. **Summarizing** The major battles fought in Texas were attempts to block supply and trade routes. Add details to the chart shown here about each of these three strategic locations.

Location	Reasons for Importance
Galveston	
Sabine Pass	
Laredo	

Critical Thinking

5. **Evaluating** Do you think that conscription laws should be passed to force people to fight in a war, even if they are opposed to fighting? Explain your answer.

TAKS PRACTICE

Summarizing the Main Idea In your own words, write the main idea of Private Dunbar Affleck's letter on page 348.

Texas LITERATURE

A.C. Greene

A.C. Greene has worked as a book reviewer, a bookstore owner, a university instructor, and a columnist. Greene also wrote a series of short biographical columns he called "Texas Sketches." One of these mentioned a powerful, fast-charging Texas & Pacific locomotive that was 90 feet long and 10 feet wide. A typographical error changed this to "90 feet long and 100 feet wide." He told another columnist, Bill Whitaker, that "one woman wrote and said, 'Well, at least it could've paid for itself—100 feet wide, going down the right-of-way, mowing down all those tall East Texas pines!'"

Read to Discover

As you read this story about an early Texas pioneer, form an opinion of how you think she must have viewed her disability. Why do you think the author felt the pioneer was a heroine?

Reader's Dictionary

mere: nothing more than

insurmountable: impossible to overcome

treadle: foot pedal that drives a machine

The following describes pioneer life for one remarkable woman born just before the Civil War.

Pioneer Heroine
by A.C. GREENE

Amanda Jane Crawford was two years old when her family moved to the Flower Mound Community. Amanda Jane Crawford Raines would have been a **mere** name on a list of settlers had it not been for an unfortunate occurrence in her childhood. When she was six years old, the little girl was stricken with polio. She was never able to walk or use her feet again.

For a 19th century farm child, the handicap would have seemed **insurmountable,** but not for Amanda Jane. As a youngster she learned to do housework on her hands and knees, sharing in all the difficult labor of a frontier farm home: she literally scooted in her work. She attended school by means of a specially built box hitched to her pony, which she drove by herself . . . After she married, to make her family's clothes, she disconnected the **treadle** so that she could operate a sewing machine with one hand and guide the cloth with the other. She drove her six children wherever they needed to go, becoming an expert with wagons and buggies . . .

Amanda Jane died in 1949, nearing the age of 95. Her surviving children agreed nothing had kept her from leading a full life—but *they* placed more emphasis than *she* did on something that happened on her 50th birthday. On that occasion, after half a century of scooting around on hands and knees, Amanda Jane Crawford Raines became the owner of a wheel chair.

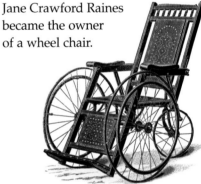

ANALYZING LITERATURE

1. **Recall and Interpret** Describe two ways that the subject of this article showed cleverness in managing her disability.

2. **Evaluate and Connect** Do you agree with the author that Amanda Jane Crawford Raines was a "pioneer heroine"? Why or why not?

Interdisciplinary Activity

Interview Write a column based upon an interview of an individual that you believe overcame a disability—physical or otherwise.

Home Front Hardships

Guide to Reading

Main Idea
Confederates took control of local and state government. All Texans were forced to make lifestyle changes and sacrifices because of the war.

Key Terms
homespun
quinine

Reading Strategy
Classifying Information As you read this section, complete a table like the one below, listing how women's roles changed during the war.

The Changing	1.
Role of Women	2.
During the War	3.
	4.

Read to Learn
- how shortages and other hardships affected Texans during the war.
- what events led to the end of the Civil War.

Section Theme
Economic Factors The war caused shortages of food, medicine, and other goods, which affected the lives of all Texans.

Preview of Events

♦1863   ♦1864   ♦1865

August — Pendleton Murrah is elected governor of Texas

April — General Robert E. Lee surrenders at Appomattox Courthouse

April — President Lincoln is assassinated

July — Andrew J. Hamilton becomes provisional governor

Civil War soldier's shoes

A
Texas Story

During the Civil War, the Union blockade of Southern ports was successful. While in Texas, Lucy Pier Stevens had to put up with high prices and shortages of many goods. In 1864, she wrote in her diary, "My $30.00 worth of paper came tonight—24 sheets of paper and 1 and 1/2 packages of envelopes." One woman is said to have paid $180.00 for twelve candles, a pair of shoes, and some cloth. Although Texans were clever in finding substitutes, the shortages produced great hardships.

Texas Confederates Take Charge

Confederate leaders were now in power at every level of state and local government. Lieutenant Governor Edward Clark completed Houston's term as governor in 1861. Clark sought reelection in August but was defeated by **Francis R. Lubbock.** Lubbock, a South Carolina native, previously had held several political offices in Texas, including lieutenant governor. In 1863 Governor Lubbock entered the Confederate army and did not seek reelection. **Pendleton Murrah,** a lawyer from Marshall, was elected governor in 1863. Murrah served as governor until the closing days of the Civil War. Both Lubbock and Murrah devoted much of their time as governor to working for the Confederate war effort.

War Changes Women's Roles

Texas suffered less physical damage than did other Confederate states because few battles were fought in the state. No Union army swept a path of destruction through Texas's farms and towns as had happened in Georgia. Life on the plantations with slaves doing the work remained much the same as before the war. On many smaller farms, however, there were no men to work the crops or tend the livestock. It is estimated that during the war, four out of five adult white men were away from home at some time. Women, children, and slaves did almost all the farm work.

Women served as nurses during the Civil War. **Rosanna Osterman** turned her luxurious Galveston home into a hospital. She and her helpers used carpets to make slippers and sheets to make bandages. In 1865 Mary Sweeny went to Matagorda to help restore the Union garrison to health. As a reward for her services, the Union commander sent a wagonload of medical supplies to Brazoria County to aid the Southern ill and wounded.

War Changes the Economy

The war brought economic changes. Farmers were encouraged to plant more corn and wheat for the war effort. As a result, cotton production declined in all the Southern states throughout the war years. Texas opened small factories in Austin and Tyler to manufacture cannons and ammunition. Other factories made needed items such as wagons, ambulances, blankets, shoes, tents, cloth, and saddles. In addition to

their work on the farms, women also contributed to the war economy by making uniforms and other clothing for the soldiers. In Austin, the Ladies Needle Battalion sewed items for the soldiers. Women also took jobs usually performed by men. They became teachers, shopkeepers, and drivers.

Shortages Make Life Difficult

The people of Texas were forced to make many sacrifices during the war. The Union blockade of Confederate ports stopped many goods from reaching the South. Clothes, manufactured in the North, disappeared from the stores. Many Texans wore a coarse, loosely woven, homemade fabric called homespun that was similar to cloth worn in colonial days. Governor Lubbock wore a homespun suit to his inauguration.

Getting coffee and tea was nearly impossible. Among the ingredients Texans used as coffee substitutes were parched sweet potato and parched corn beverages. One mixture, called

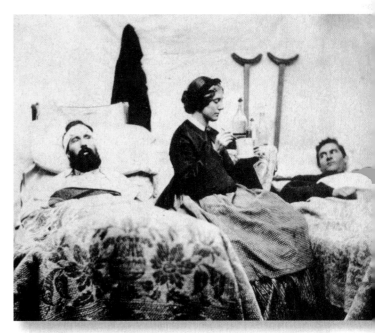

Picturing **History**

Nurses aided wounded soldiers on both sides of the war. What are some ways nursing has changed since the Civil War?

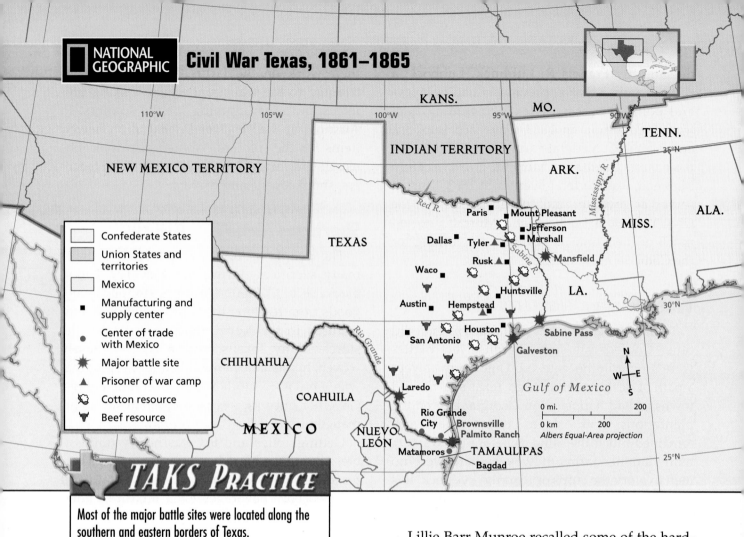

NATIONAL GEOGRAPHIC Civil War Texas, 1861–1865

Confederate States
Union States and territories
Mexico
■ Manufacturing and supply center
● Center of trade with Mexico
✳ Major battle site
▲ Prisoner of war camp
Cotton resource
Beef resource

KANS.
MO.
TENN.
INDIAN TERRITORY
ARK.
MISS.
ALA.
NEW MEXICO TERRITORY
TEXAS
LA.
CHIHUAHUA
COAHUILA
MEXICO
NUEVO LEÓN
TAMAULIPAS

Red R.
Paris
Mount Pleasant
Jefferson
Dallas
Tyler
Marshall
Rusk
Mansfield
Waco
Huntsville
Austin
Hempstead
San Antonio
Houston
Sabine Pass
Galveston
Laredo
Rio Grande City
Brownsville
Palmito Ranch
Matamoros
Bagdad

Gulf of Mexico

0 mi.   200
0 km   200
Albers Equal-Area projection

TAKS PRACTICE

Most of the major battle sites were located along the southern and eastern borders of Texas.
Explaining Why did these battles take place in these regions?

Confederate coffee, was made of rye, meal, Indian corn, and sweet potatoes. It was a common, if not well-liked, replacement. Texans tried substitutes for imported Asian tea as well. People learned to use native plants as alternatives to imported goods.

Salt, baking soda, and paper were also scarce. Some women dug up the floors of their smokehouses to recover the salt drippings from the dirt. Several newspapers suspended publication because they had no paper. Some people used wallpaper torn from walls as writing paper. Civilians often had to do without medicines and hospital supplies because these were needed on the battlefield. Quinine, an imported drug for fighting malaria and other fevers, could not be obtained. The shortages of all items became worse as large numbers of refugees fleeing the Union armies came to Texas.

Lillie Barr Munroe recalled some of the hardships caused by the war and what her family life was like in Austin during the war:

❝It was just before we left the house on the flat . . . that Civil War was declared, and I can recall many pictures in *Harper's Weekly* then of the rising of the war cloud . . .

War times began their hard pinch here and one of the clearest memories I have of them is that mother had no tea, we gathered the leaves of Upon [yaupon] shrub . . . they made a substitute, but only a substitute; then white flour was almost impossible to get, and no one had white bread but Mother and Mary—Mary because she was delicate . . . [As for clothing,] Confederate money was of little value and even if it had been, cloth was almost impossible to get.❞

Reading Check **Explaining** Name some of the ways that Texans sacrificed for the war effort.

The Civil War Ends

For four years the armies of the South fought against great odds. The North had more soldiers, more money to finance the war, and more factories making war materials. By the spring of 1865, the weary Confederate armies could hold out no longer. On April 9, 1865, **General Robert E. Lee** made a difficult decision. The Army of Northern Virginia, the largest Confederate military force, surrendered to **General Ulysses S. Grant** at **Appomattox Courthouse** in Virginia. Within weeks Confederate President Jefferson Davis was captured, and the remaining armies in the South surrendered.

The last land battle of the Civil War took place on May 13, 1865, at **Palmito Ranch,** near Brownsville. Here Confederate forces led by John S. Ford defeated a Union force trying to invade the mainland from Brazos Island. From their captured prisoners, the Texans learned that General Lee had surrendered a month earlier. The Texas troops had not yet received word of the war's end.

The end of the Civil War marked a turning point for Americans. They faced the task of rebuilding the nation. Sorrow had touched nearly every family. Millions of soldiers fought in the conflict. More than 600,000 Northerners and Southerners died. This number almost equals the number killed in all other American wars combined.

The North's victory meant the Union had been preserved. It also brought an end to slavery. During the war President Lincoln had issued the Emancipation Proclamation, freeing enslaved people in the Confederate states. Once the war ended, federal officials began to enforce the proclamation in all the defeated states. Lincoln did not live to see all the slaves freed. The Thirteenth Amendment—which abolished slavery—was not ratified until late 1865, after President Lincoln's assassination. He was shot and killed five days after Lee's surrender by **John Wilkes Booth,** an actor who believed he was helping the Confederate cause.

As Southern armies surrendered, the state government of Texas collapsed. Governor Murrah and other state officials fled to Mexico in June 1865 to escape Union troops. For some weeks Texas had no state government. Lawless armed bands roamed the countryside. Order was restored only after President Andrew Johnson appointed **Andrew Jackson Hamilton** provisional governor in July 1865. Now Texans faced the task of rejoining the Union.

TAKS PRACTICE

Evaluating Resources The North had greater amounts of resources than the South during the Civil War. *The South possessed the least amounts of which two resources?*

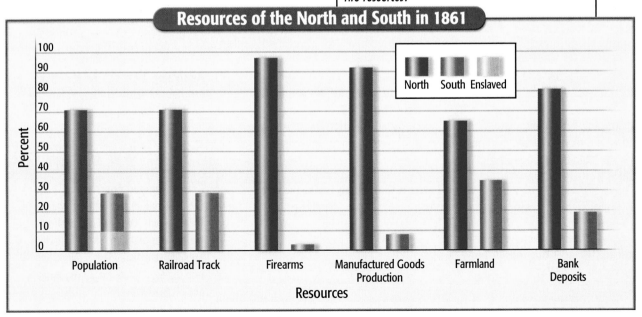

Resources of the North and South in 1861

Legend: North   South   Enslaved

Y-axis: Percent (0 to 100)

X-axis (Resources): Population, Railroad Track, Firearms, Manufactured Goods Production, Farmland, Bank Deposits

Santos Benavides 1823–1891

Santos Benavides was the highest-ranking Mexican American to serve in the Confederacy. His great-great-grandfather was the founder of Laredo, where Santos was born. As a political and military leader, Benavides worked hard to bring this region closer to the mainstream of Texas politics. When Texas seceded, he supported the Confederacy.

Benavides's greatest triumph was his defense of Laredo. However, his most important contribution to the Southern cause came when he arranged for the safe shipment of cotton along the Rio Grande to Matamoros and ports in Europe.

In recognition of his achievements, Benavides was appointed Texas delegate to the World Cotton Exposition in 1884.

A Texas Story Continued

Lucy Pier Stevens, trapped in Texas when the war broke out, could stand it no longer! She would go home no matter what the risk. In April of 1865 she wrote in her diary,

❝[M]y journey is fraught with too many dangers for me to anticipate much pleasure. I realize fully what I am undertaking. If it were not toward home I could not make up my mind to start such a trip.❞

Lucy went to Galveston and boarded a blockade runner. The ship took her to Havana, where she caught a steamer for New York City. While in Havana she learned of President Lincoln's assassination. When she arrived in New York, she knew the war was over. Both her personal ordeal and the nation's ordeal of war had come to an end.

✓**Reading Check** **Analyzing** Why did the battle at Palmito Ranch occur after the war had ended?

SECTION 3 ASSESSMENT

Checking for Understanding

1. **Using Key Terms** Use these terms in complete sentences: homespun, quinine.
2. **Reviewing Facts** Why did Texas suffer less physical damage during the war than other Confederate states?

Reviewing Themes

3. **Economic Factors** Give two reasons why there were widespread shortages of goods in Texas during the Civil War.

Organizing to Learn

4. **Summarizing** Using a chart like the one below, list the goods that were scarce in Texas during the Civil War. Describe the substitutes that were found for these items.

Items in Short Supply During the War	
Item	Substitute

Critical Thinking

5. **Analyzing** Why did the state government of Texas collapse after the Civil War? Explain your answer.

TAKS PRACTICE

Comparing and Contrasting The Civil War caused daily work to change for all Texans. Compare and contrast the changes that each of the following would have experienced: a plantation with slaves; a small, family-run farm; and a store in town.

Recognizing Ideologies

Why Learn This Skill?

An "ideology" is a set of key beliefs or values that guide the actions of a person or a group. Organizations with particular ideologies can influence important issues. People in environmental groups, for example, take certain actions such as recycling waste materials.

Learning the Skill

Here are some ways to recognize ideologies:
- Identify the values or beliefs of the group.
- Analyze statements or actions to see if they express the view of a particular ideology.
- Separate the facts from the opinions.
- Check any facts in statements for accuracy.

Practicing the Skill

Here is a short summary of some important ideologies in Texas history.

- Proslavery—Slavery is necessary for the economy; slavery is protected by the Constitution.
- Antislavery—Slavery is morally wrong and should be abolished; all people are created equal; slavery degrades both blacks and whites.
- Secession—States have the right to secede if the federal government threatens their constitutional rights.
- Pro-Union—The Union is perpetual and must be preserved at all costs; disagreements over rights must be settled by constitutional means.

Read the following primary source statements. Determine which ideology each statement is expressing.

❶ "Suppose I should seize you, rob you of your liberty, drive you into the field, and make you work without pay as long as you live, would that be justice and kindness or injustice and cruelty?"

Slavery supported an economic system.

❷ "If by your [free soil] legislation you seek to drive us from the territories of California and New Mexico . . . and to abolish slavery in [the District of Columbia], thereby attempting to fix national degradation upon half the states of this Confederacy, I am for disunion."

TAKS PRACTICE

Which opinion, proslavery or antislavery, is most probably represented below? Why do you think so?

Popular sovereignty for the territories will never work. Under this system, each territory would decide whether or not to legalize slavery. This method was tried in the territory of Kansas and all it produced was bloodshed and violence.

Glencoe's **Skillbuilder Interactive Workbook,** Level 1, provides instruction and practice in key social studies skills.

Chapter Summary
The Civil War

1860

★ Abraham Lincoln is elected president.

• South Carolina secedes from the Union.

1861

• Texas and other Southern states secede from the Union.

• The Confederate States of America is formed.

★ Sam Houston is removed as governor of Texas.

• The Civil War begins with the firing on Fort Sumter.

1862

• The Conscription Act is passed.

• Forty Texas Unionists are hanged in Gainesville.

• Union forces capture Galveston.

1863

★ Texas and Confederate forces retake Galveston.

• Union forces are defeated at Sabine Pass.

• Pendleton Murrah is elected governor.

1864

• Union forces are defeated near Red River.

1865

• General Lee surrenders to General Grant.

• President Lincoln is assassinated.

• The last Civil War battle is fought at Palmito Ranch near Brownsville.

Reviewing Key Terms

Examine each group of terms below. Explain why one term in each group does not belong with the others.

1. sovereignty, states' rights, perpetual, conscription
2. preventive strike, vigilante, blockade
3. ordinance, secede, Unionists

Reviewing Key Facts

4. Why did the Southern states support states' rights?
5. Who were the abolitionists?
6. Why did most Southerners oppose the Republican Party?
7. What was Sam Houston's belief about Texas secession?
8. Why did many German settlers fight conscription?
9. Why did Texas attack Union forces in New Mexico?
10. What was the importance of the Battle of Sabine Pass?
11. What was one way Texans on the home front suffered during the war?
12. What happened in Texas immediately after the South surrendered?

Critical Thinking

13. **Identifying Main Ideas** What political and economic changes were brought about in Texas by the Civil War?
14. **Summarizing** Describe the social effects of the Civil War on Texas.
15. **Citizenship** Why do you think Governor Houston declined President Lincoln's offer of military aid to help him stay in office? How was this action in keeping with what you have learned about Houston's character?
16. **Making Inferences** Although one-fourth of all Texans opposed secession before the Civil War began, most of them supported the Confederacy after the fighting started. Why do you think this happened?
17. **Analyzing** Why was it important for Union troops to control the flow of goods over the Rio Grande boundary?
18. **Understanding Cause and Effect** What effect did the Civil War have on enslaved African Americans in Texas? Use a web like the one below to help organize your answer.

BEFORE	**WAR**	**AFTER**
	→	

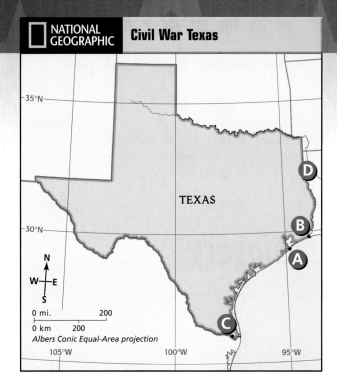

NATIONAL GEOGRAPHIC Civil War Texas

Geography and History Activity

Refer to the map above to identify where each of the events listed below took place. Place the correct letter with the military event.

19. Capture of Brownsville
20. Red River Campaign
21. Capture of Galveston in October 1862; Battle and Recapture of Galveston in January 1863
22. Battle of Sabine Pass

Portfolio /TAKS Writing Activity

23. **Making Predictions** After reflecting on the ideas and information presented in the chapter, write a paragraph describing how our lives might be different today if the South had won the Civil War. Save your work for your portfolio.

Building Technology Skills

24. **Using the Internet or Library for Research** Work with another student to research one of the battles described in this chapter. After you have completed your research, develop a multimedia presentation of the information, using charts, graphs, photos, maps, and narration. (You might use computer presentation software, if available.) Share your presentation with the rest of the class.

TEXAS HISTORY Online

Self-Check Quiz
Visit the texans.glencoe.com Web site and click on **Chapter 15—Self-Check Quizzes** to prepare for the chapter test.

Cooperative Learning Activity

25. **Journalism** As a class, produce a newspaper that describes what was going on in Texas during a critical week of the Civil War.

Economics and History Activity

26. **Wartime Economics** Review the chapter to identify two economic activities that began because of the Civil War and eventually benefited the Texas economy.

Practicing Skills

27. **Recognizing Ideologies** Ideologies, or belief systems, are a part of everyday life. Discussions of ideologies appear in newspapers, magazines, and TV programs. The belief in a democratic system of government is an ideology that is accepted by most Americans. Identify an excerpt from an article in a newspaper or magazine that is an ideology.

TAKS PRACTICE

Use your knowledge of Texas history to answer the following question.

Texas's location was important during the Civil War because

A the frontier of Texas was vulnerable to Native American attacks.

B Texas controlled the Mississippi River.

C control of the Gulf of Mexico was vital to Civil War victory.

D Texas linked supplies from western states with Confederate troops.

Test-Taking Tip:

The word *location* is important in this question. It signals that you will need to think about geography and the role it plays in history. Eliminate any answer choices that are wrong either because they are not true or because they do not offer good geographical explanations.

Economics & History

Surviving Under Slavery

The plantations of eastern Texas produced much of what Texas citizens needed for their survival. Landowners planted corn, peas, sweet potatoes, wheat, rye, and oats for their own use and for sale to others, but cotton was the main crop. Raising cotton provided cash for plantation owners, and the cotton industry created jobs for many Texans. Storeowners furnished supplies to the plantations, ranchers sold horses needed for heavy labor, and freighters hauled away the harvest.

The Slavery System in Texas

Enslaved Africans who labored on the plantations received few benefits for their contribution to the successful industry. Far from accepting slavery, many enslaved Africans fought the slave system as much as possible. They were able to control, to some extent, the pace of their work by sometimes feigning illness or breaking tools. Some enslaved men and women even risked beatings in an effort to exert some control over their lives.

Others tried to escape, but few succeeded in remaining free for long.

Carding paddles were used to separate cotton fiber.

The majority of enslaved laborers worked in the fields. These African Americans are picking cotton with an overseer behind them supervising their labor.

Taking Initiative

Within the slavery system, some African Americans sought to improve their personal condition. Slaves found ways to make money from their hard work and acquired skills. With the consent of their owners, they would "hire

362

In 2001, *Black Enterprise* magazine named Houston as the "best city" for African Americans, a fact which made Mayor Lee Brown (right) very pleased.

out" to others. Both the plantation owner and the laborer benefited from this plan. The slave paid the plantation owner part of the wages earned and kept the rest. For plantation owners, this agreement helped to provide additional income; for the slave, wages were used to buy household items. Some enslaved workers hired out to local plantations where temporary help was needed. Others took jobs in town as blacksmith helpers, carpenters' assistants, loaders at freight depots, and similar jobs. One woman described her father's attitude toward hard work:

> "My father was Jack Mickens, the hardest working slave on Major Jackson's Texas plantation. He was the blacksmith and even before the slaves was made free my father earned outside money that his master allowed him to keep. He had money when he was set free."
> —1930s interview with Alice Rawlings (age 80)

Enslaved African Americans also sought to earn income for themselves by raising farm animals for food or for trade. Additionally, they planted vegetable gardens and sold what they grew.

The greater effort that slaves put forth to improve their patches of land proved that people will work harder when they believe it will benefit them in some way. Enslaved African Americans used torchlight to tend their own garden plots past sundown. While not all slaves had the opportunity, some were motivated by knowing that the money made from their efforts belonged to them.

Economic Conditions

Because the little money they earned had to cover most of their needs, slaves economized. Basic items, like food and fabric, were provided by plantation owners. Slaves learned to be creative with the small amounts of corn and pork they were given. Out of necessity, African Americans became skilled at preparing meals to both suit their tastes and feed an entire family. From the small amount of cloth they were given, they made long-lasting work clothing, and they used leftover material for special-occasion garments. Homespun cotton they were given was put to use making shirts, pants, or dresses to use for barter.

Under slavery, African Americans had little control over their financial circumstances. They did, however, use whatever resources they could to ease their poverty and to exert some control over their lives. This resourcefulness shown by some of the enslaved African Americans is a trait that is common to many Texans, whatever their place of origin or economic condition. It is a goal of people everywhere to improve life for themselves and for their families.

TAKS PRACTICE

1. **Making Generalizations** Can you think of other kinds of workers who are not paid for their labor? Explain.
2. **Drawing Conclusions** How does your family economize to meet everyone's needs?
3. **Writing About Economics** Write a paragraph that develops the following theme: People take initiative to improve their lifestyle.

16 Reconstruction

Why It Matters

The end of the Civil War brought freedom for enslaved Texans. It was a period in which Texans would develop new social, political, and economic systems.

The Impact Today

Although African Americans were no longer enslaved after the Civil War, white Southern leaders, including those in Texas, refused them full social and economic privileges. The ongoing struggle for that equality grew stronger during this period.

1865
★ June 19, African Americans in Texas celebrated freedom
★ President Johnson appointed Andrew Hamilton governor of Texas

1866
★ Constitution of 1866 ratified in June

 Texas

United States   1865   1866   1867

 **World**

1865
• Slavery abolished in U.S.
• Andrew Johnson became president of the United States

1867
• Russia sold Alaska to U.S. for $7.2 million

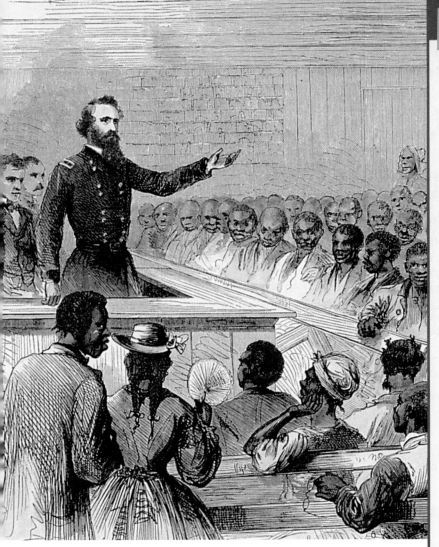

T.R. Davis created this woodcut of a Union general meeting with freed African Americans for Harper's Weekly magazine.

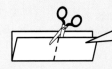
1869
★ New Texas constitution approved
★ Edmund Davis elected governor of Texas

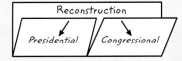

TEXAS HISTORY *Online*

Chapter Overview
Visit the texans.glencoe.com Web site and click on **Chapter 16—Chapter Overviews** to preview chapter information.

| 1868 | 1869 | 1870 |

1868
• Suez Canal opened
1868
• President Johnson impeached

1869
• Charles Darwin published his book The Descent of Man

1870
• Fifteenth Amendment ratified (right to vote)

Presidential Reconstruction

Guide to Reading

Main Idea

Reconstruction in Texas involved readmission to the Union and addressing the rights of former slaves.

Key Terms

Reconstruction
nullify
freedmen

Reading Strategy

Locating Information Create a chart like the one shown and fill in the main elements of President Johnson's Reconstruction plan.

Readmission Conditions	To Regain the Right to Vote

Read to Learn

• about the changes affecting African Americans' lives.
• about Texas's readmission to the Union.
• about the new constitution.

Section Theme

Government and Democracy Texans had to meet certain requirements to regain statehood.

Preview of Events

♦1865   ♦1866   ♦1867

June 19
All slaves in Texas are now free

June
Voters approve new Texas constitution

Singing spirituals

A
Texas Story

Enslaved African Americans derived comfort from their religions. The spiritual was a song that combined African rhythms with Christian themes. In "Go Down Moses," African Americans compared their enslavement and release to that of the Hebrews in ancient Egypt.

"Go down Moses 'way down in Egypt's land. Tell ol' Pharaoh, Let my people go.

"O let us all from bondage flee: / Let my people go / And let us all in Christ be free! / Let my people go."

Reconstruction

The end of the Civil War in 1865 was followed by a period in which the Southern states were gradually brought back into the Union. This period of rebuilding is called **Reconstruction.**

The Reconstruction era was a difficult time. Although Texas had largely been spared, much of the South lay in ruins, and money was scarce. African Americans were free, but many were without food or shelter. In addition, the differences that existed between many Northerners and Southerners continued after the war. Reconstruction created new bitterness, too.

Juneteenth

Because of distance and the war, many African Americans did not immediately learn about the **Emancipation Proclamation** of 1863 that had freed slaves in Confederate states. Union troops, however, were stationed in Southern states after the Civil War. On June 19, 1865, **General Gordon Granger** and 1,800 Union troops landed at Galveston. Granger's first act was to issue a proclamation declaring that all enslaved Texans were free:

Headquarters, District of Texas
Galveston, June 19, 1865

GENERAL ORDERS, No. 3
The people of Texas are informed that, in accordance with a Proclamation from the Executive of the United States, all slaves are free. This involves an absolute equality of rights and rights of property between former masters and slaves, and the connection heretofore existing between them becomes that between employer and free laborer. The freedmen are advised to remain at their present homes and work for wages. They are informed that they will not be allowed to collect at military posts, and that they will not be supported in idleness, either there or elsewhere.

By order of G. Granger
Major General, Commanding

For enslaved Texans, June 19, 1865, was the day they celebrated their freedom. On that evening, one observer remarked that "thousands flooded the streets of Galveston, rejoicing in their newly-announced freedom. The sweet smell of barbecue smoke filled the air. Dancing feet pounded the dirt roads and harmonic voices sang spirituals." In the immediate years

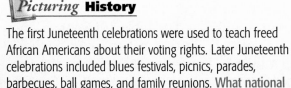

Picturing **History**

The first Juneteenth celebrations were used to teach freed African Americans about their voting rights. Later Juneteenth celebrations included blues festivals, picnics, parades, barbecues, ball games, and family reunions. What national holiday is the most similar to Juneteenth?

Galveston

to follow, Galveston and other Texas cities planned **Juneteenth** activities. The holiday was a time "to express to young and old alike the fact that African Americans are a proud people with past, present, and future contributions to American society."

✓ **Reading Check** **Summarizing** What was the significance of Granger's General Orders, No. 3?

Two Presidential Plans

Granger's troops were the first Union troops in Texas during Reconstruction, but more would come. By the end of 1865, about 50,000 Union troops were stationed in Texas. Many were ordered to the Rio Grande to patrol the Mexican border. Others were assigned to larger towns in Texas to maintain law and order. Union cavalry, with **Brigadier General George A. Custer** in command, occupied Austin, the capital.

President Lincoln had wanted to restore the Union as quickly as possible. He wanted a moderate policy of Reconstruction—one "with malice toward none, with charity for all." Some Republican leaders thought the president should be harder on the South. They argued that the Southern states had left the Union and should be treated as conquered territories. Lincoln believed that the Confederate states had never been legally out of the Union, so they still had all the rights of states. After Lincoln's assassination, the task of Reconstruction passed to the new president, Andrew Johnson.

President Johnson was from Tennessee and showed much sympathy toward the South. In May 1865 President Johnson set forth a plan of Reconstruction modeled after Lincoln's. Johnson set up a provisional government in each Southern state. He appointed officers and ordered federal troops to protect them in their offices. The provisional government would govern until the state was readmitted.

Among President Johnson's conditions for readmission were that each Southern state must prohibit slavery and must **nullify,** or cancel, its ordinance of secession. (The ordinance claimed that each state had the right to secede or withdraw from the union.) Johnson also set certain requirements for voting. To regain the right to vote, Southern citizens were required to take an oath of allegiance to the United States. In addition, leaders of the Confederacy and people who had at least $20,000 in cash or property would have to get a special pardon from the president. Once the people of the state met these requirements, they could write a new constitution and elect their own representatives.

✓ **Reading Check** **Describing** What was President Lincoln's approach to Reconstruction?

Governor Hamilton Works to Restore Statehood

President Johnson appointed Unionists, or former Union supporters, to lead the provisional Southern governments. In June 1865, he named Andrew J. Hamilton as provisional governor of Texas. Hamilton was born in Huntsville, Alabama, on January 28, 1815. He moved to Texas in 1846, joining his brother in Fayette County. Hamilton had served Texas in Congress and was against secession and expanding the territory open to slavery. He left Texas during the Civil War and went to Washington, D.C., where he supported the Union. He served on the House committee formed during the secession winter of 1860–61 to try to solve the sectional crisis. When he returned to Texas in the spring of 1861 he won a special election to the state Senate, and he remained in Austin until July 1862. Believing his life was in danger, he fled to Mexico and from there back to Washington, D.C.

Hamilton had great sympathy for the people of Texas. He wanted to return the state quickly and peacefully to the Union. Most Texans considered Hamilton honest and fair-minded. Some citizen groups pledged that they would cooperate to restore civil government to the state. Others, however, were openly hostile to Hamilton.

The Freedmen's Bureau Assists Freed Texans

While Governor Hamilton worked to restore local government, a federal agency, known as the Freedmen's Bureau, assisted many African Americans throughout the South. Former slaves were often referred to as **freedmen.** The Bureau's job was to provide relief to the thousands of people, black and white, who had been left homeless by the Civil War. It was also the Bureau's job to supervise the affairs of newly freed slaves in the Southern states and to manage Confederate land seized during the war.

Oliver O. Howard, a Union Civil War general, headed the **Freedmen's Bureau** nationally. Howard University in Washington, D.C., was named for General Howard in 1867. In Texas, **General E.M. Gregory** headed the Freedmen's Bureau. The state was divided into 18 subdistricts with an agent in charge of each.

The Freedmen's Bureau operated for 5 years. It helped find jobs for freed Texans and issued food and clothing to the sick, aged, and poor. The Freedmen's Bureau believed that education would equip African Americans with the skills they needed for economic independence. The Bureau established the first public schools in Texas for African American children. Many of the teachers in the Freedmen's Bureau schools were women from New England. Some of them had been active in the abolitionist movement before the Civil War. Most of the Bureau schools were racially segregated, but in the cities of Charleston, South Carolina, and New Orleans, Louisiana, the Bureau established schools that enrolled both African American and white children. By 1870 Texas had more than 100 schools for African Americans. Many, however, were closed after the Bureau ceased operation.

The Bureau also defended the legal rights of the freed Texans in court cases. A visitor from the North described one of the courts:

> ❝A great variety of business is brought before the Bureau. Here is a [black] man who has printed a reward offering fifty dollars for information to assist him in finding his wife and children, sold away from him in times of slavery: a small sum for such an object you might say, but it is all he has, and he has come to the Bureau for assistance.❞

The Bureau's work in Texas was made harder by the size of the state, and by its poor transportation and communication systems. The Bureau also faced the hostility of most white Texans, and Southerners in general, to the Bureau's efforts. Many Texans accused its agents of meddling in matters that local officials could handle. They also argued that the Bureau wasted taxpayers' money and that its real goal was not to help the needy but to strengthen the Republican Party.

Picturing **History**

Teachers such as Sara Barnes, shown here with her class list, helped the Freedmen's Bureau run schools for African Americans. Why were schools an important part of the Bureau's program?

369

After the Civil War, the Freedmen's Bureau protected and aided freed African Americans. **What type of aid was provided by the Bureau?**

Government Restored in 1866

In the fall of 1865, Governor Hamilton appointed hundreds of state and local officers to restore law and order in Texas. By November, many white males had taken the oath of allegiance. Then Texans elected delegates to a convention to write a new constitution for the state.

Many of the delegates who met in Austin in February 1866 had actively supported the Confederacy. Nine had served in the Secession Convention of 1861, and several others had been high-ranking officers in the Confederate army. The president had not yet pardoned four delegates. There were no African American delegates.

For two months the delegates crafted a new constitution, following President Johnson's requirements. The finished version stated that secession was illegal, slavery was abolished, and the state war debts were canceled. The constitution provided schools for African American children and also extended certain legal rights to African Americans. It did not, however, give these former slaves full legal status since they were denied the right to vote. This disappointed Governor Hamilton. He had hoped that African Americans would get broader rights.

The convention finished its work in April 1866. An election in June ratified the proposed amendments by a vote of 28,119 to 23,400, making the constitution the law of the state. The large number of people voting against ratification may have been due to the fact that the constitution raised the salaries of many officials. At the same time, Texas elected officers for the new government.

TEXAS HISTORY Online

Student Web Activity Visit the texans.glencoe.com Web site and click on **Chapter 16—Student Web Activity** to learn more about the Freedmen's Bureau in Texas.

People on the Move

The ports and roads of Texas were filled with travelers during Reconstruction. One of the tragic aspects of slavery was the separation of family members. Emancipation meant that freedmen and women could travel in search of loved ones. The reunion of husbands and wives, and parents and children produced joyful celebrations. Unfortunately, many searchers were unsuccessful.

Other travelers were looking for a better life. Texas had not experienced as much destruction as Confederate states further to the east. Texas still had public lands available for farmers. Many white Southerners and African Americans from Georgia, Alabama, and Mississippi hoped to improve their economic condition by migrating to Texas. In 1873 the Bureau of Immigration estimated that at least 125,000 persons had come to Texas since 1865, about 100,000 of them from the former Confederate states.

European immigrants came as well. Germans made up the largest group, but Irish, French, English, Austrians, Czechs, Scots, Swedes, and Swiss also arrived. Estimates show that by the end of Reconstruction, as many as a million European immigrants had landed in Texas.

People moved within the state, from country to town, from town to city. Texas was still more

Southerners on a train bound for Texas, 1870s

than 90 percent rural, but urban centers were growing. Galveston and San Antonio were the largest cities during this period.

Texas also experienced *emigration*, or people moving out of the state. Some of the most radical Confederates such as Peter Hardeman and Francis McMullan refused to take an oath of allegiance to the United States. They led groups of Texans to Brazil where slavery still existed. They founded agricultural settlements where their descendants can still be found.

✓ **Reading Check** **Examining** Why were many immigrants to Texas from the Southern states?

SECTION 1 ASSESSMENT

Checking for Understanding

1. **Using Key Terms** Write a sentence explaining the tasks required of Southern states to regain statehood. Use the terms nullify and Reconstruction.
2. **Reviewing Facts** What was the purpose of the Freedmen's Bureau, and how did it help African American children?

Reviewing Themes

3. **Government and Democracy** What was the role of each state's provisional government?

Organizing to Learn

4. **Sequencing** Create a time line like the one shown and place the following events in the correct order.

```
|-------|-------|-------|
```

   a. First annual Juneteenth celebration
   b. President Johnson's Reconstruction plan
   c. President Lincoln's Emancipation Proclamation
   d. General Granger's "General Orders, No. 3"

Critical Thinking

5. **Evaluating** What part of the new Texas constitution would most likely have disappointed President Lincoln? Why?

TAKS PRACTICE

Distinguishing Fact From Opinion
Primary sources are valuable historical documents. General Granger's orders and the account written by a visitor to the Freedmen's Bureau are primary sources. Which one of these might include opinion and bias? Why?

Expressing Problems Clearly

Why Learn This Skill?

Why do individuals or groups take certain actions? In most cases, people act to solve particular problems. By identifying these problems, and stating them clearly, actions make more sense.

Learning the Skill

When analyzing problems, first identify the main problem. By looking more closely, find the underlying, or "root," problem(s). Then, express the main problem clearly by summarizing all the root problems in one sentence.

Here are some steps to follow in expressing problems clearly:

- Identify an action and analyze the main problem by asking, "Why was this action taken?"
- Analyze each root problem by asking, "What caused this problem?"
- Combine the root problem(s) to make one clear sentence.

One mission of the Freedmen's Bureau was to help former enslaved African Americans find work because:

- Some did not want to remain on plantations.
- Former slaveholders were unwilling to pay wages.
- African Americans were competing for jobs with white Americans.
- New laws kept them out of many areas of employment.

The problem could be stated clearly like this: After the Civil War, many African Americans were jobless because they were not allowed to earn wages from their former slaveholders and were denied other employment opportunities.

The Freedmen's Bureau provided jobs through schools such as this one where sewing was taught.

Practicing the Skill

For each action listed below, determine what surface and root problem this action was intended to solve. Then write one sentence which clearly expresses all of the root problems.

1 The Texas legislature of 1866 refused to ratify the Thirteenth and Fourteenth Amendments.

2 Under Radical Reconstruction, Southern states were placed under military rule until they adopted constitutions approving political rights for African American males.

3 Many Southern legislatures passed black codes.

TAKS PRACTICE

Expressing Problems Clearly Think about a problem you have. Example: Maybe you have trouble getting up in the morning. Write 3–4 root problems that contribute to your main problem.

GO TO Glencoe's **Skillbuilder Interactive Workbook,** Level 1, provides instruction and practice in key social studies skills.

Congress Takes Control

Guide to Reading

Main Idea
In the final years of Reconstruction, Southerners were forced to accept new leaders and new political freedoms for African Americans.

Key Terms
ratify, amendment, black codes, Radical Republican, veto, impeach, scalawag, carpetbagger, compulsory

Reading Strategy
Classifying Information As you read this section, complete a chart like the one shown filling in the forces opposing each leader: Democrats, Radical Republicans, or former secessionists.

Political Leadership	Opposing Forces
President Johnson	
U.S. Congress	
Governor Davis	

Read to Learn
- how Reconstruction began and ended.
- about Reconstruction reforms by Radical Republicans.
- about the Constitution of 1869.

Section Theme
Government and Democracy Democrats and Radical Republicans fought for power.

Preview of Events

1867	1869	1874
Texas is placed under military rule	Davis is elected as governor	Richard Coke is inaugurated governor / Reconstruction in Texas ends

Freed couple from Austin, Texas

A
Texas Story

Although freedom had come, African Americans had not achieved equality. They were free, but they had a long way to go. This feeling was expressed in songs, such as this spiritual written down in 1867.

"No more driver's lash for me; No more, No more.
No more driver's lash for me; Many thousand to go."

Texas Elects Ex-Confederates to Office

Many Northern political leaders believed that the Confederate states had left the Union and must apply for readmission as new states. Because Congress alone has the power to admit new states, they argued that Congress, not the president, should control Reconstruction.

Southerners, including Texans, elected many former Confederate officials and soldiers to top state government posts. Newly elected Texas **Governor James W. Throckmorton** had served the Confederacy as commanding general of the Frontier District of Texas and commissioner to Native Americans. Every Texan elected to the federal House of Representatives in 1866 had been either a secessionist or a Confederate officer who fought against the Union. The Texas legislature sent Judge O.M. Roberts, president of the Texas Secession Convention of 1861, to the United States Senate. Now walking the halls of Congress were the leaders who had encouraged the people to secede from the Union—an act of treason, according to many Northerners.

Southern legislatures took other troubling actions. The Texas legislature refused to ratify, or approve, two amendments (changes) to the United States Constitution. It rejected the **Thirteenth Amendment,** which abolished slavery, and the **Fourteenth Amendment,** which granted citizenship to former enslaved people.

Just as troubling to many Republicans, Southern state governments restricted the rights of African Americans. **Black codes,** laws limiting the rights of African Americans, differed from state to state but had certain features in common. African Americans were not allowed to vote. They could not testify against whites in court, nor could they serve on juries. African Americans also could hold only certain types of jobs, generally in agriculture. If African Americans did not have a home or a job, the laws forced them to work for plantation owners. The Texas codes restricted African Americans less than did the laws of some other Southern states. The Texas codes, however, were still offensive to those who wanted equal rights for all citizens.

Reading Check **Summarizing** What actions by Texas politicians upset Northern lawmakers?

Radical Republicans Take Charge

Republicans in Congress who disagreed with Johnson drew up their own plan for Reconstruction. The Radical Republicans pushed several goals in their plan. The first was to set stricter standards for admitting the Southern states back into the Union. The second was to protect the freedom of African Americans in the South. Many Republicans genuinely cared about the freed slaves, but they were also aware that protecting the rights of African Americans would help the Republican Party stay in power. Freedmen who had the right to vote would likely vote for Republicans.

The Radical Republicans gained control of both the United States House and the Senate in the 1866 congressional elections. Now having the power to override any presidential **veto** (an action refusing to approve a law), they launched their own ideas for Reconstruction. Johnson's accusers argued that Congress should have the supreme power to make the laws of the land. The president believed he had

History *Through Art*

A Working Cotton Plantation by William Culleen Walker, 1884 Black codes forced African Americans without other employment to work plantations similar to this one in the South. What rights were denied to African Americans by the black codes?

Radical Republicans hoped to remove President Andrew Johnson from office by impeaching him. The attempt failed by one vote. **Why did the Radical Republicans object to President Johnson's policies?**

the right to challenge any laws he believed were unconstitutional. Johnson refused to give up and fought against the Radical program. The struggle soon came to a head. In February 1868, the House of Representatives voted to impeach Johnson by bringing charges of misconduct in office. The president was tried before the Senate. The president's accusers failed by one vote to convict him. Johnson served the rest of his term, but he had lost most of his influence.

New Requirements for Statehood

In March 1867, Congress divided the South into five districts. Texas and Louisiana made up one district, commanded by **Major General Philip Sheridan.**

Under this plan, the military would rule the districts until the states met certain requirements. Among these was the adoption of new state constitutions that gave African American men the right to vote and to hold office. Congress also required the states to ratify the Fourteenth Amendment to the U.S. Constitution. Some states, including Texas, were also required to ratify the **Fifteenth Amendment,** which guaranteed African American men the right to vote. States also had to repeal the black codes.

Under the congressional plan, many voters had to take what became known as the *Ironclad Oath.* The oath stated that they had not voluntarily served in the Confederate army or given aid to the Confederacy. This oath kept thousands of Southerners from voting.

Southerners Oppose Reconstruction

The congressional plan for Reconstruction pleased African Americans and Unionists. Most former Confederates and former secessionists considered it much too harsh. Federal officials believed that Governor Throckmorton did not put the Reconstruction laws into effect.

One of the first acts of General Sheridan was to remove Governor Throckmorton from office on July 30, 1867. **Elisha M. Pease,** Throckmorton's opponent in the 1866 election, was appointed in his place. Pease had been a Unionist and was more sympathetic to the goals of the Republicans in Congress. Pease was also well respected by the majority of Texans. During the summer and fall of 1867, military officials removed hundreds of state and local leaders who were considered opponents of Reconstruction. They were replaced with individuals more acceptable to the Radical Republicans.

Southern whites who supported Reconstruction were called scalawags. Northerners who often came to the South during this period were called carpetbaggers. This name came from the belief that carpetbaggers carried all their possessions in traveling bags made of carpet. Some were sincerely interested in helping rebuild the nation. Others were there for political or economic gain. Few carpetbaggers actually arrived in Texas, however.

Texans who supported Reconstruction worked for the rights of former slaves to vote, but organizations such as the Ku Klux Klan used violence and threats to prevent African Americans from voting. Klan members, wearing hoods and robes to hide their identities, burned crosses in the yards of African Americans. They whipped and hanged African Americans who tried to exercise their right to equality.

Reading Check Examining What goals were the Radical Republicans seeking?

A New Constitution and Elections

In February 1868, Texans who qualified to vote elected delegates to a new convention. The delegates, which included African Americans, completed a new constitution in February 1869. The Constitution of 1869 provided that no one should be excluded from voting because of race or color. It provided more support for public education than did any previous Texas constitution. It extended numerous rights to African Americans and protected public lands. It expanded the power of the governor and the legislature. In November, the voters approved the Constitution of 1869 and, at the same time, elected a governor and other state officials, including thirteen African Americans who were elected to the legislature.

The Radical Republicans' candidate for governor, **Edmund J. Davis,** defeated Andrew J. Hamilton in the 1869 election. The new state legislature contained a Radical Republican majority. It quickly ratified the Fourteenth and Fifteenth Amendments to the United States Constitution. The legislature also declared that all acts passed by the legislature during the Civil War had no binding legal force.

On March 30, 1870, President Ulysses S. Grant signed a proclamation that Reconstruction in Texas was ended. By the end of the year, all of the Southern states had rejoined the Union on the Radical Republicans' terms. From a legal point of view, Reconstruction was over. Many Texans believed, however, that Reconstruction

A Shared Past...

African Americans knew that economic freedom would come only with property ownership. They argued that because their labor had changed much of the South into productive farmland, they should now own their own farms. The slogan, "40 acres and a mule," expressed that goal. During the war, the Union army had actually designated abandoned property in Georgia and South Carolina to be given to freedmen in 40-acre tracts. Some African Americans did receive land and began farming. President Johnson reversed the decision, took the farms away, and returned the lands to the former owners.

was not over as long as Governor Davis and Radical Republicans controlled the Texas government.

A Republican Governor

Many who were against Governor Edmund J. Davis viewed his term as the darkest period of Reconstruction. Davis was an active and powerful governor and often provoked controversy. For example, Davis claimed that he only used the state police to keep law and order. He argued that there was a need to protect the freedmen and to fight crime and lawlessness. His opponents, however, charged that the state police also were used to threaten those who opposed the governor. Some white Texans resented the use of Tejanos and African Americans as state policemen.

Some critics complained that Davis and Republicans in the legislature used their powers to restrict the activities of their political opponents. The legislature gave Davis the authority to use the military forces in the event of civil disturbances. The legislature also postponed elections, giving those officials who were elected in 1869 another year in office.

Increased spending for law enforcement and public education meant the government needed to raise more money. In 1865 the state tax rate had been 15 cents on every $100 worth of property. By 1872 the combined state and county tax rate had increased to more than $2 on each $100 worth of property. Even with the increase in taxes, the state debt continued to grow.

Because Davis was so disliked, it is easy to forget that Davis and the Republicans started some worthwhile projects and completed others. Davis and the legislature improved roads, built forts, passed a new Homestead Act, and set up free public schools. Education leaders today consider that

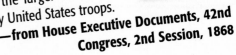

TWO VIEWPOINTS

Texas State Police

Republican Governor Edmund J. Davis created a state police force to counter Reconstruction's widespread lawlessness and to protect the rights of former slaves. Democrats strongly opposed his action. Read the two views below and then answer the questions.

A Republican Congress Supports the Need to Restore Order

In 1868 almost the entire state was [in turmoil] and in the northern half of the state hardly a white man escaped being driven from his home or suffering persecution of some kind. As for the freed people, they were robbed, outraged and intimidated systematically, and almost everywhere, except in some of the larger towns [protected] by United States troops.
—from House Executive Documents, 42nd Congress, 2nd Session, 1868

Democrats Oppose Davis's Police Bill

The terms . . . constitute an authorized violation of nearly every private right of the citizen. The police force is chosen by the Executive, and placed under his command without restriction or responsibility; it is always ready for action, with arms in hand, . . . The practical workings of this force, raised under the pretense of securing peace . . . has demonstrated . . . that it is a body of armed men, massed to overawe the citizen . . .
—Taxpayer's Convention quoted in the *Democratic Statesman*, September 23, 1871

Learning From History

1. Why do you think crime was so widespread during Reconstruction?

2. Why did the Taxpayer's Convention oppose the police force?

Analyzing *Political Cartoons*

This political cartoon shows a carpetbagger being protected by U.S. soldiers while being carried by the Solid South (white Southern Democrats). What does this cartoon suggest about the power of the carpetbaggers during Reconstruction?

🅐 Carpetbagger 🅑 the South 🅒 Union Soldier

school system to have been 50 years ahead of its time. Attendance was compulsory, or required, and the tax system provided enough money to maintain the schools.

A Democratic Challenge

In 1872 anti-Davis Democrats won a majority of seats in the state legislature. The new legislature immediately reduced the governor's power

TEXAS TODAY

The Texas governor today holds an office with limited powers, in part because of the reaction to Edmund J. Davis. The governor, who had fought on the side of the North, so angered Texans that when the Constitution of 1876 was written, the governor's office was stripped of many of its powers. Since then, however, the office of the governor has regained power in indirect ways.

and abolished the state police force. The legislature also limited the governor's authority to appoint officials.

In 1873 Davis ran for reelection against the Democratic candidate, **Richard Coke,** a former Confederate officer from Waco. The campaign was bitter. Republicans urged African Americans to support Governor Davis. During the election campaign, Davis focused on the programs he had begun, while Coke focused on states' rights issues and talked about returning Texas to the times before the Civil War and Radical Reconstruction.

Coke's platform, or outline of political goals, appealed to many of the white settlers and immigrants. Coke also appealed to businessmen who wanted to see railroads and industry expand. At the same time, Coke drew support from the farmers.

More freedmen voted in 1873 than had voted in the 1869 election for governor, but many more would have voted except for the actions of some Democratic supporters. Democrats used threats and violence to keep African Americans from voting. Richard Coke received twice as many votes as did Davis. The final count was 100,415 to 52,141. Democrats won all other state offices and added to their majority in the legislature.

Reconstruction Ends

Different interpretations of the law under which the election had been conducted plunged Texas into a crisis from December 1873 until mid-January 1874. Democrats claimed that Coke should take office in January. Republicans maintained that Davis should remain governor until April 28, 1874. The legality of the election for other officials was also questioned.

The Texas Supreme Court, whose members had been appointed by Davis, decided in favor of the Republicans, declaring the election unconstitutional. Democrats organized a new government anyway. On January 15, 1874, Democratic supporters occupied the halls of the legislature on the second floor of the capitol. Some reports claim that Governor Davis had state troops positioned on the lower floor where the executive offices were located. Soldiers brought in

Richard Coke replaced the Radical Republican governor of Texas, Edmund Davis, in 1874.

to protect Davis switched sides and joined Coke's supporters. Finally, on January 15, 1874, Coke was sworn in as governor. Militia groups armed themselves to defend each position. The potential for violence at the capitol was very real.

Governor Davis made a final appeal to President Grant asking for U.S. support to keep him in office. Two days later the attorney general of the United States wired back:

❝Your right to the office of the Governor at this time is at least so doubtful that [President Grant] does not feel warranted in furnishing United States troops to aid you in holding further possession of it.❞

The telegram was telling Davis that President Grant would not send troops to Austin. Finally, the governor left office on January 17, 1874. The period of Republican control of Texas was over. Reconstruction in Texas had come to an end.

✓ **Reading Check** **Explaining** Why was there potential for violence at the capitol?

SECTION 2 ASSESSMENT

Checking for Understanding

1. **Using Key Terms** Explain President Johnson's loss of influence using the terms Radical Republicans, veto, and impeach.

2. **Reviewing Facts** Why did Radical Republicans protect African Americans' rights?

Reviewing Themes

3. **Government and Democracy** How did the *Ironclad Oath* ensure that Confederate sympathizers could not influence elections?

Organizing to Learn

4. **Charting Information** Governor Davis used his power in office to accomplish his goals for the state. Create a chart like the one shown and describe some reactions to Governor Davis's changes.

Changes	Reactions
State Police	
Legislative Powers	
Public Schools	

Critical Thinking

5. **Explaining** Use the information in this section to write one summarizing statement that explains why so many Texans opposed Reconstruction.

TAKS PRACTICE

Making Inferences As Davis struggled to keep his governorship, he asked President Grant for military protection. Why do you think President Grant did not send troops to Texas?

Chapter Summary

Reconstruction

1865

★ June 19th—General Gordon Granger declares all enslaved in Texas are free.

★ President Johnson announces plan for Reconstruction.

• 50,000 Union troops arrive in Texas.

• Andrew J. Hamilton becomes provisional governor.

1866

• Voters approve a new constitution in June.

• Former Confederate James W. Throckmorton is elected governor.

1867

★ Congressional Reconstruction begins in Texas. Congress places the South under military rule.

• Governor Throckmorton is removed from office.

1869

• A new constitution is completed.

• Edmund J. Davis, a Radical Republican, is elected governor.

1870

• More than 100 schools for African American children are built.

• President Grant proclaims the end of Reconstruction in Texas, but policies continue under Governor Davis.

1874

★ Richard Coke becomes governor of Texas.

Reviewing Key Terms

Find the term in each group which does not belong. Explain your choice.

1. Radical Republican, scalawag, carpetbagger, secessionist
2. ratify, impeach, veto
3. compulsory, amendments, black codes
4. Confederate, nullify, ratify

Reviewing Key Facts

5. Explain the connection between General Gordon Granger and Juneteenth.
6. What were the major requirements of President Johnson's Reconstruction plan for the Southern states?
7. List four activities of the Freedmen's Bureau in Texas.
8. What about the Constitution of 1866 disappointed Governor Hamilton?
9. State the steps that Southern legislatures took that troubled the Radical Republicans.
10. List the five new provisions of the Constitution of 1869.
11. What did Governor Davis accomplish in office?

Critical Thinking

12. **Evaluating** Radical Republicans influenced the House of Representatives to impeach President Johnson. With what offense was he charged? What are the benefits and disadvantages of having such a process in our government?

13. **Citizenship** In a democracy, citizens show their preferences by voting. How did Texans show their disapproval of Governor Davis? What actions followed this in the state legislature?

14. **Understanding Cause and Effect** How did the 1866 elections lead to President Johnson's loss of power?

15. **Summarizing** Draw a chart like the one below and describe the purpose of each of the amendments to the U.S. Constitution listed.

Amendment	Purpose
Thirteenth	
Fourteenth	
Fifteenth	

Geography and History Activity

16. Many immigrants to Texas during Reconstruction came from countries that are today known as Germany, Ireland, France, Great Britain, the Czech Republic, Austria, Sweden, and Switzerland. Use the World Political Map on pages RA2 and RA3 in the Reference Atlas to determine which of the countries listed here is farthest from Texas.

Portfolio/TAKS Writing Activity

17. **Making Inferences** What can you infer about the importance of the telegraph during Reconstruction? In arriving at your answer, you might consider how this scientific advance changed people's lives. After you make your inferences, write a paragraph that states them clearly. Use standard grammar, spelling, sentence structure, and punctuation. Save this example of your writing for your portfolio.

Building Technology Skills

18. **Using the Internet or Library for Research** Working alone, or with a partner, research the life of one of the political or military leaders mentioned in this chapter. As you work, keep a record of bibliographic sources. Also keep a log of the Web sites visited. Prepare a report, complete with visuals. Your work may be written and presented orally, or it may be prepared as an interactive computer/multimedia document.

Practicing Skills

Expressing Problems Clearly *When people act to solve problems, their actions are not always clearly thought out. It is important to analyze actions to figure out what problems they are intended to solve. For Questions 19–21, explain why the action was taken. Then explain what caused the problem. Finally, write a sentence that clearly expresses the major problem or problems.*

19. Under Governor Edmund J. Davis, the tax rates increased dramatically.

20. The Texas legislature ratified the Fourteenth and Fifteenth Amendments to the United States Constitution.

21. Governor Davis's opponents in the legislature abolished the state police force.

TEXAS HISTORY *Online*

Self-Check Quiz
Visit the texans.glencoe.com Web site and click on **Chapter 16—Self-Check Quizzes** to prepare for the chapter test.

Cooperative Learning Activity

22. **Debating an Issue** Debate the appropriateness (fairness) of voting requirements established for African American voters in 1869. Divide into groups to research, prepare questions and ask questions of the debaters, and report on the progress of the debate.

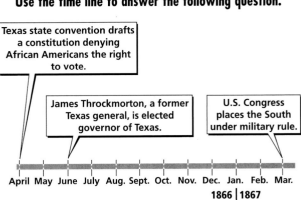

Use the time line to answer the following question.

Texas state convention drafts a constitution denying African Americans the right to vote.

James Throckmorton, a former Texas general, is elected governor of Texas.

U.S. Congress places the South under military rule.

April May June July Aug. Sept. Oct. Nov. Dec. | Jan. Feb. Mar.
1866 | 1867

Which of the following events completes the time line?

F In 1869, 2 African American senators and 12 representatives win Texas offices.

G General Albert Sidney Johnston is killed in the Battle of Shiloh.

H In late 1866, the Texas Legislature rejects the Thirteenth and Fourteenth Amendments.

J Many public schools are established by the state legislature.

Test-Taking Tip:
The correct answer must fit into this time line. Get rid of any answer choices that happened too early or too late to belong on this time line.

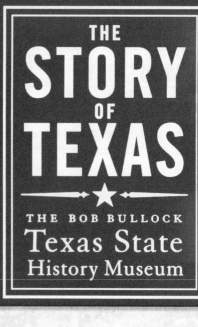

THE STORY OF TEXAS

★

THE BOB BULLOCK
Texas State
History Museum

Building the Lone Star Identity
The Civil War

*M*ost Texans were keenly aware of the bitter debate between the North and South over states' rights. They concluded that slavery was essential to the survival of the Texas economy. Even those who did not own slaves believed that their right to do so was more important than preserving the Union.

◀ **Cash Crop** Cotton could be sold or traded for ammunition, arms, and food. Stopping the cotton trade became a major Union objective. Blockade runners were ships loaded with cannon and protected from Union fire by stacked bales of cotton. They broke through Union blockades to carry cotton to Bermuda and Cuba.

Visit The Bob Bullock Texas State History Museum in Austin to see artifacts and exhibits such as these about Texas history and heritage.

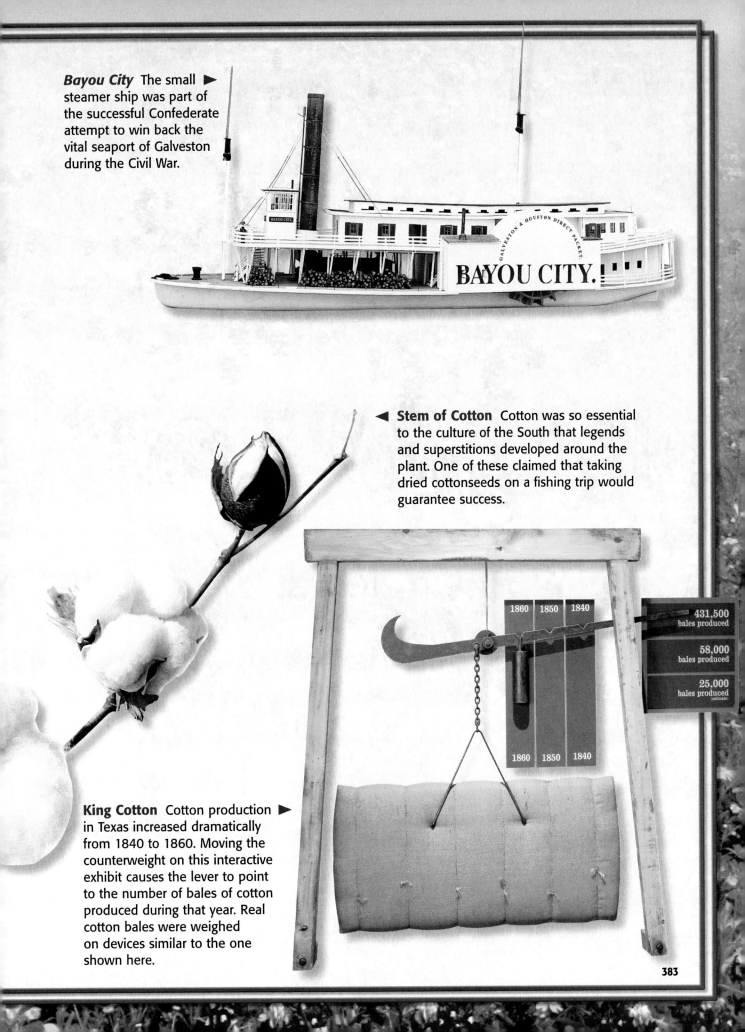

Bayou City The small ▶ steamer ship was part of the successful Confederate attempt to win back the vital seaport of Galveston during the Civil War.

◀ **Stem of Cotton** Cotton was so essential to the culture of the South that legends and superstitions developed around the plant. One of these claimed that taking dried cottonseeds on a fishing trip would guarantee success.

1860 1850 1840

1860 1850 1840

431,500 bales produced

58,000 bales produced

25,000 bales produced (estimate)

King Cotton Cotton production ▶ in Texas increased dramatically from 1840 to 1860. Moving the counterweight on this interactive exhibit causes the lever to point to the number of bales of cotton produced during that year. Real cotton bales were weighed on devices similar to the one shown here.

6 Growth and Development

1874–1900

Why It Matters

As you study Unit 6, you willl learn about Texas during the period after the Civil War and Reconstruction. During this time, people settled in almost every region and laid the foundations that would lead to a modern agricultural and industrial state.

Primary Sources Library

See pages 694–695 for primary source readings to accompany Unit 6.

It was cattle ranching more than any other activity that helped Texas become a symbol of the American West. *Watering Hole* was painted by western artist Richard Baldwin.

"Already Texas is the foremost State in the production of cotton and beef cattle."

—Governor O.M. Roberts,
Inaugural Address, January 18, 1881

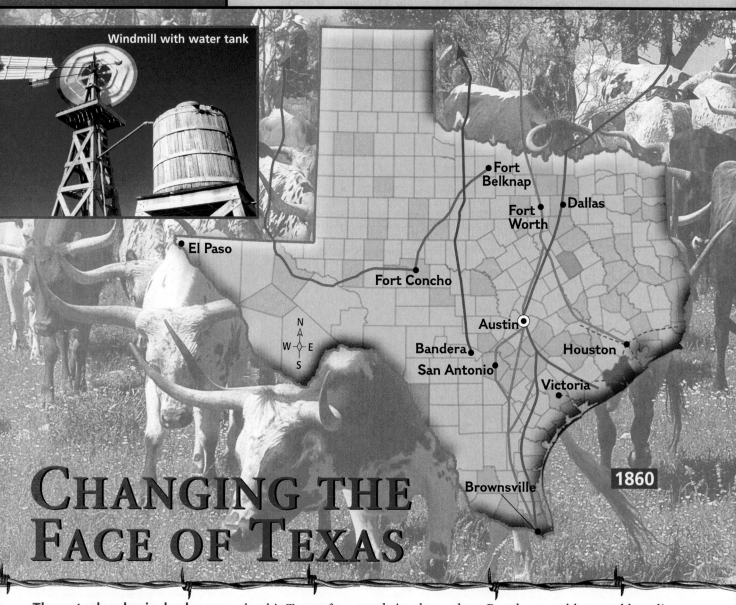

Windmill with water tank

Fort Belknap

Dallas

Fort Worth

El Paso

Fort Concho

Austin

Bandera

Houston

San Antonio

Victoria

Brownsville

1860

N W E S

CHANGING THE FACE OF TEXAS

Three technological advances that hit Texas after the Civil War changed the state's economy and population patterns forever. Barbed wire, windmills, and railroads made ranching and agriculture much more profitable than before. These technologies also opened new areas of Texas to agriculture and spurred human settlement of the almost empty western two-thirds of the state.

Fencing the Range

Barbed wire was invented in the 1870s. Perhaps no other single invention transformed Texas and the American West as much as this relatively inexpensive

and simple product. Ranchers could control breeding and produce better quality beef in greater quantities. Farmers could keep animals from trampling and eating their crops. This change—with all its benefits—also spelled the end of the seemingly endless, open range.

Bringing Water to the Surface

The dry plains and uplands of West Texas receive scant rainfall, but they do have aquifers, or large reservoirs of water underground. In the late 1800s improvements in the ancient technology of windmills made it possible to tap this underground water

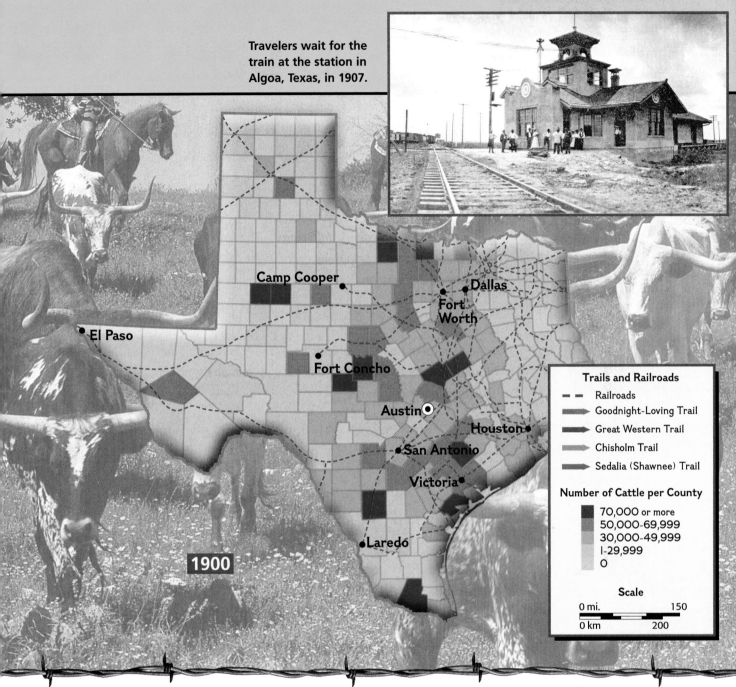

Travelers wait for the train at the station in Algoa, Texas, in 1907.

Camp Cooper

El Paso

Dallas

Fort Worth

Fort Concho

Austin

Houston

San Antonio

Victoria

Laredo

1900

Trails and Railroads

- - - Railroads
➤ Goodnight-Loving Trail
➤ Great Western Trail
➤ Chisholm Trail
➤ Sedalia (Shawnee) Trail

Number of Cattle per County

- 70,000 or more
- 50,000-69,999
- 30,000-49,999
- 1-29,999
- 0

Scale

0 mi.   150

0 km   200

supply. Windmills used the energy from the steady winds that blew over the treeless rangeland to pull water up into surface wells. Thus, windmills turned thousands of desolate acres into productive land for cattle, farms, and towns.

Moving Cattle to Market

Between 1870 and 1890 the amount of railroad track in Texas grew from 300 miles to more than 9,000 miles, providing ranchers with a cheaper, more direct link to northern markets. Before this period, cowhands on horseback drove cattle over long, punishing trails (see 1860 map) to Colorado, Kansas, or Missouri to reach the nearest rail line that connected to hungry northern cities. With the coming of the railroads, the great cattle drives passed into history and became a theme for folklore, books, and—much later—western movies.

LEARNING *from* GEOGRAPHY

1. **Describe three ways technology changed in the Texas landscape in the late 1800s.**

2. **Which technological advance do you think is changing the landscape of Texas today?**

Cultures in Conflict

Why It Matters

In the years immediately following the Civil War, more Native Americans in Texas were forced onto reservations. West Texas was settled primarily by Anglo ranchers and farmers.

The Impact Today

The removal of Native Americans from the Texas plains in the 1870s was thorough. Texas today has far fewer Native Americans than do the neighboring states of Oklahoma and New Mexico.

1875
★ Kwahadies surrendered at Fort Sill

1867
★ Treaty of Medicine Lodge Creek

1874
★ Battle of Palo Duro Canyon

Texas

United States   1865   1870   1875

World

1876
• Custer was defeated at Battle of Little Bighorn

1877
• Chief Joseph surrendered to the U.S. Army

1876
• Korea became an independent nation

Native Americans watch as covered wagons carrying pioneers cross traditional hunting grounds.

FOLDABLES™ Study Organizer

TAKS PRACTICE

Categorizing Information Study Foldable
Make this foldable to help you learn about the Native Americans' fight to keep settlers out of West Texas, and the settlers' determination to remove Native Americans from Texas lands.

Step 1 Fold a sheet of paper into thirds from side to side.

> This forms three rows.

Step 2 Open the paper and refold it into fourths from top to bottom.

> Fold it in half, then in half again.

Step 3 Unfold, turn the paper, and draw lines along the folds.

Step 4 Label your table as shown.

	West Texas after the Civil War	West Texas at War	Fighting on the Rio Grande
Native Americans			
Texans			

Reading and Writing Use your foldable table to record the actions and reactions of the Native Americans and Texans, which ultimately led to war and the settlement of West Texas.

1880
★ End of Apache wars in Texas

1880   1885   1890

1877
• All-England Lawn Tennis Championship first played at Wimbledon

1886
• Geronimo surrendered to the U.S. Army

1890
• Conflict at Wounded Knee between Sioux and U.S. soldiers

TEXAS HISTORY Online

Chapter Overview
Visit the texans.glencoe.com Web site and click on **Chapter 17—Chapter Overviews** to preview chapter information.

CHAPTER 17   Cultures in Conflict   389

West Texas After the Civil War

Guide to Reading

Main Idea
The Civil War was over, but conflict continued for Texans on their western frontier.

Key Terms
campaign
agent

Reading Strategy
Classifying Information As you read the section, complete a chart like the one shown here by listing the strengths and weaknesses of the soldiers and the Native Americans.

	Soldiers	Native Americans
Strengths		
Weaknesses		

Read to Learn
• about Native Americans in Texas after the Civil War.
• about the Treaty of Medicine Lodge Creek.
• about Native American leaders.

Section Theme
Groups and Institutions The Native Americans fought to protect their homelands.

Preview of Events

♦1866 — Federal troops in Texas frontier

♦1867 — Treaty of Medicine Lodge Creek

Rearing horse

A Texas Story

The U.S. Army invited the Seminoles to settle near Brackettville and Eagle Pass. Here, Johanna July, an expert horsewoman of African American and Seminole descent, gives her impression of army horsemanship: "I couldn't ride a horse like they do . . . I couldn't straddle them. I didn't use a bridle either, just a rope around their necks and looped over the nose . . . I don't like a saddle [or] . . . shoes. I can sure get over the ground barefooted."

—Johanna July, WPA Oral History

Native Americans Control the West

By 1850 nearly all Native Americans had been removed from the settled eastern part of Texas. In the state's western region, however, Native Americans fought to keep settlers from moving westward. During the Civil

War, federal soldiers left Texas to fight in the eastern United States. The settlements in isolated parts of western Texas were left vulnerable to the Comanches, Kiowas, and other Plains people. After the Civil War, settlers in West Texas continued to live in constant fear of raids. With little organized defense against the attacks, some pioneers packed up and moved east to safer areas, abandoning their ranches and farms.

Frontier Line 1870

To prevent further Native American raids after the Civil War, federal soldiers were stationed in the west. By the end of 1866, troops were posted at Fredericksburg, Mason, Brackettville, and Eagle Pass. More soldiers eventually were located near present-day Albany, Menard, San Angelo, Fort Stockton, Fort Davis, and El Paso.

For a time, the army was unable to prevent raids. The soldiers were too few in number and often were untrained. Some of the officers were Civil War veterans, with little experience in fighting Native Americans. The forts were built too far apart and too far to the west to provide immediate defense for the settlers. Another serious problem was the shortage of supplies. Military **campaigns,** or operations, against Native Americans sometimes had to be cancelled because there was not enough food for the soldiers and horses.

The Native Americans, on the other hand, knew their territory and were skilled fighters. Until the invention of Samuel Colt's six-shot pistol, Comanches usually had the advantage in warfare. It took one minute to reload a muzzle-loading pistol or rifle. In those 60 seconds, a Comanche warrior could ride 200 yards (183 m) and shoot 20 arrows. Warriors adopted the tactic of drawing the fire of settlers, then rushing upon them while they reloaded. By the 1870s and 1880s, most Native American warriors carried rifles too.

Reading Check **Identifying** What advantage did the Native Americans have over federal soldiers?

The Search for Peace

In 1867 federal **agents** representing the U.S. government and the chiefs of several Native American nations met in present-day Kansas and signed a peace treaty called the **Treaty of Medicine Lodge Creek.** According to its terms, Native Americans would live on reservations in the **Indian Territory** (present-day Oklahoma). The government would provide food and supplies, but the army would not be allowed on the reservations. The Native Americans who signed the treaty agreed to stop making raids on Anglo American settlements.

It was generally believed that kind, fair treatment would stop Native Americans from warring with settlers. So President Ulysses S. Grant tried to appoint federal agents who would treat the Native Americans well. Many agents were members of the Society of Friends, also known as Quakers. The Quakers did not believe

History *Through Art*

The Outlier **by Frederic Remington, 1909** By the time of this painting, most Native Americans had been forced onto reservations. What adjectives would you use to describe the mood of this painting?

in violence. **Lawrie Tatum,** the agent in Indian Territory, was a Quaker. He worked to educate the Plains people in agriculture, which would allow them to earn a living in the Anglo world.

The Peace Policy Fails

Peace, however, did not come to western Texas. Many Native American leaders did not sign the treaty. Others claimed that the government broke its promise, and that some agents for the Indian Territory cheated them and treated them badly. About one-half of the Comanches and many Kiowas refused to move to reservations.

Satanta (sah•TAHN•tah), the most famous Kiowa chief, insisted that West Texas belonged to the Comanches and Kiowas. A respected leader known for his eloquent speeches, he earned the name Orator of the Plains. Without the buffalo, Satanta believed his people could not survive very long on reservations. Speaking at the Medicine Lodge Creek peace conference, Satanta explained why he did not want to abandon the Kiowa way of life.

> ❝I love the land and the buffalo and will not part with it. I want you to understand well what I say. Write it on paper . . . I hear a great deal of good talk from the gentlemen whom the Great Father sends us, but they never do what they say. I don't want any of the medicine lodges [schools and churches] within the country. I want the children raised as I was.❞

Another important Kiowa chief was **Lone Wolf.** He called for war in part to avenge the death of his son, who had been killed in a battle with federal troops. **Ten Bears,** a Comanche chief, argued that his people must be allowed to roam freely over the plains.

> ❝I was born upon the prairie, where the wind blew free and there was nothing to break the light of the sun . . . I want no blood upon my land to stain the grass. I want it all clear and pure, and I want it so that all who wish to go through among my people may find peace when they come in.❞

Wild Horse and Black Horse were two other powerful Comanche chiefs who could not bring themselves to surrender to reservation life. Another strong Comanche chief, **Quanah** (KWAHN•ah) **Parker,** also refused to sign the treaty. Of mixed heritage, he was the son of a chief, Peta Nocona (PAY•tah noh•KOH•nah), and an Anglo American woman, Cynthia Ann Parker, who had been captured by the Comanches as a child. Quanah Parker grew up on the Texas high plains, a member of a roving band of Comanches who followed the buffalo. After he

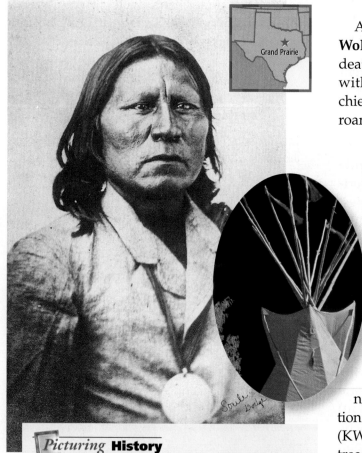

Grand Prairie

Picturing **History**

Satanta is honored today by the Kiowa peoples. Each year, Native Americans meet in Grand Prairie for an annual powwow (gathering) to celebrate their social and religious customs. Events include storytelling and constructing tepees, such as the Kiowa example shown here. What benefit is gained from these gatherings?

People of Texas

Cynthia Ann Parker c.1825-1871

On May 19, 1836, Comanche warriors captured Cynthia Ann. She was given to a Comanche couple and raised as their own daughter. Cynthia Ann played with the tribe's children and soon forgot her other life. She married Peta Nocona, a young chief, and raised a family.

Twenty-four years later, the Texas Rangers came into the camp and took Cynthia and her daughter captive. When they saw her blue eyes, one of the captains remembered the story of Cynthia Ann Parker's abduction. She was taken back to East Texas but never got used to living in the white world and tried several times to return to her Comanche family. Her attempts were unsuccessful and she died without having had further contact with her husband or sons.

---

became a chief, Parker spent 10 years trying to stop the spread of Anglo American settlements as they took over Texas land. **Victorio,** a war chief of the Apaches, was equally as determined to resist life on reservations.

Not all Native American leaders favored war. Kiowa chiefs **Kicking Bird** and **Striking Eagle** advised against war and argued that their people must accept Anglo ways. **Horseback,** a Comanche chief, led his people to a reservation. Warfare continued, however, and soon many of the conflicts became more serious.

✓**Reading Check** **Explaining** Why did the Treaty of Medicine Lodge Creek fail?

SECTION 1 ASSESSMENT

Checking for Understanding

1. **Using Key Terms** Write a paragraph in which you use the terms campaign and agent to show that you understand the meaning of these words as they are used in this chapter.

2. **Reviewing Facts** Why was the U.S. army not able to stop Native American attacks before the Treaty of Medicine Lodge Creek?

Reviewing Themes

3. **Groups and Institutions** Why was control of the land important to both Native Americans and Anglo settlers?

Organizing to Learn

4. **Categorizing** Some Native American leaders resisted any attempt to relocate them onto reservations, while others agreed that their people should move to the reservations. Create a chart like the one shown, and place an **X** in the appropriate box.

Chief	Reservation Life	
	Rejected	Accepted
Black Horse		
Horseback		
Lone Wolf		
Quanah Parker		
Striking Eagle		

Critical Thinking

5. **Making Judgments** Do you think the Native American chiefs were justified in leading their people to fight for their land? Explain your answer.

6. **Considering Options** What are some of the alternative ways Lawrie Tatum could have approached his job? How did his personal beliefs affect his choices?

TAKS PRACTICE

Analyzing Do you think war against the Texas Native Americans was necessary? Why or why not?

Texas LITERATURE

Elmer Kelton

Elmer Kelton is regarded by many as one of the best modern western writers. He was awarded the Western Heritage Award as well as the Golden Spur Award for *The Time It Never Rained.* His other award-winning novels include *The Day the Cowboys Quit, The Far Canyon,* and *The Man who Rode Midnight.* Kelton lives in San Angelo, Texas.

Reading to Discover

As you read, think of the language the author uses to take the reader into the distant and very different past.

Reader's Dictionary

pumpkin roller: slang term for a Southern farmer

tangible: real or concrete; something one can touch

mitigated: made milder or lessened in intensity

wresting: gaining by force, violence, or determined labor

interloper: intruder in a place or on rights of others

dispossessed: deprived of homes or possessions and security

The Pumpkin Rollers

by ELMER KELTON

Trey McLean left his cotton farm in East Texas to become a cattleman in West Texas.

[Trey] might ride for hours without seeing a house, a corral, any **tangible** mark of the invader's hand.

Now and then he came unexpectedly upon signs of previous tenants: old campgrounds where smoke-blackened stones lay in circles around dead fire pits, where broken and imperfect arrowheads lay discarded. Turning his ear to the wind, he could imagine he heard the lingering voices of those who so recently had fought with full heart rather than yield to new conquerors. When he allowed his mind to drift in that direction he felt sorrow for them, **mitigated** by the knowledge that it had always been so.

The Comanche himself had come as an invader, **wresting** these grounds by force from those who had conquered it earlier. Conquest had been the way of the world, not simply of the West. Hungry invaders enjoyed the spoils for the length of their season, then lost to some new **interloper** who came with greater strength, a more unyielding hunger.

Those who came to this land now would have the use of it a while, but always they would have to watch over their shoulders, for others

would come with needs of their own and want it as much. The soldier **dispossessed** the Indian and opened the way for the hunter and trapper, to be succeeded by the cattleman, who then gave way to the farmer.

Buffalo on the Plains
by Albert Bierstadt (c. 1890)

ANALYZING LITERATURE

1. **Recall and Interpret** What evidence did Trey find that Native Americans had been there before?
2. **Evaluate and Connect** What changes have taken place in your area over the past 50 years?

Interdisciplinary Activity

Writing Write a letter home to your family on the cotton farm in East Texas. Explain how you feel about your move to West Texas and what is different about your new home.

West Texas at War

Seminole woman c. 1880

A
Texas Story

Seminole men enlisted in the U.S. Army and worked as scouts. Women could not enlist, but served as trainers and handlers for horses and mules. Johanna July developed a system for breaking horses. "I'll tell you how I broke my horses . . . I would lead him down to the river and get him out in water where he couldn't stand up and I would swim up and get him by the mane and ease up on him. He couldn't pitch and when I did let him out of that deep water, he didn't want to pitch."

—Johanna July, WPA Oral History

The Peace Policy Ends

Quaker agents in the United States had worked for peace for several years, but their peaceful policies in Texas were questioned in 1871. Many complaints were made about Native American raids. In response, the

Quanah Parker *(left)* sits astride his horse in front of a tepee. As a Comanche chief, Quanah Parker had to make some difficult decisions on behalf of his people. How did he try to protect Native American rights while he lived in Texas and then on the reservation?

army sent **General William Tecumseh Sherman** from the Fort Sill, Oklahoma, reservation to West Texas to investigate the matter.

General Sherman and many other federal officials believed that the stories about the Texas frontier were exaggerated. On his two-week tour of Texas, however, Sherman became convinced that the peaceful policies of the agents were unsuccessful.

While he visited Fort Richardson at **Jacksboro** in May 1871, a group of Kiowas attacked a wagon train traveling nearby along Salt Creek. This became sensationalized and called the Warren Wagontrain Raid. Several men were wounded or killed. Satanta, one of the Kiowa chiefs who led the raid, returned to the reservation in the Indian Territory and admitted his actions to the Quaker agent, Lawrie Tatum. He and two other chiefs—**Big Tree** and **Satank**—were arrested and ordered by Sherman to be taken back to Jacksboro for a trial. While trying to escape from the transport wagon, Satank was killed along the way, but Satanta and Big Tree were tried, found guilty, and sentenced to hang.

Federal officials in Washington, D.C., believed that killing the chiefs would start a major war on the plains. Supporters of the current peace policy convinced Governor Davis to commute, or change, the death sentence for the chiefs to life imprisonment. Later Satanta and Big Tree were paroled. Texans became furious when they learned that the two chiefs were set free in the hope of peace. Later Satanta was accused of more raids, and he was sent to the state prison at Huntsville. He found prison life intolerable and is believed to have killed himself.

The real significance of the Warren Wagontrain Raid was that it changed the attitude of many of the military leaders, especially General Sherman. After Satanta's attack on the wagon train, the peace policy was abandoned. No longer would the army merely defend the settlements from attacks. Native Americans would be forced onto reservations. Upon Sherman's advice, the federal government sent expeditions to northwest Texas to locate and destroy Native American camps.

Reading Check **Contrasting** How did General Sherman's thinking change during his tour of Texas?

Mackenzie Leads the Early Texas Campaigns

During 1871 and 1872, army expeditions actively campaigned on the South Plains against the Native Americans. **Colonel Ranald S. Mackenzie,** commander of the Fourth Cavalry Regiment, led the operations. An excellent officer in the Civil War, Mackenzie was daring, aggressive, and persistent. He demanded much from his troops, but he shared their hardships and earned their respect.

Col. Ranald Mackenzie

Led by Mackenzie, the Fourth Cavalry located Comanche parties on the South Plains in the autumn of 1871. Quanah Parker, the Comanche leader, outwitted Mackenzie. Using a snowstorm for cover, Parker avoided capture by leading his people away from their camp in Blanco Canyon. The next year, however, the Fourth Cavalry defeated a large Comanche party in a battle fought near present-day Pampa. More than 100 Comanches were captured, but they were later released. By 1873, Comanche raids on West Texas had declined.

In 1873, from its base at Fort Clark, the army concentrated its efforts along the Rio Grande in South Texas. Here the Kickapoos and Apaches, who lived in northern Mexico, were attacking settlements on both sides of the border. Mackenzie and his troops crossed the Rio Grande and attacked the Native American villages. For several years after that attack, the southern border was more peaceful.

Native Americans Depend on the Buffalo

The culture of the nomadic Plains peoples depended upon open land, the horse, and buffalo. The Native Americans who lived on the plains feared that the rapidly increasing number of buffalo hunters would soon end their way of life. Although they also hunted large game such as deer, moose, and elk, the Native Americans depended on the buffalo for much of their food and many other necessities. Water bags were made from the buffalo's **paunch,** or stomach. Hoofs, horns, and bones became ornaments, cups, and other utensils. **Sinews** (tendons) and hair yielded necessities such as bowstrings, thread, and rope. Buffalo hide became clothing, saddles, robes, and covers for tepees. Even the dried manure, called buffalo chips, was used for fuel. Striking Eagle of the Kiowas explained the importance of the buffalo to his people in this way:

> 66The buffalo is our money . . . [T]he robes we can prepare and trade. We love them just as the white man does his money. Just as it makes a white man feel to have his money carried away, so it makes us feel to see others killing and stealing our buffaloes, which are our cattle given to us by the Great Father above.99

Buffalo Herds Are Slaughtered

The era of the buffalo hunt in Texas was begun by **Charles Rath** and brothers **John** and **J. Wright Mooar.** Recognizing the value of buffalo hides in the manufacture of leather goods, these men developed a market for the hides. The slaughter of the buffalo herds began early in the

A Shared Past...

The buffalo continued to provide a valuable resource for several years after their slaughter. The hide hunters had abandoned buffalo carcasses on the plains. Eventually there was nothing left but millions of pounds of buffalo bones. Those bones were gathered and hauled to railroad stations to be sent east. By this time, German chemists had discovered how fertilizers worked and had created an early form of scientific agriculture. Tons of buffalo bones were ground up and spread as fertilizer on mineral-poor soils on Eastern farms.

1870s. By 1873 the herds north of Texas had been wiped out, and the hunters began to move onto the Texas plains.

Many sympathetic Anglo Americans realized the importance of the buffalo to the Native American way of life. A law was proposed in the Texas legislature to protect the buffalo, but **General Philip Sheridan,** commander of the U.S. Military Department of the Southwest, helped to defeat the bill. He favored the slaughter of the buffalo as a means of defeating the Plains culture. Appearing before a joint assembly of the House and Senate, he spoke of the role of the buffalo hunters:

> ❝They are destroying the Indians' commissary [storehouse], and it is a well-known fact that an army losing its base of supplies is placed at a great disadvantage. Send them powder and lead, if you will; but, for the sake of a lasting peace, let them kill, skin, and sell until the buffaloes are exterminated. Then your prairies can be covered with speckled cattle, and the festive cowboy, who follows the hunter as a second forerunner of advanced civilization.❞

The buffalo hunters continued to slaughter buffalo by the thousands. The hunters wanted only the hide, which they sold for one or two dollars each. They left the land filled with rotting carcasses and white buffalo bones and destroyed the last hopes of the Plains people. Without the buffalo for food, clothing, and other necessities, Native Americans of the Plains could not sustain, or continue, their way of life. The Native Americans made plans for war.

✓ **Reading Check** **Summarizing** Why did General Sheridan want the buffalo slaughtered?

History *Through Art*

Shooting Buffalo on the Line of the Kansas–Pacific Railroad, c. **1870** Although the buffalo sustained many Native Americans on the Plains, Anglo Americans regarded the buffalo differently. What does this image suggest about Anglo American attitudes?

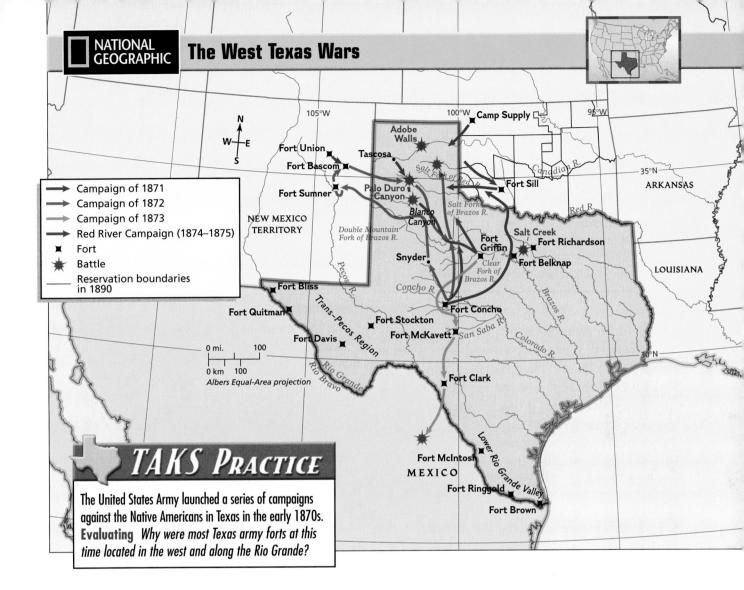

Campaign of 1871
Campaign of 1872
Campaign of 1873
Red River Campaign (1874–1875)
Fort
Battle
Reservation boundaries in 1890

TAKS PRACTICE

The United States Army launched a series of campaigns against the Native Americans in Texas in the early 1870s. **Evaluating** *Why were most Texas army forts at this time located in the west and along the Rio Grande?*

The Attack on Adobe Walls

In June 1874 Quanah Parker led several hundred warriors from 5 Native American nations in an attack on a buffalo hunters' camp at **Adobe Walls.** The camp, a settlement of sod houses, was a few miles northeast of present-day Borger, near the Canadian River. There the Texan settlers defended the camp with the help of buffalo guns designed to fire many shots in a short time. In all, 28 buffalo hunters and 1 woman withstood the attack.

Frustrated by the failure to take Adobe Walls, the Comanches, Kiowas, Cheyenne, and other Plains groups increased their attacks on West Texas settlements. Many Native Americans on the reservations left to join the fighting. The warring Plains people then spread across 5 states and territories, killing 190 Anglo Americans over the next 2 months.

The Red River Campaign

After this Native American uprising and the attack on the buffalo hunters at Adobe Walls, President Grant put the army—rather than government agents—in charge of Native American affairs in West Texas. Some Native Americans registered at agencies set up on the reservations. About 4,000—mostly Comanches, Kiowas, and Cheyenne—did not. Some of these people based their camps in canyons and valleys in the Texas Panhandle. There approximately 1,200 warriors prepared for the final defense of their land. They did not have long to wait.

An army of some 3,000 troops moved in on the camps from five different directions. The first battle of what became the **Red River campaign** was fought in late August 1874. The army did not halt its determined search for Native American camps until the following spring.

TEXAS FACT

Quanah Parker was a war chief who made the change to peacetime through his great intellect and integrity. By observing how business was transacted successfully, he became a very wealthy rancher and cattleman. He counted Theodore Roosevelt among his friends and was frequently interviewed by magazine reporters. He maintained a mansion for his seven wives and numerous children. Through it all, he kept his Native American identity and refused to cut off his long braids.

The Texas Rangers also fought in the west. **Major John B. Jones,** a veteran of Terry's Texas Rangers, led the Frontier Battalion during the Red River campaign. Forcing his troops to stay constantly alert, Jones protected the West Texas line of defense, while Mackenzie and other military leaders stormed camps even further west. In its first 6 months, the Frontier Battalion fought 15 battles against Native Americans.

The Battle of Palo Duro Canyon

The **Battle of Palo Duro Canyon,** on September 28, 1874, was the most decisive battle of the Red River campaign. The canyon was a favorite campground of many Plains groups. After a dangerous descent down sheer canyon walls, the Fourth Cavalry, under Colonel Ranald S.

Mackenzie, set fire to 5 Comanche, Kiowa, and Cheyenne villages. In the conflict that followed, few lives were lost, but the troops captured valuable supplies and 1,424 horses and mules. Mackenzie had more than 1,000 horses destroyed to prevent the Native Americans from retrieving them. Without food, horses, and shelter, the Native Americans could not survive long.

By early November most of the Native American bands were making their way to the reservations. Some defied the army and held out through an unusually harsh winter until early summer. The last remaining Comanche bands, the **Kwahadies** (kwah•HAH•deez), surrendered in June 1875 at Fort Sill in Indian Territory. Among them was Quanah Parker.

Quanah Parker continued to represent his people. He worked as a mediator to settle disputes among the various Native American nations. He fought for Native American rights and represented their interests to the federal government in Washington, D.C.

After the Red River campaign, Native Americans rarely were seen on the prairies and plains of Central and West Texas. Kickapoo and Apache warriors, however, continued their struggle for a few more years in the border country along the Rio Grande.

✓ **Reading Check** **Describing** What happened at the Battle of Palo Duro Canyon?

SECTION 2 ASSESSMENT

Checking for Understanding

1. **Using Key Terms** Use the terms paunch, sinew, and commissary in a short paragraph about the buffalo.
2. **Reviewing Facts** Why was the battle at Palo Duro Canyon significant?

Reviewing Themes

3. **Culture and Tradition** Why was it not possible for Native American and Anglo cultures to live together peacefully?

Organizing to Learn

4. **Summarizing** Create a chart like the one below. Explain the purpose of the various events listed in this chart.

Event	Purpose
Early Texas campaigns	
Buffalo hunts by Anglo Americans	
Red River campaign	

Critical Thinking

5. **Analyzing** How did the army's policy of attacking Native Americans rather than defending settlements affect the Native Americans in West Texas?

TAKS PRACTICE

Drawing Conclusions What was the most important action in the final defeat of the Native Americans of West Texas?

Using a Spreadsheet

Why Learn This Skill?

People use electronic spreadsheets to help them manage numbers quickly and easily. Formulas may be used to add, subtract, multiply, and divide the numbers in the spreadsheet. If you make a change to one number, the totals are recalculated automatically.

Microsoft® Excel spreadsheet

Learning the Skill

To understand how use a spreadsheet, follow these steps:

- Vertical columns are assigned letters–A, B, C, AA, BB, CC, and so on.
- Horizontal rows are assigned numbers–1, 2, 3, and so on.
- The point where a column and row intersect is called a *cell–C6,* for example.
- The computer highlights the cell you are in. The contents of the cell also appear on a status line at the top of the screen.
- Spreadsheets use *standard formula*s to calculate numbers. To create a formula, highlight the cell you want the results in. Type an equal sign (=) and then build the formula, step by step. If you type the formula *=B4+B5+B6* in cell **B7**, the values in these cells are added together and the sum shows up in cell **B7.**
- To use division, the formula would look like this: *=A5/C2.* This divides A5 by C2. An asterisk (*) signifies multiplication: *=(B2*C3)+D1* means you want to multiply B2 times C3, then add D1.

Practicing the Skill

Refer to the spreadsheet to answer these questions.

❶ What information is found on this spreadsheet?

❷ What cell is highlighted? What information is found in the highlighted cell?

❸ What formula would you type in which cell to calculate the average land area of the five counties listed?

❹ What formula would you type in which cell to find the number of people per lane mile in each county?

TAKS PRACTICE

Using a Spreadsheet Answer the following questions by referring to the spreadsheet above.

1. What formula would you type in which cell to calculate the average number of lane miles per county?

2. Create your own question using this spreadsheet.

3. Write a short paragraph about these five counties using the information from the spreadsheet.

Fighting on the Rio Grande

Guide to Reading

Main Idea
The Rio Grande Valley was the scene of conflict among Native Americans, Mexican Americans, and Texans in the late 1870s.

Key Term
renegade

Reading Strategy
Summarizing Information Draw a chart. As you read about the people listed below, write two important facts about each.

Person/Group	Important Facts
Victorio	
Buffalo Soldiers	
Benjamin Grierson	
Texas Rangers	

Read to Learn
• who the buffalo soldiers were.
• what problems were produced by the violence along the Rio Grande.
• about the outcome of the Anglo and Native American conflict.

Section Theme
Groups and Institutions With the Native Americans defeated, Anglo settlers moved into West Texas.

Preview of Events

1875	1876	1878
Texas Rangers in Rio Grande Valley — Wichita Falls is founded	Warfare resumes along the Mexican border	Kickapoo are subdued

A Texas Story

Seminole scout

When she was 18, Johanna July married a Seminole scout. But settling down was difficult. Her husband wanted her to stop breaking horses and devote herself to housework. Johanna was unwilling to give up the horses she loved so much. One night she slipped away and rode all night to Fort Duncan. "As I got to Fort Duncan I heard the sentry call 'Four o'clock and all is well!' I said to myself, 'All may be well, but I don't feel so well after this ride!'"

—Johanna July, WPA Oral History

Buffalo Soldiers End the Wars

After several years of peace, warfare along the Mexican border resumed in 1876. Colonel Mackenzie and his Fourth Cavalry returned from the campaigns against the Sioux to Fort Clark in 1878. Mackenzie established regular patrols and sometimes crossed the Rio Grande into Mexico in search of **Kickapoo** raiders. Mexican army units joined in the campaign. By 1878 the Kickapoo were subdued, but the Apaches continued their raids.

By the 1870s most Apaches lived in New Mexico and Arizona. At least one band, however, traveled in the mountains of West Texas. This defiant band of warriors, led by Chief Victorio, fought battles in Mexico, Texas, and New Mexico. Each time, the band of Native Americans escaped to fight again.

The war against Victorio was placed in the hands of **Colonel Benjamin H. Grierson** and the African American troops of the Twenty-fourth Infantry and Tenth Cavalry. Many African Americans were stationed in the frontier forts. The Ninth and Tenth Cavalries, made up entirely of African American soldiers, were famous throughout Texas. They became experienced campaigners, skilled in warfare on the frontier. One member of the Tenth Cavalry was **Lieutenant Henry Ossian Flipper,** the first African American graduate of West Point Military Academy.

Native Americans called the African American troops **"buffalo soldiers,"** a title of great respect. The army recognized their courage. Nineteen buffalo soldiers received Medals of Honor from Congress for service in the U.S. Army during the wars in the American West. The buffalo soldiers did not, however, receive equal treatment from the Anglo American settlers. The buffalo soldiers were sometimes harassed and abused.

Grierson and his soldiers pursued Victorio through the rough terrain of the Mountains and Basins region and forced the Apaches across the Rio Grande into Mexico. Mexican soldiers trapped Victorio and his men in northern Mexico. In the battle that followed, Victorio was killed. Some members of his band continued to

Model of a "buffalo soldier"

fight, although they no longer operated in Texas. Victorio's defeat in 1880 marked the end of the Apache wars in Texas.

Reading Check **Identifying** Who was Chief Victorio?

South Texas Renegades

West Texas was not the only area seeing conflict and violence. Renegades, or outlaws, from both sides of the Rio Grande were robbing and raiding towns and settlements. Lawlessness increased as deserters from the Civil War and outlaws crossed into Texas. These renegades instilled fear in many Texans and Mexican Americans.

Other problems in South Texas were difficult to control. Sometimes ambitious ranchers took advantage of the lack of law and order to expand their lands and herds of cattle. Many poorer people, especially those of Mexican heritage, lost their lands and were mistreated in other ways. In many cases it was difficult to determine the true ownership of cattle.

Sometimes law enforcement agents added to the problems. The Texas Rangers were sent to the lower Rio Grande in 1875 to establish peace. One unit active in the Rio Grande Valley was the **Special Force,** commanded by Captain L.H. McNelly, a veteran of the Confederate cavalry and a fearless law officer. Fearless and effective, the Rangers soon acquired a reputation for ruthlessness. Many people believed that the Rangers mistreated Mexican Americans and that innocent people suffered along with the guilty.

Juan N. Cortina was among those who clashed with law authorities. He had taken up the role of protector of the rights of Mexicans and Tejanos before the Civil War and was a hero to many families along the border. The authorities generally

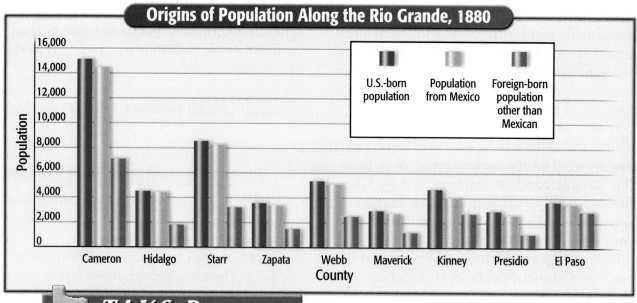

Origins of Population Along the Rio Grande, 1880

U.S.-born population

Population from Mexico

Foreign-born population other than Mexican

Population

16,000
14,000
12,000
10,000
8,000
6,000
4,000
2,000
0

Cameron Hidalgo Starr Zapata Webb Maverick Kinney Presidio El Paso

County

TAKS PRACTICE

Comparing and Contrasting By the late 1800s, people living in Texas came from the United States and Mexico, as well as other countries. *According to this bar graph, which counties had the largest and the smallest populations with Mexican origins in 1880?*

looked on him as an outlaw who was responsible for much violence along the Rio Grande.

Although he was accused of many crimes, the extent of Cortina's activities cannot be determined. Reports claimed that his followers raided Texas and Mexican ranches daily. On one occasion, Captain L.H. McNelly and his Special Force followed a party of cattle thieves across the Rio Grande into Mexico. The Rangers recovered some of the stolen cattle but were unable to find Cortina's hideout.

The Rangers were never able to capture Cortina. The Mexican army arrested him and removed him from the Valley. Cattle raids did not stop, but they did become less frequent.

The Texas Rangers' constant patrolling of the countryside north of the Rio Grande and the patrolling of the

TEXAS HISTORY *Online*

Student Web Activity
Visit the texans.glencoe.com Web site and click on **Chapter 17—Student Web Activity** to learn more about Texas soldiers and law officers.

Mexican army south of it helped reduce lawlessness. This peace did not come easily, however, and many Mexican Americans would remember these years with bitterness.

Time of Sadness for Native Americans

For Native Americans this was a time of great sadness. They would never again roam freely over the land in search of buffalo. The growing population of the Eastern states was spilling onto the Great Plains. The westward migration of settlers could not be prevented. Land once used for hunting was turned into farms and towns. To prepare them for these new conditions, many young Native Americans were taken from their homes and placed in boarding schools where they had to wear Anglo clothing, cut their long hair, and speak only English. War, disease, and starvation killed many Native Americans during the 1870s, 1880s, and 1890s. A census taken in 1875 reported only 1,597 Comanches when, just a few years earlier, there had been thousands.

A New Era Begins

What was a disaster for Native Americans was viewed differently by many Anglo settlers. With the threat of raids gone, settlers could move into West Texas and establish their farms and ranches. The forts were no longer

Henry O. Flipper 1856-1940

Born into slavery, Henry Ossian Flipper was the first African American to graduate from West Point. In 1881 Lt. Flipper's commanding officer accused him of "embezzling funds and of conduct unbecoming an officer and a gentleman." The Army found him guilty of misconduct and discharged him.

After leaving the army, he worked as an engineer in Arizona, Mexico, and Venezuela. He continued to protest his innocence throughout his life, and at the time of his death, his greatest regret was that he was not able to clear his name.

On February 19, 1999, almost 60 years after Flipper's death, President William Clinton finally ordered a full pardon of Lt. Henry O. Flipper, recognizing his achievements as an American soldier.

necessary, but several of them had attracted small settlements that survived the closing of the forts. Both San Angelo and Brackettville grew up around military posts.

Anglo American settlers poured into western Texas immediately after the removal of the Native Americans. They settled along transportation routes and quickly built new towns. Wichita Falls was founded in 1875 at the falls of the Wichita River. Two years later Vernon was surveyed on the Pease River. Coleman, Brady, Abilene, Sweetwater, and Colorado City were all established in the five years between 1876 and 1881. An indication of how rapidly the settlements grew is that both Belle Plain in Callahan County and old Clarendon in Donley County had colleges by 1881. The railroads being built west from Fort Worth and Temple brought farming communities to lands that only a few years before had been the home of the Comanche.

✓ **Reading Check** **Contrasting** What were three causes of declining Native American populations in Texas?

SECTION 3 ASSESSMENT

Checking for Understanding

1. **Using Key Terms** How is a renegade different from a vigilante?
2. **Reviewing Facts** How were the buffalo soldiers important in the frontier battles?

Reviewing Themes

3. **Groups and Institutions** With the coming of new farms and towns to the Plains, how did life change for young Native Americans?

Organizing to Learn

4. **Summarizing** Create a chart similar to this one to summarize the effects of the frontier wars on Anglo settlers, Native Americans, and Mexican Americans.

Group	Effects of Frontier Wars
Native Americans	
Anglo settlers	
Mexican Americans	

Critical Thinking

5. **Analyzing Information** As a member of the Texas legislature, would you have voted for or against the bill to protect the buffalo? Explain why you would have voted that way.

TAKS PRACTICE

Evaluating Why was the idea of moving onto a reservation not acceptable to many Native Americans?

Chapter Summary

Cultures in Conflict

1866
- U.S. troops are stationed in West Texas to prevent Native American raids.

1867
- Some Native Americans sign the Treaty of Medicine Lodge Creek, a peace treaty. Others refuse to sign.

★ Warfare and raids continue.

1871
- The U.S. government decides to use military force to place Native Americans on reservations.

1873
- U.S. soldiers subdue Native Americans in South Texas.

1874
★ Buffalo hunters destroy buffalo herds.

- Native Americans are defeated at Adobe Walls and the Battle of Palo Duro Canyon.

1875
★ Quanah Parker surrenders at Fort Sill in Indian Territory.

1876
- "Buffalo soldiers" lead campaigns against Native Americans near Mexican border.

1880
- Apaches surrender.
- Most Native Americans move to reservations.

Reviewing Key Terms

Examine each group of terms below. Explain why one term in each group does not belong with the others.

1. campaign, commissary, agent
2. paunch, bill, sinew
3. outlaw, renegade, bill

Reviewing Key Facts

4. What were the sources of the conflicts in Texas after the Civil War?
5. What did those Native Americans who signed the Treaty of Medicine Lodge Creek agree to do?
6. Why were the buffalo so important to the Plains culture?
7. Who was Quanah Parker?
8. What major change in U.S. government policy toward the Native Americans resulted from the Warren Wagontrain Raid?
9. What was the importance of the Battle of Adobe Walls?
10. Why did some Native Americans move to the Texas Panhandle after the attack on Adobe Walls?
11. What were some of the problems faced by soldiers fighting against the Native Americans?
12. Who were the buffalo soldiers? How were they important during this period in Texas history?
13. Why were the problems in South Texas so difficult to solve?
14. Why was Victorio's defeat an important event in the history of the wars with Native Americans?

Critical Thinking

15. **Analyzing** How did West Texas develop after the removal of Native Americans from the area?
16. **Identifying the Main Idea** What was the "peace policy"? How was it successful? How was it unsuccessful?
17. **Identifying Differences of Opinion** One action can cause many different reactions. Draw a chart like the one below and list the reasons why each Native American leader refused to live on the reservation as instructed by the Treaty of Medicine Lodge Creek.

Native American Leader	Reason
Satanta	
Lone Wolf	
Ten Bears	
Quanah Parker	

Geography and History Activity

Draw an outline map of Texas. Indicate the location of the following important battles and who fought there.

18. Adobe Walls

19. Palo Duro Canyon

20. Salt Creek

21. South Texas (near Fort Clark)

Cooperative Learning Activity

22. Role Playing Form groups of three. Members will assume the roles of a settler, a Texas Ranger, and a Native American. Each member will discuss his or her main concerns about living in Texas in the 1880s. After each member is finished, the other members should discuss ways to help the member address, or deal with, his or her concerns. As a group, agree on two recommendations that can be accepted by all three members.

Practicing Skills

23. Using a Spreadsheet Use a spreadsheet to enter your numerical grades and scores for one of your classes. At the end of the grading period, input the correct formula and the spreadsheet will calculate your average grade.

Portfolio TAKS/Writing Activity

24. Writing a Newspaper Article Imagine that you are a reporter attending the signing of the Treaty of Medicine Lodge Creek between the Native Americans and the federal government agents. You have been assigned to write an article about the event for your newspaper. You should present both sides in your article. Try to anticipate any potential problems with the treaty. Save your work for your portfolio.

Building Technology Skills

25. Using the Internet or the Library for Research Chief Quanah Parker spent 10 years in an attempt to stop the spread of Anglo settlements on the Texas Plains. Find a book by using your library's computer system or a Web site on the Internet to gather information about Quanah Parker. Create an illustrated time line of the most important events of his life. If you have clip art on your computer, you may use that when you are creating your time line.

TEXAS HISTORY Online

Self-Check Quiz

Visit the texans.glencoe.com Web site and click on **Chapter 17—Self-Check Quizzes** to prepare for the chapter test.

TAKS PRACTICE

The Princeton Review

Use the graph to answer the following question.

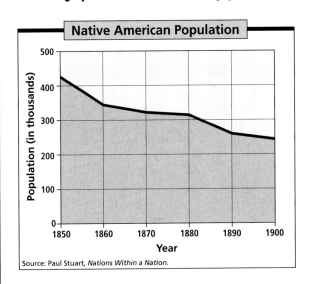

Native American Population

Source: Paul Stuart, *Nations Within a Nation.*

The population of Native Americans in the United States decreased by approximately what number from 1850 to 1900?

A 450,000

B 250,000

C 300,000

D 200,000

Test-Taking Tip:

When reading a line graph, first make sure that you identify and understand the information on both the horizontal and vertical axes. This question does not ask for the Native American population in 1850 or in 1900 but for the difference between those two years. Subtract the amount in 1900 from the amount in 1850 to come up with the correct answer.

Economics & History

Buffalo Boom and Bust

The sight of a buffalo—more correctly a bison—today brings several things to mind. Some people may remember how close the species came to extinction. Others might be reminded of Native Americans and their way of life. For citizens in many North Texas settlements during the 1870s, the mention of the term "buffalo" brought visions of instant profits and high drama.

Buffalo Hunters

By the early 1870s, American hunters had greatly reduced buffalo herds in Kansas, Nebraska, and eastern Colorado. With the northern herds nearly gone, buffalo hunters turned to the High Plains in the Texas Panhandle where buffalo still roamed freely. The region resembled the Great Plains and served as a natural grazing ground for the animals. Here, the buffalo hunters continued to make large profits shooting and skinning buffalo.

Counties that grew prosperous from buffalo hunts included Shackelford, Taylor, Haskell, Stephens, Callahan, Eastland, Jones, Scurry, and Throckmorton. Fort Griffin, a small community in Shackelford County that grew around a fort of the same name, became the center of the boom.

Towns Grow and Prosper

How did these communities—so far away from the hunting grounds in the Panhandle Plains—benefit? The answer is that developing industries need the support of existing businesses. They also lead to the creation of new jobs. Shackelford and surrounding counties lay midway between the hunting fields and the nearest railroad line in Denison, Texas. These towns were perfectly positioned to provide services to those involved in the buffalo hunt.

Men needed to recruit workers and organize expeditions to the buffalo range. They demanded "office space," as did businessmen who bought buffalo hides from the hunters. Every outsider needed sleeping accommodations. Warehouse space was essential for storing the hides until they were ready to be shipped to Denison. Further, buffalo hunters required food, gear, tobacco, and other supplies to sustain them for long periods of time.

Buffalo hunters on the plains profited from their activities for a time.

Good Times Turn Bad

The town of Fort Griffin grew to a population of nearly 3,000 during the peak buffalo hunting period on the High Plains. In the community, new general stores went up, as did boarding houses, saloons, trading posts, and the like. Other businesses essential to the buffalo trade appeared, among them blacksmith shops and livery stables.

Young men looking for extra money found no difficulty finding jobs as hunters. The task required no experience or skill; all a person needed was a rifle, a horse, and some supplies. Unskilled laborers could make more money faster from a "kill" than they could working on a farm or as a ranchhand. There were various other ways of earning a living related to the buffalo hunts. Some people became skinners, stripping the hide from the animal, preparing it for market, and stockpiling it. Others worked around the camp, cooking, caring for horses, cleaning equipment, or guarding the mounds of dried buffalo hides. Skilled wagon drivers transported equipment, supplies, and hides from the Panhandle to Fort Griffin or to Denison.

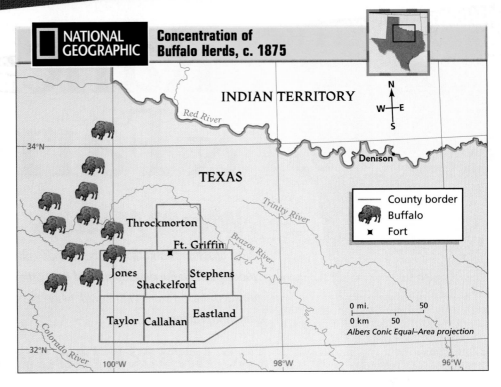

Concentration of Buffalo Herds, c. 1875

Similar to the California gold rush of 1849, the "good times" created by the buffalo hunts of the 1870s ended in a bust by the early 1880s. Prosperity was followed by a depression. There was no longer a need for hotels, office facilities, saloons, feed stores, or other enterprises that had been crucial to the success of buffalo hunting. Many workers were laid off. Because most workers had not saved their earnings or invested them, individual wealth did not last long. The once-prosperous community of Fort Griffin does not exist today.

TAKS PRACTICE

1. **Drawing Conclusions** Name an industry or occupation that exists today as a result of urbanization in Texas.
2. **Making Generalizations** How would you describe economic times today in Texas?
3. **Writing About Economics** Write a paragraph that develops one of the themes listed below. Use standard grammar, spelling, sentence structure, and punctuation. Include information and examples from the feature as details to support your argument.
   a. People work hard during boom times.
   b. Saving money during prosperous times is important.
   c. Economic cycles often go from boom to bust.

Ranching & Farming

Why It Matters

Vast grasslands and the number of wild cattle in southern and western Texas made possible the development of the Cattle Kingdom. These resources provided some Texans with wealth when the state was struggling with economic problems.

The Impact Today

Although the era of the cattle drives lasted only a few years following the Civil War, the cowboy culture, formed by a blending of Mexican and Anglo traits, continues to fascinate people.

1853
★ *King Ranch established*

1866
★ *Major cattle drives to Sedalia began*

Texas					
United States	1850	1855	1860	1865	1870
World					

1869
• *First transcontinental railroad completed*

The Stampede *by Robert Lindneux captures the excitement and tension of horses and cattle on the run.*

FOLDABLES™ TAKS
Study Organizer PRACTICE

Compare-Contrast Study Foldable
Make this foldable to help you analyze information by comparing and contrasting pre-war and post-war ranching and farming in Texas.

Step 1 Fold one sheet of paper in half from top to bottom.

Step 2 Fold it in half again, from side to side.

Step 3 Unfold the paper once and label your foldable as shown.

Step 4 Cut up the fold of the top flap only.

This cut will make two tabs.

Reading and Writing As you read the chapter, write what you learn about cattle ranching before the Civil War and farming after the war under the appropriate tabs of your foldable. Think about how ranching and farming influence the economy and culture of Texas today, and also note this on your foldable.

1880
★ *Ranchers began to use barbed wire fences*

1882
★ *XIT Ranch established*

| 1875 | 1880 | 1885 | 1890 |

1875
• *First roller skating rink opened in London*

1883
• *National time zones standardized*

1885
• *Indian National Congress established*

1889
• *Oklahoma Land Rush occurred*

TEXAS HISTORY Online

Chapter Overview
Visit the texans.glencoe.com Web site and click on **Chapter 18—Chapter Overviews** to preview chapter information.

Origins of the Cattle Kingdom

Guide to Reading

Main Idea
As farming and railroads developed, the days of the open range ended, and the cowhand image became an important part of American culture.

Key Terms
open range, *vaquero*, *ranchero*, tallow, stockyard, drive, drover, wrangler, quarantine

Reading Strategy
Locating Information As you read this section, create a chart like the one shown and fill in the missing information.

Trail Name	Where It Ended
	Abilene, Kansas
Great Western Trail	
	Colorado

Read to Learn
- who brought the first cattle to Texas.
- what made the cattle industry turn profitable after the Civil War.
- about the cattle drives.

Section Theme
Economic Factors The value of cattle changed due to supply and demand and the arrival of railroads.

Preview of Events

♦ 1853	♦ 1866	♦ 1886
Richard King buys Santa Gertrudis, later named King Ranch	First cattle drive to Sedalia, Missouri	End of trail driving

African American cowhand

A Texas Story

Many African Americans, including Tom Mills, chose to live in West Texas after the Civil War. He came from Alabama and became a cowhand on a ranch in Uvalde County. "That was the life I loved . . . We had the choicest of meats, we parched our own coffee, we drank from our own hats, we broke our own horses and done our own fightin'! We had the coffee pot hangin' 'round the hoss' neck. But we had fun, I can tell you!"

—Tom Mills, WPA Oral History

The Spanish Introduce Cattle

The cattle first brought to America arrived on the ships of Spanish explorers in the 1500s. Some of the cattle escaped from the range, and herds of wild cattle eventually grazed throughout parts of Texas.

Spanish settlers brought more cattle into the area of South Texas in the 1690s. By the late 1700s, two Spanish missions near Goliad together contained 25,000 head of cattle. Spaniards built cattle ranches along the Rio Grande, San Antonio, and Nueces Rivers. The climate, abundant water supply, and nutritious grass made Texas ideal cattle country.

The first Spanish cattle were tall, rangy, hardy animals that survived and multiplied in the semi-arid brush country. They had horns that grew six feet or more across. In time, ranchers bred these cattle with other types, giving rise to the famous Texas longhorns.

Raising cattle began on the **open range,** public land that could be used by anyone. *Vaqueros,* or cowhands, herded and drove cattle into pens they called *corrales.* Cattle were then branded with a hot iron to show ownership. The brands of early Spanish *rancheros,* or ranchers, were large designs. Later Anglo American brands were simpler and often were developed from the initials of the rancher or the name of the ranch. Spanish ranchers often drove herds to market in Louisiana.

Reading Check **Identifying** What about Texas geography made the region ideal cattle country?

Early Ranchers Use the Open Range

Anglo American ranchers moved from the southern United States into the Gulf Coast region of southeast Texas, the Piney Woods of East Texas, and the Red River region in northeast Texas. Ranchers who moved into Texas before the Civil War already were accustomed to many practices of the open range. However, they had not relied on horses, developed roping skills, worn chaps, or used saddles equipped with horns. They quickly adopted these ways and often used Spanish terms for equipment and practices. The popular image of the cowhand had its origin with the Spanish and Mexican *vaqueros.*

The ranching industry in South Texas flourished in the late 1700s and early 1800s, especially between the Nueces and the Colorado

History *Through Art*

On the Trail by J.L.T. Gentilz Cattle driving on the open range began in Spanish Texas. *Vaqueros* branded and controlled the herds. How did Spanish brands differ from later Anglo brands?

Rivers. Mexican rancheros in the region south of the Nueces River continued to operate large ranches after the Texas Revolution and the war with Mexico. Anglo American ranchers later claimed some of their lands. **Richard King,** a native New Yorker, came to Texas with **Mifflin Kenedy** during the Mexican–American War. By 1850 they had become partners in a steamboat business on the Rio Grande. In 1853 King bought the Santa Gertrudis, an old Spanish land grant of 15,500 acres in the southern Gulf Coast area, from the widow of Juan Mendiola. Eventually this holding would become the famous **King Ranch** south of the Nueces River.

Although the cattle continued to multiply, early Anglo ranchers still faced many challenges. Theft and drought were common. The major problem, however, was the lack of markets. Texas ranchers knew well a basic principle of free enterprise: a product without a market is of little value.

Most cattle were slaughtered for their hides and **tallow,** or fat, which could be shipped easily. These products brought little profit

ONLY in TEXAS

The King Ranch in southern Texas calls itself "the birthplace of American ranching." Richard King *(left)* first started the cattle ranch in 1853. The King brand *(above right)* became a well-known symbol. Today, the King Ranch produces cattle, leather goods, citrus, and grains. The ranch also breeds quality quarter horses and thoroughbreds that attract numerous buyers *(bottom right)*. Visitors to the King Ranch Museum *(bottom left)* learn about the history of ranching in Texas.

compared to what beef would bring in an eastern city. Some cattle were driven to Louisiana, Missouri, Ohio, and California in the 1840s and 1850s in an effort to find better markets.

Trail Driving Opens the Cattle Market

Several changes made trail driving profitable just after the Civil War. Cattle herds, neglected during the Civil War, roamed wild on the plains and multiplied. While the price of cattle in the Southwest was about $4 a head, people in the North and East paid $30 to $40 a head.

The expansion of the railroads after the Civil War played a major role in Texas's cattle industry. Texas ranchers needed to get their cattle to Chicago and St. Louis **stockyards,** or holding pens. When the railroads expanded westward, ranchers saw their opportunity. They would **drive,** or move, the cattle in large herds to the

railroad towns, which were connected to the stockyards by rail.

Trail driving was very economical. Twelve or fewer cowhands could drive more than 2,000 head of cattle at a cost lower than $1 per head. The longhorns were driven north in the spring, when grass was plentiful, so the animals could feed off the natural vegetation.

Reading Check **Examining** How did the railroads increase profits for the cattle industry?

Drovers Follow Major Cattle Trails

In the spring of 1866, about 260,000 head of cattle were rounded up in Texas and driven north—many to Sedalia, Missouri, where the railroad ended. The cattle path became known as the **Sedalia** or **Shawnee Trail.** All along the trail, **drovers,** or people who move cattle, found trouble. Missouri farmers complained that the herds destroyed their crops. The farmers also were afraid that the Texas cattle had a disease known as Texas Fever. The longhorns were immune to the disease, but the ticks they carried spread the deadly disease to other cattle. Angry farmers blocked the trails by building fences and barricades.

Joseph G. McCoy, from Illinois, devised a way to get cattle to market. McCoy persuaded the railroads moving westward to build towns with everything necessary to house drovers and their herds. He then persuaded Texas drovers to turn their cattle drives farther west to avoid Missouri. Thereafter, the drovers used the **Chisholm Trail** and headed their cattle for the newly built towns. For a time the trail—named after the Native American trader **Jesse**

Chisholm—was the most popular cattle trail. It began in South Texas; headed north past Austin, Waco, and Fort Worth; crossed the Red River near Nocona; and ran north to Abilene, Kansas.

The drovers later used the **Great Western Trail,** which was formed at Kerrville where the **Matamoros Trail** from Brownsville met the Old Trail from Castroville. It ran northward through Fort Griffin near present-day Albany, crossed the Red River, and headed northwest to Dodge City, Kansas. The **Goodnight–Loving Trail** moved cattle to the ranges of New Mexico, Colorado, Wyoming, and Montana. It ran west from north central Texas along the Middle Concho River, turned north along the Pecos River at Horsehead Crossing, and continued northward into Colorado.

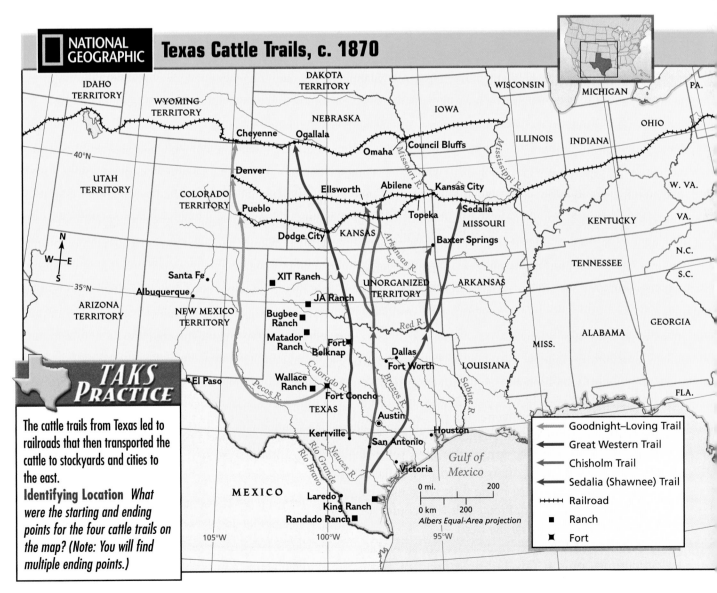

Texas Cattle Trails, c. 1870

Legend:
- Goodnight–Loving Trail
- Great Western Trail
- Chisholm Trail
- Sedalia (Shawnee) Trail
- Railroad
- Ranch
- Fort

TAKS PRACTICE

The cattle trails from Texas led to railroads that then transported the cattle to stockyards and cities to the east.

Identifying Location What were the starting and ending points for the four cattle trails on the map? (Note: You will find multiple ending points.)

Cowhands relax around the chuck wagon after working cattle. Meals were usually hearty. About how many miles did the cowhands travel in one day?

Life Along the Trail Drives

The days, which began at sunup, were long and hard. Two especially skillful cowhands rode in front of the herd to lead the cattle. Other cowhands rode on each side of the herd, while two or three had the dusty drag position behind the herd. A brief noon meal interrupted the day's travel, which ended just before sundown. The chuck wagon cook was called a "coosie," from the Spanish word for a male cook "*cocinero*," or at times was referred to as "cookie," "old lady," or "gut robber." He was usually an aging cowhand hired for his ability to drive a wagon rather than his culinary skills. He was paid more than the other hands because the success of the camp and the drive depended greatly on him.

The distance traveled each day was usually 10 to 12 miles (17 to 19 km). At night the cowhands took turns "riding herd." This meant that they each stood guard to prevent stampedes or raids by Native Americans or rustlers. Though confrontations with Native Americans were seldom violent, trail drivers often had to pay tolls to cross the Indian territory. The tolls were usually paid in the form of old, tired cattle that could not keep up with the rest of the herd.

The size of the herd could vary considerably. Sometimes only a few hundred head of cattle were driven. Herds of 2,000 to 3,000 were also common. For herds of this size, usually 8 to 12 cowhands were needed, plus a trail boss, a cook, and a **wrangler**, or ranchhand, to take care of the horses. Each cowhand had several horses because the same horse usually could not work every day.

The cattle towns of Kansas were rowdy places where cowhands "let off steam" after being paid. Many cowhands wisely saved their wages so they could buy a ranch of their own.

Charles Goodnight, one of the best known drovers, later wrote of the difficulties and dangers involved in trail driving:

❝On my first drive across the ninety-six-mile desert that lies between the Pecos and the Concho Rivers, I lost three hundred head of cattle. We were three days and nights crossing this desert, and during this time we had no sleep or rest, as we had to keep the cattle moving all the time in order to get them to the river before they died of thirst. I rode the same horse for the three days and nights, and what sleep I got was on his back.❞

Trail driving ended shortly after 1885. The supply of cattle became greater than the demand for them, so cattle prices fell. The low prices meant that cattle drives were no longer profitable. Barbed wire fences more frequently blocked the drovers' paths. Cattle that were suspected of carrying disease were kept out of Kansas and Missouri by quarantine (enforced isolation) laws, making trail driving almost impossible. By the late 1800s, railroads were built in Texas, eliminating the need for long cattle drives.

Ranching Fact and Fiction

Although the era of open range cattle ranching was brief, the cowboy became an important figure in art, literature, music, and movies. So many stories were penned about ranching that it is sometimes difficult to separate myth from reality.

At least two Texas cowboys published accounts of ranching based on experience rather than imagination. **Andy Adams** in *The Log of a Cowboy* (1903) and **Charles Siringo** in *A Texas Cow Boy, or Fifteen Years on the Hurricane Deck of a Spanish Pony* (1885) told stories based on their years as working cowhands. The reality of ranching was that it was hard, unglamorous work. Cowhands worked long hours. During roundups

A Shared Past...

The cattle drives of the 1870s and 1880s were only one of several changes that dramatically altered America's diet. Breakfast cereals became common. Improvements in canning kept many foods from spoiling. Refrigerated rail cars carried fruits and vegetables to all parts of the country. Gustavus Swift had the idea of shipping beef by refrigerated rail cars.

and trail drives, they often spent 18 hours a day in the saddle. Yet when winter came, many found themselves unemployed. They survived by doing odd jobs in the nearest towns or by shooting wolves for bounty. (Wolves were killed because they attacked cattle.)

The typical cowboy was young and single—and poor. A fortunate few made money by performing in rodeos, but these were the lucky exceptions. Nearly one-sixth of all cowhands of this period were Mexican or Mexican American. Others were African American.

✓**Reading Check** Analyzing What factors led to the end of cattle drives after 1885?

SECTION 1 ASSESSMENT

Checking for Understanding

1. **Using Key Terms** Explain the difference between a drover and a wrangler. Use the terms drive and stockyard in your explanation.
2. **Reviewing Facts** Why was South Texas considered ideal cattle country?

Reviewing Themes

3. **Economic Factors** What changes made cattle ranching profitable after the Civil War?

Organizing to Learn

4. **Sequencing** Create a time line like the one shown, and place the following events in correct order:

————|————|————|————|————

a. Cattle raised on ranches.
b. Farmers along cattle trails feared Texas Fever.
c. Spanish explorers brought cattle to Texas.
d. Early ranchers used the open range.

Critical Thinking

5. **Decision Making** Why would a Missouri farmer decide to fence his crops?

TAKS PRACTICE

Identifying Two primary sources relating to life as a cowhand are mentioned. Many movies have been made about life on the open range. Is a movie a primary or secondary source? Do movies give accurate information?

Making Generalizations

Why Learn This Skill?

When studying history, it is important to learn how to make generalizations, or general statements, from many facts and details. Making generalizations lets you use your knowledge of specific situations to understand larger concepts.

Learning the Skill

To make generalizations, follow these steps:

• Identify the subject matter.
• Gather facts and examples related to this subject.
• Identify similarities or patterns and form general ideas.
• Test your generalizations against other facts and examples.

Practicing the Skill

Read the passage below and the generalizations about the life led by a cowhand. Then answer the questions that follow.

"On one occasion we gathered eleven hundred cattle . . . [I]t fell my lot to be placed between the [strays] and the herd, which is a very hard place. One old wild cow . . . tried to run over me and get aback into the herd . . . I ran that old heifer for thirty minutes. All at once she made a break . . . I slapped my spurs into Grand Pap and wheeled around to head her off when my saddle turned under his belly and I fell . . . Jack and the boys came running to me . . . They fixed my saddle and I went on duty again . . .

"At sundown the cook prepared supper, which consisted of chili beans . . . fried calf meat, . . . biscuit bread, . . . black coffee, stewed dried apples, and molasses."

On a cattle drive

—Mrs. Jack Miles,
Texas Cowboys: Memories of the Early Days

Generalizations About Cowboy Life:

• Cowboys were excellent riders.
• Cowboys looked after the cattle no matter what.
• Cowboys ate very little fresh fruit, vegetables, or dairy products.
• Cowboys cooked their own meals.

1 Which of the generalizations above are supported by the details in this passage?

2 Write one or two statements that support each generalization mentioned in Question 1.

3 Which of the generalizations are not supported by the passage? Explain.

TAKS PRACTICE

Making Generalizations   Think about each member of your family. In what ways are they the same? Think about some positive qualities they all share. What are some generalizations you can make about them?

Glencoe's **Skillbuilder Interactive Workbook,** Level 1, provides instruction and practice in key social studies skills.

SECTION 2

The Days of the Big Ranches

Guide to Reading

Main Idea
Large cattle ranches spread throughout West Texas and the Panhandle, but open-range ranches declined as ranchers fenced their lands.

Key Terms
mustang
felony

Reading Strategy
Problem Solving As you read this section, complete a chart like the one below, showing the invention that solved the problem.

Problem	Solution
Cattle herds trampled crops	
Fences blocked access to water	

Read to Learn
- about the big ranches.
- about the use of barbed wire.
- about Europeans in ranching.

Section Theme
Continuity and Change Huge ranches formed, new types of ranching spread, and farming developed. Mexican Americans contributed to these changes.

Preview of Events

◆1876 — Charles Goodnight and John Adair establish JA Ranch

◆1883 — Most open ranges are fenced in

Mustangs

A

Texas Story

A cowhand had to have a good horse. Wild horses called "mustangs," from the Spanish *mesteño*, roamed South Texas. According to cowhand Tom Mills, mustangs were so wild that a cowhand could rarely get close enough to lasso one. "There used to be lots of wild hosses in that country below Pearsall. It was open country down there and there was thousands of mustangs runnin' over that sand . . . About the most vicious hoss I ever rode tried to eat me up . . . This horse would reach around and bite my legs. I sure had to watch 'im."

Big Ranches Bring Big Profits

Huge ranches sprawled throughout South Texas and on the rangelands to the north. When Richard King died in 1885, his ranch included 614,000 acres of land and tens of thousands of cattle, horses, mules, and sheep.

King's former partner, Mifflin Kenedy, had established another ranch of several hundred thousand acres. **Henrietta King** and King's son-in-law, **Robert Kleberg**, expanded the King Ranch to more than 1 million acres and 100,000 head of livestock by 1925.

After the buffalo were wiped out and Native Americans were removed from the Great Plains, West Texas and the Panhandle became open to ranchers. In 1876 Charles Goodnight and an Irishman named **John Adair** established the JA Ranch in Palo Duro Canyon. A former Texas Ranger, scout, and military guide, Goodnight also proved to be a skilled rancher. The partners expanded their holdings to 1 million acres (405,000 hectares) and more than 100,000 cattle. Goodnight experimented with crossbreeding his cattle and raised some of the best beef cattle in the United States. **Molly Goodnight** rescued and raised baby buffalo left to die by commercial hunters, ultimately producing the Goodnight buffalo herd.

Also in 1876, **Thomas Bugbee** began herding cattle on the Canadian River in the Panhandle. He later moved south and built his **Shoe Bar Ranch** into a spread of 450,000 acres (183,000 hectares). Two years later, Bugbee founded one of the most famous of the large ranches, the **Matador,** in the rugged country to the east of the High Plains in present-day Motley County.

The high profits of ranching attracted the attention of outside investors. The Matador Ranch was bought by the **Matador Land and Cattle Company** of Dundee, Scotland. The **XIT,** the largest ranch of the period, was financed in part by British investors. The state of Texas had granted the 3,000,000-acre (1,215,000-hectare) ranch to a Chicago company originally. In return, the company promised to build a new state capitol in Austin. To finance the building of the capitol, and to develop the ranch, the company turned to British investors.

✓ **Reading Check** **Drawing Conclusions** In what way did ranching play a part in building the state capitol in Austin?

Mustangers Catch Wild Horses

Horses also were valuable products on the ranching frontier. Catching and training mustangs, the hardy wild horses of the western plains, was the occupation of the mustangers—many of whom were Mexican American. The *mesteños,* or mustangs, were wild descendants of horses brought by the Spaniards. Before the Civil War, mustangers captured large numbers of wild horses, tamed them, and sold them to the U.S. Army or to ranchers. J. Frank Dobie wrote about an African American mustanger by the name of Bob Lemmons:

❝The most original mustanger I ever met or heard of was an ex-slave named Bob Lemmons . . . He always mustanged alone . . . After locating a bunch, he made no effort to keep up with it. He followed tracks . . . After he began following a herd of mustangs, he changed neither horse nor clothing until he led the herd into a pen. This was to keep the mustangs from getting a "foreign" scent . . . Within a week the herd he was after would usually allow him to direct their course.❞

Picturing **History**

Almost one-sixth of the cowhands during this time were African American or Mexican American. How does this information relate to Hollywood movie portrayals of cowhands?

Selling wild mustangs was an important part of the livestock industry of West Texas until the 1870s. After that, the expansion of cattle ranching significantly reduced the number of mustangs.

The Sheep Industry Booms

Sheep raising became an important part of the ranching industry about the time that catching mustangs was no longer profitable. Sheep had been raised, mostly in South Texas, for many years. There, colonists bred heavy sheep from the East with the lighter Mexican variety. This doubled the sheep's weight and tripled the amount of wool they produced.

The real boom in the sheep industry began just before the Civil War. **George Wilkins Kendall,** a newspaper reporter, set up a 5,000-acre (2,025-hectare) ranch east of Boerne. Although he had problems with disease, drought, and Native Americans, he encouraged people to come to Texas to raise sheep. Sheep ranchers came from Northern states as well as from Europe.

After the Civil War, a growing demand for wool brought even more sheep ranchers to Texas. In the 1870s ranchers west and north of San Antonio began to acquire large herds.

Ranchers who raised sheep faced the hostility of cattle ranchers and farmers. Cattle ranchers complained that sheep cropped the grass too short, ruining the range. Farmers claimed that their crops were trampled. Ranchers and farmers began to fence in their lands to protect them.

Barbed Wire Ends the Open Range

By 1873 several inventors had perfected different kinds of barbed wire fence. Small barbs that were twisted on the wire fencing pricked but did not harm the animals who came into contact with it. Barbed wire could be made cheaply and installed easily. **J.F. Glidden** was the most successful inventor.

Sales were slow at first, but by 1880 barbed wire fences were built in several Texas counties. Barbed wire, however, was a threat to law and order for a time. Cattle and sheep raisers began fencing their land, sometimes enclosing the land of others. Some ranchers cut off the water supply to other ranchers' herds. Fence-cutting wars between farmers and ranchers soon followed. Ranchers who owned no land but depended on open country for rangeland also participated in the fence cutting.

Restoring law and order required great effort. In Coleman County, landowner **Mabel Day** led the fight against those who stripped off the wires and broke the posts of newly built fences. Even the Texas Rangers found their law-enforcement skills severely tested. They

Causes and Effects of Cattle Ranching Decline

Causes

- Large profits caused ranchers to overexpand.
- Overgrazing ruined rangelands.
- Severe drought and blizzards occurred in the mid-1880s.

Effects

- Cattle prices fell.
- Ranchers forced to sell herds at low prices went bankrupt.
- Few cattle ranches survived.

Graphic Organizer → *Skills*

Due to overproduction and weather, the huge cattle ranching industry in Texas declined rapidly in the late 1880s.

Making Inferences Why do you think some of the larger cattle ranches survived?

---

were often called on to protect the fences. In a special session, the legislature made fence cutting a serious crime, or **felony.**

By the mid-1880s most ranges in South and central Texas were fenced. Panhandle and North Texas ranges rapidly were being enclosed as well. Windmills, which pumped water from wells, helped to make fenced pastures possible. Earlier the cattle had to be driven to water holes.

Reading Check **Identifying** Who was the most successful inventor of barbed wire?

The Ranching Industry Declines

The ranching industry declined rapidly in the later 1880s. The large profits earned for several years had led ranchers to expand and produce too many cattle. Too many cattle meant that rangelands were ruined due to overgrazing. Surplus cattle also caused prices to fall.

TEXAS HISTORY *Online*

Student Web Activity Visit the texans.glencoe.com Web site and click on **Chapter 18—Student Web Activity** to learn more about barbed wire.

Even nature seemed to turn against Texas ranchers. A number of severe blizzards and long droughts caused many ranchers to sell their herds. Ranches were divided into smaller units or sold as farmland. Many ranchers went bankrupt.

Nevertheless, some large cattle ranches prospered—the King Ranch in South Texas and the Matador, Pitchfork, 6666, Spur, Spade, and Waggoner Ranches in northwest Texas.

Ranching became more dependent on scientific and modern management techniques. Hereford, Angus, Shorthorn, Brahman, and other breeds of cattle replaced the rangy longhorn. Many modern ranchers today depend on computers to assist them in their ranching operations.

Cultures Meet in the Ranch Country

People of many cultures met and mingled in the dusty ranges of West and South Texas. Mexican American *vaqueros* were found most often on the ranches of South Texas. Some large ranches, particularly on the land between the Nueces River and the Rio Grande, were held by Mexican Americans. **Hipólito García's** Randado Ranch in Jim Hogg County supported 25,000 cattle on 80,000 acres (32,500 hectares). The present-day town of Randado is situated on land that was once part of Garcia's spread. Macedonio Vela's Laguna Seca and Dionisio Guerra's Los Ojuelos holdings were two additional ranching operations of significant size owned by Mexican Americans.

Mexican Americans also did much to make sheep raising possible. Most of the shepherds, or *pastores* (pahs•TOH•rays), were Mexican Americans. Practically all of the shearers, or *tasinques* (tah•SEEN•kays), who cut the wool from sheep, were also of Mexican heritage or from Mexico. Many sheep ranches were owned by Mexican Americans.

African Americans also participated in the ranching industry. Cattle drives sometimes included African American cowhands and trail bosses. **Daniel Webster "80 John" Wallace** was an African American who began life as a slave, became a trail boss, and eventually owned his own ranch near Colorado City. **"Bones" Hooks** was a pioneer African American cowhand in the Panhandle. **Bose Ikard,** an African American, was a skilled cowhand who worked for Charles Goodnight.

People of German ancestry established prosperous ranches in the Hill Country of Texas. In addition, because of the cattle-raising tradition in their homelands and the British consumer's love of beef, English, Scottish, and Irish investors used their fortunes to establish ranches on the High Plains and nearby rangelands.

Women Ranchers

Life on the ranching frontier was not only for men. Women worked with their husbands to settle the frontier and build ranches. They faced isolation and loneliness as they performed chores in the dry, dusty environment. In addition to performing ranching duties, many women would maintain a household garden. They would preserve and store the fruits and vegetables harvested from these gardens for use throughout the year.

Margaret H. Borland

Some women were i dent ranchers. **Elizabeth Williams** was an exp enced rancher who knowledge of cattle and cattle trading was widely respected. She raised her own large herd and had her own brand. Molly Goodnigh shared life with her hu band in a dirt-floor dugout in the early days of the JA Ranch in Palo Duro Canyon. Her nearest neighbor was 75 miles (121 km) away. Henrietta King carried on the development of the King Ranch after her husband's death. Margaret Heferman Borland ran her own ranch and owned over 10,000 head of cattle.

Some women actually rode the cattle trails. Experienced ranchers such as Amanda Burks and Mary Taylor Bunton drove their own cattle along trails to Kansas.

Mexican American women had their own long history of ranching. **Doña María del Carmen Calvillo** was one of Texas's earliest ranchers. Men and women of many cultures contributed to the ranching heritage of Texas and are remembered as pioneers who opened the West.

✓ **Reading Check** **Summarizing** How did the ranches contribute to the cultural diversity of Texas?

SECTION 2 ASSESSMENT

Checking for Understanding
1. **Using Key Terms** The Texas Rangers had trouble protecting fences. Use the term felony in a sentence to explain the problem.
2. **Reviewing Facts** List two reasons for the decline in cattle prices.

Reviewing Themes
3. **Continuity and Change** How did Mexican Americans contribute to cattle and sheep ranching?

Organizing to Learn
4. **Charting Information** Create a chart like the one shown and fill in the missing information.

Ranch Owners	Ranch Name	Acreage
Henrietta King, Robert Kleberg		1 million
	JA	
Thomas Bugbee		450,000
Hipólito García		

Critical Thinking
5. **Drawing Conclusions** How did the invention of barbed wire affect the development of Texas?

TAKS PRACTICE

Summarizing Reread the passage on page 420 about the method Bob Lemmons used to catch mustangs. Tell about his method in your own words.

Farming After the Civil War

Guide to Reading

Main Idea
The Texas farming industry expanded after the Civil War.

Key Terms
dry farming
tenant farmer
sharecropper

Reading Strategy
Identifying Key Factors As you read, decide how the following factors influenced the development of farming in Texas.

Factor	Effect on Farming
Cheaper land	
Dry farming	
Drought	
Railroad system	

Read to Learn
• why dry farming was significant.
• why cotton was "king."
• what hardships farmers faced.
• how two new systems of farming replaced slavery.

Section Theme
Science and Technology The railroads made an important impact on farming.

Preview of Events

♦1882	♦1900
Texas and Pacific Railroad lays tracks in west central Texas	Cotton continues to be the major crop in Texas

A cattle stampede

A
Texas Story

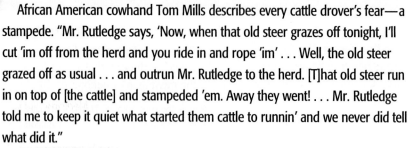

African American cowhand Tom Mills describes every cattle drover's fear—a stampede. "Mr. Rutledge says, 'Now, when that old steer grazes off tonight, I'll cut 'im off from the herd and you ride in and rope 'im' . . . Well, the old steer grazed off as usual . . . and outrun Mr. Rutledge to the herd. [T]hat old steer run in on top of [the cattle] and stampeded 'em. Away they went! . . . Mr. Rutledge told me to keep it quiet what started them cattle to runnin' and we never did tell what did it."

Farming on the Rise

After the Civil War ended, thousands of settlers pushed west in search of more and cheaper land. Farmers who moved to the drier parts of West Texas discovered that with the use of new techniques, they could produce profitable crops. Windmills pumped water from underground sources up to the surface for livestock and household use. A method of farming known as **dry farming** spread throughout West Texas and the Panhandle region. Dry farming used a manner of plowing that left loose soil on top of the ground. The layers of loose soil kept water in the ground by slowing down the rate of evaporation.

Railroads also quickened settlement by encouraging farmers to settle along their routes. Within a year after the Texas and Pacific Railroad laid its tracks through west central Texas in 1881, the towns of Abilene, Sweetwater, Colorado City, and Big Spring were encouraging farmers to settle on nearby lands. Amarillo, Quanah, Childress, and Memphis—because of the Fort Worth and Denver Railroad—also became farming centers before 1890.

Texans Rely on King Cotton

The most important crop grown in Texas was cotton. The typical Texan in the late 1800s was not a rancher but a cotton farmer. In most years the value of the cotton crop in Texas was larger than the combined value of all other crops grown. In the year 1900 alone, the revenue from the cotton crop surpassed the value of cattle and horses for the previous 25 years!

The cultivation of cotton had spread rapidly throughout the state. In South Texas, **Proceso Martínez** introduced cotton to the Rio Grande Valley. Martínez, a leader in business and agriculture, also brought the first modern plows and corn planters to the Valley.

As they did in the ranching industry, railroads played an important role in cotton farming. As tracks were built westward, farmers were provided with a cheap and efficient means

Picturing History

Cotton bales are piled high on rail cars in this Houston train station before heading to market. **What does this photograph suggest about cotton production in Texas around 1900?**

In this 1907 photograph, a supervisor looks on as African Americans pick cotton near Dallas. What economic and social conditions does this photograph reveal?

of getting their cotton to market. Better access to markets offered the chance of higher profits.

Other crops were valuable to the economy of Texas, too. Before the end of the century, Texas led the entire nation in honey production. Farmers also grew sugarcane and rice along the Gulf Coast. Elsewhere, they planted wheat, corn, and oats.

Not all farms flourished, however. Many farming families who came to Texas after the Civil War faced disappointment and failure. Many farmers did not succeed because they were unfamiliar with the land of Texas, did not know how to use the land properly, or did not know what crops were best suited for the land. Hardships included swarms of grasshoppers and droughts. A great drought in the late 1800s ruined many planters' hopes. Even a good harvest did not always mean a profit for the farmers. Cotton acreage expanded in India and Egypt, thus increasing the world supply of cotton. If there was a surplus of a crop, it could result in lower prices. Although many farmers failed, they still paved the way for others who came later and who learned from and profited by their experiences.

Reading Check **Examining** Why did many farmers fail?

The Tenant System Replaces Slavery

A new system of farm labor developed after the end of the Civil War, greatly affecting the lives of many Texans. Before the war, enslaved African Americans in East Texas produced a large part of the cash crops. After the war, many smaller farms replaced the vast plantations. Either these small farms were sold to new owners, or they were rented to **tenant farmers.** In return for a tenant's use of land, the landowner usually received a part of the crop. Landowners who provided the farming tools, seeds, and supplies would receive an even larger portion of the crop. Tenant farmers who did not provide their own tools and supplies were called **sharecroppers.** Sharecroppers received a share (usually one-half) of the value of the crop.

The tenant system was at its root an economic response to the lack of capital after the Civil War. Swapping labor for a commodity was in one sense a form of barter in an economy with too little money. The tenant system also had profound social as well as economic effects. Under slavery, men and women had often been forced to work in large gangs. Sharecropping or tenant farming meant an end to the evils of forced gang labor. On the other hand, cotton required huge

Sharecropping and Tenant Farming Compared				
	Landowner Provides	**Laborer Provides**	**Landowner Gets**	**Laborer Gets**
Sharecropper	Land, tools, seed, work animals, credit for food and other supplies	Labor	1/2 of proceeds from sale of crop	1/2 of proceeds from sale of crop
Tenant Farmer	Land	Labor, tools, seeds, work animals	1/4 of cotton, 1/3 of grain	3/4 of cotton, 2/3 of grain

Based on Neil Foley, *White Scourge: Mexicans, Blacks, and Poor Whites in Texas Cotton Culture,* U of California Press, 1997.

amounts of labor. Most tenant and sharecropper children were put to work in the fields at a very young age. A teenager was expected to do the same amount of work as an adult. Cotton farmers talked about working "From Can See to Can't." They were not exaggerating.

Many tenant farmers were former slaves who once had worked on the plantations. Although some African American farmers owned their own land, most were sharecroppers.

Life for tenant farmers, especially for sharecroppers, was difficult. Droughts, financial panics, overproduction of crops, problems with pests, and high charges by landlords often left tenants with no money. As a result, it was difficult to succeed financially. The system of sharecropping often put poor farmers into debt from which they were unable to escape. Nevertheless, the tenant system expanded during these years. In 1870 about one-third of all farmers in Texas were tenant farmers.

Whether landowner, tenant farmer, or sharecropper, these tillers of the soil brought something to the west that the ranchers could not bring: large numbers of people. Ranching simply did not require as many people as farming did. As a result, the arrival of more farmers resulted in the development of many small towns. These would grow into communities with schools, churches, roads, and businesses.

✓**Reading Check** **Explaining** Why were many sharecroppers not financially successful?

SECTION 3 ASSESSMENT

Checking for Understanding

1. **Using Key Terms** Using the terms tenant farmer and sharecropper, tell how these labor systems allowed non-landowners to make a living.
2. **Reviewing Facts** Identify the seven major cash crops produced in Texas at this time.

Reviewing Themes

3. **Science and Technology** How did the arrival of railroads change farming in Texas?

Organizing to Learn

4. **Understanding Cause and Effect** The end of slavery changed the lives of those involved in farming. Create a web like the one shown and list how former slaves farmed and the difficulties that they faced.

```
        Farming
      After Slavery
      /          \
  Types         Difficulties
of Farming
```

Critical Thinking

5. **Identifying Options** Large plantations were too vast for one family to manage by themselves. With slaves set free, what options did the plantation owner have to find necessary laborers?

Chapter Summary

Ranching and Farming

1800
- Spanish missions in Texas contain over 25,000 head of cattle.
- ★ Ranching flourishes in South Texas through the early 1800s.

1853
- ★ Richard King buys the Santa Gertrudis land grant.

1866
- ★ Cattle drives start on the Sedalia Trail. Other trails soon develop.

1870
- One-third of all farmers in Texas are tenant farmers.
- ★ More sheep ranches are established because of growing demand for wool.

1876
- Charles Goodnight and John Adair establish JA Ranch.

1880
- Many Texas ranchers use barbed wire to fence their property. Fence-cutting wars follow until the state legislature makes fence-cutting a felony.

1881
- ★ Texas and Pacific Railroad lays track through west central Texas.

1885
- Cattle driving drops sharply.
- A period of severe blizzards and droughts begins in the Great Plains and Texas.

1900
- Cotton continues to be the most important crop in Texas.

Reviewing Key Terms

Use each of the following terms in separate newspaper headlines as they might have been written in the late 1800s.

1. felony
2. open range
3. drive
4. wrangler
5. drover
6. mustang
7. *ranchero*

Reviewing Key Facts

8. How did Spanish cattle ranching first begin in Texas?
9. Explain why there was trouble between the drovers and the farmers along the Sedalia Trail.
10. Trail drives were so successful that the supply of cattle exceeded the demand. How did this change the price of cattle?
11. What did mustangers do with the horses they captured?
12. Why did sheep ranching increase after the Civil War?
13. Were most African American farmers sharecroppers or tenant farmers? Why?

Critical Thinking

14. **Resolving Conflicts** Fencing of land caused conflicts among Texans. How were these conflicts resolved?
15. **Science and Technology** How did windmills contribute to ranching and farming?
16. **Economics** Make a chart like the one below explaining how each factor affected cotton farming.

Factor	Effect on Cotton Farming
Overproduction of crop	
Railroads	

17. **Geography and Environment** Why do you think drovers followed the same trails year after year?
18. **Supply and Demand** The price of cattle in the North and East was much higher than in the Southwest. How did this affect cattle ranching in Texas?
19. **Drawing Conclusions** What factors contributed to the end of trail driving?

Geography and History Activity

Refer to the Texas Cattle Trails map on page 415 to answer the following questions:

20. Which of the large cattle ranches was located the farthest south?

21. Which ranch was located nearest to a railroad?

22. The Chisholm Trail split north of the Red River, then both trails ended at towns on the railroad line. Name the towns.

Cooperative Learning Activity

23. Culture and Traditions Songs, poems, and tall tales (stories with unlikely happenings) were made up to pass the time on trail drives. With a classmate, create one of these and share it with the class. Look in the chapter or other books to get information about the trail you are following. Include details in your piece. You may accompany your creation with music, movement, and/or visuals.

Portfolio/TAKS Writing Activity

24. Comparing and Contrasting Do you think farmers or ranchers were more important to the development of Texas? Support your answer with several reasons. Use standard grammar, spelling, sentence structure, and punctuation. Save this piece for your portfolio.

Building Technology Skills

25. Using the Internet or Library for Research Working with one other student, research one of the large cattle ranches or ranchers mentioned in this chapter. Make a list of the types of information you find. Organize this into outline form, as if you were planning a report. Now write down a minimum of three interesting facts you discovered. As you work, keep a record of bibliographic information and/or URLs.

Practicing Skills

26. Making Generalizations Making generalizations allows you to use specific details and examples to form a broader picture of situations and events. Read the excerpt below about the range wars, then answer the questions that follow:

> *The cattlemen who were determined to improve the quality of their herds soon strung miles of barbed wire. In fact, they often fenced not only land that they owned or leased, but also*

Self-Check Quiz
Visit the texans.glencoe.com Web site and click on **Chapter 18—Self-Check Quizzes** to prepare for the chapter test.

> *public land that was supposed to be open to all. Some cattle raisers even fenced off small farms and ranches belonging to others. In some places, fences blocked public roads.*
>
> *Farmers fenced their land to keep the cattle out of their crops and away from precious water sources. Ranchers were infuriated to find fences blocking their access to pasturage and water for their animals.*

—From the *Texas Almanac*

a. What generalization can you make about why ranchers and farmers fenced off land?

b. What generalization can you make about the role of water in the range wars?

TAKS PRACTICE

Use the quote to answer the following question.

Journal of Amanda Burks

> "We camped a long time in Fort Worth, waiting for the Trinity River to fall low enough to cross our cattle. I counted 15 herds waiting to cross."

Which of the following was probably true about Amanda Burks?

F She drove cattle to market.

G She was impatient and eager to cross the river.

H She did not like camping.

J She was concerned about cattle prices.

Test-Taking Tip:

The correct answer to this question is not directly stated in the quote, but clues in the quote will help you find it. Reread the quote after you read each answer choice. Ask yourself if the answer choice can be true based on the clues in the quote. If there are no clues in the quote that support the answer choice, eliminate that answer choice.

CHAPTER 19

Politics & Progress

Why It Matters

The construction of railroads through West Texas made settlement by farmers and ranchers possible. The farmers and ranchers became dependent upon railroads for both the goods they bought and the products they sold. That dependence on railroads eventually caused economic problems and discontent.

The Impact Today

Many of the important cities and towns of West Texas were settled along the railroad lines during the late 1800s. The coming of the railroads gave Texas a great economic boost.

1876
★ *Texas constitution ratified*

Texas

United States *1870*   *1880*

World

1873
• *Susan B. Anthony convicted of voting in 1872 election*

1875
• *Third Republic of France formed*

1876
• *Alexander Graham Bell invented the telephone*

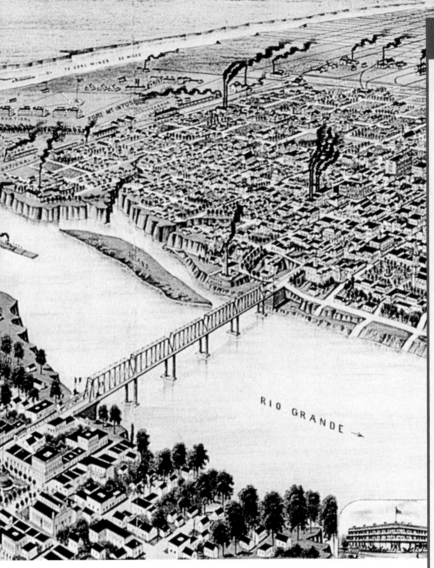

This color lithograph of Laredo (1892) reflects the growth and development that occurred in many Texas towns during this period.

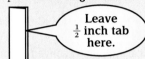

1888
★ New Capitol dedicated in Austin

1891
★ Texas Railroad Commission established

1893
★ Texas Equal Rights Association established

1890

1900

1887
• U.S. Congress created Interstate Commerce Commission

1890
• U.S. Congress passed Sherman Antitrust Act

1900
• Sigmund Freud wrote The Interpretation of Dreams

1889
• Alexander Gustave Eiffel designed the Eiffel Tower

TEXAS HISTORY Online

Chapter Overview
Visit the texans.glencoe.com Web site and click on **Chapter 19—Chapter Overviews** to preview chapter information.

Reconstruction Ends

Guide to Reading

Main Idea
A new constitution changed the political and social scene of Texas in the late 1800s.

Key Terms
suffrage
pension
vigilante

Reading Strategy
Organizing Information Complete a web like the one shown here.

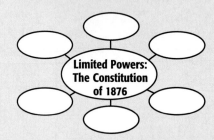

Limited Powers: The Constitution of 1876

Read to Learn
• why a new constitution was written.
• about major achievements of the Texas state government in the late 1800s.

Section Theme
Government and Democracy The Constitution of 1876 limited the powers of the Texas state government.

Preview of Events

1876	1878	1888	1893
Constitution of Texas ratified	Oran Roberts is elected governor	New capitol dedicated in Austin	Texas Equal Rights Association formed for women's suffrage

Daily journal

A Texas Story

As a child, Ethel Anna Pearce wrote in her journal of the hardships of workers' families during the westward construction of the railroads. "At sunup the wind began to blow and soon a notorious sand storm was raging. The wind and sand rocked and beat the little shack all day. The living room withstood the storm, but the roof began to rip away. [Mother] overturned an empty water barrel, climbed upon it, and just as she thought it was nailed secure, a harder gust of wind ripped away all the roof. Sand poured into the house."

A New Era Brings New Concerns

The late 1800s were a time of growth and expansion in Texas. Ambitious people spread a network of railroads throughout the state. Agriculture boomed. Existing industries expanded and new ones began.

The growing population and economy meant added wealth for the state and new problems and public concerns. Many political and social issues that remained from the Reconstruction Era also had to be addressed.

Democrats Rewrite the Constitution

In 1874 Democrats regained the governorship in Texas. One of the party's first goals was to write a new constitution. For this purpose, 90 delegates met in Austin in 1875. Many of the delegates objected to the Constitution of 1869 because it was written by Radical Republicans. Most of the delegates believed the old constitution gave too much power to a few state officials. Seventy-five of the delegates were Democrats. Six of the 15 Republican delegates were African Americans. None of the delegates had helped write the Constitution of 1869.

The new **Constitution of 1876** created a government with limited powers. The powers of the governor were reduced, the legislature was authorized to meet only once every two years, and the length of the legislators' terms were set. The Constitution also lowered the salaries of state employees, promised low taxes, and reduced the amount of money to be spent on education. The Fifteenth Amendment to the U.S. Constitution guaranteed the right of men to vote, but convention delegates ignored requests to grant **suffrage** (the right to vote) to women. The Constitution of 1876 defined voting eligibility, and those who were denied the vote included "idiots, lunatics, paupers, and felons." Women were not even mentioned.

The Constitution was ratified in 1876 by a large majority of voters. It reflected the concerns of the times and suited people's needs fairly well. As times and needs changed, however, the document had to be amended many times. The Constitution of 1876 is still the constitution of Texas, but it is long and complicated, with almost 400 amendments.

✓ **Reading Check** **Explaining** Why was the Constitution of 1869 replaced with a new constitution?

Picturing **History**

The poster at right shows the delegates to the 1875 Constitutional Convention. What characteristic do all the delegates share?

Democrats Control State Politics

Most leaders elected to public office after the end of Reconstruction were Democrats. These officials generally were cautious and conservative. To reduce public spending and lower taxes, they cut public services, such as education and hospitals for the mentally ill. They also passed laws restricting the rights of African Americans living in Texas.

Some African Americans turned to federal courts for protection. For instance, when Mary Miller was forcibly ejected from her seat in the "white ladies' circle" of the Galveston Tremont Opera House, she sued for damages in federal court. Mary Miller won her case when the opera owner was found guilty of depriving her of her civil rights. When the judge later dismissed the $500 fine, an outraged black community rallied in protest.

Norris Wright Cuney

The Republican Party continued to exist and run candidates in state and local elections, but the party had little power. Between 1868 and 1898, some 60 African Americans served in the state legislature or participated in important political conventions. African American state senators **George Ruby** and **Matt Gaines,** who served during the administration of Governor Edmund Davis, played leading roles in advocating an unsegregated public school system. (Despite their best efforts, the public schools were segregated until the 1950s.)

Many African Americans remained loyal to the Texas Republican Party. **Norris Wright Cuney** of Galveston was the most influential African American of his day. Cuney was a leading Republican, a party national committeeman, and the collector of customs for the Port of Galveston—the most important federal position in Texas. Another African American—**William "Gooseneck Bill" McDonald** of Fort Worth—became a party leader near the end of the 1800s. In counties where the African American population was large, African American men sometimes were elected to local office.

Frequently, however, efforts were made to prevent African Americans from voting. They often were threatened, denied jobs, or harmed if they tried to take part in politics or vote.

Mexican Americans were active in politics during this period and also served in the legislature. **Santos Benavides** represented Laredo, and **Gregorio N. García** was elected from El Paso. Many officeholders in South Texas were Mexican Americans.

Reading Check **Drawing Conclusions** Which party did many African Americans support and why?

Spending Cuts Reduce State Debt

The public finances of Texas were in serious trouble at the end of Reconstruction. The $3 million public debt was rising. Governor Richard Coke insisted on cutting government expenses. **Richard Hubbard,** who succeeded Coke, also tried to economize, but the public debt increased to about $5.5 million by the spring of 1879.

The budget was finally balanced as the economy improved during the administration of **Governor Oran M. Roberts,** who took office in 1879. Roberts insisted that the legislature cut veterans' pensions, or wages paid after military service, and funds for schools. He left the finances of Texas in good condition.

Lawmen Keep Order

Lawlessness was a major problem in Texas after the Civil War. Many unemployed people flocked to less settled areas of the state. Some turned to robbing trains, stagecoaches, and banks. Common but serious crimes included horse theft and cattle rustling. Bitter feuds raged in Mason, Lampasas, and Kimble Counties.

Restoring law and order was a major accomplishment for the state government and other groups during these years. Various communities

Picturing **History**

When the Texas Capitol was rebuilt (work began in 1882), the dome was deliberately made seven feet taller than the U.S. Capitol in Washington, D.C. The Texas Capitol is the largest of all the state capitols. Why was it necessary to build a new Texas Capitol in 1882?

Austin ★

formed **vigilante** committees. These volunteers punished suspected criminals quickly, but punishment was harsh and not legal. Courageous sheriffs and other local officers worked hard to enforce laws.

The **Texas Rangers,** reorganized by Governor Coke, joined local officers in the fight against crime. The Rangers pursued train bandits, bank robbers, and cattle thieves. They captured or killed outlaws like Sam Bass. The Rangers also dealt with feuding families and were active in stopping the fence-cutting wars of the 1880s.

Texas Needs a Capitol

The Constitution of 1876 included a plan for a new capitol. The need for another building became essential after the old Capitol and many valuable state records burned on November 9, 1881. A Chicago company was hired to handle the construction. For payment, the company received 3 million acres (1.2 million hectares) of land, which became the famous XIT Ranch.

Work began in 1882, and the new Capitol was officially dedicated in 1888. Modeled after the U.S. Capitol, the building was constructed of pink granite from Marble Falls. Scottish stonecutters shaped the granite blocks, each weighing as much as 16,000 pounds (7,258 kg).

Women Fight for Their Rights

By 1900, women in Texas accounted for about half the population but did not enjoy the same legal rights as men. Women's rights to own property or conduct business were limited.

It took Texas women 50 years of hard work and three different organizations to finally win suffrage. The fight began after the Civil War during the Constitutional Convention of 1868–69 and ended when women won the right to vote in Democratic Party primaries in 1918 and, later, in general elections in 1920.

In 1888 the Woman's Christian Temperance Union was the first Texas group to publicly endorse woman suffrage. It believed that if women could vote, they would help get a law passed prohibiting the sale of alcohol. In 1893, Rebecca Henry Hayes founded the **Texas Equal Rights Association** in Dallas. The 48 charter members, including 9 men, paid dues of 50 cents a year. The association grew rapidly statewide, and soon newspapers were covering its activities.

The Texas Federation of Women's Clubs, the Texas Farmers' Alliance, and the Texas Federation of Labor also supported suffrage efforts. Still, women were not immediately successful. Opponents of suffrage believed that if women voted, they would lose their femininity. "Politics are too bad for a lady to mix in," wrote one legislator. The women of Texas would not gain the right to vote until after World War I.

Women at Work

Texas women have always worked, but they have not always been paid for it. Around 1900, most continued to work in their homes as wives, mothers, and homemakers—and about half worked on family farms or ranches. But many began entering the paid labor force for the first time as farm workers, laundresses, and domestics. Hope Thompson, a former slave who became a laundress, borrowed $50 from a customer, invested it in a downtown Dallas property, then sold the property in the late 1880s for $25,000.

Teaching was one of the most accepted professions open to women at this time. Some women even founded schools. Lucy Ann Kidd-Key was principal of the North Texas Female College (later Kidd-Key College) in Sherman in 1888. In 1892, Mattie B. White established a private

Suffragist

school for African American girls in Austin. Leonor Villegas de Magnon and other Mexican American women founded *escuelitas*, or little schools, offering bilingual education and excellent academic instruction. A few women were physicians. One of these was Dr. Sofie Herzog of Vienna, Austria, mother of 14 children, who became the chief surgeon for the St. Louis, Brownsville, and Mexico Railroad in South Texas. Her specialty was digging bullets out of gunshot wounds. She also enjoyed collecting snakes.

Other women worked as journalists, artists, and merchants. Several were locomotive engineers. Women also broke ground as secretaries, telephone operators, and department store clerks. In 1872, Martha Bickler became the state government's first female worker—a clerk in the General Land Office.

Women made important contributions in the arts as well. **Elisabet Ney,** for example, was a noted European sculptor who immigrated to Texas in 1872. After living for a time near Hempstead, she established a studio in Austin. A courageous, independent artist, Ney won wide acclaim for her statues of Stephen F. Austin and Sam Houston, which were erected on the Capitol grounds. Other works by Ney are displayed in Europe, in the Art Institute of Chicago, and in the National Museum of American Art in Washington, D.C. Each year many people visit the Austin home of Elisabet Ney, which is now a museum.

✓**Reading Check** Analyzing Why were women denied the right to vote for so long?

SECTION 1 ASSESSMENT

Checking for Understanding

1. **Using Key Terms** Define suffrage, pension, and vigilante.
2. **Reviewing Facts** What constitution does Texas use today? Approximately how many amendments does it have?

Reviewing Themes

3. **Government and Democracy** How did public officials reduce public spending and lower taxes?

Organizing to Learn

4. **Creating Charts** Create a chart like the one below. Fill in the governor who was in office at the time of each budget-related event.

Event	Governor
Public debt rose to $3 million	
Public debt rose to $5.5 million	
Pensions were cut	

Critical Thinking

5. **Contrasting** How were vigilante committees different from sheriffs and local officers?

TAKS PRACTICE

Determining Supporting Details
Read the following sentence from the text: "Lawlessness was a major problem in Texas after the Civil War." Find at least three details that support this statement.

Transportation and Industry

Guide to Reading

Main Idea
Railroads, other transportation, and industry boomed in the late 1800s. Railroads impacted the growth of towns and industries.

Key Term
refinery

Reading Strategy
Organizing Information Complete a chart listing the industries that began in the counties listed.

Counties	Industry
Palo Pinto	
Rusk	
Brown	

Read to Learn
• how the railroad boom occurred.
• what other forms of transportation developed in Texas.
• what major industries contributed to the growth of Texas's economy.

Section Theme
Economic Factors Railroads moved people and goods quickly and efficiently.

Preview of Events

◆1871	◆1876		◆1900
First passenger train reaches Austin	Land Grant Law is passed		Lumber is most important industry

A Texas Story

Stagecoach bringing mail

Runnels County needed a courthouse but couldn't afford to build one. Ethel Anna Pearce's father rented rooms in his house to the county. In her diary, Ethel Anna wrote, "The court rented our front room for a court room . . . The next room was used for the Post Office and restaurant, and the family lived in the back room . . . The mail was kept in a tool chest." The rent money helped the family meet expenses.

Texans Demand Railroad Service

Before 1900 most families traveled by wagons and buggies. A 20-mile (32-km) trip into town took most of a day and usually required an overnight stay. "Going to town" for many isolated families might happen only once or twice a year.

The poor transportation system slowed the development of Texas. Farmers and merchants in many areas of the state could not market their products profitably. For example, the freight charges on cotton grown in West Texas and shipped by wagon to Galveston amounted to more than one-half the value of the crop.

Railroads could solve these problems with the promise to move people and goods quickly and cheaply. People believed that railroads would help farms, ranches, and businesses to prosper.

A Network of Steel Connects Texas

Before the Civil War, 11 railroad companies had constructed some 400 miles (644 km) of track in Texas. The war halted construction, and little was accomplished during the Reconstruction Era.

Railroad companies made rapid progress after 1870. In 1872 the first railroad connections were made with other states. Many towns paid railroad companies to build lines through their communities. To encourage the building of railroads, the state provided land grants to railroad companies. The **Land Grant Law of 1876** authorized 16 sections of land to be granted to a railroad company for every mile of track that it laid. During rail line construction, more than 32 million acres (13 million hectares) of land were given to 41 railroad companies. The railroad companies re-sold the land to ranchers and farmers. In this way, the railroad companies could make money before the railroad was ready for use. Companies built rails from the Gulf Coast northward across the state, while other lines entered Texas from the east. Three major railroads sprawled across West Texas in the 1880s.

By 1900 a network of railroads totaling some 10,000 miles (16,000 km) spread over the state. Journeys that once required days or weeks now lasted only hours. Settlers in West Texas often built their towns near the railroad lines. Cities where several railroads met became busy centers of commerce. Houston, Dallas, Fort Worth, and other cities developed rapidly because they were railroad centers. Communities such as Tascosa and Estacado, bypassed by the railroad lines, became ghost towns.

TEXAS HISTORY Online

Student Web Activity
Visit the texans.glencoe.com Web site and click on **Chapter 19—Student Web Activity** to learn more about railroads and land grants.

Picturing **History**

The coming of the railroads in the late 1800s gave Texas a great economic boost. This busy railway depot was located in Austin. What types of transportation were used in Texas before the railroads?

Austin

Major Railroads in Texas, c. 1900

NATIONAL GEOGRAPHIC

TAKS PRACTICE

After the 1870s, railroads began to crisscross Texas.
Identifying Information Name the major east-west railroads identified on the map.

Legend:
- Fort Worth and Denver City
- Gulf, Colorado, and Santa Fe
- Houston and Texas Central
- International and Great Northern
- Missouri-Kansas-Texas
- Southern Pacific
- St. Louis Southwestern
- Texas and Pacific

0 mi. 200
0 km 200
Albers Conic Equal-Area projection

When a railroad finally reached a town, it was cause for a great celebration. The first passenger trains reached Austin on December 28, 1871. The local newspaper reported:

❝On the morning of [December] 28th a telegram was received from Houston stating, that two . . . passenger trains had left that place and would arrive at Austin about 4. As the hour approached the whole city seemed [to be winding] their way to the station.

Four o'clock came, but with the hour was received the disheartening news by telegram from McDade, that the trains had just reached that point, and . . . the guests would not arrive in Austin until after dark . . . [It] was decided that the procession should [begin at once anyway] . . .

[A cannon] had been stationed on the hill near the depot, . . . in position to give a salute on the arrival of the guests. Hours passed away, and an anxious crowd waited in breathless expectation . . . [At 6:30,] a flash from the headlight down the track told that the train cars were coming, and in another instant the shrill whistle was heard, waking the darkness into renewed life. Cheer after cheer . . . arose from the assembled throng, until the trains had swept up in all their majesty, and . . . delivered their living freight of one thousand human beings.❞
—*The Democratic Statesman,* 1871

✔ Reading Check **Describing** Why did so much excitement surround the arrival of the railroads?

Transportation Improves

No road system supported by state taxes existed in the late 1800s. Each county built and maintained the roads and bridges within its own boundaries. Rainy weather turned unpaved roads into ruts and mud holes. Dust and dirt in dry weather made travel equally unpleasant.

Picturing **History**

Transportation in Dallas and other cities began to accommodate rapid growth in population and industry. What types of transportation do you see in this photograph?

Dallas

Travel did improve in some cities, however. For example, by 1887 San Antonio claimed 40 miles (64 km) of sidewalks and 8 miles (13 km) of hard-surfaced streets. In 1903 Houston had 26 miles (42 km) of pavement. Brick was probably the most common paving material, but cities experimented with other products. San Antonio even paved some streets with mesquite wood.

Streetcars appeared in the 1870s. Mules and horses pulled the first trolley cars, but electric-powered trolleys were running by the 1890s. Ten years later, an occasional automobile could be seen in Texas cities. In fact, it was the growing popularity of the automobile that ultimately led the state to improve the roads.

Telephones in Texas

Rapid communication made an important contribution to the growth of industry. In the area of cotton farming, the price of cotton was set in the cotton markets of Memphis and New Orleans. Cotton brokers traded contracts to buy and sell cotton much like investors buy and sell shares of stock today. Traders who knew the price of cotton in New Orleans before any of their competitors did could use that knowledge to a huge advantage.

The publisher of the *Galveston News*, Colonel A.H. Belo, attended the Philadelphia Centennial Exposition of 1876. While there, he saw Alexander Graham Bell's new invention—the telephone. He was determined to have one, and in 1878 Belo installed the first telephone in Texas between his home and his office. Within a year hundreds of other Galvestonians had telephones, and a centralized switchboard was necessary.

Brownsville, Palestine, Fort Worth, Waco, Denison, and Texarkana were some of the cities that had telephone service by 1882. By 1883 Galveston and Houston were linked with long distance telephone service. The equipment was crude by modern standards. Every telephone call had to be connected by employees called *operators*. The first operators were men, but in 1884 the telephone companies began hiring women. Before long all operators were women.

Industries Begin and Grow

Texas industry in 1870 was in its infancy. Less than 1 percent of the population worked in industrial jobs. Even though industries were only small shops that supplied the needs of the local communities, the shops made many products. Gristmills that ground corn and wheat made up the largest industry in the state. Other Texas products included lumber, buggies, wagons, plows, boots, harnesses, saddles, textiles, bricks, furniture, fishnets, glue, and soap.

New industries appeared in Texas following the Civil War. In 1868 the meat-packing industry began in the city of Victoria. In the next 30 years, several modern packing plants

were built in Fort Worth, and refrigerated railroad cars moved the meat to the customers. By 1900 manufacturing cottonseed into oil and other products became the second-ranking industry in the state.

Lumber and Minerals

By 1900 lumbering was the most important and valuable industry in the state. Timber companies harvested the pine forests of East Texas and built towns along the Neches and Sabine Rivers. Orange and Beaumont became major sawmill centers. Most of the lumber was used in construction.

After railroads were built to carry ore eastward, mining became an important part of the industrial economy. Coal mining began in Palo Pinto and Erath Counties. Although Thurber later became a ghost town, it was the center of coal mining operations in the state for many years. Salt came from mines at Grand Saline, and iron ore was produced at Rusk and Jefferson.

Oilmen drilled the first wells and built the first **refineries** for crude oil processing during this time. A hand-dug oil well in Brown County in central Texas in 1878 produced oil that was used as a medicine and as a lubricant. An oil field near Corsicana in East Texas in the late 1890s produced oil for use as a locomotive fuel and as an application for dusty streets. Oil would not become a major industry in Texas, however, until the twentieth century.

✓ **Reading Check** **Evaluating** What were some of the major industries in Texas near the turn of the century?

A Shared Past...

Building the railroads stimulated a tourist boom in the Great Plains and Rocky Mountains. Rich Europeans, such as princes and dukes, came to the American West in grand hunting parties. They also liked to visit and be photographed with Native Americans. Artists who had been trained in Europe came to the West and painted landscapes of the beautiful scenery. The U.S. Congress preserved some of those views when it designated Yellowstone as the first national park in 1872.

SECTION 2 ASSESSMENT

Checking for Understanding

1. **Using Key Terms** Use the word refinery in a sentence.
2. **Reviewing Facts** When were the first railroad connections made between Texas and other states?

Reviewing Themes

3. **Economic Factors** Railroads were very important to the economy of Texas in the late 1800s. How did the state encourage the building of railroads?

Organizing to Learn

4. **Creating Tables** Create a table like the one below. Fill in the years of transportation and industry milestones.

Year	Milestone
	First passenger train reached Austin
	First telephone installed in Texas
	Houston had 26 miles of pavement
	Meat-packing industry began in Victoria

Critical Thinking

5. **Describing** Railroad companies invested a huge amount of time and money before they could show any profit. How did these companies make money before their railroads were ready for use?

TAKS PRACTICE

Determining Cause and Effect
Why did some Texas cities develop rapidly while others became ghost towns?

Using a Database

Why Learn This Skill?

A computerized database program can help you organize and manage a large amount of information. After entering data in a database table, you can quickly locate the information by using key words.

Learning the Skill

An electronic database is a collection of facts that are stored in a file on the computer. The information is organized into categories called *fields*. For example, one field may be the names of your friends. Another field may be their street addresses. All the related fields make up a *record*. Together, all the records make up the database.

By using a database management system (DBMS), you can easily add, delete, change, reorganize, search for, or update information.

Practicing the Skill

Read the following passage and follow the steps to build a database on urban growth in Texas in 1890.

In 1890 Dallas had some 38,000 people; Fort Worth . . . a railhead village at the end of the Civil War, had boomed to 23,000. San Antonio was virtually the same size as Dallas; Galveston had grown to 29,000, Houston to 27,000. Austin held 14,000 residents, the same as Waco, a town halfway to Dallas that had blossomed in the wake of the cattle boom.

—James Haley, *Texas: An Album of History,* 1985

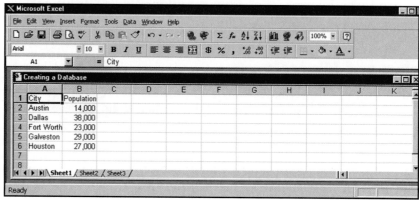

Microsoft® Excel database

① Determine what facts you want to include in your database. Research to collect that information.

② Follow the instructions in the DBMS that you are using to set up the fields. Then enter each item of data in its assigned field.

③ Determine how you want to organize the facts in the database—chronologically by the date, alphabetically, or by some other category.

④ Follow the instructions in your computer program to enter and sort the information as you choose.

⑤ Evaluate whether all the information in your database is correct. If necessary, add, delete, or change information or fields.

TAKS PRACTICE

Using a Database   Research and build a database that organizes information in this chapter concerning the delegates to the Constitutional Convention of 1875. Explain why the database is organized the way it is and how it might be used in this class.

Demands for Reform

Late-19th-century bride

★★★★★★★★★
A
Texas Story
★★★★★

Ethel Anna Pearce's penmanship was so good that she got a high paying job one summer. "[The County Clerk] wanted to make a new copy of the Runnels County Tax Rolls . . . [s]o he came to the principal of Ballinger School and asked his help in finding a girl or boy who was a good spellar [sic] and wrote a plain hand. They chose me. It took 2 months to copy them by hand. I received $25 for the job . . . I saved it nearly 2 years to buy my 'Wedding Dress.'"

—from the diary of Ethel Anna Pearce Hayley

Monopolies Use Unfair Tactics

During the years approaching the twentieth century, many large companies began operations in Texas. These companies employed people such as Ethel Anna. The companies were helpful to the growth of the

TWO VIEWPOINTS

Farmers Ask for Government Support

By the late 1880s, many Texas farmers faced serious problems. The Farmers' Alliance wanted government to step in and help. Read the two views below, and then answer the questions.

A Newspaper Editorial Is Favorable to the Farmers' Concerns

The only reason for establishing government is to utilize human effort to the advantage of the governed. It is the duty of every government, of, by, and for the people, to provide for the constant and profitable employment of its people.

—*Southern Mercury* (Dallas), December 24, 1886

A Conservative Newspaper Opposes Government Involvement

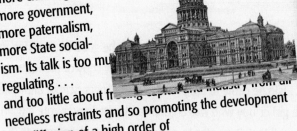

The discontented classes are told, and are only too ready for the most part to believe, that the remedy [to economic recession] is more class legislation, more government, more paternalism, more State socialism. Its talk is too mu~~ch~~ regulating . . . and too little about fr~~eeing~~ ~~capital and industry from all~~ needless restraints and so promoting the development and diffusion of a high order of hardy manhood.

—*The Dallas News*, August 19, 1886

Learning From History

1. What do you think farmers thought the role of government should be?

2. What do the writers of the *Dallas News* excerpt mean by "too much regulation"?

state because they provided valuable new services and products. As the companies became more powerful, however, problems arose.

Sometimes several companies formed arrangements known as **trusts.** A trust was usually powerful enough to prevent other companies from selling the same product or service. The trusts reduced and sometimes eliminated competition and free trade. Trusts were able to hold a **monopoly,** or exclusive control, of a business. This meant that trusts could pay low prices for the materials they bought and charge high prices for the goods they sold. Farmers, consumers, and some merchants could not protect themselves against such unfair practices.

Farmers Become Trapped in Debt

Railroads were another source of discontent. Farmers and merchants often complained that the railroad companies were unfair. They claimed that railroads charged higher rates to some farmers and merchants who had no choice but to use the local railroad to get their products to market. On the other hand, large businesses that shipped their products to other states could choose from several competing railroads. Facing competition, the railroad companies charged these larger businesses lower rates. For example, it was cheaper to ship lumber from East Texas to Nebraska than from East Texas to Dallas.

Farmers also worried about the profits they received from their crops. The prices of cotton and other farm products generally went down between 1875 and 1900. During this period, farmers plowed more land and used more farm equipment. They borrowed money to buy the land and the equipment. Farmers found it hard to repay these debts. As they planted more cotton, they increased the cotton supply, which soon exceeded the demand. This oversupply resulted in lower prices and less profit. Many farmers never got out of debt.

The rise of commercial farming in the lower Rio Grande Valley also resulted in the displacement of Mexican American ranchhands and landowners. Many became wage laborers on farms owned by others.

Reading Check **Summarizing** Why did both farmers and merchants fear monopolies?

Texans Call for Reforms

Some Texas farmers, particularly the poor ones, believed that state officials were too cautious and too timid to fight monopolies. They thought that the state was helping the trusts and the railroads and not the average Texan. Other individuals, however, argued that the **free enterprise** system allowed businesses to operate without government interference.

Farmers organized to gain support for dealing with their problems. An early organization of farmers was the Patrons of Husbandry, also called the **Grange.** The Grange was both a social organization and a group calling for economic changes. It set up stores throughout Texas where

J.B. Rayner

Picturing **History**

The Grange, the Farmers' Alliance, and the Populist Party gained members from New England to Texas. What did these groups share in common?

members could buy supplies at cheaper prices. It also pressured the state legislature to deal with unfair shipping rates charged by the railroads.

After the Grange declined in influence, many Texas farmers joined another organization, the **Farmers' Alliance.** By 1886, it had 100,000 members. They tried to eliminate the middleman's profits by negotiating sales directly with the cotton mills. Some Alliance members believed that government reforms were necessary. In August of 1891 they participated in the founding of a new political party in Dallas called the **Texas People's Party** (or the Populist Party). This party appeared in many states throughout the nation in the early 1890s. Most Texas populists were struggling farmers. African American farmers, many of whom also faced problems, sometimes joined the party ranks. One of the more talented leaders of the People's Party was **J.B. Rayner.** A former slave, Rayner was a successful writer, politician, public speaker, and educator.

Although the People's Party did not win control of the state government, some populist candidates were elected to important offices.

A Shared Past...

Many universities were founded between the years of 1876 and 1900, some by wealthy industrialists. Leland Stanford (Central Pacific Railroad) gave $24 million to create Stanford University. John D. Rockefeller (Standard Oil) gave $34 million to the University of Chicago and lesser amounts to Spellman and Morehouse Colleges in Atlanta. Vanderbilt and Tulane Universities, as well as many public universities, also began in this period. Texas A&M, Prairie View A&M, and the University of Texas all date from this important time in history.

Populist influence led other politicians to support the passage of laws that protected farmers and workers. Before 1900, however, the People's Party began to fade from Texas political affairs.

✓ **Reading Check** **Explaining** What brought about the rise of the People's Party?

New Law Prohibits Trusts

In 1889 the legislature responded to the public's concerns and passed an antitrust law. The antitrust law prohibited companies from joining together to fix prices or limit production. Although the law was later amended several times, it is still in effect. The antitrust law often has been used to prevent unfair practices. Some companies have been forced to stop doing business in Texas or have paid large fines because they violated this law.

Governor Hogg Regulates the Railroads

The regulation of railroads was another important reform of the period. In 1887 the U.S. Congress created the Interstate Commerce Commission (ICC). The ICC set rules for interstate railroads that connected two or more states. An authority to control intrastate railroads was also needed. Intrastate shipments went from one part of the state to another.

Earlier, as state attorney general, **James S. Hogg** had helped Texas become only the second state in the country to pass an antitrust law. Hogg had realized that the important question in Texas at the time was how to control the growing power of corporations. After he became governor in 1891, Hogg asked the legislature to create a state agency to regulate railroads operating in Texas. In 1891 the legislature established the **Texas Railroad Commission,** which set the rates and watched over railroad practices. John H. Reagan was appointed by Hogg to head the commission. Reagan was well liked by both Texas citizens and railroad officials, both of whom considered him to be fair.

Within a few years, many of the railroads' unfair practices were stopped. Fixing prices, demanding more money for short than for long hauls, and charging unfair rates were practices that were watched closely by the commission. Since its creation, the Railroad Commission has

Picturing **History**

Western Railway Station, Frontier Days by Oscar Edward Berninghaus, c. 1901 Railroad depots dotted the West Texas landscape in the late 1800s. How does this painting emphasize the importance of the railroad to growing Texas pioneer towns?

People of Texas

James S. Hogg 1851-1906

James Stephen Hogg, born near Rusk in East Texas, was the first native-born Texas governor. He became an orphan at age 12, but he began working and managed to support himself. He continued his education, became a lawyer, and was admitted to the Texas State Bar in 1875.

In 1891, after 15 years of public service, Hogg became governor of Texas. He was popular with the majority of citizens because he supported bills to increase funds for public schools, helped write the state's antitrust law protecting the public from monopolies, and supported the establishment of the Railroad Commission.

Texas has honored him with Jim Hogg County in South Texas and two state historical parks, one of which includes a museum featuring items that belonged to him.

been given additional power over other industries in Texas. Today it is particularly important in the regulation of the oil industry.

In part because of his efforts in creating the Railroad Commission, James Hogg is remembered as one of the most important governors of Texas. At the same time, Hogg was a very popular governor. Reform-minded Texans championed Hogg because they realized that he would not back down from a fight against big business. Small-town and rural Texans considered Hogg as "one of their own." He spoke of their hopes and dreams in language that they understood. His personality and reforms made him a favorite throughout the state.

✓ **Reading Check** **Identifying** Why is James Hogg considered one of the most important governors of Texas?

SECTION 3 ASSESSMENT

Checking for Understanding

1. **Using Key Terms** Using at least four of the six terms (trust, monopoly, free enterprise, antitrust law, interstate, intrastate), write a paragraph about an 1870s business in Texas.

2. **Reviewing Facts** What was the purpose of a trust?

Reviewing Themes

3. **Economic Factors** Why did the price of farm products generally decrease between 1875 and 1900?

Organizing to Learn

4. **Sequencing** Create a time line like the one shown here. Place the letters of the following events in the proper order.

   a. Antitrust law was passed.
   b. Interstate Commerce Commission was established.
   c. Hogg became governor.
   d. Texas Railroad Commission was established.
   e. Farmers' Alliance had 100,000 members.

Critical Thinking

5. **Analyzing Information** What are some ways that trusts affected farmers, consumers, and merchants?

6. **Understanding Supply and Demand** Why did Governor Hogg decide to establish the Texas Railroad Commission?

TAKS PRACTICE

Summarizing How did organizations such as the Grange and the Farmers' Alliance help Texas farmers?

Chapter Summary

Politics & Progress

1876
- Texans adopt a new Constitution that creates a government with limited powers.

1879
- Governor Oran Roberts begins program to balance the budget.

1886
★ The Farmers' Alliance has a membership of 100,000.

1887
★ U.S. Congress creates the Interstate Commerce Commission to set rules for interstate railroads.

1888
★ A new capitol is dedicated in Austin.

1891
- The Texas Railroad Commission is established to regulate the railroad business.
- The Texas People's Party is formed in Dallas.

1893
★ Suffragists in Dallas organize the Texas Equal Rights Association.

1900
- 10,000 miles of railroads spread across the state.
- Lumber is the most important and valuable industry in the state, providing wood for the construction of homes and buildings.

Reviewing Key Terms

Number your paper from 1 to 5. Next to each number, write the letter of the definition of each boldfaced word.

1. That company has had a **monopoly** over the production of oil in this area for many years.
2. The **vigilantes** captured the robber near the Red River.
3. The company offered a **pension** to any employee who had worked for them for 25 years.
4. Many women joined the **suffrage** movement to work for the right to vote.
5. That oil **refinery** has been operating safely in this area for nearly 10 years.

   a. the right to vote
   b. a wage paid to a person following his or her retirement
   c. private citizens organized to punish criminals
   d. exclusive control
   e. a building equipped to refine or process products such as oil, metals, or sugar

Reviewing Key Facts

6. How did the Constitution of 1876 change the government of Texas?
7. List the major accomplishments of the state government in the years following the end of Reconstruction.
8. What was the most common method of transportation in Texas before 1900?
9. Indicate why farmers and small merchants believed that the railroad companies were unfair.
10. Discuss the aims of the Grange.
11. Identify two major business reforms of the period.

Critical Thinking

12. **Determining Cause and Effect** Draw a web like the one below to show the effects of the railroad on the economy of Texas.

13. **Analyzing Government Regulation** Why did government decide to regulate big business?
14. **Drawing Conclusions** What is the danger of vigilante committees? Do you think they are ever justified?

Geography and History Activity

15. Imagine that you work for the Texas Visitors Bureau in the late 1800s. You want to bring visitors to Texas. Make a colorful brochure that includes the following information:
    • Recommended cities to visit
    • Ways to travel from Houston to Dallas and from Galveston to Amarillo
    • Information about the state capitol
    • Advice about transportation in cities

Cooperative Learning Activity

16. **Debating Issues** Working in groups of three, organize a debate among candidates for governor in 1900. Select one student to represent the Democratic Party, another the Republican Party, and the third student to be a candidate for the Populists. Candidates should each prepare a statement expressing their views regarding the budget and reform, what they will do once elected, and why voters should support them.

Practicing Skills

17. **Using a Database** Create a database of your friends' and classmates' addresses, phone numbers, birthdays, and e-mail addresses using a table, an electronic database, or a special software program.

 Portfolio/TAKS Writing Activity

18. **Writing a Paragraph** Write a one-paragraph summary about the advantages and disadvantages of the railroad coming to a small Texas town in the late 1800s. Save your work for your portfolio.

 Building Technology Skills

19. **Research on the Internet** Select one of the following topics about late-nineteenth-century Texas to research. Use the Internet and the library to find information. Choose from the following topics: Texas Equal Rights Association, the Populist Party, the 1875 Constitutional Convention, William "Gooseneck Bill" McDonald, coal mining, railroads in the late 1800s. Use at least two sources. Share your information in class. Determine which of your sources provides the best information.

Economics and History Activity

20. **Government Regulation** In the late 1800s, railroad companies often charged more for short hauls than for long hauls. Short hauls were goods that were transported only short distances, often within one state (intrastate). Long hauls were goods that were transported longer distances, usually in more than one state (interstate). Write a letter to Governor Hogg about the short-haul versus long-haul rates. Play the role of a Texas farmer or a railroad owner. Describe any economic effects that you have observed or experienced.

Use the graph to answer the following question.

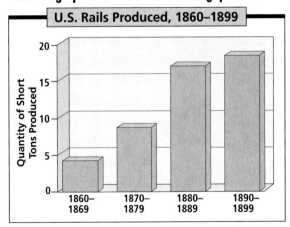

U.S. Rails Produced, 1860–1899

Which decade showed the greatest increase in production of rail short tons since 1860?

A 1860s   C 1880s
B 1870s   D 1890s

Test-Taking Tip:
Look at the graph to estimate your answer and then confirm your answer by using the numbers on the vertical axis.

THE STORY OF TEXAS

★

THE BOB BULLOCK
Texas State
History Museum

Museum Tour 6

Creating Opportunity
Ranching

*I**n time, settlers established ranches** throughout southern Texas. On the *ranchos,* Mexican cowhands called *vaqueros* (later buckaroos) adapted their equipment and methods to the particular challenges of ranching in Texas.*

Artifact The signal cannon was used on ranches to call men to the house in case of bandit or Indian raids. It was loaded with black powder and lit at the touch hole. ▶

◀ **Texas Longhorns** Longhorns were a mix of Spanish stock and English cattle. Even though immune to diseases, they carried some cattle diseases to other breeds and thus were unpopular with ranchers outside Texas.

Visit The Bob Bullock Texas State History Museum in Austin to see artifacts and exhibits such as these about Texas history and heritage.

STAN DARD

CO. LUBBOCK TEX.

▲ **Artifact** Early *vaqueros* wore shoes of soft leather that could be fitted with spurs.

◄ **Working Saddle** Equipment was adapted to the Texas landscape. Long chaps, or panels, were added to this working saddle. Chaps covered the legs and protected the *vaquero* from thorny vegetation.

Texas Cattle Drives A typical drive to get cattle to railheads for eastern markets took about 4 months. To succeed, drivers had to have courage, patience, self-reliance, and great skill. This era lasted only 25 years, but created an enduring legend. ▼

▲ **Wind Power** Railroad companies built windmills to attract settlers and ranchers to where the railroad companies planned to lay track. Texas became the largest user of windmills in the U.S. The XIT Ranch alone had 335 windmills in operation in 1900.

The
Early 20th
Century
1900–1950

Why It Matters

As you study Unit 7, you will learn about Texas in the first half of the 1900s. Texas and the United States faced economic depression and world war during the first half of the twentieth century. Texans acted boldly in response to both challenges. By doing so they provided vital national leadership necessary to solve the crises.

Primary Sources Library

See pages 696–697 for primary source readings to accompany Unit 7.

South Texas Panorama by Warren Hunter (1939) was originally painted for the walls of the Old Post Office Building in Alice, Texas. When the building was destroyed, the mural was moved to the Smithsonian Institution for preservation. A scene from that mural is shown at right.

"We are passing through a critical period . . ."

—Governor Coke R. Stevenson,
Inaugural Address, January 19, 1943

TEXAS OIL

Partially decayed plants and animals that lived hundreds of millions of years ago may be heating your home or helping your family car run. The plants and animals have been transformed, or changed, into oil and gas.

Oil Formation

1 Millions of years ago the ancient Gulf of Mexico covered what is now South Texas. Billions of tiny plants and animals living in the Gulf died and sank into the muddy ooze at the bottom of the seafloor.

2 When the sea level fell, rivers brought sand and other sediments from the mountains and covered the decaying plants and animals. As time passed the sediments gradually hardened into sandstone, a rock that has pores, or spaces.

3 When the sea level rose again, another muddy layer was deposited. It formed a seal over the porous rocks.

4 As layers built up, the weight caused the seafloor to sink and slide. Pressure, time, and heat changed the partially decayed plants and animals into oil and gas.

5 Oil and natural gas rose through the holes in the porous sandstone until they were trapped by the seal. Today geologists look for those reservoirs, or pockets of trapped oil, when they want to drill for oil.

Geologists have also discovered a lot of oil and natural gas in the western part of Texas. Rocks that contain oil and gas resources in the western region were formed in an earlier period when shallow seas covered the area.

T E X A S

Gulf of Mexico

In the Gulf of Mexico, the darker the blue, the deeper the water. Green represents land. Most oil is found in the green areas of Texas and light blue area offshore.

LEARNING from GEOGRAPHY

1. Where are the oldest oil basins in Texas and approximately how old are they? (See inset map.)

2. What conditions changed decayed plants and animals into oil and gas?

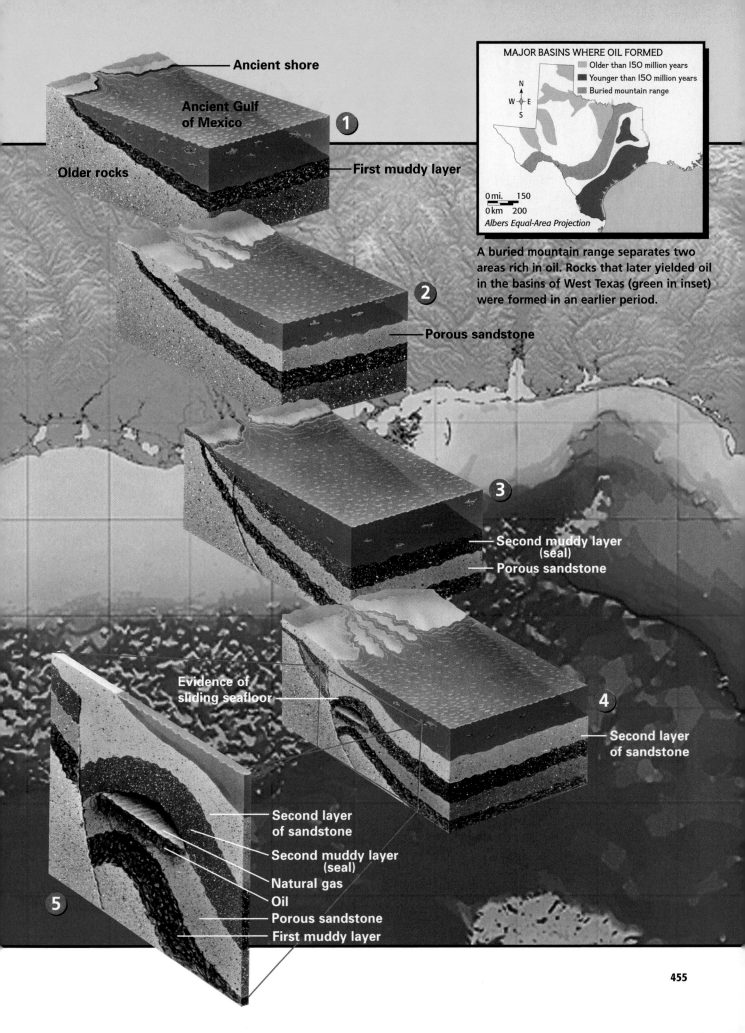

Ancient shore

Ancient Gulf of Mexico

1

Older rocks

First muddy layer

MAJOR BASINS WHERE OIL FORMED

Older than 150 million years
Younger than 150 million years
Buried mountain range

N
W E
S

0 mi.   150
0 km   200
Albers Equal-Area Projection

A buried mountain range separates two areas rich in oil. Rocks that later yielded oil in the basins of West Texas (green in inset) were formed in an earlier period.

2

Porous sandstone

3

Second muddy layer (seal)
Porous sandstone

Evidence of sliding seafloor

4

Second layer of sandstone

Second layer of sandstone
Second muddy layer (seal)
Natural gas
Oil
Porous sandstone
First muddy layer

5

Why It Matters

In the first years of the twentieth century, Texas began to change from a rural state in which most people depended upon agriculture to a state with growing industrial cities. Ranches continued to be turned into farms. Immigration from Mexico increased in response to the political unrest there and to the demand for workers in Texas.

The Impact Today

Texas's role as an energy capital for the United States began at Spindletop in 1901. Although the dependence upon oil has lessened in recent years, energy production remains an important segment of the Texas economy.

Texas

1900
★ *Galveston hurricane of 1900*

1901
★ *Spindletop gusher*

United States 1900 1905

World

1900
• *Boxer Rebellion in China*

1901
• *Theodore Roosevelt became president*

1909
• *National Association for the Advancement of Colored People formed*

By the mid 1920s, Houston had all the characteristics of a "modern" industrialized city. Shown here is a view of Texas Avenue and Main Street, the center of the retail business district.

FOLDABLES™
Study Organizer

TAKS PRACTICE

Identifying Main Ideas Study Foldable

To fully understand what you read, you must be able to identify and explain key vocabulary terms and chapter concepts. Use this foldable to identify, define, and use important terms and phrases in Chapter 20.

Step 1 Fold a sheet of notebook paper in half from side to side.

Step 2 On one side, cut along every third line.

Tabs will form as you cut.

Step 3 Label your foldable as shown.

Disaster/Galveston | Oil: Texas Gold | Lumber | Industry | Dallas | Voting Reform | Prohibition | Discrimination | Cultures Clash | Organized Groups

Reading and Writing As you read the chapter, write an explanation of each term or phrase on the back of each tab of your foldable. Then, under each tab, write an original sentence correctly using the term or phrase.

1912
★ Houston chapter of NAACP formed

1914
★ Houston Ship Channel officially opened

1915

1920

1914
• World War I began in Europe

1917
• U.S. entered World War I

1919
• Eighteenth Amendment (Prohibition) ratified

1913
• Mohandas Gandhi, leader of Indian Passive Resistance Movement, arrested

1920
• Nineteenth Amendment (Woman Suffrage) ratified

TEXAS HISTORY *Online*

Chapter Overview
Visit the texans.glencoe.com Web site and click on **Chapter 20—Chapter Overviews** to preview chapter information.

CHAPTER 20   A New Century   **457**

The Modern Era Begins

Guide to Reading

Main Idea
The new century brought many changes to Texas.

Key Terms
derrick
scrip
conservationist
retail
white-collar

Reading Strategy
Organizing Information In the early 1900s, oil was discovered in three main areas of Texas. Draw a chart like the one below and list the three oil fields and nearby towns.

Oil Field	Nearby Town

Read to Learn
• what event devastated Galveston.
• why Spindletop was important.
• how the oil industry promoted growth.

Section Theme
Economic Factors Remote areas of Texas became accessible, and economic growth occurred in every area of Texas.

Preview of Events

♦1866   **♦1900**   **♦1901**   **♦1914**

First Texas oil well drilled near Nacogdoches

Galveston struck by severe hurricane

Spindletop— first oil gusher

Houston Ship Channel opens

Hallie Crawford Stillwell

A Texas Story

By 1910 even the most remote sections of Texas—like the Big Bend region—were accessible to settlers. As did many other families, Hallie Crawford and her parents decided to make one last move. "The last move I made with my family was in 1910 to Alpine, Brewster County, Texas. It offered opportunities to make a good living, the school system was good, and Uncle Jim and his family also lived there."

—*I'll Gather My Geese* by Hallie Crawford Stillwell

Into the New Century

The beginning of the modern era is marked by two momentous events that occurred in southeast Texas in 1900 and 1901. One of these involved water, the other involved oil.

Disaster Strikes Galveston

In many ways, Galveston was the most modern Texas city. It had the first electric lights and telephones in the state. A magnificent opera house, built in 1894, hosted world-class performers.

On September 8, 1900, **Galveston** was struck by a hurricane of unbelievable force. The storm battered the city for 12 hours, with winds reaching 120 miles (194 km) an hour. High-cresting tidal waves completely covered the island. When the storm was over, dazed Galvestonians discovered that 6,000 of their neighbors had perished in the water and rubble. Half of the city lay in ruins. Thousands were left homeless. It was the worst natural disaster in U.S. history. In its wake, the **Women's Health Protective Association** organized to inspect and safeguard cemeteries, streets, markets, dairies, schools, hospitals, and parks. To cope with the emergency, a new type of city government was formed (see page 466).

The U.S. Army Corps of Engineers built a seawall to provide protection against any future hurricanes. After it was completed, all of Galveston behind the seawall had to be raised. Houses that had withstood the hurricane were jacked up, and engineers pumped sand from the bay under them. Some buildings in Galveston were raised as much as 10 feet (3 m).

After Galveston was rebuilt, it resumed its traditional role as a port of entry for immigrants.

Rabbi Henry Cohen greeted Jewish people fleeing from persecution in Russia and eastern Europe. Italians came through Galveston on their way to farms in the Brazos Valley. Italian, Lebanese, and Greek newcomers also found jobs in the growing cities of the Coastal Plains region, such as Houston and Beaumont.

✓ **Reading Check** **Explaining** Why was the Women's Health Protective Association formed in Galveston?

Oil—Texas Gold

Only four months after the hurricane and less than 100 miles away, another event occurred that changed the economy of Texas and the U.S. The event was the discovery of a major oil deposit.

People had known about oil for centuries. Native Americans had probably used it for medicine. Survivors of the de Soto expedition found deposits of sticky tar on the Texas coast. They used it to fix leaks in their boats.

In later times Anglo Americans used oil to grease the axles on their wagons. In the 1840s a Canadian scientist discovered how to make kerosene fuel from petroleum. Kerosene lamps provided much better light than did candles. As the demand for kerosene grew, operators began drilling for oil. In 1859 Edwin Drake drilled the first successful oil well in Pennsylvania, near Titusville. Soon drilling began in Ohio and West Virginia.

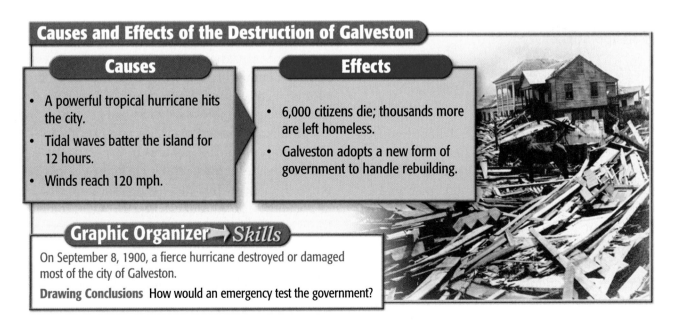

Causes and Effects of the Destruction of Galveston

Causes
- A powerful tropical hurricane hits the city.
- Tidal waves batter the island for 12 hours.
- Winds reach 120 mph.

Effects
- 6,000 citizens die; thousands more are left homeless.
- Galveston adopts a new form of government to handle rebuilding.

Graphic Organizer → Skills

On September 8, 1900, a fierce hurricane destroyed or damaged most of the city of Galveston.

Drawing Conclusions How would an emergency test the government?

In 1866 **Lyne T. Barret** drilled the first oil well in Texas, a few miles east of Nacogdoches. It produced only 10 barrels per day, but by 1890 the field at Oil Springs, as it was known, had 40 wells and a pipeline to Nacogdoches. In 1894 a driller searching for water near Corsicana found oil at a depth of 1,050 feet (320 m). Soon other wells were drilled, starting an oil boom in the area. Joseph S. Cullinan built a refinery at Corsicana to process the crude oil. Cullinan pioneered using natural gas for home heating and lighting, and using oil to power locomotives. This was the first refinery built west of the Mississippi River.

Spindletop—the First Gusher

South of Beaumont on the coastal prairie was a small hill named Spindletop. Earlier attempts to drill for oil near Spindletop had been unsuccessful, but oilmen such as **Pattillo Higgins** and **Anthony Lucas** remained optimistic. Another well was started, with Lucas in charge of the drilling. On January 10, 1901, the rotary drilling bit dug 1,139 feet (347 m) into the ground, and mud started coming up the hole. There was brief silence. Then mud, gas, and oil started shooting into the air, as high as 100 feet

(31 m). The well flowed nonstop for the next 9 days. It is estimated that 100,000 barrels of oil flowed per day until the well could be capped.

There had been nothing to compare with the **Spindletop gusher,** and the almost unbelievable flow of oil continued. In 1901 the Spindletop Oil Field yielded more than four times as much oil as had been produced the year before by all Texas oil wells combined. In 1902 Spindletop production quadrupled.

Beaumont changed overnight. Oil prospectors and drillers descended on the city. Oil companies like the Texas Company (later Texaco) were started. Within a few months, the population of Beaumont increased from 9,000 to 50,000. There were not enough places for people to stay. Hotel rooms were rented for 8-hour shifts. Barber chairs and pool tables served as beds.

Spindletop boosted overall economic development, both within Texas and beyond the state. Business leaders built a refinery in Pennsylvania to refine Spindletop oil. Others constructed refineries, pipelines, ocean tankers, and storage facilities. More important, the success of Spindletop encouraged oil drilling in other locations.

✔**Reading Check** **Examining** How did oil discoveries change Beaumont?

Boomtowns in Southeast Texas

Oil operators began drilling all around Beaumont. Within two years of the Spindletop discovery, oil fields opened at Sour Lake, Saratoga, and Batson. In 1904 drillers discovered oil near Humble, 20 miles (32 km) north of Houston. The Humble Oil Company became the multinational corporation known as Exxon–Mobil.

Early boomtowns were noisy, dirty, hazardous, and crowded. Charles Jeffries, an oil worker, recalled his days at Sour Lake:

> 66It was the gas fresh from the wells, less diffused and more highly impregnated with sulphur, that the workers dreaded. This kind had hardly any scent, but it was as deadly as a murderer. Its effect when breathed was much like that of chloroform. If a person, or any other living animal, inhaled a few strong breaths of it, he would fall over unconscious; and if he lay in it and continued to breathe it, he would die as surely as if chloroformed.99

Oil production moved nearer the Texas coast with the opening of the **Goose Creek Oil Field** in 1916. This field was unusual because some of its wells were drilled in the waters of Galveston Bay. Because of its coastal location, operators built a major refinery nearby. For many years it was one of the largest refineries in the world. A new settlement near the refinery joined with the communities of Goose Creek and Pelly to become the prosperous town of Baytown.

Houston Benefits From Oil Discoveries

Houston reaped the most benefit from the oil discoveries of the Coastal Plains. As oil fields grew around it, Houston became the center of oil business activities. Houston was prepared to become the leading city. In 1900 it had a well-developed rail network. Its city motto was "Where 17 Railroads Meet the Sea." Petroleum companies needed the banking, insurance, transportation, and legal services that Houston could provide.

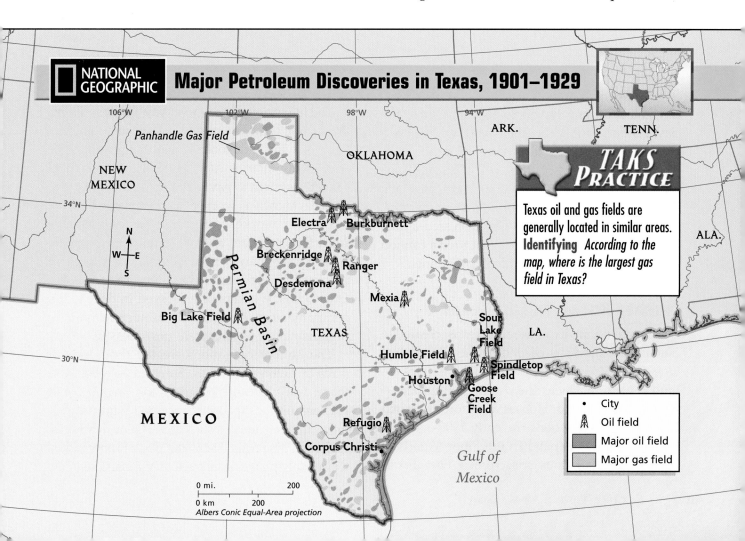

NATIONAL GEOGRAPHIC

Major Petroleum Discoveries in Texas, 1901–1929

TAKS PRACTICE

Texas oil and gas fields are generally located in similar areas. **Identifying** *According to the map, where is the largest gas field in Texas?*

Panhandle Gas Field

OKLAHOMA

NEW MEXICO

ARK.

TENN.

ALA.

Electra

Burkburnett

Breckenridge

Ranger

Desdemona

Mexia

Big Lake Field

Permian Basin

TEXAS

Sour Lake Field

LA.

Humble Field

Houston

Goose Creek Field

Spindletop Field

MEXICO

Refugio

Corpus Christi

Gulf of Mexico

• City
⚒ Oil field
▓ Major oil field
▒ Major gas field

0 mi. 200
0 km 200
Albers Conic Equal-Area projection

Houston

Opened in 1914 and completed in 1925, the Houston Ship Channel connects Houston with the Gulf of Mexico. Why was building the channel important to Houston's growth?

Particularly significant was the construction of the **Houston Ship Channel.** Small vessels had navigated Buffalo Bayou to Houston since the days of the Republic, but the bayou was not deep enough to handle modern ships. **Congressman Thomas Ball,** for whom the town of Tomball was later named, secured funds from the U.S. Congress to deepen the channel. On September 7, 1914, President Woodrow Wilson pressed a telegraph key in the White House that fired a cannon to officially open the Houston Ship Channel.

Lumber Booms in East Texas

The oil boom in southeast Texas created a demand for products needed by the oil industry. One such product was lumber. The derricks—high towers that held the drilling equipment—were made of wood. Houses and stores required large amounts of wood. The early 1900s saw the lumber industry expand in the Piney Woods of East Texas. Rail lines crisscrossed East Texas,

making it easy to get the lumber to market. Workers often lived in towns created by the lumber companies. Camden, Kirbyville, and Diboll all had their origin as company towns.

The life of a lumber worker was not easy. Every aspect of a lumber worker's job, from cutting the tree to sawing it into boards, was dangerous. There were many injuries. In 1913 the Texas legislature created a system to pay for job-related injuries that today is known as workers' compensation.

Lumber workers often rented their houses from the company and were paid in company scrip rather than currency. Scrip was "money" that could be spent only at company-run stores. Due to this, workers often stayed in debt to the company store. Attempts by lumber workers to organize labor unions were unsuccessful.

The lumber operations created thousands of acres of deforested lands. Some people believed these lands should be used for farming, but conservationists (people concerned with preserving natural resources), such as **W. Goodrich Jones,** replanted pine trees. Today the Texas timber industry actually plants more trees than it harvests.

Many leaders wanted Texas and the rest of the South to imitate the North and develop a variety of industries. A plow factory existed at Longview, and attempts were made to create a steel industry near Rusk. Brickmakers in Henderson and Harrison Counties took advantage of excellent clay deposits to produce high quality bricks.

✔**Reading Check** **Explaining** How did the oil industry contribute to the rise of other industries?

Dallas Dominates Central Texas

By 1900 Dallas had emerged as the major city in central Texas. Manufactured goods from the North were shipped by rail to Dallas, and cotton was shipped out. Companies from the northern and eastern United States that wished to have a branch office in the western part of the country often chose Dallas because of its excellent rail connections. Dallas also became a center for banking, insurance, and legal services.

About this time, Texas consumers began buying more ready-made clothes rather than making their own. Dallas became the leading retail (sold directly to the consumer in small quantities) center of Texas, Oklahoma, and New Mexico. The **Neiman–Marcus department store** was established in Dallas in 1907 by Carrie Marcus Neiman, her husband A.L. Neiman, and

Carrie Marcus Neiman

her brother, Herbert Marcus. **Sears Roebuck,** a Chicago mail-order company, was America's largest retailer. When the company's board wanted a southwestern distribution center, it chose Dallas.

Dallas's rail connections helped make it a white-collar city. Its work force included many lawyers, bankers, accountants, and business executives. These community leaders tended to support the arts and cultural activities. Dallas became known for its symphony orchestra (founded in 1900), the popular Museum of Art (founded in 1903), bookstores, and other cultural and educational attractions.

Dallas doubled its population from 1900 to 1910. By 1920 it had a population of almost 159,000. Fort Worth's growth rate was even greater. Other central Texas cities like Waco, Austin, and San Antonio also gained population.

✔**Reading Check** **Examining** How did Dallas come to be considered a "white-collar city"?

SECTION 1 ASSESSMENT

Checking for Understanding

1. **Using Key Terms** Write a sentence for each of these key terms: derrick, scrip, conservationist, retail. The meaning should be clear from the term's use in the sentence.

2. **Reviewing Facts** In what ways was Galveston the same and in what ways was it different after the hurricane of 1900?

Reviewing Themes

3. **Economic Factors** How did the discovery of oil impact the economic growth of Texas?

Organizing to Learn

4. **Analyzing** Create a web like the one below, filling in each circle with a business that was affected by the oil industry.

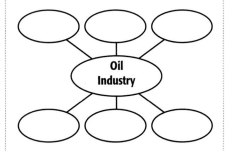

Critical Thinking

5. **Evaluating** Why was the discovery of oil at Spindletop in 1901 so important to other parts of the state?

TAKS PRACTICE

Analyzing At the top of this page, the statement was made: "Many leaders wanted Texas . . . to imitate the North and develop a variety of industries." What industries besides oil developed in Texas in the early 20th century?

TAKS Skillbuilder

Making Inferences

Why Learn This Skill?

Making inferences allows you to "read between the lines," or draw conclusions that are not stated directly in the text. Inferences should be based on logical thinking and careful analysis.

Imagine that you hear a news report of a fire near the school bus garage. When your bus arrives late, you *infer* that the fire disrupted the bus schedule. You made an inference that was not based on direct information but that was suggested by the facts.

Learning the Skill

Use the following steps to help you make inferences.

- Read carefully for stated facts and ideas.
- Summarize and list the important facts.
- Use other information you know to decide what inferences can be made.

Practicing the Skill

Read the passage below and answer the questions that follow:

> The people in Galveston had never held hurricanes in too much awe . . . a storm was an occasion for school to let out, for children to slosh in the streets . . . and for crowds to gather at the beach and watch waves crash . . . People now took the storm seriously and sought shelter . . . [B]y 4 P.M. the entire island was flooded] . . .
>
> Estimated at 120 miles per hour, the wind shifted suddenly from east to southeast, sending a five-foot tidal wave rolling over the city. It was the instant of greatest destruction. In

Galveston hurricane of 1900

> the large buildings where many had sought shelter, brick walls gave way to the wall of water or were battered down by surging debris . . . Hundreds were crushed or drowned at a time.
>
> James L. Haley, *Texas: An Album of History*

❶ Why did people wait to take shelter from this storm?

❷ What precautions or preparations might have spared lives and property? How did you infer this?

TAKS PRACTICE

Making Inferences   Write about an event or activity that you participated in recently, but leave out one or two facts. Pose two questions about the event or activity that a friend or classmate will answer by making inferences.

 GO TO

Glencoe's **Skillbuilder Interactive Workbook,** Level 1, provides instruction and practice in key social studies skills.

The Progressive Movement

Main Idea
Reformers attempted to solve the problems created as the cities grew.

Key Terms
progressivism
commission
primary election

Reading Strategy
Analyzing Draw a chart like the one below and describe changes associated with progressivism in Texas.

Issue	Changes
City government	
Voting	
Voting for women	
Prohibition	

Read to Learn
• how Galveston's form of government changed.
• about the Terrell Election Law.
• about the suffragists.
• about Prohibition.

Section Theme
Government and Democracy The Progressive Movement produced reforms in government and society.

Preview of Events

♦1903		♦1917	♦1918
Terrell Election Law is passed		Governor James Ferguson is impeached	Texas women vote in primary elections	Texas prohibition law passed

Hallie Crawford

A
Texas Story

In 1916, when Hallie Crawford graduated from high school in Brewster County, there were few job opportunities for women besides teaching. Teachers then did not have to go to college to be qualified to teach elementary school. Hallie remembered, "I started school in Alpine as a sixth grader, and by the time I graduated I not only had my high school diploma but also my teaching certificate. [T]eaching was certainly the most respectable job for a woman."

Galveston Reforms City Government

As more Texans moved to cities, they found new problems and became more aware of existing ones. The attempts of reformers to solve those problems became known as the **Progressive Movement.** Progressivism took several forms in Texas.

The storm of 1900 presented Galveston with an opportunity to set up a completely new form of city government. Galvestonians replaced their mayor and city council with a **commission** form of government. The five-member commission made the laws for the city. Each commissioner was in charge of one city department, such as police, fire, or water services. Galveston's commission form of city government worked so well that it became a model for other cities. Houston adopted it in 1905. Denison, El Paso, Greenville, and Dallas adopted this type of government in 1907. Before long, 400 cities across the nation had a commission form of government.

The Terrell Election Law

The Progressives believed that voting was the cornerstone, or fundamental basis, of democracy. In 1903 the state legislature passed the **Terrell Election Law** to ensure that elections would be carried out fairly. The law called for secret ballots and restricted campaigning near polling booths. An important provision required that major political parties hold **primary elections.** A primary election is held by a political party before a general election (in November).

Its purpose is to select that party's official candidates from a field of nominees. Those selected run in the general election. Although the Terrell Election Law has been amended, or changed, several times since it was originally passed in 1903, it remains the basic election law today.

Votes for Women

The election reforms still left women disqualified from voting. Many women were determined to change that mark of second-class citizenship. In 1893 **Rebecca Henry Hayes** of Galveston had organized the Texas Equal Rights Association. In 1903 the Finnegan sisters—Annette, Elizabeth, and Katherine—founded the **Equal Suffrage League** of Houston. Suffrage is the right to vote. Other women joined the cause, including Mary Eleanor Brackenridge of San Antonio and Minnie Fisher Cunningham of Galveston.

Picturing **History**

Austin suffragists stand in front of Travis County Court House in 1918. Jane McCallum was elected president of the Austin Women's Suffrage Association in 1915. What did Texas suffragists achieve in 1918?

Opposition to woman suffrage was strong. Many traditionalists argued that women had no need to vote because men would protect their rights. Others said that women would neglect their homes and children if they became more involved in political affairs.

Suffragists—those supporting women's right to vote—claimed that just the opposite was true. They said that if women had the right to vote, they could be even more effective in their traditional roles. They could cast their ballots in favor of better schools, more playgrounds, safe parks, and improved public health.

The suffragists also argued that if a woman failed to pay her taxes, her property could be sold; if she forged a check, she could go to jail; if she stole, she could be convicted; and if she defaulted on her contracts, she could be sued. In none of these cases would her father or her husband be punished. Therefore, the suffragists asked, why was it that the only place in the world that men wanted to represent women was at the ballot box?

From 1915 to 1918, suffragists wrote letters, signed petitions, and lobbied state legislators to let women vote. **Governor James Ferguson** fought against woman suffrage, but in the summer of 1917 he was charged with a variety of offenses (not related to woman suffrage). He was impeached, tried, and found guilty, even though he had already resigned from office.

In 1918 Texas women won the right to vote in party primaries by making a deal with the new governor, **William P. Hobby.** They promised that if he would sign a bill granting women the right to vote in primaries (which he had neither supported nor opposed), they would support him in the forthcoming election against impeached governor James Ferguson. Hobby signed the bill, and the suffragists threw their support to him, as

TWO VIEWPOINTS

Prohibition

Texans were split between Progressives who favored a statewide ban on the sale of alcohol and more traditional Democrats who opposed such a ban. Read the two views below and then answer the questions.

The Democratic Governor Opposes Prohibition as a Loss of Freedom

Civil liberty will give way to military dictatorship. Is the crime of taking a drink as a beverage so bad as to justify [the limitation of our freedoms]? Shall our constitution become a dish-rag for the convenient use of [politicians] leading a popular clamor? Or shall it remain the strong protection to the individual?
—Governor Oscar Colquitt, *Dallas Morning News,*
July 14, 1911

Religious Leaders Support Prohibition on Moral Grounds

There is but one side to the question as to the attitude . . . of any Christian man and thoughtful citizen concerning the liquor traffic. That attitude is and must ever be one of hostility against the entire liquor [power structure], local, county, state and national, root and branch.

—proceedings of the sixty-third annual session of the Baptist General Convention of Texas, 1911

Learning From History

1. Why do you think Governor Colquitt was opposed to prohibition?

2. Are the arguments above based on fact or opinion?

they voted for the first time. Hobby won in a landslide. Full voting rights for women throughout the United States were granted by the **Nineteenth Amendment** to the U.S. Constitution in 1920.

Prohibition

The one issue that aroused the most interest in Texas during the Progressive Era was the battle about alcoholic beverages. Saloons—the main business of which was selling alcoholic beverages—were a target of Progressive reformers because alcohol seemed to be at the center of so many social ills. Saloons were associated with gambling, the sale of stolen goods, and the planning of crimes. It was claimed that men who spent their money in saloons forced their families to rely on charity.

One of the groups that was most involved in trying to bring about the end of alcohol sales and close down the businesses that made alcoholic beverages was the **Woman's Christian Temperance Union** (WCTU). The organization was active across the country and had opened chapters in

Governor William P. Hobby (1878–1964)

Texas as early as the 1880s. The **Texas Anti-Saloon League** formed in 1907 and became another powerful voice in the battle to outlaw drinking in the state. Certain church groups strongly supported the efforts of these organizations.

The brewing industry opposed prohibition. German and Italian immigrants generally opposed prohibition, as did conservatives who disapproved of a strong federal government. In 1918, however, Texas approved a statewide prohibition law, and in 1919 the **Eighteenth Amendment** to the U.S. Constitution made prohibition the law of the land throughout the United States.

Prohibition was in effect nationally from 1919 to 1933. There is no doubt that many people believe the law prohibiting the manufacture of alcohol reduced the amount of alcohol that Americans drank. However, many people resented the law and some people broke it. The Eighteenth Amendment became an unpopular law that was eventually repealed in 1933. It was thought that the repeal would help to improve the economy.

✓ Reading Check **Examining** Why did religious groups generally support prohibition?

SECTION 2 ASSESSMENT

Checking for Understanding

1. **Using Key Terms** Use the terms progressivism and primary election in sentences to show you understand their definitions.
2. **Reviewing Facts** Galveston adopted the commission form of government. What other Texas cities adopted this same form of city government?

Reviewing Themes

3. **Government and Democracy** How did the Terrell Election Law make elections fairer?

Organizing to Learn

4. **Creating a Chart** Although the suffragists were determined to win the right to vote for women, others were just as determined to stop them. Draw a chart like the one below and list the arguments for and against woman suffrage.

Arguments for	Arguments Against

Critical Thinking

5. **Analyzing** Why are groups more successful in solving political problems than individuals?
6. **Evaluating** Why do you think women were denied the right to vote for so long?

TAKS PRACTICE

Making Judgments The suffragists worked to change the voting laws so that women could vote. If you could change any present voting law, which one would it be? Why?

Discrimination

Main Idea
African Americans and Mexican Americans were often the victims of discrimination.

Key Terms
Jim Crow laws
segregation
lynch
poll tax

Reading Strategy
Analyzing Discrimination was present in the early 1900s. It is also present today. Draw a chart like the one below, listing examples of discrimination in the early 1900s, and then think of possible examples of discrimination today.

Examples in 1900s	Examples Today

Read to Learn
• how African Americans experienced and challenged discrimination.
• how Mexican Americans experienced and challenged discrimination.

Section Theme
Continuity and Change
Discrimination against African Americans and Mexican Americans was present in politics, education, housing, and public services.

Preview of Events

♦1902
Poll tax law is passed

♦1912
First chapter of NAACP is founded in Texas

Mexican revolutionary soldier

A
Texas Story

Hallie Crawford found a teaching job in Presidio. Her father worried about her safety because the Mexican Revolution was still raging. "Presidio was largely populated by Texans of Mexican descent. Most of these people had fled Mexico seeking protection from Pancho Villa . . . My father thought this place was too dangerous for a young lady. He didn't want me to go . . . 'Daughter, I think you're going on a wild goose chase,' he said. Hallie replied, 'Then I'll gather my geese.'"

—*I'll Gather My Geese* by Hallie Crawford Stillwell

African Americans Fight Discrimination

Progressive Era reforms did not benefit African Americans. In fact, African Americans actually lost rights during the first years of the twentieth century.

From Reconstruction to the 1890s, the Republican Party had firmly supported rights for African Americans. Republican leaders tried to build their political party in the South with a combination of African American and sympathetic white voters. When Republicans occupied the White House, they often appointed African Americans, such as **Norris Wright Cuney,** to federal jobs in Texas.

By the 1890s the Republican Party abandoned this strategy. It was thought that the Republican Party would always be a minority party in the South if it continued to support African American rights. All across the South, the more popular Democratic Party had been passing laws discriminating against African Americans. These statutes were known as **Jim Crow laws.**

One important Jim Crow law required the **segregation** of public facilities. Hotels, restaurants, and entertainment events were closed to African Americans. Blacks were required to sit in the backs of streetcars and buses and in the balconies of public theaters. African Americans were also forced to use separate water fountains, restrooms, railway cars, and waiting rooms.

Discrimination was present in housing and education. African Americans lived in sections of town that had inadequate paving, lighting, sewage, and police protection. African American children attended separate, poorly equipped schools. African American teachers received lower salaries than did white teachers with the same qualifications.

Sometimes racial unrest led to violence. African American soldiers and local citizens clashed in riots that occurred in Brownsville (1906) and in Houston (1917). Lives were lost and property was damaged. A riot in Longview (1919) resulted in the death of one African American. During this period, blacks who were accused of even minor crimes were sometimes **lynched,** or hanged, by white mobs.

African Americans were active in politics until about 1900. Their participation began to decline after that. In 1902, Texas adopted a constitutional amendment establishing a **poll tax,** a fee for voting. The $1.50 cost kept many poor and minority citizens from voting. In addition, the primary elections in the Democratic Party soon were restricted to white people. In this way, African Americans were denied the chance to take a meaningful part in politics.

Picturing **History**

Many African Americans in Texas participated in Texas politics until Jim Crow laws restricted their rights. What were Jim Crow laws?

ONLY in TEXAS

Blue Bell Creameries Few Texans today would not be able to identify the Blue Bell ice cream label *(below center)*. The company had its beginnings in the early 1900s. It began in 1907 as the Brenham Creamery Company. Then, the ice cream was packed in large wooden tubs with ice and salt and delivered by horse and wagon to local Brenham residents. In 1936, the company—now named Blue Bell Creameries—bought its first refrigerated truck and began delivering wider afield *(left)*. Blue Bell Ice Cream was a special treat enjoyed by this Johnson Space Center crew *(right)* during a docking mission with the Mir space station.

During the first decades of the 1900s, many African Americans left farms and moved to the cities. Segregated neighborhoods, such as Acres Homes in Houston, became springboards for African American achievement in business, education, religion, and cultural affairs. African American businesses provided services to the black community. Hobart Taylor, Sr., started a taxi business and expanded into insurance. He became a millionaire. A. Maceo Smith received his education at Fisk University and New York University. He then moved to Dallas and organized an insurance company.

African Americans such as **Charles N. Love** and **W.E. King** both founded newspapers in 1893 to serve the African American community. Love's paper, the *Texas Freeman*, eventually merged with the *Houston Informer*. The *Houston Informer & Texas Freeman*, still published today, is the oldest African American newspaper west of the Mississippi River. Both it and King's *Dallas Express* fought segregation and lynching.

African Americans also created organizations to work for racial equality. Efforts to organize the first Texas chapter of the **National Association for the Advancement of Colored People** (NAACP) began in Houston in 1912. A chapter was founded in El Paso in 1915. By 1918 four more Texas chapters had been formed, and by 1930 there were more than 30 chapters in the state.

Perhaps the most important African American institution was the church. The influence of African American ministers often extended far beyond the church walls. They gave advice on political and community affairs. Church conferences and conventions searched for common solutions to problems. Private church colleges,

such as Mary Allen Junior College in Crockett, Wiley and Bishop Colleges in Marshall, and Paul

THIS PARK WAS GIVEN FOR WHITE PEOPLE ONLY. MEXICANS AND NEGROES STAY OUT. ORDER OF PARK BOARD.

Picturing **History**

Some Mexican immigrants, such as these at Fort Bliss, came to the U.S. to escape the Mexican Revolution. As the sign from elsewhere in Texas demonstrates, both Mexican Americans and African Americans experienced discrimination throughout the state at this time. How does this sign show that segregation was allowed by the government?

Quinn College in Waco, trained generations of African Americans for leadership positions. Black doctors, dentists, and lawyers had to travel out of state for training, because Texas universities at that time admitted only whites.

Other African American Texans resisted discrimination by leaving Texas and the South. During the early 1900s many went to the industrial cities of the North, where they found jobs.

Reading Check **Inferring** How did Republican Party strategy change by the 1890s?

Cultures Clash in South Texas

South Texas also experienced dramatic changes in the early 1900s. Completion of the St. Louis, Brownsville, and Mexico Railway in 1904 resulted in a wave of immigration.

Two groups of immigrants met in the Lower Rio Grande Valley. Midwestern farmers from Iowa, Wisconsin, and the Dakotas developed farms to produce fruit, vegetables, cotton, and sugarcane. The other immigrants came from Mexico. Many Mexicans fled to Texas to escape

the Mexican Revolution of 1910–1920. They took jobs on the newly established farms.

The heavy migrations strained the relationships between the Anglo and Mexican ethnic groups. People of Mexican descent made up almost half the population in South Texas. Anglo farmers from the Midwest often held anti-Mexican prejudices. Discrimination and friction became common.

Such conflict became much more serious and life threatening during the years of the Mexican Revolution. Some of the violence was caused by bandits who abused Mexicans, Mexican Americans, and Anglos. Some of it was the work of Mexican revolutionary leaders seeking support or supplies. Some of it was the result of fear caused by rumors of a great conspiracy to take Texas and other nearby states away from the U.S. Much of the violence simply reflected the hostility, distrust, resentment, and fear that Anglo and Mexican ethnic groups felt toward one another. At times, particularly between 1915 and 1918, violence along the Rio Grande was common, with many innocent citizens killed or wounded.

Citizens, seeking revenge or protection, organized vigilante groups. State officials increased the number of Texas Rangers stationed in the Valley and eventually sent the state militia to the area. Mexican officials also increased military patrols along the Rio Grande. In time, these efforts were effective, but they sometimes added to the hostile feelings among the people in the Valley. Mexican Americans claimed that Texas Rangers abused and killed innocent members of their communities. A later investigation by the state legislature revealed several instances of brutality, mistreatment, and murder involving the Rangers.

It is difficult to determine with certainty how many people died in the conflicts along the Rio Grande. Untold numbers of Anglos, Mexicans, and Mexican Americans were killed, but most of the victims were Mexican Americans or newly arrived refugees from Mexico.

Native-born Tejanos and Mexicans trying to escape the violence of the Mexican Revolution encountered the poll tax and other voting restrictions. Mexican Americans also experienced segregation. Plans for towns in the Valley included different residential sections for Anglos and Mexican Americans. Often the dividing line between the areas was the railroad track or some other readily visible landmark.

Mexican American and Anglo children generally went to different schools and played in separate parks.

Mexican Americans fought discrimination and ill treatment by joining labor unions and self-help organizations. Railroad, mining, construction, and laundry workers at times participated in strikes for better wages and working conditions during the early 1900s. Agricultural workers found it more difficult to organize.

Ethnic self-help organizations, such as the *Grán Circulo de Obreros Mexicanos*, provided assistance with weddings, baptisms, and funerals. Families often formed associations to help maintain Mexican culture. Women and men founded *mutualistas* (mutual aid societies) to provide help and community service, including low-cost funerals, low-interest loans, and aid to the poor. Groups were formed to give drought assistance or offer protection from abusive conditions.

TEXAS HISTORY Online

Student Web Activity Visit the texans.glencoe.com Web site and click on **Chapter 20—Student Web Activity** to learn more about Mexican immigration to Texas.

✓ **Reading Check** **Explaining** How did Mexican Americans fight discrimination?

SECTION 3 ASSESSMENT

Checking for Understanding

1. **Using Key Terms** Write a paragraph in which you explain the following key terms: Jim Crow laws, segregation, lynch.
2. **Reviewing Facts** What group was created to work for racial equality for African Americans?

Reviewing Themes

3. **Continuity and Change** Give an example of discrimination and how the group affected by it confronted the discrimination.

Organizing to Learn

4. **Analyzing** Draw a chart as shown, listing examples of discrimination faced by African Americans in the areas listed below.

Area	Examples of Discrimination
Education	
Housing	
Public services	
Politics	

Critical Thinking

5. **Analyzing** The "poll tax" was a way of keeping African Americans and Mexican Americans from registering to vote. Why was this so?
6. **Identifying** In what ways did Mexican Americans maintain their cultural values?

TAKS PRACTICE

Contrasting Did African Americans use various methods to resist discrimination? Explain and give examples.

Chapter Summary

A New Century

1900
★ Galveston hurricane destroys the city. The city establishes a commission form of government.

1901
★ The Spindletop gusher erupts. An oil boom begins.

1902
★ Texas establishes a poll tax, which discriminates against the poor and minorities.

1903
• The Terrell Election Law creates campaign reform.

• The Equal Suffrage League of Houston is established to fight for women's right to vote.

1912
• The NAACP establishes a chapter in Houston.

1914
• The Houston Ship Channel opens.

1916
★ Oil is discovered at Goose Creek field. Wells are drilled in Galveston Bay.

1918
• Women are allowed to vote in Texas primary elections.

• A statewide prohibition law goes into effect.

1919
• Prohibition (the Eighteenth Amendment) is ratified.

1920
★ Women gain the right to vote nationwide through the Nineteenth Amendment.

Reviewing Key Terms

1. *Make illustrated flash cards for the following vocabulary terms. On the front side of each card, write the term and make an illustration to help you remember it. On the back of the card, write the definition.*
   a. derrick, conservationist, scrip
   b. retail, progressivism, primary election
   c. Jim Crow laws, segregation, lynch

Reviewing Key Facts

2. What happened on September 8, 1900?
3. What types of jobs were available in Dallas in the early 1900s, and why?
4. How did Houston benefit from the oil discoveries?
5. How did the lumber business benefit from the oil industry?
6. What arguments were given for and against woman suffrage?
7. What arguments were given for and against prohibition?
8. Why were African American churches so important?

Critical Thinking

9. **Analyzing** How did the oil industry affect the development of Texas?

10. **Making Comparisons** Create a chart like the one below. Use your text to list early uses of oil, and then think of ways oil is used today all over the world.

Early Uses	Uses Worldwide Today

11. **Making Comparisons** Do you think rural life or urban life changed more during the early 1900s? Explain your answer.

12. **Identifying Central Issues** What conditions led to the rise of the Progressive Movement?

13. **Synthesizing Information** In what area—taxes, workers' safety, election procedures, or civil rights—did Texas Progressives make the strongest reforms? Explain.

14. **Analyzing** In what ways did Texas women work to improve their lives and society in general?

15. **Making Generalizations** What methods did the suffrage and the temperance movements use to achieve their goals?

16. **Identifying** What specific measures were taken in the early 1900s to prevent African Americans from voting?

Geography and History Activity

17. Study the Major Petroleum Discoveries map found on page 461. Compare this map with the Texas Land Use map on page RA21. According to the land use map, which of the major oil discoveries are probably still producing? You will have to transfer information from the land use map to the petroleum map.

Portfolio/TAKS Writing Activity

18. **Writing a Résumé** Find a copy of a résumé and become familiar with the parts so that you will know the important facts to find concerning the person you will research. Many individuals were important to Texas during the Age of Reform. Choose one of the individuals mentioned in this chapter. Find several sources of information and write a résumé for that person.

Cooperative Learning Activity

19. **Writing a Response** Organize into groups of four. Do additional reading about the growth and development of the oil industry in Texas. Your school or public librarian can help you find books on the subject. You may also find valuable information on the Internet. Then, write a short report on one of the following topics or a related topic that your group chooses.

- the beginning of the oil industry in Texas
- the effects of the oil industry on another Texas industry
- life in a Texas town during the oil boom

Include in your report original artwork, maps, or diagrams.

Practicing Skills

20. **Making Inferences** Read the paragraph and then answer the question that follows.

Woman suffrage groups in Texas made limited progress in the early 1900s. They often spoke to politicians and organized public parades. Most suffragists were white women, although African Americans and Mexican Americans also participated in suffrage efforts.

How might the suffragists have been more effective as a political force?

Building Technology Skills

21. **Internet Research** Do an Internet search on the words "Texas Oil Museums." Try more than one search engine

to compare your results. Write a brief explanation of each site (limit of 10 sites). Finally, decide which of the sites are the best and rate the top 5 sites.

Use the graph to answer the following question.

Which city grew the fastest between 1900 and 1920?

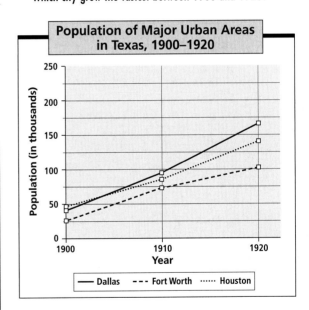

Population of Major Urban Areas in Texas, 1900–1920

Legend: — Dallas --- Fort Worth ...... Houston

F Dallas

G Fort Worth

H Houston

J Galveston

Test-Taking Tip:
Do not just pick the city with the largest population. Instead, look at the legend. Pay attention to the rate of growth or the slope of the line between 1900 and 1920.

CHAPTER 21

World War I and the 1920s

Why It Matters

Involvement in World War I, improvements in transportation, and immigration from foreign lands all contributed to an expanded view of the world for Texans. Prosperity, population growth, and modern technology meant that Texas was becoming an urban state.

The Impact Today

Many aspects of Texas today, such as the school system and the highway system, have their origins in reforms made in the 1920s. Texas women began to achieve important victories in their fight for equality, especially on the political front.

1916
★ *General Pershing chased Pancho Villa in Mexico*

Texas

United States   *1910*   *1912*   *1914*   *1916*

World

1910
• Mexican
  Revolution began

1913
• Zippers became
  popular in clothing

1914
• World War I
  began in Europe
• Panama Canal
  opened

1915
• Albert Einstein
  completed his
  Theory of
  Relativity

The painting Fifth Avenue in the Armistice Winter of 1918–1919 by Anna Richards Brewster captures the sense of patriotism felt by all America—including Texas—after the Great War.

FOLDABLES™ Study Organizer — TAKS PRACTICE

Compare-Contrast Study Foldable Make this foldable to help you collect and analyze information on the economy and progress of Texas during the first quarter of the twentieth century.

Step 1 Mark the midpoint of the side edge of a sheet of paper.

Draw a mark at the midpoint.

Step 2 Turn the paper and fold the outside edges in to touch at the midpoint.

Step 3 Label your foldable as shown.

1917 — Wartime Prosperity

1929 — Peacetime Struggles

Reading and Writing As you read the chapter, write key facts and main ideas under the appropriate tabs of your foldable. Use what you learn to compare and contrast the economy of Texas before, during, and after World War I.

1918
★ Annie Webb Blanton elected superintendent of public instruction

MIRIAM A. FERGUSON
Candidate for Governor

1924
★ Miriam "Ma" Ferguson elected governor

1920   *1922*   *1924*

1917
• U.S. entered World War I

1920
• Women granted right to vote

TEXAS HISTORY Online

Chapter Overview
Visit the texans.glencoe.com Web site and click on **Chapter 21—Chapter Overviews** to preview chapter information.

International Affairs

Guide to Reading

Main Idea

Texans were affected by the Mexican Revolution and became involved in World War I.

Key Terms

recruit
ration

Reading Strategy

Organizing Information Complete a table like the one shown here by filling in the dates of these significant events.

Historical Event	Date
Mexican Revolution	
General Pershing sent to Mexico	
World War I	
U.S. enters WWI	

Read to Learn

• about the Mexican Revolution.
• about World War I.
• about life on the home front.

Section Theme

Global Connections The U.S. involvement in World War I led to important changes for Texans.

Preview of Events

♦1916 ♦1917

General Pershing pursues Pancho Villa in Mexico

April 5
Kelly Field opens as flight training school

August 23
Race riot erupts in Houston

A
Texas Story

Bessie Coleman

Bessie Coleman was an African American who knew prejudice. Born near Atlanta, Texas, in 1893, she was one of 13 children living on a sharecropper's farm raising cotton. She finished high school and went to college for one year, but then the money ran out. Bessie moved to Chicago and became a successful manicurist. Some of her brothers went to France during World War I. They told Bessie that there was less prejudice there. They also said they saw women in France who flew airplanes. Bessie dreamed of the day she would fly.

United States Troops Enter Mexico

The outbreak of revolution in 1910 in Mexico soon became a concern for Texans. Revolutionaries replaced long-time dictator **Porfirio Díaz** with a progressive reformer named **Francisco Madero.** A military dictator,

Victoriano Huerta, soon removed Madero by having him shot and killed. **Emiliano Zapata** in the south of Mexico and **Francisco (Pancho) Villa** in the north recruited (enlisted) armies of thousands to oppose Huerta and his successor, **Venustiano Carranza.**

Pancho Villa used Ciudad Juárez, across the Rio Grande from El Paso, as his base, or headquarters. In March 1916, he and 500 men raided Columbus, New Mexico. Several Americans and Mexican raiders were killed.

President Woodrow Wilson responded to the Columbus raid by ordering **General John J. Pershing** and 6,000 troops from San Antonio to pursue Villa across northern Mexico. Pershing could never catch Villa but did keep him away from the border. The presence of American troops on Mexican soil caused anger among the Mexican people and the government.

In 1917 President Wilson ordered Pershing back to San Antonio. Accompanying the troops were more than 500 Chinese immigrants who had helped Pershing in Mexico. Even though Congress had passed laws prohibiting Chinese people from entering the U.S., these immigrants were given special permission to stay in San Antonio. They formed the largest Chinese American community in the state.

The U.S. Enters World War I

The Pershing expedition returned to the U.S. as Wilson was preparing American forces to fight in the "Great War." Later, the Great War was called **World War I.** The European nations of France, England, and Russia had been at war with Germany and Austria–Hungary since 1914. The U.S. remained neutral. But in early 1917, President Wilson found the pressures to enter the war overwhelming. German submarines sank ships carrying American passengers. In January, a German diplomat named Arthur Zimmermann sent a coded telegram to the German representative serving in Mexico. It instructed him to propose an alliance with Mexico in the event that war broke out between Germany and the United States. It further promised to help Mexico regain its lost territories of Texas, Arizona, and New Mexico in

exchange for Mexico's support of Germany. This famous telegram read, in part:

> ❝We make Mexico a proposal of an alliance on the following basis: Make war together, make peace together, generous financial support, and an understanding on our part that Mexico is to reconquer the lost territory in Texas, New Mexico and Arizona.❞

Americans, and Texans in particular, reacted angrily when newspapers published this message. In April 1917, President Wilson asked Congress to declare war on Germany.

✓ **Reading Check** **Explaining** How did Germany's actions lead the United States into war?

Picturing History

Rose Wu, a longtime Chinese American resident of San Antonio, was an active community member. In 1937, she testified in Austin against a bill that would prevent Chinese immigrants from owning property. **How do you and your family contribute to your community?**

Texas Mobilizes for War

The United States was not ready for war. New soldiers had to be trained. Texas supplied almost 200,000 of those troops. Texans served in the Army, Navy, and Marine Corps. The wide open spaces and railroad network made Texas a good place to train troops. The army established training camps at Houston, Fort Worth, Waco, and San Antonio. **Kelly Field** was built at San Antonio in 1917 as a training camp. Pilots would study aviation at other camps, but when it came time to fly, they all came to Kelly. It became the largest flight training school in the world. Pilots also trained

at Stinson Field in San Antonio, founded by **Marjorie** and **Katherine Stinson** and their mother.

Military units from Texas included the 36th Division, which was composed primarily of National Guard troops from Texas. Several thousand of its members died fighting in France. The 90th Division included soldiers from both Texas and Oklahoma. Both divisions suffered heavy casualties.

Some Texans held positions of major importance. Colonel Edward M. House of Austin was one of President Woodrow Wilson's most trusted advisers. The president appointed another Austin resident, Albert Sidney Burleson, postmaster general of the United States. Burleson directed the government's wartime operation of the national telephone and telegraph system. Thomas Watt Gregory, also of Austin, was the United States attorney general.

Approximately one-fourth of the Texans who served were African Americans. One group of African American soldiers was stationed at **Camp Logan** just outside Houston. These regular army troops were not used to restrictions on their freedoms. Tensions developed between them and Houston police enforcing the Jim Crow laws. The soldiers claimed they were mistreated, and were angry when they learned they would not be sent overseas to fight. In 1917 a riot erupted in which 17 people were killed, including 5 police officers. After the war, Camp Logan was purchased by the Hogg family and given to the city of Houston. Today it is Memorial Park.

Mexican Americans were urged by their leaders to support the war effort. Although Mexicans living in Texas who were not citizens were not required to serve in the military, many volunteered. Hundreds of Mexican Americans served with combat troops of the 141st, 125th, 325th, and 359th Infantry Regiments in France.

Several individuals were honored for bravery in battle. **Marcelino Serna,** a Mexican immigrant from El Paso, earned the Distinguished Service Cross and two Purple Hearts. He single-handedly captured 24 enemy soldiers. **Marcos Armijo,** who worked in an El Paso print shop before the war, was awarded the Distinguished Service Cross after his death.

✓ **Reading Check** Evaluating Why was Texas a good place to train new soldiers?

The War Changes Soldiers

The war caused profound changes for both the soldiers and those who remained at home. Many recruits from the farms and ranches of Texas received medical and dental care for the first time in their lives when they joined the armed services. Some recruits had never traveled outside the county of their birth. Joining the army often meant a chance for more education and training. Going to France, or even to an army base in the northern United States, provided new experiences that changed the lives of many service personnel. A new world opened up to them, and many were eager to find better lives after their service was completed. A popular song of the day captured this feeling. It asked, "How Ya Gonna Keep 'em Down on the Farm After They've Seen Paree [Paris]?"

African Americans were affected more than any other group. Europeans generally showed less racial prejudice than African Americans had known at home. Restaurants, theaters, and other public places in Europe welcomed African Americans on an equal basis. These experiences would not be forgotten.

Women and the War

Many Texas women helped the war effort as nurses, factory workers, and farmers. But Katherine Stinson of San Antonio wanted to make a different kind of contribution. She was an experienced pilot and owned her own flying service. She tried to volunteer for service in World War I. The army refused her offer and told her that women could not be military pilots. Stinson and her sister, Marjorie, however, were allowed to train male pilots. Later, Katherine was an ambulance driver in the campaigns in France.

At Home in Wartime

"Do Your Bit" advised the war posters, and the Texans who remained at home did just that. Texans took part in the Liberty Loan campaigns and bought Liberty Bonds, Victory Bonds, and

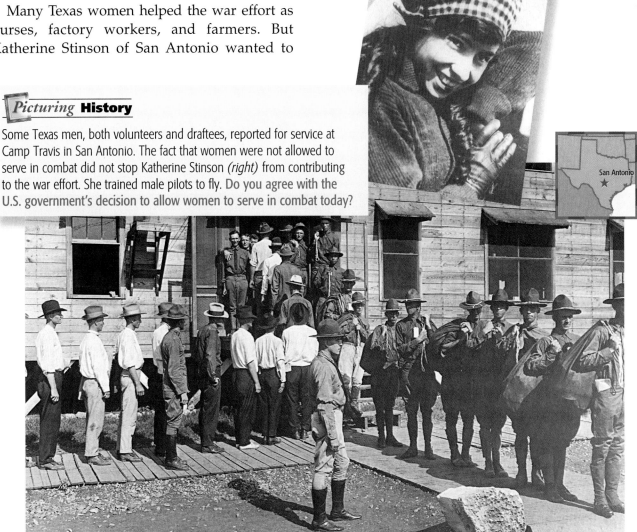

Picturing **History**

Some Texas men, both volunteers and draftees, reported for service at Camp Travis in San Antonio. The fact that women were not allowed to serve in combat did not stop Katherine Stinson *(right)* from contributing to the war effort. She trained male pilots to fly. Do you agree with the U.S. government's decision to allow women to serve in combat today?

The U.S. government printed war posters to urge citizens to buy bonds in support of the war effort. What type of support is this poster asking for?

War Savings Stamps to raise money for the war effort. They also gave generously to the Red Cross and other care-giving organizations. Texans voluntarily rationed, or cut back on, food so more could be shipped to the troops in Europe. For example, many Texans reduced the amount of sugar and fat in their diets. They ate no pork on Thursdays and Saturdays and observed meatless Tuesdays. Because wheat was scarce, Texans went without wheat products on Mondays and Wednesdays.

The war heightened strong anti-German feelings. Some German Texans were pressured into joining the army to show their patriotism. Others were forced to kneel and kiss the United States flag. Some communities banned the performance of German music, and many high schools stopped teaching German. Governor Hobby even vetoed funding for the German Language Department at the University of Texas. A favorite German food, sauerkraut, was renamed "liberty cabbage." Frankfurters briefly became known as "liberty sausages." To show loyalty to American values, the town of Brandenburg in Stonewall County changed its name to Old Glory. While some Texans spoke out against these actions and the intolerance they produced, many people believed that, in wartime, no measures could be "too drastic" to root out disloyalty.

✓**Reading Check** **Summarizing** Give some examples of anti-German attitudes and actions during World War I.

SECTION 1 ASSESSMENT

Checking for Understanding

1. **Using Key Terms** Write a sentence using the key terms ration and recruit to demonstrate your understanding of the terms.
2. **Reviewing Facts** What was the name of the world's largest flight training school built in 1917?

Reviewing Themes

3. **Global Connections** In what ways did war change the lives of Texans at home, soldiers who went to serve in other parts of the U.S., and soldiers who fought in Europe?

Organizing to Learn

4. **Sequencing** Create a time line like the one below and place the letters of the following events in the proper order.

   a. President Wilson asks Congress to declare war on Germany.
   b. World War I ends with an armistice (Nov., 1918).
   c. Pancho Villa raids Columbus, New Mexico.
   d. World War I begins.
   e. Revolution begins in Mexico.

Critical Thinking

5. **Drawing Inferences** Many Mexicans living in Texas volunteered to serve in the United States military even though noncitizens were not required to do so in World War I. What reasons might have caused them to take this action?

TAKS PRACTICE

Predicting Consequences African American soldiers found less racial prejudice in Europe than at home. How do you think they felt when they returned to the United States?

A Return to Peace

Guide to Reading

Main Idea
The 1920s were a time of social, economic, and political change in Texas and throughout the world.

Key Terms
tenant farmer
sharecropper
urban
rural

Reading Strategy
Cause and Effect As you read this section, complete a chart like the one shown here listing the effect of each cause.

Causes	Effects
Cotton prices fall	
Electricity in homes	
Ku Klux Klan forms	

Read to Learn
- what accounted for Texas's wartime prosperity.
- what postwar life was like for sharecroppers in Texas.
- whom the Ku Klux Klan targeted.

Section Theme
Economic Factors Social and economic change contributed to political outcomes in Texas.

Preview of Events

1910	1920	1924
Mexican Revolution increases Mexican immigration to Texas	Ku Klux Klan gains influence in the 1920s	"Ma" Ferguson is elected governor

Airplane, c. 1920

A Texas Story

When no flight school would let her enroll because she was African American, Bessie Coleman went to France and earned her license in 1921—becoming the only African American in the world with a pilot's license! She came back to the U.S., bought an airplane, and began flying. One night she celebrated Juneteenth by taking passengers up to view the lights of Houston. It was probably the first time African Americans in Texas had flown.

Wartime Prosperity

Soldiers returned to a Texas greatly changed by the war. Farmers and ranchers had prospered because Texas produced so many things the military needed. It had cotton and wool for tents and uniforms, leather for

Texans celebrated Armistice Day in cities and towns across the state. Citizens of Granger turned out on November 11, 1918, to celebrate together. How does this compare to celebrations of national holidays in Texas today?

Granger ★

boots, and meat and grain to feed the troops. High wartime prices encouraged Texas farmers to expand their farms and go into debt for new agricultural machinery.

The petroleum industry expanded to meet the needs of war. More gasoline and lubricants were needed by armies. Ranger Field (1917) and Burkburnett Field (1918) supplied large quantities of both.

Cotton Prices Fall

The high prices Texas cotton farmers received during World War I did not last. In 1920 farmers received $.42 per pound for their cotton. A year later the price had fallen to less than $.10 per pound. One result of the decline in cotton prices was that more Texas farmers rented their land rather than owning their own farms. By 1930 about 40 percent of farmers were tenant farmers who rented the land, but who provided their own

equipment. About 20 percent were sharecroppers who exchanged their labor for a share of the crops. Most farmers were poor, but the poverty of sharecroppers was especially severe. A group of sociologists from the University of North Carolina studied sharecropping throughout the South, including Texas. Here is how they described the system:

66 The cultural landscape of the cotton belt has been described as a 'miserable panorama of unpainted shacks, rain-gullied fields, straggling fences, rattle-trap Fords, dirt, poverty, disease, drudgery, and monotony that stretches for a thousand miles across the cotton belt' . . .

Although living on abundant land in the south temperate zone, tenant families have probably the most meager and ill-balanced diet of any large group in America . . . The diet can be . . .

strained down to the notorious three M's—meat [fat salt pork], meal, and molasses. Evidence of the slow ravages of this diet are to be found in the widespread evidence of [disease]. 🔊🔊

As farmers watched the price of cotton drop, they reacted by growing more cotton. This was not helpful, because the low prices were the result of supply exceeding demand. Often the farmers had little choice, because landlords required tenants or sharecroppers to grow only cotton. Banks and merchants would not extend credit to farmers growing other crops.

✔ **Reading Check** **Explaining** How did increasing supply lead to lower cotton prices?

The Ku Klux Klan

The 1920s was a time of reacting to the great social and political changes of the previous decade. There had been revolutions in Mexico and Russia. Millions of Americans had their lives changed by either war or employment in newly built factories. Women had, at long last,

won the right to vote. Some people resisted the rapid social change. The most visible reaction was the growth of the **Ku Klux Klan.**

The Ku Klux Klan had been formed during Reconstruction by Confederate veterans who terrorized African Americans to keep them from participating in politics. The Klan was a secret, anti-minority organization. Its members wore white hoods and robes and took part in rituals. The Reconstruction Klan died out by the 1870s, but a new Klan was formed in Georgia in 1915. After World War I the Klan became very active in Texas. Its victims were African Americans, Jews, Catholics, and "persons of low morality." Klan members used beatings, tar-and-feathering, and other forms of violence against their victims.

The Klan also engaged in politics. Klan members elected state representatives, judges, sheriffs, and other local officials. At one time or another, the Klan controlled local governments in Dallas, Fort Worth, Beaumont, Wichita Falls, and other cities. Its greatest political success came in 1922 when Klan member, Earle Mayfield, was elected to the United States Senate.

In 1924, however, **Miriam "Ma" Ferguson** won the race for governor on an anti-Klan platform. Her husband, **James Ferguson,** had been impeached and removed as governor in 1917. One of

Picturing **History**

Entire families were hired to help pick cotton. After it was picked, the cotton was immediately weighed. Why do you think the cotton was weighed?

the terms of his sentence was that he could not hold state office again. When voters voted for "Ma," they believed that "Pa" would be the governor in all but name.

Another anti-Klan politician, **Dan Moody,** succeeded "Ma" Ferguson as governor. Moody had become famous when he prosecuted Klan members for violent crimes. His victory was a sign that most Texans were fed up with Klan violence.

Texans Face Rapid Changes

Returning soldiers found a Texas that was undergoing great changes. Texas was on its way to becoming an urban state. More people were leaving the rural countryside and moving to towns and cities. In the 1920s, urban population grew by 58 percent. The average Texas family size decreased from 4.6 to 3.5 in those same years. Because of school attendance laws and better enforcement of child labor laws, fewer children worked outside the home.

Many houses in the cities were now wired for electricity. The horse-drawn ice wagon was seen less frequently as people bought refrigerators. Foods could now be kept longer without spoiling, and fewer trips to the market were necessary. Electric irons replaced the type that had to be heated on the cook stove, and so relieved a major part of household drudgery. Vacuum cleaners and washing machines also helped reshape household routines.

Picturing **History**

"Ma" Ferguson ran for governor using the slogan "two governors for the price of one" because she said she would listen to her husband's advice. **In what political ways are spouses important to politicians?**

Many of these new consumer goods were available on credit through either mail order catalogs or from department stores opening in Texas cities.

✓ **Reading Check** **Identifying** Which groups were victims of the Ku Klux Klan?

SECTION 2 ASSESSMENT

Checking for Understanding

1. **Using Key Terms** Write a short paragraph describing a sharecropper's life.
2. **Reviewing Facts** Explain how and why the Ku Klux Klan became so powerful in Texas.

Reviewing Themes

3. **Economic Factors** How did the war help farming and the oil industry?

Organizing to Learn

4. **Categorizing** Create a web like the one shown here and describe a social, an economic, and a political change after World War I.

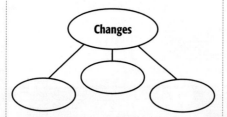

Critical Thinking

5. **Comparing and Contrasting** Family size decreased as the urban population in Texas grew. Why do you think this was a common trend?

TAKS PRACTICE

Analyzing "As farmers watched the price of cotton drop, they reacted by growing more cotton." Explain why growing more cotton was not helpful.

Identifying Assumptions

Why Learn This Skill?

Identifying a writer's assumptions is an important key to understanding a writer's point of view. Assumptions are ideas that the writer believes the reader already understands. Assumptions are usually not stated.

Learning the Skill

Here are steps in identifying assumptions:
- Read the material carefully.
- Identify the writer's point of view.
- Identify stated and unstated assumptions underlying the writer's views.
- Check the accuracy of these assumptions.

Practicing the Skill

Read the speech and answer the questions.

"Brothers and sisters, we are oppressed . . . The chains of slavery are broken and we must make our way in this world as free men and women . . . Education is the key that will unlock this door to the future.

"But how can our children get a good education in the Negro schools? These schools cannot train tomorrow's leaders. The school buildings are falling down. There are no books or supplies inside. Negro schools have the least qualified and lowest paid teachers in Texas. As long as our children go to all-Negro schools, they will never get the same education as white children. No, 'colored only' schools must go the way of the slave chains. We must break them before they break us."

❶ What is the topic of this speech?

❷ What is the speaker's opinion of segregated schools?

❸ What support does the speaker give?

❹ Why is the following statement an assumption: "Education is the key that will unlock this door to the future"?

❺ What assumption about education is made in the last paragraph?

❻ How could the accuracy of this assumption be tested?

African American children in front of their segregated school

TAKS Practice

Identifying Assumptions   People make assumptions every day about information that they hear or read. Find and read an article in one of your favorite newspapers or magazines. Answer the following questions:

1. What is the topic of the article?

2. Can you identify any assumptions in the article? If so, describe them.

   Glencoe's **Skillbuilder Interactive Workbook**, Level 1, provides instruction and practice in key social studies skills.

GO TO

Progress in the 1920s

Guide to Reading

Main Idea
The progressive spirit of the age led to great improvements in education, transportation, and leisure activities in Texas.

Key Term
appropriate

Reading Strategy
Categorizing Information As you read this section, create a chart like the one shown here to provide examples of lifestyle improvements in Texas.

Education	Transportation	Leisure and Fun

Read to Learn
• about Annie Webb Blanton.
• how transportation improved.
• about new technologies.

Section Theme
Science and Technology New technology contributed to progress and highlighted ethnic diversity in Texas.

Preview of Events

1918	1922	1926
Annie Webb Blanton is elected superintendent of public instruction for Texas	Commercial radio stations begin	More than 1 million cars and trucks are registered in Texas

Bessie Coleman is honored by the U.S. Postal Service

A Texas Story

Bessie Coleman was not just a pioneer aviator. She was also a pioneer in civil rights. In Dallas she refused to fly if African American and Anglo spectators had to use separate entrances to her show. She dreamed of establishing a flying school for African Americans, but she died in a plane crash in 1926. Even after death, Bessie continued to inspire Americans of all races. In 1995 the U.S. Postal Service issued a stamp in her honor. In 2000 she was elected to the Texas Aviation Hall of Fame.

Blanton Fights for Better Schools

Despite groups like the Ku Klux Klan, most Texans embraced progress. One of the most important areas of change was in education. In 1918 **Annie Webb Blanton** was elected superintendent of public instruction for

Texas. From that influential office, she worked tirelessly to improve Texas schools. During her administration the state raised school taxes and began providing free textbooks for children. Superintendent Blanton organized the Better Schools Campaign to influence voters to give schools more money. The constitutional amendment that allowed local school districts to collect property taxes passed 221,223 to 126,282.

Annie Webb Blanton served two terms as superintendent of public instruction before becoming a professor at the University of Texas in Austin. There she founded Delta Kappa Gamma, a national sorority designed to promote women's leadership in education. The organization now has more than 15,000 members in 14 countries.

Women and Equality

Living conditions for women improved somewhat in the 1920s as they continued their struggle for equality. Women worked in jobs outside the home in about the same proportions as they had in earlier times. More women, however, were working in business and in the professions. The number of married women who worked outside the home began to increase considerably.

Women also played a greater role in politics during the 1920s than ever before. The election of women as governor and as state superintendent of public instruction were important victories in the struggle for equality. Three women won seats in the state legislature. One of the legislators, **Senator Margie Neal** of Carthage, won passage of a law that provided money to help disabled people work and find jobs. **Jane Y. McCallum** held powerful posts in the state Democratic Party and served as secretary of state under two governors. **Adina de Zavala** was one of the leaders of an earlier crusade to protect the site of the Alamo. As a member of the Daughters of the Republic of Texas, she continued her efforts to preserve the heritage of the state in San Antonio and elsewhere. In 1929 **María Hernández** and her husband organized a civil rights group. Women also ran for and won local offices, serving as treasurers and on city councils.

Posters and flyers, similar to this one, helped Annie Webb Blanton spread her message to improve Texas schools.

Several women's clubs banded together to form the **Women's Joint Legislative Council.** This organization, also known as the Petticoat Lobby, supported the passage of laws that provided more money for education, registered births, and provided care for expectant mothers and their children. The Council also pushed for laws to regulate the use of child labor in Texas. The Council may be the most successful public interest lobby Texas has seen. The entire legislative program of this organization was adopted.

In some ways, the struggle for equality was only partly successful. Few women became physicians or attorneys or accountants. Even fewer studied to be engineers or ministers. Women still received lower wages than men for doing the same job. African American and Hispanic women were still mostly limited to low-paying domestic and service jobs. Moreover, women still did not have the same legal rights as men, particularly with respect to owning and selling property.

✓ Reading Check Evaluating How did women contribute to Texas politics in the 1920s?

Dallas ★

Improvements in Transportation

The 1920s saw the end of the "horse and buggy" era in Texas. Before World War I, automobiles rarely were seen in Texas. By 1926 more than one million cars and trucks were registered in Texas. New measures were needed to control these vehicles and their drivers. City governments enacted new ordinances setting speed limits, often of 5 or 10 miles (8 or 17 km) per hour. Cities hired police officers to enforce the new traffic laws. The growing number of drivers demanded better roads. Counties had been responsible for Texas roads, and the quality of roads varied tremendously from county to county. The U.S. Congress appropriated, or set aside, funds for highway construction but specified that the money would go only to states that had highway departments. Texas quickly created the **Texas Highway Department** so it would be eligible for those funds.

The new Highway Department was soon embroiled in politics. The Fergusons were accused of awarding profitable contracts to build highways to their political supporters. Eventually Texas was divided into districts with professional engineers—rather than politicians—overseeing highway construction and maintenance in those districts. Today, the Texas highway system is among the finest in the United States.

✓ **Reading Check** **Describing** What changes were necessary as the automobile replaced the horse and buggy?

Texans Enjoy Leisure Activities

Texas was changing from a rural, agricultural state to an urban, diversified state. One of the by-products of this shift was an increase in the amount of time spent on recreation and leisure. New technologies, such as motion pictures and radio, provided hours of entertainment and introduced Texans to a wider world.

The first radio broadcasts were from science departments of the University of Texas, Southwestern University, and Texas A&M University. In 1922, though, commercial radio stations started in Fort Worth (WBAP), Amarillo (KGNC), Dallas (WFAA), Houston (WEV and WGAB), San Antonio (KFJZ and WOAI), Galveston (KILE), and Waco (WACO). Radio stations in the 1920s broadcast a wide variety of programs. There were news shows, sporting events, church services, political speeches, drama, and comedy. Many radio stations featured musicians who provided live music from the radio studio. Many musicians who later became famous recording artists started their careers with Texas radio stations.

Texas music reflected the ethnic diversity of the state. The influence of African American jazz was so great in the 1920s that some historians refer to that decade as the "Jazz Age." African American blues stars "Blind" Lemon Jefferson and Huddie "Leadbelly" Ledbetter influenced many younger singers.

Cowboy songs that originated on the Texas plains found a wider audience because of radio. Marion Slaughter, who sang under the name of Vernon Dalhart, recorded the first country record to sell a million copies, "The Wreck of the Old 97." His recording of "The Prisoner's Song" sold 25 million copies by 1948.

Recording companies such as Columbia and RCA set up studios in Texas. Mexican American musicians such as La Familia Mendoza and Santiago Jiménez became stars in Texas, the U.S., and Mexico in the late 1920s and 1930s.

The growing motion picture industry did not ignore Texas. The San Antonio area was a popular site for filming movies. *Wings,* the first film ever to win an Academy Award for best picture, was made in San Antonio.

Sports, including hunting, fishing, and baseball, were popular by the 1920s. After that, a new sport—football—became an important part of Texas recreation. Huge crowds were attracted to high school games. Many of the best teams came from the oil boomtowns such as Wichita Falls. Universities also competed on the gridiron. Six

Picturing **History**

Today's high school football traditions can be traced back to the 1920s. What do you think are some reasons for football's great popularity in Texas?

Texas colleges (the University of Texas, Texas A&M, Baylor, Rice, Texas Christian University, and Southern Methodist University) and the University of Arkansas were members of the Southwest Conference.

Reading Check **Examining** What was a by-product of Texas's shift from a rural to an urban state?

SECTION 3 ASSESSMENT

Checking for Understanding

1. **Using Key Terms** Look up the term appropriate in the dictionary. What part of speech is the word as it is used in this section?
2. **Reviewing Facts** Name four musical recording artists of the era who reflected the ethnic diversity of Texas.

Reviewing Themes

3. **Science and Technology** Write a short paragraph explaining why Texans were beginning to have more time to spend on recreation and leisure.

Organizing to Learn

4. **Summarizing Contributions** In the 1920s women became more involved in government than ever before. Create a chart like the one shown here and describe how each of the individuals listed participated in Texas politics.

Woman	Contribution
Neal	
McCallum	
de Zavala	
Hernández	

Critical Thinking

5. **Understanding Cause and Effect** Explain how Superintendent Annie Webb Blanton's Better Schools Campaign worked.
6. **Drawing Conclusions** What is one way radio affected the development of Texas?

TAKS **Practice**

Drawing Inferences How did life change for the average Texas family as a result of improvements in education and transportation, and the increase in leisure time activities?

Chapter Summary

World War I and the 1920s

1910
- Revolution breaks out in Mexico.

1914
- ★ World War I begins in Europe.

1916
- ★ U.S. troops try to capture Pancho Villa.

1917
- The U.S. enters WWI.
- ★ Troops are trained at new army camps in Texas.

1918
- World War I ends.
- Annie Webb Blanton is elected superintendent of public instruction for Texas.

1920
- The 19th Amendment guarantees women the right to vote.

1922
- ★ Commercial radio stations are established in Texas cities.

1924
- ★ Miriam "Ma" Ferguson is elected governor.

1926
- More than one million cars and trucks are registered in Texas.

Reviewing Key Terms

Match the key term with its definition by pairing the correct letter and number. Then create your own sentences in which you use the key terms to show you know what they mean.

1. ration
2. tenant farmer
3. appropriated
4. rural
5. urban

a. does not own the land
b. relating to a city
c. a food allowance
d. country life or agriculture
e. set aside for a specific purpose

Reviewing Key Facts

6. At which point in the Mexican Revolution did the United States send troops across the border?
7. Which three European nations were at war with Germany and Austria–Hungary in 1914?
8. List three contributions that Texans on the home front made to the war effort.
9. What was the economic impact of World War I on farmers and ranchers in Texas?
10. Who won the 1924 race for governor on an anti-Ku Klux Klan platform?
11. Why did Texas create the Texas Highway Department?
12. How did population changes affect Texas in the 1920s?

Critical Thinking

13. **Analyzing Information** Why did President Wilson call the Pershing expedition back to the United States?
14. **Understanding Cause and Effect** Use a graphic organizer similar to the one below to show some of the reasons why President Wilson felt pressured to enter the war.

Causes		Effect
	→	U.S. enters World War I

15. **Drawing Inferences** What do you think caused some of the racial tension during and after World War I?
16. **Evaluating** What were some of the important social and political changes that took place in the world that also affected the lives of Texans in the first 20 years of the century?
17. **Predicting Consequences** What was the probable effect of increased school taxes on Texas's system of education during Annie Webb Blanton's administration?

Geography and History Activity

18. On a blank map of Texas, locate and label the six Texas colleges that were part of the Southwest Conference in the 1920s. Find a picture of the college or of the football uniforms (past or present) for each college. Label the pictures and place them on the map of Texas.

Economics and History Activity

19. Effects of Technology What do you think were some of the effects on the economy and the use of resources that resulted from the increase in the number of motor vehicles in Texas?

Portfolio/TAKS Writing Activity

20. Predicting Consequences Reflect on the ideas and information presented in the chapter and choose one of the lifestyle improvements that you think is important and interesting: better education, improvements in transportation, more time for and choices of recreation. Write a paragraph in which you identify your particular choice and some of its political and economic consequences. Save your work for your portfolio.

Building Technology Skills

21. Using the Internet or Library for Research Work with another student to research one of the army training camps in Texas that served to prepare soldiers for World War I. If possible, choose a military unit and trace its fate on the battlefields of Europe. After you have completed your research, develop a multimedia presentation of the information using photographs, maps, and narration. Share your presentation with the rest of the class.

Practicing Skills

22. Identifying Assumptions Read the following paragraph and answer the questions: *Every day more and more Mexicans cross the border into Texas, sometimes thousands in a week. If immigration continues at this rate, however, Texas will be unable to provide jobs for all these people. Then we will have large numbers of people in need of food, clothing, and shelter.*

  a. What is the main topic?

  b. What assumptions are made?

  c. How could the accuracy of these assumptions be checked?

TEXAS HISTORY *Online*

Self-Check Quiz
Visit the texans.glencoe.com Web site and check on **Chapter 21—Self-Check Quizzes** to prepare for the chapter test.

Cooperative Learning Activity

23. Creating a Presentation Working in groups of four, research the kinds of cars and trucks that were being manufactured in the United States in the 1920s. Each group should focus on one make of vehicle. Create an oral and visual presentation for the rest of the class featuring drawings and interesting details about each type of car or truck.

TAKS PRACTICE

The Princeton Review

Use the graph to answer the following question.

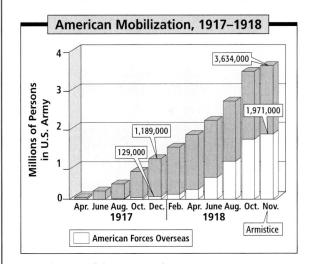

American Mobilization, 1917–1918

Millions of Persons in U.S. Army

3,634,000

1,971,000

1,189,000

129,000

Apr. June Aug. Oct. Dec. Feb. Apr. June Aug. Oct. Nov.
1917   1918

☐ American Forces Overseas   Armistice

At the time of the armistice, how many American soldiers were in the U.S. Army?

  A 129,000

  B 1,129,000

  C 1,971,000

  D 3,634,000

Test-Taking Tip:

In order to understand the information in a graph, read the title, the labels, and the legend carefully. To find the number of soldiers, look at the choices and then use the legend to make sure you locate the correct area on the graph.

Economics & History

Women on Tenant Farms

Meeting the needs of a family is not easy. Parents or guardians must find ways of paying for shelter, food, clothes, and entertainment for themselves and their children. Often, it is necessary for more than one person to work and earn money to contribute to the family budget.

Until recent times, most families had only one income earner. Women were expected to stay home to care for the children. But during the period from 1910 through the 1930s, in the cotton farms of central Texas (in counties such as Caldwell, Bastrop, Milam, McLennan, and Navarro) many women worked out of necessity.

Many of these women were wives or daughters of an earlier generation of tenant farmers. Their husbands or fathers did not have steady jobs and were always in debt. To help support the family, women worked alongside their menfolk on the tenant farms of the region.

Hard at Work

From March until November, women performed every task in the field, including the plowing at times. When the cotton seeds sprouted around May, women cultivated and chopped cotton alongside the men. Next came the "cleaning of the fields"—or weeding—a necessary step to give the cotton plants room to grow. Towards the latter part of the summer, women helped harvest the cotton. For protection, they wore gloves, bonnets, long-sleeve shirts, pants, and kneepads.

For many women, working the fields meant doing double duty, for they could not neglect their responsibilities as mothers. Somehow, they had to feed their family, nurse sick children, and take care of toddlers or infants. Sometimes they would tie one- or two-year-olds to nearby wagons to keep them from wandering off. They also placed babies on top of their cotton sacks and dragged them along to keep them close.

The mother's contribution to family did not end after long hours of working under the hot sun. There was still the cooking to be done, as

All members of the tenant farmer's family shared in the workload.

Windmills pumped water from aquifers to irrigate cotton fields on the Texas plains.

well as the washing, cleaning, and sewing. At that time, there were no modern appliances to help them. Their shabby homes often lacked electricity for lighting, washing machines, stoves, and refrigerators. Water had to be fetched from afar and carried into the home. In addition to household chores, a mother's role included all tasks relating to child care, including teaching the children proper conduct.

Paying Their Way

Women on the tenant farms of central Texas contributed a good share to the financial needs of their families. Despite all their efforts, most received no money for their fieldwork and

house duties, however, as husbands often decided how all the family's income would be spent. Usually, the money earned from working in the fields fell short of what was needed to pay off a family's back debts. The next spring, the cycle would begin again with women joining their men to work on the harvest. It took a strong woman to be a tenant farmer's wife.

TAKS PRACTICE

1. **Drawing Conclusions** What difficulties do you think working women face today to provide for the care of their children?
2. **Making Inferences** What do you think when you hear the term "women's work"?
3. **Writing About Economics** Write a paragraph that develops one of the themes below. Use standard grammar, spelling, sentence structure, and punctuation. Include information and examples from the feature as details to support your argument.
   a. Women should not work outside the home.
   b. A husband and wife should decide together how money is spent.
   c. Employers should offer on-site daycare to their working parents.

The Great Depression

Why It Matters

The 1930s brought one of the greatest challenges to Texas and the United States since the Civil War. Ideas about the role of the government in economic matters were modified as new programs such as Social Security began. Texans provided important leadership in solving the nation's problems.

The Impact Today

Many projects built with federal assistance in the 1930s continue to serve Texans. Among these are the Paseo Del Rio (the San Antonio Riverwalk), the San Jacinto Monument, Buchanan Dam, and facilities at many state parks.

1930
★ *East Texas Oil Field discovered*

Texas

United States   *1929*   *1931*   *1933*

World

1929
• *Stock market crashed; the Great Depression began*

1933
• *Prohibition ended*

Dusty Day in Texas *by Grant Tyson Reynard reflects the stark landscape of a Texas dust storm.*

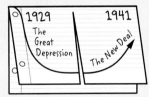

1935
★ James Allred became governor

1936
★ Texas celebrated centennial of independence

1935   1937   1939

1936
• Jessie Owens won four gold medals at the Berlin Olympics

LIMITED ENGAGEMENT
FULL LENGTH, NOTHING CUT BUT THE PRICE

DAVID O. SELZNICK'S
Production of
MARGARET MITCHELL'S
Story of the Old South

GONE WITH THE WIND
IN TECHNICOLOR, starring
CLARK GABLE

1939
• Gone With the Wind produced as a movie

1939
• Nylon stockings first commonly worn

TEXAS HISTORY
Online

Chapter Overview
Visit the texans.glencoe.com Web site and click on **Chapter 22—Chapter Overviews** to preview chapter information.

CHAPTER 22   The Great Depression   **497**

Depression Hits Texas

Main Idea
The Great Depression affected Texas in a variety of ways.

Key Terms
stock, unemployment, wildcatter, law of supply and demand, martial law, economies of scale, Dust Bowl

Reading Strategy
Organizing Information As you read this section, complete a table like the one shown here by stating how these parts of the Texas economy were affected by the Great Depression.

Factories	
Timber workers	
Oil production	
Cotton crops	

Read to Learn
• why the East Texas Oil Field was significant.
• how the cotton crisis was resolved.

Section Theme
Economic Factors Governor Sterling worked with Texans to limit production of certain products and crops during the Great Depression.

Preview of Events

♦1929	♦1930	♦1931
Stock market crashes on Wall Street	East Texas Oil Field is discovered	Texas Railroad Commission limits production in East Texas Oil Field

A
Texas Story

Emma Tenayuca Brooks

For future activist Emma Tenayuca of San Antonio, going to La Plaza de Zacate as a young girl was exciting. People sold food and newspapers and listened intently to political speeches. In an interview, Emma said, "There was one place where I used to go particularly with my grandfather . . . and that was La Plaza de Zacate, that was the square, Milam Square, right in front of Santa Rosa Hospital."

The Great Depression Begins

Republican **Herbert Hoover** became the president of the United States in 1929. He had been in office for only seven months when Wall Street stock market prices fell sharply. **Stock** shares represent ownership in companies. During the 1920s, people hoping to make quick fortunes had driven up the price of the stock of many companies. Some investors had borrowed money to buy stock. When the price of stocks fell, both they and the banks that had loaned the money were wiped out.

The economic bad news continued. Factories closed, creating widespread unemployment, or loss of jobs. Unemployed people could not buy products, so even more factories closed. As prices of agricultural products dropped, the income of Texas farmers suffered. People could not afford new houses, so East Texas timber workers were laid off from their jobs.

President Hoover greatly underestimated the severity, or depth, of the **Great Depression.** He called on local churches and charities to increase their aid to the poor. He also asked people to hire their unemployed neighbors to do odd jobs around the house. Hoover believed relief efforts should begin at the state and city levels.

Reading Check Explaining What were some results of the sharply falling stock market prices?

Too Much Oil

Texans elected an oil businessman, **Ross Sterling,** as governor in 1930. He was immediately confronted with economic crises, one of

which threatened the oil industry. In October 1930, a wildcatter named **Columbus Marion "Dad" Joiner** drilled an oil well in northern Rusk County. A wildcatter is a person who drills an oil well in an area not known to contain oil. That well, named the Daisy Bradford No. 3, was the first well of the East Texas Oil Field. This new field was so big that it was named for a whole region. Kilgore, Longview, Tyler, Henderson, Gladewater, and many smaller towns boomed as thousands of people descended upon East Texas.

Drilling in the new field provided high-paying jobs for farmers and timber workers. A driller could make as much as $10 to $12 per day. As automobile dealerships, pharmacies, and clothing stores all benefited from the East Texas Oil Field boom, the Great Depression seemed far away.

At first the major oil companies were reluctant to invest in the East Texas field, which they believed would not produce any oil. One company's geologist even offered to drink every barrel of oil that the field produced. This left opportunities for hundreds of small oil drillers—called "independents"—scattered throughout Gregg, Rusk, Smith, and Upshur Counties. They drilled wells in unlikely places. Soon the East Texas field was producing more oil than all the

People of Texas

Columbus "Dad" Joiner 1860–1947

Columbus Marion Joiner was born in Alabama. He began a law practice in Tennessee in 1883 and briefly was a member of the state legislature. In 1897 he moved to Oklahoma, where he made and lost two oil fortunes before

moving to Texas in 1926.

Joiner was convinced there were oil deposits in Rusk County, so in 1930 he began drilling. After two unsuccessful wells, he drilled a third. The Daisy Bradford No. 3 opened up the largest oil field in the

world at that time. As "father" of the field, Joiner was nicknamed "Dad."

Overwhelmed by financial problems and lawsuits, he later sold his well and leases for $1 million and retired. The city of Joinerville is named after him.

A Governor Sterling   **B** Citizen

other fields in the rest of the state combined. As the **law of supply and demand** predicted, prices went down as supply increased and demand stayed the same. With the same demand, producers were willing to lower prices to make sure they were not "stuck" with the oil. In 1931 the price of a barrel of oil fell to ten cents or even less.

Even at that low price, producers believed they had to keep drilling. If they stopped to wait for prices to go up, they feared someone else drilling elsewhere would get the oil. Finally, in April 1931, the **Texas Railroad Commission** issued an order to limit production in the East Texas field. Independent operators believed this action favored the large oil companies. There was widespread cheating. Fake valves on pipes were installed that indicated "shut" when the valve was really open. Truckers carried "hot oil" at

night on back roads without using their headlights. "Hot oil" was petroleum produced in violation of the Railroad Commission's orders and was smuggled out of the Texas boom towns.

To enforce the order, Governor Ross Sterling declared **martial law** and sent the Texas National Guard to the East Texas field. Eventually martial law ended, but overproduction continued for a time. By 1935, however, state and federal laws had successfully controlled production, and oil prices became more stable.

Crisis for Cotton Farmers

Even though cotton remained the most important crop raised by Texas farmers, its prices declined during the 1920s. The Great Depression forced them even lower. In 1931 the average price for a 500-pound bale of cotton was only $28.50. Because cotton did not spoil like other farm crops, it could be stored for years. The stored cotton and the new crop created even larger surpluses. As with petroleum, the answer was to limit production, not just in Texas but nationwide.

The Texas Department of Agriculture urged voluntary reduction in the number of acres planted in cotton, but few farmers cooperated with that suggestion. A more radical solution was proposed by the governor of Louisiana, **Huey Long.** He called the Louisiana legislature into special session and pushed through a law prohibiting the planting of cotton in Louisiana in 1932. The law, known as **"drop-a-crop,"** had a provision that other cotton-growing states must also prohibit production in order for the law to go into effect.

Because Texas was the largest cotton-producing state, everyone knew that Texas must agree if "drop-a-crop" was to become a reality. Governor Sterling did not think the idea would work. Eventually the Texas legislature passed a law calling for partial reduction. When a state court declared that measure unconstitutional, the whole plan collapsed.

☑ **Reading Check** **Explaining** Describe the "drop-a-crop" plan.

Dust Storms Blanket the High Plains

After the arrival of the railroads, many of the large ranches of the High Plains were subdivided into farms. When wheat prices were high after World War I, farmers bought tractors and expanded their production. As prices declined throughout the 1920s, farmers tried to earn more money by planting more crops. The Plains seemed perfect for the economies of scale that

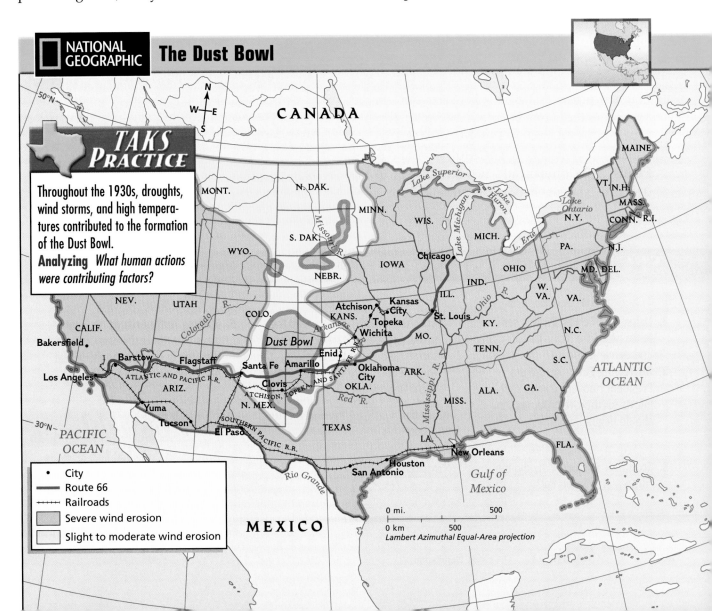

NATIONAL GEOGRAPHIC **The Dust Bowl**

TAKS PRACTICE

Throughout the 1930s, droughts, wind storms, and high temperatures contributed to the formation of the Dust Bowl.
Analyzing *What human actions were contributing factors?*

Legend:
- • City
- Route 66
- Railroads
- Severe wind erosion
- Slight to moderate wind erosion

0 mi. 500
0 km 500
Lambert Azimuthal Equal-Area projection

Dust storms such as this one could darken skies for hours and turn day into night. What were some of the effects of these storms?

came with mechanized agriculture. Economies of scale mean that the cost of operation decreases as the size of the operation increases. As with oil and cotton, however, overproduction drove prices down. In 20 years, wheat dropped from $2.19 to 39¢ per bushel.

The decline in the price of wheat was only one of the problems for High Plains farmers. When farmers plowed grasses under, there was nothing left to hold the soil when winds blew. A severe drought in the 1930s added to the problem. The soil literally blew away as the residents of the Plains watched. Dust from what came to be known as the **Dust Bowl** was reported by ship captains in the Atlantic Ocean. Motorists in Amarillo, Lubbock, Dalhart, Muleshoe, and other Plains cities often could not see 20 feet (6 m) down the street. People became ill from lung diseases. Between 1932 and 1937, the worst years of the Great Depression, many families lost their farms because of the difficult economic times.

Texans Look for Answers

At first, Texans and other Americans looked to themselves and each other for answers to their growing economic problems. As banks failed, some merchant associations printed coupons that could be used as money. Universities that could not pay salaries allowed professors and their families to eat in the university dining halls. Many rural churches paid their preachers with eggs, chickens, vegetables, and firewood.

Mexican Americans and African Americans in Texas were especially hard hit by the Great Depression. Between 1929 and 1931, large numbers of Mexicans and Mexican Americans left Texas for Mexico. Some migrated voluntarily, but many were deported, or forced to leave the United States. To open jobs for Texas citizens, some residents of Texas and some U.S. citizens were forced to go when they could not prove their citizenship. The percentage of African Americans who were unemployed was approximately twice that of the rest of the population. Many African Americans left the state looking for work.

✓ **Reading Check** **Describing** What happened to some Mexican Americans during the Great Depression?

SECTION 1 ASSESSMENT

Checking for Understanding

1. **Using Key Terms** Write a sentence using the terms law of supply and demand and unemployment.
2. **Reviewing Facts** Where did President Hoover believe relief efforts for the Great Depression should begin?

Reviewing Themes

3. **Economic Factors** Why did the "drop-a-crop" plan fail?

Organizing to Learn

4. **Creating Charts** As you read this section, create a chart like the one shown below. List the creative ways people were paid during the Great Depression.

Occupation	Payment
Professors	
Preachers	
Merchants	

Critical Thinking

5. **Making Comparisons** In what ways was the East Texas Oil Field different from other oil fields that had been discovered in Texas?

TAKS PRACTICE

Organizing The Dust Bowl made life harder for people during this time period. Find three details in the text supporting this statement.

TAKS Skillbuilder

Reading a Bar Graph

Why Learn This Skill?

Bar graphs can be used to help compare facts involving numbers. Bars, or columns, represent quantities or totals. Bar graphs can show change over time. They can compare quantities during the same time period. A bar graph might compare the number of students attending five different schools during the same year.

Bar graphs have horizontal and vertical axes that describe the information. Sometimes a bar graph compares more than one set of facts. In the graph showing the oil wells of Texas, a key uses color to distinguish productive and unproductive wells.

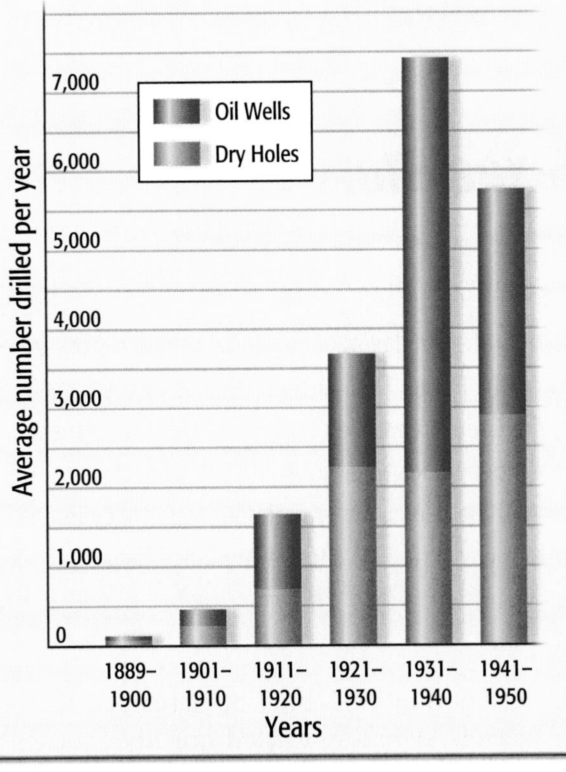

Learning the Skill

Here are some steps to follow in reading a bar graph:
- Read the title to learn the subject of the graph.
- Look at the information on the axes.
- Compare the lengths of the bars on the graph.
- Use the information to draw conclusions.

Practicing the Skill

Study the graph and answer the questions that follow.

❶ What is the subject and time period of this graph?

❷ What information is represented on the two axes?

❸ What does each color represent?

❹ Why do you think the number of wells decreased from 1941 to 1950?

❺ In what time period were the most dry holes drilled?

❻ Create your own question relating to this bar graph.

Oil Wells Drilled in Texas

Key:
- Oil Wells
- Dry Holes

Vertical axis: Average number drilled per year (0; 1,000; 2,000; 3,000; 4,000; 5,000; 6,000; 7,000)

Horizontal axis (Years): 1889–1900, 1901–1910, 1911–1920, 1921–1930, 1931–1940, 1941–1950

TAKS PRACTICE

Reading a Bar Graph Create your own bar graph. Use numbers or amounts for the vertical axis and years for the horizontal axis. Possible topics include the number of students graduating from your school in the past 10 years or the population of your city in the past 10 years. Use books, encyclopedias, or the Internet to find information. Write three questions that relate to your bar graph.

GO TO Glencoe's **Skillbuilder Interactive Workbook,** Level 1, provides instruction and practice in key social studies skills.

Texas and the New Deal

Guide to Reading

Main Idea
President Roosevelt helped Texas and the United States to begin recovering from the Great Depression.

Key Terms
alphabet agencies
mural
cooperatives
contour plowing

Reading Strategy
Classifying Information As you read this section, complete a chart like the one shown here by filling in the ways the New Deal helped Texans living in rural areas.

Rural Problem	How the New Deal Helped
Electricity	
Farming	
Soil erosion	

Read to Learn
• what the New Deal offered.
• how Texans cooperated with the Roosevelt administration.
• how rural Texans were affected by the New Deal.

Section Theme
Science and Technology Farmers used different farming methods to protect the land and raise prices.

Preview of Events

♦1933
Franklin D. Roosevelt starts New Deal

♦1936
Dallas hosts centennial celebration of Texas independence

Texas bank, c. 1930

A
Texas Story

The recollections, or stories, of everyday people can help bring history to life and give it personal meaning. Emma Tenayuca of San Antonio remembered how, as a teenager, the Great Depression hit her own family. "Times became even harder as many people lost their jobs. In 1929 Wall Street crashed. In 1932, the closing of the banks. My grandfather lost money in one of them . . . He came over to me and said, 'I've lost everything I have.'"

The New Deal Begins

President Hoover ran for reelection in 1932, but voters blamed him for the Depression. They believed Hoover had not acted quickly enough to provide help for needy people. His opponent, **Franklin D. Roosevelt,** won an overwhelming victory. Texans gave almost 90 percent of their votes to Roosevelt, who had promised "a new deal for the American people." He took office in March 1933, and his programs became part of what was called the **New Deal.**

President Roosevelt began with a flurry of activity during "the first hundred days." Among his other actions was ordering all banks to close for a short time so examiners could determine which ones were strong enough to stay in business. He also asked Congress to pass laws to help solve the economic problems.

Vice President John N. Garner, a former Texas member of the U.S. House of Representatives, helped push New Deal programs in Congress. Texans occupied some of the most powerful positions in Congress, and Roosevelt needed their cooperation. The chart below shows Texans who chaired committees in the U.S. House of Representatives during the New Deal.

New Deal Programs in Texas

The New Deal greatly increased the activity of the federal government in people's lives. Before the 1930s the government's main economic actions had been to collect taxes, print a money supply, and set up courts in which financial disputes could be settled. The New Deal created agencies to deal with the many problems faced by the nation as a result of the Depression. They were often known as the alphabet agencies because people called these organizations by their initials.

Some agencies such as the **Federal Emergency Relief Administration** (FERA) gave funds to states and local agencies for distribution directly to unemployed people. Other agencies tried to solve the unemployment problem by hiring people for various projects. The **Civilian Conservation Corps** (CCC) provided outdoor employment for young men while it helped preserve the nation's resources. Nearly 50,000 Texans participated in the CCC. Living in camps, workers planted trees, built erosion control structures, and completed other projects that helped conserve natural resources. They were paid $30 per month, $25 of which they were expected to send home to their families. Many of the state parks they developed, such as Garner, Bastrop, and Palo Duro, are still in use.

The **National Youth Administration** (NYA) hired high school and college students to perform clerical and maintenance jobs. The students often worked at schools and playgrounds. They also helped build roadside parks and spread gravel on highway shoulders. Lyndon Johnson

TEXAS HISTORY *Online*

Self-Check Quiz Visit the texans.glencoe.com Web site and click on **Chapter 22—Student Web Activity** to learn more about the Works Progress Administration.

TAKS PRACTICE

Problem Solving Each elected Texan listed in the chart helped to solve a problem facing America in the 1930s. *Consider a present-day problem that Texas or America faces and propose a possible government solution.*

Texans and the New Deal		
Member	**Hometown**	**Legislation and Contributions**
Sam Rayburn	Bonham	Proposed the Securities and Exchange Commission to restore confidence in the stock market.
		Proposed the Rural Electrification Administration to help rural residents obtain electrical service.
		Proposed the Federal Communications Commission to regulate radio broadcasting.
James P. Buchanan	Brenham	Chaired the Appropriations Committee, which approved all government spending.
Marvin Jones	Amarillo	Worked to help farmers obtain loans and worked for soil conservation.
Hatton Sumners	Dallas	Worked to modernize federal courts.

Sam Rayburn 1882-1961

Sam Rayburn was elected 24 times to the U.S. House of Representatives, spanning the terms of eight presidents. "Mr. Sam," as he was known, was raised on a cotton farm in the same rural area of Texas that he represented. That helped him understand the people who elected him and their problems, and he worked hard to bring important projects to the district to improve life there.

After working his way through college, Rayburn won his first elected position to the Texas House of Representatives in 1906. He attended law school between legislative sessions. After his 1912 election to the U.S. Congress, he never again had a Republican opponent. He was Speaker of the House for 17 years. As Speaker he was third in line for the U.S. presidency.

---

was head of the NYA in Texas. Years later, Johnson became president of the United States. Many of the programs President Johnson began in the 1960s reminded people of the New Deal.

The **Public Works Administration** (PWA) built bridges, dams, schools, and other structures of permanent value to the state. In Fort Worth alone, the PWA built 13 schools and expanded 13 more. The **Works Progress Administration** (WPA) hired 600,000 Texans during the Great Depression. Most of the jobs were in construction. Texans built swimming pools, recreation centers, stadiums, and parks. New Deal programs also involved the government in the arts. The WPA employed artists to paint murals in public buildings. Theater and musical groups were hired to provide entertainment in several Texas cities, and historians were given jobs writing community histories.

Reading Check Examining How did the New Deal help people recover from the Depression?

Rural Texans and the New Deal

Almost 60 percent of Texans lived in rural areas in 1930. The New Deal created programs for farmers, ranchers, and other rural residents. Farmers still relied on kerosene lamps and hand-powered machines long after city residents enjoyed electric lights and appliances. New Deal legislation helped rural people form cooperatives, or organized groups, that borrowed money from the government to pay for stringing electrical wires. Electricity eased the burden of house and farm work. Electric water pumps brought water into the house, and electric lights made reading possible at night. Farm families could now listen, as city families did, to the latest news broadcasts and radio programs.

Congress passed laws that paid farmers to reduce production by plowing crops under instead of harvesting them. Farmers cut down peach trees and poured excess milk into streams. The government paid them to destroy crops in an effort to drive prices up.

Dams were constructed on the Colorado River to generate electricity. The dams also provided flood control and water for rice farmers. The lakes that formed behind the dams created new economic opportunities in recreation and tourism.

New Deal programs also tried to slow down soil erosion. Farmers in the Dust Bowl regions planted alternating strips of wheat and grain sorghum. The sorghum was taller and protected the topsoil from being blown away. Farmers also plowed at right angles to the wind so ridges would collect the blowing earth. The federal government provided money to farmers to plant trees as windbreaks. By 1938, the sand dunes that had formed around Dalhart were gone.

In the cotton fields of Texas, the federal government encouraged farmers to fill up gullies with brush to slow the water as it ran downhill. Farmers plowed around hills in a method called **contour plowing** rather than going straight up and down the hills. Farmers were paid to plant crops, such as clover, that would enhance the soil.

Texas Centennial

Some of the construction projects during the Great Depression were in celebration of the 100th anniversary of Texas independence in 1936. The three largest cities in the state—Dallas, Houston, and San Antonio—competed to determine which one would host the official celebration. Dallas was chosen because it was able to contribute almost $8 million to help build the facilities. The U.S. Congress provided another $3 million. The main celebration was held at the 185-acre (75-hectare) Fair Park in Dallas. New buildings were constructed, including the Hall of State and the Hall of Negro Life. Exhibits highlighted Texas history and proudly displayed examples of Texas products and culture. Other cities joined Dallas in observing the Texas Centennial. The San Jacinto Monument was erected on the battlefield to the

Picturing **History**

The Texas Centennial in 1936 was a statewide event that celebrated Texas's past and present achievements. The state legislature provided funds for buildings, exhibitions, and special events. What is the message in this poster?

east of Houston. Museums were built at the Alamo grounds in San Antonio, on the campus of the University of Texas, and at Canyon, Huntsville, Goliad, and Gonzales.

✓ **Reading Check** **Analyzing** How did electricity change life for Texans?

SECTION 2 ASSESSMENT

Checking for Understanding

1. **Using Key Terms** Define alphabet agencies, murals, cooperatives, and contour plowing.
2. **Reviewing Facts** What percentage of Texas votes went to Roosevelt in the 1932 presidential election?

Reviewing Themes

3. **Science and Technology** How did dams built in Texas during the Great Depression contribute to the state's economic prosperity?

Organizing to Learn

4. **Creating Charts** Create a chart like the one shown here, and fill in the appropriate information for each New Deal agency.

Agencies	Full Name	Purpose
FERA		
CCC		
NYA		
PWA		
WPA		

Critical Thinking

5. **Explaining** What had been the federal government's main economic actions before the 1930s?

TAKS PRACTICE

Supporting Generalizations Some construction projects during the Great Depression were in celebration of the 100th anniversary of Texas's independence. Find three statements in the text supporting this fact.

Politics in the 1930s

Guide to Reading

Main Idea
Politics in the 1930s dealt with a variety of issues.

Key Terms
pardon
strike
arbitration

Reading Strategy
Organizing Information As you read this section, complete a table like the one shown here, outlining the significant acts of the governors in the 1930s.

Governor	Significant Acts
Ferguson	
Allred	
O'Daniel	

Read to Learn
• what Dr. Lawrence Nixon accomplished for African Americans.
• why LULAC was important for Mexican Americans.

Section Theme
Civic Rights and Responsibilities African Americans and Mexican Americans fought for their rights in court.

Preview of Events

1929	1932	1935	1938
League of United Latin American Citizens is founded	*Nixon* v. *Condon* case	James Allred becomes governor	Pecan shellers' strike

A Texas Story

Garment worker

At age 21, Emma Tenayuca was already a veteran labor organizer when she led the San Antonio pecan shellers' strike in 1938. The passion for justice she had learned from the speakers at La Plaza de Zacate inspired her. "Garment workers averaged about $3 to $4 per week . . . Sales girls earned about $6 weekly. The few Mexicans who were fortunate enough to find jobs in the cement plants and packing houses earned about 25 cents per hour."
—Emma Tenayuca Brooks, Oral History interview, 1978

1930s Governors

Despite economic problems in his term, Ross Sterling ran for re-election in 1932. His main opponent was Miriam Ferguson, who had already served a term as governor. Ferguson defeated Sterling in the Democratic primary

election by fewer than 3,800 votes out of more than 900,000 cast. She then won the general election and was sworn in shortly before Franklin Roosevelt became president.

Ferguson asked President Roosevelt to lend farmers money to help make up for lost income from lower cotton prices. She succeeded in getting the state constitution amended to allow $20 million in bread bonds to feed the poor. She also proposed a tax on oil. However, the Ferguson administration also was clouded by controversy. One of her first acts was firing several experienced Texas Rangers. She used her **pardon** power to release many criminals from state prisons. The governor and the legislature struggled unsuccessfully to meet the needs of the state when there was not nearly enough money available.

James Allred was sworn in as governor in 1935. He moved to restore confidence in law enforcement by reorganizing the Texas Rangers. They became part of the Department of Public Safety and earned high marks for their ability to solve difficult cases. Allred helped found the **Board of Pardons and Paroles** to establish an orderly system to control the release of prisoners. He also helped create retirement systems for teachers and state employees.

The governor's election of 1938 provided both politics and entertainment. At that time, W. Lee O'Daniel had been sales manager for a Fort Worth flour company. As part of his job, he hosted a daily radio show, broadcast on WBAP to several stations around the state. He had never been involved in politics, but he decided to run for governor. He campaigned around the

state, promising to raise pensions, abolish capital punishment, and veto any sales tax. His theme song, "Beautiful, Beautiful Texas," became sort of an unofficial state song. Its chorus was:

"Beautiful, Beautiful Texas, where the beautiful
    bluebonnets grow,
We're proud of our forefathers who fought at
    the Alamo,
You can live on the plains or the mountains,
Or down where the sea breezes blow,
And you'll still be in beautiful Texas,
The most beautiful place that I know."

He won an overwhelming victory. Once in office, however, he was unable to deliver on his campaign promises.

African American Voting Rights

Even after the creation of the poll tax and other devices to keep African Americans from voting, some African Americans continued to vote. In 1923 the state legislature tried to reduce African American voting even further. It passed a law declaring that only white persons could vote in the Democratic Party's primary election. Since Texas was overwhelmingly Democratic, a win in the primary meant victory in the general election. **Dr. Lawrence Nixon,** an African American

TEXAS TODAY

Michael L. Williams was appointed to the Texas Railroad Commission by former Governor George W. Bush in 1998 to serve the unexpired term of Carole Keeton Rylander. His fellow commissioners elected Williams commission chairman. In 2000, the people of Texas elected him to the term expiring in 2002. He is the first African American in Texas history to hold a nonjudicial statewide post and is the highest ranking African American in Texas state government.

Dr. Lawrence A. Nixon

physician from El Paso and a member of the NAACP, presented his poll tax receipt and tried to vote in the Democratic primary. He was turned away. Nixon then filed suit to win the right to vote. He won the case of *Nixon* v. *Herndon* (1927) in the Supreme Court of the United States when the justices declared that his rights under the Fourteenth and Fifteenth Amendments to the U.S. Constitution had been violated.

The state continued to try to exclude African Americans from voting. The legislature said that the party, not the legislature, had the power to determine who voted in the primaries. The leaders of the Democratic Party then drew up discriminatory rules. Dr. Nixon filed suit again, and in 1932 he won again in the case of *Nixon* v. *Condon*. The fight for African Americans' right to vote did not end, however. The issue would come before the Supreme Court again in 1944 when, in the case of *Smith* v. *Allwright*, the Court would rule that the all-white primary was unconstitutional. Dr. Nixon's courageous struggle was an inspiration to a younger generation who would carry on the struggle for civil rights in the 1950s and 1960s.

✔ **Reading Check** **Identifying** Which of the discriminatory laws did Dr. Lawrence Nixon challenge in the courts?

Mexican Americans Fight for Their Rights

The **League of United Latin American Citizens,** or LULAC, was founded at Corpus Christi in 1929 with **Ben Garza** as the first president. LULAC worked for Mexican American rights in the court system, in hiring, and in education.

Mexican American children attended segregated schools in the border city of Del Rio. In 1930, LULAC supported **Jesús Salvatierra** in his lawsuit against the Del Rio schools. Although Salvatierra eventually lost his suit, LULAC had

shown that it intended to be a strong voice for Mexican American rights. By the 1930s LULAC had branches in many cities and towns, including Brownsville, McAllen, San Angelo, and Roma.

Education also was an important issue for other organizations. The School Improvement League (*La Liga Pro-Defensa Escolar*) was founded in 1934 in San Antonio. **Eleuterio Escobar, Jr.,** and **María L. de Hernández,** the founders, were distressed by the inadequate school facilities for San Antonio's Mexican American children. The schools were overcrowded and poorly maintained. The League organized a rally attended by 10,000 people. It also prepared documents that proved their claims of unequal treatment.

The Pecan Shellers' Strike

San Antonio was also the place where workers organized for better working conditions. There, women at the **Finck Cigar Company** formed groups in the early 1930s to protest against poor sanitation in the company's factory and unfair work rules.

Another target of labor activists was the pecan shelling industry. More than 10,000 people, mostly Mexican Americans, were employed in

A Shared Past...

The Great Depression was especially hard on working women. Popular opinion held that the scarce jobs should be reserved for men, the traditional "breadwinners" for families. Accordingly, it was common for school boards to release women who married and for companies to fire women so men could have their jobs. On the other hand, President Roosevelt appointed Frances Perkins as the first woman cabinet member. Roosevelt was also the first president to appoint women as federal judges and as ambassadors to foreign nations.

picking the nut meats out of pecans. Working conditions were inhumane. People worked in crowded, dirty rooms. They breathed pecan dust all day. In 1938 the company cut their wages. **Emma Tenayuca Brooks** and other organizers led more than 10,000 workers on a strike (a refusal to work) that lasted three months. Police arrested more than 700 of the strikers, but eventually both sides agreed to arbitration (allowing an impartial observer to solve a dispute). The workers went back to their jobs for higher pay.

Miners and Farmers

Two other groups of workers saw their living conditions worsen during the Great Depression. New Deal farm programs that paid farmers not to grow crops specified that payment would go to the landowners. Many Texas farmers were tenants who did not own the land they farmed. Payments to the landowner meant eviction for the tenants since their labor was no longer necessary. Coal miners also suffered. The discovery of the East Texas Oil Field and low prices for petroleum meant that the demand for coal decreased. Coal mines were closed and the miners were laid off.

✓**Reading Check** **Explaining** What were the main objectives of the League of United Latin American Citizens?

Picturing **History**

San Antonio

Women who worked at the Finck Cigar Company in San Antonio went on strike in 1933 to protest working conditions and wore sashes bearing their message. Why did the workers use both English and Spanish to get their point across?

SECTION 3 ASSESSMENT

Checking for Understanding

1. **Using Key Terms** How are strike and arbitration related? Use the term pardon in a sentence that defines it in context.
2. **Reviewing Facts** What group supported Dr. Nixon in his lawsuit for the right to vote?

Reviewing Themes

3. **Civic Rights and Responsibilities** Why did LULAC support a lawsuit against the Del Rio school system in 1930?

Organizing to Learn

4. **Sequencing** Create a chart like the one shown here and add the year next to each event.

Year	Event
	Sterling loses bid for reelection.
	Allred becomes governor.
	Supreme Court rules that the all-white primary is unconstitutional.
	LULAC is founded.
	School Improvement League is founded.

Critical Thinking

5. **Evaluating Differences** What were Governor Ferguson's controversial actions involving the Texas Rangers and criminals? How did Governor Allred's actions differ from those of Governor Ferguson?

TAKS PRACTICE

Summarizing Summarize the reasons that the pecan shellers went on strike in San Antonio in 1938.

Chapter Summary

The Great Depression

1929
- President Hoover takes office.
- ★ The stock market crashes in October, and the Great Depression begins.
- The League of United Latin American Citizens is founded.

1930
- Unemployment spreads.
- ★ Oil is discovered in the East Texas field.

1931
- The price of oil, cotton, and other products decreases.
- Governor Sterling declares martial law in the East Texas Oil Field.

1932
- Franklin D. Roosevelt is elected president.
- Miriam Ferguson is elected governor.
- ★ *Nixon* v. *Condon* is decided by the U.S. Supreme Court.
- ★ The "Dust Bowl" affects Texas.

1933
- Roosevelt starts the New Deal to provide jobs and creates "alphabet agencies."

1936
- Texas celebrates centennial.

1938
- ★ Pecan shellers organize a strike in San Antonio.

Reviewing Key Terms

Number your paper from 1 to 4. Write the letter of the vocabulary term that goes with each supplied definition.

a. law of supply and demand
b. stock
c. unemployment
d. wildcatter

1. a claim representing investment in a corporation that gives the buyer a share of ownership
2. an oil operator who drills for wells in an area not known to have oil
3. having fewer jobs available than the people needing them
4. general economic principle that states if supply increases and demand stays the same or decreases, the price will go down

Reviewing Key Facts

5. Explain how independent oil operators kept producing oil in the East Texas field after the Texas Railroad Commission issued the order to limit production.
6. Which governor in the 1930s helped create retirement systems for teachers and state employees?
7. Name the U.S. vice president during the Roosevelt administration who was a former Texas member of Congress.
8. Describe how cooperatives helped Texans living in rural areas.
9. Explain why farmers destroyed some of their crops during the New Deal.
10. What happened when the pecan shellers agreed to arbitration?
11. Why was Governor Ferguson able to release many criminals from state prisons?

Critical Thinking

12. **Differentiating** Create a table like the one below to show how the Great Depression affected oil workers, cotton farmers, and Mexican Americans.

Group	Effect of Great Depression
Oil workers	
Cotton farmers	
Mexican Americans	

13. **Making Comparisons** How is contour plowing different from other plowing?
14. **Identifying** What was the result of Jesús Salvatierra's lawsuit against the Del Rio schools?

Geography and History Activity

15. Sketch a blank map of Texas. Put a dot and a symbol or image on the locations where special Texas Centennial buildings were constructed or celebrations were held. Label the buildings on the map.

Cooperative Learning Activity

16. Writing a Research Report Organize into groups of four. Choose a topic about the growth and development of the oil industry in Texas. Topics could include, but are not limited to, the beginning of the oil industry in Texas, lives of oil workers, or life in a Texas oil town. Your school or public librarian or the public information department of a large oil company can help you find information. After finding your information, write a short report. Include artwork, maps, and diagrams.

Practicing Skills

Reading a Bar Graph *Study the bar graph and answer the questions that follow.*

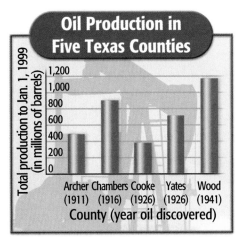

Oil Production in Five Texas Counties

17. What does the graph compare?

18. Which two counties have produced the most oil?

19. How much oil has been produced in Chambers County?

 ## Portfolio/TAKS Writing Activity

20. Descriptive Writing Imagine you are a farmer in Texas during the Hoover and Roosevelt presidencies. Write a one-page paper describing what is happening to your farm and the changes you see during the Great Depression and the New Deal. Save your work for your portfolio.

Self-Check Quiz
Visit the texans.glencoe.com Web site and click on **Chapter 22—Self-Check Quizzes** to prepare for the chapter test.

 ## Building Technology Skills

21. Using the Internet Visit the American Memory Web site hosted by the Library of Congress or another Web site to find a photograph relating to the Great Depression. Share this with your class.

TAKS PRACTICE

Use the time line to answer the following question.

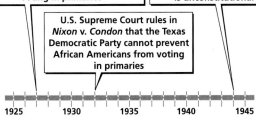

> U.S. Supreme Court rules in *Nixon* v. *Herndon* that Texas law may not prohibit African Americans from voting in primaries

> U.S. Supreme Court rules in *Smith* v. *Allwright* that the "all-white primary" is unconstitutional

> U.S. Supreme Court rules in *Nixon* v. *Condon* that the Texas Democratic Party cannot prevent African Americans from voting in primaries

1925   1930   1935   1940   1945

Selected Legal Events

Which of the following statements best summarizes the events on this time line?

F African Americans could vote in all elections between 1925 and 1945.

G The U.S. Supreme Court did not voice opinions about voting laws.

H *Nixon* v. *Herndon* ruled that segregated schools were illegal.

J Some African Americans used the court system to make sure they could vote in all elections.

Test-Taking Tip:

Read the events on the time line carefully. To summarize this time line, ask yourself how the events are similar.

CHAPTER 23

War and Peace

Why It Matters

World War II brought about considerable changes in Texas. Texans served in all branches of the U.S. armed forces. Texans also worked on the home front to supply airplanes, ships, gasoline, and other products necessary to fight the war.

The Impact Today

The Allied victory in World War II protected the freedom and democracy guaranteed in the United States and Texas constitutions.

1942
★ More available jobs for minorities and women in Texas

Texas

United States   1934   1938   1942

World

1937
• Golden Gate Bridge opened in San Francisco

1937
• Japan invaded China

1941
• United States entered World War II

This World War II battle scene of PT boats and Zero airplanes near Midway Island was painted by Lieutenant Commander Griffith Coale.

FOLDABLES™ Study Organizer

TAKS PRACTICE

Summarizing Information Study Foldable
Make this foldable and use it to help you organize information about Texas during and after World War II.

Step 1 Stack four sheets of paper, one on top of the other. On the top sheet of paper, trace a large circle. With the papers still stacked, cut out all four circles at the same time.

Step 2 Staple the paper circles together at one point around the edge.

Staple here.

This makes a circular booklet.

Step 3 Label the front cover as shown, then label the next page "Know," another page "Want to Know," and the third page "Learned."

War (1940–1945) and Peace (1945–1950)

Reading and Writing Before reading the chapter, write what you know about World War II inside your foldable on the appropriate page. Then list what you would like to know on the next page. As you read the chapter, record what you learn on the third page of your foldable.

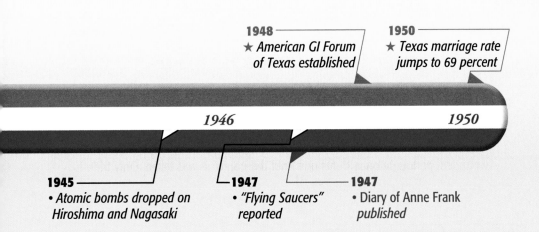

1948
★ American GI Forum of Texas established

1950
★ Texas marriage rate jumps to 69 percent

1946

1950

1945
• Atomic bombs dropped on Hiroshima and Nagasaki

1947
• "Flying Saucers" reported

1947
• Diary of Anne Frank *published*

TEXAS HISTORY Online

Chapter Overview
Visit the texans.glencoe.com Web site and click on **Chapter 23—Chapter Overviews** to preview chapter information.

Texans Support the War

Guide to Reading

Main Idea
Texans played a major role in World War II as civilian workers and as skilled military personnel.

Key Terms
dictator, Axis Powers, neutral, Allies, Lend-Lease Act

Reading Strategy
Categorizing As you read, fill in the chart with the names of the Allies and Axis Powers.

Allies	Axis Powers

Read to Learn
- how the U.S. and Texans became involved in World War II.
- how Texans responded to the war.

Section Theme
Civic Rights and Responsibilities Texans of all ethnicities and from all regions made significant contributions to the war effort.

Preview of Events

♦1939	♦1941	♦1942
Germany invades Poland	**December 7, 1941** Japan attacks Pearl Harbor	Oveta Culp Hobby recruits women to join the WAAC

World War II soldier

A Texas Story

In 1944 Army Private Macario García was a long way from his home in Sugar Land, Texas. While an acting squad leader of Company B, 22nd Infantry, near Grosshau, Germany, he single-handedly assaulted two enemy machine gun emplacements. Approaching prepared positions on a wooded hill, his company was pinned down by intense machine gun fire. Badly wounded, he fought on with his unit until the objective was taken. Only then did he allow himself to be treated.

Dictators Come to Power

The Great Depression of the 1930s was not confined to the United States. Other nations suffered economic downturns as well. In some countries, **dictators**, or absolute rulers, came to power during this time.

Military leaders in Germany, Italy, and Japan took control and began wars of expansion. These countries signed a treaty agreeing not to attack each other. They became known as the Axis Powers because the leaders believed the world would revolve around them.

Other nations watched this with great concern. When Germany invaded Poland in 1939, the European democracies such as France and England were forced into action. World War II had begun.

The Axis Powers seemed to have all the advantages. German troops conquered Belgium, Holland, Denmark, Norway, and France. Many people in Texas watched in horror at the treatment of the conquered nations.

Although the U.S. was officially neutral, or not taking sides, President Franklin Roosevelt and many American leaders favored the Allies. The Allies were the nations at war with the Axis Powers. The Allies included England, China, France, and Russia. Roosevelt made military equipment available to them through the Lend-Lease Act, even though Americans were debating whether the U.S. should be involved in the war.

The debate ended on Sunday morning, December 7, 1941. On that day, "a day that will live in infamy," Japan attacked U.S. troops based at Pearl Harbor in Hawaii. The United States was now officially at war.

Reading Check Explaining What were some of the main causes of World War II?

Texans Respond

Texans were involved in World War II from the beginning—the bombing of Hawaii. **Doris "Dorie" Miller,** an African American sailor from Waco, fired at Japanese airplanes from the U.S.S. *West Virginia* during the attack on Pearl Harbor. Later the Pacific Commander, **Admiral Chester W. Nimitz** of Fredericksburg, Texas, presented Miller with the Navy Cross. Nimitz said:

❝This marks the first time in this conflict that such high tribute has been made in the Pacific Fleet to a member of his race and I'm sure that the future will see others similarly honored for brave acts.❞

Texans of all ethnic groups and from all regions enlisted in one of the armed services. In March 1943, the War Department announced that Texas had the highest percentage of enlisted population of all the states in the nation. The total number of Texans who served was about 750,000.

Texans occupied every rank and branch of the services. William Simpson, Ira Eaker, and Lucian Truscott were 3 of 155 Texans who were generals in the war. **Dwight Eisenhower,** who was born in Denison, commanded Allied forces in Europe. Chester W. Nimitz was one of 12 admirals from the state.

Texan **Audie Murphy** fought in nine battle campaigns in North Africa and Europe. He received more medals than any other American. As "the most decorated soldier" in U.S. history, Murphy went on to a successful career as a movie actor, songwriter, and businessman. **Commander Samuel D. Dealey** of Dallas was

Picturing **History**

Audie Murphy *(inset)* was America's most decorated soldier. Dorie Miller *(below)* received the Navy Cross *(shown at right)* for bravery for his actions during the attack on Pearl Harbor. How do you define a "hero"?

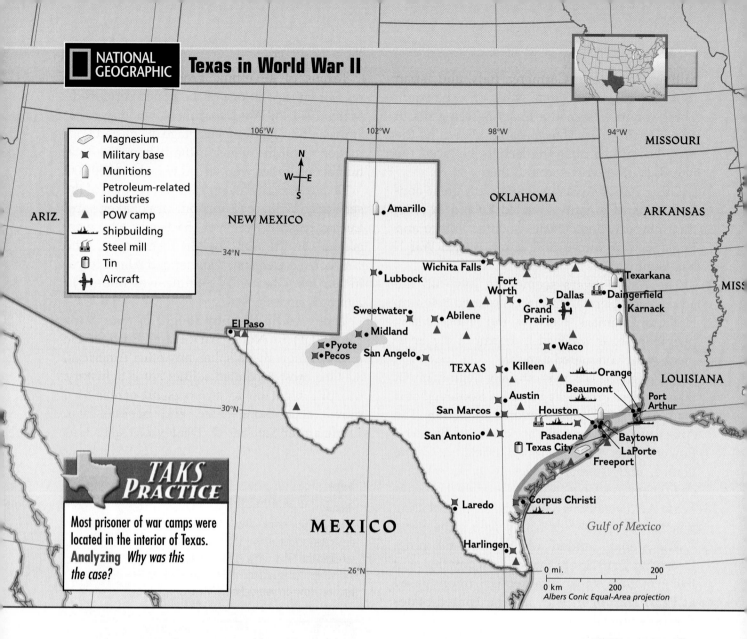

Map Legend:
- Magnesium
- Military base
- Munitions
- Petroleum-related industries
- POW camp
- Shipbuilding
- Steel mill
- Tin
- Aircraft

Albers Conic Equal-Area projection

TAKS PRACTICE

Most prisoner of war camps were located in the interior of Texas. **Analyzing** Why was this the case?

"the most decorated man" in the U.S. Navy. **Macario García** was one of 34 Texans to receive the Medal of Honor awarded by Congress. Other Hispanics who received the coveted award were José López of Brownsville, Silvestre Herrera of El Paso, and Cleto Rodríguez of San Marcos. Mike and Jimmie Cokinos, sons of a Greek immigrant in Beaumont, won medals for bravery in Germany and the Philippines.

Texan service personnel included 12,000 women, including the commander of the Women's Army Corps (WAC), **Colonel Oveta Culp Hobby** of Houston. In 1942, Congress authorized her to organize the Women's Auxiliary Army Corps (which later became the WAC). She wrote the policies and designed the uniforms, in addition to speaking to numerous groups and recruiting women all over the country.

Women Airforce Service Pilots (WASPs) received training at Avenger Field in Sweetwater. When the 1,830 trainees graduated, their main task was ferrying aircraft to places where they were needed most. WASPs also towed targets, flew tracking missions to gather information, flight-tested aircraft, gave instrument instruction, and flew practice bombing missions. Thirty-eight WASPs died in service to their country.

Katherine Luna of Dallas became director of women's recruitment for the WAVES, a unit of the United States Navy. **Marguerette Stuart** of Houston and **Antonette Bracher** of Fredericksburg became two of the first commissioned officers in that unit.

✓ **Reading Check** **Identifying** Name the three branches of service that women served in during World War II.

The Armed Forces Train in Texas

The favorable climate, location between the two coasts, and wide open spaces made Texas ideal for the establishment of military bases during World War II. Eventually more than 100 were built or enlarged to help the war effort. Every region and most cities of Texas were affected one way or another by military construction during World War II.

Soldiers, sailors, and airmen from all over the United States came to Texas for training. Carswell Field, in Fort Worth, was home to the Air Force Training Command headquarters. The Midland Army Airfield was the largest bombing crew training base in the world. Naval air stations were located in Corpus Christi, Kingsville, and Beeville. Even Dallas, far from the sea, became a site for a U.S. Navy installation where naval pilots were trained.

Prisoner of War Camps

During World War II, Texas had almost twice as many prisoner of war camps as any other state. Twenty-two base camps were located on military installations, and 48 branch, or labor, camps were constructed all over the state.

The camps housed thousands of prisoners. More than 45,000 German, Italian, and

A Shared Past...

When a family member entered the armed services, the family placed a small flag with a silver star in a window. If the family member was killed during the war, the silver star was replaced with a gold star.

Japanese prisoners were held in Texas from 1942 to 1945. The prisoners worked performing agricultural tasks, such as picking cotton, pulling corn tassels, and harvesting rice. Most of the prisoners were soldiers captured in battle, but many were civilians. They were well treated, and only a few attempts to escape from the Texas camps were made.

After the war, almost all prisoners were returned to their native countries, and many expressed their desire to return to Texas. Over 100 prisoners who died of wounds or of natural causes are still buried in the Fort Sam Houston National Cemetery in San Antonio.

✔ **Reading Check** **Summarizing** Why was Texas an ideal place to establish military bases?

SECTION 1 ASSESSMENT

Checking for Understanding

1. **Using Key Terms** Write a sentence explaining the change in the United States' involvement in the war, using the terms neutral and Allies.

2. **Reviewing Facts** Who was the commander of the Women's Army Corps? What was her role in the war effort?

Reviewing Themes

3. **Civic Rights and Responsibilities** What groups made important contributions to the war effort?

Organizing to Learn

4. **Identifying** Many Texans made important contributions to the war effort. Create a chart like the one shown, and list three Texans from this section and their accomplishment.

Individual	Accomplishment

Critical Thinking

5. **Evaluating** How did Texans feel about the way the Axis Powers treated people in the countries they invaded?

TAKS PRACTICE

Predicting Consequences Even if the United States had not entered the war, what would the result of the Lend-Lease program have been? Consider not only who might have won the war, but also future diplomatic relations between the Axis Powers, the Allies, and the U.S.

Texas LITERATURE

Audie Murphy (1924–1971)

Audie Leon Murphy was born in Kingston (Hunt County), Texas. He rose to national fame as the most decorated U.S. combat soldier of World War II, receiving every decoration for valor that his country had to offer, plus several medals from foreign countries.

After the war, Murphy was a film star, poet, and songwriter. He was killed in a plane crash at the age of 46. In 1996 the Texas legislature officially designated his birthday, June 20th, as Audie Murphy Day.

Reading to Discover

As you read the poem by Audie Murphy, imagine the feelings of a young soldier on the battlefields of World War II. Describe your feelings about the importance of freedom in a poem or paragraph.

Reader's Dictionary

implements: tools or instruments used in doing work

relics: things that have survived the passage of time

Freedom Flies in Your Heart Like an Eagle

by AUDIE MURPHY

Dusty old helmet, rusty old gun,
They sit in the corner and wait –
Two souvenirs of the Second World War
That have withstood the time, and the hate.

Mute witness to a time of much trouble.
Where kill or be killed was the law –
Were these **implements** used with high honor?
What was the glory they saw?

Many times I've wanted to ask them –
And now that we're here all alone,
Relics all three of a long ago war –
Where has freedom gone?

Freedom flies in your heart like an eagle.
Let it soar with the winds high above
Among the spirits of soldiers now sleeping,
Guard it with care and with love.

I salute my old friends in the corner,

I agree with all they have said –
And if the moment of truth comes tomorrow,
I'll be free, or by God, I'll be dead!

ANALYZING LITERATURE

1. **Recall and Interpret** What are the three relics referred to in the third stanza of the poem?
2. **Evaluate and Connect** Describe an image of war from the poem by Audie Murphy.

Interdisciplinary Activity

- Pose five interview questions you have about war and freedom. Use these questions to interview an adult who remembers American involvement in war or conflict.
- Choose a hero from Texas history and write a poem about war and freedom from his or her point of view.

The Home Front

SECTION 2

Guide to Reading

Main Idea
World War II caused many significant economic and social changes in the lives of Texans.

Key Terms
ration boards
smelter
concentration camp
Holocaust

Reading Strategy
Problem Solving Complete a chart like the one shown below. Identify solutions to the problems listed.

Problem	Solution
Loss of rubber supply	
Increased demand for magnesium	
Loss of tin supply	
Attacks on fuel shipments	

Read to Learn
• how Texas introduced rationing.
• about wartime productivity.
• about the effects of the war.

Section Theme
Economic Factors The war brought about a great increase in manufacturing and production in Texas. It also required ingenuity and sacrifice on the part of citizens.

Preview of Events

♦1941	♦1942	♦1943	♦1945
Mexican immigration increases	Expansion of wartime plant construction	Ration boards register Texans	World War II ends

Medal of Honor

A
Texas Story

Texan Macario García received the highest honor possible for his bravery in defending his squad from German machine-gun fire. On August 23, 1945, President Truman presented him with the Medal of Honor—awarded by Congress—at a ceremony at the White House. He also received the Purple Heart, the Bronze Star, and the Combat Infantryman's Badge. The following January he received the *Mérito Militar* from the nation of his birth, Mexico.

Industrial Production

President Roosevelt and his military advisers knew that an American victory could be won if the military had tanks, ships, airplanes, gasoline, explosives, and other necessary supplies and equipment. One adviser said, "This is a war of machines and of ships and airplanes powered by oil. In short, this is an oil war." United

States military planners expected Texas to provide 80 percent of the oil needed to fight the war.

Texas also possessed adequate supplies of natural gas, water, timber, and sulphur, so it was the logical site for wartime industrial expansion. The rapid rise in plant construction during the years 1942 through 1944 resembled the earlier oil booms at the Spindletop, Ranger, and East and West Texas fields. County **ration boards** registered all Texans in February 1943. When those registration figures were compared to the census figures from 1940, it was obvious that dramatic population changes had occurred in many parts of the state. Moore County, for example, had almost doubled its population because of the construction of a nitrogen-producing plant near Dumas. Many regions in Texas experienced population growth because of wartime employment opportunities.

The most pressing needs of the military were for airplanes and ships. Aircraft factories were concentrated in the Dallas–Fort Worth area. Shipyards were built along the coast at Port Arthur, Orange, Beaumont, Houston, Brownsville, and Rockport. The Houston Shipbuilding Corporation employed 35,000 workers.

Steel was produced at Daingerfield and Houston. The coastal region between the Brazos and Sabine Rivers became one of the most heavily industrialized areas of the world. Texas specialties were gasoline, aviation fuel, and petrochemicals.

New Methods of Production

Wartime demands encouraged the development of new products and better methods of production. The need for rubber, used in tires, fan belts, and dozens of other products, is a good example of such needs. The Japanese had cut off the supply of natural rubber from Southeast Asia. Scientists discovered a way to make rubber from petroleum. Plants to manufacture the synthetic rubber were built in Texas.

The war increased the demand for magnesium, a lightweight metal. Scientists devised a process to remove magnesium from seawater, and a huge plant for that purpose was built at **Freeport.** Another example of wartime problem-solving involved tin. There was no tin **smelter,** or processing plant, in the entire United States in 1941. After the Japanese

Picturing **History**

Women helped the war effort at home, in factories, and in the military. Women became Women Airforce Service Pilots *(left)* and joined other military units. On the home front, a female factory worker was often called "Rosie the Riveter." Where were many of the aircraft factories located?

conquest of Southeast Asia, the United States was without a supply of tin. The problem was solved by the construction of the largest tin smelter in the world at **Texas City.**

Shipping gasoline and aviation fuel by tanker from the refineries at Baytown, Port Arthur, and Pasadena to the East Coast ports was dangerous because German submarines were known to attack tankers in the Gulf of Mexico. Engineers planned and constructed underground pipelines to carry gases and liquids safely to their destinations.

TEXAS HISTORY *Online*

Student Web Activity Visit the texans.glencoe.com Web site and click on **Chapter 23—Student Web Activity** to learn more about rationing in World War II.

Home Front Workers

Wartime construction created a huge demand for labor. Between 1940 and 1943, at least 450,000 rural Texans moved to cities to work in the factories. There they earned high wages and worked many hours per week to meet the demands of wartime production.

The war presented new opportunities for women, African Americans, and Mexican Americans. Women found work in factories, shipyards, mills, and plants. They operated heavy equipment, welded metal, drove trucks, and proved their ability to work in jobs that had formerly been for "men only." **Olivia Rawlston,** for example, was president of an International Ladies Garment Workers Union local at a Dallas garment factory that made military garments.

War did not end discrimination and prejudice in Texas. Many African Americans found work in refineries and construction that had previously been denied them. However, they received lower wages than did others and were rarely promoted to supervisory positions. Restaurants and hotels denied service to African American sailors and soldiers and sometimes treated Mexican Americans similarly. The practice of racial and ethnic segregation changed little, if at all.

The federal government recognized that discrimination in factories made those factories less productive. It created the **Fair Employment Practices Committee** (FEPC) to reduce discrimination in war industries. The regional director of the FEPC was Carlos Castañeda, a University of Texas professor.

✔**Reading Check** Evaluating What new opportunities opened up for African Americans in Texas during the war?

Lives Touched by War

Texans at home had to make sacrifices, too. Sugar, meat, gasoline, tires, and other scarce items were distributed or rationed to Texans according to their needs and each item's value to the war effort. Texans added to their food supplies by planting "victory gardens." They collected scrap iron for use in the manufacture of war supplies. Texans contributed to the Red Cross and other agencies that served people in uniform. Cities conducted blackouts at night to protect against possible enemy air attacks. Each day Texans anxiously listened to their radios and read their newspapers for news about the war and about their many relatives and friends fighting overseas.

War brought death and hardship, but it also brought employment and rising production. Farmers plowed more land, planted more acreage, and harvested more crops. Industrial leaders built factories to supply the military. Because many Americans were in the armed forces, there was a great need for workers. Many new Mexican immigrants came to Texas to find jobs in agriculture and industry. In the early

TEXAS FACT

Two world wars made Texas into one of the nation's foremost military training centers. Bases were added in San Antonio and other cities during World War II, until the state had over 100 military bases. During the Persian Gulf War in 1991, Texas bases supplied tens of thousands of troops and planes for the war effort.

People of Texas

Oveta Culp Hobby 1905-1995

Oveta Culp Hobby was born in Killeen, Texas. She was a remarkable woman who held leadership positions and shaped major institutions.

In 1941, Col. Hobby accepted a position to head the War Department's Women's Interest Section.

She organized the Women's Auxiliary Army Corps, later known as the Women's Army Corps, and became America's first woman colonel. She commanded 100,000 women at more than 200 posts around the world. In 1953 she was named the first secretary of the Department of Health, Education and Welfare. As a result of her contributions, she was awarded the Distinguished Service Medal. She was inducted into the National Women's Hall of Fame in 1996, one year after she passed away.

1940s, more than 800,000 people of Mexican ancestry—12 percent of the total population of the state—lived in Texas.

An Allied Victory

In 1945 the long war finally came to an end. As Allied forces entered Germany, they discovered horrors beyond imagination. Millions of innocent people, especially Jews, had been killed in concentration camps. These camps were established to advance the Nazi government's idea of a superior race. The efforts to destroy these people is known as the Holocaust. Many Texas Jews lost relatives during this time.

Where great cities of Europe had once stood, there was now only rubble and ashes. Millions were homeless and starving. Thoughtful leaders looked at the destruction and resolved to work even harder to prevent another world war.

✓ **Reading Check** Comparing Although the war brought hardship, what were some of its positive effects?

SECTION 2 ASSESSMENT

Checking for Understanding

1. **Using Key Terms** Use the terms Holocaust and ration boards in sentences.
2. **Reviewing Facts** Why was the Fair Employment Practices Committee (FEPC) created?

Reviewing Themes

3. **Economic Factors** What facts would you select to show how the growth of the military in Texas brought money into the state economy?

Organizing to Learn

4. **Categorizing** Texans were called upon to produce, as well as to ration, goods. Create a chart like the one shown, listing goods produced and goods rationed.

Goods Produced	Goods Rationed

Critical Thinking

5. **Predicting Consequences** How would Texas industry be different today if the FEPC had not been formed? What other areas of Texas life would be affected?

TAKS PRACTICE

Wartime generally has a great impact on the economic patterns of production. What specific materials or goods do you think the government would encourage production of during wartime?

Reading a Line Graph

Why Learn This Skill?

Graphs can help with comparing facts. They compare numerical facts, changes over time, or differences between places, groups of people, or related events.

A line graph uses a line to connect numerical facts. Line graphs most often show change over a period of time. Different days, months, or years are usually shown along the bottom of the graph, or the horizontal axis. Numbers are usually found on the left side of the graph, or the vertical axis.

Learning the Skill

Here are some steps to follow in reading line graphs:
• Read the title of the graph.
• Become familiar with the information on the horizontal and vertical axes.
• Study the points where the line crosses the axes—vertical and horizontal.
• Study the changes over time.
• Form conclusions about the graph with other data.

Practicing the Skill

Study the line graph that appears on this page. Then answer the questions that follow.

❶ What is the subject of this line graph?

❷ What information is presented on the horizontal and vertical axes?

❸ How many students attended Texas schools in 1870?

❹ During which 20-year period did Texas have the greatest increase in school enrollment?

❺ During which 20-year period did Texas have the smallest increase in school enrollment?

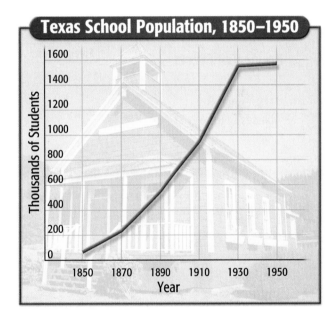

Texas School Population, 1850–1950

TAKS PRACTICE

Creating a Line Graph Listed below are Texas school population statistics for three years. Using the statistics, transfer the information to a line graph.

1991 3,460,378 students

1995 3,740,260 students

1999 3,991,783 students

1. Label the horizontal axis and vertical axis of the graph.

2. Create and answer three questions based on the information on your line graph.

 Glencoe's Skillbuilder Interactive Workbook, Level 1, provides instruction and practice in key social studies skills.

Guide to Reading

Main Idea
After the war ended, Texans experienced changes in the workplace, civil rights, education, and population.

Key Terms
consumer goods, mechanize, civil rights, GI Bill of Rights, baby boom, armies of occupation, Communist, Cold War

Reading Strategy
Summarizing Identify and summarize a significant change for each topic. Complete a chart like the one shown below.

Topic	Change
Demobilization	
Civil rights	
Education	
Population	
Foreign affairs	

Read to Learn
• how the economy of Texas changed.
• about discrimination against minorities and women.
• about the Korean War.

Section Theme
Continuity and Change
After Texans adjusted to peacetime following World War II, the U.S. became involved in another war.

Preview of Events

♦1944 — ♦1948 — ♦1950

U.S. Congress passes GI Bill of Rights

American GI Forum of Texas is established

U.S. enters Korean War

Sweatt v. *Painter* decision

Macario García

A
Texas Story

One month after receiving the Medal of Honor from President Truman, Staff Sergeant Macario García was refused service at a Richmond restaurant because he was Hispanic. He was outraged at that refusal, and a fight broke out. García was arrested. Many people who had been inspired by his heroism came to his aid. He was found not guilty. Later a Sugar Land middle school was named in his honor.

Demobilization

For four years the United States had concentrated on winning the war. Now it was time to think of peace. Dr. Florence Barns of the Texas Employment Commission summed up the situation. She wrote, "The years 1945 and 1946 were marked by [confusing changes] between war and peace economies." Many of the wartime factories that produced gasoline, rubber, and metals stayed open, because those basic materials were valuable to both civilians and soldiers.

Plants that produced ships and airplanes either closed or began producing consumer goods such as refrigerators and automobiles.

Women who had worked in factories generally were fired so returning servicemen could have their jobs. Few tenant farmers who had left for war or factory work returned to the farm. Texas agriculture had become more mechanized, or equipped with machinery, and therefore required fewer workers.

Reading Check **Explaining** Why did the Texas economy change after the war?

New Attitudes

World War II affected the lives of many African Americans and Mexican Americans. They realized the unfairness of fighting and dying for democracy when many of their civil rights (rights guaranteed by the U.S. Constitution) were denied to them at home. Mexican American service personnel, some even in uniform, were denied haircuts, restaurant service, and admission to public places. Some of the incidents, such as the case of Macario García, became well known. In another incident, the funeral home director at Three Rivers refused the family of **Félix Longoria** the use of its chapel. Longoria had died in the Philippines while serving his country. Senator Lyndon Johnson—later to become president—arranged for Longoria's body to be buried in Arlington National Cemetery with full military honors.

Many Mexican American veterans joined LULAC to work to end discrimination. Others decided to form a new organization. **Dr. Hector P. García** led 700 veterans in 1948 to form the **American GI Forum** of Texas. The organization soon became a voice in the fight for equal treatment. García's sister, Dr. Clotilde García, also became a civil rights leader.

The **National Association for the Advancement of Colored People** (NAACP) became more active during the war. In 1944 the U.S. Supreme Court ruled in *Smith v. Allwright* that all-white Texas primaries were not legal. The NAACP helped bring the case before the Court.

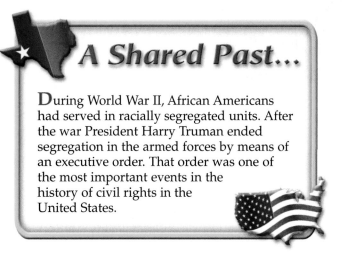

A Shared Past...

During World War II, African Americans had served in racially segregated units. After the war President Harry Truman ended segregation in the armed forces by means of an executive order. That order was one of the most important events in the history of civil rights in the United States.

The NAACP's main strategy was to file lawsuits forcing local officials to obey the U.S. Constitution. In 1950 it won a major victory in the case of *Sweatt v. Painter.* **Heman M. Sweatt** was an African American who lived in Houston and worked for the post office. He wished to become a lawyer, so he applied for admission to the University of Texas Law School. Although he was qualified, he was rejected because of his race. The Court ruled that the University must admit him. More people joined the NAACP after that victory.

Picturing **History**

Christia Adair and Heman Sweatt, both of Houston, led campaigns for equal rights for African Americans. What are some ways civil rights activists brought attention to their cause?

People of Texas

Hector P. García 1914–1996

Hector García was born in Mexico. His family left during the Mexican revolution and moved to Mercedes, Texas.

During World War II García was an officer in the infantry and later earned the rank of major. He was awarded the Bronze Star for his service. After the war, he returned to Texas and opened a medical practice. He also founded the American GI Forum, to address the health, education, and civil rights of Hispanic veterans.

Dr. García was the first Mexican American to serve on the U.S. Commission on Civil Rights, and he served as U.S. ambassador to the United Nations. In 1984 he received the highest award a civilian can receive, the Presidential Medal of Freedom. A statue and plaza honor him at Texas A&M University–Corpus Christi.

Christia Adair led the Houston NAACP in getting "Whites only" signs removed from the Houston airport and in the fight for the right of African American women to try on garments in department stores. With leaders such as Carter Wesley and Lulu B. White of Houston, and A. Maceo Smith and Juanita Craft of Dallas, the NAACP increased its membership.

Reading Check **Examining** How did minorities challenge discrimination during and after the war?

GIs Return to Civilian Life

Factories opened during the war faced closure just when returning servicemen needed jobs. People had saved their wages throughout the war but there was little to buy. Labor unions had promised not to strike during the war, but now that the war was over, they were ready to deal with long-ignored issues.

The U.S. Congress passed a law in 1944 to help returning servicemen—the **GI Bill of Rights.** The effects of this bill are still being felt. A key provision of the law paid veterans to attend college. Many veterans quickly took advantage of the opportunity. The table on page 529 shows some representative enrollments at several Texas universities.

The $13.5 billion amount spent on education for veterans between 1945 and 1955 was an excellent investment. The education these veterans received is an important reason that the United States has enjoyed economic prosperity.

Population Increases

Texas universities hurried to build more facilities for the growing number of students. More classrooms, libraries, and labs were needed. The universities also asked for something new—housing for married students.

Because "setting up housekeeping" was costly, the marriage rate had gone down during the Great Depression. Serving in the armed forces during World War II meant long separations from loved ones. When the war was over, people were eager to begin families. In 1940, 62 percent of the adult population of Texas was married. By 1950 the figure had jumped to 69 percent.

The large number of marriages led to a **baby boom.** Hospital nurseries across Texas were filled to capacity. Cribs were put in the hospital halls to accommodate the overflow. As the children grew older and began school, many school districts had to build new facilities. The "baby boomers" had arrived.

Texas GIs Return to School on GI Bill			
University	1942–43 School Year	1946–47 School Year	% Increase
University of Texas	10,854	17,242	59
Texas A&M	6,981	8,643	24
University of Houston	1,530	9,842	543
Texas Technological College	3,824	5,400	41
Southern Methodist	2,517	6,780	169
Baylor	2,198	3,711	69

TAKS PRACTICE

Summarizing The GI Bill of Rights encouraged veterans to attend college. Write a sentence summarizing the information in this chart.

Foreign Affairs

The United States did not bring all of its troops home after the war. Armies of occupation continued to serve in Germany and Japan to ensure an orderly change to peacetime for those countries. Although the war was over, new threats soon emerged. The Soviet Union, which had been a U.S. ally in the war against Germany, set up Communist dictatorships in several nations of Eastern Europe and in the northern half of Korea. Communism is an economic system in which property, including factories and farms, is owned by the government rather than by individuals. The United States was committed to containing, or stopping, the spread of communism. The U.S. government acted to prevent the Communist takeovers of Turkey and Greece.

The United States found itself involved in a new kind of conflict called the Cold War. The Cold War was a time of smaller, localized hostilities. Most of the conflicts were isolated affairs, but in 1950 the Cold War "heated up." North Korean soldiers invaded South Korea. The United States was again at war.

✓**Reading Check** **Evaluating** What new threats emerged after World War II?

SECTION 3 ASSESSMENT

Checking for Understanding

1. **Using Key Terms** Explain the changes in industrial production in the United States. Use the terms consumer goods and mechanize.
2. **Reviewing Facts** What was one important provision of the GI Bill of Rights?

Reviewing Themes

3. **Continuity and Change** Who formed the American GI Forum of Texas? Why was the group organized?

Organizing to Learn

4. **Sequencing** Create a time line like the one shown and place the following events in correct chronological order:

——+———+———+———+——

a. Baby boom
b. Korean War begins
c. GI Bill of Rights
d. WW II ends
e. University enrollment increases

Critical Thinking

5. **Evaluating** If you had been the president, how would you have justified the U.S. military presence in Japan and Germany after the war?

TAKS PRACTICE

Decision Making Becoming involved in a war is never an easy decision for a president or a country. Make a list of reasons for the United States to enter the Korean War and another list of reasons not to enter.

Chapter Summary

War and Peace

1930s
- Dictators come to power around the world.
- ★ Axis Powers unite.

1939
- Germany invades Poland and World War II begins in Europe.
- European countries enter the war.

1941
- ★ Japan bombs Pearl Harbor on December 7.
- U.S. enters World War II against the Axis Powers.

1942
- ★ Texans move to cities in large numbers to work in factories.
- More women and African Americans begin working in factories.
- ★ Colonel Oveta Culp Hobby organizes the WAAC.

1943
- Ration boards register all Texans.

1944
- Congress passes the GI Bill of Rights.

1945
- World War II ends.

1946
- The Baby Boom begins.

1950
- U.S. enters the Korean War to fight communism.

Reviewing Key Terms

Match the terms in Column 1 with their definitions (a–e). Write your answers on a separate piece of paper.

1. Allies
2. dictator
3. Axis Powers
4. consumer goods
5. Cold War

a. manufactured products bought by the general public
b. leader who holds absolute power over an area
c. conflict in which countries try to expand their power and influence by any means other than actual warfare
d. nations fighting the Axis Powers
e. Germany, Italy, and Japan

Reviewing Key Facts

6. What did the Axis Powers agree by treaty NOT to do?
7. What was the date of the Japanese attack on Pearl Harbor?
8. Besides captured soldiers, what other group of people were detained, or held, in the Texas prisoner camps?
9. Why did Texans invent synthetic rubber?
10. What was the purpose of the FEPC?
11. What was the GI Bill of Rights? Why was it important?

Critical Thinking

12. **Identifying** Identify three ways in which the war changed women's traditional position in American society.
13. **Describing** How did President Truman encourage integration in the military?
14. **Evaluating** Do you think the money spent on the GI Bill of Rights was worthwhile? Why or why not?
15. **Analyzing** What Soviet Union actions caused the U.S. government to conduct a Cold War against the superpower?
16. **Drawing Conclusions** Why did the military accept women into service? What were some possible negative reactions to women serving in the military?
17. **Identifying** The government rationed key goods like butter, sugar, meat, shoes, and gasoline. For each item, identify a possible substitute or alternative.
18. **Citizenship** How did WW II contribute to a growing awareness of civil rights for minorities?

Geography and History Activity

19. Texans served in all areas where fighting occurred during World War II. Turn to the World Map on pages RA2 and RA3. Locate where each of the following Texans served in the war: Doris Miller, Chester W. Nimitz, Dwight D. Eisenhower, Audie Murphy, and Mike and Jimmie Cokinos.

 ## Portfolio/TAKS Writing Activity

20. **Persuasive Writing** The U.S. government created recruitment posters to persuade people to help the war effort during World War II. Create a recruitment poster for World War II or for a present-day purpose. Refer to real World War II recruitment posters for ideas.

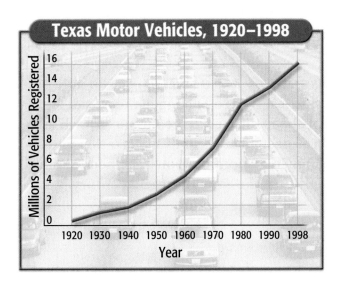

Texas Motor Vehicles, 1920–1998

Practicing Skills

Reading a Line Graph *Study the line graph above and answer the questions that follow.*

21. What is the subject of this line graph?

22. What information is shown along the horizontal axis?

23. During which decade did Texas pass the 10 million mark in number of motor vehicles?

24. Pose and answer your own question about this line graph.

Economics and History

25. **Analyzing** Why are wars often "good" for the economy of an industrialized nation?

Self-Check Quiz
Visit the texans.glencoe.com Web site and click on **Chapter 23—Self-Check Quizzes** to prepare for the chapter test.

 ## Cooperative Learning Activity

26. **Writing a Front Page** With two other students, create an original newspaper front page as it might have looked the day after either the bombing of Pearl Harbor or the U.S. entry into the Korean War. Be sure to research the facts. Make your front page as realistic as possible, using current newspapers as models.

Building Technology Skills

27. **Using the Internet or Library for Research** Locate information about the life of one of the outstanding citizens mentioned in this chapter. Record facts and gather or create visuals to prepare a complete report. Keep a record of bibliographic information and/or URLs. Your work may be presented orally, or it may be prepared as an interactive computer/multimedia document.

What did the GI Bill mean for Texas?

A It caused the massive erosion that led to the Dust Bowl.

B It paid for veterans to attend college and, as a result, university enrollment increased.

C The marriage rate in Texas rose dramatically after World War II.

D Many farmers became sharecroppers who were trapped in debt.

Test-Taking Tip:

Ask yourself when the GI Bill was passed and in what context it was discussed in class and in your textbook. Use that knowledge of chronology to get rid of answer choices that must be incorrect. Then pick the best answer from the remaining choices.

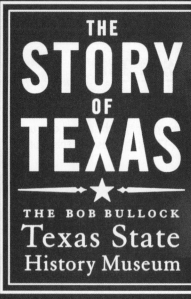

THE STORY OF TEXAS

★

THE BOB BULLOCK
Texas State
History Museum

Creating Opportunity
How Oil Changed Texas

*T*_he discovery of oil fields_ not only changed Texas, Texas oil changed the world. The availability of cheap oil spurred economic growth and expansion in almost all areas of transportation and manufacturing. That booming growth helped to shape the Texas identity in the early twentieth century.

◀ **Water Is Still Vital**
Although the oil boom changed Texas forever, farmers still needed water to grow crops. Here a farmer clears an irrigation ditch to keep the water, pumped from underground, flowing to his fields.

Visit The Bob Bullock Texas State History Museum in Austin to see artifacts and exhibits such as these about Texas history and heritage.

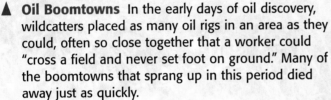

▲ **Oil Boomtowns** In the early days of oil discovery, wildcatters placed as many oil rigs in an area as they could, often so close together that a worker could "cross a field and never set foot on ground." Many of the boomtowns that sprang up in this period died away just as quickly.

Putting America on ▶ Wheels Your grandparents could have filled up their automobile at this gas pump in 1952 for about $.30 per gallon. Why do you think the trademark for Sinclair Oil was a dinosaur? Other major oil producers of the time included Esso, Texaco, and Humble.

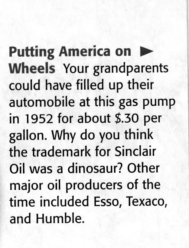

UNIT ★

8 The Modern Era

1950 to the Present

Why It Matters

As you study Unit 8, you will learn about Texas's recent history. Texans in the second half of the twentieth century continued to value their heritage while Texas underwent great changes. Its population rose to become second among the states. Women, Mexican Americans, African Americans, and Asian Americans expanded their influence in business and government. Texas became a leader in science and technology, in education, and in international trade. As the twenty-first century began, Texans looked ahead with confidence and pride.

Primary Sources Library

See pages 698–699 for primary source readings to accompany Unit 8.

The Saturn V is on display at the Johnson Space Center in Houston. It is still the largest and most powerful single-use launch vehicle ever built. It is 363 feet tall and weighs over 6 million pounds. The Roman numeral "V" stands for the five powerful F-1 engines used to lift the first stage of the rocket.

"*Manned exploration of the moon is essential.*"

—Lyndon B. Johnson,
April 28, 1961

TRADE PARTNERS

Blue jeans, computer parts, portable CD players—
what do these have in common? They are often produced in factories in the Texas–Mexico border region. The economy of the region has changed dramatically during the last decade. Most of the changes have been triggered by the North American Free Trade Agreement (NAFTA), which went into effect in 1994. NAFTA reduced taxes on goods and services traded between Mexico, Canada, and the United States.

Texas's economy has benefited from NAFTA in many ways.
• In 1999, almost half of the products shipped out of Texas went to Mexico.
• More than $112 million in merchandise made in Texas crosses the border every day.
• One out every five jobs in the state is somehow related to the trade between Texas and Mexico.

There are also some problems, however, that have resulted from the increase in trade.
• The increased number of *maquiladoras* in Mexico's northern border states has created air and water pollution on both sides of the Rio Grande.
• Some Texans lost jobs when U.S. companies closed their factories to open *maquiladoras* south of the border.
• Truck traffic has quadrupled since 1990 on eight heavily traveled bridges to Mexico. Bridge traffic has grown from one-half million trucks per year to more than 2.2 million trucks per year.
• The safety of Mexican trucks has been questioned by some. After lengthy debate, however, Congress passed laws in 2001 allowing Mexican trucks on U.S. highways. The trucks must undergo regular safety inspections and the licenses of drivers carrying high-risk cargo must be electronically checked at all border crossings.

Texas, as Mexico's neighbor, will continue to benefit from and be challenged by the interaction between NAFTA countries.

LEARNING *from* GEOGRAPHY

1. **Between which border cities is the most heavily traveled crossing between Texas and Mexico?**

2. **In which state in northern Mexico has the number of *maquiladoras* grown the most?**

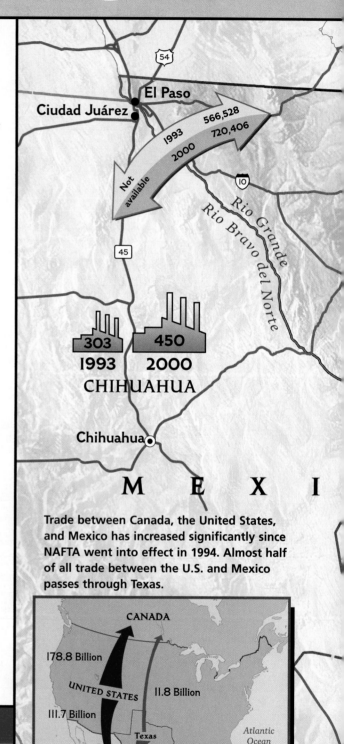

Trade between Canada, the United States, and Mexico has increased significantly since NAFTA went into effect in 1994. Almost half of all trade between the U.S. and Mexico passes through Texas.

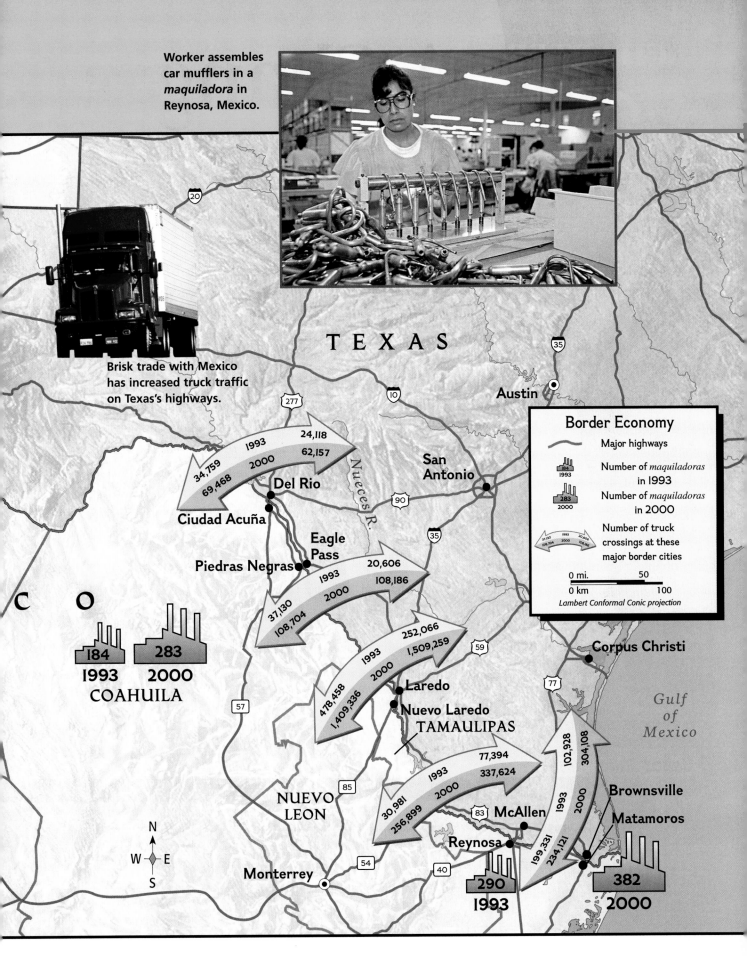

Worker assembles car mufflers in a *maquiladora* in Reynosa, Mexico.

Brisk trade with Mexico has increased truck traffic on Texas's highways.

TEXAS

Austin

San Antonio

Border Economy

Major highways

Number of *maquiladoras* in 1993

Number of *maquiladoras* in 2000

Number of truck crossings at these major border cities

0 mi.   50
0 km   100

Lambert Conformal Conic projection

Del Rio

1993   24,118
2000   62,157
34,759
69,468

Ciudad Acuña

Nueces R.

Eagle Pass

Piedras Negras

1993   20,606
2000   108,186
37,130
108,704

COAHUILA

184   283
1993   2000

1993   252,066
2000   1,509,259
478,458
1,409,336

Laredo

Nuevo Laredo
TAMAULIPAS

Corpus Christi

Gulf of Mexico

NUEVO LEON

1993   77,394
2000   337,624
30,981
256,899

McAllen

Reynosa

Monterrey

102,928
304,108

199,331
234,121

Brownsville

Matamoros

290
1993

382
2000

C   O

N
W   E
S

537

CHAPTER 24
A Changing Society

Why It Matters

World War II had a dramatic impact on Texas and altered the way its people lived and worked. In coming to terms with those changes, Texas became an urban industrial state with many international connections.

The Impact Today

Two projects from the 1950s and 1960s continue to have dramatic effects on the Texas landscape. The first was the construction of dams across almost all of the major rivers of Texas. The second was the establishment of the interstate highway system linking Texas cities to each other and to the rest of the nation.

1954
★ Women allowed to serve on Texas juries

1953
★ Texas state employees required to sign loyalty oaths

Texas

United States   *1950*   *1952*   *1954*

World

1951
• "Rock and Roll" era began

1953
• Soviet Union exploded hydrogen bomb
• Korean War ended

1954
• First McDonald's opened

1955
• Montgomery, Alabama, bus boycott

This busy freeway interchange is found in Dallas. The Texas highway system is both a cause and an effect of urbanization.

Categorizing Information Study Foldable
When you group information into categories in a table, it is easier to compare characteristics of items. Make this foldable to help you evaluate the causes and effects of the changes Texas experienced between 1952 and 1963.

Step 1 Fold a sheet of paper into thirds from top to bottom.

This forms three rows.

Step 2 Open the paper and refold it into fourths from side to side.

Fold it in half, then in half again.

This forms four columns.

Step 3 Unfold and turn paper, then draw lines along the folds.

Step 4 Label your table as shown.

	Causes	Effects
Political Issues and Changes		
Civil Rights Movement		
Technology and Economic Growth		

Reading and Writing As you read the chapter, use your foldable to record information as you learn about how Texas developed into an urban, industrial state. Write the causes and effects of the events listed on the table.

1956   1958   1960

1958
★ Jack Kilby invented the "silicon chip," first used in calculators

1957
• Jack Kerouac wrote On the Road

1959
• Charles de Gaulle became president of France

TEXAS HISTORY Online

Chapter Overview
Visit the texans.glencoe.com Web site and click on **Chapter 24—Chapter Overviews** to preview chapter information.

Politics and New Problems

Guide to Reading

Main Idea
Texas confronted many new issues involving politics and civil rights after World War II.

Key Terms
liberal, conservative, moderate, sovereignty, redistricting, unconstitutional, McCarthyism, libel

Reading Strategy
Classifying Create a chart like the one shown below. Indicate with an X each Texan's political party.

Politician	Republican	Democrat
Gov. Shivers		
Sen. Tower		
Pres. Eisenhower		
Pres. Johnson		

Read to Learn
• about post-war politics in Texas.
• about the Korean War.
• about desegregation in Texas.
• about fears of communism.

Section Theme
Government and Democracy Civil rights made Texans consider the issues of freedom and democracy.

Preview of Events

♦1948	♦1952	♦1954		♦1963
President Truman desegregates armed forces	Dwight Eisenhower is elected president	Women are allowed to serve on Texas juries	*Brown* v. *Board of Education of Topeka, Kansas*	President Kennedy is assassinated in Dallas

T.M. Moody

A Texas Story

In 1954, African American students in Mansfield had to ride a bus 15 miles and walk 20 blocks to the nearest African American high school. Then, in *Brown* v. *Board of Education of Topeka, Kansas*, the Supreme Court wrote: "We conclude that in the field of public education the doctrine of separate but equal has no place." Mansfield resident T.M. Moody celebrated the Court's decision. He and other parents prepared to ask the local school board to admit African Americans to Mansfield High.

Political Parties

Franklin Roosevelt's death in the closing days of World War II made **Vice President Harry Truman** the new president. During his years in office, both Democrats and Republicans were divided about how to respond to new, post-war conditions. Now that the Great Depression was over, what should be the role of the government in the economy? What would be the best way to deal with the Communist threat of the Soviet Union? How should the government address the demand of minority groups for equal rights?

The Republican Party was divided between those who wished to return to a policy of isolationism and those who wished to be involved in world affairs. In economic matters, some wished to eliminate New Deal programs that still existed, while others did not. The party was also divided between Republicans favoring civil rights for African Americans and others supporting continued segregation.

The Democratic Party was even more divided. In 1948 the party's platform included a strong civil rights program. With President Truman's desegregation of the armed forces, the Democrats seemed to be making a strong commitment to civil rights. Many Southerners, including Texans, began to rethink their loyalty to the Democratic Party. Southerners who favored segregation nominated ex-Democrat **Strom Thurmond** of South Carolina to head the new Dixiecrat Party and run for president against Harry Truman. He received 106,000 votes in Texas, or about 10 percent of the total.

Texas Democrats had their differences as well. Some identified themselves as liberals. They remained loyal to New Deal programs. They wanted more done to ensure equal rights and opportunities for minorities. They also supported labor unions. They were strongest in the poorer areas of Texas and also in cities with large labor union representation, such as Port Arthur and Beaumont. Conservative Democrats, such as **Texas Governor Allan Shivers,** believed that government assistance weakened the ability of people to do things for themselves. Shivers believed that "the growing tendency to look toward Washington for financial assistance can be destructive of a most important element in our

Beaumont

Port Arthur

form of government—that of responsibility." Many Democrats considered themselves neither conservative nor liberal. They called themselves moderates. Most political offices in Texas were held by moderates or conservatives.

✓ **Reading Check** **Contrasting** How did liberal and conservative Texas Democrats differ?

Texans Support Republican Eisenhower

As the 1952 elections approached, it appeared that Democrats were in trouble in Texas. The **Korean War,** which began in 1950, had not produced a decisive victory for the United States. As North Korean Communists tried to take control of South Korea, they used Soviet-supplied tanks. South Korea, the United States, and the Allies who made up the United Nations forces gained the advantage with a surprise sea-to-land invasion far behind enemy lines. The war became a political issue, however, when the Chinese entered the fight and inflicted reverses upon U.S. troops. President Truman fired **General Douglas MacArthur** after he publicly disagreed with Truman's strategy. General MacArthur enjoyed great popularity in Texas. After his dismissal and a sentimental farewell speech to Congress, MacArthur toured Texas, speaking to a crowd of 27,000 of his supporters at the Cotton Bowl in Dallas.

Even more important to many Texas voters was the so-called **"tidelands"** issue. Tidelands are areas under the ocean and near the shore but not exposed in low tides. New technology was allowing companies to drill oil wells in tideland areas. When oil and gas were found in deposits off the Texas coast, a dispute over ownership arose between the federal government and Texas.

The U.S. government had agreed with Texas on its coastal boundaries as far back as 1845, when it was admitted to the Union as a new state. After that time, opinions on the legal limits of Texas territory changed. The federal government now claimed that Texas sovereignty, or right to rule, stopped at the 3-mile (5-km) line. Texas claimed that the limit was 3 leagues, or 10.5 miles. The 7.5-mile (12-km) area between the two lines spanned 2,440,650 acres and had the potential to produce billions of dollars worth of oil and gas. President Truman vetoed bills that would have given Texas revenues from the tidelands.

History

Democratic Governor Shivers supported Republican presidential candidate "Ike" Eisenhower in the 1952 election. How did this strategy work in Shivers's favor?

The Republican nominee for president, **Dwight Eisenhower,** met with Governor Shivers and announced that he would sign a bill giving the tidelands to Texas if he was elected. Money from the tidelands would go to support Texas schools. Even though Eisenhower was a Republican, Shivers organized a "Democrats for Eisenhower" committee. In November 1952, Texans helped elect the Denison-born Republican nominee, Dwight Eisenhower. When Republican leaders in Texas saw that the Democrat Shivers was supporting Eisenhower, they declined to name a candidate to run against Shivers for governor. Instead they nominated Shivers, and his name appeared on the ballot twice—once as a Democrat and once as a Republican—and he won.

Shivers Helps Modernize Government

Allan Shivers served Texas as either the lieutenant governor or governor from 1947 to 1957. He supported several programs that made Texas government more modern. For example, he helped create the **Legislation Council** to research proposed new laws. He also established the **Legislative Budget Board** to make recommendations on how much money different state government agencies should receive. He supported funding for state hospitals, retired teachers, retired state employees, and roads and bridges. He influenced the legislature to allow women to serve on juries. In 1954 Texas women finally gained that right, largely through the efforts of the League of Women Voters. Texans endorsed the right as a constitutional amendment. Until 1954, all jurors in Texas had been male.

"One-Man, One-Vote"

For most of Texas history, voting districts had been based on land area, not population. This meant that in elections, it could take far fewer votes to win in a rural district than in a city district. As a result, each person's vote in a rural area seemed to count more than each person's vote in the city. For a long time, this did not seem that important

Causes and Effects of the Tidelands Issue

Causes

- Technology enables drilling for oil in coastal waters.
- Texas and federal government dispute oil deposits ownership.
- President Truman refuses to grant tidelands revenues to Texas.

Effects

- Eisenhower pledges to sign bill giving tidelands to Texas—if elected.
- Texans help elect Eisenhower.
- Eisenhower signs bill restoring tidelands to Texas.

Graphic Organizer → Skills

Ownership of oil-rich tidelands was an issue in the presidential election of 1952.

Drawing Conclusions Why did Eisenhower give Texas the tidelands revenue when Truman had not?

---

because there were not many big cities. By the 1960s, however, as the number and size of cities grew, this rural voting advantage became an issue of concern.

In 1962 the U.S. Supreme Court ruled that each state senator must represent about the same number of voters and that each state representative's district must be nearly equal in population. This ruling was based upon the idea that every vote should be of equal value—sometimes known as "one-man, one-vote."

The ruling meant vast changes for Texas. "One-man, one-vote" resulted in large population areas—large cities and surrounding suburbs—gaining representatives in the legislature. Less-populated areas—small towns and rural communities—lost representatives. The process of changing, or redrawing, district lines to reflect changes in population is called redistricting. The chart at right shows the inequality of some U.S. congressional districts in 1953.

National Politics

As Texas grew in wealth and population, it increased its influence in the federal government. Texans held several important committee chairmanships in the U.S. House of Representatives. **Sam Rayburn** served as the speaker of the House for all but four years between 1940 and 1961. **Lyndon Johnson** was selected as majority leader of the Senate in 1955. He ran for the Democratic Party nomination for president in 1960. Even though he lost the nomination to **John F. Kennedy,** Johnson became the vice presidential nominee. Kennedy knew that Johnson would help win votes in important Southern states. Many Southerners opposed Kennedy's election because he was a Roman Catholic. On

TAKS PRACTICE

Summarizing This chart illustrates the population of selected U.S. congressional districts in Texas in 1953. Write one or two sentences summarizing the information in this chart.

District Size in 1953 Before Redistricting

District	Representative	Home	Population of District
1	Wright Patman	Texarkana	276,945
4	Sam Rayburn	Bonham	227,735
5	J. Frank Wilson	Dallas	614,799
6	Olin Teague	College Station	228,112
8	Albert Thomas	Houston	806,701
20	Paul Kilday	San Antonio	500,460

Lyndon B. Johnson is sworn in as president of the U.S. by Judge Hughes of Dallas after the tragic assassination of President John F. Kennedy. What did Johnson promise the country in a televised address?

September 12, 1960, Kennedy came to Houston for his most important speech of the campaign. In his speech, Kennedy told the audience that his Roman Catholic beliefs would not interfere with his ability to be president. Film clips from that speech were televised in campaign commercials in other states. The Democratic Kennedy–Johnson ticket won in one of the closest presidential elections in U.S. history.

The Democratic victory indirectly helped the Texas Republican Party. When Lyndon Johnson was elected vice president, he resigned his seat in the U.S. Senate. A special election was necessary to replace Johnson. The Republican candidate, **John Tower,** surprised many Texans by winning. He was helped by a feud between conservative and liberal Democrats. The split in the Democratic vote gave the victory to the Republicans. The Republican Party continued to grow in Texas. Tower remained in the Senate until 1985.

✔ **Reading Check** **Analyzing** How did the Democrats' 1960 presidential election win help Texas Republicans?

A National Tragedy

Lyndon Johnson took on important responsibilities as vice president. One of the key assignments given to him by President Kennedy was to oversee America's space program. Johnson was named chairman of the high-level **National Aeronautics and Space Council.**

In November 1963, President Kennedy was on a tour of Texas, having visited San Antonio, Houston, and Fort Worth. Riding in an open-car motorcade in Dallas, he was shot and killed. Investigators concluded that **Lee Harvey Oswald** was the assassin. Lyndon Johnson took the oath of office as president. It was given by federal judge Sarah T. Hughes of Dallas. As the nation grieved over the tragedy, Johnson acted swiftly to calm the nation. In a televised address to Congress, Johnson promised to carry on programs that Kennedy had begun.

The Warren Court

Early in President Eisenhower's first term, he appointed **Earl Warren** to be the new chief justice of the United States. The "Warren Court" would make many important decisions. During the 1950s and 1960s, many individuals and groups worked to extend civil rights and individual liberties to all citizens. Others opposed their efforts. In the American political system, questions about rights, liberties, and justice are ultimately decided in the U.S. Supreme Court. Under Earl Warren's leadership, the Supreme Court consistently decided in favor of people and groups seeking to end discrimination. These decisions affected many Texans.

School Desegregation

Civil rights lawyers argued that segregation of the races was unconstitutional, or not legal. In 1896 the U.S. Supreme Court had said that racial segregation was legal as long as the facilities for both races were equal. In the 1954 case of *Brown v. Board of Education of Topeka, Kansas,* civil rights lawyers, including future Supreme Court Justice Thurgood Marshall, argued that schools

TEXAS HISTORY *Online*

Student Web Activity Visit texans.glencoe.com and click on **Chapter 24— Student Web Activity** to learn more about civil rights and desegregation.

that were separated by race could never be equal. The Supreme Court ruled that racial segregation in public schools was unconstitutional. The Court ordered schools to desegregate "with all deliberate speed."

Some officials in Texas began a campaign of delay and resistance. The **National Association for the Advancement of Colored People** (NAACP) had brought the school desegregation case to court. The state attorney general filed a lawsuit to prohibit the NAACP from operating in Texas.

West Texas and central Texas schools obeyed the desegregation order more quickly than did schools in East Texas. San Antonio, Austin, San Angelo, El Paso, and Corpus Christi began desegregating in 1955. **Mansfield,** about 15 miles southeast of Fort Worth, was the site of the most visible resistance to desegregation, as mobs prevented African American students from enrolling at the local high school.

More common than mob action were delaying tactics. Some school districts submitted plans that called for desegregating one grade per year so that full desegregation would take 12 years. Other districts desegregated school faculty members but not students. Still other districts created schools with African American and Mexican American but no Anglo American students. Sometimes African American students were enrolled in white schools but were grouped in segregated classrooms in one part of the building and assigned a separate lunch period. These tactics delayed segregation in many schools until the mid-1970s, twenty years after *Brown v. Board of Education of Topeka, Kansas.*

School officials also resisted court decisions guaranteeing Mexican American children access to desegregated schools. The American GI Forum and LULAC filed numerous lawsuits to make districts follow the law.

Reading Check **Summarizing** What was Thurgood Marshall's argument against "separate but equal" facilities?

Desegregation of Public Facilities

Schools were not the only focus of desegregation. African Americans also wanted access to public facilities such as parks, libraries, swimming pools, and auditoriums. These had been built with tax revenues. African Americans' taxes helped to support these facilities, but they were denied the use of them. African Americans sued to gain access to a municipal

Picturing **History**

In 1954, the principal of Linfield Elementary School refused to enroll these African American schoolchildren as students. What Supreme Court decision ended legal segregation of public schools?

ONLY in TEXAS

Aquarena Springs, called "the place of warm waters" by the Tonkawa Indians, was an important stop on the Old San Antonio Road. A popular resort grew up around the springs in the 1920s, featuring glass-bottom boats and Ralph the Swimming Pig *(left)*. The home of Eli Merriman, a founder of San Marcos, was moved to the park from its original location near the town square *(center)*. Today, the Aquarena Center is an educational park preserving the unique ecosystem of the region *(right)*.

golf course in Houston. Similar suits occurred in several Texas cities. Sometimes city officials complied with desegregation orders. Other times they resisted. A popular form of resistance was to turn the operation of city properties over to a private club organized expressly to maintain discrimination. City officials could then claim there was no longer discrimination at public facilities.

Houston

Individual Rights Versus National Security

Fears about the rise of communism led to important consequences for Americans. The Soviet threat increased when Russia tested an atomic bomb. A revolution in China installed a Communist government in 1949. The U.S. Congress reacted by making membership in the Communist Party a crime. It held hearings about Communist influence in various American industries, including the motion picture business. Entertainers, producers, writers, and directors were investigated for signs of Communist Party sympathy or affiliation. In the name of national security, many people were willing to restrict traditional American rights, such as freedom of speech, press, and assembly.

Whole groups of people, including labor unions and civil rights workers, were accused of having Communist ties. Conservatives criticized government welfare programs that had been popular during the New Deal. The Houston School District board refused to participate in a federally sponsored school lunch program. It defended its action in a newspaper ad that said in part, "Self reliance is the strongest lesson we can teach our youth." In 1953 the legislature passed a law requiring all state employees, including teachers, to sign a loyalty oath before they would be paid. Many Texans felt they were in the midst of a **"red scare."**

The Red Scare

The most famous anti-Communist was Senator Joseph McCarthy of Wisconsin. McCarthy was the featured speaker at the San Jacinto Day celebration, April 21, 1954. Some 5,000 to 9,000 people in the audience heard him accuse leaders in the United States Army of being Communists. In Washington, D.C., McCarthy led televised hearings to investigate charges that Communists were in the U.S. Army. His behavior was seen by many to be bullying and cruel. Soon afterwards, McCarthy lost most of his influence. Because of his activities, a new word—McCarthyism—entered the language. It means the act of making unfounded, sensationalist charges against persons.

Results of the "red scare" were seen in Texas in the schools, libraries, and churches, and in opposition to labor unions and the United Nations. Textbooks and school library books were examined for possibly disloyal content. Some school board committees required teachers to attend anti-Communist lectures. People who belonged to certain international organizations were often closely watched for signs of Communist activity.

John Henry Faulk, an Austin native, was a radio star for CBS in New York City. He was fired

TEXAS TODAY

First Lady Lady Bird Johnson, wife of Lyndon B. Johnson, did much to raise Americans' awareness that individual citizens should help "keep America beautiful." Before her efforts, it was not unusual to see highways cluttered with billboards, junkyards, and roadside trash thrown from car windows. In 1987 she helped create a requirement that 25 percent of the landscape budget of federally funded highway projects be devoted to planting native wildflowers. Today, Texans are benefiting from her vision of a beautiful America.

when a group claimed he was a member of the Communist Party. He sued and was awarded $3.5 million in damages—the largest libel judgment to that date. Libel is the act of printing statements known to be false and intentionally spreading them to do damage to someone's reputation. Faulk later moved back to Texas and toured the nation, speaking on the importance of protecting freedom of speech and freedom of the press.

✓**Reading Check** **Identifying** Which traditional American rights were restricted because of the "red scare"?

SECTION 1 ASSESSMENT

Checking for Understanding

1. **Using Key Terms** Write a short paragraph using the following terms: conservative, moderate, redistricting, and unconstitutional.
2. **Reviewing Facts** How did the "red scare" and McCarthyism affect the lives of many Texans?

Reviewing Themes

3. **Government and Democracy** What changes did the "one-man, one-vote" ruling bring to Texas?

Organizing to Learn

4. **Cause and Effect** Complete a web like the one shown below. Identify three responses to the 1954 Supreme Court desegregation order in *Brown* v. *Board of Education of Topeka, Kansas.*

Responses to Desegregation Order

Critical Thinking

5. **Identifying** Which groups of people were most often suspected of having Communist ties?
6. **Drawing Conclusions** Why did John Faulk value his freedom of speech?

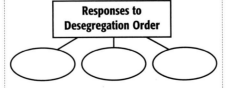

TAKS PRACTICE

Categorizing Explain the difference between liberal, conservative, and moderate Democrats in Texas at this time in history.

Demonstrating Reasoned Judgment

Why Learn This Skill?

It is often necessary to make judgments about past or current events. Sometimes it is easy to make judgments with little information or based on emotion. Those judgments are usually unfair or inaccurate.

It is important to make judgments based on facts and reasoning. To do so, there should be a standard or criteria for judging. To judge the effectiveness of a law banning teenage smoking, for example, would require information about teenage smoking habits before and after the law was passed.

Learning the Skill

Follow these steps to make a reasoned judgment:
• Carefully identify the criteria for making your judgment.

Selected Elections for Governor

Year	Percent of votes for Democrats	Percent of votes for Republicans
1946	91.2	8.8
1954	89.6	10.4
1962	54.0	46.0
1972	47.9	45.0
1982	53.2	45.9
1986	46.1	52.7
1990	49.5	46.9
1994	45.4	52.3
1998	30.0	67.5

• For each criterion, decide what facts are necessary and gather that information.
• Evaluate the event according to the criteria.
• Make a judgment based on reason and fact.

Practicing the Skill

Study the information on the chart at left about the two-party system in Texas. Answer the questions that follow.

❶ In which years did Democratic candidates receive more than 80 percent of the vote? The Republican candidates?

❷ In which election did a Republican first receive more than 40 percent of the vote?

❸ In the last four elections shown on the chart, how many times did the Democratic candidate receive more than 50 percent of the vote? The Republican candidate?

❹ Based on the information on the chart, is the two-party system in Texas today stronger or weaker than in the past? Explain.

TAKS PRACTICE

Demonstrating Reasoned Judgment Consider the following situation: You have been invited to go to a friend's house on Saturday and you are spending Sunday with your grandparents. You have tests on Monday and Tuesday. When will you study for your tests? What are your priorities? Make some reasoned judgments about the amount of time you will need to study for your tests and alternatives that you can make in your weekend plans.

Glencoe's **Skillbuilder Interactive Workbook,** Level 1, provides instruction and practice in key social studies skills.

Foundations for Growth

Guide to Reading

Main Idea
New interstate highways, the growth of suburbs, conservation, and technological developments changed Texas in the 1950s and 1960s.

Key Terms
convoy, suburb, reservoir, synthetic, vacuum tube, transistor, integrated silicon circuit

Reading Strategy
Evaluating Consequences As you read this section, create a chart like the one below of some positive and negative consequences of interstate highway construction in Texas.

Positive Consequences	Negative Consequences

Read to Learn
• about suburban life.
• about drought conditions.
• about pioneer medical and business technology.

Section Theme
Economic Factors New technologies gave Texans more choices regarding where they could live and work.

Preview of Events

♦1957	♦1958	♦1962	♦1969
Soviet Union launches *Sputnik*	Jack Kilby invents the "silicon chip"	John Glenn orbits the earth three times	Americans walk on the moon

Mansfield High School entrance

A
Texas Story

Despite *Brown* v. *Board of Education,* the integration of some Texas schools was delayed. Hearing that the Mansfield School Board had agreed to admit African American students, mobs refused to let the students enter. Mansfield High remained segregated until 1965. Many African Americans relied on spiritual values to help them through segregation. Maggie Briscoe wrote, "[African Americans] have had it very very hard and some of us it has made real real bitter, but I guess the Lord saved me, I just didn't let it make me bitter. I just kept praying."

Highway Construction

Although news headlines of the 1950s tended to focus on politics, international affairs, and civil rights, other changes were occurring that would reshape Texas and the nation.

People of Texas

Michael DeBakey 1908–

Michael DeBakey, an internationally respected physician and surgeon, turned Baylor College of Medicine into a world-renowned facility. DeBakey was born in Louisiana, the son of Lebanese immigrants. While still a medical student at Tulane University in 1932, he invented the roller pump, a device that helped make open-heart surgery possible.

Since then, DeBakey is credited with inventing or perfecting many medical devices and procedures that have become commonplace in heart surgery. He has served as an adviser to almost every president in the last 50 years, as well as to other leaders, including former Russian president Boris Yeltsin. In 1999, he received the United Nations Lifetime Achievement Award for his medical and humanitarian work.

One of Dwight Eisenhower's tasks as a young army officer was leading a military convoy (a group of vehicles) across the country. The trip took months. It convinced Eisenhower that a better highway system was needed. When he was president, he supported the creation of an interstate highway system that would connect the states with quality roads. Congress appropriated money to help build highways that would have no cross traffic, stop signs, or traffic lights. Motorists could drive safely at higher speeds on these highways than they could on regular highways. In times of crises the highways would help the military quickly move troops and equipment.

Interstate highways were built with a combination of federal and state money. The first interstate highway in Texas was the Gulf Freeway in Houston, or Interstate 45. The interstate system consisted of east-west highways I-10, I-20, I-30, and I-40 and highways that went north and south, such as I-35. Three-digit highways signified loops around cities, such as I-410 around San Antonio.

Highway construction often caused problems. Some people had to find new homes when their houses were purchased to make way for the new highways. Sometimes businesses were forced to close. On the other hand, new businesses such as gasoline stations and motels sprang up to serve travelers. Truckers were able to deliver their products much more rapidly and efficiently than before. Texans loved their automobiles more than ever.

Reading Check **Describing** What could motorists expect of the new interstate highways?

Texans Move to the Suburbs

Improved highways made it possible to live farther away from the central city and still work in a downtown office building or store. Developers purchased property located miles from the downtown business districts and began building residential areas, called suburbs, at the outskirts of cities or large towns. An increasing percentage of Texans lived in suburbs during the 1950s and 1960s, and developers built houses and shopping centers to serve these residents and attract new ones. As the suburban population grew, so did the need for new schools and religious centers. Modern recreational facilities such as Little League baseball fields and swimming pools became part of suburban life. Many suburban Texans rarely found a reason to go "downtown."

Downtown movie theaters and stores closed because they could not withstand competition from the newer, more modern suburban facilities.

Sometimes the vacant stores were boarded up. More and more affluent people moved to the suburbs, while downtown neighborhoods became home to growing numbers of lower income people. "White flight" was the name given to describe this migration because often, lower income people were members of minority groups, such as Hispanics or African Americans. City governments, struggling to provide fire, police, and waste services, often directed more of their resources to the needs of the new suburbs and their residents. Almost every major city in Texas had some downtown, or inner-city, area that housed needy people during the 1950s and 1960s.

Drought Puts a Strain on Water Resources

Suburban, urban, and rural Texans all faced the same problem during the 1950s. That problem was drought. Rainfall amounts had been less than normal since 1949, but in 1956 conditions became even worse. Towns depended upon human-made reservoirs, or open water storage areas, for their water supply. These reservoirs began drying up. Lake Dallas was only 11 percent full. Rivers slowed to a trickle, and wells that had never run dry did so. Cattle went thirsty and thousands of square miles of pasture

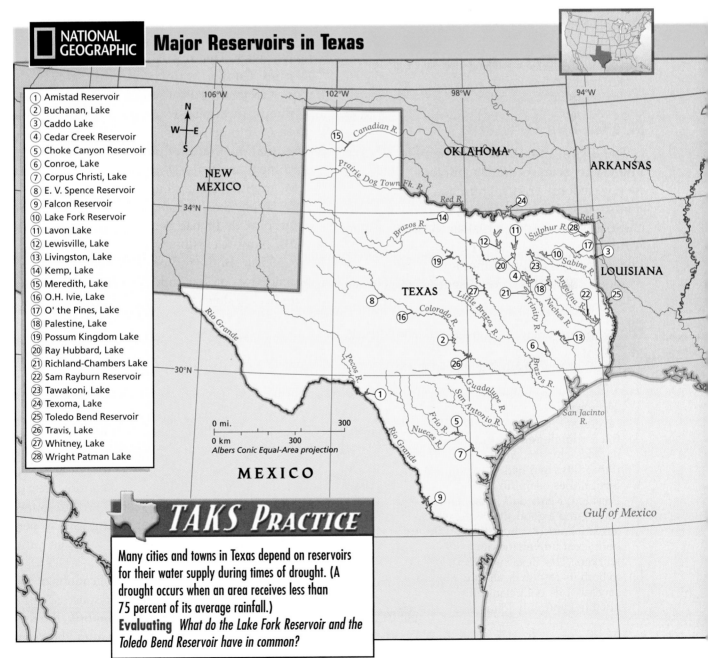

NATIONAL GEOGRAPHIC Major Reservoirs in Texas

① Amistad Reservoir
② Buchanan, Lake
③ Caddo Lake
④ Cedar Creek Reservoir
⑤ Choke Canyon Reservoir
⑥ Conroe, Lake
⑦ Corpus Christi, Lake
⑧ E. V. Spence Reservoir
⑨ Falcon Reservoir
⑩ Lake Fork Reservoir
⑪ Lavon Lake
⑫ Lewisville, Lake
⑬ Livingston, Lake
⑭ Kemp, Lake
⑮ Meredith, Lake
⑯ O.H. Ivie, Lake
⑰ O' the Pines, Lake
⑱ Palestine, Lake
⑲ Possum Kingdom Lake
⑳ Ray Hubbard, Lake
㉑ Richland-Chambers Lake
㉒ Sam Rayburn Reservoir
㉓ Tawakoni, Lake
㉔ Texoma, Lake
㉕ Toledo Bend Reservoir
㉖ Travis, Lake
㉗ Whitney, Lake
㉘ Wright Patman Lake

0 mi. 300
0 km 300
Albers Conic Equal-Area projection

TAKS PRACTICE

Many cities and towns in Texas depend on reservoirs for their water supply during times of drought. (A drought occurs when an area receives less than 75 percent of its average rainfall.)
Evaluating What do the Lake Fork Reservoir and the Toledo Bend Reservoir have in common?

withered. In desperation, ranchers burned the thorns off cactus plants so that cattle could eat the prickly pear pads. One rancher in Washington County reported chopping down a hackberry tree every morning so that cattle could reach the leaves. Spring rains in 1957 ended the drought, but thoughtful Texans knew they had to plan for the next dry spell.

City officials, industrialists, farmers, and ranchers all responded to the water crisis. Cities funded new reservoirs. Ranchers built more stock ponds. Farmers turned more to irrigation. The **U.S. Army Corps of Engineers** built more dams across Texas rivers. The whole state became more aware of the need for water conservation.

✓**Reading Check** **Explaining** How did the drought affect water supplies?

Science and Technology

The 1950s and 1960s were a time of high interest in science and technology. State tax money, federal grants, churches, and wealthy donors together founded advanced hospitals and medical centers in Dallas, Galveston, San Antonio, and Houston. The various facilities treated patients, taught medical students, and engaged in trailblazing research. Houston's

A Shared Past...

Where was NASA to be located? There were several states vying for that honor and for the economic benefits that would come with it. Massachusetts was home to great universities and had scientists and laboratories useful to NASA. Besides, it was President Kennedy's home. Florida was considered a good site because rockets were already launched from there. California had both great universities and skilled aerospace workers. That Texas was chosen is a tribute to both its resources and the political skills of several of its politicians, most notably Lyndon B. Johnson.

M.D. Anderson Hospital, for example, became known for its cancer research. Just a short distance away, **Doctors Michael DeBakey** and **Denton Cooley** were pioneering new techniques in treating heart disease. DeBakey used synthetic, or human-made, materials to replace diseased blood vessels. The technique was so new that he had to use his wife's sewing machine to make the synthetic vessels at home.

Meanwhile Dallas engineers and scientists were laying the foundation for a revolution in electronics. Radio had become widespread in the 1920s. Now television was making its mark in the 1950s. Both radios and television sets depended upon vacuum tubes, but such tubes were heavy, slow, and fragile. A device called a transistor was a great improvement. In 1954 a Dallas company called **Texas Instruments** became the first company to make a radio with transistors. It was portable and battery operated. Soon people carried radios with them to the beach and on picnics.

In 1958, **Jack Kilby,** working for Texas Instruments, invented the integrated silicon circuit, which today we call a "chip." The chip made it possible to make many electronic instruments even smaller and faster. Within a few years integrated circuits were being used in personal computers, calculators, watches, and thousands of other applications.

One of the most important applications of the chip was in the growing field of space science. The Soviet Union had launched *Sputnik,* the first artificial satellite, in 1957. Shortly after, they sent

People of Texas

Walter Cunningham 1932–

Walter Cunningham is a successful businessman in Houston today, but he is best known as America's second civilian astronaut. Cunningham knew he wanted to be a navy pilot from the time he was a child. He served as a Marine pilot from 1953 to 1956. In 1963 he became one of the third group of astronauts selected by NASA.

Cunningham specialized in systems and systems analysis of the Apollo spacecraft. In 1968 he served as lunar module pilot of *Apollo 7*, the first crewed flight of the Apollo Program. Despite catching colds during their 11-day mission, he and his fellow astronauts tested lunar docking and orbiting maneuvers and provided the first live television transmission of onboard activities to a proud and grateful nation.

the first man into space. The United States responded quickly to this threat to American scientific leadership. President John F. Kennedy announced that the national goal was to land a man on the moon before 1970. The **National Aeronautics and Space Administration** (NASA), formed during the Eisenhower administration, was given that task. After an extensive search for a suitable site, NASA announced plans to build a space center near Houston. On September 19, 1961, the NASA administrator announced that the new Manned Spacecraft Center (now called the Johnson Space Center) would be built in southeastern Harris County, about 25 miles from downtown Houston. In 1962 **John Glenn** orbited the earth three times. In July 1969 Americans walked on the moon. Texans working in the Space Center played a major role in these great accomplishments. Since then, the Center has continued to improve space satellites and develop new technology.

✓ Reading Check **Evaluating** How did Texas Instruments contribute to technological progress?

SECTION 2 ASSESSMENT

Checking for Understanding

1. **Using Key Terms** Define the following key terms and use each one in a sentence: convoy, suburbs, reservoirs, transistor.
2. **Reviewing Facts** Identify two Texans who made significant contributions in the field of science or technology.

Reviewing Themes

3. **Economic Factors** How were downtown areas of cities affected by the growth of suburbs?

Organizing to Learn

4. **Categorizing** Create a chart like the one shown below and fill in the uses for each invention.

Invention	Uses
Synthetic blood vessels	
Vacuum tube	
Transistor	
Integrated silicon circuit	

Critical Thinking

5. **Problem Solving** Refer back to the section about drought. Suggest ways in which Texans could provide additional water or conserve existing water resources.

TAKS PRACTICE

Analyzing How did the discoveries and inventions of the 1950s and 1960s mentioned in the text affect the everyday lives of Texans?

Chapter Summary

A Changing Society

1948
- President Truman desegregates the armed forces.

1949
★ Allan Shivers becomes governor.

1950
- The Korean War begins.

1953
- All Texas state employees are required to sign a loyalty oath.

1954
- U.S. Supreme Court rules racial segregation is unconstitutional in *Brown v. Board of Education*.
★ Women gain the right to serve on Texas juries.
- Texas Instruments makes a radio with transistors.

1955
★ Schools begin to desegregate in Texas.

1956
- Serious drought conditions affect Texas.

1958
★ Jack Kilby invents the "silicon chip."

1962
- John Glenn orbits the earth three times.
- U.S. Supreme Court makes "one-man, one-vote" ruling.

1963
- President John F. Kennedy is assassinated in Dallas.

1969
- Americans walk on the moon.

Reviewing Key Terms

1. *Use the following six terms to write a short paragraph about life in Texas in the 1950s and 1960s:* liberal, suburb, transistor, libel, interstate, *and* reservoir.

Reviewing Key Facts

2. After World War II, what were three of the issues that divided the Republican Party?

3. Whom did Southern Democrats who favored segregation nominate to run for president against Harry S Truman in 1948?

4. What policies did liberal Texas Democrats support at this time?

5. Why was General Douglas MacArthur, an important American general in the Korean War, fired?

6. In your own words, explain the so-called "tidelands" issue.

7. Which Texan became majority leader of the Senate, then vice president, and ultimately president?

8. What is the name of the landmark civil rights case that led to desegregation of schools?

Critical Thinking

9. **Civic Rights and Responsibilities** Why was segregation of schools and public facilities found to be unconstitutional?

10. **Understanding Cause and Effect** Even though the severe drought was a terrible hardship, especially for farmers, how could it also be seen as an opportunity for learning and creative problem solving?

11. **Drawing Inferences** Do you think that the Soviet Union's satellite *Sputnik,* launched in 1957, was the turning point that spurred the United States on to enter the "space race" to land a man on the moon? Why or why not?

12. **Economics and Politics** The U.S. Congress held hearings to find, try, and punish suspected Communists. Some people were able to go free if they "told on" others. What do you think the atmosphere was like?

13. **Drawing Conclusions** Describe some possible economic benefits to Texas from changes in the areas of medicine and technology, highways, and civil rights during the 1950s and 1960s.

14. **Making Connections** How did the Johnson Space Center connect Texas to the rest of the United States and the world?

Geography and History Activity

15. The new suburbs around cities and towns needed many services. Design and illustrate a map of a suburb. Draw and label residential, professional, recreational, and commercial areas.

Practicing Skills

Demonstrating Reasoned Judgment *Differences in computer ownership among the 50 states exist because of varying economic activities, income levels, and urbanization patterns. Study the chart below, and then answer the questions that follow.*

Household Computer Ownership (Selected States as of August 2000)		
State	% Computer Ownership	% Growth in Ownership 1999–2000
Alaska	67.0	5.8
California	56.1	19.1
Texas	48.4	15.8
Oklahoma	42.1	10.2
Arkansas	38.5	25.4

16. Which of the following data would be helpful in understanding this chart?
    a. the percentage of urbanized areas in each state
    b. the number of computers used in offices
    c. the average household income in each state

17. What prediction can you make based on the information in this chart?

Cooperative Learning Activity

18. **Creating Presentations** Assign groups to focus on one metropolitan area or city in Texas. Working in groups, find maps of the interstate highway model showing how it connects one city to the next. Each group should focus on a different part of the state. Create an oral and visual presentation to show how the highway system connects the entire state and makes travel to neighboring states easier.

Self-Check Quiz
Visit the texans.glencoe.com Web site and click on **Chapter 24—Self-Check Quizzes** to prepare for the chapter test.

Portfolio/TAKS Writing Activity

19. **Predicting Consequences** Imagine that you are an African American student who has had to endure separate and unequal education but finally can attend desegregated schools. Write one to two paragraphs in which you address some of the fears and frustrations you felt before finally gaining admission to equal, desegregated schools, and the relief you felt afterward. Save your work for your portfolio.

Building Technology Skills

20. **Using the Internet or Library for Research** Divide the class equally into two research teams to gather information about the 1960 presidential race between John F. Kennedy and Richard M. Nixon. Each team should research topics such as foreign policy, domestic policy, education, taxes, and civil rights. Develop a multimedia presentation using photographs, maps, and narration to share with the rest of the class.

TAKS PRACTICE

Directions: Use your knowledge of Texas history to answer the following question.

In post-World War II American history, Texas has played an important role in national government because

F redistricting shifted the proportion of votes allotted to urban areas.

G it joined the union as an independent country.

H it is a geographically large state.

J several U.S. presidents have come from Texas.

Test-Taking Tip:

Make sure to read **all** the answers given before choosing your answer. It is easy to recognize a term that relates to the question, but the answer containing that term might not be correct.

Economics & History

Building a Better Mousetrap

There is an old expression that says, "If you build a better mousetrap, the world will beat a path to your door." Jack Kilby proved that this is still true. Kilby developed the silicon chip in 1958 at the Texas Instruments plant in Dallas. This invention had a revolutionary effect on our daily lives. It also had economic and social consequences for the state, the nation, and the world.

Jack Kilby grew up in Great Bend, Kansas. After serving in World War II, he attended the University of Illinois and graduated in 1947 with a degree in engineering. While working at his first job, Kilby developed a famous method for solving complicated engineering problems. First, he considered all possible answers to his question. Next, he eliminated all answers that did not seem likely. Last, he pursued the most practical solution to the problem at hand. He would use this method later to develop a very important invention—the integrated circuit.

Working Smart

In 1958, Kilby was hired by Texas Instruments. His assignment was to find a way for the electronics industry to manufacture better products

to be sold at cheaper prices. At that time, transistors acted as the brains of electronic equipment. However, connecting transistors to complete a circuit required expensive hand labor and left room for error. In addition, transistor products, such as radios, were generally big, expensive, and wore out quickly.

Kilby tackled his project at Texas Instruments by using the problem-solving method he had perfected earlier. First, he considered all possible answers. Then he eliminated numerous plans that did not show promise. Finally, he decided to experiment with silicon, a substance that has the capacity to conduct, or carry, electricity. Previously, Texas Instruments had used this chemical element in its own transistors.

High Technology Discovery

Kilby's efforts led to the development of what is known as the integrated circuit. Instead of complicated circuits made up of wired-together transistors, a single chip of silicon was designed to contain an entire circuit. This computer chip, less than half the size of a dime, could house electronic units capable of retaining memory and giving commands.

Within a few years, Jack Kilby's invention changed society worldwide. The silicon chip reduced the size of new electronic products, cut

down on the cost of manufacturing them, and, as a result, increased sales figures for his company and others in the electronics industry. One of Texas Instruments' first inventions to use the

An integrated circuit on a silicon chip

integrated circuit was the hand-held calculator. It has become an indispensable product used by people everywhere.

Today, the integrated circuit is part of most military weapon systems. It is necessary to run personal computers, appliances, cameras, clocks, video games, and countless other everyday products. It is even found on spacecraft and satellites that travel far beyond our planet.

Honors and Recognition

Jack Kilby, who left Texas Instruments in 1970, has been honored with membership in the National Inventors' Hall of Fame in Washington, D.C. When inducted in 1982, he joined Thomas Edison, Henry Ford, Robert Noyce (recognized by the electronic community as the co-inventor of the integrated circuit), and other great American inventors. Will you remember the name Jack Kilby from now on?

Jack Kilby with then president George H.W. Bush

TAKS PRACTICE

1. **Making Generalizations** How do products using integrated circuits benefit your family?
2. **Making Inferences** How do you approach problems that are difficult to solve?
3. **Writing About Economics** Write a paragraph that develops one of the themes below. Use standard grammar, spelling, sentence structure, and punctuation. Include information and examples from the feature as details to support your argument.
   a. How has technology impacted the business world?
   b. Imagine a career in technology or engineering. What do you think you would or would not like about jobs in these fields?
   c. Why is it important for manufacturers to keep costs low so consumers can buy affordable products?

CHAPTER 25

Turmoil & Progress

Why It Matters

The 1960s and 1970s were a time of dynamic change in Texas. Women and members of ethnic minorities demanded and realized greater equality. Texas culture was enriched by the increasing immigration of people from Mexico, Central America, the Middle East, the northern United States, Africa, and Asia.

The Impact Today

Several trends that began in the 1960s and 1970s continue to influence Texas:
* *Elected officials began to more closely reflect the state's diverse population.*
* *New techniques and technologies increased the productivity of Texas agriculture.*
* *A concern for protecting the Texas environment became more important.*

1956
★ *Henry B. González elected to Texas State Senate*

1965
★ *Texas created the Air Control Board*

Texas

United States   *1955*   *1960*   *1965*

World

Dr. Fidel Castro
Prime Minister of Cuba

1959
• *Fidel Castro became Communist premier of Cuba*

1963
• *Lyndon B. Johnson became president of the United States*

1964
• *United States sent ground troops to Vietnam*

1964
• *The Beatles rock group began first tour of the United States*

The National Aeronautics and Space Administration at the Johnson Space Center in Houston, Texas, is responsible for managing the space shuttle program.

FOLDABLES™
Study Organizer

TAKS PRACTICE

Categorizing Information Study Foldable
Make this foldable and use it to record information about the turmoil and progress that took place in Texas between 1963 and 1974.

Step 1 Fold a sheet of paper into thirds from top to bottom.

This forms three rows.

Step 2 Open the paper and refold it into fourths from side to side.

Fold it in half, then in half again.

This forms four columns.

Step 3 Unfold, turn, and draw lines along the folds.

Step 4 Label your table as shown.

Chapter 25 1963-1974	Turmoil	Progress
Politics and Protest		
Civil Rights and Politics		
Growth and Development		

Reading and Writing As you read the chapter, write what you learn about the years of "Turmoil" and "Progress" in Texas in the appropriate places on your table foldable.

1966
★ Barbara Jordan elected to Texas State Senate

1970

1975

1966
• Indira Gandhi became prime minister of India

1973
• U.S. involvement in Vietnam ended

TEXAS HISTORY Online

Chapter Overview
Visit the texans.glencoe.com Web site and click on **Chapter 25—Chapter Overviews** to preview chapter information.

CHAPTER 25   Turmoil & Progress   559

The Politics of Protest

Main Idea

Texas and the nation confronted poverty, civil rights, and Vietnam during the 1960s. All three issues affected politics.

Key Terms

prosperous
refugee

Reading Strategy

Summarizing Information Draw a table like the one below and write at least two interesting facts about each individual listed.

Individual	Interesting Facts
Lyndon B. Johnson	
Martin Luther King, Jr.	
Richard Nixon	

Read to Learn

• about "The Great Society."
• about the upheavals of 1968.
• about the conflict in Vietnam.

Section Theme

Government and Democracy Political parties, special interest groups, and governments struggled in an age of change.

Preview of Events

♦1963	♦1964	♦1968	♦1974
Lyndon B. Johnson becomes president	Civil Rights Act is passed	Dr. Martin Luther King, Jr., and Robert Kennedy are assassinated	Richard Nixon resigns the presidency

Refugees fleeing Saigon

A Texas Story

Dai Huynh knew her family had to leave Vietnam when American forces pulled out. The new Communist government would deal severely with the relatives of South Vietnam officers. "My dad, a major in the army . . . was gone most of the time, leaving my mother, my two sisters, my brother, and me at home." When the Viet Cong seized control of Saigon's airport, it became impossible for Dai Huynh and her family to leave by air. They seemed to be trapped.

A Texan in the White House

Judge **Sarah T. Hughes** administered the oath of office to Lyndon B. Johnson hours after President John F. Kennedy died. A Texan was now president. In a speech to Congress, President Johnson challenged the grief-stricken nation to honor the memory of President Kennedy by supporting the programs he had favored. In 1964 American voters showed their continued approval by electing Johnson to a full term as president.

The Great Society

Johnson believed in a federal government that was deeply involved in the lives of citizens. Accordingly, Congress passed so many laws during Johnson's presidency that it has been compared to Franklin Roosevelt's New Deal. Johnson's programs were called the **Great Society.** He declared a **"war on poverty."** Although the nation as a whole was prosperous, some regions and groups of people had not shared in that general wealth. Johnson believed that education was the best way to solve problems of poverty. He told his cabinet, "I want—and I intend—education to be the cornerstone on which we build this administration's program and record." When the **Elementary and Secondary Education Act** was passed, Johnson went back to Stonewall, Texas, to sign the bill in the small,

one-room schoolhouse where he had started school. His first teacher, Mrs. Katie Deadrich Looney, was with him.

Johnson also supported laws that created **Head Start, Job Corps,** and federal aid for college students. A major Job Corps installation at San Marcos provided vocational education to 3,000 students by 1967.

Johnson was a strong supporter of civil rights. As president, he helped push the **Civil Rights Act of 1964** through Congress. Then he turned his attention to the **Voting Rights Act.** This law protected the rights of all people, regardless of race, to vote. In March 1965, he addressed Congress while the nation watched on television. He said,

> ❝A century has passed . . . since the Negro was freed. And he is not fully free tonight . . . A century has passed . . . since equality was promised. And yet the Negro is not equal . . . The real hero of this struggle is the American Negro . . . he has called upon us to make good the promise of America.❞

Picturing **History**

Dr. Martin Luther King, Jr., (*second from right*) and supporters march for civil rights in Memphis, Tennessee. Marches also took place in Texas. What two major pieces of civil rights legislation did President Johnson help move through Congress?

People of Texas

Barbara Jordan 1936–1996

Born into a poor family in Houston, Barbara Jordan used education as her means to success, leading to a number of impressive "firsts." Jordan was the first African American student at Boston University Law School. She was the first African American woman elected to the Texas Senate (and the first African American since 1883). Jordan was the first African American Texan (and Southern African American woman) in the U.S. Congress, and the first African American woman to give a keynote address at a major political party's national convention.

Throughout her political career, Jordan was respected and admired by both her public and politicians. In 1994, she was awarded the Presidential Medal of Freedom—the highest award given to a civilian.

Foreign Affairs

Johnson wanted to focus on economic and civil rights programs, but foreign affairs began to occupy more of his attention. New difficulties were developing in Southeast Asia. Since the 1950s, the country of **Vietnam** had been divided into two parts. North Vietnam had a Communist government. The United States supported South Vietnam in its fight against communism. When Johnson became president, there already were Americans in South Vietnam acting as military advisers. The situation changed by the mid-1960s when Johnson ordered combat troops to the country. Many of these were Texans.

As the number of Americans killed and wounded in Vietnam grew, so did the number of Americans opposed to the war. The war divided the country. Although many people in the United States felt the war was necessary to stop communism, a large number believed the war was immoral and unnecessary. Some Texans opposed the war and some did not. Sometimes there were protest demonstrations in the streets of states all across the country. Occasionally these demonstrations turned violent.

Opposition to the war in Vietnam grew, and conflict over civil rights spread across the nation. Riots in cities such as Los Angeles, Detroit, and Washington, D.C., created a fearful mood. Violence occurred in Texas in 1967 when a riot at Texas Southern University took the life of a Houston policeman.

A Critical Year

The year 1968 was critical. On March 31, 1968, President Johnson announced he would not run for another term. Less than a week later, on April 4, **Dr. Martin Luther King, Jr.,** a leader in the civil rights struggle, was assassinated in Memphis, Tennessee. His message of nonviolence attracted a wide following of people of all ethnic groups united in their belief that racism was immoral. Only two months later, on June 5, **Robert Kennedy,** President Kennedy's brother, was assassinated while campaigning in Los Angeles.

These and other turbulent events of the 1960s produced a sense of crisis by election day in 1968. Many Americans longed for an end to the turmoil. In the election they turned to the Republican candidate, **Richard Nixon.** Texans, however, supported **Hubert Humphrey,** the Democratic candidate, by a small margin.

✓ **Reading Check** **Explaining** Why did President Johnson declare a "war on poverty"?

Nixon as President

Once in office, Richard Nixon struggled to end the war in Vietnam. His efforts did not bring peace, however, and opponents of the war increased their efforts to "bring the boys home." In 1972, Nixon was involved in a scandal, now known as **"Watergate."** Taped conversations and other evidence revealed that he conspired in a cover-up of a burglary of the Democratic Party's headquarters in the Watergate Hotel. Two Texans, **Jack Brooks** and **Barbara Jordan,** served on the Judiciary Committee of the House of Representatives investigating Nixon. In the opening address to the committee, Representative Jordan stated her belief in the power of American law:

> ❝My faith in the Constitution is whole, it is complete, it is total. I am not going to sit here and be an idle spectator to the diminution, the subversion, the destruction of the Constitution.❞

Knowing he could not continue to lead, Nixon resigned from office on August 8, 1974.

Refugees Seek Homes in Texas

Both those who had supported the war and those who had opposed it were relieved when the last U.S. troops left Vietnam in 1973. Thousands of Vietnamese **refugees** (persons who flee for safety, especially to a foreign country)

A Shared Past...

Lyndon Johnson's becoming president created a vacancy in the office of vice president. Because President Johnson had a history of heart disease, many people were concerned about his health. If Johnson were to die in office, they feared an elderly speaker of the House of Representatives might have to assume the office of president as called for by the Constitution. The problem was solved for future generations by the ratification of the Twenty-fifth Amendment in 1967. That change in the Constitution made it possible for a president to name a new vice president subject to the Senate's approval.

immigrated to the U.S. Texas became home to many of them. Some Vietnamese immigrants found work in the shrimping industry on the Texas coast and lived in cities such as Rockport, Port Aransas, and Kemah. Most, however, relocated to cities such as Houston, Beaumont, Port Arthur, and Galveston. By the 1980s, the population of several schools in west and southwest Houston was more than 10 percent Vietnamese.

✓ **Reading Check** **Explaining** Why did President Nixon resign?

SECTION 1 ASSESSMENT

Checking for Understanding

1. **Using Key Terms** Write a sentence using the term refugee(s).
2. **Reviewing Facts** What were two major areas of President Johnson's Great Society?

Reviewing Themes

3. **Government and Democracy** In 1968, several events occurred in the nation that had an impact on Texas government. Identify two of these and explain their importance.

Organizing to Learn

4. **Evaluating Effects** Create a chart like the one below and list the effects of the war in Vietnam on people in the U.S. and people in Vietnam.

Effects on Americans	Effects on Vietnamese

Critical Thinking

5. **Using Oral History** Prepare questions to interview someone who was an adult at the time of the war in Vietnam. After the interview, write a brief summary and share it with the class.

TAKS PRACTICE

Making Judgments What part of President Johnson's "Great Society" had the most lasting impact? Why?

Identifying Alternatives

Why Learn This Skill?

Texans face many problems that will require solutions now and in the years ahead. Citizens and state and local government leaders will have to take actions to solve these problems. One way to make decisions is to identify alternative, or other, solutions. Decision makers can then try to predict which alternative is the best solution.

Learning the Skill

Follow these steps when identifying alternatives.
- State the problem.
- List all the possible alternatives for solving the problem.
- Gather information about each alternative.
- Predict the positive and negative consequences of each alternative.

Practicing the Skill

When public schools are funded by property taxes, not all students receive the same quality of education. Study the chart and then answer the following questions.

❶ What are the alternatives for funding schools?

❷ Which effect(s) of A are advantages? Which are disadvantages?

❸ Which effect(s) of B are advantages? Which are disadvantages?

❹ Which effect(s) of C are advantages? Which are disadvantages?

❺ Which alternative would you choose? Why?

Alternatives for Funding Schools

Alternative	Effects
A. State income tax on individuals and businesses	• Might drive some business out of state • Might be unpopular with voters
B. Increase student fees for activities	• Would put unfair financial burden on lower-income students • Would save tax money for other areas of education
C. Increase the sales tax	• Would affect lower-income families more significantly than higher-income families • Might upset voters • Would raise costs of all consumer items • Might be easier for voters to accept since the sales tax already exists

Identifying Alternatives Read the excerpt below and answer the questions that follow.

SAN ANTONIO (AP) – Legislators are looking at proposals that could generate millions, if not billions, of dollars for [Texas] state highway needs, but experts say it won't be enough to relieve traffic congestion in cities or on the border.
—*Amarillo Globe News*, February 5, 2001

1. Describe the problem.
2. List at least two possible solutions for the problem.
3. Identify an advantage and disadvantage for each alternative.

 Glencoe's **Skillbuilder Interactive Workbook,** Level 1, provides instruction and practice in key social studies skills.

Civil Rights and Politics

Guide to Reading

Main Idea
The struggle for civil rights was a result of individuals and groups who worked to ensure equality for all citizens.

Key Terms
boycott
sit-in
freedom ride
keynote address

Reading Strategy
Analyzing Information As you read this section, draw a table like the one below and fill in the accomplishments of each group.

Group	Accomplishments
African Americans	
Mexican Americans	
Women	

Read to Learn
• how African Americans and Mexican Americans worked for racial justice.
• how women participated in politics.

Section Theme
Civic Rights and Responsibilities
Through the turmoil of the 1960s and 1970s, thoughtful citizens looked for ways to ensure equality for all.

Preview of Events

♦1958 ♦1961   ♦1972   ♦1998

Hattie Mae White is the first African American on Houston School Board

Henry B. González is elected to U.S. House of Representatives

Barbara Jordan is elected to U.S. House of Representatives

James Farmer receives Presidential Medal of Freedom

Vietnamese refugees

A
Texas Story

In the early 1970s, thousands of refugee families searched frantically for an escape from war-torn Vietnam. Robbed of their few remaining possessions, the Huynhs were left with only their birth certificates. Dai Huynh remembers, "All the fishing boats had left . . . In a last effort, Dad took off his white shirt and started waving. 'Wait, over here. Please, don't leave us behind.' By a miracle, the captain saw us. He yelled back, 'Come quickly. I can't go back, but I'll slow down for you.'"

Growing Involvement of African Americans

Congressional hearings in the Watergate affair were broadcast on national television. Those broadcasts made America familiar with Representative Barbara Jordan of Houston. That she was there at all was a tribute to the growing political power of African Americans in Texas. In 1966 she became the first African American elected to the state Senate since Reconstruction. She worked effectively with the 30 white men who made up the rest of the Senate. Houston voters in 1972 elected her to the U.S. House of Representatives.

In Representative Jordan's first term, the House investigated the Watergate scandal. Jordan was a member of the investigating committee. When she spoke, she had the attention of the room and the nation. She said,

> ❝But when [the Constitution] was completed, on the seventeenth of September in 1787, I was not included in that *We, the people.* I felt somehow for many years that George Washington and Alexander Hamilton just left me out by mistake. But through the process of amendment, interpretation, and court decision, I have finally been included in *We, the people.*❞

Civil Rights Achievements, 1950–1970

Public Facilities	• Parks and pools are integrated.
Business and Work	• Bus terminals, restaurants, theatres, and railroads are integrated. • Equal pay is required for white and African American teachers.
Legal and Judicial	• Police departments and juries are integrated.
Education	• Public schools, universities, athletic teams, cheerleading squads, and drill teams are integrated.
Personal	• Newspapers add Mr. and Mrs. to African American names.
Housing	• Restrictive covenants (provisions preventing house sales to African Americans) are removed.

TAKS PRACTICE

Evaluating Integration was not always a smooth process but it was accomplished. *How did integration benefit Texas society?*

So impressive was her statement that the Democratic Party invited her to give a major speech at its 1976 convention.

Another leader in the struggle for equality was a Texan named **James Farmer.** Early in his career, Farmer became attracted to the ideas of Mohandas Gandhi, who had led a nonviolent movement for the independence of India. Farmer founded the **Congress of Racial Equality** (CORE), dedicated to the idea of peaceful change. He was the director during the 1960s when the group organized several nonviolent methods of opposition to segregation. In boycotts, people would protest by refusing to use a certain product or service. During sit-ins, demonstrators physically sat down inside or in front of businesses or offices, interfering with the process of work. Freedom rides took integrated buses through segregated areas of the South to draw attention to civil rights. In January 1998, Farmer received the Presidential Medal of Freedom in a White House ceremony.

✓**Reading Check** **Evaluating** Why was it significant that Barbara Jordan was elected to the Texas Senate?

Mexican Americans and Politics

During the same period, Mexican Americans also sought fair treatment from school officials, employers, and state and local governments. LULAC and the American GI Forum continued their work for civil rights, and others individually became more politically involved. In 1956 San Antonio voters elected **Henry B. González** to the state Senate. He was the first Mexican American to serve in modern times. In 1958 González ran for governor. Two years later Hector P. García and others formed "Viva Kennedy" clubs to campaign for John Kennedy. People who had volunteered in the elections for González and Kennedy later formed the Political Association of Spanish-Speaking Organizations (PASSO). In 1961 González was elected to the U.S. House of Representatives. By the mid-1960s, Mexican American candidates were winning seats on several school boards and city councils.

Henry B. González 1916-2000

Henry B. González was born in San Antonio. When he was young, he was barred from attending local restaurants and public swimming pools because he was of Mexican descent. Henry did not let that stop him. He overcame poverty and adversity, graduated from college and law school, and later ran for public office. In 1956 he became the first Mexican American to be elected to the Texas Senate in 110 years and, in 1961, he was the first Mexican American elected to the U.S. Congress from Texas.

González fought for civil rights and better housing. He served as chairman of the House Banking Committee, writing the laws that ended the savings and loan scandals of the 1980s. His career in politics spanned a period of 42 years.

Forming New Groups

In the summer of 1966, a dramatic incident inspired many Mexican Americans to even greater political involvement. Farm workers in the Rio Grande Valley toiled under harsh conditions. They often were exposed to dangerous agricultural chemicals without the aid of safety equipment. In protest, the field hands went on strike. Demands included a minimum wage, decent housing, provision of toilets and drinking water, and the banning of the short-handled hoe. Labor leaders organized a march from the Rio Grande Valley to Austin to make their case before state government leaders. **Governor John Connally** met with them in New Braunfels. His actions did not satisfy the unhappy workers, and many became more active in politics.

New groups during the 1960s that stressed more activism came out of this 1966 incident. One such group was the **Mexican American Youth Organization** (MAYO). It was founded in San Antonio by José Ángel Gutiérrez, William "Willie" Velásquez, Mario Compeán, Ignacio Pérez, and Juan Patlán. MAYO embraced the Mexican American link to Mexico's heritage enthusiastically and adopted an Aztec warrior as its symbol. Its greatest strength was among high school and college youth. Educational issues were among the most visible of MAYO's causes. It wanted more Mexican American teachers, Mexican American studies in the curriculum, and an end to discriminatory school policies. MAYO led walkouts in several high schools, including Edcouch, Elsa, and Crystal City.

MAYO members founded a new political party, *La Raza Unida* **Party** (RUP), to represent their interests. It placed its candidate for governor on the ballot for the 1972 election. It was also successful in winning city offices in Crystal City and Cotulla. Another group formed during the period was the **Mexican American Legal Defense and Education Fund** (MALDEF). Its main purpose was to end discriminatory practices through lawsuits.

The increased activity resulted in more Mexican Americans being elected to local and state offices. By the end of the 1970s, Irma Rangel, Raúl Longoria, and Hugo Berlanga had been elected to the state legislature. In addition, a Houstonian, Leonel Castillo, served as head of the Immigration and Naturalization Service in Washington, D.C. Reynaldo Garza became a federal judge in Brownsville.

Reading Check **Identifying** What organizations were created as a result of the farm workers' march in 1966?

Mexican American Heritage

Many Mexican Americans in the 1960s and 1970s found renewed pride in their Mexican roots. There was increased interest in art and literature that reflected Mexican American experiences. Mexico's **Diego Rivera** and **José Clemente Orozco** inspired artists such as **Manuel Acosta** of El Paso. He and others created murals in San Antonio, Houston, and other Texas cities to tell the story of their culture. Writers such as Abelardo Delgado, Raúl Salinas, Rolando Hinojosa-Smith, Tomás Rivera, Ricardo Sánchez, and Estela Portillo produced novels, short stories, poems, and plays reflecting the Mexican American experience. Also during this era, many younger Mexican Americans began referring to themselves as *Chicanos* or *Chicanas* as a way to express pride in their heritage.

Women and Politics

During the 1960s and 1970s, women became more active at all levels of Texas political life. They increased their numbers on school boards, city councils, and in the state legislature.

In 1958 **Hattie Mae White** became the first African American to serve on the Houston School Board. Anita Martínez was elected to the Dallas City Council in 1969. When Barbara Jordan was in the state Senate and **Frances "Sissy" Farenthold** was in the state House, they

Picturing History

Frances Farenthold represented Corpus Christi in the Texas House of Representatives from 1969 to 1973. In her 1972 run for Texas governor, she was supported by the Texas Women's Political Caucus. What was one of the aims of the Texas Women's Political Caucus?

were the only two women in the legislature. The Texas Women's Political Caucus, the National Organization for Women (NOW), and the *Mujeres por la Raza* encouraged more women to run for office. Farenthold ran for governor twice, although she did not win. By 2000, 86 women had served in the Texas legislature.

In 1972, as women's political power kept growing, Anne Armstrong became the first woman to give a **keynote address** at a national political party convention. (A keynote address is a speech that presents the main issue of interest to an audience and often inspires unity and enthusiasm.) A few years later, San Antonio and Austin elected women mayors.

✓ **Reading Check** Evaluating How did women's participation affect politics in Texas?

SECTION 2 ASSESSMENT

Checking for Understanding

1. **Using Key Terms** Write a sentence to show that you understand the definition of the terms boycott, sit-in, and keynote address.
2. **Reviewing Facts** Identify influential Mexican American artists and writers.

Reviewing Themes

3. **Civic Rights and Responsibilities** Why are civil rights important in a democracy?

Organizing to Learn

4. **Describing** Create a chart like the one below, and describe the purpose of each organization that is listed.

Organization	Purpose
CORE	
MAYO	
MALDEF	
NOW	
Mujeres por la Raza	

Critical Thinking

5. **Analyzing** Why did various minorities form special groups?
6. **Evaluating** Were civil rights groups successful in achieving their goals? Explain.

TAKS PRACTICE

Identifying Who was James Farmer, and how did he contribute to the civil rights movement?

Growth and Development

Dai Huynh today

A Texas Story

It was hard for the Vietnamese refugee family at first. The Huynhs had settled in Texas. Both mother and father worked at two jobs. They encouraged their children to do well in school. The older children had gone to college by the time the youngest daughter, Dai, graduated from high school in Houston. The entire family was filled with pride at her accomplishment: Not only did she graduate first in her class, she also led the 5,000-person audience in singing "The Star-Spangled Banner" at her graduation ceremony.

Agriculture

Texas experienced increased economic growth during the 1960s and 1970s. Although oil and agriculture remained important to the state's economy, other industries also became prominent.

Fewer Texans worked in agriculture than ever before but continued to produce large quantities of food and cotton. Greater productivity was based on several factors. First—and most important—increased mechanization, expansion of irrigation, increased use of fertilizers, and more effective insecticides significantly increased yields per acre. The U.S. Department of Agriculture and agents of the Texas A&M University Extension Service provided information about the use of these new products and methods.

Second, Texas agriculture became more productive as cotton planting moved westward. Following World War II, the lands that were poor cotton producers, such as the sandy soils of East Texas, were converted to cattle pastures and pine plantations. Cotton continued to be grown in the regions that were best suited for that crop, such as the High Plains, the Rio Grande Valley, and the Blackland Prairie.

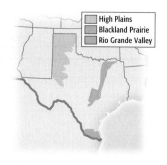

High Plains
Blackland Prairie
Rio Grande Valley

A third reason for the increased productivity was that farmers and ranchers took advantage of economies of scale. Factory methods were applied to raising both cattle and poultry. Young steers were placed in feedlots, large outdoor facilities. There they ate grain until they were large enough to be processed into meat. Because the grain was produced mainly on the High Plains, feedlots were built there. The High Plains experienced a boom in the cattle feed industry. In 1973 alone, 4.8 million cattle were fattened in Texas feedlots. In that same year President Nixon imposed a price freeze on beef. Ranchers withheld their cattle from the market. When they finally sold their cattle, the oversupply made prices drop. The result was a "bust" after a "boom." Several feedlots went out of business. These boom and bust cycles would appear in other Texas industries as well.

New developments also occurred in the raising of chickens and turkeys. Farmers, especially in Gonzales and Shelby Counties, constructed large poultry houses and raised thousands of fowl each year. Chicken became more popular in the diets of Texans and other Americans. The greater availability of chickens made it possible for fast-food chicken restaurants to expand their operations.

Environmental Concerns

The use of feedlots and changes in poultry farming increased productivity and lowered costs, but new techniques raised new issues. When many animals were concentrated in one place, the result was offensive odors and waste products. Texas also had other industries that were possible sources of pollution. Cotton gins, smelters, foundries, paper mills, steel plants, petroleum refineries, and petrochemical plants were all suspect. It was noted by one investigative reporter that the air quality was worse in the regions of Texas where those facilities were concentrated, such as El Paso and Houston. For a time, pollution in the Houston Ship Channel became so severe that tests showed almost no

Picturing **History**

Panhandle

Cattle feed on grain at a large feedlot in the Panhandle. How did the use of feedlots contribute to increased agricultural productivity?

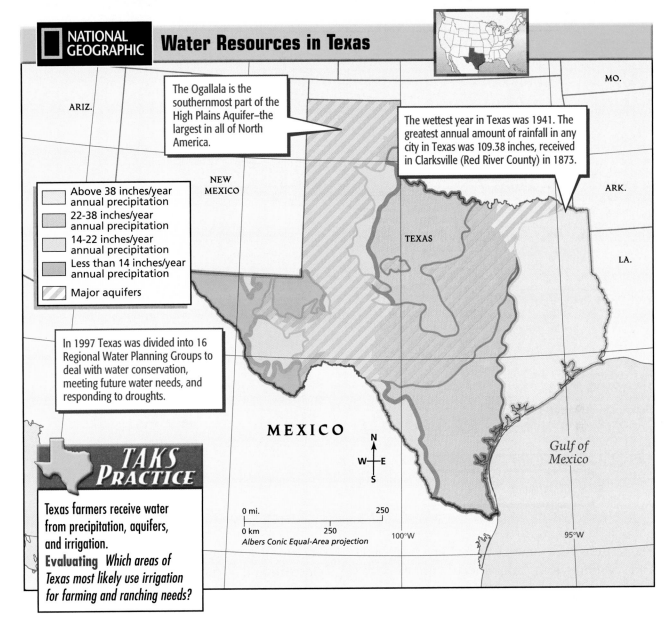

NATIONAL GEOGRAPHIC — Water Resources in Texas

The Ogallala is the southernmost part of the High Plains Aquifer–the largest in all of North America.

The wettest year in Texas was 1941. The greatest annual amount of rainfall in any city in Texas was 109.38 inches, received in Clarksville (Red River County) in 1873.

Above 38 inches/year annual precipitation

22-38 inches/year annual precipitation

14-22 inches/year annual precipitation

Less than 14 inches/year annual precipitation

Major aquifers

In 1997 Texas was divided into 16 Regional Water Planning Groups to deal with water conservation, meeting future water needs, and responding to droughts.

TAKS PRACTICE

Texas farmers receive water from precipitation, aquifers, and irrigation.
Evaluating Which areas of Texas most likely use irrigation for farming and ranching needs?

0 mi. 250
0 km 250
Albers Conic Equal-Area projection
100°W
95°W

MEXICO

Gulf of Mexico

---

oxygen in the water. Without oxygen, aquatic life—fish and plants—could not survive.

Steps were taken at both the state and federal levels to clean up Texas's air and water. Many concerned officials and citizens-action groups that included young people became involved in pollution issues. In 1965 the state created an **Air Control Board,** and in 1968 the state prohibited cities from burning garbage. Industries along the Houston Ship Channel worked to reduce their pollutants. By 1980 scientists found that fish, shrimp, and crabs had returned to those waters. Today, water quality in the channel is closely watched.

✓ Reading Check **Contrasting** What was a result of cleaning up the Houston Ship Channel?

Oil Economics

Events of the 1960s and 1970s showed Texans that their involvement in the oil industry connected them to international affairs. A group of foreign nations had created a cartel, or association to limit competition, called the **Organization of Petroleum Exporting Countries** (OPEC). The cartel was able to drive up the price of oil. In 1973 the Arab nations that supplied much of the OPEC oil ended shipments of oil to the United States because of U.S. support for Israel.

TEXAS HISTORY Online

Student Web Activity Visit the texans.glencoe.com Web site and click on **Chapter 25—Student Web Activity** to learn more about environmental concerns.

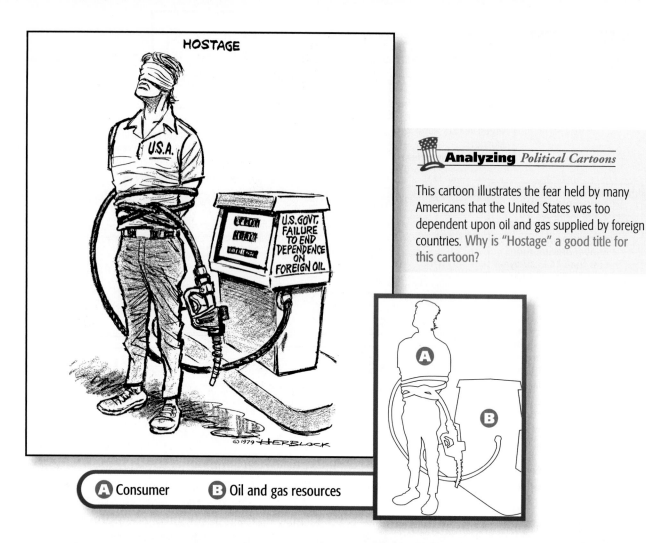

HOSTAGE

U.S.A.

U.S. GOVT. FAILURE TO END DEPENDENCE ON FOREIGN OIL

© 1979 HERBLOCK

Ⓐ Consumer　　Ⓑ Oil and gas resources

Analyzing *Political Cartoons*

This cartoon illustrates the fear held by many Americans that the United States was too dependent upon oil and gas supplied by foreign countries. Why is "Hostage" a good title for this cartoon?

The result was an "energy crisis." The price of oil and gasoline rose dramatically. To ease the demand, motorists could buy gasoline only on Monday–Wednesday–Friday or Tuesday–Thursday–Saturday, depending upon whether their license plates ended with an odd or even number. All gas stations were closed on Sundays.

Higher oil prices caused problems for many Texans, yet the high prices stimulated the drilling of more oil wells and increased activity in other areas of the oil industry. Texas oil companies hired more employees at high wages, and prosperity spread throughout other businesses, including real estate and banking. High oil prices lasted into the 1980s. When prices finally did fall, they brought down other parts of the economy as well.

The oil industry helped make Texas more global in its outlook. Texans traveled throughout the world because their skills and knowledge were in demand in "oil patches" everywhere. Indonesia, Saudi Arabia, Scotland, Nigeria, and

Venezuela were only some of their destinations. Once there, they might be called upon to perform a variety of jobs. Some Texans were geologists and geophysicists who looked for oil. Others were drillers and pipeline builders. Some were engineers who built refineries and petrochemical plants. If disaster struck in the oil fields, Texas companies were called to put out the raging oil well fires. The oil industry has used the talents and expertise of Texans all over the world.

Reading Check **Examining** How did the energy crisis of 1973 affect the Texas oil industry?

New Construction for a Modern State

A sure sign that Texans were looking to the future was the increase in construction projects during the 1960s and 1970s. Perhaps the most dramatic was the **Harris County Domed Stadium (Astrodome),** built in 1963–1964. The

Astrodome was the first enclosed, domed, air-conditioned, multipurpose sports stadium in the world. Since 1966 it has been the site of the Houston Livestock Show and Rodeo.

Texas's growing interdependence with the rest of the world encouraged both Dallas and Houston to build new airports. Soon developers built housing developments nearby. The north side of Houston sprouted developments in places such as Kingwood, Spring, Klein, and Conroe. Meanwhile NASA provided the stimulus for development around Clear Lake. The suburbs near the Dallas–Fort Worth Airport, such as Arlington, Grapevine, Grand Prairie, and Irving, also grew.

In San Antonio there was a special construction project that showed Texas pride in its past and confidence in its future. A 92-acre (37-hectare) site in downtown San Antonio was transformed into a setting for **HemisFair '68**—the first officially designated international exposition to be held in the southwestern United States. The fair, championed by Congressman Henry B. González, marked the 250th anniversary of the founding of San Antonio. Although it was designed to celebrate the cultural heritage shared by San Antonio and the nations of Latin America, more than thirty nations participated. Exhibits educated and entertained the 6 million visitors who came between

A Shared Past...

Concern for the environment was both a state and federal issue. Americans had been alarmed by Rachel Carson's book, *Silent Spring,* about the use of pesticides. Increased concern about air and water pollution prompted Congress to create the Environmental Protection Agency in 1970. It also passed the Clean Air Act. One provision of the Clean Air Act encouraged electric-generating companies to shift from coal to natural gas. The law thus had the indirect effect of helping Texas's natural gas producers.

April and October 1968. The 622-foot (190-m) Tower of the Americas was the most impressive building, but the most important was the **Institute of Texan Cultures.** In that building Texans and world visitors came to appreciate the rich ethnic diversity of Texas. Though not a museum, the institute displays relics, artifacts, and personal memorabilia with a direct connection to the people of each ethnic group represented.

✓ **Reading Check** **Identifying** What was the HemisFair?

SECTION 3 ASSESSMENT

Checking for Understanding

1. **Using Key Terms** Create illustrated flash cards for the following key terms: productivity, feedlot, boom and bust cycle, and cartel.

2. **Reviewing Facts** In addition to oil and agriculture, what other economic activities became important for Texas?

Reviewing Themes

3. **Science and Technology** Give examples of how technology affected the economy of Texas.

Organizing to Learn

4. **Identifying** Create a web like the one shown here, and identify reasons for increased productivity of food and cotton in Texas.

Increased Productivity

Critical Thinking

5. **Identifying Solutions** Environmental concerns have become particularly important to Texans. What can be done today to improve our environment?

TAKS PRACTICE

Identifying Technological innovations and scientific discoveries often have economic, social, or environmental consequences. Predict some consequences of a technological or scientific development.

Chapter Summary

Turmoil and Progress

1956
★ Henry B. González is elected to Texas Senate.

1958
• Hattie Mae White becomes first African American to serve on Houston School Board.

1961
• Henry B. González is elected to U.S. House of Representatives.

1963
★ Lyndon B. Johnson becomes president of the United States.

1964
★ Congress passes the Civil Rights Act.

1965
• Texas creates an Air Control Board.

1966
• Rio Grande Valley farm workers organize a protest march.
• MAYO is formed.
★ Barbara Jordan is first African American elected to Texas Senate since Reconstruction.

1968
• April 4, Dr. Martin Luther King, Jr., is assassinated.
• Richard Nixon is elected president.

1972
• *La Raza Unida* Party candidates win city offices.
• Barbara Jordan is elected to the U.S. House of Representatives.

1980s
• Houston Ship Channel pollution is greatly reduced.
★ Vietnamese immigrate to Texas in significant numbers.

Reviewing Key Terms

1. *Using graph paper, make a crossword puzzle using the following key terms:*

   refugee
   boycott
   sit-in
   freedom ride
   keynote address
   productivity
   feedlot
   boom and bust cycle
   cartel
   interdependence

Reviewing Key Facts

2. What did President Lyndon B. Johnson believe was the best way to solve problems of poverty?

3. What two Texans served on the Judiciary Committee investigating President Nixon in the Watergate scandal?

4. Name the Marshall, Texas, native and Presidential Medal of Freedom honoree who founded CORE (Congress of Racial Equality).

5. Who was the first Mexican American elected to the Texas state Senate in modern times? To what office was he later elected?

6. What factors led to increased productivity in Texas agriculture during the 1960s and 1970s?

7. How did the oil crisis of 1973 affect motorists? What plan was put in place to regulate purchases of gasoline?

Critical Thinking

8. **Summarizing** How did President Lyndon Johnson attempt to solve the problems related to education?

9. **Analyzing** Why was the war in Vietnam controversial?

10. **Evaluating** How did Barbara Jordan impress the Democratic Party?

11. **Describing** In what ways did Mexican Americans in Texas become more involved politically?

12. **Drawing Conclusions** How has the Texas oil industry made Texans more global in their outlook?

13. **Understanding Cause and Effect** How did falling oil prices bring down other parts of the economy?

Geography and History Activity

Using books available in your library or from information on the Internet, find the following information about Vietnam and Texas. As you find the information, complete a chart like the one shown below.

	Vietnam	Texas
Land area (sq. mi.)		
Population		
Per capita yearly income		

14. How does Vietnam compare to Texas in land area and population?

15. How could you explain the difference in per capita yearly income?

Cooperative Learning Activity

16. Role Playing Divide into groups of five. One person will be the moderator, and the other four will each choose to role-play one of the following individuals: Lyndon B. Johnson, Barbara Jordan, Henry B. González, or James Farmer. Research that person's views and activities concerning civil rights. The moderator will pose questions that will be used in a forum-type interview. Your classmates may also ask questions.

 ## Building Technology Skills

17. Using the Internet for Research Using several Internet sources, find additional information about one of the individuals mentioned in the Cooperative Learning Activity above. Keep a record of the Web sites you use.

 ## Portfolio/TAKS Writing Activity

18. Summarizing Look at the obituary section of your local newspaper. Read several of the obituaries to see what information is included. Choose a person from this chapter and write an obituary for that person.

Practicing Skills

19. Identifying Alternatives An important part of making decisions is identifying alternatives. Imagine you are on a commission to improve air quality in Texas. Come up with two alternatives that would help the commission accomplish its goal. For each alternative, list one advantage and one disadvantage.

TAKS PRACTICE

Use the line graph to answer the following question.

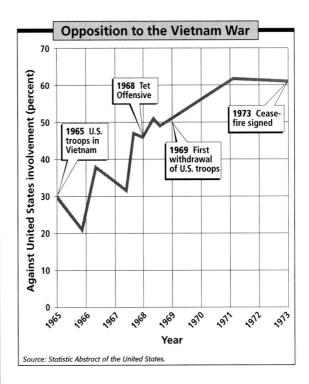

Opposition to the Vietnam War

Source: Statistic Abstract of the United States.

In 1968, approximately what percentage of Americans opposed United States involvement in the Vietnam War after the Viet Cong attack known as the Tet Offensive?

A 30%   **B** 40%   **C** 50%   **D** 60%

Test-Taking Tip:

In order to answer the question correctly, read the title and the labels carefully. Make sure to look at the section of the line graph that follows the Tet Offensive. Since this question asks for "approximately what percentage," you need to identify what percentage on the line graph most closely matches one of the answers.

CHAPTER 26

Texas Today

Why It Matters

New challenges faced Texas in the 1980s, 1990s, and the opening years of the twentieth-first century. International trade and new information technologies created a demand for better schools. State, county, and city governments increased law enforcement, transportation, and public welfare. Texans assumed more leadership positions in the federal government.

The Impact Today

- *Two Texans have been elected president of the United States during this time period.*
- *Increasing trade among the United States, Mexico, and Canada as a result of NAFTA has resulted in more goods being transported through Texas.*

1980
★ *Law prohibiting children of undocumented aliens from attending public schools ruled unconstitutional*

1982
★ *Kathy Whitmire elected mayor of Houston*

Texas

United States | *1980* | *1982* | *1984* | *1986* | *1988* | *1990*

World

1981
- *Sandra Day O'Connor appointed to United States Supreme Court*

1988
- *George H.W. Bush elected president of the United States*

1989
- *Berlin Wall came down in Germany*

Identifying Main Ideas Study Foldable
Make and use this foldable to identify and describe different aspects of life in Texas today.

Step 1 Fold two sheets of paper in half from top to bottom. Cut the papers in half along the folds.

Cut along the fold lines.

Step 2 Fold each of the four papers in half from top to bottom.

Step 3 On each folded paper, make a cut 1 inch from the side on the top flap.

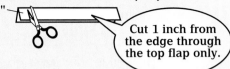

1"

Cut 1 inch from the edge through the top flap only.

Step 4 Place the folded papers one on top of the other. Staple the four sections together and label each of the tabs as you read the chapter.

Staple here.   Politics

Reading and Writing Label the sections of your foldable: Politics, Economics, Education, and Transportation. As you read, write key facts under each appropriate tab.

The Texas Capitol makes quite an impression during a laser light show, while Texas itself makes an increasingly large impact on the country and the world.

1993
★ Kay Bailey Hutchison elected to United States Senate

1995
★ George W. Bush became governor of Texas

2000
★ Rick Perry became 47th governor of Texas

1993   1995   1997   1999   2001

1992
• UN Earth Summit held in Rio de Janeiro

1995
• Use of Internet became more widespread

1997
• Pathfinder *landed* on Mars

2001
• September 11, terrorists attacked U.S. World Trade Center and Pentagon

• U.S. launched effort to wipe out international terrorism

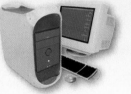

TEXAS HISTORY *Online*

Chapter Overview
Visit the texans.glencoe.com Web site and click on **Chapter 26—Chapter Overviews** to preview chapter information.

Guide to Reading

Main Idea
Women, African Americans, and Mexican Americans have influenced politics in Texas and the U.S.

Key Terms
urban dweller
cabinet
third-party
bill

Reading Strategy
Organizing Information As you read this section, complete a table like the one shown here. Fill in the positions of these Texans.

Person	Position
George H.W. Bush	
George W. Bush	
Henry González	
Phil Gramm	

Read to Learn
• about the two-party system in Texas.
• what accomplishments women, African Americans, and Mexican Americans made in Texas politics.

Section Theme
Individual Action Many public officials have made important contributions to Texas and the U.S.

Preview of Events

1988	1990	1993	2000

George H.W. Bush elected 41st president of the U.S.

Ann Richards elected governor of Texas

Henry Cisneros appointed to President Clinton's cabinet

George W. Bush elected 43rd president of the U.S.

Neglected classroom

A Texas Story

Demetrio Rodríguez, a sheet metal worker living in San Antonio, was troubled. The buildings in which his children attended school had broken windows and inadequate restroom facilities. Just a few miles away, children went to school in modern, well-equipped buildings. Rodríguez believed that this was unfair. He took the school board to court.

"The kids who attend school in my district still have classrooms in portable buildings," he wrote. "Many Texas teachers are forced to buy crayons and other supplies out of their own pockets."

—Demetrio Rodríguez, quoted in "Education and Equality: The Battle for School Funding Reform"

A Broader Political Base

The Texas political scene continues to undergo many changes. The events of the 1960s and 1970s so transformed Texas politics that, by the 1980s and 1990s, groups that had been excluded from political power were now included. The political power of minorities, women, and **urban dwellers** (those who live in cities) grew significantly.

Republicans

By the year 2000, the Republican Party held all major statewide elective offices. The "one-man, one-vote" rule of the U.S. Supreme Court made it difficult to draw districts that favored a particular party. People moving into Texas included many Northerners who often voted with the Republicans. The Republican Party became identified with oil producers, and the Democratic Party became associated with oil consumers and environmentalists. Supporters of the Republican Party favored less government regulation of businesses and industry. They also championed free enterprise.

For many years Senator John Tower was the most prominent Texas Republican. In 1978 Texas elected **William Clements** the first Republican governor of Texas since Reconstruction. Clements was a successful oil man but had never run for political office. Many voters, disillusioned with politicians after the Watergate scandal, found Clements' lack of political experience appealing.

Women

Both parties welcomed women into greater political participation. Democrats nominated **Ann Richards** for state treasurer in 1982. She held the office until 1991, when she became governor for a term. Democratic women such as **Sheila Jackson Lee** and **Eddie Bernice Johnson** were African Americans

who represented Texas in the U.S. House of Representatives. Republican women also became more prominent in their party. **Kay Bailey Hutchison** was elected to the U.S. Senate in 1993 and reelected in 1994 and 2000. In 1996 **Kay Granger** became the first Republican woman to be elected to the U.S. House of Representatives from Texas. She was reelected from her district in 1998 and 2000.

At the end of the 1990s, 29 members of the state House of Representatives and 3 members of the state Senate were women. At the local level, too, women increasingly served in numerous capacities. **Kathy Whitmire** was the mayor of Houston from 1982 to 1992. **Annette Strauss** was elected to the same position in Dallas in 1987. **Suzie Azar** served as mayor of El Paso in the late 1980s. In fact, by the 1990s women had been elected mayor of more than 100 Texas towns. In 2001, there were 27 female county judges serving across the state. Women also became city council members and county commissioners. In the 1990s more than 50 percent of the school board members in the state were women.

![Exploring Government]

Exploring **Government**

Texans Mickey Leland (*seated right*), Ann Richards (*center*), and Kay Bailey Hutchison (*left*), have chosen to serve Texas and the U.S. as public officials. **Why do people choose to run for public office?**

People of Texas

George W. Bush 1946–

George W. Bush grew up in Midland and Houston. He received a bachelor's degree from Yale and a master of business administration from Harvard. Before beginning his career in the oil and gas business, he was an F-102 pilot for the Texas Air National Guard. After working on his father's successful presidential campaign in 1988, he invested in the Texas Rangers baseball franchise.

In 1994 Bush was elected the 46th governor of the state of Texas and was reelected in 1998—the first Texas governor to be elected to consecutive four-year terms. George W. Bush was elected the 43rd president of the United States in 2000, becoming only the second son of a president to serve as president. He is married to Laura Welch Bush, a former schoolteacher and librarian.

Mexican Americans

The civil rights struggle of the 1960s involved Mexican American Texans in politics. However, *La Raza Unida*, formed in 1970 by those who had rejected the Democratic and Republican Parties, had disappeared by 1978. Mexican Americans now worked in the Democratic and Republican Parties. The educational gains of prior decades resulted in many well-educated Mexican American professionals becoming politically active. In 2001, Russ Garcia was elected the first Hispanic mayor of Austin, with nearly 60 percent of the vote. For the first time in the city's history, two Hispanics served on the city council at the same time. In the 77th session of the state legislature, 7 Mexican Americans served in the Senate, and 26 held seats in the House. In many Texas communities, Mexican Americans held local offices, including sheriff, judge, commissioner, and mayor. In the mid-1990s former San Antonio mayor **Henry Cisneros** served in President Clinton's cabinet, or group of top advisers, as secretary of housing and urban development.

✓ **Reading Check** Describing How did Mexican Americans become involved in Texas government?

African Americans

African Americans also increased their political involvement throughout the 1980s and 1990s. After serving from 1973 to 1979 in the state Senate and the U.S. House of Representatives, **Barbara Jordan** retired to Austin to become a professor at the LBJ School of Public Affairs. She was awarded the Presidential Medal of Freedom in 1994 and had an airport terminal in Austin named after her. Jordan's place in Congress was taken by **Mickey Leland.** During his six terms in Congress, Representative Leland worked diligently to fight world hunger. He died in an airplane crash while carrying food relief to starving people. A federal office building and an airport terminal in Houston are named in his honor.

In 2000, Sheila Jackson Lee was reelected to her fourth term in the U.S. House of Representatives and Eddie Bernice Johnson was reelected to her fifth. African Americans also gave distinguished service in state and local government. In 1999, 14 African Americans served in the state House of Representatives, and 2 served in the state Senate. As the new century began, Dallas had an African American mayor. Voters elected African American mayors in other cities, and many held positions on city councils.

Influential Texans in Washington, D.C.

Texans had held great power in Washington, D.C., when Democrats dominated the state. When Texas became a two-party state, Texas politicians remained powerful. Republican **George H.W. Bush** served as vice president of the United States for eight years and as president from 1989 to 1993. Some observers believed that another Texan on the ballot, H. Ross Perot, who ran as a third-party (neither Republican nor Democrat) candidate, may have contributed to Bush's defeat in 1992. Bush's son, **George W. Bush,** also a Republican, was elected president in 2000.

When Democrats were in the majority in Congress, they were led by **Jim Wright** of Fort Worth who was speaker of the House of Representatives. Henry B. González of San Antonio and **Eligio de la Garza** of Mission were chairmen of powerful committees in the House of Representatives. When Republicans replaced Democrats as the majority party in the House in 1995, Richard Armey of Irving, Tom DeLay of Sugar Land, and Bill Archer of Houston became leaders in Congress.

Men from Texas were very influential in setting the nation's finance policy in the 1980s and 1990s. As a Democratic member of the U.S. House of Representatives, **Phil Gramm** co-authored

A Shared Past...

The number of women holding political office grew during the 1980s and 1990s. In 1984 the Democrats picked a woman as their candidate for vice president of the United States. California and Washington elected two women to the Senate. Maryland, Louisiana, Arkansas, Maine, New York, and Illinois also elected women senators. Several women, such as Elizabeth Dole and Janet Reno, were appointed to head cabinet departments.

President Reagan's economic program, prompting the Democratic leadership to remove Gramm from his seat on the House Budget Committee. Gramm resigned from the House, but ran again in a special election as a Republican and won. Later, Gramm was elected to the U.S. Senate, where he continued to write important bills, or proposed laws, dealing with taxation, spending, and banking. In the early 1990s, former **U.S. Senator Lloyd Bentsen** served as secretary of the Treasury Department.

✓ Reading Check **Identifying** Which Texan ran for president of the U.S. on a third-party ballot in 1992?

SECTION 1 ASSESSMENT

Checking for Understanding

1. **Using Key Terms** Define urban dweller, cabinet, third-party, and bill, and use each term in a sentence.
2. **Reviewing Facts** What office did Henry Cisneros hold in Texas? What national position did he hold?

Reviewing Themes

3. **Individual Action** What is named in honor of Representative Mickey Leland?

Organizing to Learn

4. **Creating Charts** Create a chart like the one shown here and identify the office each woman held.

Person	Office Held
Ann Richards	
Eddie Bernice Johnson	
Kay Bailey Hutchison	
Kathy Whitmire	
Suzie Azar	

Critical Thinking

5. **Explaining** How have politics in Texas changed from the 1960s and 1970s to the present?
6. **Evaluating** Who are Phil Gramm and Lloyd Bentsen? How did these two Texans become so influential in national finances?

TAKS PRACTICE

Analyzing Why did voters support William Clements in the election of 1978?

Critical Thinking
TAKS Skillbuilder

Predicting Consequences

Why Learn This Skill?

Every decision or action produces logical results, or consequences. We can try to predict consequences by identifying each possible outcome and analyzing each outcome to see how likely it is to occur.

After the Galveston hurricane of 1900, the citizens of Galveston built a huge seawall to prevent flooding in the case of another large hurricane. Because of the seawall, future hurricanes did not impact Galveston nearly as much. Thus, predicting consequences accurately served Galveston well.

How can we make accurate predictions? Try to find information about past events and the present situation. Making accurate predictions helps us to prepare for the future.

Learning the Skill

Follow the steps listed in the next column to help you accurately predict consequences.

Present-day Galveston seawall

- Gather information about the decision or action.
- Use your knowledge of history and human behavior to identify possible consequences.
- Analyze each consequence by asking: How likely is it that this will occur?

Practicing the Skill

Pages 578 through 581 discuss the impact of a broadened political base on Texas politics. Use this information to answer the questions below.

1 What trend does the section show?

2 Do you think this trend is likely to continue?

3 On what do you base this prediction?

4 What are three possible consequences of this trend?

5 What are possible consequences of this trend for politicians?

6 What are possible consequences of this trend for young people who want to enter the Texas political process?

TAKS PRACTICE

Predicting Consequences Perhaps there is one class in particular in which you would like to earn a higher letter grade. How can you do this? You will need to make a plan. Start by identifying your current letter grade. Make a list of actions that you can take in order to achieve your goal. Identify the possible consequences of your actions depending on whether you do or do not follow your plan.

 Glencoe's **Skillbuilder Interactive Workbook,** Level 1, provides instruction and practice in key social studies skills.

SECTION 2 International Events

Guide to Reading

Main Idea
Texans adapt to a changing economy and a stronger role in world trade.

Key Terms
deactivation
appropriate
mortgage
National Guard

Reading Strategy
Classifying Information As you read this section, complete a web like the one shown here identifying the problems with *maquiladoras*.

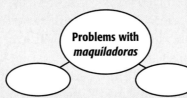

Problems with *maquiladoras*

Read to Learn
• how the end of the Cold War affected Texas.
• why the border trade between Mexico and Texas is so important.
• how Texas was affected by NAFTA.

Section Theme
Global Connections Texas has influenced world economic and political developments.

Preview of Events

1989	1991	1994	2001
Berlin Wall is torn down	Operation Desert Storm is fought in Persian Gulf	NAFTA goes into effect	Terrorists attack U.S. World Trade Center and Pentagon

U.S. Supreme Court

A Texas Story

After losing his lawsuit for equal schooling in San Antonio in state court, Demetrio Rodríguez took his case to the U.S. Supreme Court. He lost in a 5–4 decision. Rodríguez, however, kept fighting. His lawyer said, "No matter whether the lawyers come and go . . . Demetrio just stays right where he was. He doesn't care who's in office . . . He doesn't care whether they've helped some or none at all, unless they're for absolute equality he doesn't like 'em."
—*The Merrow Report,* copyright PBS, 1995

The End of the Cold War Affects Texas

After World War II, U.S. foreign policy focused on limiting Soviet expansion, but the Soviet threat virtually disappeared while George H.W. Bush was president. The tearing down of the Berlin Wall on November 9, 1989, signaled the end of the Cold War.

Barrier	Definition	Effect
Tariff	Tax on imported goods	Price of foreign goods increases
Embargo	Prohibits goods from another country	Causes a political or economic consequence
Standards	Qualifications placed on goods	Prevents goods from entering country for health or safety reasons

TAKS PRACTICE

Analyzing Trade barriers are imposed for different reasons. Why would the U.S. impose a high tariff on another country's goods?

Foreign policy changed, and the changes affected Texas. A series of treaties reduced the number of missiles owned by the Soviet Union and the United States. **Karnack,** in Harrison County, became world famous as the site where Pershing missiles that had been built during the Cold War were destroyed. In 1992 the **Pantex Plant** near Amarillo, where many U.S. nuclear weapons were constructed, began the process of weapon **deactivation.** Here the nuclear material was removed. Texas was home to numerous bases that no longer were needed. Many were closed, but several were converted to civilian use. For example, **Bergstrom Air Force Base** in Austin became a badly needed city airport.

The collapse of the Communist-controlled Soviet economy meant new opportunities in the petroleum industry. In the former Soviet Union there were vast reserves of oil, natural gas, and minerals. Development of these reserves created a demand for geologists, geophysicists, and petroleum engineers. Many companies that could fill that demand for services were based in Texas.

Reading Check **Examining** What important event happened in Karnack, Texas, and why did it occur?

The Expansion of Trade

Texas and Mexico share a long, common border. Because Texas is halfway between the two coasts of the United States, it is perfectly located to serve as Mexico's gateway to U.S. markets. Texas–Mexico border trade always has been important. Mexican citizens cross the border into Texas in large numbers. Many stores along the border depend upon shoppers from Mexico for most of their business. Some establishments on the Texas side accept Mexican *pesos,* and many on the Mexican side accept U.S. dollars.

A recent development in trade with Mexico was the establishment of *maquiladoras,* factories near the border that use Mexican labor and U.S. materials. Goods made at these plants are shipped to and sold in the U.S. Many companies, attracted by low labor costs and tax breaks from both nations, have set up such factories. Thousands of plants with hundreds of thousands of employees now are located along the border. El Paso is the Texas city most closely linked with this industry. As many as 100,000 jobs in El Paso and its sister city, Ciudad Juárez, depend on *maquiladoras.*

There are, however, serious problems associated with *maquiladoras.* By U.S. standards, wages are low and working conditions are poor. Many workers are young women who make little more than $1 per hour. *Colonias* (neighborhoods) on both sides of the border where workers often live were built without proper streets, water, or sewage facilities. The Texas legislature has recognized the problems of the *colonias* in Texas. It **appropriated,** or officially set aside, money to help provide basic services to these neighborhoods. Cities in both Mexico and Texas also suffer from polluted air and water caused by factories and cars on both sides of the border. Pollution is a regional problem, and solutions will come only after cooperative efforts by both nations.

Many Americans were encouraged by the successes of the European Union, a cooperative agreement among the major nations of Europe. Political leaders in Mexico, Canada, and the

United States realized that increased cooperation among their countries also could produce benefits. The result was the **North American Free Trade Agreement** (NAFTA), which became effective January 1, 1994. NAFTA removed many barriers to the shipment of goods between the three nations of North America.

Because of its location, Texas was affected by NAFTA more than any other state. Companies that wished to increase trade with Mexico set up offices in Dallas, San Antonio, and Houston. The trucking and warehouse industries of Texas boomed. Laredo and El Paso received most of the traffic. It became necessary to build new international bridges, such as the one in Hidalgo County. When Houston leaders pointed out that one good route between Mexico and Canada would be Highway 59 through their city, plans to widen the highway and connect it to the Port of Houston were proposed immediately.

Reading Check Evaluating Why was the North American Free Trade Agreement (NAFTA) created?

Boom and Bust Oil Cycle

Texans had seen oil prices go up and down. The **Organization of Petroleum Exporting Countries** (OPEC) and the oil shortages of the 1970s had driven up the price of oil, raising it as high as $40 per barrel. High oil prices meant that the petroleum industry boomed. Drilling companies, pipe manufacturers, and oil well service companies all shared in the resulting prosperity. Government tax revenues increased as well. Banks issued mortgages (loans to purchase property) for the construction of office buildings, shopping centers, and housing. People moved to Texas in large numbers to find employment. Lending them money to buy houses and to start businesses seemed like good business practice during such boom times.

As often happens, "bust" followed "boom." Economic prosperity gave way to hard times. The weakening of the OPEC cartel and overproduction lowered the price of oil to $10 a barrel. The effect on Texas was swift and dramatic. Companies cut back on drilling and fired employees. Drilling rigs were put in storage. When borrowers could not repay loans, mortgage companies, banks, and other lending institutions found themselves with millions of dollars worth of bad loans. In 1986 and 1987 Texas's lending institutions lost $3.7 billion. Many banks and savings and loan institutions closed or were acquired by banks with headquarters in other states.

The Persian Gulf War

In August 1990 Iraq invaded its oil-rich neighbor, Kuwait. Iraq seemed to desire not only Kuwait's oil, but also that of nearby Saudi Arabia. By January 1991 President George H.W. Bush had assembled a coalition of nations to drive Iraq out of Kuwait and protect the oil resources of the region. The coalition did so in a military operation called **Desert Storm** by the military and the Gulf War by the media.

Many Texans were involved in Desert Storm. **Fort Hood** in central Texas was a major staging area where troops and equipment were assembled for transport to Saudi Arabia. The military used a higher percentage of troops from the National Guard (a reserve military force available in times of crisis) in Desert Storm than in previous wars. Many of those National Guard troops were Texans who had skills necessary for fighting a war in the desert. For example, one Texas unit specialized in laying pipelines to supply water to troops. The **Gulf War** lasted slightly over a month, but it reemphasized how Texas was connected to the rest of the world.

Texas soldiers served in the Gulf War.

Texans Respond to Terrorism

The disastrous events of September 11, 2001, showed that threats to world peace continue to exist. On that day, terrorists hijacked four U.S. airplanes. Two of them were crashed into the World Trade Center in New York City. The third was flown into the Pentagon across the Potomac River from Washington, D.C. The fourth plane crashed in a field in rural Pennsylvania. In all, several thousand people were killed.

Texans, like other Americans, responded to the events with anger and grief, but also with an outpouring of cash and relief supplies. So many Texans wanted to donate blood that people were turned away. Houses of worship hosted prayer vigils and memorial services. Texans united in their desire to bring the terrorists to justice. They rallied behind fellow Texan President George W. Bush as he led the country in the time of crisis. Terrorists had committed acts of war against the United States, the president explained. In response, the U.S. government began a campaign against terrorism and vowed to fight to victory.

In the following weeks, anonymous letters containing deadly anthrax bacteria arrived at some government and media offices. Several people died as a result. Security was increased at airports and along the Texas coast. At El Paso, Brownsville, Laredo, and other entry points from Mexico, Customs and Immigration and Naturalization agents looked for possible threats.

Texas school children show their patriotism.

On October 7, 2001, the United States launched air attacks against Afghanistan. The Taliban government in that country had refused repeated demands to surrender accused terrorist Osama bin Laden for trial. By the end of the year, the Taliban government was forced to abandon power. The United States and its allies had won their first victory in the campaign against terrorism.

Reading Check **Examining** How did Texans respond to the terrorist attacks?

SECTION 2 ASSESSMENT

Checking for Understanding

1. **Using Key Terms** Use each of these key terms in a sentence: appropriate, mortgage, National Guard.

2. **Reviewing Facts** How did Karnack become famous?

Reviewing Themes

3. **Global Connections** Why were many National Guard troops from Texas used in Desert Storm?

Organizing to Learn

4. **Categorizing** Create a web like the one shown here, showing the various ways that NAFTA affects Texas.

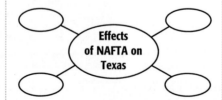

Effects of NAFTA on Texas

Critical Thinking

5. **Evaluating** Is the Texas economy likely to experience another oil boom in the near future? Explain the reasons for your answer.

TAKS PRACTICE

Drawing Inferences How was the Texas economy helped by the fall of the Soviet Union?

Texas LITERATURE

About the Author
Sandy Sheehy

Sandy Sheehy has lived in Texas since 1967. She considers herself a "naturalized" Texan. She now lives in Houston and has contributed as an editor for *Town and Country* and *Ultra*. She has also written for *Working Woman*, *Forbes*, and *House Beautiful*.

Reading to Discover

As you read this selection on Jack Grimm's adventurous searches, imagine how you would spend your money if you had an unlimited amount.

Reader's Dictionary

quixotic: caught up in the legend of noble deeds and striving to achieve impossible goals

elusive: difficult to capture

recoup: to make up for

wildcatting: the act of mining or drilling in an area that is not known to have oil

Texas Big Rich

by SANDY SHEEHY

Chapter 17 deals with Jack Grimm's perpetual interest in hunting for treasure and the near impossibility of finding any.

Jack Grimm liked finding things. When he wasn't digging for oil or prospecting for precious metals, he was mounting a number of **quixotic** expeditions: one to capture Bigfoot, the **elusive** man-ape of British Columbia; another to photograph the legendary Loch Ness Monster; another to locate evidence that Noah's Ark had landed on the rocky summit of Turkey's Mount Ararat; yet another to mine for emeralds . . . in Colombia, where [he] had to defend his treasure from bandits. In 1980 he made the first of his three attempts to find the *Titanic* . . . and in 1983 he came up with the cash to allow three wheelchair-bound paraplegic Vietnam vets to climb the highest mountain in Texas—8,751-foot Guadalupe Peak. In 1984 Grimm set out on yet another quest, one to locate and salvage a paddle wheeler that sank off Charleston in 1850 with at least five million dollars in gold coins . . .

To **recoup** some of the costs, Grimm turned [his expeditions] into real-life cinematic adventures.

. . . Grimm didn't foot the bills for his enterprises alone. He had a knack for getting others to

Jack Grimm

invest in his adventures even though all the most glamorous ones lost money . . . As with the oil **wildcatting,** only part of the appeal was in the enormous potential for profit. Grimm's investors were mostly fellow Cowboy Capitalists who preferred to make or lose money in things they could brag about.

ANALYZING LITERATURE

Evaluate and Connect Jack Grimm was interested in intriguing, historical events. Which exploration do you find the most interesting and why?

Interdisciplinary Activity

Writing If you were to explore something you are interested in, what would it be? Write a short autobiography of yourself in the future, after your "expedition" has been successful.

Reforms Come to Texas Schools

Guide to Reading

Main Idea
Many education reforms occurred as Texans and their leaders came to recognize the need for a better educated workforce.

Key Terms
extracurricular
bilingual education

Reading Strategy
Classifying Information As you read, create a web like the one shown here, outlining the recommendations of the commission to study schools.

Read to Learn
• why the Texas economy moved away from manufacturing.
• what changes were made in the educational system.

Section Theme
Continuity and Change Texans reform the system of education and provide educational opportunities for all students.

Preview of Events

♦ *1973*
└ Bilingual education becomes state law

♦ *1984*
└ Texas makes reforms in public school system

Children eating lunch in a school cafeteria

A Texas Story

Demetrio Rodríguez's campaign to achieve equality in public schools through the court system failed, but he could not accept that poor neighborhoods should be content with poor schools. The struggle he had begun for his children in 1968 finally bore fruit for his grandchildren. In the 1980s, the state devised a plan to help poor school districts build better classrooms.

—*The Merrow Report,* copyright PBS, 1995

The Reforms of 1984

Even before the oil, banking, and real estate crises of the late 1980s, forward-thinking Texans predicted that the Texas economy no longer could depend upon agriculture and oil as it had through the twentieth century. More and more products were manufactured overseas. Workers in poorer countries accepted much lower wages than did U.S. laborers. The nation moved away from an economy based on manufacturing. Providing services and information increasingly became important. This "new economy" was driven by many advancements in technology. Personal computers demonstrated their usefulness in practically every profession. Advances in medical technology, fiber optic communications, cellular telephones, and satellite communications were only a few of the new developments.

Clearly, Texas needed more highly skilled, better educated people to work in the emerging industries. Even the traditional industries, such as ranching, farming, saw mills, and oil well drilling, required workers with new skills. For example, farmers and ranchers began using computers, lasers, and satellite photographs for many tasks.

Mark White, the governor of Texas from 1983 to 1987, appointed a commission headed by a successful businessman, **H. Ross Perot,** to study the schools of Texas. In June 1984, Governor White submitted the commission's recommendations to the legislature, which enacted many of them. The legislature increased the amount of money the state gave to poorer school districts. It increased teacher salaries, provided for merit pay, and reduced class sizes. It also created free summer classes for young children whose English skills were limited.

There were two very controversial parts of the new education laws. The first required teachers to

TEXAS HISTORY *Online*

Student Web Activity Visit the texans.glencoe.com Web site and click on **Chapter 26—Student Web Activity** to learn more about school reform.

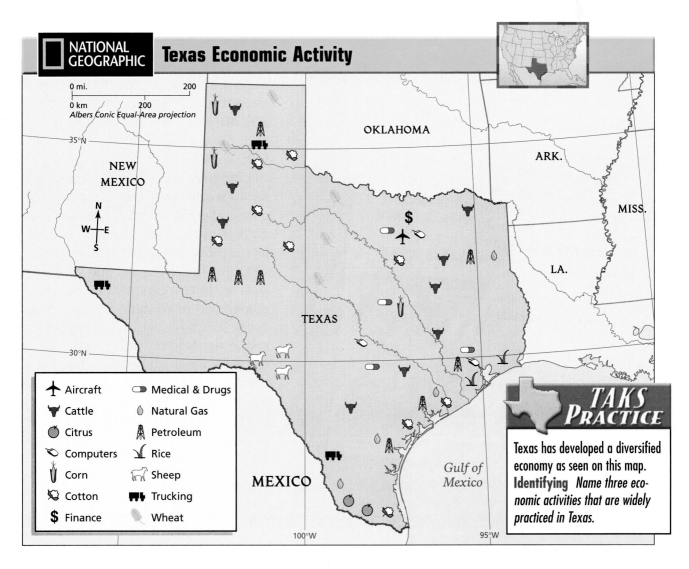

NATIONAL GEOGRAPHIC Texas Economic Activity

0 mi. 200
0 km 200
Albers Conic Equal-Area projection

35°N

NEW MEXICO

N
W—E
S

OKLAHOMA

ARK.

MISS.

LA.

TEXAS

30°N

MEXICO

Gulf of Mexico

Legend:
- ✈ Aircraft
- 🐂 Cattle
- 🍊 Citrus
- 🖱 Computers
- 🌽 Corn
- Cotton
- $ Finance
- Medical & Drugs
- Natural Gas
- Petroleum
- Rice
- Sheep
- Trucking
- Wheat

100°W   95°W

TAKS PRACTICE

Texas has developed a diversified economy as seen on this map. **Identifying** *Name three economic activities that are widely practiced in Texas.*

TWO VIEWPOINTS

No Pass, No Play

Reforms to improve education in Texas were approved by the legislature in the 1980s. Included was a measure requiring high school athletes to pass all their courses in order to play sports. Read the two views below and then answer the questions.

A Business and Political Leader Supports the Requirement

Any time someone has a problem, they can come up with an alibi or an excuse. That's all it is. If a student doesn't have a learning disability, passing all his classes in school is not that difficult. There's a solution to all this: study. All we want is to keep a balance and set the proper priorities.

—Ross Perot, quoted in *Dallas Morning News,* November 10, 1985

A Coaches' Organization Worries About Effects on Small-School Athletics

Small schools are certainly affected more. The percentage of failures is not higher, but they have fewer players. Some of the smaller schools are having enrollment problems, too, so it's kind of a double whammy of them. I can see in three or four years, if schools keep losing a few players every grading period, the [football programs] could be in jeopardy.

—Eddie Joseph, executive director, Texas High School Coaches Association, quoted in *Dallas Morning News,* November 10, 1985

Learning From History

1. Describe the two opinions given here and explain which view you support and why.

2. Suggest a reform that might help improve education in your school.

---

pass a test to remain employed. Many veteran teachers resented this. Some expressed their dissatisfaction by voting against Governor White's reelection. The other controversial provision was called "no pass, no play." It raised the minimum passing score for students to 70 and disqualified students with even one failing grade from participating in **extracurricular** activities, such as sports or band. Athletic coaches argued that extracurricular activities were one of the best ways to prevent students from dropping out. Courts upheld legal challenges to the law, and schools adapted to the new rules. Later changes reduced the penalty for loss of eligibility.

✓**Reading Check** **Summarizing** What were some of the new education laws in Texas?

Immigrant Schoolchildren

As far back as the 1940s, **Jovita González de Mireles** and her husband **E.E. Mireles** wrote bilingual textbooks and promoted them in the Corpus Christi schools.

Bilingual education, a program that serves students who speak a native language other than English, began in Texas schools in the 1960s and became state law in 1973. Immigration from Mexico, Central America, India, and Southeast Asia in later years meant that more schools had more students who did not speak English. Because there was a severe shortage of teachers qualified to teach bilingual education, some school districts offered bonuses to teachers who would train for bilingual education.

The emphasis on bilingual education caused many parents to believe that the traditional U.S. curricula were threatened. Some Texans joined an "English only" political movement, trying to put an end to bilingual education. A law was passed that prohibited the children of undocumented aliens from attending public schools in Texas. In 1980, however, **Judge Woodrow Seals** of Houston ruled that the law was unconstitutional. In his decision, which the U.S. Supreme Court later supported, Seals said, "Children are the basic resource of our society."

Educational Testing

More educational reforms occurred as Texans and their leaders recognized the need for a better educated workforce. Students had to take more tests, including the **Texas Assessment of Academic Skills** (TAAS) and end-of-course exams. (Today, these tests are known as the **Texas Assessment of Knowledge and Skills, or TAKS.**) High schools were encouraged to offer more Advanced Placement courses so students could receive college credit. Programs such as Gifted and Talented Education and School-to-Work instruction received more state funding. Students were encouraged to take more college preparatory classes and fewer lower level courses.

The Texas Academic Skills Program (TASP) is an important step for many students interested in higher education. The program, established in 1989, requires that all students entering public colleges and universities must take tests to identify any weaknesses in their basic academic skills. There was a dramatic increase in the number of students attending community colleges. Those

A Shared Past...

The increased need for bilingual education teachers was not confined to Texas. Spanish-speaking immigrants moved to places such as Iowa, North Carolina, and Arkansas to work in food processing plants. Arabic speaking immigrants moved to Michigan. The breakup of the Soviet Union allowed Russians more freedom to emigrate. Many of them moved to New York and New Jersey. Southern Florida was a favorite destination for Caribbean people, many of whom spoke Spanish or French. All of these states are addressing the issues of how to best educate the children of immigrants.

institutions provided a good transition between high school and college and offered training in technical skills. Graduates of community colleges often found employment in fields such as medical technology, communications, and electronics. The state legislature passed a law ensuring that high school students who graduated in the top 10 percent of their class could gain admission to state universities.

✓ Reading Check **Identifying** What ruling concerning schools did Judge Seals make in 1980?

SECTION 3 ASSESSMENT

Checking for Understanding

1. **Using Key Terms** List some extracurricular activities in your school.
2. **Reviewing Facts** Which high school students are guaranteed admission to state universities?

Reviewing Themes

3. **Continuity and Change** What were the two controversial parts to the new education laws passed in Texas in the mid-1980s?

Organizing to Learn

4. **Evaluating** Create a chart like the one shown here and use the text and your own reasoning to identify three or four advantages and disadvantages of bilingual education.

Advantages	Disadvantages

Critical Thinking

5. **Analyzing Information** Is equal funding for school districts important in providing equal educational opportunity? Why or why not?

TAKS PRACTICE

Distinguishing Fact From Opinion
Athletic coaches argued that extracurricular activities were important in preventing students from dropping out of school. Is this a fact or an opinion? Explain.

Chapter Summary

Texas Today

1973
* ★ Bilingual education becomes state law.

1978
* • William Clements is elected the first Republican Texas governor since Reconstruction.

1984
* • Texas makes school reforms to improve education.

1986
* • Many Texas banks close as a result of the "oil bust."

1988
* ★ George H.W. Bush is elected president of the United States.

1990
* ★ Many Texans participate in the Persian Gulf War to defend Kuwait from Iraq.

1991
* ★ Ann Richards becomes the second woman governor of Texas.

1992
* • The Pantex Plant begins to disassemble nuclear weapons from the Cold War.

1993
* • Kay Bailey Hutchison becomes a U.S. senator for Texas.

1994
* • NAFTA goes into effect.
* • Many U.S. companies build maquiladoras in Mexico at the Texas border.

2001
* ★ Texans donate to relief efforts after terrorists attack.
* • The U.S. fights back against terrorism.

Reviewing Key Terms

Number your paper from 1 to 7. Next to each number, write the letter of the term that goes with the phrase provided.

1. neither Republican nor Democrat
2. set aside money
3. group of advisers
4. sports, clubs, cheerleading
5. a loan to pay for a house or building
6. proposed law
7. part-time military force

a. mortgage
b. third-party
c. National Guard
d. extracurricular
e. cabinet
f. appropriate
g. bill

Reviewing Key Facts

8. What political party identifies more strongly with reducing government regulation of businesses?
9. Who was the first Republican governor of Texas since Reconstruction?
10. Which third-party presidential candidate from Texas ran in the 1992 election?
11. Explain how making goods in *maquiladoras* helps keep costs of buying many products down.
12. How has the Texas legislature helped the *colonias* in Texas?
13. How did Texans respond to the terrorist attacks of September 11, 2001?
14. Describe the purpose of bilingual education.
15. How do school districts deal with the shortage of bilingual education teachers?
16. What types of technology do some farmers and ranchers now use?

Critical Thinking

17. **Predicting Consequences** How would an increase in factories along the Texas–Mexico border affect the environment?
18. **Drawing Conclusions** Should only students with passing grades be allowed to take part in extracurricular activities? Explain.
19. **Evaluating** Does a two-party system benefit citizens more than a system in which one party dominates? Explain the reasons for your answer.
20. **Drawing Inferences** How have technological advancements of the "new economy" changed the lives of Texans?

Geography and History Activity

After the Berlin Wall came down in 1989, the Cold War ended. As a result, the United States closed many military bases such as the Bergstrom Air Force Base in Austin, Texas.

21. What did Bergstrom Air Force Base become after it was closed?

22. What are some other ways to convert military bases into civilian uses?

Cooperative Learning Activity

23. Making Predictions Organize into small groups in order to research possible future changes in technology. Research one of the following topics: career, family, or education. Discuss your findings with your group, and agree on three important technology changes that might occur. Share your findings with other groups.

Practicing Skills

24. Predicting Consequences Imagine that you are a member of the Texas state legislature. You must vote on many bills to decide whether they will become laws. To make these decisions, you have to predict the consequences of each bill. Read the description of the bill below. Then write the following:

> Bill to lengthen the school year by 30 days:
>
> *This bill would add 30 days to the current school schedule. Its purpose is to improve the quality of education and reduce the amount of time spent in review at the beginning of each school year.*

a. three consequences of the bill

b. the consequence that is most likely and least likely to occur

c. two ways in which the bill could affect different groups of people

Portfolio/TAKS Writing Activity

25. Defending a Position Judge Woodrow Seals of Houston ruled that prohibiting children of undocumented aliens from attending public schools was unconstitutional. He said, "Children are the basic resource of our society." Take the position that you agree with Judge Seal. Write a paragraph defending Judge Seals's positions. Save your work for your portfolio.

Self-Check Quiz

Visit the texans.glencoe.com Web site and click on **Chapter 26—Self-Check Quizzes** to prepare for the chapter test.

Building Technology Skills

26. Using a Spreadsheet Place this information about NAFTA on a spreadsheet program such as Excel. Create appropriate formulas to answer the questions below.

Year	U.S.–Mexico Trade ($ million)	Increase in Trade
1994	100,000	
1995	110,000	
1996	130,000	
1997	160,000	
1998	170,000	

a. Determine the increase in U.S.–Mexico trade for each year between 1994 and 1998.

b. Create your own question based on this information.

c. Draw a line or bar graph based on the chart.

Use your knowledge of the information in this chapter to answer the following question.

The end of the Cold War offered new opportunities for Texas because

F the United States closed many military bases.

G many Texas companies could perform work in countries free from the control of the former Soviet Union.

H no new wars would occur.

J more nuclear weapons would be built.

Test-Taking Tip:

Always delete any answers that you know are incorrect.

The Texas Heritage

Why It Matters

Every ten years the United States conducts a census, or a count, of the population. Comparing data from different time periods is a good way to determine how the states and nation are changing. Census 2000 showed important shifts had taken place in Texas. Even in the midst of change, Texans find ways to preserve their rich cultural heritages.

The Impact Today

States use census numbers to draw the boundaries of electoral districts. Where the lines are drawn influences who will be elected to Congress, the state legislature, county commissioners courts, and city councils. Each census, therefore, has a direct political impact that lasts for 10 years.

	1850 ★ First U.S. census to include Texas	1907 ★ Heart of the West by O. Henry published	

Texas

United States 1789 1850 1900 1950

World

1789
• French people stormed the Bastille on July 14 (Bastille Day)

1790
• United States took first census

1886
• Statue of Liberty dedicated

1946
• United Nations held first session

Bluebonnet Field, *by Julian Onderdonk. Texas possesses both a natural beauty and a rich multicultural heritage.*

FOLDABLES™
Study Organizer

TAKS
PRACTICE

Compare-Contrast Study Foldable Make the following foldable to collect information to help you determine how Texas's past has affected the lives of Texans today.

Step 1 Fold a sheet of paper from side to side, leaving a 2-inch tab uncovered along the side.

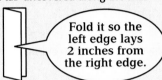

> Fold it so the left edge lays 2 inches from the right edge.

Step 2 Turn the paper and fold it in half.

Step 3 Unfold and cut along the inside fold line.

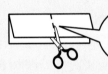

> Cut along fold on the front flap to make 2 tabs.

Step 4 Label the foldable as shown.

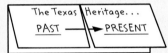

The Texas Heritage...
PAST ⟶ PRESENT

Reading and Writing As you read the chapter, record what you learn about the heritage of Texas under the appropriate tabs. Use this information to compare and contrast Texas—past and present.

2000
★ U.S. census counted 20.8 million people in Texas

2001
★ Texan Lance Armstrong won third straight Tour de France race

1975   *2000 2001 2002*

1970
• First celebration of Earth Day held on April 22

1999
• Worldwide New Year's millennium celebrations

2000
• U.S. census counted 281.4 million people in the nation

2000
• World population just over 6 billion people

TEXAS HISTORY Online

Chapter Overview
Visit the texans.glencoe.com Web site and click on **Chapter 27—Chapter Overviews** to preview chapter information.

Turn-of-the-Century Texas

Guide to Reading

Main Idea
The United States census provides important information about population changes in Texas.

Key Terms
census
growth rate
ethnicity

Reading Strategy
Identifying Connections Texas is developing global economic connections. Complete a chart like the one shown here by listing the countries related to each economic link.

Economic Link	Countries
Spanish language	
Petroleum	

Read to Learn
• how the population of Texas compares to the rest of the U.S. in ethnicity and age.
• about populated areas.
• about the future of Texas's economy.

Section Theme
Continuity and Change Census results help to predict future needs in Texas.

Preview of Events

1790	1850		1994	2000

First census in the U.S. — First U.S. census to include Texas — Texas becomes second most populous state — 28 percent of Texas population under 18 years old

Michael Dell

A
Texas Story

When Michael Dell was a freshman at the University of Texas in 1984, he had already traded stamps and sold newspaper subscriptions. His attention turned to electronics. Instead of building computers to sell, he decided to sell computers first, then build them. He formed Dell Computer. The company soon had sales of over $2 billion with more than 4,800 employees. Census 2000 data showed that Williamson County was Texas's second-fastest growing county in the 1990s. Dell Computer, located in Round Rock, is one reason.

The Census

Every 10 years the United States is required by the Constitution to count its people, or conduct a **census.** The first U.S. census was in 1790, but Texas was included for the first time in 1850. The writers of the U.S.

Constitution ordered the census to determine how many members each state could send to the U.S. House of Representatives. States with large populations send more members than do states with small populations. The census also provides information concerning how Texas and other states change. By comparing census data from various years, historians can note trends.

Population

In April 2000, census takers throughout Texas and the United States gathered information for the 22nd U.S. census. The data showed that in some ways Texas was similar to the rest of the United States, and in some ways it was different. According to the census, the population of the United States was 281,421,906. Texas's population was 20,851,820, or about 7 percent of the U.S. population. In 1994 Texas passed New York to become the second most populous state. Only California has more people than Texas.

Texas grew by 3.8 million people in the 1990s. This was a 22 percent increase for the decade. The percentage increase in population is called the growth rate. A growth rate is positive if more people are born or move into the state than die or leave the state. Nevada had the highest growth rate in the nation, and Texas ranked eighth. The net increase in population meant that Texas gained two members in the U.S. House of Representatives. Because the number of representatives in the House is frozen at 435, this means that other states lost members.

Ethnicity

The census asked people to identify themselves by race and ethnicity (national or cultural heritage). The chart on this page compares the ethnic makeup of Texas and the United States.

The percentages do not add up to 100 percent because for the first time people answering the census were allowed to select more than one category, thus reflecting a multicultural heritage. Nationally, about 4 percent of the population claimed membership in more than one race or culture. Texans claimed mixed heritages at a much higher rate—almost 18 percent.

If you divide the population by the land area, you can determine how many people there are per square mile. In an interesting coincidence, the figures for Texas and the United States are the same. There are 79.6 people per square mile in both Texas and the United States as a whole.

Where Do Texans Live?

Census 2000 showed that 4 counties—Harris, Dallas, Tarrant, and Bexar—have populations greater than 1 million. The combined populations of those counties account for 40 percent of the state population. The next 4 largest counties in population are Travis, El Paso, Hidalgo, and Collin. The combined populations of the 8 most

TEXAS HISTORY Online

Student Web Activity Visit the texans.glencoe.com Web site and click on **Chapter 27—Student Web Activity** to learn more about Census 2000.

Comparing Ethnic Distributions

Census 2000 Category	Texas	United States
White persons	71.0%	75.1%
Black or African American persons	11.5%	12.3%
American Indian persons	0.6%	0.9%
Asian persons	2.7%	3.6%
Persons of Hispanic or Latino origin	32.0%	12.5%
Total	117.80%	104.4%

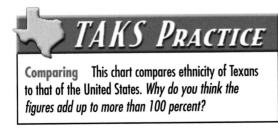

TAKS PRACTICE

Comparing This chart compares ethnicity of Texans to that of the United States. *Why do you think the figures add up to more than 100 percent?*

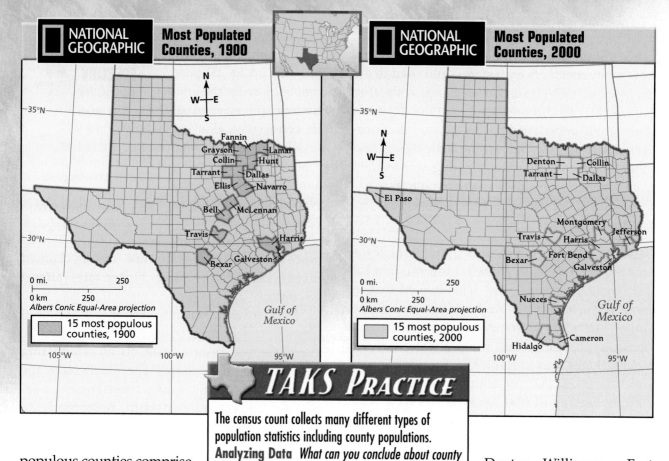

NATIONAL GEOGRAPHIC Most Populated Counties, 1900

NATIONAL GEOGRAPHIC Most Populated Counties, 2000

TAKS PRACTICE

The census count collects many different types of population statistics including county populations.
Analyzing Data *What can you conclude about county population changes in Texas between 1900 and 2000?*

populous counties comprise 52 percent of the population of the state. Out of 254 counties in Texas, more than half of the population lives in only 8 of them. From these figures, it is easy to see that the population is not evenly distributed. In fact, 51 Texas counties have fewer than 5,000 people. Only 2 of these 51 counties—Kenedy and McMullen—are east of Interstate 35. The least populated county in Texas—and in the entire United States—is Loving County. It has a population of 67.

The Growth Rate

Population growth rate is one of the most important statistics learned from the census. City and county governments, school districts, the Texas Department of Transportation, health care providers, and businesspeople all need to know which areas are growing and which are not.

Census 2000 revealed that some areas are growing very rapidly. The greatest growth has been in the suburbs of Dallas, Fort Worth, Austin, San Antonio, and Houston. Collin County, in the eastern part of the state, was the fastest growing of all Texas counties in the 1990s. It grew by 86 percent.

Denton, Williamson, Fort Bend, and Montgomery Counties also experienced rapid growth, especially in suburban areas.

The U.S.–Mexican border areas also saw significant growth. The lower Rio Grande Valley and El Paso experienced increases in population primarily as a result of people moving there to take advantage of new business opportunities.

Other parts of the state experienced either population declines or flat growth rates. Those counties were mainly in the Lower Plains, High Plains, and western Edwards Plateau. Several mid-size cities such as Wichita Falls, Abilene, Beaumont, San Angelo, and Orange grew at rates less than the overall state growth rate.

✓ Reading Check **Identifying** Who benefits from knowing the growth rate from the latest census?

How Old Are Texans?

The Texas population is younger than is the overall U.S. population. On April 1, 2000, 28.2 percent of Texans were under 18 years of age. The figure for the United States was 25.7 percent.

These Texas teens reflect some of the many ethnicities that make up the state's population. What percentage of Texans were under 18 years of age in 2000?

It is important for business, education, and government planners to know the age distribution of the population because older and younger populations need different services. For example, areas with a younger population need more elementary schools, baseball and soccer fields, and pediatricians. An older population usually requires more retirement homes, bus services, and medical facilities.

Knowing the age distribution in the workplace is important in planning for the future. If a large percentage of the workers are between the ages of 55 and 65, it is safe to predict that in the next 10 years companies will have to recruit new employees to take the place of people who retire.

Looking Ahead

Both an increase in population and an increase in the diversity of Texas's population seem likely in the future. Population increases often follow strong economic conditions. Texas is large enough that economic downturns in one sector of the economy often can be offset by strengths in other areas. In addition, growing international trade can lead to increases in diversity. Because of Texas's historical and cultural ties to Mexico, many Texans speak Spanish and are able to conduct business in Latin America. Texas's petroleum heritage means that it has ties to the Middle East, Indonesia, and Africa. As trade increases to those areas of the world, Texans are certain to be involved.

Texas recently has recognized the importance of human resources in commerce and industry. Experience has shown that economic progress occurs when people of diverse cultural backgrounds share their talents and work together.

✓ **Reading Check** **Evaluating** Why would a healthy economy lead to an increase in population?

SECTION 1 ASSESSMENT

Checking for Understanding

1. **Using Key Terms** Use the terms census and ethnicity in a sentence that shows you understand their meanings.
2. **Reviewing Facts** Which counties experienced the greatest growth rate in the state in the 1990s?

Reviewing Themes

3. **Continuity and Change** In what way did Michael Dell's business success cause a change in Williamson County's population?

Organizing to Learn

4. **Organizing Information** Create a chart like the one shown below and draw on your experiences to list the services that are important to younger and older populations in Texas.

Younger Population	Older Population

Critical Thinking

5. **Predicting Consequences** Congress is limited to 435 representatives. Since Texas gained 2 seats, what must have happened to other states' representation?

TAKS PRACTICE

Problem Solving Starr County reports a total population of 53,597. Of this number, 52,000 are of Hispanic heritage. Calculate the approximate percentage of Hispanics in the county.

SECTION 2 Texas and the Arts

Guide to Reading

Main Idea
The diversity of Texas provides a rich artistic heritage.

Key Terms
folklore
los corridos
pictograph
petroglyph

Reading Strategy
Classifying Information As you read this section, complete a chart like the one shown below, filling in names of artists for each art form.

Art Form	Artist
Folklore	
Historical literature	
Fiction and poetry	
Theater	

Read to Learn
• about different types of art.
• about famous Texans.
• how artists reflect their heritage and experiences in their creations.

Section Theme
Culture and Traditions Whether factual or fictitious, realistic or abstract, the arts of Texas represent enormous diversity and beauty.

Preview of Events

1892	1926	1941	1991
Elisabet Ney finishes life-size marble statue of Sam Houston	"Blind" Lemon Jefferson records "Long Lonesome Blues"	J. Frank Dobie's *The Longhorns* is published	Sandra Cisneros's "Woman Hollering Creek" is published

Peanut plant

A
Texas Story

"My grandfather had farmed in the north part of the county and even further to the west, toward Freer . . . [H]e farmed mostly grain sorghum and a few acres of watermelons. He raised peanuts one year. He told us to pick all the peanuts we could find . . . We never found any, not knowing they grew underground, and he laughed so much and told the story many years."

—Lionel G. García,
I Can Hear the Cowbells Ring, Arte Público Press, Houston, 1994

Folklore

Texas's ethnic diversity has created a rich literary and artistic heritage. Folklore, or stories told orally and passed down from generation to generation, is especially valuable in preserving the history and culture of Texas. Some of the stories are true, while others are fiction. Many are legends, blending fact with fiction. These interesting stories might be told in verse, song, or ballad.

Many of these stories have been collected. **J. Frank Dobie,** probably the best known of Texas folklorists, collected and published a large number of folktales and legends from many cultural groups in Texas. Some of his books look at cowhands and ranching, including *The Longhorns* (1941) and *The Voice of the Coyote* (1949). Dobie once noted that the African American folklorist and historian **J. Mason Brewer** was "the best storyteller of [African American] folklore anywhere in America." Brewer was born in Goliad County and moved to Austin. He recorded stories in *The Word on the Brazos,* and poetry in *Heralding Dawn.* African American poet **Bernice Love Wiggins** self-published *Tuneful Tales* in 1925.

Américo Paredes preserved much Mexican American folklore. He was most noted for his work on *los corridos,* or Mexican American folk ballads. Among his many publications is *With His Pistol in His Hand,* a study of Gregorio Cortéz, a heroic victim of injustice. Another folklorist and novelist was **Jovita González de Mireles.**

Reading Check **Explaining** What are *los corridos?*

Historical Literature

The first traveler to write of his experiences in Texas was Cabeza de Vaca. The Spanish explorer was shipwrecked on the coast of Texas in 1528. The first written report of buffalo in Texas was recorded in Cabeza de Vaca's journal. Members of the de Soto (1539–1543) and Coronado (1540–1541) expeditions also wrote accounts of their travels.

Many travelers in Texas documented their experiences during the time when Texas was a part of Mexico. **Mary Austin Holley,** a cousin of Stephen F. Austin, wrote the first book in English about Texas. **George W. Kendall** wrote one of the most colorful and popular descriptions of Texas during the time of the republic. Ferdinand Roemer, a German scientist, and Frederick Law Olmsted, a keen observer, reported their impressions of Texas and Texans in the two decades before the Civil War.

Historians have told the story of Texas many times and in many ways. Henderson Yoakum, who published his *History of Texas* in 1855, was one of the most knowledgeable early historians. Another widely read Texas historian was **Anna Pennybacker,** who wrote *A New History of Texas for Schools.* For many years students learned about Texas through her books.

Some historians have written about particular periods, regions, and topics. Herbert E. Bolton, Carlos Castañeda (kahs•tah•NYAY•dah), and Charles W. Hackett are remembered for their works about the Spanish period in the history of Texas. Eugene Barker has told in heroic style the story of the Austins, colonization, and the Texas Revolution. Ralph Steen and S.S. McKay wrote about Texas during the twentieth century.

The exciting and perilous adventures of the West have interested many historians. Among the many books about cowhands and the cattle industry are works by J. Evetts Haley, W.C.

J. Frank Dobie collected many Texas folktales and legends.

Novels can be rich sources of historical information. *Old Yeller* by Fred Gipson portrayed the dangers of the wild Texas frontier and the bravery of a pioneer family. The Disney studios produced a film based on the book. How are historical novels and films different from primary sources?

Holden, Tom Lea, and Wayne Gard. Two of **Walter Prescott Webb's** books, *The Texas Rangers* and *The Great Plains*, are considered classics. More recently, Rupert N. Richardson's *Texas, The Lone Star State* and Robert A. Calvert's, Arnoldo De Leon's, and Gregg Cantrell's *A History of Texas* have presented a comprehensive Texas history. Ruthe Winegarten's books about Texas women include *Black Texas Women: 150 Years of Trial and Triumph.*

Fiction and Poetry

Texans have used their talents to write memoirs, novels, short stories, and poems. Good writers often draw upon their personal experiences and observations. For example, **Lionel García** used his childhood experiences in San Diego in Duval County to write amusing stories in *I Can Hear the Cowbells Ring* (1994). **Norma Cantú** used family photographs to interpret life in Laredo in *Canícula: Snapshots of a Girlhood en la Frontera* (1997). **William A. Owens** in *This Stubborn Soil* writes about growing up in northeastern Texas. **John Graves** wrote *Goodbye to a River* (1960), telling about his adventures on the Brazos River.

The Texas experience has been portrayed in novels, too. **Katherine Anne Porter** of Indian Creek published several novels, including the Pulitzer Prize winner *Ship of Fools*. **Rolando Hinojosa's** novels, including *The Valley* (1983), have received much praise. **William Humphrey** described a northeast Texas family in his novel *The Ordways* (1964). **Larry McMurtry** of Archer City wrote novels set in both the 1800s and the modern era. Many of McMurtry's novels, such as *The Last Picture Show, Lonesome Dove,* and *Terms of Endearment,* have been made into successful motion pictures. **James Michener's** novel *Texas* tells the Texas story from Spanish times to the present.

The Texas heritage also is prominent in the works of many short-story writers. **William Sydney Porter** lived in Texas in the late 1800s and used **O. Henry** as his pen name. He based most of his stories in *Heart of the West* on Texas scenes. "The Ransom of Red Chief" and "The Gift of the Magi" are widely read O. Henry stories. El Paso's **Dagoberto Gilb** has extended the short story tradition in Texas with "The Magic of Blood" (1993). **Sandra Cisneros** dealt with modern issues in "Woman Hollering Creek" (1991).

The Texas Poetry Society recognizes outstanding poets each year. Every two years, Texas selects a **poet laureate,** its most outstanding or representative poet. Many Texas poets have achieved distinction. Among them is **John P. Sjolander,** a Swedish American who has been called the "greatest pioneer poet of the Southwest."

Another area of importance is children's literature. Family, Mexican American culture, and the desert are all important themes for **Pat Mora,** a popular children's author from El Paso. In 1998 she was one of the Texas Institute of Letters Award winners.

Reading Check Examining Which of Larry McMurtry's novels were made into motion pictures?

Theater, Film, and Television

Since the days of the Texas Republic, Texans have shown a special interest in the theater. Touring companies of performers visited the state, and many Texas cities had opera or theater houses by the late 1800s. Lon Morris College in Jacksonville became known as a training ground for Texans such as actors Sandy Duncan and Tommy Tune. Tune has received nine Tony Awards, Broadway's highest honor. Theater departments across the state have been helped by donations from successful artists such as Bob Hope and Greer Garson, a Dallas resident.

Both amateur and professional theater groups have performed scripts by Texas playwrights. **Preston Jones's** *Texas Trilogy* examined the confrontation between traditional values and the modern world. **Horton Foote,** from Wharton, became nationally recognized for plays such as *Driving Miss Daisy* and *A Trip to Bountiful* that drew their inspiration from Texas history.

Texas has produced many television and film celebrities. Debbie Allen and Patrick Swayze are both from Houston. Tommy Lee Jones, originally from San Saba County, is a Harvard graduate who captured starring roles in the films *The Fugitive* and *Men In Black.* Comedian Steve Martin hails from Waco, while Matthew McConaughey is a Longview native. Dallas was the birthplace of Aaron Spelling, one of the most successful television producers of all time. Spelling has a string of hit shows to his credit, including *Charlie's Angels* and *Beverly Hills 90210.* Often these famous Texans donate their time to support special benefits and fundraisers for Texas causes.

Music

The music of Texas is the creation of many cultures. African Americans have contributed much to the music of the state, especially with spirituals and blues—an expressive and emotional African American folk music. Blues musicians **"Blind" Lemon Jefferson** and **Huddie "Leadbelly" Ledbetter** are African Americans

Picturing **History**

This student production of *Godspell* is a retelling of parts of the Christian gospel. What benefits are gained by students involved in the arts?

who have greatly influenced music. They set the stage for jazz, an American music that blends African rhythms and scales and European harmony and instruments. **Scott Joplin,** born the son of a former slave in Cave Springs near Linden, became known as the "father of ragtime." Joplin also wrote an opera and composed tunes that are still popular. His music was featured in the hit movie *The Sting.*

Country western is the most popular radio format in America today, with more than 2,600 stations playing country music. Texan **Willie Nelson** developed his talent while working at a Fort Worth radio station. His popularity helped lead a new explosion of interest in country music in the 1970s and 1980s. In the 1990s, Pearsall native **George Strait** was credited with taking country back "to its roots."

Some of Texas's more familiar ballads and folk songs originated as well-known Mexican tunes. They were sung by artists like **Lydia Mendoza,** who was called *"La Alondra de la Frontera,"* the "Lark of the Border." Today many Mexican American musicians play popular music known as **Tejano,** a sound that varies from country to pop. Performers such as Freddie Fender, Tish Hinojosa, and,

more recently, Selena, David Lee Garza, and Los Chamacos have attracted the attention of the nation.

Texans have made important contributions to rock music as well. One of rock and roll music's earliest stars was **Buddy Holly** of Lubbock. Janis Joplin's "Me and Bobby McGee" rocketed her from Port Arthur to national fame. Roy Orbison of Wink, Texas, was a favorite of the "King of Rock and Roll"—Elvis Presley. Although not a Texan himself, Elvis got his start singing in Gladewater, Texas. Rock musician **Don Henley,** formerly of the Eagles, was awarded the National Endowment for the Humanities Award in 1997. The Linden native was recognized for his efforts to preserve the environment and promote knowledge and culture. Texas rock trio **ZZ Top** is best known for its roots in the "Texas blues" sound.

Classical music fans also have reason to be proud of their Texas heritage. Symphonies are found in major cities across the state. The Morton H. Meyerson Symphony Center in Dallas is one of the finest musical centers in the nation. Here, Texans can enjoy, among other things, German and Czech compositions. Whatever the type of music, the performers draw on their Texas heritage to entertain.

Artists of Texas

The first artists of Texas were prehistoric people who left pictographs (ancient drawings or paintings on rock walls) and petroglyphs (rock carvings) on rocks and cave walls. Examples of these works are on view in the lower Pecos River region, near Hueco Tanks in far west Texas, along the Concho River near Paint Rock, and in other locations.

Europeans contributed their artistry in the days of the Spanish colonial era. Mission artists often blended Spanish and Native American patterns in their works. Mission buildings were decorated with carved figures and finely crafted windows and doors. **The Rose Window of Mission San José** in San Antonio is an outstanding example of mission artistry. Many historians credit **Pedro Huizar** with the carving. The Rose Window is considered one of the finest works of its kind in the United States.

Throughout history, talented artists painted Texas scenes. The Mexican painter **José Sánchez y Tapia** toured Texas in 1828. Two gifted German painters moved to Texas in the 1850s. They were Hermann Lungkwitz, who often painted landscapes and city scenes, and **Friedrich Richard Petri,** known for his paintings of Native Americans and rural scenes.

At about the same time, two French painters added their talents to the artwork of Texas. **Eugenie Lavender** braved life on the frontier in the 1850s and sometimes made her paints from the juices of Texas herbs and flowers. **Theodore Gentilz** (zhahn•TEELZ) lived in Castroville and San Antonio. His paintings are of San Antonio and of the Mexican people in the mid-1800s.

Later artists—**H.A. McArdle, William H. Huddle, Robert Jenkins Onderdonk, Julian Onderdonk,** and **Frank Reaugh**—made

History *Through Art*

The Posse by Theodore Gentilz Though not an eyewitness to much of what he painted, Gentilz used his artist's skill to produce a valuable record of events, characters, customs, and landscapes of early Texas. Would Gentilz's paintings be considered primary or secondary sources?

important contributions. McArdle gained fame for his mural-like paintings of historical scenes. *Dawn at the Alamo* and *Battle of San Jacinto* are just two of them. Huddle also painted historical scenes as well as portraits of important people in Texas history. His *Surrender of Santa Anna* hangs in the entrance hall of the Capitol at Austin. **Mary Bonner** was known as the "Texas Girl Etcher of Cowboys." **Chelo Amezcua** used ballpoint pens to perfect her filigree art.

Landscape Painters

Although Robert J. Onderdonk painted portraits, both he and his son Julian are better known for their paintings of Texas landscapes. Another landscape artist, Frank Reaugh, depicted mostly ranch scenes and is known for his portrayals of longhorn cattle.

Porfirio Salinas has won national acclaim for his striking paintings of the Texas Hill Country, particularly for scenes featuring bluebonnets. **José Cisneros** of El Paso is noted for his numerous pen-and-ink illustrations of the borderlands. Works by talented African Americans such as **John Thomas Biggers** and **Carroll Simms** are on display in major galleries.

Georgia O'Keeffe was the first American woman painter to gain major recognition from art critics. She painted more than 50 watercolors while living in Canyon, Texas, in the early 1900s. She wrote about Texas at that time that "there was a quiet and an untouched feel to the country and I could work as I pleased." The watercolors were the subjects of her first solo show in 1917.

Sculpture

Well-known sculptors such as **Elisabet Ney** (see page 436), **Bonnie MacLeary, William McVey,** and **Charles Umlauf** are linked to Texas. Two Italians, **Pompeo Coppini** (pohm•PAY•oh kop•PEE•nee) and **Enrico Cerracchio** (ehn•REE•koh cheh•RAH•kee•oh), have contributed many famous works. Coppini created the Littlefield Memorial in Austin and the Alamo Cenotaph in San Antonio's Alamo Plaza. El Paso-born sculptor **Luís Jiménez, Jr.,** is also known for his vibrant drawings. Other noted sculptors include **Octavio Medellin,** who was from Dallas, and **James Surls.** Born in Terrell, Surls is known for his wood carvings.

✓ **Reading Check** **Describing** What is the difference between historical and landscape painting?

SECTION 2 ASSESSMENT

Checking for Understanding

1. **Using Key Terms** Use the key terms folklore, *los corridos,* pictograph, and petroglyph in sentences to demonstrate your understanding of the terms.
2. **Reviewing Facts** What is a poet laureate? How often is one chosen?

Reviewing Themes

3. **Culture and Traditions** Throughout history, painters have depicted famous events, making important contributions to the historical record. What two paintings by H.A. McArdle commemorate historical events?

Organizing to Learn

4. **Charting Information** The music of Texas reflects many cultures and ethnic backgrounds. Create a chart like the one shown below and fill in the missing information.

Types of Music	Performer or Location
Ragtime, blues	
Rock and roll, country western, orchestra, opera	
Ballads, folk songs, Tejano	

Critical Thinking

5. **Evaluating** Choose one artist, musician, actor, or author mentioned in the chapter and tell how he or she has influenced you.

TAKS PRACTICE

Identifying the Main Idea Choose the statement below that best reflects the main idea of this section and explain why.

A. People from many different countries have influenced the music of Texas.

B. Cultural and ethnic diversity have enriched every art form in Texas.

Writing a Paragraph

Why Learn This Skill?

Writing is usually organized into paragraphs—groups of sentences that express one main idea. Well-written paragraphs help the reader more easily follow the writer's ideas.

Paragraphs take many forms. They can be long or short. Some are factual statements. Others are poetic descriptions. Effective paragraphs, however, usually share four common characteristics.

- Each paragraph expresses one main idea.
- The main idea can be stated in a topic sentence.
- The other sentences in the paragraph support the main idea.
- The sentences are clear, easy to read, and arranged in a logical order.

Learning the Skill

Here are some steps that you can follow in writing a paragraph:

- Identify the main idea of your paragraph and write it as a topic sentence.
- Choose details that support the main idea.
- Arrange the topic sentence and the details in a logical order.
- Add transition words to make the relationship between the sentences clear. Some useful transition words are: *first, next, finally, before, after, but, therefore, however, also, for example,* and *because.*

Practicing the Skill

Read the group of sentences in the next column about O. Henry's stories. Organize the sentences into a paragraph that has a topic sentence and supporting details. Add transition sentences if necessary.

❶ The plan backfires because the boy is such a troublemaker that the bandits have to pay the father to take his son back!

❷ Often, he wrote about the common people of the western frontier.

❸ O. Henry's short stories were known for their interesting characters, humor, and surprise endings.

❹ In his story, "The Ransom of Red Chief," two bumbling bandits kidnap the young son of a wealthy man in order to get some ransom money.

William Sydney Porter
(O. Henry)

TAKS PRACTICE

Writing a Paragraph Write a four- or five-sentence paragraph on a topic of your choice. For example, you could write about a favorite book, movie, or TV show. Begin with a topic sentence. The topic sentence should provide general information. The sentences that follow should include supporting details.

Glencoe's Skillbuilder Interactive Workbook, Level 1, provides instruction and practice in key social studies skills.

GO TO

Texans Create a Unique Culture

Guide to Reading

Main Idea
A wide variety of celebrations and festivals promote community pride and help Texans maintain their rich and diverse cultural heritage.

Key Term
reenactment

Reading Strategy
Identifying Regions As you read this section, complete a chart like the one shown below by identifying the area where each festival is celebrated.

Festival	General Location
St. Patrick's Day	
Cajun Festival	
Buccaneer Days	
Rose Festival	

Read to Learn
• why celebrations and festivals take place and why they are important.
• about Texas festivals.

Section Theme
Culture and Traditions Texans' lives are connected and enriched by a wide variety of events that celebrate their heritage and history.

Preview of Events

One Year

March 2	April 21	May 5	June 19	July 4	October
Texas Independence Day	San Jacinto Day	*Cinco de Mayo,* Mexican victory over the French	Juneteenth, freedom from slavery	American independence from England	Oktoberfest, harvest by German community

Irish cowboy practicing his roping skills

A Texas Story

In 1832 Irish immigrants celebrated the completion of the road from San Patricio to Matamoros. Local resident Susanna O'Docharty wrote a poem about it.
"The Mexican and Irish were friends.
Did we not meet the *alcalde* and the merchants of Matamoros
In 1832 and sing and dance beside a creek
Still named Banquete because we had a banquet there?"

Ethnic Celebrations

Throughout Texas history, people from different cultures have met and celebrated together. Spanish explorers and Native Americans often had feasts of thanksgiving and fellowship. Later Texans celebrated on religious holidays and at events connected with cattle roundups, sheep shearings, and crop harvests. These traditions are honored throughout the state with rodeos and county fairs. These events are far more than just recreation. They contribute to the social and economic landscape of Texas as well. They promote community pride, encourage family interaction, and help maintain a rich and diverse cultural heritage.

Recent increases in population have brought increased diversity and ethnic pride as well. During the 1960s African Americans and Mexican Americans boldly proclaimed a renewed public pride in their heritage. Inspired by their example, people of other ethnic groups began celebrating their past. One expression of the renewed interest in ethnic heritage was the expansion of existing festivals and the creation of new ones. The festivals featured music, food, crafts, dance, art, games, and other forms of entertainment. These events have become so popular that since the 1990s a different one is held almost every week of the year.

Some of the celebrations, such as the Vietnamese holiday Tet or New Year's Day on the Chinese calendar, reflect immigration from new lands. Others such as *Cinco de Mayo, Diez y Seis de Septiembre,* July 4, Juneteenth, Brenham's Maifest, and Fredericksburg's Oktoberfest long have been observed in Texas. Czech Texans have the Westfest at West, the *Czhilispeil* at Flatonia, and the *Kolache* Festival at Caldwell. German Texas is

reflected in the Wurstfest at New Braunfels and Fredericksburg's Easter fires. That particular event was inspired by the story of immigrant German children who were frightened by Native American campfires in the hills. Their mothers told them that the fires were being used to boil Easter eggs.

Irish heritage is emphasized on St. Patrick's Day. Texans dress in green and march in parades. The towns of Dublin, in Erath County, and Shamrock, located in the Panhandle, hold major celebrations. **Acadians** (also referred to as **Cajuns**) have a French heritage and celebrate mainly in southeast Texas. A highlight of most Cajun festivals is a crawfish race. Cajun bands feature fiddles and accordions playing vigorous dance tunes. African Americans with French heritage have developed a truly unique musical style called *zydeco* that adapts everyday objects for use as musical instruments. A grand ethnic celebration is held on the grounds of the Institute of Texan Cultures in San Antonio each summer.

Reading Check Evaluating What is the importance of traditional celebrations?

Other Festivals

Festivals also celebrate an important crop or economic activity related to a community's past. Tyler hosts a Rose Festival. Gilmer celebrates its

Picturing **History**

The Ukrainian folk dancers *(left)* are an example of cultural diffusion—the blending of elements from different cultures. The Indian dancers *(right)* performing at the San Antonio folk festival recall their culture with intricate dance steps and motions. What dances reflect your own cultural heritage?

sweet potato harvest with a "Yamboree." Athens has the Black-Eyed Pea Jamboree. Poteet residents put on a Strawberry Festival, and Luling is home to the Watermelon Thump. Brownsville has Charro Days. Both Dalhart and Stamford host reunions for cowhands who once worked on ranches in the area. Corpus Christi has its Buccaneer Days in late spring and its Bayfest in September. In early December, Galveston celebrates Dickens on the Strand.

Texas celebrates its musical heritage with a variety of events. Bob Wills, a bandleader of the 1930s and 1940s, grew up in the town of Turkey, so each year Turkey celebrates with a Bob Wills Reunion. Each summer at Palo Duro, visitors to the Canyon State Park can watch *Texas*, an outdoor musical drama by Pulitzer Prize winner Paul Green. Folk music and jazz festivals occur in several cities. In addition, Mexican American musical traditions are observed. For example, the *conjunto*, a musical style that relies on the accordion, drum, and *bajo sexto*, or 12-string guitar, remains popular.

Historical Festivals and Celebrations

Among Texas's state holidays are Texas Independence Day (March 2), San Jacinto Day (April 21), Emancipation Day (June 19), and Lyndon Baines Johnson's Birthday (August 27). In addition, many Texas cities organize celebrations around historic events and buildings. People who visit Jefferson during its celebration are taken back in time to the 1800s, when it was a thriving cotton port. Events of the Texas Revolution are commemorated with the "Come and Take It" Festival at Gonzales, a celebration in San Antonio at the Alamo, and ceremonies on the San Jacinto battleground in Houston.

Importance of Celebrations

There are two important conclusions we can draw from examining the hundreds of celebrations Texans hold each year. The first is that ethnic diversity is one of Texas's most important strengths. The presence of so many celebrations shows that pride in one's ethnic heritage does not prevent appreciation of other people's cultures. Texans enjoy the music, food, and dance of many traditions and learning about other people's ideas and values. When individuals from different cultures come together, they share the

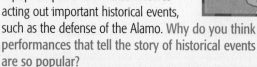

Picturing **History**

A popular pastime in Texas involves acting out important historical events, such as the defense of the Alamo. Why do you think performances that tell the story of historical events are so popular?

BIG TEX

Analyzing Political Cartoons

When this cartoon was drawn in 1977, Texas was 3rd in population. Today, the Census 2000 puts Texas in 2nd place, just behind California. The increase in population is partly because of immigration from Hispanic and Asian countries. Why do you think the cartoonist drew a look of suprise on the face of the smaller figure?

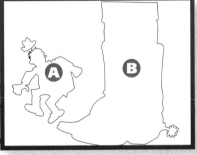

Ⓐ Average state population   Ⓑ Texas population

things they cherish. Respecting other cultures and beliefs is part of the democratic process.

Texans are proud of their unique history. Historical reenactments and "living histories" are often part of celebrations. In reenactments, participants dress in historic costumes, camp in tents similar to those of the period, and eat only foods available during that time. They put aside modern conveniences such as wristwatches, radios, and air conditioners. They do this because Texas history is unique and inspiring. To understand how Texas is today, we need to look back and learn about our heritage.

✓ **Reading Check** **Examining** Why does Texas have so many different celebrations?

SECTION 3 ASSESSMENT

Checking for Understanding

1. **Using Key Terms** Write a sentence using the term reenactment.
2. **Reviewing Facts** List three crop festivals that are held in Texas, and name the city or town in which each takes place.

Reviewing Themes

3. **Culture and Traditions** How are religious holidays, cattle roundups, sheep shearing, and harvests significant to communities?

Organizing to Learn

4. **Identifying Locations** The following festivals arrived in Texas with immigrants. Create a chart like the one shown below and identify the country of origin for each festival.

Festival	Country of Origin
Tet	
St. Patrick's Day	
Cinco de Mayo	
Wurstfest	

Critical Thinking

5. **Decision Making** Choose a Texas festival or celebration that you would like to attend. Give at least two reasons for your interest in the event you select.

TAKS PRACTICE

Drawing Inferences What other reasons, not mentioned in the text, might exist for cities and towns to host celebrations and fairs?

Chapter Summary

The Texas Heritage

Census 2000
- Determines the number of representatives per state in the U.S. Congress
- Reflects multicultural heritage
- Helps local governments plan for the future
- Points industry toward international business links

Literature
- Folklorists preserve tales and legends
- Historians record and analyze the past
- Historical novelists describe themes of the West
- Writers draw on personal experiences and Texas past

Music
- Blues and jazz music have strong roots in Texas
- Music reflects cultural diversity
- New and blended forms of music are created

Graphic Arts
- Ancient rock art is preserved
- Art is influenced by many cultures
- Painters record historical scenes, portraits, and landscapes

Celebrations
- Rodeos and county fairs celebrate ranching and farming activities
- Festivals celebrate diverse ethnic heritage
- Cities celebrate historical places, people, and events
- Celebrations serve to unify Texas

Reviewing Key Terms

Number your paper from 1 to 5. Next to each number, write the letter of the group of words that correctly defines the term.

1. growth rate
2. folklore
3. ethnicity
4. petroglyph
5. reenactment

   a. a repeat of the actions of an earlier event
   b. traditional customs, beliefs, or stories
   c. national or cultural heritage
   d. a carving on a stone
   e. percentage by which the population increases

Reviewing Key Facts

6. Explain why the writers of the U.S. Constitution required a census every 10 years.
7. According to Census 2000, which Texas county was the fastest growing? What was the growth rate (percent of growth)?
8. According to Census 2000, what areas showed population declines or flat growth rates?
9. What was storyteller O. Henry's real name?
10. Name two of the first people to write about their experiences in Texas.
11. Identify the unique musical style developed by African Americans of French heritage.
12. Name the musical style that relies on the accordion, drum, and 12-string guitar.

Critical Thinking

13. **Evaluating** Do you think the census should be taken every 10 years, as it is now, or at some other interval? Why?
14. **Making Comparisons** In the past, people used folklore as a means of passing on history to their descendants. Does folklore serve the same purpose today? In what ways do people today pass on information?
15. **Drawing Conclusions** Spirituals are often sung in churches even when there are no African American members. People with no African American heritage enjoy jazz, the blues, and ragtime. From these facts, what can you conclude about music's place in society?
16. **Explaining** How do celebrations serve the communities of Texas?

Geography and History Activity

17. Organize in groups of two or three. Discuss and list the celebrations attended by your group members in Texas and elsewhere. Categorize events by type, using the following headings: Ranching and Farming, From a Foreign Country, Historical, Related to the Arts. Note where and in what season these events occur. Create a database of your information to share with the class. Each member should recommend their favorite event and tell why. Your group may want to interview parents, relatives, neighbors, or visit the local chamber of commerce for information.

 ## Building Technology Skills

18. Using the Internet or Library for Research Working alone, or with one partner, research the works of one writer, artist, or musician mentioned in Section 2. As you work, keep a record of bibliographic information and/or URLs. Prepare a written or multimedia report, complete with visuals. What does this person's work tell about him/her? Why is this body of work important to society?

Practicing Skills

19. Writing a Paragraph Review the information in the Skillbuilder on page 607. Organize the sentences below into a paragraph that has a topic sentence, supporting details, and transition words, if necessary.

a. Buddy Holly was born and raised in Lubbock, Texas.

b. He recorded several hit songs including "Peggy Sue," "That'll Be the Day," and "True Love Ways."

c. The plane was also carrying rock and roll stars Ritchie Valens and the Big Bopper, who also died in the crash.

d. Buddy Holly was a musician who made important contributions to the development of rock and roll.

e. Holly's career ended suddenly in a tragic plane crash.

 ## Portfolio/TAKS Writing Activity

20. Literature and History Today, folktales and legends are found in children's books. Which ones do you remember? What characteristics do they have in common? What value do these stories have for young children? Answer these questions in a three-paragraph essay, using standard grammar, spelling, sentence structure, and punctuation. Save this for your portfolio.

TEXAS HISTORY Online

Self-Check Quiz
Visit the texans.glencoe.com Web site and click on **Chapter 27—Self-Check Quizzes** to prepare for the chapter test.

Economics and History Activity

21. Texas's increasing population means the state sends more representatives to the U.S. Congress than it did in the past. Use the library or Internet to research other ways an increasing population may benefit the economy of a state.

Use the graph to answer the question that follows.

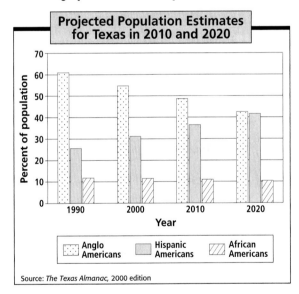

Projected Population Estimates for Texas in 2010 and 2020

Source: *The Texas Almanac,* 2000 edition

What is the difference in the percentage of Hispanic American population in Texas between the year 2000 and the year 2020?

A 5%   **B** 10%   **C** 30%   **D** 40%

Test-Taking Tip:
Be careful when you answer questions from a bar graph with many bars. Use the legend to make sure you identify the correct information. Read the labels to confirm that you have the correct year. Finally, read the question carefully.

THE STORY OF TEXAS

THE BOB BULLOCK
Texas State
History Museum

Museum Tour **8**

Creating Opportunity
Texas and the Nation

Texans played an active role in the nation's history. Key military bases and defense-related industries were located in Texas. By the end of World War II, Texas was poised to become a major international force in economics, politics, and technology.

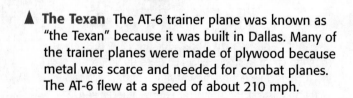

▲ **The Texan** The AT-6 trainer plane was known as "the Texan" because it was built in Dallas. Many of the trainer planes were made of plywood because metal was scarce and needed for combat planes. The AT-6 flew at a speed of about 210 mph.

Visit The Bob Bullock Texas State History Museum in Austin to see artifacts and exhibits such as these about Texas history and heritage.

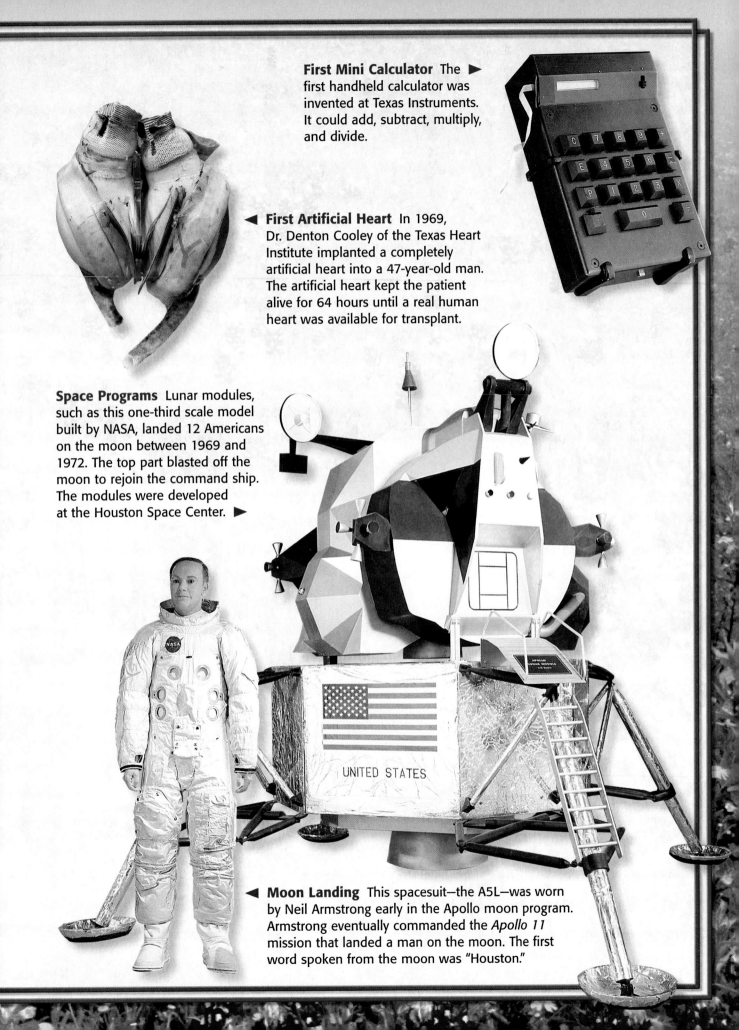

First Mini Calculator The ▶ first handheld calculator was invented at Texas Instruments. It could add, subtract, multiply, and divide.

◀ **First Artificial Heart** In 1969, Dr. Denton Cooley of the Texas Heart Institute implanted a completely artificial heart into a 47-year-old man. The artificial heart kept the patient alive for 64 hours until a real human heart was available for transplant.

Space Programs Lunar modules, such as this one-third scale model built by NASA, landed 12 Americans on the moon between 1969 and 1972. The top part blasted off the moon to rejoin the command ship. The modules were developed at the Houston Space Center. ▶

◀ **Moon Landing** This spacesuit—the A5L—was worn by Neil Armstrong early in the Apollo moon program. Armstrong eventually commanded the *Apollo 11* mission that landed a man on the moon. The first word spoken from the moon was "Houston."

UNIT
9

The
Government
of Texas

hy It Matters

As you study Unit 9, you will learn about Texas government. Texans have created a system of state, county, and local governments to protect freedom and ensure justice.

Primary Sources Library

See pages 700–701 for primary source readings to accompany Unit 9.

New members of the Texas Senate are sworn in at the Capitol on the opening day of the 77th legislative session in Austin.

"All political power is inherent in the people."

—Article 1, Section 2, Texas Constitution
of 1876, Governor Richard Coke

Scientists are banding elf owls in West Texas so they can keep track of the tiny birds. Researchers are setting up nest boxes to see if the owls will use them when their natural homes have been destroyed.

Students get ready to plant a tree in Austin. Trees contribute to clean air by removing carbon dioxide and releasing oxygen.

Amarillo

Lubbock

Dallas/Ft. Worth

El Paso

Austin

San Antonio

Port Arthur

Houston

Corpus Christi

Lights at Night: Urban Sprawl
Existing development as of 1993
Development since 1993

McAllen/Brownsville

A student closely examines a beaker of pond water. Learning about plants and animals is key to understanding our environment.

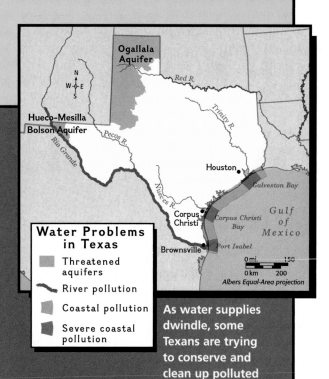

Water Problems in Texas

■ Threatened aquifers

~ River pollution

▨ Coastal pollution

◆ Severe coastal pollution

As water supplies dwindle, some Texans are trying to conserve and clean up polluted waterways.

Volunteers help protect coastal wildlife and the beauty of the beach by picking up trash on Padre Island.

CARING FOR THE EARTH

Bright lights spread across the night sky of Texas, one of the fastest growing states in the country. Between 1993 and 2000, Texas grew by more than two and a half million people. Today there are 21 million Texans, and the population is expected to double in the next 50 years. Growth puts a strain on the environment, but many people are trying to preserve the air, water, and wildlife.

Water

Water, which sustains people, crops, animals, and industry, is getting scarce in some regions of Texas. During recent droughts, roaring rivers like the Rio Grande slowed to a mere trickle. Many Texans depend on aquifers, or natural underground reservoirs, for water. As more and more people need water, aquifers like the Ogallala and the Hueco–Mesilla Bolson are being drained faster than they can refill. To save water, some cities are asking residents not to water yards on certain days.

Air

Some Texas students are trying to clean the air and beautify the environment by planting trees. Pollutants from cars, oil refineries, chemical plants, and other industries may contribute to poor air quality. People can improve the air by walking, riding bikes, carpooling, or using public transportation when possible instead of using their own car.

Wildlife

As people clear land to grow crops or build houses, stores, factories, and roads, they destroy many animal homes. Some Texans are making an effort to provide water, nest boxes, and local plants for wildlife on their own property.

Trash

More people generally means more garbage, but cities like Austin have actually reduced the amount of garbage people generate. Austin has encouraged its residents to recycle paper, plastics, glass, and aluminum.

Maintaining a healthy environment is a challenge, but many Texans are cleaning up, recycling, saving water, and trying to protect the natural resources of the state.

LEARNING *from* GEOGRAPHY

1. In what areas of Texas does the map show the greatest growth since 1993? Are there many new lights near your community? How would you describe the rate of development in your region?

2. What environmental problems are there in your area?

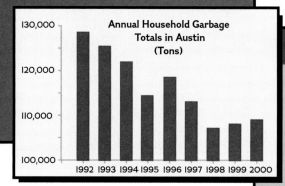

619

Democracy & Constitutions

Why It Matters

The organization of a government and a justice system are made possible through a document called a constitution. Texans live under a state constitution adopted in 1876.

The Impact Today

The writers of the Texas Constitution of 1876 provided that many important decisions would be made by the voters. Texans, therefore, frequently vote on amendments to the constitution.

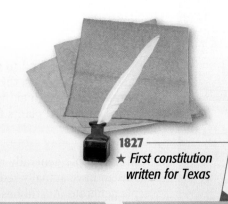

1827
★ First constitution written for Texas

1836
★ Republic of Texas adopted constitution

Texas

United States   1780   1790   1820   1840   1860

World

1788
• U.S. Constitution ratified

1789
• France adopted its first constitution

1791
• Bill of Rights added to U.S. Constitution

1821
• Simón Bolívar freed Venezuela from Spanish control

1861
• Russian serfs emancipated

1865
• Thirteenth Amendment abolished slavery

Article 1, Section 27, of the Texas constitution guarantees that *"citizens shall have the right, in a peaceable manner, to assemble together for their common good."*

FOLDABLES™ Study Organizer

TAKS PRACTICE

Summarizing Information Study Foldable
Make this foldable to help you collect and analyze information about the history of the Texas constitution and democracy in Texas.

Step 1 Mark the midpoint of the side edge of a sheet of paper.

Draw a mark at the midpoint.

Step 2 Turn the paper and fold the outside edges in to touch at the midpoint.

Step 3 Turn and label your foldable as shown.

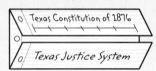

Texas Constitution of 1876

Texas Justice System

Reading and Writing As you read the chapter, record information under each tab of your foldable. For example, under the top flap, write about the constitutions of Texas. Use a time line to record significant developments. Under the bottom flap, include information on the Texas system of justice.

1876
★ Current Texas constitution adopted

1880   *1900*   *1920*   *1940*

1920
• Nineteenth Amendment gave women the right to vote

1944
• Women in France gained right to vote

TEXAS HISTORY Online

Chapter Overview
Visit the texans.glencoe.com Web site and click on **Chapter 28—Chapter Overviews** to preview chapter information.

Texas Constitutions

Guide to Reading

Main Idea
The Texas constitution establishes a framework of government for today.

Key Terms
constitution, amendment, bill of rights, federalism, separation of powers, legislature, executive, judiciary, checks and balances, bond

Reading Strategy
Classifying Information As you read this section, create a web like the one below and fill in the three branches of Texas government.

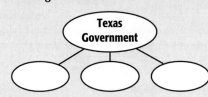

Texas Government

Read to Learn
• about the Texas constitution.
• what three branches make up the state government.
• how to amend the constitution.

Section Theme
Government and Democracy The current constitution of Texas emphasizes that political power belongs to the people.

Preview of Events

| ♦1827 | ♦1836 | ♦1845 | ♦1861 | ♦1866 | ♦1869 | ♦1876 |

First constitution for Coahuila y Tejas — Second constitution (after declaring independence) — Third constitution (after becoming part of the U.S.) — Fourth, fifth, and sixth constitutions — Seventh constitution, still used today

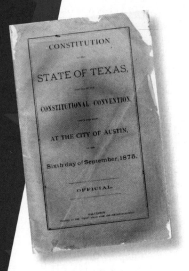

Constitution of 1876

A
Texas Story

When the delegates to the state's Constitutional Convention of 1876 met, their goal was to create a document that would meet the needs of Texans for many years. Their experiences must have told them this would be a difficult task. Since 1824—a little over 50 years—Texans lived under seven different constitutions. Yet, without the benefits of electricity, computers, or telephones, the diverse group of men produced a constitution that is still in use today, more than 125 years later.

The Texas Constitution in Early Government

What exactly is a **constitution**, and why is it important? A constitution is a document that outlines fundamental laws and principles of law. It describes the nature, functions, and limits of government. Citizens of

Texas live under the laws of both the United States and the Texas constitutions.

In 1827 the legislature of Coahuila y Tejas wrote the first of Texas's seven constitutions. Modeled after the Mexican constitution, it strictly controlled regional and individual rights. After gaining independence from Mexico in 1836, Texas wrote another constitution. This served Texas until it became part of the U.S. in 1845, when a third constitution was written. During the Civil War and Reconstruction, three more constitutions were written. Another constitution, adopted in 1876, was written at the end of Reconstruction. That document is Texas's present constitution. (See pages 710 and 711 for summaries of these constitutions.)

The Role of Constitutions

Each Texas constitution has had four important purposes. They have outlined parts of the government and described the duties of each. Officials and governmental bodies were given various powers. The constitutions described the rights of citizens. They provided a method for making changes, or adding amendments.

Each constitution reflected the times in which it was written. The earliest Texas constitutions permitted slavery. Women were not even mentioned in the early constitutions. They struggled for the right to vote until 1920. Today all Texas citizens 18 years of age or older who have not been convicted of serious crimes are eligible to vote.

Constitutions reflect the ideals and values of citizens. Later Texas constitutions were modeled after the United States Constitution. Defining citizen rights and powers became important. Most constitutions emphasize that political power belongs to the people, a concept known as **popular sovereignty,** and that citizens' voices must be heard at all levels of government. Sometimes a bill of rights, specifically listing individual freedoms, is included.

Reading Check **Contrasting** How do the earliest Texas constitutions differ from later constitutions?

Federalism

As a state within the United States, Texas is part of a federal system of government, which means that some powers belong to the federal government and others belong to state governments. This sharing of powers and duties is

Article 1 – Bill of Rights
The Texas Constitution

1. Texas is a free and independent state.

2. All political power is inherent in the people.

3. All free men have equal rights.

4. No religious test is required to hold office.

5. Oaths are administered according to the conscience of the individual.

6. Freedom of worship is guaranteed.

7. No money shall be appropriated for sectarian (religious) purposes.

8. Freedom of speech and the press is guaranteed.

9. No unreasonable search and seizure is permitted.

10. Rights of persons accused of crime are protected.

called federalism. Powers given to the states are **reserved** powers. Examples are a state's right to regulate commerce within its borders, provide for a state militia, establish the legal age for marriage without parental permission, and create public school systems. On the other hand, Texas does not have the right to create its own money, declare war, or sign treaties with other countries, because those are specific powers of the federal government. Thus, the Texas constitution and other laws address all powers that do not belong to the federal government.

Three Branches of Government

The Texas Constitution of 1876 requires that the three branches of government be separate. In Article II, the constitution states that "the powers of the government of the State of Texas shall be divided into three distinct departments." This separation of powers prevents any branch from having too much power. These divisions are known as the *legislative,* the *executive,* and the *judicial* branches of government.

TEXAS HISTORY *Online*

Student Web Activity Visit the texans.glencoe.com Web site and click on **Chapter 28—Student Web Activity** to learn more about the three branches of government.

The legislature, with its power vested in the Senate and House of Representatives, makes the laws of the state. The legislature also is given the responsibility of approving the state's budget. The **Constitution of 1876** set the limit of the Senate at 31 members. The House of Representatives consisted of one representative for every 15,000 inhabitants in the state, never to exceed 150 members. Today, the House has reached that limit. Texas has a population of nearly 20.8 million, so a member now represents many more than 15,000 people.

The executive department is responsible for seeing that the laws of the state are carried out. It consists of the chief executive (the governor), lieutenant governor, secretary of state, comptroller of public accounts, commissioner of the General Land Office, commissioner of agriculture, and attorney general. The office of treasurer was eliminated in 1996.

The judicial branch, or judiciary, interprets the laws of the state and decides how the laws should be applied. The judiciary also may try people accused of crimes and may settle other disputes. It consists of several courts, including the supreme court and courts of appeals.

The writers of the Texas constitution also believed it was important for each branch of government to act as a check on the powers of the other two. This is called the principle of checks and balances. The legislature, for example, makes the laws. The governor, who heads the executive branch, can check this power through the veto power. The legislature, with a two-thirds vote, can pass a law over a veto. At the same time, the **supreme court**—the final authority of the judicial branch—can rule that laws passed by the legislature and signed by the governor are unconstitutional.

The Bill of Rights Protects Citizens

Protecting the rights of citizens is so important to Texans that the constitution begins with a bill of rights, similar to the one in the United States Constitution. The Texas Bill of Rights protects freedom of speech, religion, and the press. It guarantees the right to bear arms, forbids unreasonable searches and seizures, and assures accused people a speedy trial. The bill of rights also lists special rights for crime victims. These freedoms are essential for a free and democratic society that relies on free speech and open debate to create sound public policy.

The Constitution of 1876

The Constitution of 1876 is considered by some historians to be a reaction to the Reconstruction administration of Governor Davis. The Constitution of 1869 gave the executive branch more power than previous constitutions. The 1876 Constitution prevented a strong governor from controlling all the branches of government.

Adopted on February 15, 1876, the current Texas constitution established a system of public schools. It separated government into three branches and strengthened the system of checks and balances. While the constitution guaranteed that race could not prevent a person from voting, women were not mentioned. The Constitution of 1876 also removed much of the governor's power and cut salaries for state officials. Terms of office were shortened. To reduce costs and limit powers, legislative sessions were scheduled to meet once every two years instead of annually.

Many argue the constitution is badly outdated because so many changes have been made to it since 1876 to address shifting times. Several tries to adopt a new constitution have failed. Instead, Texans have updated the existing constitution by voting on amendments.

Amending the Constitution

Amendments are formal additions to a constitution. During every legislative session, amendments are considered to keep the state current with changing times. Amendments have been passed to authorize the issuing of bonds (guarantees from the government to repay money it borrows), to abolish political offices, to exempt school districts or other entities from taxes, and to deal with other issues.

Adopting an amendment requires approval by two-thirds of both the House and Senate, followed by voter approval. The governor cannot veto amendments to the Texas constitution.

✔ **Reading Check** **Describing** Name three types of amendments that have been passed.

SECTION 1 ASSESSMENT

Checking for Understanding

1. **Using Key Terms** Use the words constitution and amendment in a sentence that explains how state laws are changed.
2. **Reviewing Facts** Summarize some key rights granted by the Texas Bill of Rights.

Reviewing Themes

3. **Government and Democracy** How is the Texas constitution similar to the United States Constitution?

Organizing to Learn

4. **Identifying Central Issues** Create a chart like the one shown and identify the major area of responsibility of each of the branches of government.

Branch of Government	Responsibility
Executive	
Legislative	
Judicial	

Critical Thinking

5. **Analyzing** How does the current Texas constitution reflect the ideals and values of Texans?
6. **Predicting** Since the Texas constitution limits the power of the executive, what factors might affect a governor's influence or power?

TAKS PRACTICE

Determining Cause and Effect Why did the framers of the 1876 Constitution limit the powers of the state government?

Developing Multimedia Presentations

Why Learn This Skill?

A multimedia presentation is a different way to learn and to share material. It combines many types of media. Multimedia presentations can hold your classmates' attention. They also enable you to familiarize yourself with some interesting learning tools.

Learning the Skill

A multimedia presentation involves using several types of media, including photographs, videos, or sound recordings. The equipment can range from simple cassette players, to overhead projectors, to VCRs, to computers, and beyond.

Multimedia, as it relates to computer technology, is the combination of text, video, audio, and animation in an interactive computer program. You need certain tools to create multimedia presentations on a computer, including computer graphic tools and drawing programs, animation programs, and authoring systems that tie everything together. Your computer manual will tell you which tools your computer can support.

Practicing the Skill

Plan and create a multimedia presentation on a topic found in the chapter, such as Texas constitutions or the Department of Criminal Justice. After selecting your topic, list three or four major ideas you would like to cover. When you decide on your topic, consider whether the topic has enough resources available. If you choose a unique or unusual topic, it will be more difficult to find resources, so choose your topic wisely. Use the questions listed in the next column as a guide when planning your presentation.

❶ Which forms of media do I want to include? Video? Sound? Animation? Photographs? Graphics?

❷ Which kinds of media equipment are available at my school or local library?

❸ What types of media can I create to enhance my presentation?

❹ Which of the media forms does my computer support?

TAKS PRACTICE

Developing Multimedia Presentations Choose an individual in Texas history and create a multimedia presentation about his or her contributions. Use as many multimedia materials as possible, and share your presentation with the class.

SECTION 2

The Texas System of Justice

Guide to Reading

Main Idea
The Texas court system protects citizens' rights.

Key Terms
civil law, criminal law, felony, misdemeanor, grand jury, indictment, no bill, petit jury, plea bargain, juror, mediate

Reading Strategy
Classifying Information As you read this section, create a chart like the one shown and list the types of cases heard in each court.

Courts	Cases Heard
Municipal	
Justice of the Peace	
County	
District	

Read to Learn
• about civil law and criminal law.
• about juvenile justice.
• about Texas law enforcement.

Section Theme
Civic Rights and Responsibilities Through the system of trial and appeals courts, disputes can be settled, and people accused of crimes can be fairly tried.

Preview of Events

♦1967 — Fourteenth appeals court is added in Houston

♦1989 — Texas Department of Criminal Justice is formed

♦2001 — Over 62,000 attorneys hold licenses to practice law in Texas

Texas citizens participating in state government

A
Texas Story

By the year 2001, almost 400 amendments had been added to the original Constitution of 1876 in an effort to keep the document current. Although some argue that the constitution is outdated even with the changes, the last time a constitutional convention was called to rewrite the document was back in 1974. After meeting for seven months, the convention failed by three votes to approve a new version of the constitution to submit to Texas voters—the Constitution of 1876 was to remain the law of the land.

The Judicial System

The judicial branch is made up of courts and judges throughout the state. It serves three purposes. It supports a system by which those accused of crimes may be tried and, if found guilty, punished; it provides a system

The Texas Court System

Trial Courts	Appeals Courts
What they do:	**What they do:**
Hear civil and criminal cases and render verdicts	Determine whether trials held in trial courts were fair; can order new trials
Who they are:	**Who they are:**
• Municipal/Justice of the Peace • County Courts • District Courts	• Courts of Appeals • Court of Criminal Appeals (for criminal cases) and Supreme Court (for civil cases)

TAKS PRACTICE

Identifying The Texas court system allows for an appeals process. *What is the major role of the appeals courts in Texas?*

in which disputes can be settled; and it decides what the laws of the state mean and how they should be enforced. Texas, like the United States, has two general areas of law—civil and criminal. With the exception of some local judges, Texas judges are elected by voters.

Texas Civil Law

The word *civil* comes from the Latin word for *citizen.* Civil law pertains to legal disputes between private citizens, businesses, and governments. Lawsuits between citizens are known as civil suits and are based on civil laws.

Most civil cases concern disputes about property, money, child custody, or insurance claims. Civil cases may be decided either by a judge or by a judge and a jury. Judge and jury trials can be very expensive and time consuming. Because of this, parties to civil cases are encouraged to try to work out agreements in out-of-court settlements. Still, about one-third of the civil cases filed in Texas actually go to trial.

✓ Reading Check Evaluating Why are parties in civil cases encouraged to seek out-of-court settlements?

Criminal Law

Criminal law is the set of laws that describe what people can and cannot do. It is concerned with crimes and punishments. Criminal laws protect the public and help maintain order. Criminal codes make it illegal for someone to break into your home and steal your video game or television. Punishments for such crimes are also included in the criminal codes.

A criminal case is one in which a person or people are accused of breaking the law. In a criminal case, the government brings court action against the accused. A private citizen cannot file a criminal suit but may bring a civil suit resulting from a criminal action. Sometimes people have been found not guilty in criminal cases and at fault in a related civil case.

Two types of offenses are recognized under criminal law—**felony** and **misdemeanor.** A felony is a very serious crime, such as murder, arson, or kidnapping. A misdemeanor is a less serious crime, such as disorderly conduct, gambling, or dangerous traffic violations.

If convicted of a felony, the accused person usually goes to prison and, depending on the nature of the crime, might be given the death penalty. Texas leads the nation in the number of executions of violent criminals. As a result, the state has been criticized by some groups. People convicted of misdemeanors may pay fines, serve terms in county jails, or both.

✓ Reading Check Identifying Who is responsible for bringing court action in a criminal case?

Justice for Juveniles

Much of the effort of the juvenile justice system is directed at preventing child and adolescent legal problems. Programs try to get youths involved in families, schools, and communities. When these programs are not enough, however, the state must intervene for the protection of both the youth and the public.

The **Texas Youth Commission** (TYC) is the state's juvenile corrections agency. The TYC provides for the care, custody, and rehabilitation of Texas's most chronically delinquent or serious juvenile offenders. Young people between the ages of 10 and 17 who have committed serious offenses are the responsibility of the TYC. While in this system, offenders receive a medical evaluation, educational testing and assessment, and a psychological evaluation. Special treatment for problems such as drug dependency or violent behavior is provided. If the crimes are serious enough, a youth may be transferred to the adult prison system (Texas Department of Criminal Justice) to complete the sentence.

✓Reading Check **Describing** What kind of offenders are the responsibility of the Texas Youth Commission?

The Jury System

Whenever a person is accused of a felony, a group of people called a grand jury considers the case. If 9 or more of the 12 members of the grand jury believe there is evidence that the person might have committed the crime, an indictment, called a "true bill," is issued. If the grand jury decides there is not enough evidence to justify a trial, it can issue a "no bill." In most cases grand juries agree with the recommendations of the prosecuting attorney.

A petit jury decides the criminal cases that go to court. After the attorneys present the evidence, all members of the jury must agree on a decision of "guilty" or "not guilty." If the jury decides that the accused person is guilty, either the judge or the jury decides on a sentence.

Some cases are settled by plea bargaining. Usually, in such cases, the defendant agrees to plead guilty to a lesser charge. Why is plea bargaining used? Many times, both sides have something to gain. The courts cannot handle all the cases that come up for trial. When a plea bargain occurs, the government saves the money and time involved in a trial. The guilty plea also ensures that the accused will receive some punishment.

Working for Justice

Many state and local agencies work together to enforce the laws of Texas. **The Texas Department of Public Safety** (DPS) conducts criminal investigations, supervises highway traffic, and licenses drivers. County sheriffs and city police departments conduct local law enforcement. The **Texas Department of Criminal Justice** administers the state prisons for adults. The Texas Youth Commission oversees juvenile correctional facilities.

One key individual who works on behalf of justice is the state attorney general, considered to be the state's lawyer. He or she provides advice to the governor, the legislature, and all the agencies, boards, and commissions of state government. If a case goes to court, the attorney general's office represents the state.

Attorneys are often consulted in legal matters. In 2001, 62,000 attorneys were licensed to practice law in Texas. To be licensed, a Texan must complete law school, pass an examination, and become a member of the State Bar of Texas.

When a case comes to court, jurors have a great responsibility to determine the facts. They also may have to decide the punishment for a person found guilty. To serve on a jury, one must be a Texas citizen, be at least 18 years old, and be able to read and write. Jurors must also be of sound mind, and they cannot have any felony convictions or be under indictment for committing any felony.

Exploring **Government**

An attorney addresses a jury during a trial. What important job do jurors have?

The Three Branches of Texas Government

Legislative Branch	Judicial Branch	Executive Branch
What they do:	**What they do:**	**What they do:**
Make the laws of the state	Interpret the laws of the state	Enforce the laws of the state
Who they are:	**Who they are:**	**Who they are:**
• Senate (31 members) • House of Representatives (150 members)	• Supreme Court • Court of Criminal Appeals • District Courts • County Courts • Justice of the Peace Courts	• Governor • Lieutenant Governor • Secretary of State • Comptroller of Public Accounts • Commissioner of the General Land Office • Commissioner of Agriculture • Attorney General

TAKS PRACTICE

Analyzing   The Texas constitution divided the government into three separate branches. This is known as "separation of powers." *How does the Texas government benefit from this structure?*

The Court System of Texas

There are two kinds of courts in Texas—trial and appeals. Trial courts hear cases and reach a decision called a verdict. Appeals courts decide if trials held in trial courts were fair. They can order a new trial if proper procedures were not followed.

Trial Courts

Trial courts are courts where witnesses are heard, evidence is presented, and a verdict (in a jury trial) or a decision (in a case tried by a judge) is reached. Trial courts in Texas are concerned with civil and criminal cases. Civil cases—such as divorce settlements, personal injuries, and uncollected taxes—comprise most of these cases. Criminal cases include burglary, assault, driving while intoxicated (DWI), theft, and more serious offenses. Texas has three levels of trial courts—**municipal** and **justice of the peace, county courts,** and **district courts.** Larger cities have municipal courts that deal with violations of city ordinances, such as fire-safety infractions, traffic offenses, and zoning violations. They also hear misdemeanor cases in which the maximum fine is less than $2,000.

For small towns and rural areas without municipal courts, justice of the peace courts try civil and minor criminal cases. Justices perform several roles, such as performing marriages, issuing search warrants, setting bail, and determining the cause of death. Justices can also send cases to a higher court.

County courts are the second level of trial courts. The Texas constitution requires that each of Texas's 254 counties have at least one county court. Called constitutional county courts, they hear civil cases in which the amount of the dispute is between $500 and $5,000. They also hear criminal misdemeanor cases in which the fine is greater than $200. Where needed, the legislature has the power to create additional county courts, called county courts at law. In fast-growing cities like Austin, new county courts are established every few years to handle increasing caseloads. County courts hear criminal misdemeanor cases and civil cases in which the amount in dispute is less than $5,000.

District courts are considered important trial courts in Texas. District courts hear criminal felony cases and other serious criminal matters such as murder. Civil cases and those involving juveniles or disputes of over $500 may also be heard in district courts.

Appeals Courts

People who file lawsuits hope to win. However, in almost every court case, one party wins and one party loses. The loser has to pay attorneys' fees and court costs.

In some cases the loser may believe that the trial was unfair. He or she may believe that evidence was illegally obtained or that the judge was not fair in making decisions. The losing party has the right to file an appeal, or a request to have the decision of a court set aside. Except for divorce cases, lower court decisions can be appealed in Texas. Appeals usually begin in the district courts of appeals but can reach the two highest courts—the Court of Criminal Appeals (for criminal cases) and the Supreme Court of Texas (for civil or juvenile cases). Texas is one of two U.S. states with more than one highest court.

Both of these high courts are composed of nine justices. In the case of the Supreme Court, the presiding justice is called the chief justice. All of the justices must be elected to a full term of six years. However, many justices begin to serve after being appointed by the governor to fill vacancies.

Divorce cases cannot be appealed. There is, however, an alternative for resolving divorce cases. Several county courts in Texas now require that people going through a divorce first *mediate*, or meet with an unbiased professional

A Shared Past...

Two elements of Spanish law were so popular in Texas that they were retained after Texas became independent. The homestead law protected one's land and tools from creditors. The other was the law of community property. This law says that husband and wife share equally in property they acquire during their marriage. Both laws were so popular that other states adopted them. The other community property states are Arizona, California, Idaho, Louisiana, Nevada, New Mexico, Washington, and Wisconsin.

who helps the couple come to an agreement on the terms of their divorce. This frees the courts from having to divide a couple's property and decide who gets custody of the children. It also spares couples the additional strain of having to argue their cases in court. Mediation is fair, has a good success rate, and is becoming widely used to resolve business, workplace, neighborhood, and public policy disputes.

✓ **Reading Check** **Evaluating** What type of court, civil or criminal, would hear a case about a bank robbery?

SECTION 2 ASSESSMENT

Checking for Understanding

1. **Using Key Terms** Use the terms grand jury and indictment to describe what might happen in a criminal court.
2. **Reviewing Facts** Name four state or local agencies that work together to enforce the laws of Texas.

Reviewing Themes

3. **Civic Rights and Responsibilities** What is one way that cases can be decided out of court?

Organizing to Learn

4. **Comparing and Contrasting** Create a chart like the one shown below and compare the differences between civil law and criminal law.

	Civil Law	Criminal Law
Definition		
Who decides case?		
Example of typical case		
Highest appeals court		

Critical Thinking

5. **Analyzing Information** Why are juvenile offenders usually handled by a different justice system than that which deals with adults?
6. **Drawing Inferences** Why does the law forbid anyone with a felony conviction from serving on a jury?

TAKS PRACTICE

Evaluating Information Why are district trial courts considered important courts in Texas?

Chapter Summary

Democracy and Constitutions

Important Features of the Texas Constitution

- Outlines the branches of government
- Describes the powers of officials
- Protects the rights of citizens
- Provides a method for making changes

Three Branches of Government

- Legislative—makes the laws
- Executive—sees that the laws are carried out
- Judicial—interprets the laws

Judicial System

- Civil law—disputes between citizens, business, and government
- Criminal law—people accused of breaking the law, either felony or misdemeanor

Jury and Court System

- Grand jury and petit jury
- Trial courts and appeals courts

Reviewing Key Terms

Write a sentence for each pair of terms.

1. indictment, no bill
2. legislature, judiciary
3. amendment, bond
4. felony, misdemeanor
5. plea bargain, mediate

Reviewing Key Facts

6. What are the four purposes of the Texas constitution?
7. How is Texas part of the federal system of government?
8. Why are there three branches of state government?
9. What are the duties of each branch of state government?
10. What does the Texas Bill of Rights guarantee to all Texans?
11. Why and how are amendments added to the constitution?
12. What is the difference between civil and criminal law?
13. What is the difference between a felony and a misdemeanor?
14. How do a grand jury and a petit jury differ?
15. How do a trial court and an appeals court differ?
16. Name the two highest courts in Texas.

Critical Thinking

17. **Identifying Central Issues** In your opinion, which of the four purposes of a constitution discussed in the chapter is the most important? Explain.
18. **Drawing Conclusions** If you were chosen for jury duty, would you rather serve on a civil or a criminal case? Why?
19. **Evaluating Information** What purpose do appeals courts serve? What are their benefits? What are their disadvantages? Do the benefits outweigh the disadvantages? Be sure to explain your reasoning.
20. **Summarizing** Create a web like the one below. Use knowledge you have gained from reading earlier chapters to explain why the Texas constitution was written or rewritten in the years indicated.

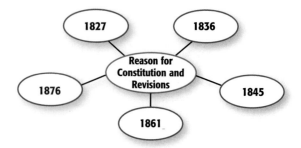

Geography and History

21. The Capitol in Austin is the seat of Texas government. Hopefully you will visit the Capitol in the future if you have not already done so. For this activity, you will learn about the Capitol through the Internet. Go to the Texas State Preservation Board Web site at www.tspb.state.tx.us and click on the Maps/Floorplans link. Choose two maps or floorplans. Describe four or more interesting facts that you learned from the maps or floorplans. What would you like to see if you visited the Capitol or area?

Cooperative Learning Activity

22. **Studying the Amendments** Organize into groups of three. Your task is to study an amendment to the Texas constitution and explain the reasons this particular amendment became law. Your group may choose any amendment. It is important to research background information about the issues and events that led to the amendment's adoption (see **Building Technology Skills** below). Explain why your group thinks that the amendment accomplished or did not accomplish what it was supposed to do. Present your findings to the rest of the class.

Practicing Skills

23. **Multimedia Presentations** Choose a past or present-day topic about Texas. Possible topics could be immigration, the oil industry, Texas independence, education, sports, art, or transportation. Depending on which topic you choose, think about which multimedia resources would be best for your presentation. Share your multimedia presentation with your class.

 Portfolio/TAKS Writing Activity

24. **Supporting a Point of View** Think of an amendment that you think should be added to the Texas constitution. Write a paper explaining what the amendment would be, why you think it is necessary, and how you would get it approved.

 Building Technology Skills

25. **Using the Internet for Research** Use the Internet or library resources to find the current Texas constitution with all of the latest amendments. Focus on one amendment and look for articles that explain the reasons it was added to the constitution. Find out whether it had

 **TEXAS HISTORY** *Online*

Self-Check Quiz
Visit the texans.glencoe.com Web site and click on **Chapter 28—Self-Check Quizzes** to prepare for the chapter test.

positive, negative, or no results. Use this information in your **Cooperative Learning Activity** or your **TAKS Writing Activity.**

Law and History Activity

26. **Knowing Your Public Officials** Learn more about one of the justices on the Texas Supreme Court—the state's highest appeals court for civil cases. Use at least two sources for your research. You can access information through www.supreme.courts.state.tx.us or newspapers and magazine articles. Write a brief biography about the justice you have chosen.

The Princeton Review
TAKS PRACTICE

Use the quotation to answer the following question.

The Texas Constitution

Article 1—The Bill of Rights, Section 8

Every person shall be at liberty to speak, write or publish his opinions on any subject, being responsible for the abuse of that privilege; and no law shall ever be passed curtailing the liberty of speech or of the press.

Section 8 of the bill of rights of the Texas Constitution protects which of the following rights?

F It outlines the rights of citizens to practice any religion they wish.

G It protects citizens from discrimination on the basis of race.

H It provides for the separation of church and state.

J It describes the rights of citizens to express their ideas.

Test-Taking Tip:

Read the quotation and test question carefully. Compare each answer choice to the quotation. Eliminate any answer choices that are not mentioned in this article of the bill of rights.

Texas State Government

Why It Matters

The state legislature makes laws, and the governor administers them. This division of responsibilities is called "separation of powers."

The Impact Today

The amount of money the state spends on services such as education, highways, parks, and health care is decided by the legislature with the approval of the governor.

1991
★ Ann Richards inaugurated as governor

★ Dan Morales, first Hispanic attorney general, sworn in

1995
★ George W. Bush inaugurated as governor

Texas

United States *1988* *1990* *1993*

World

1988
• Benazir Bhutto became prime minister of Pakistan

1990
• Violetta de Chamorro became president of Nicaragua

1993
• Bill Clinton inaugurated as president of the United States

The dome of the Texas State Capitol is a well-known and inspiring landmark in Austin.

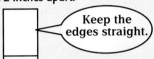

FOLDABLES™ Study Organizer

TAKS PRACTICE

Categorizing Information Study Foldable
Make this foldable to categorize what you learn about the state government of Texas.

Step 1 Collect two sheets of paper and place them about 2 inches apart.

Keep the edges straight.

Step 2 Fold up the bottom edges of the paper to form 4 tabs.

This makes all tabs the same size.

Step 3 When all the tabs are the same size, crease the paper to hold the tabs in place and staple the sheets together. Turn the paper and label each tab as shown.

Texas Government
Executive
Legislative
Judicial

Staple together along the fold.

Reading and Writing As you read about the executive, legislative, and judicial branches of the Texas state government, ask yourself what facts are important. Record these key facts under each appropriate tab of your foldable.

2000
★ Rick Perry became governor

1997   1999   2001

1997
• Kofi Annan chosen as secretary general of the United Nations

2000
• George W. Bush elected president of the United States

2001
• Terrorists attacked the U.S. World Trade Center in New York

2001
• Condoleezza Rice appointed head of the National Security Council

TEXAS HISTORY Online

Chapter Overview
Visit the texans.glencoe.com Web site and click on **Chapter 29—Chapter Overviews** to preview chapter information.

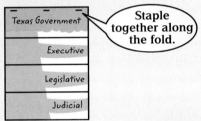

The Texas Legislature

State Senator Rodney Ellis

A Texas Story

State Senator Rodney Ellis represented one of the poorest Senate districts in the state, but that did not keep him from being an effective member of the legislature. After one legislative session, a reporter for *The Texas Observer* wrote the following about him. "[As] the driving force behind a package of criminal justice reform bills, Ellis has had a hand in most of the legislature's major accomplishments." Dedicated public servants like Rodney Ellis are one group of people who help create the laws to determine how we live.

The Function of the Legislative Branch

Like the United States legislature, the Texas **bicameral** legislature is composed of a Senate and House of Representatives. *Bicameral* means having two rooms, or chambers. Several Senate committees oversee the affairs of the state, including education, criminal justice, and health and human services. The House is concerned with many of the same matters as is the Senate. Its committees are responsible for agriculture and livestock, economic development, environmental regulation, higher education, natural resources, public health, and other matters.

Lawmakers from both chambers decide how much money should be spent on education, whether taxes should be raised or lowered, and how to help the economy.

Duties

The Texas **legislature** makes the laws that govern Texas. Other duties include approving or rejecting the governor's appointments and using the power of oversight to review the actions of other branches of government. The legislature also discusses how state monies should be spent and what to do about prison overcrowding, taxes, education, and the environment.

Because legislators represent the people of Texas, they listen to voters' concerns about current issues. For example, some members of the House met with hundreds of concerned Austin residents about the proposed use of a 50-year-old pipeline through which a private company wanted to pump gas. Because the pipeline ran near residential neighborhoods, the citizens expressed their concerns about potential hazards.

✓ Reading Check **Questioning** What is one way citizens share their concerns with their legislators?

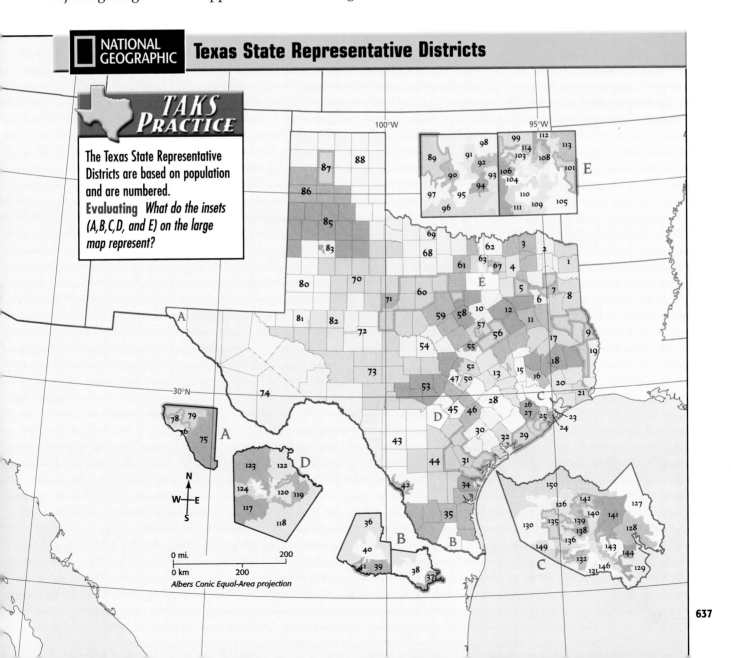

NATIONAL GEOGRAPHIC **Texas State Representative Districts**

TAKS PRACTICE

The Texas State Representative Districts are based on population and are numbered.
Evaluating *What do the insets (A, B, C, D, and E) on the large map represent?*

Albers Conic Equal-Area projection

Running the State Government

The Texas legislature is composed of 31 members in the **Senate** and 150 members in the **House of Representatives.** It meets every two years. Sometimes special sessions are necessary to handle problems needing immediate solutions. The governor may call one or more special sessions when the legislature is not in regular session.

The **lieutenant governor,** elected by voters of the state, serves as the Senate's president. The House of Representatives elects a **Speaker of the House.** These leaders have a great deal of power.

Committees help the legislature carry out tasks such as studying problems and drafting bills. Appointing legislators to committees is an important responsibility for the Speaker and lieutenant governor. Committee chairpeople are powerful. They can "kill" any proposed law they do not agree with by not scheduling it for discussion in the House or Senate.

One important duty of the legislature is redrawing legislative and congressional districts as the population changes. This is known as **redistricting** and may determine which party controls the state legislature. Redistricting occurs after a census is completed. Redistricting creates many arguments in the Texas legislature because it changes the distribution of political power.

✓ **Reading Check** **Explaining** Why is redistricting important to political parties?

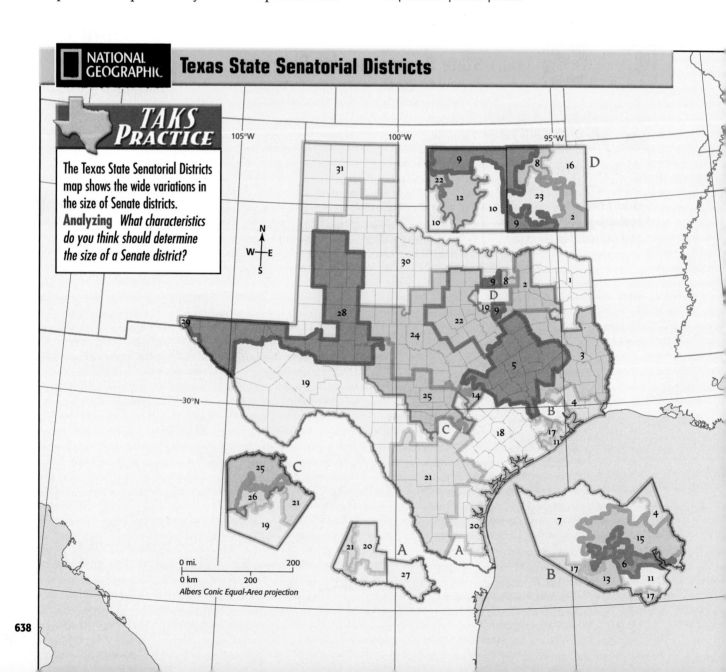

NATIONAL GEOGRAPHIC **Texas State Senatorial Districts**

TAKS PRACTICE

The Texas State Senatorial Districts map shows the wide variations in the size of Senate districts. **Analyzing** *What characteristics do you think should determine the size of a Senate district?*

0 mi. 200
0 km 200
Albers Conic Equal-Area projection

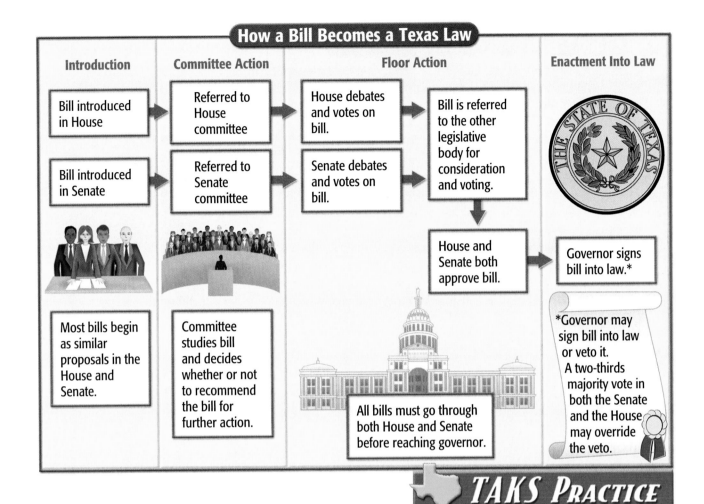

How a Bill Becomes a Texas Law

Introduction

Bill introduced in House

Bill introduced in Senate

Most bills begin as similar proposals in the House and Senate.

Committee Action

Referred to House committee

Referred to Senate committee

Committee studies bill and decides whether or not to recommend the bill for further action.

Floor Action

House debates and votes on bill.

Senate debates and votes on bill.

Bill is referred to the other legislative body for consideration and voting.

House and Senate both approve bill.

All bills must go through both House and Senate before reaching governor.

Enactment Into Law

THE STATE OF TEXAS

Governor signs bill into law.*

*Governor may sign bill into law or veto it. A two-thirds majority vote in both the Senate and the House may override the veto.

TAKS PRACTICE

Evaluating A bill goes through a specific process before becoming a law. *At what point do most bills "die" in the process?*

How a Bill Becomes a Law

There are two major types of proposals that can be considered by the state legislature. The first of these is a **resolution.** A resolution officially expresses the legislature's opinion about a subject. Resolutions are used to propose amendments to the Texas or U.S. Constitutions or to set rules of conduct. They might proclaim certain days to honor individuals or special groups, like veterans. For example, your school might be honored for a sport-related or academic achievement.

The second type of proposal is a "bill," which is a proposed law. Thousands are considered each legislative session, but few become law. A bill that is approved by both the House and Senate and signed by the governor becomes a **law.**

A bill is first "read" before the entire House or Senate and assigned to a committee. Just a summary is read aloud. Committee members listen to testimony from people who favor the bill and from people who oppose it. Then the committee members decide whether the rest of the House or the rest of the Senate should consider the bill. Most bills are not recommended for further consideration. Those bills are said to have "died in committee."

A bill that is recommended for further consideration must be debated by the entire House or by the entire Senate. After a debate, the representatives or senators vote. If a majority votes in favor of the bill, then that bill usually will be considered by the legislators in the other house. The bill must be approved in the same form by a majority of the House and the Senate.

Sometimes the House and the Senate approve different forms of the same bill. Then the Speaker of the House and the lieutenant governor appoint a conference committee, made up of

Causes and Effects of Redistricting

Causes

- Census results show a shift in population to cities.
- U.S. Supreme Court ruled each senator or representative must represent the same number of voters.

Effects

- Large cities and surrounding suburbs gain representation.
- State government now spends more money on urban areas.
- Minorities are more easily elected.

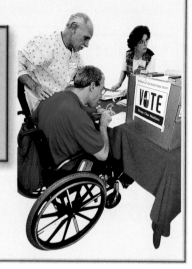

Graphic Organizer → Skills

Before the U.S. Supreme Court passed the "one-man, one-vote" ruling, Texas's large cities were "underrepresented" in the legislature.
Analyzing How did minorities benefit from redistricting?

---

members from both houses, to work out the differences. Conference committees sometimes change a bill so thoroughly that the new version may not look very much like either bill when it arrived at the conference committee. After the committee members agree on the bill, it must then be passed by both the House of Representatives and the Senate another time.

Once a bill has been approved by both the House and the Senate, it goes to the governor. If the governor signs the bill, it becomes law. If the governor vetoes the bill, it does not become law unless two-thirds of the House and two-thirds of the Senate vote to override the veto.

The legislature considers thousands of proposals each session, but few become law. One bill that passed during a recent legislative session was the **Hate Crimes Bill.** This bill increases penalties for crimes committed because of hatred or bias against personal characteristics of the victim, such as age, race, or gender.

✓**Reading Check** **Evaluating** What reasons might prevent a bill from reaching the governor's desk?

SECTION 1 ASSESSMENT

Checking for Understanding

1. **Using Key Terms** Use the terms bicameral, oversight, redistricting, and resolution in sentences to demonstrate your understanding of the terms.
2. **Reviewing Facts** What is the difference between a bill and a resolution?

Reviewing Themes

3. **Government and Democracy** Identify three main responsibilities of the Senate.

Organizing to Learn

4. **Sequencing** Create a flow chart like the one shown here. For each stage shown, describe the steps a bill passes through to become a law.

> Committee
> ↓
> Legislature
> ↓
> Governor

Critical Thinking

5. **Analyzing** How does a census influence the political makeup of the Texas legislature?

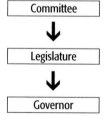

TAKS PRACTICE

Distinguishing Fact From Opinion
Imagine that you are writing a bill that would widen roads to add more bike lanes. Write two facts and two opinions that would attract support for your bill.

The Executive Branch

Guide to Reading

Main Idea

The executive branch carries out the laws. The governor is the state's chief executive.

Key Terms

line-item veto
commander in chief

Reading Strategy

Identifying The governor appoints certain officials; others are elected. Create a chart like this one and place an X in the appropriate column.

	Appointed	Elected
Comptroller		
Judges		
Board of Pardons and Paroles		

Read to Learn

• what the governor's powers are.
• about the duties of other officials.

Section Theme

Government and Democracy
Though the governor is the chief executive of the state, the executive powers are checked and balanced by the legislative branch, and shared with other elected officials.

Preview of Events

♦1924	♦1932		♦1978	♦1990
Miriam Ferguson is elected governor	Miriam Ferguson is reelected governor		Governor's term is changed from two years to four years	Ann Richards is elected governor

Sometime acting governor Rodney Ellis

A
Texas Story

When the governor is out of the state, the lieutenant governor is the acting governor. When both the governor and the lieutenant governor are out of the state at the same time, the president *pro tempore* of the Senate is the acting governor. In 1999–2000 Senator Rodney Ellis was acting governor of Texas for a total of 50 days.

The Function of the Executive Branch

The **executive branch** of state government carries out the laws passed by the legislature. It also conducts the business of the state. Executive agencies account for 99 percent of the state's budget and are required to "execute," or carry out, policy set by the legislative branch. Executive power is shared by elected officials and those appointed by the governor.

Elvira Reyna 1950–

Elvira Reyna (Dallas) has the distinction of being the first Hispanic American Republican to be elected to the state legislature. Prior to her election in 1992, Reyna participated in numerous civic groups such as the PTA, the local library board, and the school board. As a state representative, Reyna has served on the Higher Education Committee and the Juvenile Justice and Family Issues Committee.

Reyna has overcome many obstacles and challenges on her way to the State Capitol. She is proud of her success, but she also wants to motivate others to excel. In a speech, she urged the audience to "find [their] own steps to success" and not to define themselves by another's achievements. She also believes that education is fundamental to success.

The Governor of Texas

The **governor** is the head of the executive branch of Texas government. Although elected to terms of four years, there is no limit to the number of terms a governor may serve. Prior to 1978, governors were elected to two-year terms. To qualify for the office, one must be at least 30 years old, a U.S. citizen, and a resident of Texas for at least five years before the election.

A campaign for governor is very expensive. Candidates for governor must raise large sums of money to pay for advertising and other expenses. Third-party candidates sometimes run for office, but campaign costs make their elections unlikely.

Two women have served as governors of Texas. The first was Miriam "Ma" Ferguson, elected in 1924 and 1932. Her husband, Governor Jim Ferguson, had served as governor between 1915 and 1917, but had been impeached and removed from office. Ann Richards, a Democrat, was elected to a four-year term in 1990.

Governors and their staffs have much work to do. By the end of 2001, **Governor Rick Perry** had received almost 1,500 bills for review by staff members. After review, senior staff members recommend that bills be signed or vetoed.

✓ **Reading Check** **Identifying** How many years make up one term in office of a governor?

Executive Powers of the Governor

One **executive power** is to make appointments to **boards** and **commissions.** In a four-year term, the governor may make more than 4,000 appointments, each of which must be approved by two-thirds of the Senate.

The governor also has the power to remove certain officials, such as a judge engaged in serious misconduct. With the approval of the Senate, the governor can remove anyone he or she has appointed to a board or commission.

The governor's residence in Austin

Legislative Powers of the Governor

In addition to executive powers, the governor of Texas holds three important **legislative powers.** One is the power to send messages to the legislature. The governor speaks to the legislature at the opening of each regular session. In addition, the governor may send messages throughout the session. These speeches or documents usually explain the governor's policy goals. The legislature does not have to act on the governor's recommendations, however.

The veto power is one of the governor's legislative powers, providing an important check over the legislature. Just by threatening to veto a bill, the governor can influence the legislature to change a piece of legislation in a way that would make the governor's approval of the final version more likely. An important part of the governor's veto power is the line-item veto. This type of veto is allowed by the constitution and gives the governor the power to reject particular items in appropriations bills. Appropriations bills itemize how state money will be spent.

The governor also has the power to call special sessions of the legislature for emergency business. The governor decides what business needs to be done, and the legislature cannot consider any other topics unless the governor approves them. Because regular sessions are short and are held only every two years, a significant amount of business is completed during special sessions.

Making Predictions The top elected officials in Texas oversee the activities of numerous state agencies. *When might new state agencies be created?*

Other Powers of the Governor

The governor has certain powers that influence the judicial system. The governor appoints the members of the **Board of Pardons and Paroles,** the **Board of Criminal Justice,** the **Texas Youth Commission,** and other commissions that deal with offenders. The governor also can delay the execution date of prisoners or grant pardons. He or she can appoint judges to fill vacancies until regular elections are held.

The governor also serves as the **commander in chief** of Texas. This means that the governor is in charge of the Texas Guard, except when units are called into action for the National Guard. The Texas Guard includes the Army National Guard, the Texas Air National Guard, and the Texas State Guard.

Duties of Top Elected Officials of Texas	
Official	**Duties**
Governor	• Acts as chief executive of Texas • Makes appointments to boards and commissions • Removes officials when necessary • Signs or vetoes bills • Calls special sessions of the legislature • Serves as commander in chief • Represents Texas
Lieutenant Governor	• Acts as chief executive in governor's absence • Carries out duties as requested by governor • Serves as president of Texas Senate
Attorney General	• Acts as the state's lawyer • Represents Texas or Texas agency in court • Advises the legislature • Explains regulations to agencies and local governments
Comptroller of Public Accounts	• Serves as chief tax collector • Makes expenditures according to state regulations • Provides budget estimates to legislature
Commissioner of the General Land Office	• Manages the land and mineral rights owned by Texas
Commissioner of Agriculture	• Enforces agricultural laws • Provides educational and research services to farmers, ranchers, and consumers • Promotes Texas products • Protects the environment

Because the governor's presence lends importance to an occasion, hundreds of requests are received every year for his or her attendance at various functions. The governor represents Texas at meetings, celebrations, and ceremonies. The governor, for example, may attend the openings of new schools and present awards to honored citizens. With technology, the governor now can "attend" meetings without being present. In April 2001, Governor Rick Perry made history when his image was beamed from Austin to the University of Texas at Dallas using new "teleportation" technology. "I can't shake your hand, but I'm there with you," Perry told the audience.

Other Elected Members

In addition to the governor, five other members of the executive branch are chosen in statewide elections. Being elected rather than appointed means these officials are not as dependent on the governor. They are directly responsible to the people who voted for them. This is one reason the office of the governor of Texas is weaker than in many other states.

Texas's lieutenant governor is unique in that he or she is part of both the executive and the legislative branches of government. Unlike in most other states, he or she is elected separately from the governor and can belong to a different political party. The lieutenant governor assumes the powers and duties of the governor when the governor is not able to serve or is absent from the state. Most of the power of the lieutenant governor, however, comes from the fact that he or she is also president of the Texas Senate. In the Senate, the lieutenant governor can set state policy and influence the law-making process.

Other elected offices include the **attorney general,** the **comptroller of public accounts,** the **commissioner of the General Land Office,** and the **commissioner of agriculture.**

Boards and Commissions

The heads of boards and commissions are appointed by the governor or elected. The **State Board of Insurance,** the **Texas Transportation Commission,** the **Business and Economic Development Council,** and the **Railroad Commission** are some of the larger agencies. The **State Board of Education** manages and invests the $20 billion **Permanent School Fund** used to finance education in Texas public schools.

✓ **Reading Check** **Analyzing** Why is the office of the governor of Texas weaker than in many other states?

SECTION 2 ASSESSMENT

Checking for Understanding

1. **Using Key Terms** Write a news brief, using the terms commander in chief and line-item veto.
2. **Reviewing Facts** List three requirements necessary to become governor of Texas.

Reviewing Themes

3. **Government and Democracy** Name one reason why third-party candidates are usually not elected.

Organizing to Learn

4. **Creating Charts** Create a chart like the one shown here. List three legislative powers of the governor and three powers of the governor that influence the judicial branch.

Legislative	Judicial

Critical Thinking

5. **Evaluating** Why do some people say "the governor's most important power is the power to persuade"?
6. **Analyzing** How does the State Board of Education help finance the education of Texas students?

TAKS PRACTICE

Summarizing Make a list that summarizes the ways in which the governor represents the state.

Interpreting Political Cartoons

Why Learn the Skill?

Unlike a block of text that may take several minutes to read, a cartoon has an immediate impact on the viewer. This is one reason why newspapers regularly use cartoons to support or criticize current issues and public figures.

In political cartoons, artists use humor and satire to express opinions about political issues. The purpose of most political cartoons is to inform and influence public opinion in an entertaining way. Political cartoons often appear on the editorial pages of newspapers.

To interpret the meaning of a political cartoon, study its pictures, words, and symbols to discover the main idea and point of view. Cartoonists often exaggerate their drawings to make their points more forcefully. Cartoonists also use symbols. The figure of Uncle Sam, for example, is a symbol for the United States government.

Learning the Skill

Here are some steps to follow in interpreting political cartoons.

- Read the title and information in the cartoon to identify the topic.
- Analyze the symbols in the cartoon.
- Identify the main idea and the cartoonist's point of view.

Practicing the Skill

Study the cartoon on this page and answer the questions that follow.

1 How is Texas represented?

2 What is the title of the cartoon?

3 What is the man in the bottom right corner about to do?

4 How does the cartoonist portray the man?

5 What is the main point of this cartoon?

6 What is the cartoonist's point of view?

Tough Bird to Carve, 1964

TAKS PRACTICE

Interpreting Political Cartoons   Look in your local newspaper to find a political cartoon. They are often located in the news or opinion (editorial) sections. Decide what the main point is of the cartoon. Summarize the main point in a paragraph. Explain any symbols or figures and what you think they represent.

GO TO Glencoe's **Skillbuilder Interactive Workbook,** Level 1, provides instruction and practice in key social studies skills.

Financing State Government

Guide to Reading

Main Idea

The government of Texas requires a network of officials to plan and carry out the state's budget policies.

Key Terms

budget
fiscal
franchise tax
windfall

Reading Strategy

Identifying As you read this section, complete a web like the one shown here and indicate in which three areas most money is spent.

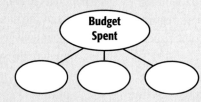

Budget Spent

Read to Learn

• what the state budget includes.
• which programs receive the largest share of the money.
• where the money comes from.

Section Theme

Government and Democracy The state legislature decides what share of the budget various state programs will receive.

Preview of Events

July	September	January	May	June
State agencies create budget requests for the next two years	Budget requests are discussed	Comptroller gives revenue estimate to legislature; general budget is submitted to legislature for approval	Legislature passes budget bill	Governor signs budget bill

College students on graduation day

A Texas Story

One of the most important decisions of the legislature is how to spend the money it collects in taxes. In the 77th Legislature, Senator Rodney Ellis used his power as chair of the Senate Finance Committee to "fund four priority items: a major Medicaid expansion, state employees' pay raises, teacher health insurance, and financial aid for college students."

—*The Texas Observer*, June 8, 2001

Setting the State Budget

Running a state government as large as that of Texas requires careful planning and budgeting. The state's budget sets economic and social priorities. It also estimates how much revenue the state expects to take in and how much it may spend. The budget determines which programs will grow, shrink, or be eliminated. If the state does not manage its money wisely, services essential to the citizens of Texas may not get adequately funded. For example, roads and schools can deteriorate, neighborhoods can suffer the effects of decreased spending on law enforcement, and the economy can weaken.

The Budget Process

A budget is a plan for how much one expects to earn and how one proposes to spend the earnings. In most states, the governor draws up the budget. In Texas, the governor shares this power with a legislative committee that has the job of proposing a budget to the legislature. Except in unusual circumstances, two-year budgets for Texas government are set during the regular session of the legislature. Budget planning begins long before that, however. Usually, 12 months before the legislature meets, every agency that spends state funds reports to the **Legislative Budget Board** and to the **Governor's Office of Budget and Planning.** The agencies list their past expenses and estimate what they will need for the next two years. This can be very difficult because the demand for government services may change over time. Agencies must anticipate those changes. After the agencies' requests have been

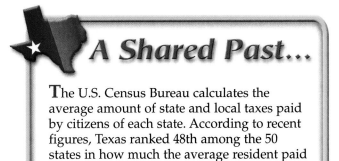

studied and other groups have weighed in with their requests, a budget bill is submitted to the legislative committee for consideration. The bill then follows the legislative process.

How the State Spends Money

In the 77th Legislature, a House–Senate budget committee created a 2002–2003 state budget of nearly $114 billion that was 11.6 percent larger than the prior budget. For the 2002–2003 fiscal (financial) year, education accounted for 31 percent of the budget. This budget included money for state employees' raises, improving Medicaid

People of Texas

Rick Perry 1950–

Former lieutenant governor Rick Perry became governor of Texas in 2000 when George W. Bush left the governor's office to become president. Before taking office as lieutenant governor, Perry served in the Texas House of Representatives and as

Texas commissioner of agriculture. Perry believes that he has achieved success in his life because of his education. As governor, he wants to expand educational opportunities for all school children in Texas.

Rick Perry did not start his career in politics. He

came from a ranching and farming family. He attended Texas A&M University and earned a degree in animal science. After graduating, he served in the U.S. Air Force as a pilot. After leaving the service, he worked on the family ranch near Abilene.

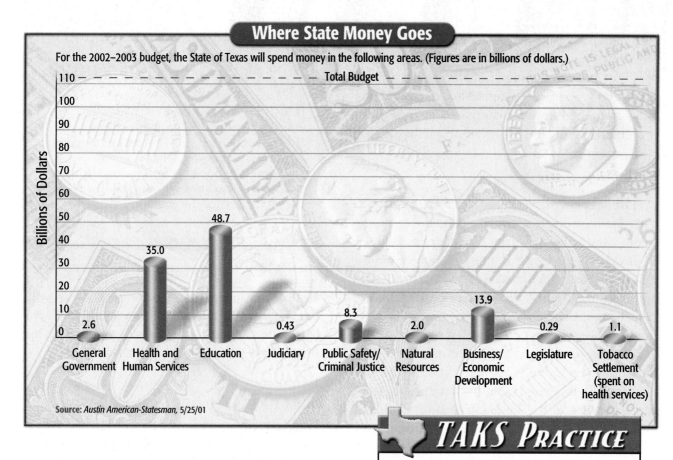

Where State Money Goes

For the 2002–2003 budget, the State of Texas will spend money in the following areas. (Figures are in billions of dollars.)

Billions of Dollars

Total Budget

General Government	2.6
Health and Human Services	35.0
Education	48.7
Judiciary	0.43
Public Safety/Criminal Justice	8.3
Natural Resources	2.0
Business/Economic Development	13.9
Legislature	0.29
Tobacco Settlement (spent on health services)	1.1

Source: *Austin American-Statesman*, 5/25/01

eligibility for children, and an insurance plan for some teachers. Funds for health, economic development, and criminal justice programs are also major expenses.

Reading Check **Describing** What are some of the items in the state budget?

Where the State Gets Its Money

A general sales tax produces the most revenue. The amount of the tax varies with the price of the item or services sold. Food and medicine are not taxed. The tax on motor fuels, such as gasoline and diesel, makes up the second largest source of tax revenue. Taxes on the sale of motor vehicles and manufactured housing are third. Taxes on utility services, alcoholic beverages, and tobacco products provide revenue as well.

The major tax on business in Texas is the franchise tax. This tax is based on the value of machinery and equipment that businesses use to produce income. Businesses that provide only services pay little or no franchise tax. Texas's change to a service economy has made the franchise tax less important.

Texas also receives money from sources other than taxes. A major source of revenue for education spending is the Texas Lottery. From the sale of the first ticket in May 1992 through the end of 2000, over $8 billion in revenue was raised through the lottery. In addition, Texas receives many grants from the federal government. Revenue also comes from the sale, rental, and leasing of land and mineral rights. The investment of state funds yields additional revenue. Fees for state services and permits are another source.

Sometimes the state receives money from unexpected sources. A 1998 tobacco lawsuit settlement will give Texas millions of dollars over 25 years. This kind of windfall, though, does not happen every day.

People of Texas

Bill Ratliff 1936-

Former state senator Bill Ratliff became lieutenant governor of Texas in 2000 when Rick Perry left the office to become the governor. It was the first time in Texas history that the state Senate elected one of its own members to become lieutenant governor. As a state senator, Ratliff proposed the "Robin Hood" bill in 1993, which then became law. It forced the state's wealthiest school districts to share their wealth with the poorest districts.

Bill Ratliff graduated from the University of Texas with a degree in civil engineering. He has practiced as an engineer for over 35 years. He has also served as an engineering professor and has shared his expertise on civil engineering matters with the United States Congress.

Influences on the Process

Many people and factors influence the budget process. Federal decisions affect state budgets. For example, if the federal government set a water pollution standard different from the state standard, Texas may have to put more money into cleaning waterways than it would otherwise. Court decisions at the federal and state levels also may direct what the state can and cannot do. In a famous case, a federal judge required Texas to spend more money to build more prisons after a Texas prisoner had filed suit protesting overcrowded prison cells. The state courts might say that the legislature may not use money in certain ways. In addition, individuals and groups through special lobby efforts work to promote their interests with legislators. They pressure budget officials on many important issues.

✓ **Reading Check** **Identifying** List the major types of taxes that provide revenue for Texas.

SECTION 3 ASSESSMENT

Checking for Understanding

1. **Using Key Terms** Use the term franchise tax in a sentence to demonstrate your understanding of the term.
2. **Reviewing Facts** Identify the two principal items on which Texas spends the majority of its money.

Reviewing Themes

3. **Government and Democracy** Identify three or more of the factors influencing the budget process.

Organizing to Learn

4. **Identifying** Create a web like the one shown and identify which taxes bring in the largest amount of revenue.

```
        (        )
    (        )        (        )
            ( Taxes )
    (        )        (        )
```

Critical Thinking

5. **Evaluating** Refer to the "Where State Money Goes" chart on page 648. If you wanted to increase the money given to education, explain whose budget you would decrease and why.

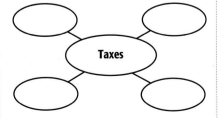

TAKS PRACTICE

Considering Options The state budget is regularly reviewed and changed. If you could change amounts of money the budget allows next year, what would you change and why would you do so?

Chapter Summary

Texas State Government

The Legislative Branch

Structure
- Made up of House of Representatives and Senate
- Speaker of the House heads the House of Representatives
- Lieutenant Governor heads the Senate
- Meets every two years

Function
- Approves or rejects governor's appointments
- Reviews actions of other branches of government
- Redraws legislative and congressional districts
- Considers resolutions and bills
- Estimates revenue and expenses for the state and creates budget
- Receives money from sales taxes, the federal government, land leases, and mineral rights

The Executive Branch

Structure
- Governor is the head of the executive branch
- Serves for four years

Function
- Carries out approved legislation
- Conducts business of the state
- Appoints boards and commissions
- Serves as commander in chief
- May veto or line-item veto bills
- Calls special sessions of the legislature when necessary

Reviewing Key Terms

Create a crossword puzzle, complete with numbered clues. Hint: start with the longest words.

1. bicameral
2. commander in chief
3. franchise tax
4. line-item veto
5. oversight
6. redistricting
7. resolution

Reviewing Key Facts

8. Identify the two governing bodies in the state legislature.
9. List three important state matters that are overseen by committees of the Texas Senate.
10. Why does redistricting cause so many arguments in the Texas legislature?
11. How many four-year terms of office may a governor serve?
12. When may the governor NOT command the Texas Guard?
13. What might happen if the state does not manage its money wisely?
14. What must state agencies submit as part of the budget process?

Critical Thinking

15. **Evaluating** If you were developing a budget for Texas, what would be your number one budget concern? Why?
16. **Categorizing** Create a web like the one shown below. Describe three ways that the governor can influence a bill before it reaches a vote.

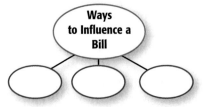

Ways to Influence a Bill

17. **Developing Citizenship Skills** Why is it important for each citizen to pay his or her share of taxes?

Refer to the graph on page 648, "Where State Money Goes," to answer the following questions.

18. **Making Inferences** What departments might provide funds for protecting our water supply?
19. **Making Inferences** Which fund supplies money to support people in need?

Geography and History Activity

Research and answer the questions below about Texas legislative districts:

20. In what House and Senate legislative districts do you live?

21. Who are your representatives in the House and in the Senate?

Portfolio/TAKS Writing Activity

22. Persuasive Writing Politicians usually need to campaign during an election. Press releases, speeches, posters, brochures, and advertisements promote the politician as a worthy candidate. Choose a political position that interests you and, through a press release, poster, brochure, speech, or advertisement, explain how and why you would be an ideal candidate for that office.

Cooperative Learning Activity

23. Sequencing Working in groups of two to four, create a board game to illustrate how a bill becomes a law. Hint: look at commercially prepared games for ideas.

Practicing Skills

Interpreting Political Cartoons *Study the political cartoon below and answer the questions that follow.*

24. What do the figures in the cartoon represent?

25. What is the woman in the middle picture doing?

26. Are the cooks doing a good job? Explain.

TEXAS HISTORY Online

Self-Check Quiz
Visit the texans.glencoe.com Web site and click on
Chapter 29—Self-Check Quizzes to prepare for the chapter test.

Use the chart below to answer the following question.

Texas Tax Revenues in 1997 and 1998

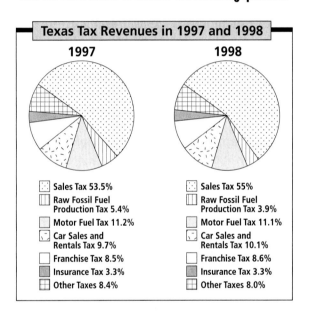

1997	1998
Sales Tax 53.5%	Sales Tax 55%
Raw Fossil Fuel Production Tax 5.4%	Raw Fossil Fuel Production Tax 3.9%
Motor Fuel Tax 11.2%	Motor Fuel Tax 11.1%
Car Sales and Rentals Tax 9.7%	Car Sales and Rentals Tax 10.1%
Franchise Tax 8.5%	Franchise Tax 8.6%
Insurance Tax 3.3%	Insurance Tax 3.3%
Other Taxes 8.4%	Other Taxes 8.0%

Which taxes raised a smaller portion of Texas's tax revenues in 1998 than they did in 1997?

A Taxes on the sale of goods

B Taxes on franchises

C Taxes on insurance

D Taxes on petroleum products

Test-Taking Tip:

Compare the 1997 tax percentage to the 1998 tax percentage for each answer choice. Eliminate answer choices in which the tax percentage was not lower in 1998 than it was in 1997. Make sure you consider all of the choices in order to avoid making a careless mistake. The answer choice that remains is the correct answer.

Economics & History

Preserving Our Past

City governments are responsible for a variety of services that affect people's daily lives. Law enforcement officials make sure that all laws are enforced. Transportation departments maintain city roads, traffic signals, and highway signs. In addition to many duties that meet the needs of its citizens, many city governments also raise funds to promote cultural life in their communities. Some, like the city government of San Angelo, Texas, become involved in preserving history.

In San Angelo, the current city council makes available more than $300,000 for the upkeep of the buildings that are part of Fort Concho. The fort was established in 1867, even before the town existed. When the federal government closed the fort down in 1889, citizens of the town began to use the buildings for houses and businesses. In 1930, however, a local resident by the name of Ginevra Wood Carson opened a museum in one of the historic buildings.

History Is Preserved

Five years later, the San Angelo city government decided to help Mrs. Carson preserve old Fort Concho. By then, the fort was located inside the city limits close to the downtown area. Over the years, through fundraisers and special events, private citizens of the town had raised money to buy the fort's original buildings. Finally, in 1967, the city council got involved. A staff of professional artists and historians was hired to see that the fort was restored to how it looked in the 1870s and 1880s.

Why would the San Angelo city government take an interest in something so old? Like Texans all over, San Angeloans have pride in their heritage. They believe in preserving their links with the past. Today, the fort is used for civic programs and local festivities. The city also uses the fort as a cultural center.

Tourist Attraction

San Angelo sees the fort as a way to raise money for the town's citizens. Many tourists come to visit Fort Concho and spend money in the area. During the annual festival called "Christmas at Old Fort Concho," visitors stay at

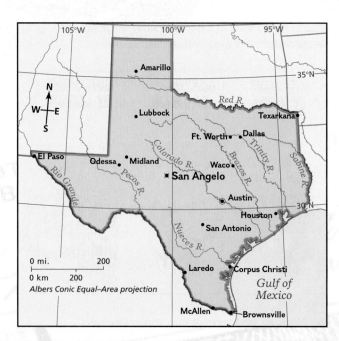

Fort Concho is located in the town of San Angelo. The frontier fort is one of the best preserved in the United States.

Fort Concho was established before the town of San Angelo was founded.

Today, the preserved fort is a source of civic pride for citizens of San Angelo.

local hotels and eat at the city's many restaurants. The chamber of commerce proudly shows off Fort Concho to companies thinking of moving to San Angelo.

City employees run the fort. They perform many duties to ensure that it serves as a symbol of civic pride. They also work hard to see that the fort is profitable for the city. They prepare exhibits, organize special events throughout the year, and maintain the grounds and buildings in attractive condition. With money received from fundraisers, the staff sponsors education programs, including a living history program that features stories about the buffalo soldiers.

Using What They Know

Many of those employed at the fort studied history in college and apply what they learned in school to the study and preservation of Texas's frontier heritage. Several people have the job of preserving original records and maintaining the fort library. They help researchers working on books about life in West Texas. They also assist those who cannot come to the fort in person but who want to access information through the Internet.

A city council can play a role in society besides governing. To undertake historic

preservation as San Angelo has, governments must use part of their budget for salaries for staff members. Fort Concho staff, for example, receives most of the benefits other city workers do, including health care and retirement benefits. Out-of-town travel expenses are also covered by the city when necessary. The real "pay off"—according to those who work there—is that Fort Concho professionals get paid while doing something they love.

TAKS PRACTICE

1. **Making Generalizations**   What responsibility does city government have to preserve a city's history?
2. **Making Inferences**   What civic projects might your city consider?
3. **Writing About Economics**   Write a paragraph that develops one of the themes below. Use standard grammar, spelling, sentence structure, and punctuation.
   a. Studying history can lead to an exciting present-day career.
   b. People go to school to learn a craft or a profession.
   c. City governments should spend money on cultural projects that involve preserving their cities' histories.

Local Government

Why It Matters

Government services such as education, law enforcement, street maintenance, and public health are usually provided by local units of government such as cities, counties, and school boards.

The Impact Today

Although counties were established when Texas was mainly a rural state, county governments have adapted to meet the new problems and challenges of urban Texas. Cities, too, have developed different ways to organize themselves to ensure the highest level of service for their citizens. Governments at every level work best when citizens keep informed and get involved.

Texas

1929
★ League of United Latin American Citizens founded

1947
★ Houston adopted strong mayor-council city government

United States

1923

1947

1963

World

1923
• Equal Rights Amendment first proposed

1945
• United Nations organization formed

1963
• Martin Luther King, Jr., organized March on Washington

Houston, Texas's largest city, boasts a strong mayor-council city government and an impressive skyline.

2001
★ *Bob Bullock Texas State History Museum opened in Austin*

1982   1989   1995   2002

1982
• *Equal Rights Amendment defeated*

1989
• *Chinese students protested at Tiananmen Square*

1994
• *Nelson Mandela elected president of South Africa*

TEXAS HISTORY Online

Chapter Overview
Visit the texans.glencoe.com Web site and click on **Chapter 30—Chapter Overviews** to preview chapter information.

SECTION 1

Types of Local Government

Guide to Reading

Main Idea

Local government affects everyday life in neighborhoods and cities.

Key Terms

general-law city, home-rule city, mayor-council, ordinance, council-manager, commission, appraise, commissioners court, precinct, real estate

Reading Strategy

Organizing Information Complete a chart like the one shown here. Fill in three of the services provided by each type of local government.

County Government	City Government	Special Government Districts

Read to Learn

- about the different types of local governments.
- about county officials.
- about special districts.

Section Theme

Government and Democracy Types of local government include county government, city government, and special government districts.

Preview of Events

1901 — Sweetwater incorporates as a commission city

Dallas becomes a council-manager city government

1931

Houston adopts a strong-mayor-council form of city government

1947 — San Antonio becomes a council-manager city government

1951

Marcus Puente

A Texas Story

After two years working for the Yorktown school district in Dewitt County and hearing co-workers' complaints, Marcus Puente decided to take action. With three seats on the school board up for election, Puente threw his hat in the ring. He was one of six candidates. A 2000 honors graduate at Yorktown High School, Puente had no political experience. With help from friends and family, he hit the campaign trail. "People started listening to me because nobody else really knew how everybody in the community felt," he said.

Local Governments at Work

Local government affects people on a day-to-day basis. Services provided by local government include police protection, garbage collection, water and sewer services, education, and fire protection. If your house is on fire, you call your local fire department, not someone in Washington, D.C. When garbage is not picked up, local government is responsible for restoring service. There are three basic types of local governments in Texas—city, county, and special districts.

Two Kinds of City Government

Some cities and towns are called **municipalities.** If a city government incorporates by citizen request, it is considered a **municipal** government. Cities in Texas operate under one of two types of law—general law or home rule. Small cities with populations of less than 5,000 may incorporate as a general-law city. As of 2002, there were nearly 1,000 general-law cities in Texas. These cities function under the general laws of Texas and often provide basic services such as police, fire protection, and water and sewer service.

A home-rule city may organize itself and conduct its business in any way its citizens see fit, as long as no state or federal laws are violated. Approximately one-fourth of Texas cities are home-rule cities. Such cities try to increase their tax bases by becoming larger. One way to do this is to annex, or take over, nearby land. Texas law, however, states that city services must be provided to newly added areas within four and one-half years. This is to ensure that people living in the newly annexed areas fully share in the benefits that the city government already provides to those living in the longer established parts of the city. Some annexations are not popular with the residents. Efforts are being made to change the state laws so that people living in an area have more to say about what happens to their town.

TEXAS HISTORY Online

Student Web Activity Visit the texans.glencoe.com Web site and click on **Chapter 30—Student Web Activity** to learn more about a mayor's duties.

Organization of City Governments

Three common forms of city governments in Texas include **mayor-council, council-manager,** and **commission.**

The mayor-council city government is used by some cities in Texas. This model gives the mayor executive authority. There are strong-mayor and weak-mayor types of this form. In a **strong-mayor city,** the mayor is responsible for day-to-day operations, hiring and firing department heads, and vetoing city council actions. Houston and El Paso are strong-mayor cities.

Exploring **Government**

Firefighters provide valuable services to city and county residents. What are some of the ways that firefighters assist local communities?

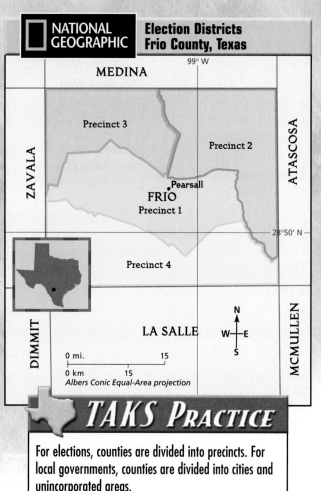

NATIONAL GEOGRAPHIC Election Districts
Frio County, Texas

MEDINA

99° W

ZAVALA

Precinct 3

Precinct 2

ATASCOSA

•Pearsall
FRIO
Precinct 1

28°50' N

Precinct 4

DIMMIT

LA SALLE

MCMULLEN

N
W—E
S

0 mi.   15
0 km   15
Albers Conic Equal-Area projection

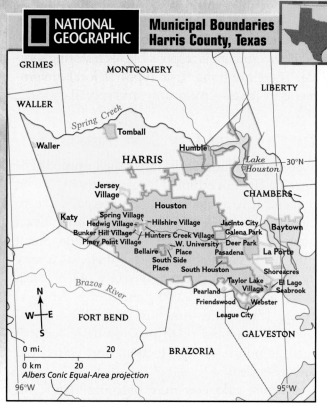

NATIONAL GEOGRAPHIC Municipal Boundaries
Harris County, Texas

GRIMES

MONTGOMERY

LIBERTY

WALLER

Spring Creek

Tomball

Waller

Humble

HARRIS

Lake Houston

30°N

Jersey Village

CHAMBERS

Houston

Katy

Spring Village
Hedwig Village
Bunker Hill Village
Piney Point Village

Hilshire Village

Hunters Creek Village

Jacinto City
Galena Park

Baytown

W. University Place

Deer Park

Bellaire
South Side Place

Pasadena

La Porte

South Houston

Brazos River

Taylor Lake Village

Shoreacres
El Lago
Seabrook

Pearland
Friendswood

Webster

N
W—E
S

FORT BEND

League City

GALVESTON

0 mi.   20
0 km   20
Albers Conic Equal-Area projection

BRAZORIA

96°W

95°W

TAKS PRACTICE

For elections, counties are divided into precincts. For local governments, counties are divided into cities and unincorporated areas.
Analyzing Do you think Harris County would have fewer or more election districts than Frio County? Why?

Houston first started using this model in 1947. In **weak-mayor cities,** the mayor shares administrative duties with the city council. City councils regularly consider ordinances, or local laws, that address health and public safety.

In council-manager cities, generally home-ruled ones, the mayor has less power, presiding over council meetings and having only one vote, like the other council members. Dallas is the largest city in the United States to use this type of local government, having adopted it in 1931. San Antonio changed to this structure in 1951. In these cities, the city council hires a professional city manager to manage the day-to-day affairs of the city and prepare the city budget. He or she can hire and fire city employees.

In commission cities, voters elect commissioners to operate the government. The commissioners serve as a city council, yet each member is

also head of a department, such as public safety or human services. The mayor has little power, presiding over meetings and acting as a spokesperson for the council. If commissioners follow different goals, it is difficult to coordinate city policies. Commission city government is the least common form of local government in Texas. It was often used in the early part of the century. Both Galveston and Sweetwater adopted this form in 1901.

City Governments Need Funds

Local governments need money to operate and provide services for their citizens. Cities have several sources of revenue, the most important of which is **property taxes.** These taxes are paid by the owners of land, houses, and other buildings and depend on the financial worth of the property. Tax assessors inspect the property, appraise, or determine the value, and make recommendations to the city.

Cities can also charge a sales tax on the value of goods sold within the city. Other sources of revenue include fees for services such as garbage collection, hospital care, and use of parks. Building permits and fines collected from traffic violations are also a source of money.

Local governments in Texas spend their money on police and fire protection, jail maintenance, parks, streets, sanitation, recycling, storm drainage, bridges, animal shelters, libraries, museums, and airports. When money is needed for special long-term projects, such as building a convention center or sports arena, governments may issue **bonds,** certificates that guarantee payment plus interest, or ask for state or federal assistance.

✓ **Reading Check** **Identifying** Name five services that taxes pay for in local governments.

County Government

The county level of government was originally created to establish laws and procedures for rural areas. The county remains the most important unit of local government. All 254 counties in Texas exist as administrative areas of the state and are staffed by locally elected officials.

One of the most important responsibilities of county governments is to help the state government fulfill its duties. County officials help collect state taxes, handle important election matters, and issue licenses. County courthouses maintain records of births, deaths, marriages, and property ownership. Every Texas county works with state and federal agencies to provide a wide variety of services and programs for its citizens.

TAKS PRACTICE

Describing County department heads oversee many important functions. *Which county official would hear minor criminal or civil cases?*

County Officials

The Texas constitution requires that the government be set up the same way in every county. The most important governing body is the commissioners court, responsible for determining the county's budget, setting the property-tax rate, and deciding how tax monies are spent.

Each county in Texas is divided into four districts, or precincts, that elect one county commissioner each. The commissioners serve four-year terms. The county judge, responsible for the day-to-day administration of the county, is elected in a county-wide election and also serves a four-year term. The county judge heads the commissioners court.

The commissioners court does not conduct trials. Instead, it makes policies and directs

Elected County Officials

County Official	Job Description and Duties
Commissioner	Four commissioners comprise each commissioners court. They make policies and direct county business, including approving budgets and setting tax rates.
County Judge	The chief administrator of the court. Heads the commissioners court, prepares budgets for approval, serves as judge of the county court, performs special election duties.
Sheriff	A county's chief law-enforcement officer. Along with deputies (in larger counties), manages county jails and prisoners.
County Attorney	Serves as legal adviser to other county officials and represents the county in criminal cases.
County Clerk	Maintains records of the county courts and registers births, deaths, marriages, divorces, and property transfers. Prepares election ballots. Registers voters.
District Clerk	Keeps the records of the state district courts.
Treasurer	Acts as the county's banker, receives money, and pays the county's bills.
Tax Assessor	Collects property taxes and license fees. Issues automobile titles.
Justice of the Peace	Larger counties have four to eight justices of the peace who hear minor criminal and civil cases. Small counties may have only one.
Constable	Serves official papers issued by the courts.

county business. Among the projects the commissioners court works on are building and repairing roads and bridges, operating the courthouse and jail, and maintaining county hospitals, museums, libraries, parks, and airports. The chart on page 659 shows the major county officials in Texas and their duties.

Financing County Government

Counties rely on two important sources of revenue—property taxes and bonds. The state permits counties to collect taxes on most **real estate** property (buildings and land). Property taxes are the most important source of county revenue. Personal property, such as automobiles and airplanes, may also be taxed. The commissioners court sets the tax rate for the county. Counties also can raise money by issuing bonds after voter approval. Bonds pay for long-term construction projects. Other sources of income for counties include fees for various permits, taxes on fuel, and fees for vehicle registration.

County budgets, drawn up by the county judge and approved by the commissioners court, address the needs of each particular county. Fast-growing counties may set aside more funds for roads and bridges. Counties with high crime rates may spend more on law enforcement, courts, and jails.

Special Districts

Special districts are created to meet a specific need. They are the most numerous of all government units. School districts, rapid transit authorities, municipal utility districts, river authorities, and water control and improvement districts are all types of special districts.

School districts are the most common kind of special district. Each of the 1,000-plus school districts in Texas is directed by an elected board of trustees, commonly called the **school board.** The trustees have the power to select school superintendents, make school policies, hire teachers, set salaries, maintain school buildings, and provide transportation to and from schools.

Money for school districts comes from federal, state, and local funds. In the 1990s, Texas was under court order to change its method of distributing state funds to schools. The changes were intended to shift money available per student from richer school districts to poorer ones. Critics of this program called this the "Robin Hood Plan," named after the legendary outlaw who "took from the rich and gave to the poor."

Community college districts support the development of junior or community colleges. These districts have a separate board of trustees.

✓ **Reading Check** **Explaining** Where do school districts get their funding?

SECTION 1 ASSESSMENT

Checking for Understanding

1. **Using Key Terms** Use the words **appraise** and **real estate** in one sentence that shows you understand what they mean.
2. **Reviewing Facts** What are the duties of the county treasurer?

Reviewing Themes

3. **Government and Democracy** How does county government help the state government?

Organizing to Learn

4. **Summarizing** Create a chart like the one below. List the sources of money for local government and how local governments spend the money.

Sources of Money	How Money Is Spent

Critical Thinking

5. **Contrasting** How are general-law cities different from home-rule cities?
6. **Analyzing** Why do some cities choose to incorporate?

TAKS PRACTICE

Analyzing Why can special districts often meet the needs of citizens better than a city or county government can?

Analyzing Newspaper Articles

Why Learn This Skill?

Newspaper articles are important sources of information about today's events. In addition, they are important primary sources about the past.

News articles begin with a headline, which is a short phrase that tells the main point; a byline, which is the writer's name; and often a dateline, which tells where and when the story was written. The first paragraph is the "lead." It addresses the main topic of the article. Other paragraphs add details. The writer will often quote people who have differing views. Newswriters try to be objective, writing only facts and not their own personal opinions.

Learning the Skill

- Read the headline, the byline, and the dateline
- Read the "lead" to determine the main topic
- Identify other important details

Practicing the Skill

Read this article from the April 16, 2001, *New York Times,* then answer the questions.

At a time when nearly every major city in Texas is desperate for more water to meet runaway population growth, Mr. [T. Boone] Pickens is proposing to pump tens of billions of gallons—to the highest bidder . . .

"Water is the lifeblood of West Texas," said Mr. Pickens, 72, who is courting Fort Worth, Dallas, San Antonio, and El Paso as potential customers and estimates that a deal could reap $1 billion . . .

"For decades the gold beneath the ground in Texas was oil. But if oil built modern Texas, water is now needed to sustain it."

. . . "You're going to devastate a large part of the state of Texas," said Tom Beard, a rancher. He feared that arid West Texas could be pumped dry by water ranches owned by distant cities . . .

❶ What is the main subject of the article?

❷ What two sources does the writer quote and what arguments do those sources make?

Nearly dry riverbed in the Rio Grande system

GO TO

TAKS PRACTICE

Analyzing Newspaper Articles   Read this paragraph from the same article, and then answer the questions below.

The political debate is complicated. Environmentalists want more conservation and tougher regulation, as opposed to new dams and aggressive pumping of groundwater. There are the competing demands of agriculture and urban areas. There are also differing needs and climates in the state's various regions . . .

1. Identify the main issues in the paragraph.
2. Decide your view of the issue and share with the class.

Glencoe's **Skillbuilder Interactive Workbook,** Level 1, provides instruction and practice in key social studies skills.

Participation in Government

Main Idea

Many opportunities exist for Texans to participate in government and politics.

Key Terms

nonpartisan election
watchdog role
special interest groups

Reading Strategy

Organizing Information As you read this section, complete a web to show how Texas residents can participate in government.

Ways to Participate

Read to Learn

• about citizen participation.
• about political parties and special interest groups.
• about the election process.

Section Theme

Civic Rights and Responsibilities All Texans have the right and duty to participate in government on some level.

Preview of Events

♦1919 — League of Women Voters of Texas forms

♦1929 — League of United Latin American Citizens is founded

A
Texas Story

Yorktown school board, 2000

Marcus Puente received the second-highest vote total among the field of six candidates in the school board election. The University of Texas at San Antonio sophomore is now a member of the school board for Yorktown, which has 700 students from kindergarten to 12th grade. Puente, who turned 19 when elected, is one of the youngest—if not *the* youngest—school trustee in the state. By law, school board members in Texas must be at least 18.

Democratic Principles

Both the United States and Texas were founded on the principle that citizens should govern themselves. The founders fought for and established democratic governments for the nation and the state. Today Texans have the right and duty to support their democratic government. This right too often is taken for granted.

A democratic government is founded on three important beliefs. One is that the needs and opinions of each citizen are important. Another is that citizens have different needs, values, and experiences that government should consider if it is to serve all the people. Third, a democratic government is founded on the belief that citizens should participate in government.

Individual Participation

Government officials perform their jobs more effectively when they know what the people want. Citizens can learn about their government from many sources. They can watch television, listen to the radio, read newspapers and magazines, and talk to their friends and neighbors. People can then express the views they formed by talking to or writing to government officials and employees. An important way to express concerns is by voting. Citizens help make many important decisions when they vote. Voters elect individuals to carry out specific government tasks. To vote in Texas elections, a person must be a native-born or naturalized citizen of the United States and 18 years or older on election day. He or she must also be a resident of the state and county and be registered to vote for at least 30 days before election day.

Many people are involved in government through volunteer work, an important activity in which citizens can make a difference. Volunteers read to young children at public libraries, help in city cleanup campaigns, answer phones at crisis hot lines, and volunteer in political campaigns.

✓ **Reading Check** **Examining** How is voting an expression of individual participation in government?

Running for Political Office

Any Texan who wants to serve as an elected official must campaign to win voter support. Campaigns are excellent opportunities for candidates and voters to express their opinions and concerns. Some officials in government receive salaries, while others donate their time to help meet the needs of other citizens. While serving as state treasurer, Ann Richards spoke about citizens becoming involved:

❝People come up to me and want me to teach them what I know. As if what I know is something in that great magical beyond. It is nothing more than establishing a goal, taking the risk to go after that goal, and putting the money together to pay for it.❞

Political Parties in Texas

Voting is one of the most important ways to participate in a democracy. The chart on page 664 describes the four types of elections that take place in Texas—**primary elections, general elections, special elections,** and **local elections.** In nonpartisan elections, candidates are not identified by any particular party.

One of the most important ways citizens can affect government decision making is by taking part in **political parties.** The ideas and actions of each individual citizen are important. Today there are many opportunities for citizens to become involved and to influence government.

Political parties serve several functions. One of the most important is to nominate people to run for public office. Political parties campaign for their candidates both in general elections and in special elections. They encourage volunteers to campaign, to participate in party activities, and to conduct voter registration drives.

A Shared Past...

A key event in expanding political participation occurred in 1971. That was the year of the passage of the Twenty-sixth Amendment to the Constitution of the United States. Under the provisions of the amendment, persons who are 18 years of age or older cannot be excluded from voting because of age.

Once elections have been held, political parties play an important part in organizing government. Political parties help to staff the government by recommending qualified candidates for positions that need to be filled.

The parties work to unite government leaders so they can better carry out their duties. Members of Congress who belong to the same party meet regularly to choose leaders and to decide new policy strategies. They discuss common problems and possible plans of action.

Another activity of political parties is to monitor, or keep track of, other parties. This is called the watchdog role. Each party tries to keep informed about the work of others, reporting practices or decisions with which it disagrees. This process helps to keep the citizens informed.

Until recently, the **Democratic Party** was dominant in Texas. Now both the **Republican Party** and the Democratic Party compete for voter support. Texans benefit from having active political parties. The parties work hard to recruit good candidates and to publicize important issues. The political parties also encourage citizens to participate in campaigns and elections. In addition to the Democratic and Republican Parties, other parties have appeared on Texas ballots in recent years, including the Reform Party, Libertarian Party, and the Green Party.

✓ **Reading Check** **Summarizing** What are the roles of political parties?

Special Interest Groups

Special interest groups (SIGs) are organizations of people who share a common interest and seek to exert influence over a particular aspect of government. SIGs might be formed to promote a particular industry, or to influence a particular political matter like civil rights for minorities or environmental protection.

Although SIGs are similar to political parties, their focus is generally narrower and more specific. Another important difference between SIGs and political parties has to do with their activities. One of the main functions of political parties is to nominate and elect

Types of Elections and What You Should Know About Them

Primary elections	Candidates from the same political party compete against each other. Each party's primary winner runs in the general election.
General elections	Held on the first Tuesday after the first Monday of November in even-numbered years. Voters elect government leaders at the national and state levels. Statewide officials are elected in nonpresidential years. Citizens may be asked to vote on proposed laws or special issues.
Special elections	Held to fill vacancies in the Texas legislature or the U.S. Congress. Held to approve local bond proposals, taxes, and constitutional amendments. Held to fill vacancies of city councils, school boards, and community college boards
Local elections	Held to elect city council members, mayors, school board members, and special district boards; usually nonpartisan

TAKS PRACTICE

Identifying Elections are a very important part of the democratic process. Citizens express their opinions about candidates and issues through their votes. *Name the school board members who were most recently elected in your school district.*

candidates to office. Although SIGs may support candidates, their main goal is to influence public officials.

People are motivated to join SIGs if they think there is a potential benefit. For example, labor groups work to advance their rights or increase wages. Racial and ethnic groups promote political, economic, and social equality for their members.

Political interest groups focus on a variety of issues. Women's groups, such as the **Texas League of Women Voters,** founded in 1919, publish reliable voter information. Religious groups promote government policies in agreement with their beliefs. Groups like the Sierra Club seek to achieve and maintain clean air and water. The oldest and largest Hispanic group, the **League of United Latin American Citizens** (LULAC), founded in 1929, has worked hard to ensure social justice and equal educational opportunities for Latinos. The **NAACP Texas State Conference** formed in 1937 to help its local branches continue their work in registering African American voters and working for civil rights legislation.

Exploring **Government**

These citizens met at the State Capitol to lobby against a motorcycle helmet law. **How else can citizens show their support or opposition to a bill or law?**

Directly Influencing Government

An important way interest groups work toward their goals is by electing government leaders whose views agree with their own. Interest groups may recruit or encourage particular candidates, publicly endorse candidates, contribute money to campaigns, or encourage members to serve as campaign volunteers.

Interest groups also work for their goals by gaining public support. They may purchase advertisements on radio and television and in magazines and newspapers. Interest groups might hold public events to make their point and shape public opinion. Another way interest groups work toward their goals is through lobbying, trying to persuade government leaders to favor a certain cause. **Lobbyists** may appear before legislative committees, testify in court hearings, and visit legislators and other officials. Some interest groups hire professional lobbyists. In other groups, members volunteer. Any lobbyist who spends a certain amount of time or money must register with the secretary of state, and all lobbyists must follow certain regulations.

✓ **Reading Check** **Identifying** What is a lobbyist?

SECTION 2 ASSESSMENT

Checking for Understanding

1. **Using Key Terms** Write a sentence for each of the following terms: **nonpartisan, watchdog role, special interest group.**
2. **Reviewing Facts** When are general elections held?

Reviewing Themes

3. **Civic Rights and Responsibilities** On which three important beliefs is a democratic government founded?

Organizing to Learn

4. **Categorizing** Create a chart like the one shown here and fill in the blanks to show the purpose of each type of election (why it is held).

Type of Election	Purpose
Primary	
General	
Special	
Local	

Critical Thinking

5. **Drawing Inferences** Why do we consider voting not just a right but also a duty?
6. **Evaluating** Why would lobbyists need to register with the secretary of state?

TAKS PRACTICE

Analyzing Write a paragraph that describes the role of a lobbyist.

Chapter Summary

Local Government

Types of Cities
- General-law
- Home-rule

Types of City Governments
- Mayor-council
  - strong-mayor city
  - weak-mayor city
- Council-manager
- Commission

Sources of Revenue for Cities and Counties
- Taxes
- Fees
- Bonds
- State government
- Federal government

Types of Special Districts
- School districts
- Water districts
- Transportation districts

Types of Elections
- Primary elections
- General elections
- Special elections
- Local elections

Types of Political Groups
- Volunteer groups
- Political parties
- Special Interest Groups (SIGs)

Reviewing Key Terms

Choose from the following words to fill in the blanks in the three spaces below: appraise, nonpartisan, special interest group, bonds, ordinance, commissioners court.

1. Local governments often receive funding from _____.
2. Elections for local government offices usually are _____.
3. Tax assessors _____ property.

Reviewing Key Facts

4. Describe the differences between the council-manager, mayor-council (strong and weak), and commission forms of city governments.
5. What conditions must be met in order for a person to be allowed to vote in elections in Texas?
6. How is county government financed other than by property taxes and bonds?
7. List three functions of political parties.
8. Name three political parties other than the Democratic and Republican Parties.

Critical Thinking

9. **Identifying Options** Create a web like the one shown below. Give two reasons why you would participate in your local or state government.

10. **Civic Rights and Responsibilities** Imagine if junior high schools in Texas required that all students put in a certain number of volunteer hours working for the party of their choice before and during elections. How might that affect the way that those students understand the democratic process?
11. **Comparing and Contrasting** Explain the differences between a political party and a special interest group. What do you think would happen if every special interest group became a political party?
12. **Understanding Democracy** Would there be any benefits if special interest groups (SIGs) were eliminated from political life? In what ways might it be helpful? In what ways might it be harmful?

Self-Check Quiz
Visit the texans.glencoe.com Web site and click on
Chapter 30—Self-Check Quizzes to prepare for the
chapter test.

Geography and History Activity

Research and answer the following questions.

13. Where would you find a copy of your birth certificate? (Name the building and/or address.)

14. What is the name of your local school district, and where is the district office located? (Name the building and/or address.)

Portfolio/TAKS Writing Activity

15. **Identifying Options** Reflect on the ideas and information presented in the chapter. Imagine that you are running for the school board of your local school district. You have some very strong opinions and ideas about what is working well in the schools and what needs to be changed. Write a paragraph that summarizes your ideas. Keep your campaign promises realistic yet optimistic. Save your work for your portfolio.

Citizenship and History Activity

16. **Researching a Current Issue** Choose a special district that interests you, such as a water district or soil conservation district. Use the Internet or go in person to the special district office to collect information about a current issue under discussion in the district. Write a one-page paper on your findings.

Building Technology Skills

17. **Using the Internet or Library for Research** Work with another student to research one of the special interest groups (SIGs) that represents a concern presented in *Texas and Texans.* Choose a special interest topic such as civil rights, environmental protection, the oil industry, the beef or dairy industry. Focus on explaining the SIG's purpose—why it was formed in the first place—and the advertising and lobbying strategies it uses to make its concerns heard. After you have completed your research, develop a multimedia presentation. Share your presentation with the rest of the class.

Practicing Skills

18. **Analyzing Newspaper Articles** Find a newspaper article that interests you. Read the headline, byline, and dateline. Determine the main topic. Distinguish different views on the topic. Identify any other important details. Summarize the article in your own words.

Government and History Activity

19. **Attending a City Council Meeting** As a citizen and resident of a town or city and county in Texas, you have the opportunity to participate in local government. Attend a city council meeting or, if you do not live in a city, attend a county commissioners meeting. Some cities broadcast the council meetings on local cable TV channels. Take notes on the meeting or pick up an agenda. Write a paragraph about your observations.

Cooperative Learning Activity

20. **Identifying Local Issues** Working in groups of four, identify and follow a current local issue or problem that affects your town or Texas by reading about it in the newspaper, watching local TV news, and talking to friends and neighbors. Evaluate the possible solutions that are being offered by officials and the public in general. Create an oral and visual presentation for the rest of the class featuring videotaped news clips, newspaper articles, or interviews with people you spoke to.

Use the information in this chapter to answer the following question.

Which of the following is NOT the responsibility of your local government?

F Running the public schools

G Collecting recyclables and trash

H Paying for the police department

J Creating and passing state laws

Test-Taking Tip:

Read questions carefully and pay attention to key words such as **not** or **except**. These key words can change the entire meaning of a question.

Appendix

Contents

What Is an Appendix and How Do I Use One?

An appendix is the additional material you often find at the end of books. The following information will help you learn how to use the appendix in **Texas and Texans**.

TAKS Preparation Handbook

This handbook provides you with examples of critical social studies concepts. Mastery of these skills is necessary for graduation from Texas state schools. Understanding concepts explained here will improve your performance on all assessments.

Primary Sources Library

The **Primary Sources Library** provides additional first-person and secondary accounts of historical events. Primary sources are often narratives by a person who actually experienced what is being described.

Texas Counties

The chart of Texas Counties provides important information on all counties in Texas, including location, population, area, county seat, and major economic activities in the county.

Texas Declaration of Independence

The **Texas Declaration of Independence** is one of the most important documents in Texas history. It is unique among all the states in that it establishes the principles upon which the Republic of Texas was founded.

Texas Constitutions

The **Texas Constitutions** provide brief summaries and descriptions of the most important elements of the eight constitutions in Texas history. Compare and contrast the historical influences on these significant documents.

Governors and Presidents of Texas

Beginning with the Spanish royal governors, progressing to the Mexican leaders, through the presidents of the Republic, and up to the present day, this time line lists influential Texan politicians.

Glossary

A **glossary** is a list of important or difficult terms found in a textbook. Since words sometimes have other meanings, you may wish to consult a dictionary to find other uses for the term. The glossary gives a definition of each term as it is used in the book. The glossary also includes page numbers telling you where in the textbook the term is used.

Spanish Glossary

A **Spanish glossary** does everything that an English glossary does, but it does it in Spanish. A Spanish glossary is especially important to bilingual students, or those Spanish-speaking students who are learning the English language.

Index

An **index** is an alphabetical listing that includes the subjects of that book and the page numbers where those subjects can be found. The index in this book also lets you know that certain pages contain maps, graphs, illustrations, or quotations.

Credits and Acknowledgements

This sections lists photo credits and literary credits for the book. You can look at this section to find out where the publisher obtained the permission to use a photograph or to use excerpts from other books.

Test Yourself

Find the answers to these questions by using the Appendix on the following pages.

1. **What does the term *presidio* mean?**
2. **Who was the first signer of the Texas Declaration of Independence?**
3. **On what page can I read about Spindletop?**
4. **How many counties are there in Texas?**
5. **When was George W. Bush elected governor of Texas?**

TAKS
Preparation Handbook

The Texas Assessment of Knowledge and Skills, or TAKS, test is one way educators in Texas measure what you have learned. This TAKS Preparation Handbook is designed to help you prepare for the 8th grade TAKS test in Social Studies. On the pages that follow, you will find a review of major Social Studies concepts included in the Texas Essential Knowledge and Skills (TEKS) that are tested at Grade 8.

TAKS Objectives

Grade 8 Social Studies

There are five objectives for the Social Studies TAKS. These objectives are listed below.

For the test the student will be expected to:

1. Demonstrate an understanding of issues and events in United States history.

2. Demonstrate an understanding of geographic influences on historical issues and events.

3. Demonstrate an understanding of economic and social influences on historical issues and events.

4. Demonstrate an understanding of political influences on historical issues and events.

5. Use critical thinking skills to analyze social studies information.

Author
Tara Musslewhite
Humble I.S.D.
Humble, Texas

Reviewed by

TEKS Covered:
Obj. 1 – 8.1ABC, 8.2B
Obj. 2 – 8.6E, 8.10B, 8.11AB
Obj. 5 – 8.30ABC

British Colonies in America

*By completing and understanding the activities on this page, you will practice for **TAKS Objectives 1, 2,** and **5.***

Skills Practice: Reading a Map

Christopher Columbus's voyages of exploration to the Americas for Spain led to further exploration of North and South America. Drawn by stories of gold and wealth, the Spanish conquered both the Aztec and Inca Empires, seizing their wealth. News of these conquests inspired other European nations to claim lands in the Americas. The first permanent English colony in America was Jamestown, founded in 1607. By the mid-eighteenth century, the British had established 13 colonies along the Atlantic coast of North America.

Historians use maps to learn about places and events in history. Political maps show the boundaries between cities, states, countries, or regions. The map below shows the areas known as the New England, Middle, and Southern Colonies. Study the map and answer the following questions on a separate sheet of paper.

1. List the Southern Colonies.
2. Which were the Middle Colonies?
3. Which is the northernmost group of colonies?
4. In which New England Colony was the settlement of Plymouth located?
5. Which Middle Colony bordered Pennsylvania to the north?
6. Name the body of water that formed the eastern border of the colonies.
7. Where was Charles Town located?
8. Which New England Colony covered the largest land area?

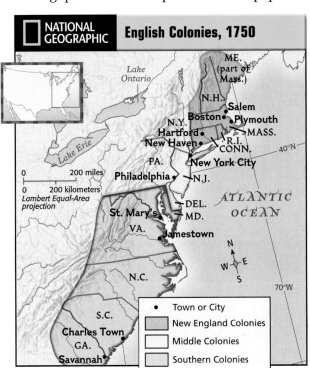

NATIONAL GEOGRAPHIC — **English Colonies, 1750**

- • Town or City
- New England Colonies
- Middle Colonies
- Southern Colonies

The Princeton Review **Test Practice**

DIRECTIONS: Use the map and your knowledge of social studies to answer the following questions on a separate sheet of paper.

1. The first permanent English settlement in North America was located in
   A Plymouth.
   B the New England Colonies.
   C Virginia.
   D the Middle Colonies.

2. This political map shows the boundaries of
   F cities.
   G countries.
   H regions.
   J states.

3. The Southern Colonies consisted of all of the following places EXCEPT
   A Georgia.
   B Pennsylvania.
   C South Carolina.
   D Virginia.

TAKS Practice Lesson 2

Colonial Growth

By completing and understanding the activities on this page, you will practice for TAKS Objectives 1, 2, and 5.

Skills Practice: Interpreting Bar Graphs

Settlers in the 13 English colonies came to North America for many reasons. Some sought religious freedom. Others looked to gain land and new opportunities for their families. Not all colonists came to the English settlements of their own free will, though. Africans were taken from their homelands and brought to America as slaves. Indentured servants as well as criminals and war prisoners were forced to work without pay for several years before gaining their freedom.

Bar graphs are used to compare facts and numbers. Information presented in the graph is described along the vertical and horizontal axes. Bars of different lengths represent different quantities. Study the bar graph below and answer the following questions on a separate sheet of paper.

The Princeton Review

TAKS Test Practice

DIRECTIONS: Use the graph and your knowledge of social studies to answer the following question on a separate sheet of paper.

1. Which of the following generalizations best reflects information shown on the graph?
   A New York had the smallest African American population.
   B Maryland's total population was twice as large as the population of New York.
   C Massachusetts had the largest total population.
   D Fewer African Americans lived in the New England Colonies than in the Southern Colonies.

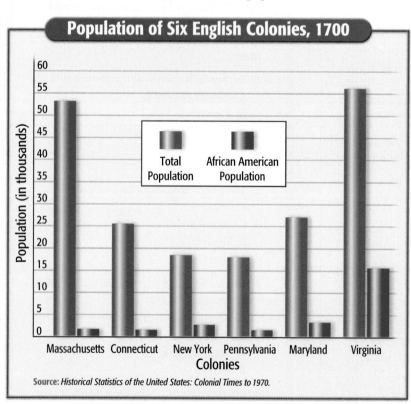

Population of Six English Colonies, 1700

Population (in thousands)

Total Population   African American Population

Massachusetts Connecticut New York Pennsylvania Maryland Virginia

Colonies

Source: *Historical Statistics of the United States: Colonial Times to 1970.*

1. What does the bar graph compare?

2. What time period is reflected by the graph?

3. What information is presented by the numbers along the vertical (left) axis?

4. What information is shown along the horizontal (bottom) axis?

5. Which colony had the largest total population in 1700? The smallest?

6. Which colony had the largest African American population in 1700?

TAKS Preparation Handbook

Triangular Trade Routes

*By completing and understanding the activities on this page, you will practice for **TAKS Objectives 1, 2, 3,** and **5.***

TEKS Covered:
Obj. 1 – 8.1A, 8.2B, 8.4A
Obj. 2 – 8.10B, 8.11ABC, 8.12A
Obj. 3 – 8.13B   Obj. 5 – 8.30BC

Skills Practice: Reading a Special Purpose Map

Mercantilism is the economic idea that a nation's power depended on trade and gold reserves. British leaders viewed their colonies in America as sources of wealth. The New England Colonies became the center of the shipping trade, linking the colonies to Great Britain and other parts of the world. The map below is a special purpose map. It shows the triangular-shaped trade routes that developed among Great Britain, America, and Africa.

Read the labels on the map to determine what information is presented. Then answer the following questions on a separate sheet of paper.

1. What did the colonies export to Africa?

2. What did the colonies import from Africa through the West Indies?

DIRECTIONS: Use the map and your knowledge of social studies to answer the following question.

1. Triangular trade routes benefited colonial merchants by allowing them to
   A import goods from Great Britain.
   B visit Africa.
   C make a profit from the goods they traded.
   D establish new colonies.

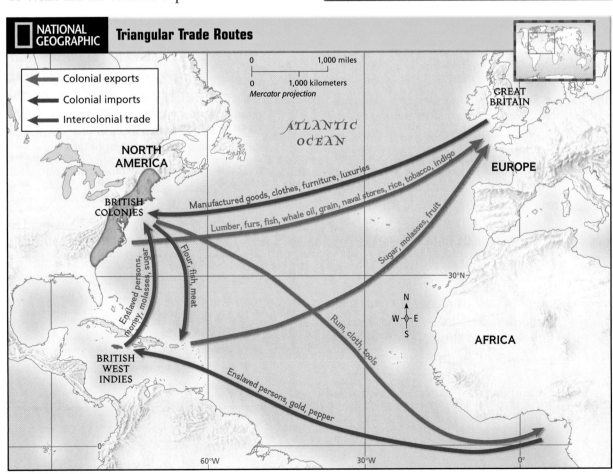

Triangular Trade Routes

TAKS Practice Lesson 4

Americans Move Toward Independence

By completing and understanding the activities on this page, you will practice for TAKS Objectives 1, 4, and 5.

Skills Practice: Identifying the Main Idea

While the Spanish were trying to colonize Texas, American colonists east of the Mississippi River were protesting against unfair taxation and attempts by the British to limit their rights. These protests eventually led to the American Revolution.

The Horse America, Throwing His Master

In January 1776, an American Patriot named Thomas Paine published a pamphlet called *Common Sense*. In it, Paine urged Americans to break away from Great Britain. He argued that it was simply "common sense" to stop following the "royal brute," King George III. Paine told his fellow colonists that their struggle was not just a struggle against unfair taxes, but it was a struggle for freedom. *Common Sense* inspired thousands of Americans.

You can identify the main ideas of visuals, like political cartoons, and passages of text. Finding the main idea helps you to understand the whole story. Study the political cartoon and read the primary source excerpt on this page, then answer the following questions on a separate sheet of paper.

> ❝*Every thing that is right begs for separation from Britain. The Americans who have been killed seem to say 'TIS TIME TO PART. England and America are located a great distance apart. That is itself strong and natural proof that God never expected one to rule over the other.*❞
>
> *– Thomas Paine*, Common Sense, *1776*

1. What is the title of the cartoon?
2. What symbols does the cartoonist use?
3. Whom does the horse represent?
4. What actions are taking place in the cartoon?
5. What is the message of the cartoonist?
6. What is the main idea of the excerpt?
7. What details are given to support the main idea?

The Princeton Review

TAKS Test Practice

DIRECTIONS: Use the political cartoon, the primary source, and your knowledge of social studies to answer the following questions on a separate sheet of paper.

1. The creator of the political cartoon was most likely protesting against the
   A American colonists.
   B British government.
   C Spanish government.
   D colonial governments.

2. What is Paine's proof that Americans should break away from Great Britain?
   F America is strong.
   G Taxation is unfair.
   H Americans need to beg for separation.
   J England and America are located a great distance apart.

TAKS Preparation Handbook

TAKS Practice Lesson 5

Growth of a Nation

By completing and understanding the activities on this page, you will practice for TAKS Objectives 1, 3, and 5.

Skills Practice: Reading a Circle and a Bar Graph

The United States is a place where people of many backgrounds have come together to form a new, uniquely American culture. Our country was founded as a nation of immigrants. Throughout its history, people have journeyed to the United States seeking new opportunities. During the nineteenth century, the population of the United States grew rapidly. Immigrants contributed to the great increase in population.

The graphs on this page present information about the population of the United States. Graphs show statistics in a clear, easy-to-read way. Bar graphs compare characteristics of items, and circle graphs show parts of a total. To read the graphs, read the title and labels to identify the subject of the graph, then compare the bars or the parts of the circle to draw conclusions or identify trends. A *trend* is the tendency to move in a certain direction. Bar graphs oftentimes identify trends. Study the graphs and answer the following questions on a separate sheet of paper.

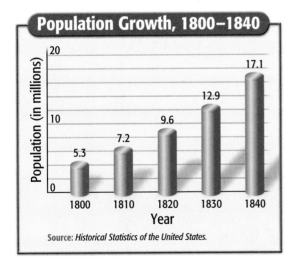

Population Growth, 1800–1840

Population (in millions)

20

17.1

12.9

10

9.6

7.2

5.3

0

1800 1810 1820 1830 1840

Year

Source: *Historical Statistics of the United States.*

1. What is the subject of each of the graphs?

2. What time period is reflected in each?

3. What was the population of the United States in 1810?

4. During which year was the population the greatest?

Urban and Rural Population, 1820

Rural
92.8%

Urban
7.2%

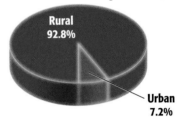

The Princeton Review

TAKS
Test Practice

DIRECTIONS: Use the bar and circle graphs and your knowledge of social studies to answer the following questions on a separate sheet of paper.

1. Which of the following trends does the bar graph reflect?

   A The U.S. population increased between 1810 and 1840.

   B The U.S. population decreased between 1810 and 1840.

   C The U.S. population doubled between 1820 and 1830.

   D The U.S. population was greatest in the year 1840.

2. One inference that can be made from information found on the circle graph is that in 1820

   F America's population was predominately urban.

   G more Americans lived in cities than in the countryside.

   H America's population was predominately rural.

   J fewer Americans lived in country areas than in cities.

TAKS Practice Lesson 6

TEKS Covered:
Obj. 1 – 8.1ABC, 8.4C 8.6BCD
Obj. 2 – 8.6E, 8.10B, 8.11A
Obj. 5 – 8.30ABCD

Changing Boundaries of the United States

By completing and understanding the activities on this page, you will practice for TAKS Objectives 1, 2, and 5.

Skills Practice: Sequencing Information

The Treaty of Paris, signed in 1783, officially ended the American Revolution. According to the terms of the treaty, Great Britain recognized the United States as an independent nation and agreed upon its borders. After that, the boundaries of the United States expanded greatly. New lands were acquired in a variety of ways. The widespread belief in the idea of Manifest Destiny led to the westward expansion of the country in the 1800s.

Sequencing information involves placing facts in the order in which they occurred. Use the map below to list the areas acquired by the United States in chronological order (on a separate sheet of paper). Then answer the following questions.

1. What is the subject of the map?

2. What land purchase in 1803 doubled the size of the United States?

3. In what year was the American goal of Manifest Destiny accomplished?

The Princeton Review

TAKS
Test Practice

DIRECTIONS: Use the map and your knowledge of social studies to answer the following questions on a separate sheet of paper.

1. In 1783 the treaty ending the American Revolution established the western border of the United States as
A the Mississippi River.
B Canada.
C Florida.
D the Oregon Country.

2. Which of the following areas became part of the United States first?
F Texas
G the Oregon Country
H Louisiana
J California

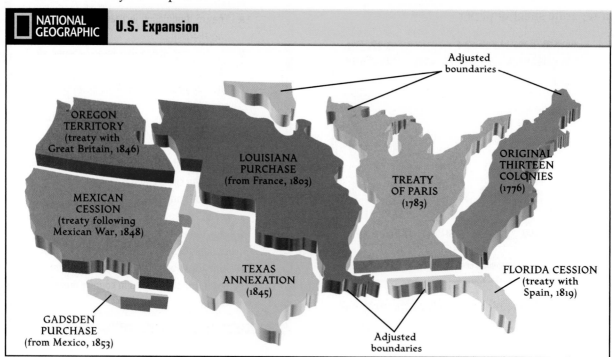

NATIONAL GEOGRAPHIC **U.S. Expansion**

Adjusted boundaries

OREGON TERRITORY
(treaty with Great Britain, 1846)

LOUISIANA PURCHASE
(from France, 1803)

TREATY OF PARIS
(1783)

ORIGINAL THIRTEEN COLONIES
(1776)

MEXICAN CESSION
(treaty following Mexican War, 1848)

TEXAS ANNEXATION
(1845)

FLORIDA CESSION
(treaty with Spain, 1819)

GADSDEN PURCHASE
(from Mexico, 1853)

Adjusted boundaries

King Cotton in the South

*By completing and understanding the activities on this page, you will practice for **TAKS Objectives 1, 3,** and **5**.*

Skills Practice: Making Comparisons

By the 1850s the North had developed a manufacturing economy. Industry, though, played a limited role in the South. The economy of the South was mainly agricultural. The invention of the cotton gin in the late eighteenth century led to an increase in the production of cotton. This, in turn, led to a demand for more slave labor in the South. As a result, the plantation system became a symbol of Southern society.

The circle graphs below compare items. When you compare two or more items, you examine the items to identify any similarities and differences. When comparing visual graphics, be sure to read the title to determine what information the graphs display. Study the graphs below and answer the following questions on a separate sheet of paper.

Cotton Production as a Percentage of U.S. Exports

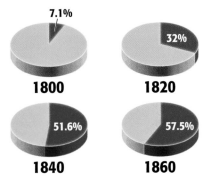

7.1%   32%   51.6%   57.5%
1800   1820   1840   1860

Source: *Historical Statistics of the United States.*

1. What are the circle graphs comparing?

2. What percentage of total U.S. exports did cotton make up in 1800?

3. In what year did cotton production first make up more than half of all U.S. exports?

4. In 1860 what percentage of U.S. exports did cotton production represent?

The Princeton Review

TAKS
Test Practice

DIRECTIONS: Use the graphs and your knowledge of social studies to answer the following questions on a separate sheet of paper.

1. Which statement best explains the increase in cotton as a percentage of U.S. exports between 1800 and 1860?
   A There was a decrease in the demand for cotton in the United States.
   B Trade between the United States and Europe decreased.
   C The United States imported more cotton than it could use.
   D The use of the cotton gin increased the amount of cotton production in the United States.

2. By 1860 the economies of the Deep South profited mainly from the production of cotton. What percentage of the South's exports did NOT consist of cotton?
   F 57.5 percent
   G 51.6 percent
   H 5.75 percent
   J 42.5 percent

3. Because the cotton gin processed cotton fibers so quickly, farmers could grow more cotton. Which of the following statements reflects an effect of this situation?
   A Eli Whitney invented the cotton gin in 1793.
   B Southern planters demanded more workers, especially enslaved workers.
   C Rice, indigo, and tobacco became the South's main crops.
   D Southerners demanded the establishment of more industry.

The Civil War

TEKS Covered:
Obj. 1 – 8.1ABC, 8.7C
Obj. 2 – 8.10B, 8.11BC Obj. 3 – 8.13A
Obj. 4 – 8.18B   Obj. 5 – 8.30ABCD

TAKS Preparation Handbook

By completing and understanding the activities on this page, you will practice for TAKS Objectives 1, 2, 3, 4, and 5.

Skills Practice: Interpreting Maps and Graphs

The immediate cause of the Civil War was the election of Abraham Lincoln as the nation's sixteenth president. He was a member of the newly formed Republican Party, which had vowed to stop the spread of slavery. Some Southern leaders threatened to secede, or withdraw, from the Union if Lincoln became president. Shortly after his election, 11 Southern states, including Texas, carried out their threat.

During the Civil War the North and the South had strengths and weaknesses. The circle graphs on this page compare the resources of the two sides. Examine the graphs and map below, then answer the following questions.

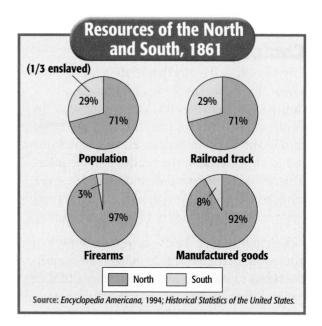

Resources of the North and South, 1861

(1/3 enslaved)

29% / 71% — **Population**

29% / 71% — **Railroad track**

3% / 97% — **Firearms**

8% / 92% — **Manufactured goods**

North   South

Source: *Encyclopedia Americana, 1994; Historical Statistics of the United States.*

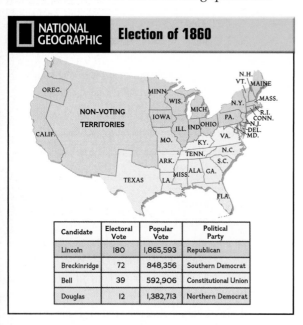

NATIONAL GEOGRAPHIC — **Election of 1860**

NON-VOTING TERRITORIES

Candidate	Electoral Vote	Popular Vote	Political Party
Lincoln	180	1,865,593	Republican
Breckinridge	72	848,356	Southern Democrat
Bell	39	592,906	Constitutional Union
Douglas	12	1,382,713	Northern Democrat

1. Who was the Republican candidate for president in 1860? In what region of the United States was the Republican Party strongest?

2. What do the graphs compare? What time period is represented?

3. What percentage of goods was manufactured in the South?

The Princeton Review

TAKS
Test Practice

DIRECTIONS: Use the map, graph, and your knowledge of social studies to answer the following questions on a separate sheet of paper.

1. Information on the map suggests that just prior to the Civil War, the region most opposed to the spread of slavery was
   A the North.   C the East.
   B the South.   D the Southwest.

2. Which of the following statements best reflects information shown by the circle graphs?
   F The North had better leaders than the South.
   G The North had a greater population from which to build an army.
   H The South had more railroad mileage than the North.
   J The North had less ability to produce farm products than the South.

Rebuilding the Nation

TEKS Covered:
Obj. 1 – 8.1AC, 8.8A
Obj. 3 – 8.24D   Obj. 4 – 8.17AB
Obj. 5 – 8.30ABCD

By completing and understanding the activities on this page, you will practice for TAKS Objectives 1, 3, 4, and 5.

Skills Practice: Identifying Central Issues

After four long years of bloodshed, Confederate General Robert E. Lee and his troops surrendered to Union General Ulysses S. Grant. Following the bitter war, the United States faced the huge task of rebuilding the nation. The effort to reorganize the seceded states and bring them back into the Union is known as Reconstruction.

Congress devised a Reconstruction plan that included amending, or changing, the Constitution. The Thirteenth, Fourteenth, and Fifteenth Amendments are known as the Reconstruction amendments.

Understanding the central issue of material allows you to see the whole picture or story. To find the central issues, read or study the material and ask yourself: What is the purpose of this information? This will help you identify the central issue. Study the information below and answer the following questions on a separate sheet of paper.

Reconstruction Amendments

Amendment	Date Ratified	Description
Thirteenth	1865	Abolished slavery in the United States
Fourteenth	1868	Granted citizenship to African Americans
Fifteenth	1870	Guaranteed African American men the right to vote

1. What was the goal of government Reconstruction policies?

2. Why are the Thirteenth, Fourteenth, and Fifteenth Amendments called the Reconstruction amendments?

3. Which Reconstruction amendment was ratified during the Civil War?

4. In what year were African American men given the right to vote?

5. Which amendment officially ended slavery in the United States?

6. When were African Americans granted citizenship rights?

7. What was the purpose of the Fourteenth Amendment?

 The Princeton Review **TAKS** Test Practice

DIRECTIONS: Use the chart and your knowledge of social studies to answer the following questions on a separate sheet of paper.

1. By 1870 all of the following groups of Americans had suffrage, or the right to vote, EXCEPT
   A African American men.
   B white men.
   C former male slaves.
   D women.

2. Even after the Thirteenth, Fourteenth, and Fifteenth Amendments were passed, African Americans were prevented from voting in many Southern states because of all of the following EXCEPT
   F Jim Crow laws.
   G poll taxes.
   H literacy tests.
   J grandfather clauses.

3. Which amendment would a lawyer most likely use to argue against punishment without due process of the law?
   A Thirteenth
   B Fourteenth
   C Fifteenth
   D Sixteenth

TAKS Practice Lesson 10

We, the People

*By completing and understanding the activities on this page, you will practice for **TAKS Objectives 1, 4,** and **5.***

Skills Practice: Analyzing Information

The first three words of the United States Constitution have become one of many proud symbols of American democracy. Written in 1787, the Constitution remains the nation's most important document. In the Constitution, powers of the federal government are divided among three branches. The first 10 amendments, or additions, to the Constitution are called the Bill of Rights. These amendments guarantee basic freedoms of Americans. The First Amendment protects rights necessary in a democracy. Study the charts on this page and answer the following questions on a separate sheet of paper.

★ **Freedoms Protected** ★
by the First Amendment

★ Freedom of the Press
★ Freedom of Assembly
★ Freedom to Petition the Government
★ Freedom of Religion
★ Freedom of Speech

1. What is the major function of the executive branch of the U.S. government?

2. Which branch of government makes decisions about the law?

DIRECTIONS: Use the charts and your knowledge of social studies to answer the following questions.

1. The major purpose of the first 10 amendments to the U.S. Constitution is to
   A ensure economic growth for Americans.
   B protect the government from criticism.
   C divide the powers of the government among three branches.
   D protect individual rights.

2. To keep any one branch of government from becoming more powerful than the others, the Constitution set up a system called
   F federalism.
   G checks and balances.
   H the Bill of Rights.
   J the Preamble of the U.S. Constitution.

Branches of the United States Government

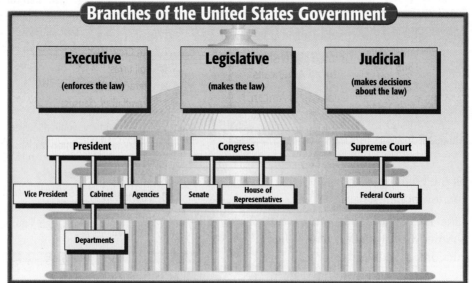

Executive	Legislative	Judicial
(enforces the law)	(makes the law)	(makes decisions about the law)
President	Congress	Supreme Court
Vice President Cabinet Agencies	Senate House of Representatives	Federal Courts
Departments		

TEKS Covered:
Obj. 1 – 8.1AB, 8.7C
Obj. 4 – 8.16AD, 8.17AB
Obj. 5 – 8.30ABCDE

Extending the Right to Vote

*By completing and understanding the activities on this page, you will
practice for TAKS Objectives 1, 4, and 5.*

Skills Practice: Making Inferences

Suffrage, or the right to vote, has not always been extended to all groups of Americans. In the early years of the nation, only white male landowners could vote. Since that time, amendments to the United States Constitution that guarantee voting rights to virtually all adult Americans have been adopted.

Barbara Jordan became the first African American woman from Texas to serve in the United States Congress. Elected in 1972, she became a powerful voice in the House of Representatives.

When you make inferences, you use your reasoning skills. Making an inference involves combining the available facts and your general knowledge to form a reasonable conclusion. Read the chart on this page and the statement made by Congresswoman Jordan, then answer the following questions on a separate sheet of paper.

> **❝**I felt somehow for many years that George Washington and Alexander Hamilton just left me out by mistake. But through the process of amendment, interpretation, and court decision I have finally been included in 'We, the people.'**❞**
>
> –Barbara Jordan, 1974

1. What men does Jordan refer to? Why does she refer to these men?

2. What did Jordan mean by the phrase "left me out by mistake"?

3. Through what processes have African Americans and women been included in "We, the people"?

4. What is the purpose of the Twenty-sixth Amendment?

Suffrage Amendments

Amendment	Date	Description
Fifteenth	1870	Extended voting rights to African Americans by outlawing denial of the right to vote on the basis of race, color, or previous condition of servitude
Nineteenth	1920	Extended the right to vote to women
Twenty-Sixth	1971	Extended the right to vote to 18 year olds

DIRECTIONS: Use the information on this page and your knowledge of social studies to answer the following questions on a separate sheet of paper.

1. Which of the following groups of United States citizens gained suffrage rights before the twentieth century?

A 18-year-old males

B 18-year-old females

C African American males

D African American females

2. To which historical document does Congresswoman Jordan indirectly refer?

F the Texas Constitution

G the United States Constitution

H the Declaration of Independence

J the Bill of Rights

3. Barbara Jordan refers to all of the following ways of changing the U.S. Constitution EXCEPT

A passing amendments.

B the interpretation of laws by the Supreme Court.

C the enforcement of laws by the executive branch.

D appealing a law to the Supreme Court.

Working With Primary Sources

Suppose that you have been asked to write a report on changes in your community over the past 25 years. Where would you get the information you need to begin writing? You would draw upon two types of information—primary sources and secondary sources.

Definitions

Primary sources are often first-person accounts by someone who actually saw or lived through what is being described. In other words, if you see a fire or live through a great storm and then write about your experiences, you are creating a primary source. Diaries, journals, photographs, and eyewitness reports are examples of primary sources.

Secondary sources are secondhand accounts. For instance, if your friend experiences the fire or storm and tells you about it, or if you read about the first or storm in the newspaper, and then you write about it, you are creating a secondary source. Secondary sources are often accounts that are put together, or compiled, by using many different primary sources. Textbooks, biographies, and histories are examples of compiled secondary sources.

Settler's diary

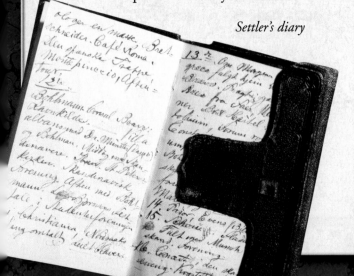

Checking Your Sources

When you read primary or secondary sources, you should analyze them to figure out if they are reliable. Historians usually prefer primary sources to secondary sources, but both can be reliable or unreliable, depending on the following factors.

Time Span

With primary sources, it is important to consider how long after the event occurred the primary source was written. Chances are the longer the time span between the event and the account, the less reliable the account is. As time passes, people often forget details and fill in gaps with events that never took place. Although we like to think we remember things exactly as they happened, the fact is we often remember them as we wanted them to occur.

Validity

Another factor to consider when evaluating a primary source is the writer's background and experiences. First, try to determine how this person knows about what he or she is writing. How much does he or she know? Is the writer being truthful? Is the account convincing?

Bias

When evaluating a primary source, you should also decide whether the account has been influenced by emotion, opinion, or exaggeration. Writers can have reasons to distort the truth to suit their personal purposes. Ask yourself: Why did the person write the account? Do any key words or expressions reveal the author's emotions or opinions? You may wish to compare the account with one written by another witness to the event. If the two accounts differ, ask yourself why they differ and which is more accurate. (Your response, of course, will be influenced by your own individual bias.)

Interpreting Primary Sources

To help you analyze a primary source, use the following steps:

- **Examine the origins of the document.**
  You need to determine if it is a primary source.

- **Find the main ideas.**
  Read the document and summarize the main ideas in your own words. These ideas may be fairly easy to identify in newspapers and journals, for example, but are much more difficult to find in poetry.

- **Reread the document.**
  Difficult ideas are not always easily understood on the first reading.

- **Use a variety of resources.**
  Form the habit of using the dictionary, the encyclopedia, and maps. These print and electronic resources are tools to help you discover new ideas and knowledge and check the validity of sources.

Opera glasses, late 1800s

Classifying Primary Sources

Primary sources fall into different categories:

Printed Publications

Printed publications include books such as autobiographies. Printed publications also include newspapers and magazines.

Songs & Poems

Songs and poems include works that express the personal thoughts and feelings, or political or religious beliefs, of the writer, often using rhyming and rhythmic language.

Visual Materials

Visual materials include a wide range of forms: original paintings, drawings, sculptures, photographs, film, and maps.

Oral Histories

Oral histories are chronicles, memoirs, myths, and legends that are passed along from one generation to another by word of mouth. Interviews are another form of oral history.

Personal Records

Personal records are accounts of events kept by an individual who is a participant in, or witness to, these events. Personal records include diaries, journals, and letters.

Artifacts

Artifacts are objects such as tools or ornaments. Artifacts present information about a particular culture or a stage of technological development.

Geography

The land that would become Texas was full of resources. It had water, grasslands, timber, minerals, and fertile soils. Many people who traveled through Texas commented on the geography of the region. Nations and people wanted to claim the land for their own. As you read the following selections, think about how important the land and its resources have been to the development of Texas.

Reader's Dictionary

frontage: land bordering a street or river

grantee: someone given land by the king

heir: someone who receives property through inheritance

parallel: a line of latitude

South Sea: the Pacific Ocean

Spain and the United States Determine the Eastern Boundary of Texas

Printed Publications

In 1819 Spain and the United States agreed on the boundary between their territories. When Mexico became independent from Spain, Mexico and the United States agreed to respect the same boundary. The current border between Texas and Louisiana, Texas and Arkansas, and most of Texas and Oklahoma is based on this treaty.

Article 3. The boundary line between the two countries, west of the Mississippi, shall begin on the Gulph [Gulf] of Mexico, at the mouth of the river Sabine, in the sea, continuing north, along the western bank of that river, to the 32nd degree of latitude; thence, by a line due north, to the degree of latitude where it strikes the Rio Roxo of Nachitoches, or Red River; then following the course of the Rio Roxo westward, to the degree of longitude 100 west from London and 23 from Washington; then crossing the said Red River, and running thence, by a line due north, to the river Arkansas; thence following the course of the southern bank of the Arkansas; to its source, in latitude 42 north; and thence, by that **parallel** of latitude to the **South Sea.**

Ouachita Mountains

An Immigrant's Description of Texas

Personal Records

The following description of Texas geography encouraged many Germans to immigrate to Texas. Many other German immigrants also wrote home in what were called "Texas Letters."

Settlement on Mill Creek
In Austin's Colony
State of Texas,
Republic of Mexico
February 1, 1832

The ground is hilly and alternates with forest and natural grass plains. Various kinds of trees. Climate like Sicily. The soil needs no fertilizer. Almost constant east wind. No winter, almost like March in Germany. Bees, birds, and butterflies the whole winter through . . . Birds of all kinds from pelicans to hummingbirds. Wild horses and buffalo in hordes; wolves, but of a feeble kind; also panthers and leopards, of which there is no danger; rich game, delicious roasts. Meadows with the most charming flowers. Many snakes, also rattlesnakes; each planter knows safe means against them . . .

On account of the yellow fever, one should arrive some weeks before the month of July or after the first of October . . .

Your friend,
Fritz Ernst

Dividing the Land

Printed Publications

The following appeared in a 1939 National Geographic Magazine *article about the Rio Grande. It mentions property that had been held by the same family for 178 years.*

Another survival from old days is land grants, dating from the Spanish kings. I was in a Brownsville law office when one such tract was being sold by **heirs** of the original **grantee,** its first transfer since 1761! Such grants usually faced the river for one league and extended far inland. As one generation after another inherited this land, each heir took his share in the form of a strip, always with river **frontage** so he might water his cattle. On record today is one such strip which is actually only thirty-six inches wide at the river and runs inland twelve miles! It is, however, not fenced off, but farmed by neighbors.

As I write, Brownsville is one of the busiest cities in the United States. Grapefruit made it so. Air travel helps. Here the giant skyliners of Pan American Airways halt to satisfy international border rules. Weary passengers alight to rest their ringing ears and stretch their cramped legs. Men in uniform rummage through baggage, turning out knickknacks bought in Buenos Aires, Lima, or Guatemala. With microscopes, the Department of Agriculture men paw over orchids, gardenias, and other costly cut flowers shipped from Mexico City . . .

Analyzing Primary Sources

1. Which boundaries established by the Treaty of 1819 are still in effect?
2. What motive would Fritz Ernst have in encouraging other Germans to immigrate to Texas?

TAKS PRACTICE 3. **Identifying Geographic Factors** Write a letter to someone in another country describing where you live. Include information about the landscape, the weather, types of homes, businesses, and recreation areas.

**For use with Unit 2
"Explorers and Settlers"**

Explorers and Settlers

*Europeans and Native
Americans encountered each
other in what was later to
become Texas in the 1500s,
1600s, and 1700s. The
Europeans came to explore,
trade, and teach the Native
Americans about their religion.
As you examine these
documents, think about what
changes occurred when the two
groups of people met.*

Reader's Dictionary

bowmen: people armed with bows
and arrows

fanega: a Spanish unit of measurement

granary: a structure designed to store grain

ingratiate: to make friends with

placate: to please

rampart: a wall built for defensive purposes

sombrero: a hat designed to shade the face

standard: flag

venerated: worshiped

wrought: carved or shaped by hand

Native Americans and Spaniards Meet on Galveston Island

Personal Records

*The earliest account of Texas written by a European
was Cabeza de Vaca's description of his shipwreck
and life in Texas among Native Americans.*

After we ate, I ordered Lope de Oveido, our
strongest man, to climb one of the trees not
far off and ascertain the lay of the land. He
complied and found out from the treetop that we
were on an island. He also said that the ground
looked as if cattle had trampled it and therefore
that this must be a country of Christians . . .

They saw three Indians with bows and arrows
following him (Oveido). The Indians were calling
to him and he was gesturing them to keep coming. When he reached us, the Indians held
back and sat down
on the shore.

Half an hour later
a hundred **bowmen**
reinforced the first
three individuals.
Whatever their
stature, they looked
like giants to us in
our fright. We could
not hope to defend
ourselves; not half a
dozen of us could
even stand up.

The inspector and I walked out and greeted
them. They advanced, and we did our best to
placate and **ingratiate.** We gave them beads and
bells, and each one of them gave us an arrow in
pledge of friendship. They told us by signs that
they would return at sunrise and bring food,
having none.

The Alamo in 1785

The following description of Mission San Antonio de Valero comes from an official report.

The mission is situated across the [San Antonio] river from San Antonio de Béxar. It is built to form almost a square, surrounded by a single stone

Mission San Antonio de Valero

and mud wall that stands about 300 paces from the center. The same **rampart** serves as a wall for most of the fifteen or sixteen houses, with ample capacity for lodging the Indians. Nearly all the houses are covered with wood and mortar, as a protection against the rain, and have hand-carved wooden doors and iron keys. Within the square is the **granary,** made of stone and lime, which has enough room to hold two thousand *fanegas* (4000 bushels) of corn, two hundred more *fanegas* of beans, etc. Next is the house or living quarters, adequate for the missionary and the officers of the community, made of stone and lime, with good roofs, doors, windows, and locks . . . The mission has under construction a church . . . In the front, its beautiful façade of **wrought** stone has been completed to the same height as the walls. At this point the construction has been stopped many years ago for lack of qualified workmen.

A Spanish Priest Describes Meeting With Native Americans

Isidro Felix de Espinoza was a priest who traveled to East Texas in 1716 to establish missions among the Native Americans who lived there. He wrote the following account.

. . . the Captain bearing a **standard** on which were painted the images of Christ Crucified and of Our Lady of Guadalupe . . . Our Captain delivered the standard into my hands, and kneeling **venerated** and kissed the Holy Images and we embraced each other. All the others did likewise . . . Then we seated ourselves on the carpets of the preceding day. The Indians conversed among themselves for a little while, and each chief bringing a handful of ground tobacco they mixed it together to show the unity of their wills, then handed it to the Captain. Afterwards they brought their gifts of ears of corn, watermelons, tomales [tamales], and cooked beans with corn and nuts. To them were distributed, in the name of His Majesty, the blankets, **sombreros,** tobacco, and flannel for undergarments. And that night they demonstrated their joy with dances.

Analyzing Primary Sources

1. Describe the meeting between the Native Americans and the Spaniards.
2. Why were gifts important when Spanish and Native Americans met?

TAKS Practice **3. Organizing Information** Make a list of items you think would be necessary in establishing a colony in Texas in the 1600s.

Mexican Texas

When Mexico became independent from Spain, it adopted a policy of encouraging settlement of Anglo Americans in Texas. In 1836 tensions between those settlers and the Mexican government resulted in a revolution which ended with the victory for the Texas revolutionaries on the banks of the San Jacinto River. As you read these documents consider the issues of colonization and revolution.

Reader's Dictionary

adornment: decoration

alcalde: local official

bar: sand deposit blocking a river's mouth

bovine: relating to cattle

ecclesiastical: relating to church affairs

lighter: small boat that takes people from a large boat to the shore

sheep's head: a type of fish

solemnize: to preside at a wedding

vermilion: a red paint

The Alabamas

Personal Records

On his inspection trip to East Texas in 1828, General Mier y Terán described the Alabamas.

Six or eight families of the Alabama tribe live in the rancheria where we are staying. The very fertile land they cultivate is well fenced. They keep large herds of domesticated **bovine** stock and pigs and are supplied with good horses and arms. The tribe distinguishes itself, as do they all, by its hairstyle: on either side of the head they have a triangular patch without hair which they shave to the skin. On the top there is a strip of hair two inches wide, and to flatten it out in either direction they use grease. On the forehead and down the neck the hair hangs evenly like a fringe. They have white metal **adornments** in every shape and paint their faces heavily with **vermilion.**

Mary Austin Holley

Personal Records

Traveling in 1835 had its own special dangers.

May 3—Morning a fair breeze sprung up—went on beautifully.

May 4—At night, reached the mouth of the Brazos with great rejoicing.

May 5 Morning—all the passengers but Mrs. Pharis & self went ashore amid the breakers in a small **lighter.** I preferred my chance in the vessel. Red fish, **Sheep's head** & mullet and crabs for supper and breakfast.

May 6—Crossed the **bar** with difficulty. The *Elizabeth* after us broke her rudder & stuck fast.

A Marriage Bond

Printed Publications

Couples who wished to marry in Texas in the 1820s would sign a contract promising to marry the next time a priest came through. Here is an example of such a contract.

Know all Men by these Presents: That we, John Oliver . . . and Nancy Curtis . . . are held and firmly bound to the other in the penal sum of ten thousand dollars,

Whereas the said John Oliver and Nancy Curtis have mutually agreed to enter in the solemn bonds of matrimony; and there being as yet no church erected in this colony, or **ecclesiastical** authority established in said colony, and it being a great distance to San Antonio de Bexar, and no **alcalde** yet appointed before whom this bond should have been taken, Now, therefore, it is fully understood by and between the said parties, that if they do faithfully appear before some priest or person legally authorized to **solemnize** marriage as soon as circumstances will permit, and be married as the laws of this government may require, why, then this bond to be forever void. And it is further to be understood by and between the said parties, that if either of the said parties shall fail or refuse to comply with the conditions of this bond . . . [T]he party so failing or refusing shall forfeit and pay the penalty in the said bond mentioned.

The Law of April 6, 1830

Printed Publications

The Mexican government was concerned that the Anglo colonists in eastern Texas were not following the law and were growing so numerous that they might rebel against the government. The government passed the Law of April 6, 1830, to end immigration from the United States and reinforce the law against slavery.

Article 9. The introduction of foreigners across the northern frontier is prohibited under any pretext whatsoever, unless the said foreigners are provided with a passport issued by the agent of the republic at the point whence the said foreigners set out.

Article 10. No change shall be made with respect to the slaves now in the states, but the Federal government and the government of each state shall most strictly enforce the colonization laws, and prevent the further introduction of slaves.

"Dogtrot" or double log cabin

Analyzing Primary Sources

1. How did the Alabama people make a living?
2. What was the penalty if one of the parties to the marriage bond changed his or her mind?

   TAKS PRACTICE **3. Understanding Cultures** Use Mier y Terán's description to draw a typical Alabama person's hairstyle.

Independence

Texas independence brought both opportunities and challenges. The new government concentrated on land policy, military affairs, and finances. Meanwhile immigrants came to Texas in increasing numbers. By 1845 most Texans were eager to become part of the United States. As you examine these documents, consider problems and opportunities the Republic of Texas faced.

Reader's Dictionary

creditor: a person owed money to

commonwealth paper: paper money issued by the Republic of Texas

procure: to obtain

rced: common abbreviation for "received"

tender: something offered in payment

Texas Postal Service

 **Personal Records**

Postmaster General John Rice Jones had trouble providing enough equipment for the postmasters. He explains his problem in a letter to David Ayres, the postmaster at Center Hill.

Post Office Department
Austin, March 13, 1840

David Ayres, Esqr.
P. M. Center Hill

Sir—[your letter of the 29th of last month] has been **rced.** I have just rced a letter from Houston informing me that the mail bags &c which I wrote to the Post Office agent at New Orleans for, have been rced so soon as I can get them every route in the country will be furnished with a pair. For the future, whenever an "old salt bag, full of holes," comes to your office it will be your duty to furnish a better one, that the mail may not be received in the "wretched state" you so much complain of. Thank you for telling me it was my duty to **procure** leather mail bags, which duty I was aware of, and performed immediately after my arrival here.

I am yours with respect
Jno [John] Rice Jones
            Post Master General

Early telegraph key

Lack of Money

Personal Records

The Republic of Texas never had enough money in circulation to satisfy the needs of the people. Noah Smithwick described how some Texans dealt with the lack of money.

Coin there was absolutely none, and the constantly downward tendency of the **commonwealth paper** kept it moving lively . . . Under these circumstances we established a currency of our own, a kind of banking system as it were, which though thoroughly unauthorized by law, met the local requirements . . . we settled on the cow and calf . . . Mrs. H., a widow living near me, having need of merchandise, . . . offered a cow and a calf . . . a cow and a calf being rated at ten dollars. The **tender** was accepted, Mrs. H. reserving the use of the cow during milking season. The bill of sale being made out, the merchant paid off a debt with it and the **creditor** likewise passed it on. That bit of paper passed from hand to hand, . . . till it paid about one hundred dollars . . . We all felt satisfied that the cow was safe in the widow's keeping . . . the only possible risk being the possible death of the cow.

Texans Vote for Annexation

Printed Publications

In October 1845, a referendum was held to answer the question of Texas's annexation. Few people bothered to vote since the outcome of the referendum was never in doubt. Elections results on annexation appear below by county.

Counties	Annexation	
	For	**Against**
Austin	114	1
Bastrop	166	0
Bexar	138	17
Colorado	168	0
Fayette	287	3
Fort Bend	166	1
Galveston	287	125
Goliad	16	0
Harrison	498	5
Jackson	58	0
Jasper	200	1
Lamar	238	7
Liberty	297	3
Matagorda	140	0
Montgomery	534	25
Robertson	271	22
San Patricio	56	35
Shelby	286	3
San Augustine	227	13
Travis	107	6
TOTAL	**4,254**	**267**

Analyzing Primary Sources

1. What were some disadvantages of using livestock for currency?
2. About what percent of the voters approved Texas's annexation?

TAKS PRACTICE 3. **Supporting a Point of View** Pretend you are David Ayres. Write a letter back to Postmaster General Jones in reply to the one he has written to you.

Statehood

In spite of the turmoil brought about by the war with Mexico, the Civil War, and Reconstruction, Texans in the 1840s, 1850s and 1860s raised families, established towns, planted crops, and earned a living. As you read these documents, think about everyday life in the Lone Star state.

Reader's Dictionary

furrier: a merchant who deals with furs

hospitable: welcoming to strangers

manifestation: something that is easily seen or obvious

rouanne: roundup (from the French)

sheath: a protective covering

startling: causing surprise or fright

subsided: lessened

Union: the United States of America

A Traveler Describes Houston

 **Personal Records**

A German traveler visited Texas in 1848. When he returned to Europe, he wrote about his adventures in the Lone Star state.

Houston was about the same size as Galveston but had more brick buildings than the latter and a great many more stores. In my opinion, the most interesting of these stores was the **furrier** establishment belonging to the Torrey brothers who owned a trading post located on the northern reaches of the Brazos River where they bought from the Indians . . . The streets of this town were terribly dirty and completely impassable during or after a rain. In the market square the stumps of trees, which had been cut down only recently, could be seen.

In general, Houston was not as **hospitable** in appearance as Galveston because the lovely gardens that lined the streets of that port were lacking in Houston. Also an attitude of small-mindedness seemed to prevail more in Houston.

I did not doubt, however, that Houston would far outstrip Galveston in terms of business activity if it had not already done so. This was because the location of Houston was more suited for such growth. Farmers from all over the state brought their cotton here loaded in large wagons pulled by teams of ten to twelve oxen. Their crops were either sold here or traded for wares, and from here their cotton, hides, or other commodities would then be shipped elsewhere. I saw a local businessman trade a variety of brightly colored cloths for a whole bundle of bear hides brought in by two Indians.

The mockingbird is the state bird of Texas.

Texas Language in 1869

Oral Histories

A journalist toured Texas in 1869 and wrote a magazine article about how Texans spoke.

It may be doubted if there is any other state in the **Union** which pretends to rival Texas in the **startling** originality of its slang.

A Texan never has a great quantity of anything, but he has "scads" of it, or "oodles," or "dead oodles," or "scadoodles," or "swads."

But it is in geography that this gift gives forth its most amazing **manifestations** . . . Read these [place names] from Texas: Lick Skillet, Buck Snort, Nip and Tuck, Jimtown, Rake Pocket, Hog Eye, Fair Play, Seven League, Steal Easy, Possum Trot, Flat Heel, Frog Level, Short Pone, Gourd Neck, Shake Rag, Poverty Slant, Black Ankle, Jim Ned.

One [man named] Maverick formerly owned such immense herds that many of his animals unavoidably escaped his **rouanne** in the spring were taken up by his neighbors, branded, and called "mavericks."

During the [Civil] War we all heard enough of "we-uns" and "you-uns," but "you-alls," was to me something fresh.

A San Antonio Mother Describes Her Son's Accident

Personal Records

Many Texans looked forward to autumn when pecans were ripe. Gathering the pecans sometimes involved risk. Mary Maverick described how her son was injured by a fall from a pecan tree.

Saturday October 5 Lewis was gathering pecans, when a rotten limb broke with his weight and he fell to the ground breaking both bones in his right arm just above the wrist. Dr. Dignowity set his arm. Lewis suffered much pain and I sat by him all night pouring cold water over the arm. Sunday, Dr. Dignowity put the arm in a tin **sheath** and he slept little—Monday night no sleep—Tuesday night the same. Wednesday he was better . . . Thursday he walked some with his arm in a sling. Friday the pain returned and sleeplessness . . . The swelling **subsided** and he slowly got over his suffering—but not before the 30th of November did he have any use of his arm—and it is not straight.

Pecan tree

Analyzing Primary Sources

1. Compare the advantages of geography possessed by Houston and Galveston that helped them become major cities.
2. How can place names show the way settlers thought?

TAKS PRACTICE 3. **Maintaining Cultural Heritage** Describe some slang words or terms that are special or unique to your culture or ethnic heritage.

People of Texas

*The last years of the 1800s
brought more immigrants to
Texas, an expanding economy,
new industries, and transportation
routes. Some people, such as
Native Americans, suffered from
changes during the period while
others found new opportunities.
As you read the following
documents, think about who was
helped and who was hurt by
changes in the late 1800s.*

Reader's Dictionary

burdensome: causing hardship

enclosure: a place surrounded by a fence or wall

gray-backs: biting insects

jurisdiction: the right and power to interpret and apply the law

oppressive: difficult to bear; harsh

tariff: a tax on goods entering the country

tender: offer

Buffalo Skinners

Songs & Poems

*Buffalo hunters hired crews to remove the hide
from the buffalo. As they worked, they
made up songs such as this one.*

Twas in the town of Jacksboro in the spring of
    seventy-three,
A man by the name of Crego came stepping up
    to me,
Saying, "How do you do, young fellow, and how
    would you like to go
And spend the summer pleasantly on the range of
    the buffalo?"

And not having any job, to old Crego I did say
"This going out on the buffalo range depends
    upon the pay.
But if you will pay good wages, give
    transportation too,
I think I will go with you to the range of the
    buffalo."

Our meat was of buffalo hump, like iron was our
    bread,
And all we had to sleep on was a buffalo for a
    bed;
The fleas and **gray-backs** worked on us, and boys,
    they were not slow;
I tell you there's no worse place on earth than the
    range of the buffalo.

Buffalo hunters on the Plains

Governor Hogg Writes to Senator Reagan

Personal Records

Asking a senator to resign to take a seat on the Texas Railroad Commission may seem like a strange request. Governor James Hogg asked Senator John H. Reagan to do exactly that. He explained why in a letter written on April 21, 1891.

Executive Office
Austin
April 21, 1891

My Dear Sir,

I hearby **tender** to you a position on the Railroad Commission of Texas. To accept this trust I know you must make unusual sacrifices, but considering public interests, I feel impelled to ask you to do so.

Continuously and for many years our agricultural and commercial interests have been severely depressed for which there are three causes: 1st **Burdensome** and unnecessary federal taxes, called the **tariff,** 2nd the want of money as a circulating medium, 3rd **Oppressive** local freight rates. With the evils of the first two, the federal government alone can deal. The third is within the exclusive jurisdiction of the state government. The time has come for it to be handled.

Ten Bears Speaks

Oral Histories

Comanche chief Ten Bears spoke at the Medicine Lodge Council when his people agreed to go to a reservation.

You said that you wanted to put us upon a reservation, to build us houses, and make us medicine lodges. I do not want them. I was born on the prairie, where the wind blew free and there was nothing to break the light of the sun. I was born where there were no **enclosures** and everything drew a free breath. I want to die there and not within walls. I know every stream and every wood between the Rio Grande and the Arkansas. I have hunted and lived over that country. I live like my fathers before me and like them I lived happily.

If the Texans had kept out of my country, there might have been peace. But that which you now say we must live in, is too small. The Texans have taken away the places where the grass grows the thickest and the timber was the best . . . The Whites have the country which we loved . . .

Comanche tepee

Analyzing Primary Sources

1. Why would the life of a buffalo skinner be a hard one?
2. Describe how Ten Bears felt about the idea of moving onto a reservation.

TAKS PRACTICE 3. **Diversity** Research ways in which minority religious groups in Texas, such as Jews, Muslims, or Buddhists, preserve their cultures and traditions.

A Changing Texas

The early 20th century brought about many changes to Texans. Women organized to win the right to vote. Cities were growing. New demands were being made of the educational system. African American and Mexican American Texans were adding to the cultural variety of the state. Petroleum discoveries were adding to the economic base of the state. As you read these documents, think about how groups and individuals were responding to the changes around them.

Reader's Dictionary

cyclone: an intense windstorm

fault: a structure in underground rocks that may trap oil

geology: study of Earth's physical systems

A Suffrage Leader's Busy Schedule

Personal Records

Jane Y. McCallum of Austin was one of the leaders in the fight for voting rights for women. Her diary shows how hard she worked.

Juneteenth, 1918

Tomorrow paper day, have been sick with cold; got breakfast; worked all morning in outskirts explaining registering & voting to those poor, poverty stricken women. Pretty good success. Been sewing all aft. On K.'s dress. How *am* I to get a magazine article off that I have been asked to write. Tomorrow *last day* and not a line. Hobby Club meeting in a.m. Conference with Mrs. C. *before*—then work for paper. And I'm so hot and tired—tired.

Sat. July 7, 1918

Doing organizing, sending "Women in Politics" to paper nearly every day besides Sunday. And speaking & 'phone'phone'phone—Company—oh Gee! Last Tuesday spoke at High S. at 4:30—to Confederate Veterans at 7:00. Spent Wed. aft. At Court house where women registering. Thursday did paper work and lived in a **cyclone** until left to speak at a school house beyond Del Valle at 8 o'clock. Got home not until 2:00 next morning and I had to break & refuse engagements until just this minute I've promised to go to Manor tonight.

Austin suffragists

Violin for a Saxophone

Oral Histories

One of the great jazz saxophonists of all time was Arnett Cobb of Houston. In 1988 he told an interviewer about his introduction to the saxophone.

[Question] Mr. Cobb, . . . when and where were you born?

Cobb: I was born in Houston in 1918 on August 10.

[Question] Were you introduced to music at an early age?

Cobb: Yes, My grandmother taught piano, so I had basic piano. I was around it all the time. My mother, an aunt, and two uncles played piano. When they got off the piano, I wanted to play it myself. Then I went into violin. The lessons every Saturday were a dollar; I got the violin free. I was the only violinist in the Phyllis Wheatley band, and eighty-piece brass band. The instructor told me, "Son, I can't hear you!" I said, "I can't hear me either." He said, "Would you like to have a horn?" I have one horn left: a C-melody saxophone." It was strictly a band instrument, but I was happy to get it. I had to bring a note from my parents that they would stand for it. I asked my mother. She sent the note, and I got the horn. The main thing I had to learn was the fingering of the horn. I knew the notes. I just put the two together.

Saxophone

A Wildcatter Looks for Oil

Oral Histories

Wildcatters were people who drilled for oil where none had been found before. A famous wildcatter named Glenn McCarthy describes how he looked for oil.

[Question] Well, I was wondering how you went about deciding where to drill?

[Answer] Through a certain amount of **geology,** first formations, and various other rules. For instance, the Goose Creek field. I guess you know where that is, at Baytown, in that area. Goose Creek was what it was called then. It was discovered because it's on lowland, swampland, and some of the first people to discover Goose Creek used funnels. They'd stick a funnel in the ground over a bubbling condition in the marsh. And they'd light it with a match, and if it would burn, it was making some gas from the surface . . .

[Question] It has been said that some of your biggest wells were found on land that the oil companies had abandoned. Was anything learned from their attempts?

[Answer] . . . Many years ago, most companies didn't believe there were any **faults** in the Texas Gulf Coast. But we find that it's full of faults. There are hundreds of faults on the Texas Gulf Coast.

Analyzing Primary Sources

1. List three ways Jane McCallum promoted the cause of woman suffrage.
2. What was one way wildcatters knew where to drill oil wells?

TAKS PRACTICE 3. **Explaining** How did Arnett Cobb's performances help reflect Texas cultural diversity?

Continuity and Change

In the modern era Texans have witnessed social and economic progress. Groups that had been excluded from politics now participated by holding office, voting, and campaigning. More and more Texans received a high quality education and found good jobs. Even in the middle of great change, many Texans continued to hold on to traditional values of family and community that had served so well in the past. As you read these documents look for things that changed and things that stayed the same.

Reader's Dictionary

communal: relating to the group rather than the individual

potent: powerful and strong

suppress: to hold down

Mexican American youth

Football Lessons

Don Meredith of the Dallas Cowboys talks about lessons he learned from football.

I can honestly say that football was always fun for me . . . Then as I got older and started playing high school ball I bumped into new emotional things . . . you realize that it's become much more than that, it's bigger than that, it becomes a **communal** thing. In a small town everyone sort of gets involved. I think it's the first time that a young kid feels all the different responsibilities of belonging to a group, being a real member of the community.

Mexican American Youth Organization

On May 4, 1970, Mario Compean, one of the founders of MAYO, spoke to a political gathering in San Antonio.

The time has come when the Chicanos cannot be taken for granted any longer. Politicians of all kinds will have to keep reminding themselves that the Chicanos are a **potent** political force. Therefore, the worst mistake any politician can make is to forget the Chicano. (Applause)

La Raza Unida Calls for Women's Equality

 **Printed Publications**

The La Raza Unida *Platform for 1972 contained a strong statement in favor of women's rights.*

B. La Familia y La Raza Unida

La Raza Unida Party believes that the strength of unity begins with the family. Only through full participation of all members of the family can a strong force be developed to deal with the problems which face *La Raza*.

This total family involvement is a basic foundation of *La Raza Unida* Party—men, women, and youth working together for a common cause. However, acting in good faith, and realizing that, as a group, women are **suppressed**, *Raza Unida* Party resolves that:

1. The amendment to the U.S. Constitution providing equal protection under the law for women be endorsed and supported.
2. All laws which maintain a double standard such as the "protective legislation" be amended or repealed to give women equality . . .

Hispanic women on strike

Civil Rights

 **Oral Histories**

Reverend Claude Black used an amusing story to help prevent violence in San Antonio.

So I got up and asked for the floor, and I made a statement. Said, "Let me tell you a story." I said, "Two men were standing beside a railroad track, and they watched a big bull standing in the middle of the track with the train coming. The train was blowing smoke and chugging and moving. The bull was standing in the middle of that track, pawing and hooking his horns and snorting and going on and digging into the gravel with his paws. This train was coming, and finally the train hit the bull and broke his neck and knocked him off the track. One of them turned to the other one and said, 'Man, did you see that bull?' Said, 'Didn't that bull have a lot of courage? Did you watch that bull, how he stood up against that train?' Said, 'Didn't he have a lot of courage?' And the other fellow said, 'Yeah, he had a lot of courage, but his judgment was poor.'" [laughter] So I said, "Now listen, there are a lot of policemen around this place; what you got—sticks? rocks?" I said, "It's one thing to have a lot of courage, but it's also another thing to have good judgment. Don't let bad judgment get us killed out here. And we'll win nothing." I think that turned them around.

Analyzing Primary Sources

1. How do sports help young people prepare for adult responsibilities?
2. How does full participation of all family members help to solve problems?

TAKS Practice **3. Categorizing Information** Sports can bring people together. Make a list of other cultural activities that bring people together.

Government

Women were excluded from full participation in Texas government for many years. When women did achieve political office as senators, governors, mayors, and many other offices, they made notable contributions to both Texas and the United States. As you read these documents, think about the importance of including both women and men in government.

Reader's Dictionary

belligerent: aggressive

eloquent: able to speak gracefully and persuasively

intern: someone who works to obtain experience rather than for pay

privileged: having advantages that are not available to most people

shelved: put aside, not used

Women in Government

Salado native and University of Texas graduate Liz Carpenter has a distinguished career in journalism and politics. In this statement she reminds her audience of how Texas women have become involved in government.

WHO IS THE WOMAN IN PUBLIC LIFE?

She is the voter, volunteer, and rising new voice at the City Hall and the Capitol.

She is the **eloquent** congresswoman from Houston, conscience of the constitution. She is the [college] girls who came home with a lot of uppity ideas, raised their families, ploughed their energies and brains into the vivid politics of South Texas and made an impact on their political parties.

She is the avid political science student, the **intern** learning the ropes. She's young and determined to be her own person; she is old and determined not to be **shelved.** She's the homemaker determined to have a say in how her town is run.

She's Democrat, Republican, a member of La Raza Unida. She's a **belligerent** independent. She thinks the country's moving too slowly. She fears it will move too fast. She is Black, Brown, Anglo. Her roots are **privileged.** They are humble. She's married, singled, widowed, divorced. Mother of five children. Or none.

She's you. And me. Our mothers. Our daughters. Our granddaughters. Qualified by centuries of struggle, she stands ready to run for public office or help administer public policy.

She's the most overwhelming, awe-inspiring, refreshing political force to come along in 100 years. And she's ready for action. Now. And for all time to come.

San Angelo Municipal Building

Texas, Our Texas

Words by
GLADYS YOAKUM WRIGHT
and WILLIAM J. MARSH

Music by
WILLIAM J. MARSH

NOT FAST

1. Tex — as, our Tex — as! All hail the might — y State!
2. Tex — as, O Tex — as! Your free — born Sin — gle Star
3. Tex — as, dear Tex — as! From ty — rant grip now free;

Tex — as, our Tex — as! So won — der — ful, so great!
Sends out its ra — diance To na — tions near and far.
Shines forth in splen — dor Your Star of Des — ti — ny!

Bold — est and grand — est, With—stand — ing ev — 'ry test; O
Emb — lem of Free — dom! It sets our hearts a — glow, With
Moth — er of He — roes! We come, your chil — dren true, Pro—

Em — pire, wide and glo — rious, You stand su — preme — ly blest.
tho'ts of San Ja — cin — to And glo — rious A — la — mo.
claim — ing our al — le — giance, Our Faith, our Love for you.

CHORUS Repeat ff

God bless you, Tex—as! And keep you brave and strong, That you may grow in

2nd time   1st time   2nd time

pow'r and worth Thru — out the a — ges long.   out the a — ges long.

Copyright © 1925 by W. J. Marsh. Copyright renewed 1953 by William J. Marsh.

Used by permission of Southern Music Co.

Analyzing Primary Sources

1. According to Liz Carpenter, how do women participate in government?
2. What is the emblem of freedom referred to in the Texas state song?

TAKS PRACTICE 3. **Practicing Citizenship** Explain why a free press is an essential part of a democratic society.

Texas Counties

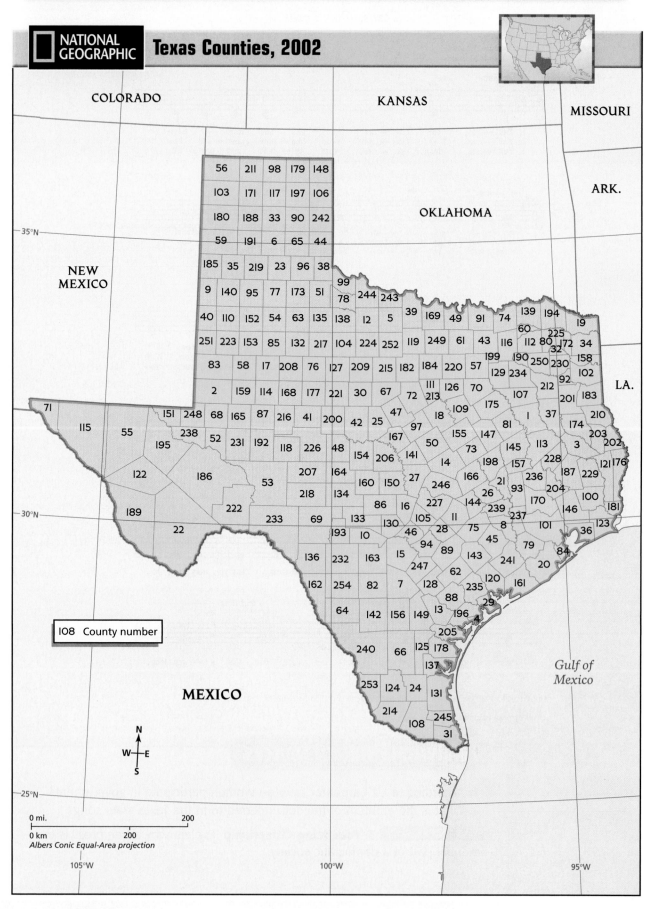

NATIONAL GEOGRAPHIC Texas Counties, 2002

COLORADO

KANSAS

MISSOURI

ARK.

OKLAHOMA

NEW MEXICO

35°N

| 56 | 211 | 98 | 179 | 148 |

| 103 | 171 | 117 | 197 | 106 |

| 180 | 188 | 33 | 90 | 242 |

| 59 | 191 | 6 | 65 | 44 |

| 185 | 35 | 219 | 23 | 96 | 38 |

| 9 | 140 | 95 | 77 | 173 | 51 | 99 78 | 244 | 243 |

39 169 49 91 74 139 194 19

40 110 152 54 63 135 138 12 5 60 225 32 172 34

251 223 153 85 132 217 104 224 252 119 249 61 43 116 112 80 158 102

LA.

83 58 17 208 76 127 209 215 182 184 220 57 199 190 250 230 92

2 159 114 168 177 221 30 67 72 111 126 70 129 234 212 201 183

30°N

71

115

55

151 248 68 165 87 216 41 200 42 25 47 18 109 175 107 1 37 210 174 203 202

238 52 231 192 118 226 48 97 155 147 81 113 3 228 187 229 121 176

195

122 186 53 207 164 154 206 141 14 50 73 198 145 157 236 204 100

189 222 233 69 218 134 160 150 27 246 166 21 93 170 146 181

22 193 10 133 86 16 227 144 26 239 237 101 36 123

136 232 163 15 105 11 28 75 8 79 84

162 254 82 7 128 94 89 143 45 20

64 142 156 149 3 196 62 235 120 161 29 4

240 66 125 178 205 88

137

253 124 24 131

214

108 245

31

25°N

MEXICO

Gulf of Mexico

108 County number

N
W E
S

0 mi.   200
0 km   200
Albers Conic Equal-Area projection

105°W   100°W   95°W

County	Map No.	2000 Population	Area (sq. mi.)	County Seat	Economy
Anderson	1	55,109	1,071	Palestine	Manufacturing, agribusiness
Andrews	2	13,004	1,501	Andrews	Oil, agribusiness
Angelina	3	80,130	802	Lufkin	Timber, manufacturing
Aransas	4	22,497	252	Rockport	Tourism, fishing, oil production, refining
Archer	5	8,854	910	Archer City	Cattle, oil services
Armstrong	6	2,148	914	Claude	Agribusiness, tourism
Atascosa	7	38,628	1,232	Jourdanton	Agribusiness, oil well supplies and services
Austin	8	23,590	653	Bellville	Agribusiness, steel, manufacturing, tourism
Bailey	9	6,594	827	Muleshoe	Farm supply manufacturing, food processing
Bandera	10	17,645	792	Bandera	Tourism, hunting, fishing, ranching supplies
Bastrop	11	57,733	888	Bastrop	Government/services, tourism, agribusiness
Baylor	12	4,093	871	Seymour	Agribusiness, retail/service, health services
Bee	13	32,359	880	Beeville	Oil supplies, agribusiness, feedlots
Bell	14	237,974	1,059	Belton	Fort Hood, manufacturing, tourism
Bexar	15	1,392,931	1,247	San Antonio	Government center, military bases, tourism
Blanco	16	8,418	711	Johnson City	Tourism, agribusiness, manufacturing
Borden	17	729	899	Gail	Oil, agribusiness
Bosque	18	17,204	989	Meridian	Agribusiness, tourism, small industries
Bowie	19	89,306	888	Boston	Government/services, agribusiness
Brazoria	20	241,767	1,387	Angleton	Petroleum/chemical industry, fishing, tourism
Brazos	21	152,415	586	Bryan	University, agribusiness, computers, tourism
Brewster	22	8,866	6,193	Alpine	University, ranching, tourism, government
Briscoe	23	1,790	900	Silverton	Agribusiness
Brooks	24	7,976	943	Falfurrias	Oil, gas, cattle
Brown	25	37,674	945	Brownwood	Agribusiness, manufacturing
Burleson	26	13,625	666	Caldwell	Oil, tourism, agribusiness, manufacturing
Burnet	27	34,147	996	Burnet	Stone processing, manufacturing, agribusiness
Caldwell	28	32,194	546	Lockhart	Petroleum, agribusiness, manufacturing
Calhoun	29	20,647	512	Port Lavaca	Manufacturing, agribusiness, oil, tourism
Callahan	30	11,859	899	Baird	Feed and fertilizer, hunting leases
Cameron	31	260,120	906	Brownsville	Agribusiness, tourism, seafood processing
Camp	32	11,549	198	Pittsburg	Agribusiness, chicken processing, timber
Carson	33	6,516	923	Panhandle	Manufacturing, Pantex plant
Cass	34	30,438	937	Linden	Government/services, timber, agribusiness
Castro	35	8,285	898	Dimmitt	Agribusiness
Chambers	36	26,031	599	Anahuac	Oil, chemicals, manufacturing, agribusiness
Cherokee	37	46,659	1,052	Rusk	Manufacturing, agribusiness, tourism
Childress	38	7,688	710	Childress	Cotton, government/services, tourism
Clay	39	11,006	1,098	Henrietta	Oil, agribusiness, varied manufacturing
Cochran	40	3,730	775	Morton	Agribusiness, oil
Coke	41	3,864	899	Robert Lee	Oil-well supplies, agribusiness, tourism
Coleman	42	9,235	1,273	Coleman	Agribusiness, oil, manufacturing
Collin	43	491,675	848	McKinney	Manufacturing, agribusiness, retail
Collingsworth	44	3,206	919	Wellington	Agribusiness, manufacturing
Colorado	45	20,390	963	Columbus	Agribusiness, manufacturing, processing
Comal	46	78,021	561	New Braunfels	Manufacturing, tourism, government/services
Comanche	47	14,026	938	Comanche	Agribusiness, manufacturing
Concho	48	3,966	991	Paint Rock	Agribusiness
Cooke	49	36,363	874	Gainesville	Agribusiness, oil industries, manufacturing
Coryell	50	74,978	1,052	Gatesville	Fort Hood, agribusiness, state prison
Cottle	51	1,904	901	Paducah	Chiefly agribusiness

County	Map No.	2000 Population	Area (sq. mi.)	County Seat	Economy
Crane	52	3,996	786	Crane	Oil-based economy
Crockett	53	4,099	2,808	Ozona	Ranching, oil and gas, hunting leases
Crosby	54	7,072	900	Crosbyton	Agribusiness, tourism, food processing
Culberson	55	2,975	3,813	Van Horn	Agribusiness, tourism, talc mining, oil
Dallam	56	6,222	1,505	Dalhart	Agribusiness, tourism, small manufacturing
Dallas	57	2,218,899	880	Dallas	Manufacturing, government/services
Dawson	58	14,985	902	Lamesa	Agriculture, manufacturing
Deaf Smith	59	18,561	1,497	Hereford	Sugar, meat packers, agribusiness
Delta	60	5,327	277	Cooper	Agribusiness, tourism, manufacturing
Denton	61	432,976	889	Denton	Colleges, tourism, government/services
De Witt	62	20,013	909	Cuero	Wood, manufacturing, agribusiness
Dickens	63	2,762	904	Dickens	Services/prison, agribusiness, hunting leases
Dimmit	64	10,248	1,331	Carrizo Springs	Agribusiness, oil products, manufacturing
Donley	65	3,828	930	Clarendon	Agribusiness, distribution, manufacturing
Duval	66	13,120	1,793	San Diego	Ranching, petroleum, tourism
Eastland	67	18,297	926	Eastland	Agribusiness, education, petroleum
Ector	68	121,123	901	Odessa	Oil field operations, rubber and plastics
Edwards	69	2,162	2,120	Rocksprings	Ranching, hunting leases, tourism, oil, gas
Ellis	70	111,360	940	Waxahachie	Manufacturing, agribusiness
El Paso	71	591,610	1,013	El Paso	Military, distribution center, manufacturing
Erath	72	33,001	1,086	Stephenville	Agriculture, industry, education
Falls	73	18,576	769	Marlin	Manufacturing, agribusiness
Fannin	74	31,242	892	Bonham	Agribusiness, distribution, meat packing
Fayette	75	21,804	950	La Grange	Agribusiness, tourism, electricity, minerals
Fisher	76	4,344	901	Roby	Agribusiness, electric co-op, oil, gypsum
Floyd	77	7,771	992	Floydada	Agribusiness, manufacturing
Foard	78	1,622	707	Crowell	Agribusiness, manufacturing, government
Fort Bend	79	354,452	875	Richmond	Agribusiness, petrochemicals, sulfur
Franklin	80	9,458	286	Mt. Vernon	Agribusiness, tourism, retirement center, oil
Freestone	81	17,867	886	Fairfield	Mining, manufacturing, agribusiness
Frio	82	16,252	1,133	Pearsall	Agribusiness, oil-field services
Gaines	83	14,467	1,502	Seminole	Oil and gas production, agribusiness
Galveston	84	250,158	399	Galveston	Port, insurance and finance, petrochemical
Garza	85	4,872	896	Post	Cotton, oil, tourism
Gillespie	86	20,814	1,061	Fredericksburg	Agribusiness, tourism, food processing
Glasscock	87	1,406	901	Garden City	Farming, ranching, hunting leases, oil and gas
Goliad	88	6,928	854	Goliad	Oil, agribusiness, tourism, electricity
Gonzales	89	18,628	1,068	Gonzales	Agribusiness
Gray	90	22,744	928	Pampa	Oil, agriculture, feedlot, chemical plant
Grayson	91	110,595	934	Sherman	Manufacturing, distribution, trade
Gregg	92	111,379	274	Longview	Oil, manufacturing, tourism, conventions
Grimes	93	23,552	794	Anderson	Manufacturing, agribusiness, tourism
Guadalupe	94	89,023	711	Seguin	Manufacturing, agribusiness, tourism
Hale	95	36,602	1,005	Plainview	Agribusiness, food processing, manufacturing
Hall	96	3,782	903	Memphis	Agribusiness
Hamilton	97	8,229	836	Hamilton	Agribusiness, manufacturing, tourism
Hansford	98	5,369	920	Spearman	Agribusiness, mineral operations
Hardeman	99	4,724	695	Quanah	Agribusiness, some manufacturing, tourism
Hardin	100	48,073	894	Kountze	Manufacturing, wood processing, minerals
Harris	101	3,400,578	1,729	Houston	Industry, petrochemicals, port
Harrison	102	62,110	899	Marshall	Oil and gas, manufacturing

County	Map No.	2000 Population	Area (sq. mi.)	County Seat	Economy
Hartley	103	5,537	1,462	Channing	Agriculture, gas, manufacturing
Haskell	104	6,093	903	Haskell	Agribusiness, oil-field operations
Hays	105	97,589	678	San Marcos	Education, tourism, retirement area
Hemphill	106	3,351	910	Canadian	Petroleum, livestock
Henderson	107	73,277	874	Athens	Manufacturing, agribusiness, minerals, tourism
Hidalgo	108	569,463	1,570	Edinburg	Food processing, shipping, agribusiness
Hill	109	32,321	962	Hillsboro	Agribusiness, varied manufacturing, tourism
Hockley	110	22,716	908	Levelland	Oil and gas, manufacturing, varied agribusiness
Hood	111	41,000	422	Granbury	Agribusiness, tourism, nuclear power plant
Hopkins	112	31,960	785	Sulphur Spr.	Dairies, agribusiness, manufacturing
Houston	113	23,185	1,231	Crockett	Livestock, timber, manufacturing, tourism
Howard	114	33,627	903	Big Spring	Oil and gas, agribusiness, manufacturing
Hudspeth	115	3,344	4,571	Sierra Blanca	Agribusiness, mining, tourism, hunting leases
Hunt	116	76,596	841	Greenville	Education, manufacturing, agribusiness
Hutchinson	117	23,857	887	Stinnett	Oil, gas, petrochemicals, manufacturing
Irion	118	1,771	1,052	Mertzon	Ranching, oil, gas production
Jack	119	8,763	917	Jacksboro	Petroleum, livestock, manufacturing, tourism
Jackson	120	14,391	829	Edna	Petroleum, manufacturing, agribusiness
Jasper	121	35,604	937	Jasper	Timber, oil, tourism, fishing, agriculture
Jeff Davis	122	2,207	2,265	Fort Davis	Tourism, ranching, nurseries, small business
Jefferson	123	252,051	904	Beaumont	Petrochemical, shipbuilding, steel, port activity
Jim Hogg	124	5,281	1,136	Hebbronville	Oil, cattle operations
Jim Wells	125	39,326	865	Alice	Oil, gas production, sorghum and cattle
Johnson	126	126,811	729	Cleburne	Agribusiness, railroad, manufacturing
Jones	127	20,785	931	Anson	Agribusiness, manufacturing
Karnes	128	15,446	750	Karnes City	Agribusiness, minerals, tourism, manufacturing
Kaufman	129	71,313	786	Kaufman	Manufacturing, trade, government, antiques
Kendall	130	23,743	662	Boerne	Tourism, agribusiness, manufacturing
Kenedy	131	414	1,457	Sarita	Oil, ranching, hunting leases
Kent	132	859	902	Jayton	Agribusiness, oil, hunting leases
Kerr	133	43,653	1,106	Kerrville	Tourism, agribusiness, manufacturing, hunting
Kimble	134	4,468	1,251	Junction	Livestock, tourism, cedar oil and wood products
King	135	356	912	Guthrie	Minerals, ranching
Kinney	136	3,379	1,363	Brackettville	Agribusiness, tourism, government service
Kleberg	137	31,549	871	Kingsville	Naval air station, ranch, chemicals and plastics
Knox	138	4,253	854	Benjamin	Agribusiness, government services
Lamar	139	48,499	917	Paris	Manufacturing, agribusiness, tourism
Lamb	140	14,709	1,016	Littlefield	Agribusiness, distribution center, denim textiles
Lampasas	141	17,762	712	Lampasas	Fort Hood, industry, tourism, agribusiness
La Salle	142	5,866	1,489	Cotulla	Agribusiness, hunting leases, tourism
Lavaca	143	19,210	970	Hallettsville	Manufacturing, leather, agribusiness, oil and gas
Lee	144	15,657	629	Giddings	Manufacturing, agribusiness, oil and gas
Leon	145	15,335	1,072	Centerville	Oil, gas production, agribusiness
Liberty	146	70,154	1,160	Liberty	Agribusiness, manufacturing, tourism
Limestone	147	22,051	909	Groesbeck	Manufacturing, agribusiness, tourism, minerals
Lipscomb	148	3,057	932	Lipscomb	Agribusiness, government, oil and gas
Live Oak	149	12,309	1,036	George West	Oil, government, tourism, agribusiness
Llano	150	17,044	935	Llano	Tourism, retirement, ranch trading
Loving	151	67	673	Mentone	Petroleum operations, some cattle
Lubbock	152	242,628	900	Lubbock	Agribusiness, manufacturing, education
Lynn	153	6,550	892	Tahoka	Agribusiness

County	Map No.	2000 Population	Area (sq. mi.)	County Seat	Economy
McCulloch	154	8,205	1,069	Brady	Agribusiness, manufacturing, tourism, hunting
McLennan	155	213,517	1,042	Waco	Distribution, manufacturing, agribusiness
McMullen	156	851	1,113	Tilden	Livestock, hunting leases, hay
Madison	157	12,940	470	Madisonville	Agribusiness, oil, manufacturing
Marion	158	10,941	381	Jefferson	Tourism, timber, food processing
Martin	159	4,746	915	Stanton	Petroleum production, agribusiness
Mason	160	3,738	932	Mason	Ranching, hunting, tourism, soft-drink bottling
Matagorda	161	37,957	1,114	Bay City	Oil, agribusiness, manufacturing, tourism
Maverick	162	47,197	1,280	Eagle Pass	Oil, agribusiness
Medina	163	39,304	1,328	Hondo	Agribusiness, tourism, manufacturing
Menard	164	2,360	902	Menard	Agribusiness, tourism, oil, gas production
Midland	165	116,009	900	Midland	Oil, distribution, manufacturing
Milam	166	24,238	1,017	Cameron	Manufacturing, lignite mining, agribusiness
Mills	167	5,151	748	Goldthwaite	Agribusiness, hunting leases
Mitchell	168	9,698	910	Colorado City	Agribusiness, oil, some manufacturing
Montague	169	19,117	931	Montague	Agribusiness, oil, manufacturing
Montgomery	170	293,768	1,044	Conroe	lumber, oil, government/services
Moore	171	20,121	900	Dumas	Oil and gas, agribusiness
Morris	172	13,048	255	Daingerfield	Manufacturing, tourism, livestock, timber
Motley	173	1,426	989	Matador	Government/services, ranching, cotton, oil
Nacogdoches	174	59,203	947	Nacogdoches	Agribusiness, timber, manufacturing, education
Navarro	175	48,124	1,071	Corsicana	Manufacturing, agribusiness, oil, distribution
Newton	176	15,072	933	Newton	Forestry, tourism
Nolan	177	15,802	912	Sweetwater	Manufacturing, ranching, oil and gas production
Nueces	178	313,645	836	Corpus Christi	Oil, port, agriculture, tourism, manufacturing
Ochiltree	179	9,006	918	Perryton	Oil, agribusiness, feedlot, hunting leases
Oldham	180	2,185	1,501	Vega	Ranching center
Orange	181	84,966	356	Orange	Petrochemicals, shipping, agribusiness
Palo Pinto	182	27,026	953	Palo Pinto	Manufacturing, tourism, petroleum, agribusiness
Panola	183	22,756	801	Carthage	Gas and oil, agribusiness, manufacturing, forests
Parker	184	88,495	904	Weatherford	Agribusiness, manufacturing, government
Parmer	185	10,016	882	Farwell	Agribusiness
Pecos	186	16,809	4,764	Fort Stockton	Agribusiness, oil, gas, tourism, government
Polk	187	41,133	1,057	Livingston	Timber, lumber, tourism, manufacturing
Potter	188	113,546	909	Amarillo	Petrochemicals, gas, transportation, distribution
Presidio	189	7,304	3,856	Marfa	Ranching, government/services, tourism
Rains	190	9,139	232	Emory	Oil, tourism, agribusiness, manufacturing
Randall	191	104,312	914	Canyon	Agribusiness, education, manufacturing, tourism
Reagan	192	3,326	1,175	Big Lake	Oil production, natural gas, ranching
Real	193	3,047	700	Leakey	Tourism, hunting leases, ranch supplies
Red River	194	14,314	1,050	Clarksville	Agribusiness, lumbering, manufacturing
Reeves	195	13,137	2,636	Pecos	Oil, agribusiness, tourism, feedlots
Refugio	196	7,828	770	Refugio	Petroleum, petrochemical, agribusiness
Roberts	197	887	924	Miami	Agribusiness, oil-field operations
Robertson	198	16,000	855	Franklin	Agribusiness, manufacturing, power plant
Rockwall	199	43,080	129	Rockwall	Industry, tourism
Runnels	200	11,495	1,054	Ballinger	Agribusiness, oil, manufacturing
Rusk	201	47,372	924	Henderson	Oil, lumber, agribusiness, government/services
Sabine	202	10,469	490	Hemphill	Tourism, broilers, timber industries
San Augustine	203	8,946	528	San Augustine	Lumbering, shipping, varied manufacturing
San Jacinto	204	32,246	571	Coldspring	Timber and oil

County	Map No.	2000 Population	Area (sq. mi.)	County Seat	Economy
San Patricio	205	67,138	692	Sinton	Oil, manufacturing, agribusiness, tourism
San Saba	206	6,186	1,134	San Saba	Agribusiness, stone processing, tourism
Schleicher	207	2,935	1,311	Eldorado	Oil and ranching
Scurry	208	16,361	903	Snyder	Oil, agribusiness, manufacturing, tourism
Shackelford	209	3,302	914	Albany	Oil and ranching, some manufacturing
Shelby	210	25,224	794	Center	Broiler, egg production, cattle, timber, tourism
Sherman	211	3,186	923	Stratford	Agribusiness
Smith	212	174,706	928	Tyler	Agribusiness, oil, distribution, tourism
Somervell	213	6,809	187	Glen Rose	Commanche Peak Power Station, tourism, agribusiness
Starr	214	53,597	1,223	Rio Grande City	Agribusiness, oil, tourism, government/services
Stephens	215	9,674	895	Breckenridge	Oil, agribusiness, recreation, manufacturing
Sterling	216	1,393	923	Sterling City	Oil and ranching, hunting leases
Stonewall	217	1,693	919	Aspermont	Agribusiness, fabrication, government/services
Sutton	218	4,077	1,454	Sonora	Oil and gas, agribusiness, hunting leases
Swisher	219	8,378	900	Tulia	Agribusiness, manufacturing, tourism, prison
Tarrant	220	1,446,219	863	Fort Worth	Tourism, industry, airport
Taylor	221	126,555	916	Abilene	Dyess Air Force Base, agribusiness, manufacturing
Terrell	222	1,081	2,358	Sanderson	Ranching, tourism, oil and gas, hunting leases
Terry	223	12,761	890	Brownfield	Agribusiness, petroleum
Throckmorton	224	1,850	912	Throckmorton	Oil, agribusiness, hunting leases
Titus	225	28,118	411	Mt. Pleasant	Agribusiness, manufacturing, lignite mining
Tom Green	226	104,010	1,522	San Angelo	Agribusiness, manufacturing, trade, education
Travis	227	812,280	989	Austin	Education, government, tourism, industry
Trinity	228	13,779	693	Groveton	Forestry, tourism, cattle, government/services
Tyler	229	20,871	923	Woodville	Lumbering, government, manufacturing, tourism
Upshur	230	35,291	588	Gilmer	Manufacturing, agribusiness, oil, lumber mill
Upton	231	3,404	1,242	Rankin	Oil, power plant, cotton, ranching
Uvalde	232	25,926	1,557	Uvalde	Agribusiness, manufacturing, tourism
Val Verde	233	44,856	3,171	Del Rio	Agribusiness, tourism, trade, military
Van Zandt	234	48,140	849	Canton	Oil, tourism, agribusiness, light manufacturing
Victoria	235	84,088	883	Victoria	Petrochemical, government, oil, manufacturing
Walker	236	61,758	787	Huntsville	Prison system, education, tourism, timber, beef
Waller	237	32,663	514	Hempstead	Agribusiness, oil, manufacturing, education
Ward	238	10,909	836	Monahans	Oil, gas, sand and gravel produced
Washington	239	30,373	609	Brenham	Agribusiness, oil, tourism, manufacturing
Webb	240	193,117	3,357	Laredo	Trade, tourism, oil and gas, manufacturing
Wharton	241	41,188	1,090	Wharton	Oil, minerals, agribusiness, hunting leases
Wheeler	242	5,284	914	Wheeler	Oil, agribusiness, tourism
Wichita	243	131,664	628	Wichita Falls	Retail, air base, government, manufacturing, oil
Wilbarger	244	14,676	971	Vernon	Agribusiness, oil
Willacy	245	20,082	597	Raymondville	Oil, agribusiness, tourism, shipping
Williamson	246	249,967	1,124	Georgetown	Agribusiness, manufacturing, education
Wilson	247	32,408	807	Floresville	Agribusiness
Winkler	248	7,173	841	Kermit	Oil, natural gas, ranching
Wise	249	48,793	905	Decatur	Agribusiness, oil, recreation, hunting leases
Wood	250	36,752	650	Quitman	Oil, natural gas, agribusiness, tourism
Yoakum	251	7,322	800	Plains	Oil, agriculture
Young	252	17,943	922	Graham	Oil, agribusiness, tourism, hunting leases
Zapata	253	12,182	997	Zapata	Tourism, oil, ranching, reservoir activities
Zavala	254	11,600	1,299	Crystal City	Agribusiness, oil, gas, hunting leases

Texas Declaration of Independence

The Unanimous Declaration of Independence Made by the Delegates of the People of Texas in General Convention at the Town of Washington on the 2nd day of March, 1836.

When a government has ceased to protect the lives, liberty and property of the people, from whom its legitimate powers are derived, and, for the advancement of whose happiness it was instituted; and so far from being a guarantee for the enjoyment of those inestimable and inalienable rights, becomes an instrument in the hands of evil rulers for their oppression: When the Federal Republican Constitution of their country, which they have sworn to support, no longer has a substantial existence, and the whole nature of their government has been forcibly changed, without their consent, from a restricted federative republic, composed of sovereign states, to a consolidated central military despotism, in which every interest is disregarded but that of the army and the priesthood—both the eternal enemies of civil liberty, the ever-ready minions of power, and the usual instruments of tyrants: When, long after the spirit of the constitution has departed, moderation is, at length, so far lost by those in power that even the semblance of freedom is removed, and the forms, themselves, of the constitution discontinued; and so far from their petitions and remonstrances being regarded, the agents who bear them are thrown into dungeons, and mercenary armies sent forth to force a new government upon them at the point of the bayonet: When, in consequence of such acts of malfeasance and abdication, on the part of the government, anarchy prevails, and civil society is dissolved into its original elements; in such a crisis, the first law of nature, the right of self-preservation, the inherent and inalienable right of the people to appeal to first principles and take their political affairs into their own hands in extreme cases, enjoins it as a right towards themselves and a sacred obligation to their posterity to abolish such government and create another in its stead, calculated to rescue them from impending dangers, and to secure their future welfare and happiness.

Nations, as well as individuals, are amenable for their acts to the public opinion of mankind. A statement of a part of our grievances is, therefore, submitted to an impartial world, in justification of the hazardous but unavoidable step now taken of severing our political connection with the Mexican people, and assuming an independent attitude among the nations of the earth.

The Mexican government, by its colonization laws, invited and induced the Anglo-American population of Texas to colonize its wilderness under the pledged faith of a written constitution, that they should continue to enjoy that constitutional liberty and republican government to which they had been habituated in the land of their birth, the United States of America. In this expectation they have been cruelly disappointed, inasmuch as the Mexican nation has acquiesced in the late changes made in the government by General Antonio López de Santa Anna, who, having overturned the constitution of his country, now offers us the cruel alternative either to abandon our homes, acquired by so many privations, or submit to the most intolerable of all tyranny, the combined despotism of the sword and the priesthood.

It has sacrificed our welfare to the state of Coahuila, by which our interests have been continually depressed through a jealous and partial course of legislation, carried on at a far distant seat of government, by a hostile majority, in an unknown tongue; and this, too, notwithstanding we have petitioned in the humblest terms for the establishment of a separate state government, and have, in accordance with the provisions of the national constitution, presented to the general congress a republican constitution which was, without just cause, contemptuously rejected.

It incarcerated in a dungeon, for a long time, one of our citizens, for no other cause but a zealous endeavor to procure the acceptance of our constitution and the establishment of a state government.

It has failed and refused to secure, on a firm basis, the right of trial by jury, that palladium of civil liberty, and only safe guarantee for the life, liberty, and property of the citizen.

It has failed to establish any public system of education, although possessed of almost boundless resources (the public domain) and, although it is an axiom, in political science, that unless a people are educated and enlightened, it is idle to expect the continuance of civil liberty or the capacity for self-government.

It has suffered the military commandants, stationed among us, to exercise arbitrary acts of oppression and tyrrany; thus trampling upon the most sacred rights of the citizen and rendering the military superior to the civil power.

It has dissolved, by force of arms, the State Congress of Coahuila and Texas, and obliged our representatives to fly for their lives from the seat of government; thus depriving us of the fundamental political right of representation.

It has demanded the surrender of a number of our citizens, and ordered military detachments to seize and carry them into the Interior for trial; in contempt of the civil authorities, and in defiance of the laws and the constitution.

It has made piratical attacks upon our commerce, by commissioning foreign desperadoes and authorizing them to seize our vessels, and convey the property of our citizens to far distant ports for confiscation.

It denies us the right of worshiping the Almighty according to the dictates of our own conscience, by the support of a national religion, calculated to promote the temporal interests of its human functionaries, rather than the glory of the true and living God.

It has demanded us to deliver up our arms, which are essential to our defense, the rightful property of freemen, and formidable only to tyrannical governments.

It has invaded our country, both by sea and by land, with intent to lay waste our territory and drive us from our homes; and has now a large mercenary army advancing to carry on against us a war of extermination.

It has, through its emissaries, incited the merciless savage, with the tomahawk and scalping knife, to massacre the inhabitants of our defenseless frontiers.

It hath been, during the whole time of our connection with it, the contemptible sport and victim of successive military revolutions, and hath continually exhibited every characteristic of a weak, corrupt, and tyrannical government.

These, and other grievances, were patiently borne by the people of Texas until they reached that point at which forbearance ceases to be a virtue. We then took up arms in defense of the national constitution. We appealed to our Mexican brethren for assistance. Our appeal has been made in vain. Though months have elapsed, no sympathetic response has yet been heard from the Interior. We are, therefore, forced to the melancholy conclusion that the Mexican people have acquiesced in the destruction of their liberty, and the substitution therfor of a military government—that they are unfit to be free and incapable of self-government.

The necessity of self-preservation, therefore, now decrees our eternal political separation.

We, therefore, the delegates, with plenary powers, of the people of Texas, in solemn convention assembled, appealing to a candid world for the necessities of our condition, do hereby resolve and declare that our political connection with the Mexican nation has forever ended; and that the people of Texas do now constitute a free, sovereign, and independent republic, and are fully invested with all the rights and attributes which properly belong to independent nations; and, conscious of the rectitude of our intentions, we fearlessly and confidently commit the issue to the decision of the Supreme Arbiter of the destinies of nations.

[The names of the signers below are shown in the style in which they were written on the document.]

RICHARD ELLIS, *PRESIDENT*

CHARLES B. STEWART	SAM^L A. MAVERICK
THO^S BARNETT	SAM P. CARSON
JOHN S.D. BYROM	A. BRISCOE
FRAN^{CO} RUIZ	J.B. WOODS
J. ANTONIO NAVARRO	JA^S COLLINGSWORTH
JESSE B. BADGETT	EDWIN WALLER
W^M D. LACEY	ASA BRIGHAM
WILLIAM MENEFEE	GEO. C. CHILDRESS
JN^O FISHER	BAILEY HARDEMAN
MATHEW CALDWELL	ROB. POTTER
WILLIAM MOTTLEY	THOMAS JEFFERSON RUSK
LORENZO DE ZAVALA	CHAS. S. TAYLOR
STEPHEN H. EVERITT	JOHN S. ROBERTS
GEO W. SMYTH	ROBERT HAMILTON
ELIJAH STAPP	COLLIN MCKINNEY
CLAIBORNE WEST	ALBERT H. LATIMER
W^M B. SCATES	JAMES POWER
M.B. MENARD	SAM HOUSTON
A.B. HARDIN	DAVID THOMAS
J.W. BUNTON	EDW^D CONRAD
THO^S J. GASLEY	MARTIN PARMER
R.M. COLEMAN	EDWIN O. LEGRAND
STERLING C. ROBERTSON	STEPHEN W. BLOUNT
BENJ. BRIGGS GOODRICH	JA^S GAINES
G.W. BARNETT	W^M CLARK, JR.
JAMES G. SWISHER	SYDNEY O. PENINGTON
JESSE GRIMES	W^M CARROL CRAWFORD
S. RHOADS FISHER	JN^O TURNER
JOHN W. MOORE	
JOHN W. BOWER	H.S. KIMBLE, *SECRETARY*

Texas Constitutions

Constitution of 1824

The 1824 constitution of the Republic of Mexico was adopted by a constituent assembly. Erasmo Seguín represented Texas in this assembly. The constitution was patterned after the United States Constitution and the Spanish Constitution of 1812. Under this constitution a president and vice president were chosen for four-year terms by the legislative bodies of the states of Mexico. A national congress, consisting of a house of deputies and a senate, was created. Judicial power was delegated to a supreme court and superior courts of departments and districts. The Roman Catholic faith was recognized as the state religion.

Constitution of 1827

Under the Constitution of 1824, each Mexican state was required to adopt a state constitution. The state of Coahuila y Tejas published its constitution in March 1827. The 1827 constitution divided the state into three departments; Texas was one of the three departments and was given 2 of 12 seats in the one-house congress of the state. A governor and vice governor were elected by popular vote for four-year terms. State courts were provided with limited authority, but trial by jury, as promised by the constitution, was never established. The Roman Catholic faith was recognized as the religion of the state.

Manuel de Zavala,
first vice president of the Republic of Texas

Constitution of 1836

The Constitution of the Republic of Texas was adopted by delegates to the convention that declared independence from Mexico. The constitution provided for a popularly elected president and vice president who would serve three-year terms. Presidents were ineligible to succeed themselves. The congress was divided into a house of representatives and a senate. Judicial powers were vested in a supreme court and such lesser courts as congress wished to establish. Congress was instructed to divide the Republic into counties and the counties into justice precincts. A Declaration of Rights consisting of 17 articles guaranteed freedom of speech, press, and religion.

Constitution of 1845

The first state constitution was twice as long as the Constitution of 1836. It was modeled upon both the Louisiana Constitution of 1845 and the Constitution of the Republic of Texas. The Constitution of 1845 provided for a popularly elected governor who would serve a two-year term. The governor was ineligible to serve for more than four years in any six-year period. The legislature was divided into a house of representatives and a senate. The judiciary consisted of a supreme court, district courts, and such inferior courts as the legislature wished to establish.

Constitution of 1861

This was an amended version of the Constitution of 1845. The words "Confederate States of America" were substituted for "United States of America." Officials were required to take an oath to support the Constitution of the Confederate States of America. Greater protection to the institution of slavery was provided.

Constitution of 1866

This constitution was adopted in compliance with the Johnson plan of Reconstruction. The governor's term was increased to four years, and the governor was given the power to veto individual items in appropriations bills. The governor was also forbidden from serving more than eight years in any twelve-year period. The composition and powers of the legislature remained about the same as under the Constitution of 1845, although the salaries of legislators were increased somewhat. The supreme court was increased from three to five members.

Constitution of 1869

The Constitution of 1869 was drafted by the convention of 1868 in compliance with the congressional Reconstruction acts of 1867. The governor was elected for a four-year term as under the Constitution of 1866, but the powers of the office were increased. The term of state senators was increased from four to six years. Permission for the legislature to call a new constitutional convention was withheld, but the amendment procedure was unchanged. Annual sessions of the legislature were provided for. The Supreme Court was reduced from five to three judges and the term reduced to nine years, one new judge to take office every third year. All judicial offices became appointive, and county courts were abolished. Generous support was provided for public schools. A poll tax was authorized and funds collected were assigned to support education. For the first time, African Americans were given the right to vote.

Constitution of 1876

The present state constitution was adopted following the end of Reconstruction. The governor's powers and salary were reduced, and the term of office set at two years with no prohibition to reelection. The senate was enlarged to 31 members, and the house of representatives was enlarged so that it might increase to 150 members as the population grew. Legislative salaries were reduced, and a ceiling was set on state debt. Biennial sessions of the legislature were provided for. District and supreme court judges were to be chosen by popular vote. County courts were reestablished. Since 1876 more than 300 amendments to the constitution have been adopted, including one in 1972 that extended the governor's term to four years.

There have been several unsuccessful attempts to adopt a new constitution for Texas. In 1974 and 1975, voters of Texas rejected attempts to revise the constitution.

Members of the 1875 Texas Constitutional Convention

The Governors and Presidents of Texas

Spanish Royal Governors of Texas

1691–1692	Domingo Terán de los Ríos
1693–1716	Texas unoccupied but included in Coahuila
1716–1719	Martín de Alarcón, appointed governor of Coahuila in August 1716; governor of Texas in December 1716
1719–1722	The Marqués de San Miguel de Aguayo, governor of Coahuila and Texas
1722–1727	Fernando Pérez de Almazán
1727–1730	Melchor de Media Villa y Azcona
1730–1734	Juan Antonio Bustillo y Ceballos
1734–1736	Manuel de Sandoval
1736–1737	Carlos Benites Franquis de Lugo
1737–1741	Prudencio de Orobio y Basterra
1741–1743	Tomás Felipe Wintuisen
1743–1744	Justo Boneo y Morales
1744–1748	Francisco García Larios
1748–1751	Pedro del Barrio Junco y Espriella
1751–1759	Jacinto de Barrios y Jáuregui, appointed governor of Coahuila in 1757; retained in Texas until 1759 to complete a task
1759–1766	Angel Martos y Navarrete
1767–1770	Hugo Oconór
1770–1778	The Barón de Ripperdá
1778–1786	Domingo Cabello
1786	Bernardo Bonavía, appointed July 8; apparently did not serve
1787–1790	Rafael Martínez Pacheco, appointed February 27, 1787; removal approved October 18, 1790
1788	Governorship suppressed; province under presidial captain
1790–1798	Manuel Muñoz
1798(?)	José Irigoyen, apparently appointed but did not serve
1800(?)–1805	Juan Bautista de Elguézabal
1805–1810	Antonio Cordero y Bustamante
1810–1813	Manuel de Salcedo
1811	Juan Bautista de las Casas (revolutionary governor, January 22–March 2)
1814–1817	Cristóbal Domínguez
1817	Ignacio Pérez and Manuel Pardo (governors ad interim)
1817–1822	Antonio Martínez

Mexican Governors of Texas

1822–1823	José Felix Trespalacios
1823(?)–1824	Luciano García

Mexican Governors of Coahuila y Tejas

1824–1826	Rafael Gonzales
1826–1827	Victor Blanco
1827–1830	José María Viesca
1830–1831	Ramón Eca y Músquiz
1831–1832	José María Letona
1832	Ramón Eca y Músquiz
1832–1833	Juan Martín de Beramendi (Veramendi)
1833–1834	Juan José de Vidaurri y Villasenor
1834–1835	Juan José Elguézabal
1835	José María Cantú
1835	Agustín Viesca
1835	Marciel Borrego
1835	Ramón Eca y Músquiz

Provisional Governors During the Texas Revolution

November 1835–March 1836
Henry Smith

January 1836–March 1836
James W. Robinson

Presidents of the Republic of Texas

March 1836–October 1836
David G. Burnet

October 1836–December 1838
Sam Houston

December 1838–December 1841
Mirabeau B. Lamar

December 1841–December 1844
Sam Houston

December 1844–February 1846
Anson Jones

Sam Houston

Governors Since Annexation

George W. Bush

February 1846–December 1847	J. Pinckney Henderson
December 1847–December 1849	George T. Wood
December 1849–November 1853	P. Hansborough Bell
November 1853–December 1853	J.W. Henderson
December 1853–December 1857	Elisha M. Pease
December 1857–December 1859	Hardin R. Runnels
December 1859–March 1861	Sam Houston
March 1861–November 1861	Edward Clark
November 1861–November 1863	Francis R. Lubbock
November 1863–June 1865	Pendleton Murrah
July 1865–August 1866	Andrew J. Hamilton (provisional)
August 1866–August 1867	James W. Throckmorton
August 1867–September 1869	Elisha M. Pease
January 1870–January 1874	Edmund J. Davis
January 1874–December 1876	Richard Coke
December 1876–January 1879	Richard B. Hubbard
January 1879–January 1883	Oran M. Roberts
January 1883–January 1887	John Ireland
January 1887–January 1891	Lawrence Sullivan Ross
January 1891–January 1895	James S. Hogg
January 1895–January 1899	Charles A. Culberson
January 1899–January 1903	Joseph D. Sayers
January 1903–January 1907	S.W.T. Lanham
January 1907–January 1911	Thomas M. Campbell
January 1911–January 1915	Oscar Branch Colquitt
January 1915–August 1917	James E. Ferguson
August 1917–January 1921	William P. Hobby
January 1921–January 1925	Pat M. Neff
January 1925–January 1927	Miriam A. Ferguson
January 1927–January 1931	Dan Moody
January 1931–January 1933	Ross S. Sterling
January 1933–January 1935	Miriam A. Ferguson
January 1935–January 1939	James V. Allred
January 1939–August 1941	W. Lee O'Daniel
August 1941–January 1947	Coke R. Stevenson
January 1947–July 1949	Beauford H. Jester (died in office)
July 1949–January 1957	Allan Shivers
January 1957–January 1963	Price Daniel
January 1963–January 1969	John Connally
January 1969–January 1973	Preston Smith
January 1973–January 1979	Dolph Briscoe
January 1979–January 1983	William P. Clements
January 1983–January 1987	Mark White
January 1987–January 1991	William P. Clements
January 1991–January 1995	Ann W. Richards
January 1995–December 2000	George W. Bush
December 2000–present	James Richard Perry

Honoring America

For Americans, the flag has always had a special meaning. It is a symbol of our nation's freedom and democracy.

Flag Etiquette

Over the years, Americans have developed rules and customs concerning the use and display of the flag. One of the most important things every American should remember is to treat the flag with respect.

- The flag should be raised and lowered by hand and displayed only from sunrise to sunset. On special occasions, the flag may be displayed at night, but it should be illuminated.

- The flag may be displayed on all days, weather permitting, particularly on national and state holidays and on historic and special occasions.

- No flag may be flown above the American flag or to the right of it at the same height.

- The flag should never touch the ground or floor beneath it.

- The flag may be flown at half-staff by order of the president, usually to mourn the death of a public official.

- The flag may be flown upside down only to signal distress.

- When the flag becomes old and tattered, it should be destroyed by burning. According to an approved custom, the Union (stars on blue field) is first cut from the flag; then the two pieces, which no longer form a flag, are burned.

★ ★ ★ ★ ★ ★ ★ ★

The Star-Spangled Banner

O! say can you see, by the dawn's early light,
What so proudly we hail'd at the twilight's last gleaming,
Whose broad stripes and bright stars through the perilous fight,
O'er the ramparts we watched, were so gallantly streaming?
And the Rockets' red glare, the Bombs bursting in air,
Gave proof through the night that our Flag was still there;
O! say, does that star-spangled banner yet wave
O'er the Land of the free and the home of the brave!

The Pledge of Allegiance

I pledge allegiance to the Flag of the United States of America and to the Republic for which it stands, one Nation under God, indivisible, with liberty and justice for all.

Glossary

A

abolitionist a person who works to end slavery (p. 328)

absolute location the exact position of a place on earth's surface expressed in latitude and longitude (p. 27)

ad interim serving for the intervening time; temporarily (p. 217)

adobe building material made of sun-dried earth and straw (p. 91)

agent a person acting or doing business for another by that person's authority; a representative (p. 391)

agribusiness large-scale commercial farming (p. 59)

alcalde the chief official of a Spanish town (p. 132)

alliance an agreement by two or more nations, people, or groups to work together (p. 139)

Allies the nations fighting the Axis powers, England, France, China, and Russia; later to be joined by the United States when it entered World War II (p. 517)

alluvial soil soil that has been deposited from river (running) water (p. 54)

alphabet agencies government agencies that came to be known by the first initials of their names (p. 505)

amend change (p. 323)

amendment an addition to a formal document such as a constitution (pp. 374, 623)

annexation to incorporate a country or territory into another country or territory (p. 271)

anthropologist a scientist who studies the origin, movement, and way of life of humans (p. 83)

antitrust law a law forbidding companies joining together to fix prices or limit production (p. 446)

appraise to determine the value (p. 658)

appropriate to set aside by formal action for a specific use (usually money) (pp. 490, 584)

aquifer an underground water reservoir (p. 34)

arbitration the process of allowing an impartial observer to resolve a dispute (p. 511)

archaeologist a scientist who studies the material remains of past human life (p. 81)

archives official government documents (p. 282)

armies of occupation foreign troops that remain in a conquered nation to ensure an orderly changeover to peacetime activities (p. 529)

artifact an object made or altered by humans (p. 81)

Axis Powers the countries of Germany, Italy, and Japan—the three dictatorships that formed an alliance to fight World War II (p. 517)

ayuntamiento city council (p. 132)

B

baby boom a period with a marked rise in birthrate—notably in the U.S. immediately following the end of World War II (p. 528)

barrier island an island that protects the main body of land from ocean waves (p. 32)

basin a sunken area in a plateau found between mountain ranges (p. 67)

bicameral composed of two legislative chambers or branches (House of Representatives and Senate) (p. 636)

bilingual education a program that serves students who speak a native language other than English (p. 590)

bill a proposed law presented to a legislature for consideration (pp. 398, 581)

bill of rights a series of laws in a constitution that protect specific rights of citizens (p. 623)

black codes laws limiting the rights of African Americans passed by Southern governments after the Civil War (p. 374)

blockade to isolate a particular enemy area (as a harbor) by a warring nation using troops or warships to prevent the passage of supplies and people (p. 350)

bombard to attack, usually with cannons (p. 233)

bond a note or guarantee issued by the government, promising to repay money it borrows, with interest (p. 625)

boom and bust cycle an economic cycle in which high demand and production leads to prosperity followed by depression (p. 570)

boycott to refuse to buy goods as a statement of opposition (p. 566)

budget a financial plan based on expected earnings and proposals for spending the money (p. 647)

butte a flat-topped hill, smaller than a mesa (p. 58)

C

cabinet the heads of departments of the executive branch appointed by the president and confirmed by the Senate; a group of advisers to a political head of government (pp. 276, 580)

campaign a connected series of military operations (p. 391)

capitol a building where a legislative body of a republic, state or country meets (p. 271)

carpetbagger Northerner in the South working for a Reconstruction government (p. 376)

cartel an association of independent commercial or industrial enterprises formed to limit competition (p. 571)

cavalry soldiers that are mounted on horseback (p. 253)

cede to give up, especially by treaty. A *cession* is the transfer of land from one country to another. (p. 327)

census a counting of the population done by the government at regular intervals (pp. 332, 596)

Centralist a person who believes power should be concentrated in the national government (p. 172)

charter to establish by a state contract or a guarantee (p. 309)

checks and balances a system whereby each branch of government has the ability to limit the actions of the other branches (p. 624)

cholera a disease caused by bacteria in food and water (p. 194)

civil law a set of laws pertaining to disputes between private citizens, businesses, and governments (p. 628)

civil rights the rights of personal liberty guaranteed to U.S. citizens by the Constitution and acts of Congress (pp. 216, 527)

Cold War a conflict in which each side uses any means except military action to expand its power and influence (p. 529)

commander in chief a top government official who holds supreme command of a military force (p. 643)

commerce large-scale trade (p. 190)

commissary a storehouse of food and other goods (p. 398)

commission a form of city government in which citizens elect officers to head departments such as public safety and human services; the mayor has little power (pp. 466, 658)

commissioners court the most important governing body in county government; responsible for determining the budget, setting the property-tax rate, and deciding how tax monies are spent (p. 659)

committees of correspondence local groups formed to share political and military information with other communities (p. 205)

Communist adhering to *communism,* a theory advocating the elimination of private property (p. 529)

compulsory required (p. 378)

concentration camp a camp where people (as prisoners of war, political prisoners, or refugees) are detained or confined. During World War II, these camps were often the sites of unspeakable crimes against humanity. (p. 524)

confederacy a union of people or groups (p. 87)

conquistador one of the Spanish soldiers who sought riches and power for themselves, and wealth and glory for Spain, in the conquest of the Americas (p. 103)

conscription the forced enrollment of people into military service (p. 348)

conservationist a person concerned with replacing renewable resources such as trees or soil (p. 462)

conservative a person who is strict in observance of traditional or established forms, ways, or beliefs (p. 541)

constitution a document that outlines fundamental laws and principles of law; it describes the nature, functions, and limits of government (p. 622)

consumer goods products such as washing machines, cars, and refrigerators, which the general public buys (p. 527)

contour plowing plowing around the contour of a hill, rather than up and down, to conserve water (p. 507)

convention a meeting of delegates of a political party to form policies and select candidates (p. 324)

convoy a group of vehicles that travel together (p. 550)

cooperatives organized groups that borrowed money from the government to pay for installing electrical services (through New Deal legislation) (p. 506)

council a group of advisers (p. 123)

council-manager a form of city government in which the city council hires a professional city manager to manage city affairs and prepare the budget; the mayor is mostly a figurehead (p. 658)

criminal law a set of laws that describes what people can and cannot do; laws concerned with crime and punishment (p. 628)

cultural diffusion borrowing and integrating ideas specific to one group of people into the culture of another group (p. 28)

culture the way of life developed by a group of people to satisfy its needs (p. 83)

customs duty a tax placed on goods coming into the country (p. 189)

deactivation the act of making inactive or ineffective (p. 584)

decree an order that has the force of law (p. 188)

department a land division within Texas: a large administrative unit, similar to a territory (p. 177)

depression a period of low economic activity, often marked by high unemployment (p. 165)

derrick a framework or tower that supports the drill over a deep hole (p. 458)

descendant proceeding from an ancestor (p. 337)

diameter the length of a straight line through the center of a circle (p. 30)

dictator a leader who controls an area through absolute power (pp. 198, 516)

dispatch to send off or away with promptness or speed on official business (p. 238)

dowry the money, property, and goods a bride gives her husband upon marriage (p. 176)

drive to move cattle in large herds to a stockyard or market (p. 414)

drought dry period in which little, if any, precipitation falls, often causing extensive damage to crops (p. 62)

drover a person who moves cattle to market (p. 414)

dry farming a method of farming that used a manner of plowing that left loose soil on top of the ground, which kept water in the ground by slowing evaporation (p. 425)

Dust Bowl the geographic area, including the Texas Panhandle, hardest hit by the drought during the 1930s where the soil was so dry it blew away in great clouds of dust (p. 502)

economies of scale a reduction in unit costs brought about especially by increased size of production facilities (p. 502)

empresario the Spanish word for a land agent whose job it was to bring in new settlers to an area (p. 168)

endowment fund income derived from donations that is set aside for a specific purpose (p. 276)

environment surroundings that include physical, social, and cultural conditions (p. 27)

erosion the wearing away of the earth's surface by the movement of water, wind, ice, and gravity (p. 63)

escarpment a steep cliff (p. 32)

ethnicity the national or cultural heritage to which one belongs (p. 597)

executive having to do with the chief officer of a government (pp. 216, 624)

exempt excuse; to free from a rule that others must obey (p. 188)

expenditure money paid out (p. 274)

extracurricular relating to activities offered by a school but not part of the course of study (p. 590)

fault a weak place in the earth's crust (p. 32)

federalism a type of government in which powers and duties between the states and the national government are shared (p. 624)

Federalist a person who believes in sharing power between the states and the national government (p. 172)

feedlot (feedyard) a large outdoor facility where cattle are fed grain before being slaughtered (p. 570)

felony a serious crime for which punishment may be imprisonment or death (pp. 422, 628)

fiesta festival or religious celebration (p. 310)

filibuster an individual who carries out rebellious activities in a foreign country (p. 142)

fiscal of or relating to financial matters (taxation, public revenue, public debt) (p. 647)

flank the right or left side of a formation (p. 255)

folklore traditional customs, beliefs, stories, and sayings of people handed down orally (p. 600)

fortify to strengthen (p. 231)

franchise tax a tax based on the value of machinery and equipment that businesses use to produce income (p. 648)

free enterprise the freedom of private businesses to compete with other businesses to make a profit without government interference (p. 445)

freedmen freed slaves (p. 369)

freedom ride a ride made by civil rights workers to desegregate public facilities, such as bus terminals or lunch counters (p. 566)

friar a member of a Catholic religious order (p. 103)

general-law city a city with a government that functions under the general laws of Texas and often provides basic services such as police, fire protection, and water and sewer services (p. 657)

geography the study of the spatial aspects of earth and the people who live on it (p. 26)

GI Bill of Rights a law passed by the U.S. Congress in 1944 which helped veterans financially to attend college (p. 528)

grand jury a group of citizens who determines whether there is enough evidence to charge someone with a crime (p. 629)

grassland an area where the natural vegetation is grass (p. 36)

growth rate the percentage by which the population increases (p. 597)

Holocaust the name given to the Nazis' mass murder of European Jews in World War II (p. 524)

home-rule city a city with a government that has freedom to govern unless prohibited by state or federal laws (p. 657)

homespun a coarse, loosely woven, homemade fabric (p. 355)

human-environment interaction how people use, adapt to, or change their surroundings and how the physical environment often affects humans (p. 28)

I

immigrant agent a person licensed to bring settlers into a country, paid in land or money to do so (p. 297)

impeach bring charges against (p. 375)

import bring in from a foreign country (p. 191)

indictment a formal statement charging a party with the commission of a crime (p. 629)

infantry soldiers that fight on foot (p. 255)

integrated silicon circuit a tiny group of electronic devices and their connections manufactured on a small slice of material (p. 552)

interdependence the act of two or more groups relying on each other for support (p. 573)

interstate connecting or existing between two or more states (p. 446)

intrastate connecting or existing in areas within a state (p. 446)

J

Jim Crow laws laws discriminating against African Americans (p. 470)

joint resolution a statement passed by both houses of a legislature that has the force of law (p. 288)

judicial having to do with courts of law or the justice system (p. 216)

judiciary the judicial branch of government, it tries cases involving government and administers justice (p. 624)

juror a member of a jury sworn to hear testimony, review facts, and hand down a verdict on a case (p. 629)

K

keynote address a speech that presents the main issue of interest to an audience and often inspires unity and enthusiasm (p. 568)

L

lariat a long light rope (as of hemp or leather) used with a running noose to catch livestock, or without the noose to tether grazing animals (p. 153)

law of supply and demand general economic principle that expresses the relationship between the quantity and supply of a product and its price (p. 500)

legislative having to do with a lawmaking body; congressional (p. 216)

legislature elected officials who make the laws for the state (pp. 323, 624)

Lend-Lease Act a 1941 program in which the United States loaned military equipment to the Allied powers (p. 517)

libel an intentionally written statement that unjustly gives an unfavorable impression (p. 547)

liberal a person who is not strict in observance of traditional or established forms, ways, or beliefs (p. 541)

liberation setting something free (p. 145)

line-item veto the power of the governor to veto individual items in a spending bill (p. 643)

location the position of a place on the earth's surface (p. 27)

los corridos Mexican American folk ballads (p. 601)

lynch to put to death (as by hanging) without a legal trial (p. 470)

M

malaria a disease caused by mosquitoes implanting parasites in the blood (p. 196)

manifest destiny the view that it was fated that the United States should expand its borders from coast to coast (p. 288)

maquiladoras factories in Mexico that assemble parts made in the United States (p. 69)

martial law the law applied by government military forces in an emergency (p. 500)

massacre to kill many at one time (p. 248)

matrilineal tracing descent through the mother (p. 87)

mayor-council a form of city government in which the mayor has full executive authority (There are strong-mayor and weak-mayor types of this form. In the weak-mayor type, the mayor shares administrative duties with the city council.) (p. 657)

McCarthyism the act of making unfounded exaggerated charges against a person (p. 547)

mechanize to equip with machinery, especially to replace human or animal labor (p. 527)

mediate to solve a problem or legal dispute through discussion and compromise rather than through the court system (p. 631)

mestizo a person of mixed blood, usually Spanish and Native American (p. 132)

middle latitudes the area approximately midway between the Equator and the North Pole or South Pole (p. 38)

middlemen dealers or agents acting as go-betweens for the producers of goods and the retailers or consumers (p. 90)

militia a group of citizens acting as a military force, usually all able-bodied men (p. 169)

Glossary

misdemeanor an offense of lesser gravity than a felony (p. 628)

mission a religious settlement (p. 103)

moderate a person who holds views that are not extreme (p. 541)

monopoly exclusive possession or control (p. 444)

mortgage a loan from a bank or lending institution to purchase a home or business property (p. 585)

movement people interacting across the globe—includes migration, transportation, and trade (p. 28)

municipality a city or other district that has local self-government (p. 208)

mural artwork applied to a wall or ceiling (p. 506)

mustang the small, hardy horse of the western plains, descended from horses brought by the Spaniards (p. 420)

National Guard part-time military forces organized by the states but available for national defense in a time of crisis (p. 585)

neutral favoring neither side in a conflict; not aligned with a political or ideological group (p. 517)

no bill a grand jury's decision that the evidence does not warrant an indictment (p. 629)

nomad a member of a group that wanders from place to place (p. 83)

nonpartisan election an election in which candidates are not identified by any particular party (p. 663)

norther icy wind that blows in quickly from the North (p. 39)

nullify cancel (p. 368)

open range public land that could be used by anyone, usually for grazing cattle (p. 413)

ordinance a local law (pp. 345, 658)

override to overrule, or set aside, another action (p. 212)

oversight the power of the legislature to review the activities of the executive branch (p. 637)

pardon to excuse from punishment (p. 509)

paunch the belly (p. 397)

pension a wage paid to a person following his or her retirement from service (p. 434)

perpetual continuing forever (p. 346)

petit jury a group of 12 people who listen to evidence and decide on a verdict; also known as a trial jury (p. 629)

petition to formally make a request (p. 215)

petrochemical substance made from petroleum or natural gas (p. 51)

petroglyph a carving or inscription on a rock (p. 605)

pictograph an ancient or prehistoric drawing or painting (p. 605)

place a geographic location, usually a town or city, and its physical and human characteristics (p. 28)

plain a landform that generally is level (p. 32)

plateau a broad, level landform that has steep cliffs—called escarpments—on at least one side and higher elevation than the surrounding land (p. 32)

plea bargain an agreement between a prosecutor and a defendant whereby the defendant is permitted to plead guilty to a lesser charge (p. 629)

poll tax a tax of a fixed amount so a person could vote (p. 470)

precinct one of four districts that each Texas county is divided into (p. 659)

presidio a Spanish military outpost (p. 121)

preventive strike an action taken to prevent a possible future attack (p. 350)

primary election an election in which party members choose the party's candidates for the general election (p. 466)

productivity rate of production (p. 570)

progressivism a reform movement in the early twentieth century that sought to correct social and political problems (p. 465)

prosperous marked by success or economic well-being (p. 561)

province one district of a country (p. 126)

provisional government temporary government (p. 208)

pueblo a Native American village with joined, flat-roofed buildings (p. 108)

quarantine a state of enforced isolation designed to prevent the spread of disease or pests (p. 417)

quinine a drug used for fighting malaria and other fevers (p. 356)

Radical Republican Republican who believed that Congress should direct Reconstruction (p. 374)

raft a floating mass of tangled driftwood that often blocks transportation (p. 308)

ranchero a rancher (p. 413)

ratify to approve formally (p. 374)

ration to limit food or goods to ensure adequate supplies to soldiers (p. 482)

ration boards groups of people (during wartime) who determined how essential goods would be allotted to the general public after military needs were met (p. 522)

real estate property in buildings and land (p. 660)

Reconstruction the effort to reorganize the seceded states and bring them back into the Union (p. 366)

recruit to enlist people into the armed services (pp. 226, 479)

redback additional money issued during Mirabeau B. Lamar's presidency to help in easing the large public debt (redbacks quickly shrank in value) (p. 279)

redistricting redrawing the boundaries of legislative districts depending on population changes (pp. 543, 638)

reenactment to repeat the actions of an earlier event or incident (p. 611)

refinery a building equipped to refine or process products such as oil, metals, or sugar (p. 441)

refugee a person who flees for safety, especially to a foreign country (p. 563)

region an area that is unified by one or more common characteristics (p. 28)

regular army an army of full-time, paid soldiers (p. 208)

relative location the location of a place in relation to other places (p. 27)

renegade a person who rejects lawful behavior (p. 403)

repeal recall or do away with a law (p. 195)

republic a government in which the power lies with the citizens, who vote for people to represent them (p. 145)

reservoir an artificial lake where water is collected as a water supply (p. 551)

resolution a formal expression of opinion voted by an official group (pp. 191, 639)

retail to sell in small quantities directly to the consumer (p. 463)

revenue money that a nation or state collects (p. 274)

rural of or relating to the country, country people or life; agricultural (p. 486)

savanna grassland with scattered trees and drought-resistant undergrowth (p. 36)

scalawag white Southerner who supported Reconstruction after the Civil War (p. 376)

scrip nongovernment currency that could be spent only at a company store (p. 462)

secede withdraw (p. 343)

segregation the act of segregating, or setting apart, from the general population (p. 470)

separation of powers the term for the fact that the powers of government are divided into three separate branches: legislative, executive, and judicial (p. 624)

shaman a person who is believed to have the power to cure the sick and forecast and control the future (p. 88)

sharecropper a tenant farmer who is provided with seed, tools, living quarters, and food and receives a share of the value of the crop (pp. 426, 484)

siege a military blockade of a city or fortress (p. 206)

sinew a tendon (p. 397)

sit-in occupying seats in a racially segregated establishment in protest against discrimination (p. 566)

skirmish a small fight, usually during wartime (p. 191)

smelter an establishment for melting or fusing ore in order to separate the metal (p. 522)

sovereignty the state of being free from outside control; self-governing (pp. 343, 542)

special interest groups (SIGs) organizations of people who share a common interest and seek to exert influence over a particular aspect of government (p. 664)

states' rights the belief that the federal government should have limited power over states (p. 343)

stock shares of ownership in a corporation (p. 498)

stockade an enclosure of posts made to form a defense (p. 114)

stockyard a place where livestock are penned before they are slaughtered or shipped (p. 414)

strike a refusal to work as protest against the employer (p. 511)

subsistence crop a crop grown to be used on the farm where it was raised (p. 303)

suburb a residential community close to a city or large town (p. 550)

suffrage the right to vote (p. 433)

survey measure for size and for boundaries (p. 167)

synthetic produced artificially or human-made (p. 552)

S

sandbar a ridge of sand built up by currents in a river or coastal waters (p. 114)

T

tallow the fat of cattle and sheep, used in the manufacture of soap, margarine, candles, and lubricants (p. 413)

tariff a tax on imported goods (p. 274)

teamster a person who drives or directs a team of animals (p. 333)

Tejano a person of Mexican heritage who considers Texas as home (p. 133)

tenant farmer a farmer who works land owned by another and pays rent either in cash or in shares of the crop (pp. 426, 484)

tepee a shelter made of tanned hides fastened to a framework of poles (p. 95)

third party an organized political group that is neither Republican nor Democrat (p. 581)

transistor a solid state electronic device used to control the flow of electricity in electronic equipment with at least three electrodes (p. 552)

trust a combination of companies formed by agreement to reduce competition (p. 444)

unconstitutional not following the U.S. Constitution and therefore not legal (p. 544)

unemployment loss of jobs—having fewer jobs available than the people needing them (p. 499)

Unionist a person who supported the Union cause during the Civil War era (p. 349)

urban of or relating to a city (p. 486)

urban dweller a person who lives in the city (p. 579)

vacuum tube an electron tube with a high degree of vacuum; used to control the flow of electricity in televisions and radios before the invention of the transistor (p. 552)

vaquero a cowhand (pp. 153, 413)

veto to reject, as to reject a bill and prevent it from becoming a law; a refusal by a president or governor to approve a law (pp. 213, 374)

viceroy a governor who rules as a representative of a king or sovereign (p. 108)

vigilante a member of a volunteer committee organized to punish criminals (pp. 349, 435)

watchdog role an activity of political parties: monitoring, or keeping track of and informed about, other parties' practices and decisions (p. 664)

white-collar generally, jobs not requiring physical labor (p. 463)

wildcatter an oil operator who drills for wells in territory not known to contain oil (p. 499)

windfall an unexpected or sudden gift, gain, or advantage (p. 648)

wrangler a ranchhand who takes care of saddle horses (p. 416)

A

abolitionist/abolicionista alguien que favorece la eliminación de la esclavitud (pág. 328)

absolute location/posición absoluta punto único sobre la tierra que se expresa en latitud y longitud (pág. 27)

ad interim/ad interim sirviendo por el tiempo intermedio; temporario (pág. 217)

adobe/adobe material de construcción hecho de barro y paja secos al sol (pág. 91)

agent/agente persona que actúa o hace negocios para otra persona; un representante (pág. 391)

agribusiness/agriindustria agricultura comercial de gran escala (pág. 59)

alcalde/alcalde funcionario administrativo de un pueblo español (pág. 132)

alliance/alianza unión entre dos o más naciones, personas, o grupos para trabajar juntos (pág. 139)

Allies/Aliados las naciones que luchaban contra las potencias del Eje, Inglaterra, Francia, China, y Rusia; a las que luego se les unió Estados Unidos al iniciarse la Segunda Guerra Mundial (pág. 517)

alluvial soil/suelo aluvial suelo que ha sido depositado del agua (corriente) (pág. 54)

alphabet agencies/agencias alfabeto agencias gubernamentales que se hicieron conocidas por las iniciales de sus nombres (pág. 505)

amend/enmendar cambiar (pág. 323)

amendment/enmienda adición a un documento formal como por ejemplo un acta orgánica (págs. 374, 623)

annexation/anexión el acto de incorporar un país o territorio a otro país o territorio ya existentes (pág. 271)

anthropologist/antropólogo científico que estudia el origen, distribución, y comportamiento de los seres humanos (pág. 83)

antitrust law/ley antimonopolio una ley que prohíbe a las compañías unirse para fijar precios o limitar la producción (pág. 446)

appraise/valuar poner precio (pág. 658)

appropriate/consignar ahorrar por medio de una acción formal para un uso determinado (generalmente dinero) (págs. 490, 584)

aquifer/depósito de agua reserva de agua subterránea (pág. 34)

arbitration/arbitraje proceso de poner fin a una disputa sometiéndola a una tercera parte imparcial (pág. 511)

archaeologist/arqueólogo científico que estudia los seres humanos del pasado a través de reliquias fósiles (pág. 81)

archives/archivos documentos oficiales del gobierno (pág. 282)

armies of occupation/ejércitos de ocupación tropas extranjeras que permanecen en una nación conquistada para asegurar un cambio disciplinado a actividades de paz (pág. 529)

artifact/artefacto objeto construido alterado por humanos (pág. 81)

Axis Powers/Potencias del Eje los países de Alemania, Italia, y Japón—las tres dictaduras que formaron una alianza para luchar en la Segunda Guerra Mundial. Fueron conocidos como las potencias del "eje" porque Benito Mussolini de Italia dijo que el mundo giraría en torno a ellas (pág. 517)

ayuntamiento/ayuntamiento alcaldía (pág. 132)

B

baby boom/auge de los bebés un período marcado por el aumento en tasa de nacimientos, en especial en los Estados Unidos, inmediatamente después del término de la Segunda Guerra Mundial (pág. 528)

barrier island/isla de barrera isla que bloquea el paso de las olas del océano hacia tierra firme (pág. 32)

basin/cuenca una depresión en una meseta entre cadenas montañosas (pág. 67)

bicameral/bicameral compuesto de dos cámaras o ramas legislativas (Cámara de Representantes y Senado) (pág. 636)

bilingual education/educación bilingüe un programa que sirve a los estudiantes que hablan en su idioma nativo que no sea el Inglés (pág. 590)

bill/proyecto de ley ley propuesta presentada a una legislatura para ser considerada (págs. 398, 581)

bill of rights/declaración de derechos una serie de leyes en una constitución que protege derechos específicos de los ciudadanos (pág. 623)

black codes/códigos negros leyes aprobadas por los gobiernos sureños después de la Guerra Civil, con el objeto de restringir los derechos de los africanos-americanos (pág. 374)

blockade/bloqueo acción y efecto de aislar un área enemiga determinada (como una bahía) por una nación en guerra con tropas o barcos de guerra de manera de impedir la entrada o salida de mercancías y personas (pág. 350)

bombard/bombardear atacar continuamente, especialmente con artillería (pág. 233)

bond/bono un certificado o garantía emitido por el gobierno con la promesa de devolver con interés el dinero prestado (pág. 625)

boom and bust cycle/ciclo de auge y depresión económica in ciclo económico en que la alta demanda y la producción llevan a la prosperidad seguida por la depresión (pág. 570)

boycott/boicot rechazo a comprar ciertos productos como protesta por alguna acción (pág. 566)

budget/presupuesto plan financiero que se basa en las ganancias esperadas y los gastos propuestos (pág. 647)

butte/otero colina cuya parte superior es plana, más pequeña que una meseta (pág. 58)

cabinet/gabinete jefes de departamentos de la rama ejecutiva designados por el presidente y confirmados por el Senado; grupo de consejeros de un jefe político de gobierno (págs. 276, 580)

campaign/campaña serie combinada de operaciones militares (pág. 391)

capitol/capitolio edificio en el cual se reúne un cuerpo legislativo de una república, un estado, o un país (pág. 271)

carpetbagger/aventurero político persona del norte en el sur buscando ganancias privadas bajo los gobiernos de Reconstrucción (pág. 376)

cartel/cartel asociación de empresas comerciales o industriales independientes formada para regular la competencia (pág. 571)

cavalry/caballería cuerpo de soldados a caballo (pág. 253)

cede/ceder rendirse, especialmente a través de un tratado. *Cesión* es la transferencia de tierra de un país a otro (pág. 327)

census/censo conteo de la población hecho por el gobierno cada cierto tiempo regularmente (págs. 332, 596)

Centralist/Centralista persona que cree que el poder debe concentrarse en el gobierno nacional (pág. 172)

charter/constituir establecer por medio de un contrato fiscal o garantía (pág. 309)

checks and balances/controles y balances sistema en que cada rama de gobierno tiene la capacidad de limitar las acciones de las otras ramas (pág. 624)

cholera/cólera enfermedad causada por bacterias que se encuentran en la comida y el agua (pág. 194)

civil law/ley civil ley que se ocupa de las disputas entre ciudadanos, empresas, y gobiernos (pág. 628)

civil rights/derechos civiles derechos de libertad personal garantizados a los ciudadanos de los Estados Unidos por la Constitución y actas del Congreso (págs. 216, 527)

Cold War/Guerra Fría conflicto en que ambas partes utilizan cualquier medio excepto acciones militares para expandir su poder e influencia (pág. 529)

commander in chief/comandante en jefe oficial superior del gobierno quien tiene el comando supremo de una fuerza militar (pág. 643)

commerce/comercio compra y venta a gran escala (pág. 190)

commissary/comisariato tienda de alimentos y otros bienes (pág. 398)

commission/comité forma de gobierno local en que los ciudadanos eligen oficiales para manejar departamentos como la seguridad pública y los servicios a las personas; el alcalde no tiene todo el poder (págs. 466, 658)

commissioners court/tribunal de comisionados el cuerpo gobernante más importante en un gobierno de distrito; responsable de determinar el presupuesto, fijar la tasa de impuestos sobre los bienes, y decidir el gasto del dinero de los impuestos (pág. 659)

committees of correspondence/comités de correspondencia grupos formados a nivel local para compartir noticias políticas o militares conotros pueblos o ciudades (pág. 205)

Communist/Comunista partidario del *comunismo,* teoría que aboga por la eliminación de la propiedad privada (pág. 529)

compulsory/obligatorio acción que se exige realizar (pág. 378)

concentration camp/campo de concentración campo donde se detiene o confina a grupos de personas (como prisioneros de guerra, prisioneros políticos, o refugiados). Durante la Segunda Guerra Mundial, estos campos fueron el escenario de abominables crímenes contra la humanidad (pág. 524)

confederacy/confederación alianza de personas o grupos (pág. 87)

conquistador/conquistador soldado español que buscaba riquezas y poder para sí mismo, y prosperidad y gloria para España, en la conquista de América (pág. 103)

conscription/conscripción eclutamiento de individuos por la fuerza para servicio militar (pág. 348)

conservationist/conservacionista persona preocupada de reemplazar recursos renovables tales como árboles o suelo (pág. 462)

conservative/conservador persona que obedece estrictamente a formas, maneras o creencias tradicionales o establecidas (pág. 541)

constitution/constitución documento que compendia leyes y principios fundamentales de la ley; describe la naturaleza, funciones, y limitaciones del gobierno (pág. 622)

consumer goods/bienes de consumo productos tales como lavadoras, autos, y refrigeradores, comprados por el público en general (pág. 527)

Spanish Glossary

contour plowing/surcado en contorno surcado alrededor del contorno de una colina, en lugar de en forma ascendente y descendente, para mantener el agua (pág. 507)

convention/convención reunión de delegados de un partido político para decidir políticas y seleccionar candidatos (pág. 324)

convoy/convoy grupo de vehículos que viajan juntos (pág. 550)

cooperatives/cooperativas grupos organizados que pedían dinero prestado al gobierno para pagar la instalación de servicios eléctricos (por medio de la legislación del Nuevo Trato) (pág. 506)

council/junta grupo de gente que da consejos (pág. 123)

council-manager/gobierno de ayuntamiento-administrador forma de gobierno local en el cual una junta contrata un administrador profesional que dirija los asuntos locales y prepare el presupuesto; el alcalde es mas bien un testaferro (pág. 658)

criminal law/ley criminal ley que señala las acciones que los individuos o grupos pueden o no pueden hacer; ley que tiene relación con el crimen y el castigo (pág. 628)

cultural difusion/difusion cultural adquirir e integrar ideas específicas de un grupo de gente en la cultura de otro grupo (pág. 28)

culture/cultura forma de vida desarrollada por un grupo de gente para satisfacer sus necesidades (pág. 83)

customs duty/pago de aduana impuesto que se paga por artículos importados (pág. 189)

deactivation/desactivación acción de hacer inactivo o ineficaz (pág. 584)

decree/decreto orden que tiene la fuerza de la ley (pág. 188)

department/departamento división territorial dentro de Tejas: una grande unidad administrativa, parecido a un territorio (pág. 177)

depression/depresión período de baja actividad económica, generalmente con desempleo difundido (pág. 165)

derrick/torre de perforación armazón o torre sobre un hueco profundo para sostener la maquinaria de perforación (pág. 458)

descendant/descendiente que procede de un ancestro (pág. 337)

diameter/diámetro segmento de una línea recta que pasa a través del dentro de un círculo (pág. 30)

dictator/dictador líder que gobierna un área con autoridad absoluta (págs. 198, 516)

dispatch/despachar enviar rápidamente para un propósito oficial (pág. 238)

dowry/dote dinero, propiedad, y bienes que lleva la mujer a su marido en el matrimonio (pág. 176)

drive/arrear guiar el ganado en grandes manadas hacia un corral o mercado (pág. 414)

drought/sequía período de poca o ninguna lluvia causando extenso daño a las cosechas (pág. 62)

drover/pastor persona que guía el ganado hacia un mercado (pág. 414)

dry farming/cultivo seco método de cultivo que utilizaba una forma de surcado que dejaba tierra suelta sobre la superficie del suelo, manteniendo el agua en éste demorando la evaporación (pág. 425)

Dust Bowl/Región de Sequía área geográfica que incluye el Brazo de Tejas golpeado en forma más severa por la sequía durante los años 30, en que el suelo estaba tan seco que se producían grandes ventarrones de polvo (pág. 502)

economies of scale/economías de escala reducción en los costos unitarios causada especialmente por un aumento en el tamaño de las instalaciones de producción (pág. 502)

empresario/empresario término español para contratista agrícola; persona cuyo trabajo consistía n traer pobladores a una área (pág. 168)

endowment fund/fondo de dotación ingresos derivados de donaciones destinados a un propósito específico (pág. 276)

environment/ambiente condiciones físicas, sociales, y culturales circundantes (pág. 27)

erosion/erosión el desgaste progresivo de la superficie de la tierra debido a la acción del agua, viento, hielo, y la gravedad (pág. 63)

escarpment/risco acantilado inclinado (pág. 32)

ethnicity/etnicidad patrimonio nacional o cultural al que se pertenece (pág. 597)

executive/ejecutiv el que tiene que ver con el oficial en jefe de un gobierno (págs. 216, 624)

exempt/exceptuar dispensar; liberar de un requerimiento que otros deben cumplir (pág. 188)

expenditure/desembolso dinero que se gasta (pág. 274)

extracurricular/fuera del plan de estudios relativo a actividades ofrecidas por una escuela pero que no forman parte de las materias de estudio (pág. 590)

fault/falla punto débil en la corteza de la tierra (pág. 32)

federalism/federalismo tipo de gobierno en que los poderes y deberes son compartidos por los estados y el gobierno central (pág. 624)

Spanish Glossary

Federalist/Federalista persona que cree en compartir el poder entre los estados y el gobierno central (pág. 172)

feedlot (feedyard)/lote de alimentación (patio de alimentación) grandes instalaciones al aire libre donde se alimenta al ganado con grano antes de ser sacrificados (pág. 570)

felony/felonía delito serio que se castiga con prisión o la muerte (págs. 422, 628)

fiesta/fiesta festival o celebración religiosa (pág. 310)

filibuster/filibustero persona en un país extranjero que incita sublevaciones (pág. 142)

fiscal/fiscal que pertenece a o se relaciona con asuntos financieros (tributación, ingresos fiscales, deuda pública) (pág. 647)

flank/flanco la izquierda o derecha de una formación militar (pág. 255)

folklore/folklore costumbres, creencias, cuentos, y dichos tradicionales de un grupo de personas transmitidos oralmente de generación en generación (pág. 600)

fortify/fortificar reforzar (pág. 231)

franchise tax/impuesto de patente impuesto que se basa en el valor de la maquinaria y el equipo que utilizan las empresas para producir ingresos (pág. 648)

free enterprise/libre comercio se refiere a la libertad de negocios privados para competir con otros negocios con el fin de obtener ganancias sin la intervención del gobierno (pág. 445)

freedmen/personas liberadas personas que una vez fueron esclavos pero que ahora son libres (pág. 369)

freedom ride/caminata de la libertad caminata que hacen los trabajadores por los derechos civiles para abolir la segregación en instalaciones públicas, tales como terminales de buses o restaurantes (pág. 566)

friar/fraile miembro de una orden religiosa católica (pág. 103)

general-law city/ciudad con leyes generales ciudad con un gobierno que opera bajo las leyes generales de Tejas y que generalmente cuenta con servicios básicos tales como policía, protección contra incendios, y servicios de agua potable y alcantarillado (pág. 657)

geography/geografía estudio de la ubicación de la tierra y los seres vivientes que la habitan (pág. 26)

GI Bill of Rights/Declaración de Derechos emitida por el gobierno ley aprobada por el Congreso de los Estados Unidos en 1944 que ayudaba financieramente a los veteranos de guerra para que estos asistieran a la universidad (pág. 528)

grand jury/gran jurado grupo de ciudadanos quienes determinan si existe suficiente evidencia sobre una persona para acusarla formalmente de un crimen (pág. 629)

grassland/tierra de pasto área donde la vegetación natural corresponde a grama (pág. 36)

growth rate/tasa de crecimiento porcentaje por medio del cual aumenta la población (pág. 597)

Holocaust/Holocausto nombre que recibe el asesinato en masa de los judíos europeos por los nazis durante la Segunda Guerra Mundial (pág. 524)

home-rule city/ciudad con autonomía local ciudad con un gobierno que tiene la libertad de gobernar a menos que los prohíba el estado o las leyes federales (pág. 657)

homespun/tela de fabricación casera tela ordinaria tejida sueltamente, hecha en casa (pág. 355)

human-environment interaction/interacción hombre-ambiente manera en que la gente usa, se adapta, o altera sus alrededores y la forma en que el ambiente físico afecta generalmente a los seres humanos (pág. 28)

immigrant agent/agente inmigrante persona que tiene licencia para traer inmigrantes a un país y a la que se le paga con tierras o dinero por el servicio (pág. 297)

impeach/censurar acusar (pág. 375)

import/importar traer desde un país extranjero (pág. 191)

indictment/acusación sumaria acusación formal de que el acusado ha cometido el crimen (pág. 629)

infantry/infantería soldados que pelean a pie (pág. 255)

integrated silicon circuit/circuito integrado de silicona grupo diminuto de dispositivos electrónicos y su conexiones fabricados sobre una pequeña lámina de material (pág. 552)

interdependence/interdependencia acción de confianza mutua entre dos o más grupos (pág. 573)

interstate/interestatal que conecta o existe entre dos o más estados (pág. 446)

intrastate/intraestatal que conecta o existe en áreas dentro de un estado (pág. 446)

Jim Crow laws/leyes de discriminación contra los negros leyes que discriminan contra los africanos-americanos (pág. 470)

joint resolution/resolución conjunta declaración formal aprobada por ambas cámaras de un cuerpo legislativo que tiene fuerza de ley (pág. 288)

judicial/judicial relativo a los tribunales de ley o el sistema de justicia (pág. 216)

Spanish Glossary

judiciary/poder judicial rama judicial del gobierno, trata casos que involucran al gobierno y administra la justicia (pág. 624)

juror/jurado miembro de un jurado que jura oír testimonios, revisar hechos, y emitir un veredicto en un caso (pág. 629)

keynote address/piedra angular un discurso que presenta el tema principal de interés ante el público y que frecuentemente inspira a la unidad y el entusiasmo (pág. 568)

lariat/mangana cuerda liviana larga (hecha de cáñamo o cuero) que se usa con un lazo corredizo para atrapar el ganado, o sin el lazo para atar animales que pastan (pág. 153)

law of supply and demand/ley de oferta y demanda principio económico general que expresa la relación entre la cantidad y oferta de un producto y su precio (pág. 500)

legislative/legislativo relativo al cuerpo legislativo que tiene la misión de hacer leyes; del congreso (pág. 216)

legislature/legislatura oficiales elegidos que tienen la autoridad para formular leyes (págs. 323, 624)

Lend-Lease Act/Ley de Préstamo-Arriendo programa de 1941 en que los Estados Unidos prestó equipo militar a las potencias Aliadas (pág. 517)

libel/libel escrito intencional que difama injustamente (pág. 547)

liberal/libera persona que no obedece estrictamente a formas, maneras o creencias tradicionales o establecidas (pág. 541)

liberation/liberación acto de liberar algo (pág. 145)

line-item veto/veto línea-asunto poder del gobernador para vetar asuntos individuales en una propuesta de ley (pág. 643)

location/posición ubicación general de un lugar sobre la superficie de la tierra (pág. 27)

los corridos/**corridos** baladas folclóricas mexicanas-americanas (pág. 601)

lynch/linchar causar la muerte (como en el caso de los ahorcamientos) sin un juicio legal (pág. 470)

malaria/malaria enfermedad causada por parásitos en la sangre introducidos por mosquitos (pág. 196)

manifest destiny/manifiesto de destino el punto de vista de que los Estados Unidos estaban predestinados a expandir sus fronteras de costa a costa (pág. 288)

maquiladoras/**maquiladoras** fábricas en México que ensamblan piezas provenientes de Estados Unidos (pág. 69)

martial law/ley marcial la ley aplicada por las fuerzas militares del gobierno en caso de una emergencia (pág. 500)

massacre/masacre asesinato violento y cruel de un número de personas (pág. 248)

matrilineal/línea materna que traza el origen de una familia a través de la madre (pág. 87)

mayor-council/consejo de alcaldes una forma de gobierno local donde el alcalde tiene autoridad ejecutiva total (Existen para esta forma dos tipos de alcalde, fuerte y débil. En el caso del alcalde débil, éste comparte las labores administrativas con el consejo local.) (pág. 657)

McCarthyism/McCartismo el acto de levantar cargos infundados, exagerados contra una persona (pág. 547)

mechanize/mecanizar equipar con maquinaria, en especial para reemplazar el trabajo humano o animal (pág. 527)

mediate/mediar resolver un problema o disputa legal por medio de discusiones y compromisos en lugar de a través de un sistema judicial (pág. 631)

mestizo/mestizo persona de sangre mixta, generalmente española y nativa americana (pág. 132)

middle latitudes/latitudes medias el área a mitad de camino entre el Ecuador y los Polos Norte o Sur (pág. 38)

middlemen/intermediarios negociantes o agentes intermedios entre los productores de los bienes y los minoristas o consumidores (pág. 90)

militia/milicia grupo de ciudadanos que actúa como fuerza militar, por lo general todos de buena salud (pág. 169)

misdemeanor/violación menor un delito menos serio que una felonía (pág. 628)

mission/misión asentamiento fundado por un grupo religioso (pág. 103)

moderate/moderado persona que mantiene puntos de vista que no son extremos (pág. 541)

monopoly/monopolio posesión o control exclusivos (pág. 444)

mortgage/hipoteca un préstamo de un banco o institución financiera para comprar una casa o un negocio (pág. 585)

movement/movimiento personas que interactúan a través del planeta—incluye inmigración, transporte, y comercio (pág. 28)

municipality/municipalidad ciudad o pueblo con sistema de gobierno propio (pág. 208)

mural/mural ilustraciones aplicadas a un muro o techo (pág. 506)

mustang/mesteño (caballo salvaje) potro pequeño, robusto de los llanos occidentales, que desciende directamente de los caballos traídos por los españoles (pág. 420)

National Guard/Guardia Nacional fuerzas militares a tiempo parcial organizadas por los estados pero disponibles para la defensa nacional en tiempo de crisis (pág. 585)

neutral/neutral que no favorece ningún sector específico durante un conflicto; que no se une a ningún grupo político o ideológico (pág. 517)

no bill/no cargos la decisión de un gran jurado de que no hay suficiente evidencia para justificar un juicio (pág. 629)

nomad/nómada miembro de un grupo que va de un lugar a otro (pág. 83)

nonpartisan election/elección fuera de partido elección en la cual los candidatos no están nominados por algún partido (pág. 663)

norther/viento del norte viento helado que sopla repentinamente desde el Norte (pág. 39)

nullify/anular cancelar (pág. 368)

open range/pradera extensa terrenos públicos que pueden ser utilizados por cualquiera, normalmente para que paste el ganado (pág. 413)

ordinance/ordenanza una ley local (págs. 345, 658)

override/pasar por encima de (políticamente) invalidar, o anular, la acción de otro (pág. 212)

oversight/vigilancia el poder de la legislatura de supervisar las actividades de la rama ejecutiva (pág. 637)

pardon/indulto liberar a una persona del castigo (pág. 509)

paunch/panza la barriga (pág. 397)

pension/pensión suma que se le paga regularmente a una persona que se ha retirado del trabajo (pág. 434)

perpetual/perpetuo que dura siempre (pág. 346)

petit jury/pequeño jurado grupo de 12 personas que escuchan las evidencias y deciden un veredicto; conocido también como jurado procesal (pág. 629)

petition/petición hacer una solicitud formal por escrito (pág. 215)

petrochemical/petroquímicos productos químicos obtenidos del petróleo o gas natural (pág. 51)

petroglyph/petroglifo tallado o inscripción sobre una roca antigua (pág. 605)

pictograph/pictografía dibujo o pintura antigua o prehistórica (pág. 605)

place/lugar ubicación geográfica, por lo general un pueblo o ciudad, y sus características físicas y humanas (pág. 28)

plain/llano forma terrestre que generalmente es plana (pág. 32)

plateau/meseta forma terrestre ancha plana que tiene acantilados inclinados—llamados riscos—al menos en un lado que se eleva abruptamente sobre la tierra circundante (pág. 32)

plea bargain/declaración de culpabilidad en menor grado acuerdo hecho entre el acusado y el fiscal para declararse culpable de cargos menores (pág. 629)

poll tax/impuesto al voto impuesto cobrado a cada persona que debe pagar para poder votar (pág. 470)

precinct/distrito uno de los cuatro distritos en que se divide el condado de Tejas (pág. 659)

presidio/fuerte puesto militar español (pág. 121)

preventive strike/ataque preventivo acción tomada para evitar un posible ataque futuro (pág. 350)

primary election/elección primaria elección en la cual los miembros de un partido nominan candidatos para las elecciones generales (pág. 466)

productivity/productividad tasa de producción (pág. 570)

progressivism/progresivismo movimiento de reforma de principios del siglo veinte que buscaba corregir los problemas sociales y políticos (pág. 465)

prosperous/próspero marcado por el éxito o el bienestar económico (pág. 561)

province/provincia división mayor de un país (pág. 126)

provisional government/gobierno provisional gobierno que sirve temporalmente (pág. 208)

pueblo/pueblo aldea nativo americana con casas de techos planos las cuales están unidas en grupos (pág. 108)

quarantine/cuarentena estado de aislamiento forzado con la intención de prevenir la propagación de una enfermedad o peste (pág. 417)

quinine/quinina droga que se utiliza para combatir la malaria y otras fiebres (pág. 356)

Spanish Glossary

Radical Republican/Republicano Radical Republicano quien creía que el Congreso debía apoyar la Reconstrucción (pág. 374)

raft/balsa una gran masa flotante de leña de playa enmarañada que generalmente bloquea el transporte (pág. 308)

ranchero/**ranchero** hacendado (pág. 413)

ratify/ratificar dar aprobación formal (pág. 374)

ration/racionar limitar el alimento o los bienes para asegurar un suministro adecuado a los soldados (pág. 522)

ration boards/juntas de racionamiento grupos de personas (en tiempo de guerra) que determinaba la forma en que se distribuirían los bienes esenciales al público general después de satisfacer las necesidades militares (pág. 522)

real estate/bienes raíce propiedades en un terreno o edificios (pág. 660)

Reconstruction/Reconstrucción esfuerzo para reorganizar e incorporar en la Unión los estados separados (pág. 366)

recruit/reclutar enlistar a las personas en las fuerzas armadas (págs. 226, 479)

redback/soporte rojo dinero adicional emitido durante la presidencia de Mirabeau B. Lamar para ayudar a aliviar la gran deuda pública (soportes rojos disminuyeron su valor rápidamente) (pág. 279)

redistricting/dividir de nuevo los distritos reorganizar los límites de los distritos legislativos según los cambios de la población (págs. 543, 638)

reenactment/restablecimiento repetir las acciones de un evento o incidente previo (pág. 611)

refinery/refinería edificio donde se refinan o procesan productos como el petróleo, los metales, o el azúcar (pág. 441)

refugee/refugiado persona que se escapa buscando seguridad, especialmente a un piad extranjero (pág. 563)

region/región un área unificada por una o más características comunes (pág. 28)

regular army/ejército regular ejército de soldados que sirve a tiempo completo y recibe paga (pág. 208)

relative location/posición relativa localización de un lugar en referencia a otros lugares (pág. 27)

renegade/renegado persona que rechaza los comportamientos convencionales (pág. 403)

repeal/revocación anular o eliminar con una ley (pág. 195)

republic/república gobierno en el cual el poder supremo pertenece a los ciudadanos, a través del derecho a votar por quienes serán las personas que los representen (pág. 145)

reservoir/embalse lago artificial donde el agua se almacena para abastecimiento de agua (pág. 551)

resolution/resolución declaración formal de la opinión votada por un grupo oficial (págs. 191, 639)

retail/vender al por menor vender en pequeñas cantidades directamente al consumidor (pág. 463)

revenue/ingreso público ingreso que recoge una nación o estado para uso público (pág. 274)

rural/rural de o relativo al campo, gente o ida del campo agrícola (pág. 486)

sandbar/banco de arena un lomo de arena construido por las corrientes en un río o aguas costeras (pág. 114)

savanna/sabana llanura con grupos de árboles esparcidos y maleza resistente a la sequía (pág. 36)

scalawag/scalawag individuo blanco del Sur que apoyaba la Reconstrucción después de la Guerra Civil (pág. 376)

scrip/papel moneda moneda no gubernamental que podía gastarse sólo en una tienda de una compañía (pág. 462)

secede/secesión separarse oficialmente de una compañía (pág. 343)

segregation/segregación separación o aislamiento (pág. 470)

separation of powers/separación de poderes el mandato para el hecho de que los poderes del gobierno estén divididos en tres ramas separadas: legislativo, ejecutivo y judicial (pág. 624)

shaman/shaman persona de quien se cree que utiliza la magia para curar a los enfermos, revelar y controlar el futuro (pág. 88)

sharecropper/compartidor de cosecha arrendatario al cual el propietario de la tierra le proporciona semillas, herramientas, alojamiento y alimentos y quien recibe una porción del valor de la cosecha (págs. 426, 484)

siege/asedio bloqueo militar sobre una ciudad o lugar fortificado (pág. 206)

sinew/fibra tendón (pág. 397)

sit-in/ocupación de asientos ocupar asientos en un establecimiento racialmente segregado en protesta contra la discriminación (pág. 566)

skirmish/escaramuza combate pequeño, generalmente en tiempo de guerra (pág. 191)

smelter/fundición establecimiento que se usa para derretir o fundir mineral con el fin de separar el metal (pág. 522)

sovereignty/soberanía libertad de controles externos; autogobernado (págs. 343, 542)

special interest groups (SIGs)/**grupos de interés especial** (GIEs) organizaciones de personas que tienen un interés común y buscan ejercer influencia sobre un aspecto específico del gobierno (pág. 664)

states' rights/derechos de los estados la creencia que el gobierno federal debe tener poderes limitados sobre los estados (pág. 343)

stock/acciones acciones de propiedad en una corporación (pág. 498)

stockade/empalizada cercado de postes hecho para formar una defensa (pág. 114)

stockyard/corrales de ganado área cercada en donde se guarda temporalmente el ganado para matanza o mercadeo (pág. 414)

strike/huelga negativa a trabajar como protesta contra el empleador (pág. 511)

subsistence crop/cosecha de subsistencia cosecha para usarse en la granja donde fue cultivada (pág. 303)

suburb/suburbio comunidad residencial cercana a una ciudad o pueblo grande (pág. 550)

suffrage/sufragio derecho a voto (pág. 433)

survey/agrimensura medida del tamaño y los límites (pág. 167)

synthetic/sintético producido artificialmente o hecho por el hombre (pág. 552)

tallow/sebo grasa de ganado y ovejas, que se usa en la fabricación de jabón, margarina, velas, y lubricantes (pág. 413)

tariff/arancel impuesto sobre los bienes importados (pág. 274)

teamster/tronquista persona que conduce o dirige un grupo de animales (pág. 333)

Tejano/tejano persona de descendencia mexicana que vive en Tejas (pág. 133)

tenant farmer/granjero arrendatario granjero que trabaja una tierra poseída por otro y paga la renta bien sea en efectivo o compartiendo lo que produce (págs. 426, 484)

tepee/tepee refugio hecho de pieles curtidas aseguradas a un armazón de postes (pág. 95)

third party/tercer partido grupo político organizado que no es ni republicano ni demócrata (pág. 581)

transistor/transistor dispositivo electrónico sólido que se usa para controlar el flujo de electricidad en equipo electrónico con al menos tres electrodos (pág. 552)

trust/trust combinación de compañías formada por acuerdo para reducir la competencia (pág. 444)

unconstitutional/inconstitucional que no está de acuerdo con la Constitución de los Estados Unidos y en consecuencia no es legal (pág. 544)

unemployment/desempleo pérdida de trabajos—hay menor cantidad de trabajo disponible que la gente que los necesita (pág. 499)

Unionist/Unionista persona que apoyaba la causa de la Unión durante la Guerra Civil (pág. 349)

urban/urbano de o relativo a la ciudad (pág. 486)

urban dweller/habitante urbano persona que vive en la ciudad (pág. 579)

vacuum tube/tubo al vacío un tubo de electrones con un alto grado de vacío; que se usaba para controlar el flujo de electricidad en los televisores y las radios antes de la invención del transistor (pág. 552)

vaquero/**vaquero** un "cowboy" en las áreas de América pobladas por españoles (págs. 153, 413)

veto/veto rechazar, como impedir que una propuesta de ley se convierta en ley; el rechazo de un presidente o gobernador a aprobar una ley (págs. 213, 374)

viceroy/virrey gobernador que gobierna como representante de un rey o soberano (pág. 108)

vigilante/vigilante miembro de un comité voluntario organizado para castigar criminales (págs. 349, 435)

watchdog role/rol de vigilante actividad de partidos políticos: monitorear, o seguir la pista de e informar sobre, las prácticas y decisiones de otros partidos (pág. 664)

white-collar/oficinista generalmente, trabajos que no requieren de labor física (pág. 463)

wildcatter/wildcatter individuo que perfora pozos con la esperanza de encontrar petróleo en un territorio que no es conocido como un campo petrolero (pág. 499)

windfall/ganga regalo, ganancia o ventaja inesperada o repentina (pág. 648)

wrangler/encargado de caballos persona que ayuda a cuidar caballos de silla (pág. 416)

Spanish Glossary

Index

Italicized page numbers refer to illustrations. The following abbreviations are used in the index:
m = map; c = chart; p = photograph or picture; g = graph; crt = cartoon; ptg = painting; q = quote

Index

Index

Index

Index

Index

Index

Index

Acknowledgements and Photo Credits

Acknowledgments

Glencoe would like to acknowledge the artists and agencies who participated in illustrating this program: Morgan Cain & Associates; Ortelius Design, Inc.; QA Digital. 44 Carey McWilliams, *Ill Fares the Land: The Spanish Speaking People of the United States* (Boston: Little, Brown and Company, 1942) George O. Coalson, *The Development of the Migratory Farm Labor System in Texas, 1900–1954* (San Francisco: R & E Research Associates, 1977) 55 Excerpt from *Explorations of the Big Witchita, etc.* by Dale Terry from "Captain R.B. Marcy's Report," © 1962 by Terry Bros. Printers. Reprinted by permission. 98 Nancy Parrott Hickerson, *The Jumanos: Hunters and Traders of the South Plains* (Austin: University of Texas Press, 1994) David La Vere, *The Caddo Chiefdoms: Caddo Economics and Politics, 700–1835* (Lincoln: University of Nebraska Press, 1998) 149 Excerpt from *The Tarnished Halo*, by Robert Carter © 1973 by Franciscan Herald Press. Reprinted by permission. 182 Gregg Cantrell, *Stephen F. Austin: Empresario of Texas* (New Haven: Yale University Press, 1999) 229 Excerpt from *All for Texas* by Gary Clifton Wisler, © 2000 by Jamestown Publishers, a division of NTC/Contemporary Publishing Group. Reprinted by permission. 280 Excerpt from Chapter 22 of *The Bugles Are Silent, A Novel of the Texas Revolution* by John R. Knaggs, © 1997 by School Creek Publishers, Inc. Reprinted by permission of the author. 292 Charles M. Robinson, *The Men Who Wear the Star: The Story of the Texas Rangers* (New York: Random House, 2000) 353 Excerpt titled "Pioneer Heroin" taken from *Texas Sketches*, (c) 1985 by A.C. Green, (Taylor Publishing, Dallas) 362 Randolph B. Campbell, *An Empire for Slavery: The Peculiar Institution in Texas* (Baton Rouge: Louisiana State University Press, 1989) 394 Excerpt from Chapter 13 of *The Pumpkin Rollers* by Elmer Kelton © 1996 by Forge, A Tom Doherty Associates Book. Reprinted by permission. 408 T.J Cashion, *A Texas Frontier: The Clear Fork Country and Fort Griffin 1849–1887* (Norman: University of Oklahoma Press, 1996) 494 Neil Foley, *The White Scourge: Mexicans, Blacks, and Poor Whites in Texas Cotton Culture* (Berkeley: University of California at Berkeley, 1997) Rebecca Sharpless, *Fertile Ground, Narrow Choices: Women on Texas Cotton Farms, 1900–1940* (Chapel Hill: The University of North Carolina Press, 1999) 520 Excerpt from "Freedom Flies in Your Heart Like an Eagle" by Audie Murphy © 1948, Audie Murphy Research Foundation. Reprinted by permission of the Estate of Audie Murphy. 556 T.R. Reid, *The Chip: How Two Americans Invented the Microchip and Launched a Revolution* (New York: Simon and Schuster, 1984) 587 Excerpt from Chapter 17 of *Texas Big Rich* by Sandy Sheehy © 1990 by William Morrow and Company, Inc. Reprinted by permission.

Photo Credits

Abbreviation Key: AP=AP/Wide World Photos; AR=Art Resource, NY; BAL=Bridgeman Art Library; BB=The Bob Bullock Texas State History Museum; BD=Bob Daemmrich; BT=Bettmann; CB=CORBIS; GI=Getty Images; HA=Hulton Archive; ITC=UT Institute of Texan Cultures at San Antonio; NG=National Geographic Maps; NW=North Wind Picture Archives; PD=PhotoDisc; PQ=PictureQuest; PR=Photo Researchers; SM=Stock Montage; TD=Texas Department of Highways & Public Transportation; THC=Barker Texas History Center, University of Texas at Austin; TSL=Texas State Library & Archives Commission.

Cover (l)BD/Stock Boston/PQ, (r)Harvey Lloyd/GI; iv Smithsonian Institution; v (t)SuperStock, (c)Austin History Center, (b)TSL; vi (t)BAL, (b)Culver Pictures; vii BD; viii Kansas State Historical Society, Topeka; ix HA/GI; x ITC; xiv PD; xvi Phil Schermeister/CB; xvii (t)Eliot Cohen, (b)Larry Lee Photography/CB; 0 (t)Jeremy Woodhouse/PD, (r)Richard Stockton/Index Stock, (b)Laurence Parent; 0–1 Laurence Parent; 1 Dennis Flaherty/PR; 2 (l)PD, (r)"Just Married" by Velox Ward, courtesy Kevin Vogel; 2–3 Michael Javorka/GI; 3 (l)TSL, (r)Michael Dwyer/Stock Boston; 4 (tl)Tim Hall/PD, (tr)CMCD/PD, (c)Michael Freeman/PhotoLink/PD, (bl)Patrick Ray Dunn, (blc)Colin Paterson/PD, (brc)Siede Pries/PD, (br)CMCD/PD; 5 (tl)Jeremy Woodhouse/PD, (tr)PhotoLink/PD, (cl)F. Schussler/PhotoLink/PD, (c)Don Farrall/PD, (cr)Doug Menuez/PD, (bl)Duncan Smith/PD, (bc)Cartesia/PD, (br)PD; 12 13 CB; 15 Culver Pictures/PQ; 18 PD; 18–19 (t)Greg Kuchik/PD, (b)Tomi/PhotoLink/PD; 20–21 Laurence Parent; 21 THC; 22 (t)BD/Stock Boston/PQ, (b)Milepost 92½/CB; 22–23 NG; 23 (t)Mark Segal/GI, (c)Kit Kittle/CB, (b)NG; 24 (l)Francois Gohier/PR, (r)Laurence Parent; 24–25 Laurence Parent; 25 Provided by the SeaWiFS Project, NASA/Goddard Space Flight Center, and ORBIMAGE; 26 TSL; 27 Douglas Kirkland/CB; 29 (t)courtesy Church of the Visitation Catholic Church, Westphalia TX/photo by Doris Voltin, (b)AP; 30 Center for American History, University of Texas at Austin; 31 David Muench/CB; 34 Laurence Parent; 35 (l)Kelly-Mooney/CB, (r)Charles O'Rear/CB; 38 Jack Jackson, Illustrator; 39 Alan R. Moller/GI; 40 Jim Watkins/AP; 44 J.R. Eyerman/TimePix; 45 (l)Joseph Scherschel/TimePix, (r)Dennie Cody/GI; 46 (l)Craig Kramer, (r)Agnew & Sons, London/BAL; 46–47 TD; 47 NW; 48 George Heinhold; 52 Keith Wood/GI; 53 PD; 54 ChromoSohm/PR; 55 (l)CB, (r)Texas Department of Transportation; 56 Laurence Parent; 57 Donna McWilliam/AP; 59 Laurence Parent; 61 HA/GI; 62 BD/Stock Boston; 64 (t)BD, (bl)courtesy Scenic Art, Temecula CA, (br)NW; 65 BD/The Image Works; 66 Buddy Mays/CB; 67 Laurence Parent; 68 Stephen Ferry/The Image Works; 69 PD; 72 (tl)collection of Roger Sanders/photo by Ken Walker, (tr)Bob & Clara Calhoun/Bruce Coleman, Inc./PQ, (c)Allan Kaye/Index Stock, (bl)C Squared Studios/PD, (br)Erwin C. Nielson/Visuals Unlimited; 73 TD; 74–75 Witte Museum, San Antonio; 75 SM; 76 (tl tr)NG, (c)Gregory A. Harlin, (others)BD; 76–77 NG; 77 Texas Historical Commission; 78 (t)NW, (bl)Buddy Mays/CB, (br)Werner Forman Archive/AR; 78–79 SM/SuperStock; 79 BT/CB; 80 ITC; 84 CB; 85 Alan Carey; 86 Mural by George S. Nelson, courtesy ITC; 88 The Art Archive; 90 George Ranalli/PR; 91 Edward Moore; 92 National Museum of American Art, Smithsonian Institution/AR; 93 Museum of Fine Arts, Houston/BAL; 94 (l)Smithsonian Institution, (r)CB; 98 Andrew Hall; 99 BD/Stock Boston/PQ; 100 (t)Joel W. Rogers/CB, (b)Bibliotheque Nationale, Paris, France/BAL; 100–101 Giraudon/AR; 101 (t)Culver Pictures/PQ, (b)Mark Downey/PD; 102 Academy of Natural Sciences of Philadelphia/CB; 103 (l)Charles & Josette Lenars/CB, (r)courtesy Edward E. Ayer Collection, Newberry Library, Chicago; 106 HA/GI; 107 SM; 108 Private collection/BAL; 109 Amanita Pictures; 110 BT/CB; 112 Laurence Parent; 114 Culver Pictures/PQ; 116 (from top)Joel W. Rogers/CB. Bibliotheque Nationale, Paris, France/BAL. HA/GI. Private collection/BAL. Culver Pictures/PQ; 118 NW; 118–119 Witte Museum, San Antonio; 119 NW; 120 David Muench/CB; 122 TD; 124 National Museum of American Art, Smithsonian Institution/AR; 127 NW; 128 TD; 130 TD; 131 Gift of the Yanaguana Society, Daughters of the Republic of Texas Library; 133 ITC; 134 (from top)CB. Jack Jackson, Illustrator. BD. NW. Texas Western Press, University of Texas at El Paso; 136 Smithsonian Institution; 136–137 Courtesy Bexar County, San Antonio Museum Association; 137 (l)Leonard de Selva/CB, (r)Dagli Orti/National Palace, Mexico City/The Art Archive; 138 TSL; 139 BT/CB; 140 ITC; 144 BT/CB; 145 National History Museum, Mexico City/Dagli Orti/The Art Archive; 146 ITC. Original owned by Winston Farber, Houston; 147 THC; 149 (l)courtesy Robert Carter, (r)Granitsas/The Image Works; 150 TSL; 151 The Thomas Gilcrease Institute of American History & Art, Tulsa OK; 152 (t bc)courtesy Justin Boot Company, (bl)BT/CB, (br)NW; 154 (from top)BD. Geoffrey Clements/CB. ITC. National History Museum, Mexico City/Dagli Orti/The Art Archive. THC. 156 Witte Museum, San Antonio/photo by Ken Walker; 157 (tl tc tr)Texas Historical Commission, Austin/photo by Ken Walker, (bl)Texas Memorial Museum, Austin/photo by Ken Walker, (br)Witte Museum, San Antonio/photo by Ken Walker; 158–159 D. Boone/CB; 159 Daughters of the Republic of Texas, The Alamo; 160 (tl tc b)Dorling Kindersley, Ltd., (tr)Carson Baldwin Jr./Earth Scenes, (cl)Patti Murray/Animals Animals, (cr)Bob Krist/CB; 160–161 NG; 161 (tl)Mary Eaton, (tc)courtesy Pilgrim Hall Museum, Plymouth MA, (tr)George Ranch Historical Park Collection, (cl)Leo Keeler/Animals Animals, (cr)CMCD/PD/PQ, (bl)Mickey Gibson/Animals Animals, (br)Duane Raver/Wildlife Illustrated; 162 (t)Gonzales County Historical Commission and Gonzales County Records Center and Archives, (bl)NW, (br)BAL; 162–163 Witte Museum, San Antonio; 163 PD; 164 Gianni Dagli Orti/CB; 165 ITC; 166 CB; 169 (l)William Johnson/Stock Boston, (r)Laurence Parent; 171 PD; 172 175 ITC; 176 Bruce Marshall, Illustrator/ITC; 178 (l)THC, (r)PD; 179 TSL; 180 (from top)CB. William Johnson/Stock Boston. ITC. ITC. Gonzales County Historical Commission and Gonzales County Records Center and Archives; 182 183 BD; 184 BT/CB; 184–185 Schalkwijk/AR; 185 Guildhall Library, Corporation of London/BAL; 186 187 ITC; 188 SM; 190 file photo; 191 BD; 193 BT/CB; 194 ITC; 195 (l)Amon Carter Museum of Western Art, Fort Worth, (r)Center for American History, University of Texas at Austin/photo by Ken Walker; 197 (l)Rosenberg Library, Galveston TX, (r)TSL; 198 BT/CB; 199 Courtesy Anita McLean/ITC; 200 (from top)ITC. BD. BT/CB. Amon Carter Museum of Western Art, Fort Worth TX. BT/CB; 202 Tarlton Law Library, School of Law, The University of Texas at Austin; 202–203 TD; 203 (l)SuperStock, (r)The Stapleton Collection/BAL; 204 Jefferson Historical Society and Museum, Jefferson TX; 205 Bruce Marshall, Illustrator; 206 TSL; 207 THC; 210 NW; 211 Daughters of the Republic of Texas, The Alamo; 212 Kermit Oliver/ITC; 213 TSL; 214 BD; 216 Collection of Mrs. Artie Futz Davis, courtesy Star of the Republic Museum; 217 ITC; 219 THC; 220 (from top)Bruce Marshall, Illustrator. Daughters of the Republic of Texas Library, The Alamo. TSL. Collection of Mrs. Artie Futz Davis, courtesy Star of the Republic Museum. Tarlton Law Library, School of Law, The University of Texas at Austin; 222 (t)The Art Archive, (b)BT/CB; 222–223 SuperStock; 223 SM; 224 Imaginary portrait of Herman Ehrenberg by José Cisneros from *Ehrenberg: Goliad Survivor, Old West Explorer,* ©1997 Natalie Ornish, Texas Heritage Press; 225 226 TSL; 227 (l)TSL, (r)BT/CB; 229 (l)courtesy Gary Clifton Wisler, (r)Aaron Haupt; 230 ITC; 233 H.A. McArdle/TSL/photo by Eric Beggs; 234 (t)Vince Streano/CB, (b)John Hayes/AP; 235 TSL; 236 SM; 237 ITC; 239 TD; 240 TSL; 241 Daughters of the Republic of Texas Library, The Alamo; 242 (t)ITC, (cl)TSL, (cr)Vince Streano/CB, (b)TSL, (br)H.A. McArdle/TSL/photo by Eric Beggs; 244 BT/CB; 244–245 TSL; 245 (t)photo by Frank Lerner ©1975 Time-Life Books/courtesy the Showers-Brown Collection/The Star of The Republic Museum, Washington TX, (b)BT/CB; 246 Jack Jackson, Illustrator; 247 TSL; 248 San Jacinto Museum of History, LaPorte TX; 252 SuperStock; 253 CB; 254 THC; 255 Henry Arthur McArdle/TSL/photo by Bill Malone; 256 (t)BT/CB, (b)TSL; 258 (l)Lake County Museum/CB, (c r)Curt Teich Postcard Archive/Lake County Museum; 259 BD; 260 (from top)TSL. BT/CB. Photo by Frank Lerner ©1975 Time-Life Books/courtesy the Showers-Brown Collection/The Star of The Republic Museum, Washington TX. San Jacinto Museum of History, LaPorte TX. Henry Arthur McArdle/TSL/photo by Bill Malone; 262 Collection of Marlene Wagner/photo by Ken Walker; 262–263 TSL/photo by Ken Walker; 263 (tl tr)San Jacinto Museum of History, LaPorte TX/photo by Ken Walker, (bl br)Rosenberg Library, Galveston TX/photo by Ken Walker;

264–265 Texas Memorial Museum, Austin/Collection of Russell Fish III; 265 TSL; 266 (t b)BD/Stock Boston/PQ; 267 (tl tc)BD, (tr)BD/Stock Boston/PQ, (cl)NG, (cr)Eric Gay/AP, (bl br)NG; 268 (t)Hulton-Deutsch Collection/CB, (r)NW; 268–269 Archives Division, Texas State University Library; 269 (t)NW, (b)SEF/AR; 270 BAL; 271 TSL; 273 SM; 275 The Stapleton Collection/BAL; 276 THC; 277 (t)TSL, (b)CB; 278 NW; 279 Bruce Marshall, Illustrator; 280 (l)courtesy John R. Knaggs, (r)Nik Wheeler/CB; 281 SM/SuperStock; 282 TSL; 283 Museum of Fine Arts, Houston/BAL; 285 BD/Stock Boston; 286 Sam Houston Memorial Museum, Huntsville TX; 287 NW; 288 BT/CB; 292 (l)CB, (r)The Library of Congress; 293 (l)Texas Ranger Hall of Fame and Museum, (r)BD; 294 (t)TSL, (b)BT/CB; 294–295 The Library of Congress; 295 BT/CB; 296 ITC, courtesy The Kilman Studio; 297 Sophienburg Museum & Archives, New Braunfels TX; 298 file photo; 299 ITC, courtesy *Harper's Weekly*; 301 TSL; 302 CB; 303 "Just Married" by Velox Ward, courtesy Kevin Vogel; 305 Jim Strawser from Grant Heilman Photography; 306 Mark Thayer; 307 TSL; 309 (t)NW, (b)Dave Bartruff/CB; 310 (t)Stan Williams/Texas Department of Transportation, (bl)Collection of Margaret Guenther Gideon, courtesy ITC, (br)C.H. Guenther & Son, Inc.; 312 (from top)"Just Married" by Velox Ward, courtesy Kevin Vogel. TSL. Sophienburg Museum & Archives, New Braunfels TX. ITC, courtesy *Harper's Weekly*. TSL; 314 (l)BB/photo by Ken Walker, (r)Sophienburg Museum & Archives, New Braunfels TX/photo by Ken Walker; 315 (t)Witte Museum, San Antonio/photo by Ken Walker, (bl)collection of Jonas Perkins/photo by Ken Walker, (br)BB/photo by Ken Walker; 316–317 National Museum of American Art, Smithsonian Institution/AR; 317 BAL; 318 NG; 318–319 Tom Bean/CB; 319 (l r)NG, (c)The Library of Congress; 320 (l)TSL, (r)Matt Meadows; 320–321 Collection of Margaret Guenther Gideon, courtesy ITC; 321 BT/CB; 322 CMCD/PD; 323 SM; 324 TSL; 326 K.D. Swan/CB; 327 (t)BT/CB, (b)Collection of David J. & Janice L. Frent; 329 Historical Art Prints; 331 SuperStock; 332 Chuck Woodbury/*Out West* Newspaper; 333 ITC; 335 Courtesy San Antonio Museum Association; 337 CB; 338 (from top)TSL. SuperStock. BT/CB. Courtesy San Antonio Museum Association. ITC. CB; 339 PD; 340 (t)TSL, (bl br)Mark Burnett; 340–341 THC; 341 BAL; 342 Archivo Iconografico, S.A./CB; 343 (l)BT/CB, (r)The Charleston Museum, Charleston SC; 345 (t)HA/GI, (b)The Library of Congress; 346 SM/SuperStock; 347 Don Troiani/Historical Art Prints; 350 Frank & Marie-Therese Wood Print Collections; 351 ITC; 352 Lawrence T. Jones Collection, Austin, courtesy Texas Historical Foundation; 353 (l)Judy Greene, (r)SM; 354 Tria Giovan/CB; 355 CB; 358 ITC; 359 HA/GI; 360 (from top)BAL. SM/SuperStock. Frank & Marie-Therese Wood Print Collections. Lawrence T. Jones Collection, Austin, courtesy Texas Historical Foundation; 362 (l)Bob Mullenix, (r)BT/CB; 363 Pat Sullivan/AP; 364 (t)Still Picture Branch, National Archives at College Park MD, (b)Chicago Historical Society; 364–365 NW; 365 Key Color/Index Stock Imagery/PQ; 366 Culver Pictures/PQ; 367 Austin History Center, Austin Public Library; 369 Rosenberg Library, Galveston TX; 370 BT/CB; 371 NW; 372 The Library of Congress; 373 Center for American History, University of Texas at Austin; 374 CB; 375 BT/CB; 377 (t)NW, (b)ITC/Hendrick-Long Publishing; 378 CB; 379 HA/GI; 380 (from top)CB. Austin History Center, Austin Public Library. Chicago Historical Society. NW. ITC. HA/GI; 382 BB/photo by Ken Walker; 382–383 Grant Heilman from Grant Heilman Photography; 383 (t)collection of Andrew W. Hall/photo by Ken Walker, (b)BB/photo by Ken Walker; 384–385 Richard Baldwin/Wood River Gallery/PQ; 385 Daughters of the Republic of Texas Library, The Alamo; 386 (l)Richard Cummins/CB, (r)NG; 386–387 (t)David Woo/Stock Boston/PQ, (b)Joseph H. Bailey; 387 (t)CB, (b)NG; 388 (t)BAL, (b)Medford Historical Society Collection/CB; 388–389 SM; 389 Hulton-Deutsch Collection/CB; 390 Hugh Beebower/CB; 391 The Brooklyn Museum of Art, New York/BAL; 392 (l)Smithsonian Institution, (r)Lindsay Hebberd/CB; 393 Texas Collection, Baylor University; 394 (l)Cynthia Farah, (r)Christie's Images/BAL; 395 396 CB; 397 Western Historical Collections, University of Oklahoma Library; 398 NW; 402 Courtesy Joe Williams/ITC; 403 BB/photo by Ken Walker; 405 ITC; 406 (from top)The Brooklyn Museum of Art, New York/BAL. Lindsay Hebberd/CB. NW. CB; 408–409 Francis G. Mayer/CB; 410 (t)Jim Strawser from Grant Heilman Photography, (b)Eliot Cohen; 410–411 BAL; 411 (t)The Purcell Team/CB, (b)Culver Pictures; 412 Paul W. Stewart Collection/TimePix; 413 Witte Museum, San Antonio; 414 (tl)TSL, (tr)King Ranch, Inc., Kingsville TX, (bl)TD, (br)Richard Stockton; 416 Southwest Collection, Texas Tech University; 418 Estate of Mary Ellen O'Connor/ITC; 419 Wood River Gallery/PQ; 420 ITC; 421 (t)Western History Collections, University of Oklahoma Library, (b)Kansas State Historical Society, Topeka; 422 Jim Strawser from Grant Heilman Photography; 423 ITC; 424 BT/CB; 425 Austin History Center, Austin Public Library; 426 (l)The Library of Congress, (r)PD; 428 (from top)Witte Museum, San Antonio. Richard Stockton. Southwest Collection, Texas Tech University. Western History Collections, University of Oklahoma Library. Austin History Center, Austin Public Library; 430 (t)THC, (b)BAL; 430–431 Published by American Publishing Co./Amon Carter Museum of Western Art, Fort Worth; 431 (t)Historiches Museum der StadtWien, Vienna, Austria/AR, (b)Hulton-Deutsch Collection/CB; 432 Brown Brothers; 433 TSL; 434 ITC; 435 TSL; 436 The Library of Congress; 437 NW; 438 TSL; 440 THC; 443 Culver Pictures; 444 (t)Panhandle Plains Historical Museum, Canyon TX, (b)Archive Photos/PQ; 445 (l)University of Texas, (r)The Library of Congress; 446 BAL; 447 ITC; 448 (from top)ITC. The Library of Congress. BAL. THC. The Library of Congress; 450 (l)BB/photo by Ken Walker, (r)Collection of Enrique Guerra/photo by Ken Walker; 451 (tl)American Wind Power Center, Lubbock TX/photo by Ken Walker, (tr)Donald & Louise Yena Collection, Witte Museum, San Antonio/photo by Ken Walker, (c)collection of Enrique Guerra/photo by Ken Walker, (b)BB/photo by Ken Walker; 452–453 National Museum of American Art, Smithsonian Institution/AR; 453 Bernard Hoffman/TimePix; 454 NG; 454–455 NOAA/National Geophysical Data Center; 455 (tr)NG, (others)Stephen R. Wagner; 456 (t)TSL, (b)National Portrait Gallery, Smithsonian Institution/AR; 456–457 Underwood & Underwood/CB; 457 Culver Pictures; 458 Texas A&M University Press; 459 CB; 460 HA/GI; 462 TSL; 463 Texas Fashion Collection at North Texas State University; 464 BT/CB; 465 Courtesy Texas A&M University Press; 466 TSL; 467 (t)Brown Brothers, (b)BAL; 468 Alfred Eisenstaedt/TimePix; 469 Culver Pictures; 470 Austin History Center, Austin Public Library; 471 (l c)courtesy Blue Bell Creameries, (r)NASA; 472 (l)CB, (r)Houston Metropolitan Research Center, Houston; 474 (from top)CB. Dudley Woodward/Wood River Gallery/PQ. Austin History Center, Austin Public Library. HA/GI. TSL; 476 (t)BT/CB, (bl)CB, (br)AR; 476–477 Museum of the City of New York/CB; 477 (t)TSL, (b)HA/GI; 478 National Air and Space Museum, Smithsonian Institution; 479 Courtesy Rose Wu/ITC; 481 (t)San Antonio Light Collection/ITC, (b)CB; 482 RH Parteous/Wood River Gallery/PQ; 483 BT/CB; 484 Courtesy Dan Martinets/ITC; 485 Arthur Rothstein/CB; 486 TSL; 487 THC; 488 Matt Meadows; 490 BT/CB; 491 Joe Raedle/ GI; 492 (from top)HA/GI. BT/CB. CB. PD. TSL; 494–495 Dorothea Lange/CB; 495 (l)HA/GI, (r)Panhandle-Plains History Museum, Canyon TX; 496 (t)BD/Stock Boston, (b)Culver Pictures; 496–497 Francis G. Mayer/CB; 497 (l)Culver Pictures, (r)George Kleiman/CB; 498 San Antonio Light Collection/ITC; 499 East Texas Oil Museum, Kilgore College, Kilgore TX; 500 *Dallas Morning News*; 502 HA/GI; 504 Arthur Rothstein/The Library of Congress/HA/GI; 506 BT/CB; 507 Dallas Historical Society; 508 ITC; 510 Houston Public Library; 511 ITC; 512 (from top)Arthur Rothstein/The Library of Congress/HA/GI. BD/Stock Boston. Houston Public Library. HA/GI. San Antonio Light Collection/ITC; 513 CB; 514 (t)Image Bank, (bl)Amos Zezmer/Omni-Photo Communications, (br)Culver Pictures; 515–516 Naval Historical Foundation; 516 BT/CB; 517 (t)Culver Pictures, (bl)BT/CB, (br)National Archives; 520 (l)Culver Pictures, (r)Jeff Lepore/PR; 521 Imperial War Museum, London/BAL; 522 Culver Pictures; 524 BT/CB; 525 CB; 526 United States Department of the Army/ITC; 527 Houston Public Library; 528 Larry Rubenstein/CB; 530 (from top)Pat LaCroix/Image Bank. Culver Pictures. National Archives. Culver Pictures. BT/CB; 531 CB; 532 BB/photo by Ken Walker; 532–533 Collection of Jim Adkins/photo by Ken Walker; 533 (t)HA/GI, (c)Texas Energy Museum, Beaumont/photo by Ken Walker, (bl)collection of Jim Adkins/photo by Ken Walker, (br)Houston Museum of Natural History/photo by Ken Walker; 534–535 Kunio Owaki/CB Stock Market; 535 file photo; 536 NG; 536–537 CB; 537 (l)BD, (r)NG; 538 (t)CB, (b)Robert Landau/CB; 538–539 Jim Wark/Index Stock; 539 Courtesy Texas Instruments; 540 Courtesy Rev. Floyd Moody Sr.; 542 (l)HA/GI, (r)BT/CB; 543 Tim Holt/PR; 544 HA/GI; 545 BT/CB; 546 TD; 549 BT/CB; 550 David J. Phillip/AP; 553 BT/CB; 554 (from top)BT/CB. HA/GI. CB. BT/CB. Marcy Nighswander/AP; 556 Donna McWilliam/AP; 557 (t)BT/CB, (b)Marcy Nighswander/AP; 558 (t)Grey Villet/ TimePix, (b)AP; 558–559 NASA/GI; 559 (t)Nancy R. Schiff/HA/GI, (b)BT/CB; 560 BT/CB; 561 AP; 562 Yoichi R. Lkamoto/CB; 565 567 AP; 568 Wells College Archives, Louis Jefferson Long Library, Aurora NY; 569 *Houston Chronicle*; 570 Michael Dwyer/Stock Boston; 572 Herblock Cartoons/*The Washington Post*; 574 (from top)AP. Culver Pictures. AP. Yoichi R. Lkamoto/CB. *Houston Chronicle*; 576 Courtesy The White House/HA/GI; 576–577 BD; 577 (t)Spencer Platt/GI, (b)Amy C. Etra/PhotoEdit; 578 Andrea Pistolesi/The Image Bank; 579 (l c)BD/Stock Boston, (r)TSL; 580 BD/Stock Boston; 582 BD; 583 Dean Brown/Omni-Photo Communications; 584 PD; 585 David Turnley/CB; 586 Kevin Bartram/*The Galveston County Daily News*/AP; 587 (t)Tom Curtis, (r)Pam Francis; 588 Paul S. Howell/GI; 590 (t)Alex Wong/GI, (b)Brett Coomer/AP; 592 (from top)Paul S. Howell/GI. Courtesy The White House/HA/GI. David Turnley/CB. BD/Stock Boston. Kevin Bartram/*The Galveston County Daily News*/AP; 594 (t)BT/CB, (b)The Military Picture Library/CB; 594–595 Witte Museum, San Antonio/San Antonio Museum Association; 595 (l)Ken Cavanaugh/PR, (bl)HA/GI, (br)Michel Lipchitz/AP; 596 University of Texas; 599 BD/Stock Boston; 600 R. Boll/Wood River Gallery/PQ; 601 Center for American History, University of Texas at Austin; 602 Walt Disney Productions/Photofest; 603 Tony Freeman/PhotoEdit; 604 (tl)San Antonio Light Collection/ITC, (tc)Cheryl Gerber/AP, (tr)Mitchell Gerber/CB, (b)BT/CB; 605 Daughters of the Republic of Texas Library/BAL; 607 BT/CB; 608 Jerry W. Hoefer/AP; 609 BD; 610 Joe Raedle/GI; 611 Reprint courtesy *Fort Worth Star-Telegram*; 614 Chris Sorensen; 615 (t)Smithsonian Institution/photo by Ken Walker, (tr)Texas Instruments/photo by Ken Walker, (bl)private collection/ photo by Ken Walker, (br)NASA/photo by Ken Walker; 616–617 Joe Raedle/GI; 617 HA/GI; 618 (t)Ross Dawkins, (tr)BD/Stock Boston/PQ, (c br)NG, (bl)BD; 619 (tl tr)NG, (c)BD/Stock Boston/PQ, (b)NG; 620 (t)Aaron Haupt, (b)Michael St. Maur Sheil/CB; 620–621 BD; 621 BT/CB; 622 Tarlton Law Library, School of Law, The University of Texas at Austin; 623 AP; 626 Richard T. Nowitz/CB; 627 BD/ Stock Boston/PQ; 629 Jeff Cadge/Image Bank; 634 (t)Aaron Haupt/PR, (b)Bill Gentile/CB; 634–635 Larry Lee Photography/CB; 635 (t)BD/Stock Boston, (b)J. Scott Applewhite/AP; 636 BD/The Image Works; 640 BD/Stock Boston; 641 Harry Cabluck/AP; 642 (t)BD/The Image Works, (b)BD/Stock Boston; 645 *Dallas Morning News*; 646 Shelley Rotner/Omni-Photo Communications; 647 BD/Stock Boston; 648 CB; 649 Harry Cabluck/AP; 651 Courtesy Ben Sargent; 653 Courtesy Fort Concho; 654 (l)Smithsonian Institution, (r)Hulton-Deutsch Collection/CB; 654–655 Chris Salvo/GI; 655 (t)BD/Stock Boston, (b)Jan Lukas/PR; 656 Courtesy Marcus Puente; 657 (t)PD, (bl)BD/Stock Boston, (br)PD; 661 BD/Stock Boston; 662 Courtesy Marcus Puente; 665 BD/The Image Works; 668 (tl)file photo, (tlc)David Chasey/PD, (trc)Siede Preis/PD, (tr)BD, (c)BD/Stock Boston/PQ, (bl)Smithsonian Institution, (bc)BD/The Image Works, (br)HA/GI; 674 By permission of the Huntington Library, San Marino CA; 682 Archivo Iconografico, S.A./CB; 683 The Oakland Museum; 684 Francois Gohier/PR; 686 HA/GI; 687 NW; 688 ITC; 689 William Johnson/Stock Boston; 690 SEF/AR; 691 Austin History Center, Austin Public Library; 692 Bob & Clara Calhoun/Bruce Coleman, Inc./PQ; 693 Erwin C. Nielson/Visuals Unlimited; 694 Francis G. Mayer/CB; 695 BB/photo by Ken Walker; 696 TSL; 697 C Squared Studios/PD; 698 San Antonio Light Collection/ITC; 699 ITC; 700 Courtesy www.sanangelotexas.org; 701 (background)Jeremy Woodhouse/PD, (foreground)file photo; 710 711 TSL; 712 BAL; 713 BD/Stock Boston.